Praise for *Che Guevara: A Revolutionary Life:*

"A masterly and absorbing account of Latin America's famous guerrilla leader . . . Anderson's book, easily the best so far on Guevara, is a worthy monument to a flawed but heroic Utopian dreamer."

—*The Sunday Times* (London)

"Remarkable . . . Anderson's account is well rounded and far from uncritical . . . [his] journalistic flair and hard legwork are evident."

—*Foreign Affairs*

"Exceptional and exciting . . . Anderson's up-close look, with beauty marks and tragic flaws so effortlessly rendered, brings the reader face to face with a man whose unshakable faith in his beliefs was made more powerful by his unusual combination of romantic passion and a coldly analytical mind. . . . An invaluable addition to the literature of American revolutionaries."

—*Booklist*

"A solidly documented biography that succeeds, with brilliant effect, in stripping away the layers of demonization and hero worship that for so long have concealed the human core of this legendary figure . . . Thanks to Jon Lee Anderson, we now have the true story, the real man, a portrait of exceptional substance to confound the myth and enhance our understanding of the facts."

—*The Kansas City Star*

"Jon Lee Anderson . . . draws upon an unprecedented wealth of new information . . . [an] assiduously researched and perhaps definitive biography."

—*San Francisco Chronicle*

"A skillful interviewer, Anderson elicited information from dozens of participants in Guevara's life. . . . Combining contradictory sources and an immense amount of detail, Anderson produces a multifaceted view of Guevara as a person, seething with ambiguities and complexities. This is an achievement that makes *Che Guevara* essential for anyone seriously interested in Guevara or the Cuban revolution."

—*The Nation*

"*Che Guevara: A Revolutionary Life* gives an admirably balanced account of the Argentine adventurer, his real achievements and glamorous Robin Hood appeal. . . . An excellent guide to the myth behind the martyr."

—*The Independent* (London)

"Five years of research and unprecedented access to friends, family, and unpublished archives have allowed Anderson to fulfill his stated aim, to present the truth about Che Guevara." —*Literary Review*

"A massive, painstaking biography of the Argentine guerrilla leader who devoted his life to the ideal of a unified Latin American revolution." —*Buzz*

"A revealing portrait of the many Ches: the quixotic, freewheeling youth rambling around South and Central America in search of the good fight; the willful, asthmatic 'Jacobin of the Cuban Revolution'; and finally . . . the holy martyr of armed rebellion at age thirty-nine . . . Che lives on as a paradox of his own time and ours." —*Time Out New York*

"Jon Lee Anderson's authoritative new biography shows both the passionate idealist and the cold-hearted disciplinarian." —*Newsweek*

"Vividly detailed . . . Anderson weaves a compelling psychological profile of Guevara." —*The Buffalo News*

"*Che Guevara* by Jon Lee Anderson may still be the best [biography of Che] for its deft style and its details of Che's post-Cuba adventures. It is also the only one to carry interviews with Che's widow, Aleida." —*Publishers Weekly*

"His biography appears to be definitive. . . . Obviously a reporter of great energy and enterprise, he scored at least two major scoops in his research: obtaining Che's uncensored diary of the guerrilla war in Cuba and discovering more or less where Che's body was buried in Bolivia . . . genuinely gripping." —*Harper's*

"[Anderson] manages to reflect his subject's 'special gleam,' the mix of qualities that made the Argentine-born adventurer irresistible to those of his contemporaries bent upon the violent overthrow of governments, and a durable icon for succeeding generations of revolutionaries. *Che Guevara* is the best treatment of its subject to date . . . because the patient reader can distill from it a vivid sense of Che the man." —*The Philadelphia Inquirer*

"Exhaustive and convincing." —*The New York Review of Books*

Che Guevara

The Guvnor

Che Guevara

A REVOLUTIONARY LIFE

Revised Edition

Jon Lee Anderson

Grove Press
New York

Published simultaneously in Canada
Printed in the United States of America

FIRST REVISED EDITION

ISBN-13: 978-0-8021-4411-9

Grove Press
an imprint of Grove/Atlantic, Inc.
154 West 14th Street
New York, NY 10011

Distributed by Publishers Group West

www.groveatlantic.com

22 23 24 25   15 14 13 12 11 10

For Erica

And in memory of my mother,
Barbara Joy Anderson,
1928–1994

Contents

Contents

Che Guevara

Ernesto "Che" Guevara, 1960.

Introduction to the Revised Edition

I became interested in Che Guevara in the late 1980s, while researching a book about modern-day guerrillas. Nearly a generation had elapsed since the poster bearing Alberto Korda's portrait of Che in the black beret with the star pin first adorned so many college dorm walls. That era had drawn to a raggedy end with the demise of the student protest movement, when the Vietnam War was over. But in the insurgent backwoods of Burma, El Salvador, the Western Sahara, and Afghanistan, Che endured as a role model and as an almost mystical symbol of veneration. He inspired new generations of fighters and dreamers because of the revolutionary principles he represented—fearlessness, self-sacrifice, honesty, and devotion to the cause.

There were few books about Che still in print then. Most were twenty years old and were either official Cuban hagiographies or equally tiresome demonizations written by his ideological foes. Che's life had yet to be written because much of it was still cloaked in secrecy, not least the mysterious circumstances of his final hours in Bolivia in 1967. Even the whereabouts of his body was unknown.

Who was this man who had given up everything he cherished in order to fight and die on a foreign battlefield? At the age of thirty-six he left behind his wife and five children and his ministerial position and commander's rank in order to spark off new revolutions. And what had compelled a well-born, intellectual Argentinian with a medical diploma to try to change the world in the first place? Unravelling the mysteries of Che's life story would shed light on some of the most fascinating episodes of the Cold War and bring into sharper focus one of its central characters.

It seemed to me that the answers to most of the questions about Che lay in Cuba, and in 1992 I went to Havana, where I met with his widow, Aleida March. I told her of my plan to write a biography of her late husband,

and I asked for her cooperation and assistance. She eventually agreed. A few months later I moved to Havana with my wife and three young children for a stay that stretched into nearly three years. It was a bleak moment for Cubans. The Soviet Union had suddenly ceased to exist, bringing to an abrupt end the generous financial subsidies that had sustained Cuba for the past three decades. But even as his country's economy disintegrated, Fidel Castro held the social-ist banner stubbornly aloft and, invoking Che's example, demanded revolu-tionary fortitude and sacrifices from his countrymen.

The biggest challenge for me was to break through the sanctimonious atmosphere that surrounded Che's memory. Che was virtually the patron saint of Cuba, and the reminiscences of people who had once known him were often cravenly laudatory or unabashedly politically deterministic. It wasn't until I spent several months roaming around Argentina in the com-pany of Che's boyhood friends that the man—the young Che Guevara— began to emerge as a believable figure. Finally, back in Havana, I was given privileged access to some of his then unpublished diaries, which helped ex-plain the boy's transfomation into the legendary Che.

One morning in November 1995, when I was in Bolivia to interview everyone I could find who had had anything to do with Che's guerrilla ef-forts there, I went to Santa Cruz to see Mario Vargas Salinas, a retired gen-eral in his early fifties. As a young army officer in 1967, Vargas Salinas became famous for leading an ambush on the Masicuri River that wiped out Che's second column. Che's German companion, Tania, and eight other fighters were killed. The massacre on the Masicuri marked the beginning of the end for Che. A little over a month later, on October 8, 1967, he was cornered in a canyon by a large number of army troops. Che was wounded and taken captive. The next day, on the orders of the Bolivian military high command, and in the presence of a CIA agent, he was shot dead. After an-nouncing that Che had died in battle, the army displayed his body to the public for a day in the nearby town of Vallegrande. Photographs were taken of the shirtless, bullet-riddled corpse. Che lay on his back with his head propped up, his eyes open. A resemblance to images of the dead Christ was apparent to everyone. That night, Che's body, and those of several of his comrades, vanished. His enemies intended to deny him a burial place where admirers might pay homage. One army officer later said, vaguely, that Che's body had been tossed out of an airplane into the jungle. Another officer claimed that the corpse had been incinerated.

Mario Vargas Salinas turned out to be an unusually amiable and can-did man. We ended up spending over three hours talking in his walled gar-den in Santa Cruz, and I discovered that he was willing to discuss subjects that were controversial. At one point he acknowledged that his soldiers had executed one of Che's wounded fighters. Vargas Salinas's frankness prompted me to ask him about Che's body, although I did not really expect an honest answer. I was stunned when he replied that he wanted to come clean with the past. He said that after Che was killed, his hands were amputated. Fingerprints were made to preserve physical proof of the body's identity, and the hands were placed in formaldehyde and hidden away. Then a nocturnal burial squad, which Vargas Salinas was part of, secretly dumped the bodies of Che and several of his comrades into a mass grave. The grave had been bulldozed into the dirt airstrip at Vallegrande.

When I wrote an article about Vargas Salinas's confession for *The New York Times,* the effect in Bolivia was both immediate and dramatic. President Gonzalo Sanchez de Lozada said he had heard that I had invented the whole story after getting Vargas Salinas drunk. Vargas Salinas, meanwhile, went into hiding and issued a statement denying everything. At a press conference in La Paz, I pointed out that I had a tape recording of the interview and suggested that the former general might be under duress of some sort. Vargas Salinas soon recanted his statement and verified the accuracy of my story, but he remained in hiding. Then, in a remarkable turnaround, President Sanchez de Lozada announced that he was reversing decades of official secrecy, and he ordered that a commission be formed to look for the bodies.

Over the weeks to come, the spectacle of former guerrillas, soldiers, and forensic experts digging holes in and around Vallegrande opened many old wounds and revealed the nastier details of an era in which Bolivia's powerful military had gotten away, quite literally, with murder. From the 1960s and into the 1980s, a succession of dictators had run the country. Under their hamfisted and often brutal rule, hundreds of citizens had been "disappeared." Now, encouraged by the hunt for Che Guevara's body, people began clamouring for justice and for information about their loved ones. There were also angry demonstrations by former soldiers who had fought against Che's band as youthful conscripts, men who in some cases had suffered grievous wounds and received no disability pensions, or any pensions at all. They too demanded their rights.

The past had been stirred up. Bolivia's military chiefs complied with the president's order, but they were furious with Vargas Salinas over his betrayal. He was flown into Villegrande on a small plane, and as he strolled around the airstrip, flanked by two unsmiling army generals, a scrum of reporters crowded close to him. After about thirty minutes, he declared that he could not pinpoint Che's burial spot. It had been "too many years." He and his escorts then climbed back into their plane and flew away. Days later, word spread that the army had placed Vargas Salinas under house arrest. It was several years before he was heard from again.

The search effort in Vallegrande yielded nothing at first. After several fruitless weeks, the generals in charge of the commission made it clear they wanted to stop looking, and they headed off to La Paz to make their case to the president. A few hours after they left, however, some local peasants, who had until then been too terrified to come forward, revealed the location of a burial site they had known about for years. It was a lonely spot in the forest a couple of miles out of town. It did not take long to confirm what they said. There, in several shallow graves, lay the remains of four of Che's comrades.

The eleventh-hour discovery put an end to the military's brinksmanship. The search resumed with renewed vigor, but, before long, the trail went cold again. It wasn't for another sixteen months, in July 1997, that Che's skeleton was finally discovered by a Cuban-Argentine forensic team. The thirty-year conspiracy of deception was finally over. The skeleton lay together with six others at the bottom of a pit dug under the Vallegrande airstrip—just as Vargas Salinas had said. Che was stretched out full length at the base of the pit, face up, as if special care had been taken in laying him there. The other bodies had been dumped in a promiscuously tangled heap next to him. Che's hands had been amputated at the wrists.

The remains were exhumed and placed in coffins and flown to Cuba, where they were received in an emotional private ceremony that included Fidel and Raúl Castro. Three months later, on October 10, 1997, at the beginning of a week of official mourning in Cuba, Fidel and Raúl paid their respects formally. The coffins of Che and his six comrades lay in state at the José Martí monument, an obelisk in the center of the Plaza de la Revolución in Havana. For the next few days, an estimated 250,000 people waited in line for hours to file past. Children left letters to Che. Weeping men and women recited poems and sang revolutionary songs. Then the flag-draped coffins were driven slowly in a motorcade to the city of Santa Clara, which Che had conquered in the final and most decisive battle of Cuba's revolutionary war, almost forty years earlier. He and his comrades were interred there in a mausoleum that had been built to honor the Heroic Guerrilla.

I revised this edition of my book on the fiftieth anniversary of the Cuban revolution. It seemed a fitting moment to polish and refresh Che's biography and to think about what he means to a new generation of readers. His surviving comrades are old men now, and Cuba is nearing the end of an era. For better or for worse, the revolution is part of Che's legacy, although he has already transcended it.

Che's face and his name have been emblazoned on snowboards and wristwatches and millions of T-shirts. But what, exactly, does the mythologized and commodified Che represent? More often than not, whatever the image signifies has little to do with Che himself. The resurrected Che Guevara—handsome and long-haired, with flashing eyes—is in many ways as unreal as the virtual heroes and villains of a video game. The real Che Guevara, who was only thirty-nine when he died, has been both canonized and demonized. However much the facts of his life are documented, I suspect that his paradoxes and his place in popular culture will ensure that that is always so. But neither school of opinion will ever be able to claim him entirely.

Part One
Unquiet Youth

I

A Plantation in Misiones

I

The horoscope was confounding. If Ernesto "Che" Guevara had been born on June 14, 1928, as stated on his birth certificate, then he was a Gemini—and a lackluster one at that. The astrologer doing the calculations, a friend of Che's mother, repeated her work and got the same result. The Che who emerged from her analysis was a gray, dependent personality who had lived an uneventful life. But this was in the early 1960s, and Che was already one of the most famous people in the world. He had been on the cover of *Time* magazine. He was a highly visible, charismatic figure renowned for his independent spirit.

When the puzzled astrologer showed Che's mother the dismal horoscope, she laughed. Then she confided a secret she had guarded closely for more than three decades. Her son had actually been born one month earlier, on May 14. He was no Gemini, but a headstrong and decisive Taurus. The deception had been necessary, she explained, because she was three months' pregnant when she married Che's father. Immediately after their wedding, the couple had left Buenos Aires for the remote jungle backwater of Misiones, 1,200 miles up the Paraná River, on Argentina's northern border with Paraguay and Brazil. There, as her husband set himself up as a *yerba mate* planter, she went through her pregnancy away from the prying eyes of Buenos Aires society. A doctor friend falsified the date on the birth certificate, moving it back by one month to help shield them from scandal.

When their son was a month old, the couple notified their families. They said that they had tried to reach Buenos Aires, and that Che's mother had gone into labor prematurely. A baby born at seven months, after all, is not unusual. There may have been doubts, but their story and their child's official birth date were quietly accepted.

It seems fitting that a man who spent most of his adult life engaged in clandestine activities and whose death involved a conspiracy should have begun life with a subterfuge.

II

In 1927, when Ernesto Guevara Lynch met Celia de la Serna, she had just graduated from an exclusive Catholic girls' school, Sacré Coeur, in Buenos Aires. She was a dramatic-looking young woman of twenty with an aquiline nose, wavy dark hair, and brown eyes. Celia was well read but unworldly, devout but questioning. Ripe, in other words, for a romantic adventure.

Celia de la Serna was a true Argentine blue blood of undiluted Spanish noble lineage. One ancestor had been the Spanish royal viceroy of colonial Peru; another a famous Argentine military general. Her paternal grandfather had been a wealthy landowner, and Celia's own father had been a renowned law professor, congressman, and ambassador. Both he and his wife died while Celia was still a child, leaving her and her six brothers and sisters to be raised by a guardian, a religious aunt. The family had conserved its revenue-producing estates, and Celia was due a comfortable inheritance when she reached the age of twenty-one.

Ernesto Guevara Lynch was twenty-seven. He was moderately tall and handsome, with a strong chin and jaw. The glasses he wore for astigmatism gave him a clerkish appearance that was deceptive, for he had an ebullient, gregarious personality, a hot temper, and an outsize imagination. He was the great-grandson of one of South America's richest men, and his ancestors included members of both the Spanish and the Irish nobility, although over the years his family had lost most of its fortune.

In the mid-nineteenth century, when Argentina was controlled by the tyrannical warlord Juan Manuel de Rosas, the male heirs of the wealthy Guevara and Lynch clans fled Argentina to join the California gold rush. After returning from exile, their American-born offspring, Roberto Guevara Castro and Ana Isabel Lynch, married. Ernesto, who would become Che's father, was the sixth of Roberto and Ana Isabel's eleven children. The family lived well, but they were no longer landed gentry. While her husband worked as a geographical surveyor, Ana Isabel raised the children in Buenos Aires. They summered at a rustic country house on the slice of the old family seat she had inherited. To prepare Ernesto for a working life, his father sent him to a state-run school, telling him, "The only aristocracy I believe in is the aristocracy of talent."

But Ernesto belonged by birthright to Argentine society. He had grown up on his mother's stories of California frontier life and his father's terrifying tales of Indian attacks and sudden death in the high Andes. His family's illustrious and adventurous past was a legacy too powerful to overcome. He was nineteen when his father died, and although he went to college, studying architecture and engineering, he dropped out before graduation. He wanted to have his own adventures and make his own fortune, and he used his modest inheritance to pursue that goal.

By the time he met Celia de la Serna, Ernesto had invested most of his money with a wealthy relative in a yacht-building company, the Astillero San Isidro. He worked in the company for a time as an overseer, but it was not enough to hold his interest. Soon he became enthusiastic about a new project. A friend had convinced him he could make his fortune by growing *yerba mate,* the stimulating native tea drunk by millions of Argentinians.

Land was cheap in the *yerba*-growing province of Misiones. Originally settled by Jesuit missionaries and their Guaraní Indian converts in the sixteenth century, annexed only fifty years earlier by Argentina, the province was just then opening up to settlement. Land speculators, well-heeled adventurers, and poor European migrants were flocking in. Ernesto went to see it for himself, and caught *yerba mate* fever. His own money was tied up in the yacht-building company, but with Celia's inheritance they would be able to buy enough land for a plantation and, he hoped, become rich from the lucrative "green gold."

Unsurprisingly, Celia's family closed ranks in opposition to her dilettante suitor. Celia was not yet twenty-one, and under Argentine law she needed her family's approval to marry or receive her inheritance. She asked for it, and they refused. Desperate, for by now she was pregnant, she and Ernesto staged an elopement to force her family's consent. She ran away to an older sister's house. The show of force worked. The marriage was approved, but Celia still had to go to court to win her inheritance. She was granted a portion of it, including title to a cattle and grain-producing *estancia* in central Córdoba province, and some cash bonds from her trust fund— enough to buy the *mate* plantation in Misiones.

On November 10, 1927, Celia and Ernesto were wed in a private ceremony at the home of her sister Edelmira Moore de la Serna. *La Prensa* of Buenos Aires gave the news in its "Día Social" column. Immediately afterward, they fled the city for the wilderness of Misiones. "Together we decided what to do with our lives," Ernesto wrote in a memoir published years later. "Behind lay the penitences, the prudery and the tight circle of relatives and friends who wanted to impede our marriage."

III

In the Argentina of 1927, political and social change seemed inevitable, but had not yet come. Charles Darwin, who had witnessed the atrocities perpetrated against Argentina's native Indians by Juan Manuel de Rosas, had predicted that "the country will be in the hands of white Gaucho savages instead of copper-coloured Indians. The former being a little superior in education, as they are inferior in every moral virtue." But while the blood flowed, Argentina spawned a pantheon of civic-minded heroes, from General José de San Martín, the country's liberator in the struggle for independence from Spain, to Domingo Sarmiento, the crusading journalist, educator, and president. Sarmiento's *Facundo,* published in 1845, was a clarion call to his compatriots to choose the path of civilized man over the brutality of the archetypal Argentine frontiersman, the gaucho. Yet even Sarmiento had wielded a dictator's authority. Caudillismo, the cult of the strongman, would remain a feature of politics well into the next century, as governments swung back and forth between caudillos and democrats. Indeed, there was an unreconciled duality in the Argentine temperament. Argentinians were in a state of perpetual tension between savagery and enlightenment. At once passionate, volatile, and racist, they were also expansive, humorous, and hospitable.

In the late nineteenth century, when the conquest of the southern pampas was finally secured after an officially sponsored campaign to exterminate the native Indian population, vast new lands had opened up for colonization. The pampas were fenced in as grazing and farming lands; new towns and industries sprang up; railroads, ports, and roads were built. By the turn of the twentieth century, the population of Argentina had tripled, swollen by the influx of more than a million immigrants from Italy, Spain, Germany, Britain, Russia, and the Middle East who had poured into the rich southern land of opportunity. A dismal colonial garrison on the vast Río de la Plata estuary only a century before, the city of Buenos Aires now had a melting pot's combustive quality, epitomized by the sensuous new culture of tango. The dark-eyed crooner Carlos Gardel gave voice to a burgeoning national pride.

Ships carried Argentina's meat, grains, and hides off to Europe while others docked, bringing American Studebakers, gramophones, and the latest Paris fashions. The city boasted an opera house, a stock exchange, and a fine university; rows of imposing neoclassical public buildings and private mansions; landscaped green parks with shade trees and polo fields, as well as ample boulevards graced with heroic statues and sparkling fountains. Electric streetcars rattled and zinged along cobbled streets past elegant *confiterías* and *wiskerías* with gold lettering on etched glass windows. In their mirrored and marble interiors, haughty white-jacketed waiters with slicked-down hair posed and swooped.

But while Buenos Aires's *porteños,* as they called themselves, looked to Europe for their cultural references, much of the interior still languished. In the north, despotic provincial caudillos held sway over vast expanses of cotton- and sugar-growing lands. Diseases such as leprosy, malaria, and even bubonic plague were still common among their workers. In the Andean provinces, the indigenous Quechua- and Aymara-speaking Indians known as *coyas* lived in extreme poverty. Vigilante justice and indentured servitude were features of life in much of the hinterland.

For decades, two parties, the Radical and the Conservative, were in power. Hipólito Yrigoyen, the Radical who was reelected president in 1928, the year Ernesto and Celia's first child was born, was an eccentric, sphinxlike figure who rarely spoke or appeared in public. Workers still had few rights, and strikes were often suppressed by gunfire and police batons. Criminals were transported by ship to serve terms of imprisonment in the cold southern wastes of Patagonia. But—with immigration and twentieth-century political changes—feminists, socialists, anarchists, and now Fascists were making their voices heard. New ideas had arrived.

IV

With Celia's money, Ernesto had bought about 500 acres of jungle along the banks of the Río Paraná. On a bluff overlooking the coffee-colored water and the dense green forest of the Paraguayan shore, they erected a roomy wooden house on stilts, with an outdoor kitchen and outhouse. They were a long way from the comforts of Buenos Aires, but Ernesto was enraptured. With an entrepreneur's eager eye, he looked into the jungle around him and saw the future.

Perhaps he believed he could restore the family fortunes by intrepidly striking out into new and unexplored lands. Whether or not he was consciously emulating his grandfathers' experiences, it is clear that for Ernesto, Misiones provided an adventure. It was not just another backward Argentine province to him, but a thrilling place full of "ferocious beasts, dangerous work, robbery and murders, jungle cyclones, interminable rains and tropical diseases." He wrote that "in mysterious Misiones . . . everything attracts and entraps. It attracts like all that is dangerous, and entraps like all that is passionate. There, nothing was familiar, not its soil, its climate, its vegetation, nor its jungle full of wild animals, and even less its inhabitants. . . . From the moment one stepped on its shores, one felt that the safety of one's life lay in the machete or revolver."

Their homestead was in Puerto Caraguataí. A *caraguatí* is a beautiful red flower in the Guaraní language. This *puerto,* however, was just a small wooden jetty. Caraguataí was reached by a two-day river journey up from the old trading port of Posadas. They traveled on the *Ibera,* a Victorian paddle-wheel steamer that had done prior service carrying British colonials up the Nile. The nearest outpost was the small German settlers' community of Montecarlo, five miles away, but the Guevaras found they had a friendly neighbor, Charles Benson, a retired English railway engineer who lived a few minutes' walk through the forest. Benson was an avid angler, and just above the river he had built himself a white, rambling bungalow with an indoor water closet imported from England.

For a few months, the couple had an enjoyable time settling in and exploring the area. They fished, boated, rode horses with Benson, and drove into Montecarlo on their mule-drawn buggy. To eight-year-old Gertrudis Kraft, whose parents ran a little hostel on the Montecarlo road, the Guevaras appeared to be, as she recalled many years later, "rich and elegant people." Their rustic home by the river was a mansion to her.

The Guevaras' honeymoon idyll, such as it was, did not last long. Within a few months, Celia's pregnancy was well advanced and it was time to return to civilization, where she could give birth in greater comfort and security. The couple set out downriver. Their journey ended in Rosario, an important Paraná port city of 300,000 inhabitants, where Celia went into labor and where their son Ernesto Guevara de la Serna was born. His doctored birth certificate, drawn up at the civil registrar's office, was witnessed by a cousin of his father who lived in Rosario and a Brazilian taxi driver evidently drafted at the last minute. The document says the baby was delivered at 3:05 A.M. on the morning of June 14, in his parent's "domicile" on Calle Entre Ríos 480.*

The Guevaras remained in Rosario while Celia recovered from the delivery of the baby they called Ernestito. They rented a spacious, three-bedroom apartment with servants' quarters in an exclusive new residential building near the city center, at the address given on the birth certificate. Their stay was prolonged when the baby contracted bronchial pneumonia. Ernesto's mother, Ana Isabel Lynch, and his unmarried sister Ercilia came to help out.

V
After a whirlwind round of visits with their families in Buenos Aires to show off their infant son, the Guevaras returned to the homestead in Misiones.

*See Notes section regarding birth date.

Ernesto now made a serious attempt to get his plantation off the ground. He hired a Paraguayan foreman, or *capataz,* named Curtido, to oversee the clearing of his land and the planting of the first crop of *yerba mate.*

Loggers and owners of *yerbatales* in Misiones usually hired itinerant Guaraní Indian laborers called *mensu,* who were given binding contracts and advances against future work. It was a form of labor bondage. *Mensu* received not cash but private bonds, valid only to purchase basic essentials at the overpriced plantation stores. Their wages were low, and the system virtually ensured that they could never redeem their original debts. Armed plantation guards called *capangas* kept vigilant watch over the work crews to prevent escapes, and violent deaths by gunshot and machete were frequent occurrences. *Mensu* who escaped the *capangas* but fell into the hands of police were invariably returned to their *patrones.* Ernesto Guevara Lynch was horrified at the stories he heard about the fate of the *mensu,* and he paid his workers in cash. It made him a popular *patrón.* Many years later he was remembered by local workers as a good man.

While Ernesto worked his plantation, his young son was learning how to walk. Ernesto would send him to the kitchen with a little pot of *yerba mate* to give the cook. Whenever he stumbled along the way, Ernestito would angrily pick himself up and carry on. Another routine developed as a consequence of the pernicious insects that infested Caraguataí. Every night, when Ernestito lay sleeping in his crib, Ernesto and Curtido crept quietly into his room. While Ernesto trained a flashlight on the boy, Curtido carefully used the burning tip of his cigarette to dislodge the day's harvest of chiggers burrowed into the baby's flesh.

In March 1929, Celia became pregnant again. She hired a young Galician-born nanny, Carmen Arias, to look after Ernestito, who was not yet a year old. Carmen proved to be a welcome addition to the family; she would live with the Guevaras until her own marriage eight years later, and she remained a lifelong family friend. Freed from having to mind her child, Celia began taking daily swims in the Paraná. She was a good swimmer, but one day, when she was six months' pregnant, the river's current caught her. She would probably have drowned if two of her husband's axmen clearing the forest nearby hadn't seen her and thrown out liana vines to pull her to safety.

Ernesto Guevara would recall, reprovingly, many such near-drowning episodes involving Celia in the early years of their marriage. Their very different personalities had already begun to collide. She was aloof, a loner, and seemingly immune to fear, while he was an emotionally needy man who liked having people around him, a chronic worrier whose vivid imagination magnified the risks he saw lurking everywhere. But while the early signs of their future marital discord were in evidence, the couple had not yet pulled apart. The Guevaras took family excursions together: horseback rides on forest trails, with Ernestito riding on the front of his father's saddle; and river excursions aboard the *Kid,* a wooden launch with a four-berth cabin that Ernesto had built at the Astillero San Isidro. Once, they traveled upriver to the famous Iguazú falls, where the Argentine and Brazilian borders meet, and watched the clouds of vapor rise from the brown cascades that roar down from the virgin jungle cliffs.

In late 1929, the family packed up once more for the long trip downriver to Buenos Aires. Their land was cleared and their *yerbatal* had just been planted, but Celia was about to give birth to their second child, and Ernesto's presence was urgently needed at the Astillero San Isidro. During his absence, business had gone badly, and now one of the company's investors had withdrawn. They planned to be away only a few months, but they would never return as a family to Puerto Caraguataí.

VI

Back in Buenos Aires, Ernesto rented a bungalow on the grounds of a large colonial residence owned by his sister María Luisa and her husband, located conveniently near his troubled boatbuilding firm in the residential suburb of San Isidro. They had not been there long when Celia gave birth, in December, to a little girl named after her. For a time, while Ernesto went to work at the shipyard, family life revolved around outings to the San Isidro Yacht Club, near the spot where the Paraná and Uruguay rivers join to form the Río de la Plata estuary.

The yacht-building company was on the edge of bankruptcy, purportedly because of the incompetence of Ernesto's second cousin and business partner, Germán Frers. For Frers, who was independently wealthy and a sailing regatta champion, the shipyard was a labor of love. Such was his enthusiasm for nautical works of art that he had poured money into fine craftsmanship and expensive imported materials, which often cost the company more than the agreed-to selling prices of the boats it produced. Ernesto's investment was in serious risk of evaporating. Then, soon after his return, a fire destroyed the shipyard. Boats, timber, and paint all went up in flames.

If the shipyard had been covered by insurance, the fire might have been a fortunate event. But Frers had forgotten to pay the insurance premium, and Ernesto lost his inheritance overnight. All he had left from his investment was the launch *Kid.* As partial compensation, Frers gave Ernesto the *Alá,* a twelve-meter motor yacht. The *Alá* was worth something, and Ernesto and Celia still had their Misiones plantation, which Ernesto had placed in the hands of a family friend to administer in his absence. It was hoped that they would soon see annual revenues from its harvests. In the meantime, they had the income from Celia's Córdoba estate. Between them, they had plenty of family and friends. They weren't going to starve.

In early 1930, Ernesto certainly didn't seem unduly worried about the future. For some months he lived the sporting life, spending weekends cruising with friends aboard the *Alá,* picnicking on the myriad islands of the delta upriver. In the hot Argentine summer (November to March), the family spent the days on the beach of the San Isidro Yacht Club, or visited rich cousins and in-laws on their country *estancias*.

One day in May 1930, Celia took her two-year-old son for a swim at the yacht club, but it was already the onset of the Argentine winter, cold and windy. That night, the little boy had a coughing fit. A doctor diagnosed him as suffering from asthmatic bronchitis and prescribed the normal remedies, but the attack lasted for several days. Ernestito had developed chronic asthma, which would afflict him for the rest of his life and irrevocably change the course of his parents' lives.

Before long, the attacks returned and became worse. The boy's bouts of wheezing left his parents in a state of anguish. They desperately sought medical advice and tried every known treatment. The atmosphere in the home became sour. Ernesto blamed Celia for imprudently provoking their son's affliction, but he was being less than fair. Celia herself was highly allergic and suffered from asthma. In all likelihood, her son had inherited the same propensity. His siblings also developed allergies, although none was to suffer as severely as he did. Exposure to the cold air and water had probably only activated his symptoms.

Whatever its cause, the boy's asthma ruled out a return to the damp climate of Puerto Caraguataí. It was also evident that even San Isidro, so close to the Río de la Plata, was too humid for him. In 1931, the Guevaras moved again, this time into Buenos Aires itself, to a fifth-floor rented apartment near Parque Palermo. They were close to Ana Isabel, Ernesto's mother, and his sister Beatriz, who lived with her. Both women showered affection on the sickly boy.

Celia gave birth for the third time in May 1932, to another boy. He was named Roberto after his California-born paternal grandfather. Little Celia was now a year and a half old, taking her first steps, and four-year-old Ernestito was learning how to pedal a bicycle in Palermo's gardens.

For Ernesto Guevara Lynch, his elder son's illness was a kind of curse. "Ernesto's asthma had begun to affect our decisions," he recalled in his memoir. "Each day imposed new restrictions on our freedom of movement and each day we found ourselves more at the mercy of that damned sickness." Doctors recommended a dry climate to stabilize the boy's condition, and the Guevaras traveled to the central highlands of Córdoba province. For several months, they made trips back and forth between the provincial capital of Córdoba, Argentina's second-most important city, and Buenos Aires, living briefly in hotels and temporarily rented houses, as Ernestito's attacks calmed, then worsened again, without any apparent pattern. Unable to attend to his affairs or get a new business scheme going, Ernesto senior became increasingly frustrated. He felt "unstable, in the air, unable to do anything."

Doctors urged them to stay in Córdoba for at least four months to ensure Ernestito's recovery. A family friend suggested they try Alta Gracia, a spa town in the foothills of the Sierras Chicas, a small mountain range near Córdoba. It had a fine, dry climate that had made it a popular retreat for people suffering from tuberculosis and other respiratory ailments. Thinking of a short stay, the family moved to Alta Gracia, little imagining it would become their home for the next eleven years.

2

The Dry Climate of Alta Gracia

I

In the early 1930s, Alta Gracia was an appealing little resort town of several thousand people, surrounded by farms and unspoiled countryside. The mountain air there was fresh, pure, and invigorating. At first, the family stayed in the Hotel de La Gruta, a German-run sanatorium on the outskirts of town. The Hotel de La Gruta took its name from a nearby chapel and grotto built to venerate the Virgin of Lourdes. Most of its clients suffered from lung ailments.

Life in Alta Gracia was an extended holiday for Celia and the children. She took them on hikes to swimming holes or on mule rides and began meeting the locals. Her husband didn't go with them. As their funds began to dwindle, his sense of frustration at being unable to work deepened to despair. He felt isolated, hemmed in by the surrounding hills. He suffered from insomnia. During the long nights awake in the hotel, he grew increasingly depressed.

Young Ernesto's asthma improved in Alta Gracia, but he still had attacks, and the Guevaras' concern for his health would continue to chart their path as a family, dominating their lives to an extraordinary degree. Before long, they had decided to stay on in Alta Gracia indefinitely. The attacks had become intermittent rather than the chronic affliction they had been in Buenos Aires. Ernestito was now a lively, willful five-year-old who joined in the *barras,* the gangs of local children who played games of trench warfare and cops and robbers and rode their bicycles pell-mell down Alta Gracia's hilly streets.

Ernesto Guevara Lynch found an unoccupied villa to rent, on Calle Avellaneda, in the neighborhood of Villa Carlos Pellegrini, only five minutes' walk from the town's social hub, the opulent Sierras Hotel, an imitation

Ernesto Guevara de la Serna with his parents, Ernesto Guevara Lynch and Celia Guevara de la Serna, in Alta Gracia, Argentina, in 1935.

of a landmark Raj hotel in Calcutta. The family's new home was called Villa Chichita. It was a two-story Gothic chalet that Ernesto senior likened to a lighthouse. Virtually surrounded by overgrown fields, it looked out to the sierras on one side and the open yellow plains spreading toward Córdoba on the other.

In January 1934, Celia gave birth to her fourth child, a girl they named Ana María after her paternal grandmother. Although he fought frequently with his sister Celia and his brother, Roberto, young Ernesto would become solicitous of his youngest sister, taking her for walks when she was still a toddler and telling her stories. When his wheezing fatigued him, he rested his weight on her shoulder.

Family photographs show Ernestito as a full-faced, stocky five-year-old with pale skin and unruly dark hair. He was dressed invariably in short pants and sandals with socks, wearing a variety of hats to shield him from the mountain sun. His expressions were private and intense, his moods not easy to capture on camera. In photos taken two years later, he has thinned out, and his face is sallow and drawn, no doubt as a result of a prolonged bout of asthma.

When Ernesto was seven, the Guevaras moved from Villa Chichita to a more comfortable house directly across the lane. Their new home, Villa Nydia, was a one-story chalet shielded by a tall pine tree, with three bedrooms, a study, and servants' quarters. It was set in two and a half acres of land. Their landlord was "El Gaucho" Lozada, the owner of Alta Gracia's church and mission house. During their years in Alta Gracia, the Guevaras would live in several seasonally rented villas, but Villa Nydia was where they lived longest, and it was the place they most considered home. The rent was low, only seventy pesos a month, the equivalent of about twenty dollars. Even so, Ernesto Guevara Lynch, who was broke much of the time, frequently found himself unable to pay it. He was in a real bind. Because of Ernestito's health, he couldn't return to Buenos Aires, but he hadn't been able to find work locally. His main hope for an income had been the Misiones plantation, but the market prices for *yerba mate* had plummeted, and a prolonged drought had adversely affected the revenues from Celia's *estancia* in southern Córdoba province.

Over the coming years, the Guevaras would continue to depend upon the revenues from their farms, but climate and market conditions fluctuated, and the income the farms produced was erratic and generally small. According to both family and friends, it was Celia's money, presumably what remained of her cash bonds, that carried the family through the 1930s. "They were really bad times for us," Ernesto Guevara Lynch wrote in his memoir. "So full of economic difficulties. The children were getting bigger; Ernesto still had his asthma. We spent a lot on doctors and remedies. We had to pay for domestic help, because Celia couldn't manage alone with the kids. There was school, rent, clothes, food, trips. It was all outgoing costs, with little coming in."

But at least some of their economic woes were due to the fact that neither Ernesto nor Celia was practical with money. They insisted on maintaining a lifestyle that was far beyond their means. They gave dinner parties, owned a riding trap and an automobile, and employed three servants. Each summer, depending on the condition of their pocketbook, they spent time at Mar del Plata, the exclusive Atlantic seaside resort favored by Argentina's wealthy, or at Ernesto's mother's *estancia* at Santa Ana de Irineo Portela.

The Guevaras became fixtures of the social scene at the Sierras Hotel. They may not have had money, but they belonged to the right social class and had the right bearing and surnames. The Guevaras had "style." They were blessed with the innate confidence of those born into affluence. Things would turn out all right in the end. When they didn't, friends and family bailed them out. Carlos "Calica" Ferrer, the fun-loving son of a well-to-do lung physician in Alta Gracia who treated young Ernesto's asthma, recalled going on a holiday with the Guevaras one summer. Ernesto Guevara Lynch had brought no money with him, and he asked Calica to lend him the pocket money *his* parents had given him for the vacation.

It was some time before Ernesto senior made good on his newfound social connections in Alta Gracia and obtained paying work. In 1941, using his brother Federico's credentials as an architect and his own as a "master of works and general contractor," he won a contract to expand and improve the Sierras Golf Course. Money came in while the job lasted, but apart from this enterprise there is no record of Ernesto working during the family's long stay in Alta Gracia.

II

Because of his asthma, young Ernesto didn't go to school regularly until he was nearly nine years old. Celia patiently tutored him at home, teaching him to read and write. This period undoubtedly consolidated the special relationship that formed between them. The symbiosis between mother and son was to acquire dramatic resonance in the years ahead as they sustained their relationship through a rich flow of soul-baring correspondence that lasted until Celia's death in 1965. Indeed, by the age of five, Ernesto had begun to reveal a personality that reflected his mother's in many ways. Both enjoyed courting danger; were naturally rebellious, decisive, and opinionated; and developed strong intuitive bonds with other people. Already, Ernesto had

The Guevara family in the Sierras Hotel swimming pool, Alta Gracia, 1936. From left, eight-year-old Ernesto; his father, holding his sister Celia; his mother with Ana María.

his "favorite" parent, and he had favorite relatives as well—his unmarried aunt Beatriz and his paternal grandmother, Ana Isabel. The childless Beatriz was especially fond of Ernesto, and she spoiled him by sending him gifts. One of Ernesto's first letters, in which he tells Beatriz that his asthma has improved, dates from 1933. Obviously written by one of his parents, it was signed laboriously in a five-year-old's scrawl, "Teté." That was Beatriz's pet name for Ernesto, and it had been adopted by the family as his nickname.

Ernesto's asthma continued to be a source of anxiety. Desperate to isolate the causes of his ailment, his parents noted down his daily activities, documenting everything from the humidity and the type of clothing he wore to the foods he ate. In his father's notebook for one of ten-year-old Ernesto's "good days" in November 1938, the entry reads: "Wednesday 15: Semi-cloudy morning—dry atmosphere—he awoke very well. Slept with the window open. Doesn't go to the swimming pool. Eats with a good appetite, the same as previous days. He is fine until five in the afternoon." They changed his bedclothes, as well as the stuffing of his pillows and mattress, removed carpets and curtains from his bedroom, dusted the walls, and banished pets from the house and garden.

In the end, the Guevaras realized that there was no pattern to Ernesto's asthma. The most they could do was find ways to contain it. Having seen that the condition seemed to diminish after he swam, for instance, they joined the Sierras Hotel swimming pool club. Certain foods—such as fish—were permanently banned, and he was placed on strict diets during his attacks. He showed unusually strong self-discipline by adhering to these diets, but once his attacks had subsided, he gorged himself, and became known for his ability to consume huge quantities of food at a single sitting.

Often unable even to walk, and confined to bed for days at a time, Ernesto spent long solitary hours reading books or learning to play chess with his father. During his asthma-free spells, however, he was understandably impatient to test his physical boundaries. It was here, in the physical realm, that he first felt the need to compete. He threw himself into sports, playing soccer, table tennis, and golf. He learned to ride horseback, went shooting at the local target range, swam at the Sierras Hotel or in the dammed-up pools of local streams, hiked in the hills, and took part in organized rock fights between the warring *barras*.

Over her husband's opposition, Celia encouraged these outdoor activities, insisting that their son be allowed to grow up as normally as possible. But the consequences were sometimes disastrous, with Ernesto being carried home prostrate and wheezing by his friends. Such episodes didn't deter the boy from doing exactly the same thing again, however, and this too became a routine over which his father eventually lost all control.

Ernesto Guevara Lynch was never able to discipline his eldest son, and Celia never tried. The result was that the boy became increasingly wild and disobedient. To escape punishment for a transgression, he would run off into the brushy countryside, returning only when his parents' fears for his safety had long since overcome their anger. Carlos Figueroa, a friend whose family had a summer villa just down the street, claimed that Ernesto's escapes to the bush were his way of fleeing his parents' arguments, which Figueroa remembered as "terrible."

Whether the emotional upset caused by these arguments helped provoke young Ernesto's asthma isn't clear, but both family and friends agree that Celia and Ernesto Guevara Lynch began to have regular shouting matches in Alta Gracia. Each of them had an extremely hot temper, and the stories of their domestic disputes are legion. No doubt their perennial economic woes were partly to blame. In Ernesto senior's mind, his inability to find work stemmed ultimately from Celia's "imprudence" and the

Celia Guevara with her children in Alta Gracia, 1937. From left, her daughter Celia, Roberto, Ernesto, and Ana María.

Ernesto and his childhood gang in Alta Gracia in 1939 or 1940. Ernesto is second from the right, in the vest. His younger brother Roberto is at the far right and his sister Ana María is at the far left.

swimming incident at San Isidro, which led to his son's asthma and the move to Alta Gracia. But the real source of the rift, according to Celia's closest friends, was Ernesto Guevara Lynch's affairs with other women— affairs that, in a small place such as Alta Gracia, must have been impossible to conceal. With divorce still not legal in Argentina, or perhaps for the children's sake, the Guevaras stuck it out.

Ernestito's days of running free were finally curbed when Alta Gracia's education authorities visited his parents and ordered them to send him to school. He was now nearly nine years old, and Celia had little choice but to relinquish him. Thanks to her tutoring, he already knew how to read and write, so he was able to skip the first and "upper first" grades of Argentina's primary school system. In March 1937, he entered the second-grade class at the Escuela San Martín. He was nearly a year older than most of his classmates.

Ernesto's grades for the 1938 school year are summed up as "satisfactory" in his report card. He received high marks in history and was said to show "steady improvement" in natural sciences, reading, writing, geography, geometry, morals, and civics, but demonstrated little interest in drawing, organized athletics, music, or dance. His conduct was termed "good" throughout the year, although it was "deficient" in the third semester. This change in behavior coincides with an abrupt change in his attendance. After missing only about four days in the first two semesters, he was out of school for twenty-one days during the third, a lapse probably caused by a prolonged attack of asthma.

Elba Rossi de Oviedo Zelaya, who was the school's headmistress and his third-grade teacher, remembered him as a "mischievous, bright boy, undistinguished in class, but one who exhibited leadership qualities on the playground." Years later, Che told his second wife, Aleida, that Elba Rossi had been a strict disciplinarian and was forever spanking him. One day, facing his customary punishment, he had gotten even with her by placing a brick in his shorts. When she hit him, she hurt her hand instead.

Ernesto was an incorrigible exhibitionist during his primary school years. Whether by inclination or to compensate for his ill health, he developed a fiercely competitive personality, engaging in attention-getting high jinks that confounded adults and awed his peers. His former classmates recalled that he drank ink out of a bottle, ate chalk during class, and climbed the trees in the schoolyard; hung by his hands from a railroad trestle spanning a chasm; explored a dangerous abandoned mine shaft; and played torero with an irascible ram. He and his *barra* companions once went around Alta Gracia shooting out the streetlights with their slingshots. Ernesto and a friend, Juan Míguez, settled a score with a member of a rival gang by defecating onto the ivory keys of his parents' grand piano. And then there was the glorious occasion when Ernesto shot burning firecrackers through an open window into a neighbor's formal dinner party, scattering the guests.

Ernesto's antics earned the Guevaras some local notoriety, but the family stood out in other ways. "Bohemian" is the term most often used to describe their buoyant, disorderly household. They observed few social conventions in their home. Neighborhood youngsters who arrived at teatime or supper were invited to stay and eat, and there were always extra mouths to feed at the dinner table. The Guevara children made friends indiscriminately. They played with the sons of golf caddies and others whose homes were in "lower" Alta Gracia.

It was Celia *madre,* however, who made the greatest impression as a free-thinking individual. Elba Rossi, the headmistress, recalled that Celia set the record for many "firsts" for women in the socially stratified community. She drove a car and wore trousers, for instance. Others cited Celia's smoking of cigarettes as a direct challenge to social norms of the day.

Celia got away with these radical-seeming gestures because of her social standing and her displays of generosity. She regularly drove her own children and their friends to and from school in the family car they had dubbed La Catramina (The Heap), a massive old 1925 Maxwell convertible with a jump seat in back. She inaugurated the practice of giving each child in school a cup of milk by paying for it herself, a custom later adopted by the local school board to ensure that poorer children had some nutrition during the school day.

Unlike most of their neighbors, the Guevaras espoused anticlerical views. Ernesto Guevara Lynch's mother was an atheist, and he had had a secular upbringing. The religiously schooled Celia's views were less certain, and throughout her life she retained a penchant for the spiritual. When they first arrived in Alta Gracia, Celia had attended Sunday Mass, taking the children with her, but according to her husband she did so for "the spectacle" more than out of any residual religious faith.

Yet, for all their libertarian views, the Guevaras shared with many other lapsed Catholics a contradiction between belief and practice, never entirely forsaking the traditional rituals that ensured social acceptance in their conservative society. Although they no longer attended church, the Guevaras had their children baptized as Catholics. Ernestito's godfather was the wealthy Pedro León Echagüe, through whom Celia and Ernesto Guevara Lynch had met, and who had persuaded Ernesto to seek his fortune in Misiones.

By the time Ernesto junior entered school, however, Celia had stopped going to Mass, and the Guevaras asked for their children to be excused from religion classes. Roberto remembered playing after-school soccer games formed by opposing teams of children: those who believed in God and those who didn't. Those who didn't invariably lost because they were so few in number.

Ernesto's fellow students in Alta Gracia recalled, unanimously, his quickness in class, although he was rarely seen studying. He didn't seem to have a competitive urge for grades, and his own were usually mediocre. It was a phenomenon that mystified his father. This theme was a constant refrain during Ernesto's formative years. His father never seems to have understood what made his eldest son tick, just as he never completely understood his wife, Celia. To him, Celia was "imprudent from birth" and "attracted to danger," and she was at fault for passing these traits on to their eldest son. Ernesto Guevara Lynch, meanwhile, who admitted to being "overly cautious," was fretful, and forever worrying about the dangers and risks in life. In some ways, he was the more maternal of the two parents, while Celia was her son's confidante and coconspirator.

Ernesto Guevara Lynch's friends from Alta Gracia all had memories of his tantrums, especially when he perceived an affront to a member of his family. This was something he passed on to his eldest son. Ernestito became uncontrollable with rage if he felt he had been unjustly reprimanded or punished, his father wrote, and he got into frequent fistfights with his *barra* rivals. His temper never left him, but by the time he reached college he had learned to bring it under control, usually substituting a razor-sharp tongue for the threat of physical violence. Only on rare occasions did he strike out physically.

Ernesto senior was an intelligent man, but he looked across a perceptual divide at his wife and son, who were far more intellectually akin. Although he read books of adventure and history, and passed on his love for these works to Ernestito, he had little scholarly patience or discipline. Celia, on the other hand, was an avid reader of fiction, philosophy, and poetry, and it was she who opened their son's mind to these interests.

They would evolve and mature in the coming years, but the character traits that later acquired legendary proportions in the adult Ernesto Guevara were already present in the boy. His physical fearlessness, inclination to lead others, stubbornness, competitive spirit, and self-discipline—all were clearly manifest in the young "Guevarita" of Alta Gracia.

III

Between 1932 and 1935, Paraguay and Bolivia fought an intermittent, bloody conflict over control of the parched *chaco* wilderness shared by the two countries. Ernesto Guevara Lynch followed the Chaco War closely in the newspapers, and because he had spent time among Paraguayans in Misiones, he sided with their country. At one point, he declared that he was willing to take up arms to help defend Paraguay. Caught up in his father's enthusiasm, the eldest son began following the war's progress. Before long, Ernesto senior later recalled, the conflict had found its way into the local children's games, with one side playing at being Paraguayans, their opponents at being Bolivians.

Ernesto Guevara Lynch later sought to portray his son's interest in this war as influential in shaping his political consciousness. This seems unlikely, since Ernesto junior was only seven years old when the war ended. But the adult Che did recall his father's passion for the conflict and, in tones that were both affectionate and sarcastic, told Argentine friends about his father's bombastic threats to join the fighting. For the son, it summed up one of the bittersweet truths about his father, a well-intentioned man who spent his life coming up with schemes, but who rarely managed to achieve anything concrete.

The Spanish Civil War was probably the first political event to impinge significantly on Ernesto Guevara's consciousness. Indeed, its effect was inescapable. Beginning in 1938, as the war in Spain turned in favor of Franco's Fascists, a number of Spanish Republican refugees began arriving in Alta Gracia. Among them were the four González-Aguilar children, who showed up with their mother. Their father, Juan González-Aguilar, the republic's naval health chief, had remained behind at his post but joined them after the fall of Barcelona in January 1939. The children of the two families were roughly the same ages, attended the same school, and sat out religion classes together. For a time the Guevaras shared their home with Celia's eldest sister, Carmen, and her two children while their father, the Communist poet and journalist Cayetano "Policho" Córdova Iturburu, was in Spain covering the war for the Buenos Aires newspaper *Crítica*. When Policho's letters and dispatches arrived in the mail, Carmen read them aloud to the gathered clan, bringing the raw impact of the war home in a way no newspaper article could do.

In the early 1930s, there had been little in Argentina's domestic politics to engage the liberal Guevaras. Argentina had been ruled by a succession of conservative military regimes in coalitions with factions of the traditional "liberal" party, the Unión Cívica Radical, which had splintered and foundered in ineffectual opposition since President Hipólito Yrigoyen's overthrow in 1930. The war for the Spanish Republic, a dramatic stand against the growing threat of international Fascism, was something one could become passionate about.

Ernesto Guevara Lynch helped found Alta Gracia's own little Comité de Ayuda a la Republica, part of a national solidarity network with

Republican Spain, and he befriended the exiled Spanish newcomers. He particularly admired General Jurado, who had defeated Franco's troops and their Italian Fascist allies in the battle for Guadalajara, and who now had to support himself by selling life insurance policies. General Jurado dined with the Guevaras and held them in thrall with war stories. Young Ernesto followed the war by marking the Republican and Fascist armies' positions on a map with little flags. According to family lore, he named the family's pet dog, a schnauzer-pinscher, Negrina—because she was black and in honor of the republic's prime minister, Juan Negrín.

When Hitler invaded Poland in September 1939 and World War II began, the inhabitants of Alta Gracia began choosing sides. Ernesto Guevara Lynch threw his energies into Acción Argentina, a pro-Allies solidarity group. He rented a little office from the Lozada family that was built into the exterior stone wall of the Jesuit mission overlooking Tajamar Lake. He traveled around the province, speaking at public meetings and following up tips about "Nazi infiltration." He and his colleagues feared an eventual Nazi invasion of Argentina and monitored suspicious activities in Córdoba's sizable German community. Now eleven, Ernesto joined the youth wing of Acción Argentina. His father recalled that "all the free time he had outside his playtime and studies, he spent collaborating with us."

In Córdoba, one of the chief targets of concern was the German settlement in the Calamuchita valley, near Alta Gracia. In late 1939, after inflicting damage on British warships in the Atlantic, the crippled German battleship *Admiral Graf Spee* was chased into the Río de la Plata, where its captain scuttled it in the waters off Montevideo. The ship's officers and crew were interned in Córdoba. Ernesto Guevara Lynch recalled that the internees were observed conducting military training exercises with dummy wooden rifles and that trucks loaded with arms from Bolivia were discovered headed for the valley. A German-owned hotel in another town was suspected of providing cover for a Nazi spy ring and of housing a radio transmitter that communicated directly to Berlin.

Alarmed at what they believed to be evidence of a flourishing Nazi underground network in Córdoba, Ernesto Guevara Lynch and his colleagues sent a detailed report to the headquarters of Acción Argentina in Buenos Aires, expecting prompt action to be taken by the pro-Allied administration of President Roberto Ortiz. But Ortiz was in ill health and was effectively replaced in his duties by his vice president, Ramón Castillo, who was strongly pro-Axis. Thus, according to Guevara Lynch, no substantive measures were taken against the Nazi network.

Argentina's ambiguous position throughout the war—it remained officially neutral until the eve of Germany's defeat in 1945—owed as much

Ernesto (on the front fender, third from left) with fellow students. The bus took them from Alta Gracia to the Colegio Nacional Dean Funes, their high school, in Córdoba.

to its economic concerns as to the considerable pro-Axis sentiments within its political and military establishment. Traditionally dependent on Europe as an export market for its beef, grain, and other agricultural products, Argentina was devastated by the wartime blockade. In return for supporting the Allies, the Ortiz administration had sought guarantees for its surplus exports from the United States, which supplied most of Argentina's manufactured goods. But Ortiz was unable to get what the Argentinians considered a fair deal from the United States, and during the Castillo regime Argentina's ultranationalists looked to Germany as a potential new market for Argentine exports and as a military supplier.

     In Ernesto Guevara Lynch's rendition of his wartime activities, there is an inescapable sense of the Walter Mitty in him. He desperately wished for a life of adventure and daring, but he was destined to be, for the most part, at the periphery of the large events of his time. He had trumpeted his willingness to fight for Paraguay, but he had not gone. The Spanish Civil War and World War II gave him new issues to champion, and later he would take up others, but he did so from the sidelines. In the end, it was not these

activities he would be remembered for, but his role as the father of Che
Guevara.

IV

Young Ernesto Guevara became a teenager while war raged abroad and
Argentinian politics grew increasingly volatile. Although his physical development was slow—he remained short for his years and didn't experience a growth spurt until he was sixteen—he was intellectually curious,
questioning, and prone to answering back to his elders. His favorite books
were the adventure stories of Emilio Salgari, Jules Verne, and Alexandre
Dumas.

In March 1942, just before his fourteenth birthday, Ernesto began attending high school, or *bachillerato*. Since Alta Gracia's schools offered only
primary school education, he traveled by bus each day to Córdoba, twenty-
three miles away, to attend one of the best state-run schools, the Colegio
Nacional Dean Funes. One morning someone took a photograph of Ernesto
posed on the front fender of the bus. Impishly grinning into the camera,
wearing a blazer and tie but still in shorts and crumpled kneesocks, he is
surrounded by older students attired in button-down collars, suits, ties, and
trousers.

During the summer holidays in early 1943, the Guevaras moved to
Córdoba. Ernesto Guevara Lynch had found a partner there to launch a
building firm. With Ernesto already commuting to school, and his sister
Celia about to enter a girls' high school in Córdoba, the move from Alta
Gracia seemed a practical choice.

3

The Boy of Many Names

The Guevaras' move to Córdoba was buoyed by a brief upswing in their economic fortunes, although it was also the beginning of the end of their days as a united family. Ernesto and Celia's attempt at a reconciliation resulted in the birth, in May 1943, of their fifth and last child, Juan Martín, who was named for Celia's father, but the strains between them deepened, and by the time they left for Buenos Aires four years later, their marriage would be finished.

As before, according to family friends, the problem was Ernesto's chronic womanizing. "The father had pretensions of being a playboy," Tatiana Quiroga, a friend of the Guevara children, recalled. "But he was a disorderly playboy, because when he worked and earned money, he spent it all . . . on going out with 'young ladies,' on clothes, on stupidities, nothing concrete . . . and the family would get nothing."

Ernesto's business partner in Córdoba was an eccentric architect who was known as the Marqués de Arias because of his extreme height and aloof, aristocratic air. The Marqués came up with the building contracts, usually houses, and Ernesto oversaw their construction. "We lived divinely, and all the money just went; they never thought in terms of investments," Ernesto's elder daughter, Celia, recalled. But before the crunch came, he bought a country chalet in the hills outside Córdoba at Villa Allende and joined Córdoba's exclusive Lawn Tennis Club, where his children swam and learned to play tennis. The Guevaras settled into a two-story rented home at Calle Chile 288, near the end of the street, where it met with Avenida Chacabuco, a boulevard lined with bulbous shade trees known as *palos borrachos*. Across the avenue lay the clipped green expanse and woods of Parque Sarmiento, the city zoo, the Lawn Tennis Club, and beyond, the University of Córdoba.

The Guevara home at Calle Chile retained the free, open atmosphere their friends had so enjoyed in Alta Gracia. Dolores Moyano, a new friend from one of Córdoba's richest families, found it all very exotic. The furniture could barely be seen because of the books and magazines piled everywhere, and there were no fixed mealtimes that she could discern—one just ate when one felt hungry. The children were allowed to ride their bicycles from the street, through the living room, into the backyard.

Dolores soon discovered that the Guevaras exacted a price for their open-house policy. Once they sensed any pomposity, pedantry, or pretense in a visitor, they would tease him or her mercilessly. Young Ernesto led these attacks, and more than once Dolores found herself a target. His mother was just as provocative and could be exceedingly stubborn. His father, on the other hand, seemed immensely likable. Dolores remembered him as a man who exuded warmth and vitality. "He spoke in a booming voice, and was rather absentminded," she wrote later. "Occasionally, he sent the children on errands which he had forgotten by the time they returned."

II

The move to Córdoba coincided with the onset of young Ernesto's adolescence. He began increasingly to assert himself, questioning the values of his bickering parents and forming the first glimmerings of his own worldview.

In his first year at the Colegio Nacional Dean Funes, Ernesto made new friends. The closest of these was Tomás Granado, the youngest of three sons of a Spanish emigré who worked as a railway conductor. At fourteen, Ernesto was still short for his years, but he was now slim instead of stocky. The bigger, huskier Tomás wore his hair stylishly slicked back, but Ernesto had an unfashionable buzz cut that earned him the nickname El Pelao (Baldy), one of several he acquired during his adolescence. (Latin Americans have a propensity for nicknames, and Argentinians, who love wordplay, are especially keen on them.)

Before long, Tomás's older brother Alberto had entered their circle as well. A first-year student of biochemistry and pharmacology at the University of Córdoba, the twenty-year-old Alberto, or Petiso (Shorty), was barely five feet tall and had a huge beaked nose, a barrel chest, and a footballer's sturdy bowed legs. He also possessed a good sense of humor and a taste for wine, girls, literature, and rugby. He and Ernesto were separated by age, but in time their friendship became stronger than that between Ernesto and Tomás.

Alberto Granado was the coach of the local rugby team, Estudiantes, and Ernesto wanted desperately to try out for it, although Alberto was doubtful about his potential. "The first impression wasn't very favorable," Alberto recalled. "He wasn't robust, with very thin arms." But he decided to give the boy a try, and accepted him for training. Soon the wheezing lad was practicing with Estudiantes two evenings a week. He earned a reputation for his fearless attacks on the pitch, which he accomplished by running headlong at the player with the ball, yelling: "Look out, here comes El Furibundo Serna!" (*Furibundo* means furious, and Serna was an abbreviation of his maternal surname.) The war cry led Alberto to give Ernesto a new nickname, Fuser, while Alberto became Mial, for *"mi Alberto."*

Alberto Granado took a special interest in Ernesto. He noticed that often, while his team waited for its turn on the practice field, the boy would sit on the ground reading, his back propped against a light post. Ernesto was already reading Freud, enjoyed the poetry of Baudelaire, and had read Dumas, Verlaine, and Mallarmé—in French—as well as most of Émile Zola's novels, Argentine classics such as Sarmiento's epic *Facundo,* and the latest work of William Faulkner and John Steinbeck. A zealous reader himself, Granado couldn't comprehend how the teenager could have gotten through so much. Ernesto explained that he had begun reading to occupy himself during his asthma attacks, when his parents made him stay at home. As for his reading in French, this was the result of Celia's influence. She had tutored him during his absences from school.

For all their new friends and comforts in Córdoba, Alta Gracia remained dear to the Guevaras, and the family returned there often, sometimes renting cottages during the holidays. Ernesto was able to keep up his friendships with Calica Ferrer, Carlos Figueroa, and other members of his old *barra*. The González-Aguilars had also moved to Córdoba, and they lived in a house not far from the Guevaras.

The new family home on Calle Chile turned out to have some disadvantages that had been overlooked by Ernesto senior in his initial enthusiasm over its proximity to Parque Sarmiento and the Lawn Tennis Club. Their neighborhood of Nueva Córdoba, built on a hill rising up from the city center, was still in the process of being urbanized. It was a hodgepodge of residential homes surrounded by undeveloped vacant lots called *baldíos*. On these lots, and in the dry creeks that ran through the area, poor people had built shanties. One of the shantytowns lay directly across from where the Guevaras now lived. It was inhabited by colorful personalities, among them a man with no legs who rode around on a little wooden cart pulled by a team of six mongrel dogs that he urged on with a long, cracking whip.

Dolores Moyano, who had become a close friend of Ernesto's youngest sister, Ana María, was now a constant visitor in the Guevara household. Moyano recalled that one of their pastimes was to sit on the curb of the "safe

side" of the street and watch the goings-on among the slum dwellers of the
baldío. One of them was a woman in black who nursed her baby under a
paraíso tree and spit phlegm over his head. Another was a dwarfish twelve-
year-old called Quico who had no eyebrows or eyelashes. They bribed him
with sweets to show them his strange white tongue.

Although they were much better off than their poor neighbors in the
hovels of cardboard and tin, the Guevaras soon discovered that their own
home was built on a shaky foundation. Before long, huge cracks began appearing in the walls, and from his bed at night, Ernesto senior could see stars
through a crack in his ceiling. Yet, for a builder, he was remarkably casual
about the dangers. In the children's room, where another crack appeared,
he remedied the situation by moving their beds away from the wall in case
it collapsed. "We found the house comfortable and we didn't want to move,
so we decided to stay as long as we could," he recalled.

The sharp contrasts of urban life may have been new to the Guevaras
but were becoming increasingly typical in Argentina and throughout Latin
America. Since the late nineteenth century, changing economics, immigration, and industrialization had brought about a radical rural-to-urban population shift, as poor farmworkers migrated from the countryside to the cities
in search of jobs and a better way of life. Many of them ended up in the
shantytowns, or *villas miserias,* that sprang up in Córdoba and Argentina's
other large cities. In a span of only fifty years, Argentina's demographics
had reversed completely, from an urban population of 37 percent in 1895 to
63 percent in 1947. During the same period, the population as a whole had
quadrupled from 4 million to 16 million. Despite this ongoing social transformation, Córdoba retained a placid, provincial air in the 1940s. Surrounded by the limitless yellow pampa, its horizons broken only by the blue
ranges of the sierras, Córdoba was still mostly untouched by the industrialization and construction boom that was rapidly turning Buenos Aires into
a modern metropolis.

As the site of the country's first university, founded by Jesuits, and with
many old churches and colonial buildings, Córdoba had earned a reputation as a center of learning, and *cordobeses* were proud of their cultural heritage. The city's leading role in education had been secured in 1918 when
Radical Party students and teachers at the University of Córdoba spearheaded the University Reform movement that guaranteed university autonomy. The movement had spread beyond Córdoba to Argentina's other
universities and throughout much of Latin America. Dolores Moyano recalled the Córdoba of her youth as "a city of bookstores, religious processions, student demonstrations, and military parades; a city gentle, dull,
almost torpid on the surface but simmering with tensions."

Those tensions burst out shortly after the Guevaras arrived. On June 4, 1943, in Buenos Aires, a cabal of military officers banded together and overthrew President Castillo, who had named as his successor a wealthy provincial strongman with ties to British corporate monopolies. Early reaction to the coup was guardedly positive among both liberal Argentines who regarded Castillo's pro-German administration with suspicion and nationalists fearing further encroachment by foreign economic interests.

Within forty-eight hours a leader had emerged: the war minister General Pedro Ramírez, representing the military's ultranationalist faction. Very quickly, he took measures to silence all domestic opposition. Declaring a state of siege, his regime postponed elections indefinitely, dissolved the congress, gagged the press, intervened in the country's universities, and fired protesting faculty members. In a second wave of edicts at the year's end, all political parties were dissolved, compulsory religious instruction in schools was decreed, and even stricter press controls were established. In Córdoba, teachers and students took to the streets in protest. Arrests followed, and in November 1943 Alberto Granado and several other students were imprisoned in Córdoba's central jail, behind the colonnades of the old whitewashed *cabildo* on the city's Plaza San Martín. Granado's brothers and Ernesto visited him there, bringing him food and news of the outside world.

The weeks dragged by, with no sign that the students were to be charged or released any time soon. An underground "prisoners' committee" asked Córdoba's secondary school students to march in the streets and demand that the detainees be freed. Alberto asked the fifteen-year-old Ernesto if he would join, but he refused. He would march, he said, only if given a revolver. He told Alberto that the march was a futile gesture that would accomplish little.

In early 1944, after a couple of months in detention, Alberto Granado was released. Despite Ernesto's refusal to demonstrate on his behalf, their friendship remained intact. In light of his penchant for daredevil stunts, Ernesto's unwillingness to help his friend is striking. And, given his extreme youth and apparent unconcern with Argentine politics, his "principled" stance seems dubious. This paradoxical behavior of making radical-sounding declamations while displaying complete apathy about political activism was a pattern during Ernesto's youth.

III

As yet unknown to most of the public, a key figure behind the political changes taking place in Argentina was an obscure army colonel with a fleshy face and Roman nose whose name—Juan Domingo Perón—would soon be very familiar. After returning from a posting in Mussolini's Italy, where he became a fervent admirer of Il Duce, Perón had briefly been a troop instructor in the province of Mendoza before going to work at military headquarters in Buenos Aires. There, he had made his move as the driving force behind the shadowy military group calling itself the Grupo de Oficiales Unidos, which had launched the coup of June 1943.

Over the next three years, Perón maneuvered his way to the top. After the coup he became undersecretary for war, serving under his mentor, General Edelmiro Farrell. When Farrell became vice president in October 1943, Perón asked for and was given the presidency of the National Labor Department. It quickly became his power base. Within a month, he had transformed his seemingly obscure job into a ministry renamed the Department of Labor and Welfare and was answerable only to the president.

A sweeping series of reformist labor decrees began to flow from Perón's office. The measures were aimed at appealing to disenfranchised workers while organized labor groups linked to the traditional political parties were being destroyed. Before long, Perón had brought the country's workforce to heel under his own centralized authority. The phenomenon that would be known as *peronismo* had begun. Very soon, it would radically alter Argentina's political landscape.

By late 1943, with the United States in the war, Nazi Germany was on the defensive throughout Europe and North Africa, and Mussolini had been overthrown in Italy. Suspecting the Argentine regime, and Perón in particular, of serving as thinly disguised representatives for the Third Reich in Latin America, the United States stepped up pressure on Argentina to abandon its official neutrality in the war. Many Argentines shared the Americans' suspicions. Perón's populist appeals to the social "underclass" in rhetoric reeking of Fascism had alienated Argentina's liberal middle classes. They were joined by the traditional oligarchy, which saw the status quo in danger. Most people of the Guevaras' social class had become virulent *antiperonistas*. But their opposition did not stop Perón from becoming even more powerful.

In March 1944, Farrell became president. Perón was war minister, and by July he was vice president as well. Of the three high-level positions he now held, however, the most important was still his post as Secretary of the Department of Labor and Welfare. Perón was known to everyone in Argentina.

Ernesto Guevara Lynch remained active in Acción Argentina, and he and Celia also joined Córdoba's Comité Pro–De Gaulle, a solidarity network aimed at helping the French Resistance in Nazi-occupied France. Unbeknownst to them, young Ernesto had resumed the old Nazi-hunting activities his father had left unfinished. With a school friend, Osvaldo Bidinost

Payer, he stealthily returned to the small mountain community of La Cumbre, where his father's group had conducted surveillance of the hotel suspected of being the headquarters for Nazi operations in Argentina's interior. Ernesto senior had warned his son against sniffing around, telling him that of the two government investigators sent there, only one had returned, the other presumably having been murdered. But the boys went anyway. They approached the hotel at night. Through an open window, Bidinost recalled later, they caught a glimpse of a couple of men busy at "a long table with lots of metal boxes and things." But before they could see more, their presence was detected. "They heard us, someone came out with lanterns, and they fired two shots at us. We left and never returned."

In spite of such escapades, Ernesto's commitment to political causes fell far short of active militancy during his high school years. He and his friends, who included children of Spanish Republican refugees such as the González-Aguilars, were, like their parents, politically "anti-Fascist," and given to arguing precociously over what had "really happened" in Spain. But they had much less notion of, or even interest in, the events taking place in Argentina at the time. When young Ernesto did espouse a political opinion, it was usually provocative, designed to shock his parents or peers. For instance, when Córdoba's *peronista* militants were rumored to be preparing to attack, with stones, the local Jockey Club, a symbol of the conservative landed oligarchy, Ernesto declared his willingness to join them. "I wouldn't mind throwing some stones at the Jockey Club myself," some of his friends heard him say. They assumed this was a sign of his pro-*peronista* sentiments, but it was just as likely he was being a bloody-minded teenager.

When Argentina's government finally broke off diplomatic relations with the Axis powers, Ernesto's parents were overjoyed. But his young friend Pepe González-Aguilar had never seen Ernestito so angry as the moment when he confronted his celebrating parents. "I couldn't understand how he, who had always been anti-Nazi, didn't share our happiness," he said. Later, Pepe surmised that Ernesto's anger was due to the fact that the decision had been made not on principle, but because of U.S. pressure, and he shared Argentine nationalists' sense of shame that their country had buckled under to the Americans. Nevertheless, when the Allied forces liberated Paris in September 1944, Ernesto joined the celebrating crowd in Córdoba's Plaza San Martín, accompanied by several of his school friends, their pockets stuffed with metal ball bearings, ready to hurl at the hooves of the horses of the mounted police called in to keep order. (In recognition of his own efforts, Ernesto senior received a certificate signed by de Gaulle himself, thanking him for the support he had given to the people of France in their hour of need. For the rest of his life, he kept it with him as one of his proudest possessions.)

Despite some retrospective attempts to see an early hint of socialist ideals in the teenage Ernesto Guevara, virtually all his Córdoba schoolmates recalled him as politically uninterested. To his friend José María Roque, Ernesto didn't have "a defined political ideal" at the time. "We all loved to argue politics, but I never saw Guevara get involved in any sense." Nor did Ernesto let his antifascism get in the way of friendship. One of his classmates was Domingo Rigatusso, a poor Italian immigrant's son who worked after school selling sweets to the patrons of the local cinemas. Rigatusso steadfastly supported Mussolini in the war, as did his father, and Ernesto referred to him affectionately as a *tano fascio,* a slang term meaning "Italian Fascist."

Raúl Melivosky, the son of a Jewish university professor, recalled briefly belonging to a "cell" of the Federación Estudiantil Socialista (FES) with Ernesto in 1943, at a time when the militant youth wing of the pro-Nazi Alianza Libertadora Nacionalista was intimidating students sympathetic to the Allies. Melivosky, who was a year younger than Ernesto and in his first year at the school, had heard about him before they were introduced. Ernesto was pointed out as the only student in school who had stood up in class to a notoriously pro-Nazi history professor over a factual inaccuracy.

When the FES decided to form three-man units as a defensive measure against the students of the Alianza Libertadora Nacionalista, Ernesto was assigned to be the leader of a group that included Melivosky and another first-year student. "We were cells in name only," Melikovsky recalled. "We didn't meet, and practically the only thing we did was to call ourselves cells." But, one afternoon, when he and some other students were blocked from leaving the school grounds by some Alianza bullies who were brandishing penknives embossed with their group's condor insignia, Ernesto hurled himself at the throng, whirling his school satchel around his head. To the grateful Melivosky, Ernesto seemed "more than brave. He was absolutely fearless."

The only other time their "cell" was activated was the day when, making use of his authority as leader, Ernesto ordered Melivosky and the other boy under his tutelage to skip school the following day. It was an exploit that could get them expelled, and Melivosky knew it. "He didn't order us only to skip school, but to go to a movie that was prohibited to minors. We were thirteen and fourteen, and you had to be eighteen, so we weren't going to be able to fool anybody. None of us was very tall or robust. But he ordered us to each come wearing a hat, with a cigarette, and with the money we needed for the tickets."

Such were Ernesto's earliest incursions into "politics." Twenty years later, in a letter to a sycophantic editor who intended to publish a hagiography about him, he wrote, bluntly: "I had no social preoccupations in my adolescence and had no participation in the political or student struggles in Argentina."

IV

Ernesto was now a full-fledged teenager, and along with his voracity for books he had developed a strong curiosity about the opposite sex. He managed to satisfy both interests when he discovered and read the unabridged and highly erotic original edition of *A Thousand and One Nights* at a friend's home.

In the provincial Argentina of the mid-1940s, prevailing values concerning sex and marriage were still very much those of a traditional Catholic society. Women didn't have the right to divorce, and "good" girls were expected to retain their virginity until marriage. "We were little angels," recalled Tatiana Quiroga, who went out with Ernesto and other friends on double dates. "We went to dance, to converse, to drink a coffee, and at twelve-thirty you had to be back, or they would kill you. That was the period when you could barely go out. How could we little girls go to some boy's house, all alone? Never! The most we ever did was to escape the parties and go drink some *mate*."

For sex, boys of Ernesto's social milieu either visited brothels or looked for conquests among girls of a lower class, where their social and economic differences gave them advantages. Their first sexual experience was often with the family *mucama,* the servant girl, usually an Indian or poor mestiza from one of Argentina's northern provinces. Ernesto was introduced to sex when he was fourteen or fifteen. Rodolfo Ruarte and several other youths spied on him during a liaison with "La Negra" Cabrera, the servant girl in the house of Calico Ferrer. The boys watched through the keyhole of the bedroom door. They observed that, while Ernesto conducted himself admirably on top of the pliant maid, he periodically interrupted his lovemaking to suck on his asthma inhaler. The spectacle had them in stitches and remained a source of amusement for years afterward. But Ernesto was unperturbed, and his sessions with La Negra continued as a regular pastime.

Along with his discovery of sex, Ernesto nurtured a love of poetry, and he enjoyed reciting passages he had memorized. With the aid of the seventeenth-century Spanish poet Francisco de Quevedo's *Picaresque Sonnets and Romances,* he began displaying a sense of the ribald. One day, he employed it to effect on a blushing Dolores Moyano. He had overheard her pedantically discussing the poetry of the Spanish-Arab mystics, and when he challenged her knowledge of the topic, she found herself gullibly explaining: "The lover and the mystic in St. John's poetry have this double vision.

The inner eye and the outward eye, the lover-mystic sees both ways. . . ."
At that point, she recalled, Ernesto interrupted her, and affecting an exaggerated Cordoban accent, he recited a profane couplet about a one-eyed nun and a cross-eyed saint.

The incident highlights the schism that existed between male and female adolescents of Guevara's social class and generation. The girls, virginal and innocent, steeped themselves in romantic poetry, saving themselves for true love and marriage, while boys like Ernesto, bursting with hormones, sought out the real world of sex as best they could in bawdy poems and brothels, or by bedding the family *mucamas.*

During the summer holidays of 1945 and 1946, Ernesto's pretty cousin Carmen Córdova Iturburu de la Serna reappeared. She was three years younger than Ernesto, on whom she developed a crush. Carmen's father, the poet Cayetano Córdova Iturburu, always brought a trunkful of newly published books from Buenos Aires with him, and she would rummage through it for books of poetry. It was her passion, one that she found she shared with Ernesto, and he recited to her from Pablo Neruda's *Twenty Poems of Love and a Desperate Song,* which he had recently discovered. "In the full bloom of adolescence, Ernestito and I were a little more than friends," she recalled years later. "One day we were playing on a terrace of my house and Ernesto asked me if I was now a woman. . . ." A lover's tryst ensued, and later on, when the Guevaras moved to Buenos Aires, Ernesto and Carmen continued to see each other. She often stayed in the Guevaras' home, where she recalled romantic interludes with Ernesto in the stairwell, talking "of literature . . . and of love because, as often happens between cousins, we too had our idyll. Ernesto was so handsome!"

And he was. By the age of seventeen, Ernesto had developed into an extremely attractive young man: slim and wide-shouldered, with dark brown hair, intense brown eyes, clear white skin, and a self-contained, easy confidence that made him alluring to girls. "The truth is, we were all a little in love with Ernesto," confessed Miriam Urrutia, another wellborn Córdoba girl.

At an age when boys tend to try hard to impress girls, Ernesto's insouciance regarding appearances was especially compelling. One evening, he showed up with an elegantly attired society girl at the Cine Opera, where his *fascio* friend Rigatusso worked. Ernesto had come dressed, as usual, in an old, oversize trench coat, its pockets stuffed with food and a thermos of *mate.* When he spotted Rigatusso, he pointedly left his date standing on her own while he chatted to his "socially inferior" friend.

Ernesto's devil-may-care attitude, contempt for formality, and combative intellect were all now visible traits of his personality. Even his sense of humor was confrontational, although it was often expressed in a self-mocking guise. His friend Alberto Granado became very familiar with Ernesto's penchant for shocking people. "He had several nicknames," Granado recalled. "They called him El Loco Guevara. He liked to be a little bit of a terrible lad. . . . He boasted about how seldom he bathed, for example. They also called him Chancho [The Pig]. He used to say, 'It's been twenty-five weeks since I washed this rugby shirt.'" One day Ernesto stopped wearing short pants to school and arrived dressed in trousers. No doubt to forestall the ribbing he was bound to receive from the older boys about suddenly growing up, he announced that the reason he wore trousers was that his shorts were so dirty he'd had to throw them away.

Throughout his five years at the Colegio Nacional Dean Funes, Ernesto cultivated the image of an irrepressible rascal. He would wordlessly light up his pungent antiasthma cigarettes in the middle of class and debate openly with his mathematics and literature teachers about inaccuracies he'd caught them in. He organized weekend outings to the outlying mountains or back to Alta Gracia, where he engaged in the same kinds of daredevil stunts that had so horrified his parents when he was a child: balancing on pipelines over steep chasms, leaping from high rocks into rivers, bicycling along train tracks.

Ernesto's behavior was duly noted by the school authorities. On the first of June 1945, his fourth year at Dean Funes, he received "ten admonishments [twenty-five meant expulsion] by rectoral order, for acts of indiscipline and for having entered and left the establishment outside of hours, without the corresponding permission."

His grades, on the whole, were good. They continued to reflect his interest in subjects such as mathematics, natural history, geography, and history, although with each year he showed a gradual improvement in French, Spanish, writing, and music. His extracurricular reading was unabated. His friend Pepe Aguilar noticed, as had Alberto Granado, that Ernesto's tastes were eclectic and often advanced for his years. "He read voraciously, devouring the library of his parents," Aguilar recalled. "From Freud to Jack London, mixed with Neruda, Horacio Quiroga, and Anatole France, even an abbreviated edition of *Das Kapital* in which he made observations in tiny letters." Ernesto found the dense Marxist tome incomprehensible, however. Years later, he confessed to his wife in Cuba that he "hadn't understood a thing" in his early readings of Marx and Engels.

V

In the 1945 school year, a more serious side of Ernesto began to emerge. He took a course in philosophy. It engaged his interest, as his "very good" and "outstanding" grades reveal. He also began writing his own "philosophical dictionary." The first handwritten notebook, 165 pages in length, was ordered alphabetically, and carefully indexed by page number, topic, and author. Consisting of pocket biographies of noted thinkers and a wide range of quoted definitions, its entries include such concepts as love, immortality, hysteria, sexual morality, faith, justice, death, God, the devil, fantasy, reason, neurosis, narcissism, and morality. The quotations on Marxism were culled from *Mein Kampf* and featured passages revealing Hitler's obsession with a Jewish-Marxist conspiracy. For his sketches of Buddha and Aristotle, he used H. G. Wells's *Short History of the World*. Bertrand Russell's *Old and New Sexual Morality* was the source on love, patriotism, and sexual morality. But Sigmund Freud's theories also obviously fascinated him, and Ernesto quoted Freud's *General Theory of Memory* on everything from dreams and libido to narcissism and the Oedipus complex. Jack London provided the gloss on society and Nietzsche on death. For revisionism and reformism, Ernesto drew definitions from a book written by his uncle Cayetano Córdova Iturburu.

This notebook was the first in a series of seven that he continued to work on over the next ten years. He would add new entries and replace older ones as his studies deepened and his interests became more focused. Future notebooks reflected his reading of Jawaharlal Nehru and also his intensified reading on Marxism, quoting not Hitler but Marx, Engels, and Lenin.

Ernesto's choice of fiction began to shift to books with more social content. Indeed, in the opinion of his friend Osvaldo Bidinost Payer, "everything began with literature" for him. Around this time, Osvaldo and Ernesto were reading Faulkner, Kafka, Camus, and Sartre. In poetry, Ernesto was reading the Spanish Republican poets García Lorca, Machado, and Alberti, and the Spanish translations of Walt Whitman and Robert Frost. But his overall favorite remained Pablo Neruda. Among Latin American writers, he had also delved into Ciro Alegría, Jorge Icaza, Rubén Darío, and Miguel Ángel Asturias. Their novels and poetry often dealt with Latin American themes—including the unequal lives of marginalized Indians and mestizos—ignored in fashionable literature and virtually unknown to Ernesto's social group. Bidinost believed that such literature gave Ernesto an inkling of the society he inhabited but did not know firsthand. "It was a kind of advance glimpse of what he wanted to experience, and what was around him was objectively Latin America and *not* Europe or Wyoming."

As Ernesto's friends in Alta Gracia had been, Bidinost was bewitched by the Guevara household's informality and by the influence of Ernesto's mother. The home seemed to shelter a cult of creativity, and of what he called "the discovery of the world through the service entrance." Celia collected all kinds of colorful people, irrespective of their social status. One met itinerant painters who worked as bootblacks, wandering Ecuadorean poets, and university professors, who sometimes stayed a week or a month, depending on their level of hunger. "It was a fascinating human zoo," Bidinost recalled.

While Celia presided over her all-hours salon, Ernesto's father came and went on an old motorbike he had named La Pedorra (The Farter), for the sputtering noise it issued from its exhaust. He and Celia slept in the same house but were estranged, and they lived increasingly separate lives.

Another Córdoba youth who found himself caught up in the Guevara magic was Roberto "Beto" Ahumada, a school friend of Ernesto's brother Roberto. Ahumada recalled many occasions when the family members unblinkingly divided up their meal into smaller portions so that he could join them. "Nobody was worried about eating a little less because one of the kids had brought friends," he said. "They brought who they wanted and nobody cared." Not surprisingly, in this rollicking home replete with children, itinerant guests, and conversation, Ernesto found it difficult to read or study undisturbed, and he acquired the habit of reading for hours on end in the bathroom.

One day, an old childhood *barra* mate named Enrique Martín bumped into Ernesto in Alta Gracia. Enrique was surprised to see him there: it was a weekday, and the school year was not over. Swearing Enrique to secrecy, Ernesto said he had rented a small back room in the Cecil Hotel, near the bus station, a place where nobody knew him. "I'm here to isolate myself from everybody," he said. Exactly what Ernesto wanted isolation for, Enrique Martín didn't ask, and he loyally guarded his friend's secret for many years. Whether Ernesto wanted a place to think and study, or to rendezvous with one of Alta Gracia's promiscuous *mucamas,* remains unknown. In any case, this was clearly not the extroverted madcap Loco, Chancho, or Pelao known to his friends in class and on the rugby pitch, but a distinctly private youth.

VI

By the beginning of 1946, Juan Perón had survived a brief ouster from office by rival military officers and a brief exile on Martín García island in the Rio de La Plata estuary. Then, after a huge popular demonstration demanding his release, he made a triumphant comeback to win the presidency in the general elections.

Perón was no longer on his own. Months earlier he had married his mistress, a young, blond radio actress named Eva Duarte.

Nineteen-forty-six was Ernesto Guevara's final year of high school. He celebrated his eighteenth birthday in June, just ten days after the Peróns assumed office. While continuing with his studies, he also had a paying job for the first time in his life, in the laboratory of Córdoba's Dirección Provincial de Vialidad, a public works office that oversaw road construction in the province. His friend Tomás Granado was with him. The two youths, similarly adept in subjects such as math and science, were already discussing plans to study engineering at the university the following year. They had obtained their jobs, which offered useful practical experience for future engineers, after Ernesto's father asked a friend to allow them into a special course given for field analysts at Vialidad. They successfully passed the course and now they were "soils specialists," examining the quality of materials used by the private companies contracted to build roads. In the lab, where they worked part-time, Ernesto made everyone fruit shakes in the blender used for mixing soils.

When they graduated from Dean Funes, Ernesto and Tomás began working full-time and were assigned to jobs in different parts of the province. Ernesto was sent to inspect the materials going into roadworks at Villa María, ninety miles to the north. His contract came with a modest salary, the use of a company truck, and free lodging.

In March 1947, with Ernesto still in Villa María, his family moved back to Buenos Aires after an absence of fifteen years. It was not a triumphant return. Ernesto senior and Celia had decided to split up, and they were once again in very bad shape economically. Ernesto senior's building business had floundered, and he had been forced to sell the summer house in Villa Allende. Soon he would have to sell the Misiones plantation as well. There was little money coming in from it, and for the last couple of years he had fallen behind in paying the property taxes.

In Buenos Aires, the family moved into the fifth-floor apartment owned by Ernesto senior's ninety-six-year-old mother, Ana Isabel, at the corner of Calles Arenales and Uriburu. In early May, Ana Isabel fell ill, and the Guevaras sent a telegram to Ernesto to advise him of her delicate state. On May 18, he wrote back, asking them to send another telegram with more details of her condition, and saying that if she worsened, he was prepared to resign his job and come immediately to Buenos Aires.

Within days, the bad news came. Ernesto's grandmother had suffered a stroke. He quit his job and raced to Buenos Aires, getting there in time for the deathwatch. He was with her for seventeen days. "We could all see that her illness was fatal," his father wrote. "Ernesto, desperate at seeing that his grandmother didn't eat, tried with incredible patience to get her to take food. He entertained her and didn't leave her side. He remained there until my mother left this world."

When his grandmother died, Ernesto was disconsolate. His sister Celia had never seen her self-contained older brother so grief-stricken. "He was *very* sad," she recalled. "It must have been one of the great sadnesses of his life."

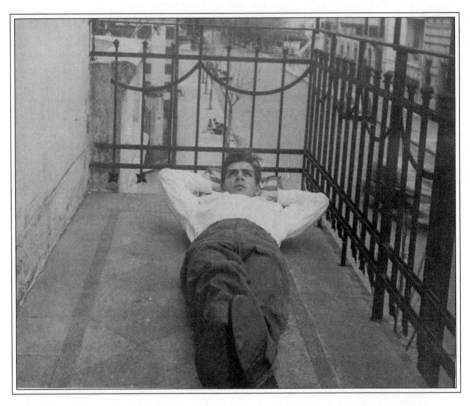

Ernesto on the balcony of his family's home on Calle Araoz in Buenos Aires, 1948 or 1949.

4

His Own Man

I

Immediately after his grandmother's death, Ernesto informed his parents that he had decided to study medicine instead of engineering. He applied for admission to the Faculty of Medicine at the University of Buenos Aires.

The Faculty of Medicine building is an early modern monolith: unremittingly gray, all straight lines and small box windows. Here and there, bronze bas-reliefs on stone tablets depict surgeons operating on patients. A chilly monument to medical science, the building thrusts fifteen stories into the sky in an otherwise elegant district of late-nineteenth-century town houses with vaulted ceilings, ornately grilled balconies, and French windows. It overlooks an open square that is dominated by the handworked dome of an old Catholic chapel.

Ernesto never spelled out his reasons for having chosen a medical career, except to say, years later, that he had been motivated by a desire for a "personal triumph": "I dreamed of becoming a famous researcher . . . of working indefatigably to find something that could be definitively placed at the disposition of humanity." He had shown himself to be adept at sciences, and a career in engineering had been an easy choice, but he wasn't passionately interested in engineering. In medicine, at least, he could do something that was worthwhile. His family thought his decision was due to his frustration at the inability of doctors to lessen the agonies of his dying grandmother. The shock of her death, despite her advanced age, may have helped spur Ernesto's decision to switch careers, but as his choice of specialties soon revealed, he was also obsessed with finding a cure for his own medical condition.

Along with his studies, Ernesto held a number of part-time jobs, but of all of them, the work he did at the Clínica Pisani, an allergy-treatment clinic, was the most absorbing as well as the longest-lasting. He had met Dr. Salvador Pisani as a patient, and his quick intelligence and curiosity led to a post as an unpaid research assistant. It was a privilege for a young medical student to be involved in a new field of medical research. Pisani had pioneered a system for treating allergies with vaccines concocted from partially digested food substances. Ernesto was so pleased with the positive results of his own treatment and his laboratory work that he decided to specialize in allergies.

The Pisani clinic became a kind of surrogate home. Dr. Pisani, his sister Mafalda, and their mother lived together next door, and they quickly developed a strong affection for Ernesto. The women fed him a special diet of carrot juice, corn bread, and oat cakes and put him to bed when he suffered asthma attacks. Ernesto responded favorably to the mothering, and Dr. Pisani began looking upon him as a protégé who might go far one day. To his father, meanwhile, Ernesto became a fleeting figure, always in a hurry, with never enough time. "Active and diligent, he ran from one place to the other to fulfill his obligations," Ernesto senior wrote. "And how could he not be in a hurry? He had to work to support himself, because I helped him little, and also because he didn't want me to give him a cent. He took care of things as best he could."

Ernesto's industrious outward appearance concealed an inner world of turmoil. Months earlier, back in Villa María, he had confronted his crowded feelings in a free-verse poem written on four pages of small notepaper. The poem provides a rare look into the unsettled emotions of Ernesto Guevara at a crucial moment in his life. On January 17, 1947, he wrote:

> *I know it! I know it!*
> *If I get out of here the river swallows me. . . .*
> *It is my destiny: Today I must die!*
> *But no, willpower can overcome everything*
> *There are the obstacles, I admit it*
> *I don't want to come out.*
> *If I have to die, it will be in this cave.*
> *The bullets, what can the bullets do to me if*
> *my destiny is to die by drowning. But I am*
> *going to overcome destiny. Destiny can be*
> *achieved by willpower.*
> *Die, yes, but riddled with*
> *bullets, destroyed by the bayonets, if not, no. Drowned, no . . .*
> *a memory more lasting than my name*
> *Is to fight, to die fighting.*

Ernesto is writing not about anxieties over family problems or about which college to choose but about questions of inner strength. The references to drowning, "the deep well," may have been allusions to his asthma, which had imposed limitations on his life and must have seemed to pose a predetermined route to death. It was a condition he had to fight to overcome. Without his own explanation, however, it is probably best to accept this piece of writing for what it certainly was: a melodramatic outpouring by a confused and self-absorbed eighteen-year-old.

The previous months had been traumatic for Ernesto. His parents' marital and economic collapse, the forced move to Buenos Aires, and then the death of his beloved grandmother had brought his sense of family security crashing down around him. As the eldest son, he must have felt an obligation to help out. His future was suddenly mortgaged. Even before the news about his grandmother had brought him to Buenos Aires, he had expressed a new sense of family duty. Just before leaving Villa María, he had written to his mother: "Tell me how you have sorted out the question of housing, and if the kids have schools to go to."

Now they were all in Buenos Aires, but because they had no money, finding a home remained a problem. For the time being they were stuck, and for the next year, the entire family lived in the late Ana Isabel's apartment. Then Ernesto senior sold the Misiones plantation and gave Celia the money it brought in to buy a house. She found an ugly old place at 2180 Calle Araoz that came with unwelcome elderly tenants who occupied the ground floor, but it was well situated, at the edge of the parklands and playing fields of the Palermo district. They had their own home again, but things were different. The older children had to find paying jobs. Ernesto senior still lived with them, but now he slept on a sofa in the living room.

The altered family circumstances brought about a fundamental shift in the relationship between Ernesto and his father. "We joked with one another as if we were the same age," Ernesto senior wrote. "He teased me continuously. As soon as we found ourselves at the table in our house, he would goad me with arguments of a political character. . . . Ernesto, who at the time was twenty years old, surpassed me in this area, and we argued constantly. Those who overheard us might have thought we were fighting. Not at all. Deep down there existed a true camaraderie between us."

II

During his first year at the university, Ernesto was called up by Argentina's military draft, but he was rejected on grounds of "diminished physical abilities"—his asthma. He was overjoyed, telling friends he "thanked his shitty lungs for doing something useful for a change."

One of the first friends Ernesto made at the school was a young woman named Berta Gilda Infante, the daughter of a Córdoba lawyer and politician whose family had recently moved to the capital. Tita, as she was known, was immediately attracted to Ernesto. She recalled later that he was "a beautiful and uninhibited young boy." A rather gruesome photograph from 1948 shows Ernesto and Tita, one of only three girls, standing among a group of white-coated medical students arrayed behind the naked body of a man lying on a slab. The cadaver's shaved head hangs over the edge of the slab and his chest cavity gapes open. Most of the students in the picture look grave. Ernesto is the only one beaming toothily straight at the camera.

Ernesto and Tita had a deep, platonic friendship. She was someone he could trust and confide in at an emotionally unstable time in his life, and it was a role she was glad to fulfill. Both of them were lonely and hungry

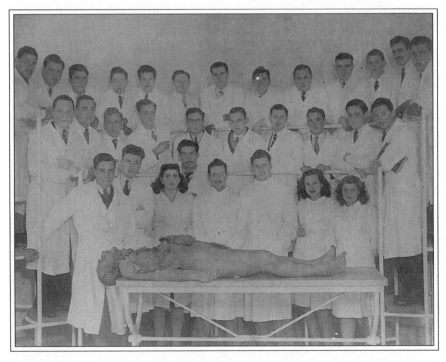

Students at the Medical Faculty of Buenos Aires University in 1948. Ernesto is in the top row, sixth from right, grinning incongruously.

for affection; both came from broken homes—Tita's father had died three years earlier—and were relative newcomers to the city. Every Wednesday, they met in the Museum of Natural Sciences for a class on the nervous system, cutting up fish under the guidance of an elderly German professor. They sat in cafés and at her home, talking about their classes or personal problems; they swapped books and discussed them; and they recited favorite poems to each other. Their relationship was long-lasting; after Ernesto left Argentina, the two maintained contact through a stream of letters almost rivaling the correspondence that he carried on with his mother and his aunt Beatriz.

Ernesto spent a great deal of time at Beatriz's apartment, which was twenty blocks from his family's new house on Calle Araoz. Beatriz had mothered him in ways Celia never did, sending him books, gifts, and new asthma remedies; encouraging him at his studies; and worrying about him. Now she prepared food and clucked over him. "My sister didn't sleep while Ernesto studied," his father wrote. "She always had his *mate* ready and accompanied him when he took a break. She did all this with the greatest affection."

Ernesto's special relationship with Beatriz was witnessed firsthand by Mario Saravia, a cousin seven years younger than Ernesto. In 1951, Saravia came from Bahía Blanca in southern Argentina, where his family lived, to attend a school in the capital. He lived with the Guevaras for the next two years, sharing Ernesto and Roberto's bedroom. As Beatriz's other pet nephew, Saravia often joined Ernesto for his meals at her house.

Beatriz was so fastidious that she wore gloves to handle money, Saravia recalled. If she shook hands with a stranger, she washed her hands afterward. Skeptical about the morals of the lower classes, she would put pincers on the service door so that the doorknob couldn't be turned when the *mucama* who cooked for her went to bed at night. Ernesto loved to shock this woman who loved him so unconditionally, although he never got into an acrimonious confrontation. He would tease her with hints about unsavory activities. According to Saravia, some of those activities would have made Beatriz "drop dead on the spot from a heart attack" if she knew about them, for they included seducing the maid she so carefully locked into her room at night. At one lunch, between servings, Saravia watched in astonishment from his place in the dining room as Ernesto had quick sex with the *mucama* on the kitchen table, which was visible through open doors directly behind their unsuspecting aunt's back. When he was finished, Ernesto returned to the dining room and continued eating, his aunt none the wiser. "He was like a rooster," Saravia observed. "He mated and then continued with his other functions."

III

Not surprisingly, Ernesto was an elusive figure to his classmates on campus. He gave the impression of being a young man in a great hurry. And he was. In some respects, Buenos Aires was merely a base for the progressive expansion of his geographical horizons as he set out hitchhiking, first on weekend or holiday jaunts back to Córdoba and to his late grandmother's *estancia* at Santa Ana de Irineo Portela, but gradually extending his radius farther afield and for longer periods.

In spite of the changes that had occurred in Ernesto's life, some things had remained constant. He still had his asthma; he continued playing chess—now one of his favorite hobbies—and rugby; he read assiduously and worked on his philosophical notebooks. He also wrote poetry. One of his earliest surviving poems, scribbled on the back inside cover of his fifth philosophical notebook, dates from this period. A short, unpolished ode, it appears to be an evocation of a grave site. As with most of the poems he wrote in his twenties, it is both awkward and pretentious:

> *Inconclusive tombstone of abstract garden,*
> *With your archaic architecture,*
> *You strike at the cubic morality of man.*
> *Horrible figurines dye your verse with blood*
> *and panegyric façades stain your front with light,*
> *Portentous whims sully your dark name*
> *Dressing you like all the rest.*

Ernesto's private world of study and reflection began to dominate more and more of his time. His brother Roberto was astounded to find him systematically reading through their father's collection of the twenty-five-volume *Contemporary History of the Modern World;* his philosophical notebooks are full of references to these tomes. With the same methodical approach, he began compiling an index of the books he read. In a black, clothbound notebook with alphabetically ordered pages, he made entries for authors, their nationalities, the book titles, and genres. The selection is lengthy and eclectic. It includes popular modern novels; European, American, and Argentine classics; medical texts; poetry; biographies; and philosophy. There are oddities scattered throughout the index, such as *My Best Chess Games* by Alexandr Aleksei, the *1937 Socialist Yearbook,* and *The Manufacture and Use of Celluloid, Bakelite, Etc.* by R. Bunke. But adventure classics predominate, especially the work of Jules Verne. A three-volume leather-bound set of Verne's collected works was one of Ernesto's prized possessions. A decade later, as a revolutionary *comandante* in Cuba, he had it brought to him from Argentina.

Ernesto continued to study Freud and Bertrand Russell, and he displayed a growing interest in social philosophy. He was now reading everyone from the ancient Greeks to Aldous Huxley. There is a great deal of cross-referencing between his literary index and his philosophical notebooks. His exploration into the concepts and origins of socialist thought was gathering momentum. He consulted Benito Mussolini on Fascism; Josef Stalin on Marxism; Alfredo Palacios, the flamboyant founder of the Argentine Socialist Party, on justice; Zola for a critical definition of Christianity; and Jack London for a Marxist description of social class. He had read a French biography of Lenin, *The Communist Manifesto,* and some speeches by Lenin; and he had dipped again into *Das Kapital.* In his third journal, he began to show a special interest in Karl Marx, filling dozens of pages with a thumbnail biography culled from R. P. Ducatillon's *Communism and Christianity.* (The figure of Marx became an enduring fascination. In 1965, while living clandestinely in Africa, he found the time to sketch an outline for a biography of Marx he intended to write.) He also copied out a portrait of Lenin from Ducatillon's book that describes Lenin as someone who "lived, breathed and slept" socialist revolution and sacrificed all else in his life to its cause. The passage presages to an uncanny degree the way Che Guevara would be described by his revolutionary comrades. Yet for all his curiosity about socialism, now, as before, Ernesto showed no inclination to become formally affiliated with the left. In fact, throughout his university years, he remained on the political sidelines—observing, listening, and sometimes debating, but studiously avoiding active participation.

By 1950, the populist-nationalist *peronismo* movement had evolved. With Juan Perón as "conductor" and Evita as messianic avenging angel, the movement possessed its own quasi-spiritual social philosophy, officially defined as *justicialismo.* Its goal was an "organized community" of men living in harmony. Against this backdrop of high-minded rhetoric, however, Perón had stepped up the repression of his opponents. Political adversaries were silenced by intimidation or with jail terms under toughened laws for *desacato,* disrespect of public officials. The *descamisados* (shirtless ones), or working masses, were won over with gifts and public works projects sponsored by Evita, who was president of the Eva Perón Foundation.

Perón defined the international posture of this new Argentina as the "third position," an opportunistic and intentionally ambiguous balancing act between the capitalist West and Communist East. "It is an ideological position which is in the center, left, or the right according to circumstances," Perón said. "We obey the circumstances." His cynicism was all too transparent, yet his desire to reinvent Argentina as a sovereign state beholden to no foreign power could generate a kind of grudging respect. Ernesto had dubbed him, somewhat ambiguously, *el capo,* but he avoided expressing sympathy for either Perón or his opponents.

The opposition to Perón was not attractive. Argentina's established parties displayed little social vision and had shown a woeful inability to counter Perón's momentum. The Argentine Communist Party was still a legal political organization, but its power base in the unions and the Central General de Trabajadores (CGT) workers' confederation had been weakened by Perón's ability to co-opt the working class. The Party responded by allying itself with the centrist Radical Party and a grouping of smaller left-of-center parties in strategic opposition to Perón. The Party was doctrinaire, bogged down in theoretical wranglings; it lacked charismatic leadership and a popular base of support.

Ernesto knew some of the militants in the Federación Juvenil Comunista, the Communist Youth, at the university. One of them, Ricardo Campos, recalled their talks on politics as "brusque and difficult." He said that he persuaded Ernesto to attend a "Fede" meeting, but that Ernesto stalked out while it was still in progress. "He had very clear ideas about certain things," Campos said. "Above all from an ethical perspective. More than a political person, I saw him at that time as someone with an ethical posture." To Tita Infante's brother Carlos, another Communist, Ernesto was a "progressive liberal" whose main interests seemed to be medicine and literature. They discussed the works of the Argentine Marxist writer Aníbal Ponce, but Ernesto was very critical of the Party's sectarianism.

Ernesto's emerging worldview began to reveal itself in personal encounters. At the funeral of an uncle in 1951, he argued with his cousin Juan Martín Moore de la Serna, pitting his interpretations of Marx and Engels against Moore's defense of French Catholic philosophers. On a visit to Córdoba, he mortified Dolores Moyano with a Nietzschean put-down of Jesus Christ. The Korean conflict sparked strong arguments between Ernesto and his father, with Ernesto opposing the Americans' role— accusing them of imperial designs—and his father supporting them. But none of his friends or relatives thought of Ernesto as a Marxist; and indeed, neither did *he,* at the time. They attributed his outspoken espousal of unfashionable positions to his "bohemian" upbringing and his iconoclastic personality, in keeping with his informal dress and his gypsy penchant for travel. Many of them probably assumed he would grow out of it in time.

There were parallels between Ernesto's uncompromising posture and the political environment of Argentina. Perón's Machiavellian exercise of power illuminated a formula for effecting radical political change *in spite of* the powerful opposition of a conservative oligarchy, the Catholic clergy, and sectors of the armed forces. Perón was a political master who could manipulate situations by knowing the mood of the people, knowing who his real friends and enemies were, and knowing when to act. The lesson was clear: what was required to make political headway in a place such as Argentina was strong leadership and a willingness to use force to meet one's goals.

Another politician who figured in the formation of Ernesto's worldview was Jawaharlal Nehru. Ernesto read Nehru's 1946 book *The Discovery of India* with great interest, underlining and scribbling comments about passages he found thought-provoking, and he talked about the book admiringly to his friends. Perón and Nehru may seem like strange bedfellows, but there are similarities between Nehru's effort to "decolonize" India and Perón's program to make Argentina economically self-sufficient. They were both strong and charismatic leaders who promoted the rapid industrialization of their overwhelmingly agrarian nations as an essential step in gaining fuller independence from the powerful countries—principally Great Britain and the United States—upon whom their fortunes rose and fell.

Perón's platform of "social justice, economic independence, and political sovereignty" for Argentina was promulgated at a time when foreign interests—in particular British, but increasingly American as well—held significant monopolies in the country's utilities, transportation, and railroad sectors, and supplied most of its manufactured goods. In his first year in office, Perón had embarked on an ambitious "import-substitution" program of industrial expansion, and in 1947 he moved to nationalize foreign-owned utilities and railroads and to pay off the country's foreign debt. This was a fertile field politically. There was widespread distrust of foreign capital interests, due principally to the economic hardships caused by repeated decreases in the price of Argentine agricultural exports during the global Depression of the late 1920s and early 1930s, and during both world wars. The ignominious Roca-Runciman Pact of 1933, which was renewed in 1936, had forced Argentina to buy British goods and grant concessions to British investors in return for Britain's continuing purchase of Argentine wheat, wool, and beef. Foreign capital investment had become symbolic of foreign interference and was a rallying point for Argentine nationalist sentiments.

"Yankee" interference had become onerous during the period leading up to the 1946 general election in which Spruille Braden, briefly the American ambassador to Buenos Aires, and then assistant secretary of state for Latin America, openly campaigned against Perón. With characteristic panache, Perón had turned the American's interference around to his favor, appealing to nationalist sentiments with counter-slogans suggesting that the election was not between Argentines at all, but a case of "Braden or Perón."

Many Argentines took umbrage when the Truman administration began lobbying for a hemispheric "mutual defense treaty" between the United States and its Latin American neighbors. Nevertheless, such a treaty, an outrowth of the recently announced "Truman Doctrine" of hard-line global containment of Soviet Communism, was signed in Rio de Janeiro in 1948 amid speeches extolling pan-Americanism. Latin American Communists denounced the U.S.-sponsored "brotherhood" as a warmed-over update of the old Monroe Doctrine, claiming that it gave Latin America to the colonialist interests of "Wall Street and the 'capitalist monopolies.'" In effect, the Rio Treaty gave Washington the right to intervene militarily in neighboring states "to support free peoples who are resisting attempted subjugation by armed minorities or by outside pressures." Ernesto remarked on the Rio conference and wrote an entry for *panamericanismo* in a notebook.

During the early 1950s, Ernesto's strongest political emotion was a deep-seated hostility toward the United States. "In his eyes, the twin evils in Latin America were the native oligarchies and the United States," Dolores Moyano recalled. The only things he liked about the U.S. were its poets and novelists. "I never heard him say one good thing about anything else," Moyano said. "He would disconcert both nationalists and Communists by being anti-American without subscribing to either of their points of view. With much bad luck, since my mother was American, I would often rally to the defense of the United States. I was never able to convince him that United States foreign policy was, more often than not, the bumbling creature of ignorance and error rather than the well-designed strategy of a sinister cabal. He was convinced of the dark princes of evil who directed every United States move abroad."

In the Latin America of the postwar years, there was plenty of evidence to nurture such perceptions. Ernesto was coming of age at a time when the United States was at an imperial apogee, aggressively pursuing its own economic and strategic interests in the region. In the anticommunist atmosphere of the Cold War, U.S. support of right-wing military dictatorships— Anastasio Somoza in Nicaragua, Rafael Trujillo in the Dominican Republic, Manuel Odría in Peru, and Marcos Pérez Jiménez in Venezuela—at the expense of outspoken nationalists or left-wing regimes was rationalized in the name of national security.

While Soviet expansion in postwar Europe was the main focus of alarm in Washington, by late 1950, the new Central Intelligence Agency felt sufficient concern about the hemispheric threat posed by Communism to prepare a secret assessment entitled *Soviet Capabilities and Intentions in Latin America*. "With respect to Latin America," the report said, "the objective of the U.S.S.R. must be presumed to be to reduce support of the U.S. as greatly as possible until the sovietization of the area becomes possible and its resources become available directly to augment Soviet strength." The CIA was especially concerned about the potential for coordination between pro-Soviet Latin American Communist parties and Moscow if a war broke out between the two superpowers. It noted the potential for Communist exploitation of existing anti-American sentiments, commenting that already in Argentina "the Communists, playing upon Argentine isolationism, found a ready response among non-Communists to their incitement against the sending of Argentine troops to Korea," while in Cuba, a recent incident in which American servicemen urinated on a statue of the Cuban nationalist hero José Martí had been "magnified" by local Communists, "thereby seriously, if temporarily, lowering popular esteem of the U.S." The CIA also warned that the Communists could exploit "liberal democratic aversion to dictatorial rulers" in some nations, straining relations between their countries and dictatorships friendly to Washington.

Ernesto was in his fourth year of medical school when, citing his own Communist threat, Perón began cracking down on the left. During the purge, a Córdoba acquaintance of Ernesto's, Fernando Barral, was arrested for "Communist agitation" and held in police custody for seven months. Barral was a Spanish Republican exile whose father, a famous sculptor, had been killed while defending Madrid. As a foreign national, he was to be deported back to an uncertain fate in Franco's Spain, but after the Argentine Communist Party secured Hungary's offer to receive him as a political exile, he was allowed to go there instead.

Except for random encounters, Barral and Ernesto had not had much contact since the Guevaras' move to Buenos Aires. Barral had meanwhile fallen in love with Ernesto's cousin Carmen Córdova Iturburu. Although his romantic feelings were unrequited, Barral and Carmen were close friends. Perhaps Ernesto viewed Barral as a rival for his cousin's affections; perhaps he simply disliked Barral's "dogmatism," a speculation later made by Barral himself. Whatever the case, throughout Barral's imprisonment, Ernesto remained unmoved. Ernesto neither visited Barral in prison nor (in a repetition of his behavior during Alberto Granado's detention) joined the efforts to secure a release.

One friend recalled Ernesto advising his maids to vote for Perón because Perón's policies favored their social class. According to Mario Saravia, Ernesto joined a Peronist youth organization on campus in order to use its extensive library facilities and check out books otherwise unavailable to him. Another time, on the suggestion, half in jest, of Tatiana Quiroga, prior to an ambitious trip through Latin America he was planning, he drafted a letter to Evita, asking her for a jeep. Tatiana helped him write it, and she remembers that they had fun doing it. They never received a reply.

IV

By the time he was in his early twenties, Ernesto stood out socially as an attractive oddball. Indeed, he defied definition and was oblivious of ridicule. Most of his peers dressed impeccably in ties, blazers, pressed slacks, and polished shoes, but he wore grimy jackets and odd-fitting, old-fashioned shoes that he bought at remainder sales.

Ernesto had perfected this untended image. As Dolores Moyano recalled, his sloppiness was a favorite topic of conversation among her friends. "One has to know the mentality of the provincial oligarchy to appreciate the remarkable effect of Ernesto's appearance," she wrote. "All the boys we knew put a great deal of effort and money into obtaining the latest fads: cowboy boots, blue jeans, Italian shirts, British pullovers, etc., back then in the early fifties. Ernesto's favorite piece of clothing in those days was a nylon shirt, originally white but gray from use, which he constantly wore and called La Semanera, claiming he washed it once a week. His trousers would be wide, floppy, and once, I recall, held up by a piece of clothesline. With Ernesto's appearance into a party, all conversation would cease, while everyone tried to look nonchalant and unimpressed. Ernesto, enjoying himself hugely and perfectly aware of the sensation he was creating, would be in complete command."

He was hopelessly tone-deaf and learned to dance only when his friends taught him the steps and pacing of the beat. At the beginning of each dance, he would ask whether it was a tango, a waltz, or a mambo. Then he would clumsily guide his partner around the dance floor. "Dancing didn't interest him in the slightest," his close friend Carlos Figueroa recalled. Ernesto was a relentless seducer of girls, and the only reason he danced was to get close to his prey.

Only a few of his closest male friends and relatives were privy to his dalliances. Mario Saravia recalled Ernesto's liaison with his family's maid, a Bolivian Indian woman in her late thirties named Sabina Portugal, with whom Ernesto slept regularly. "She was the ugliest woman I have ever seen," said Saravia. "But when she invited him, he would go to her room."

Ernesto was informal with his parents, calling them affectionately *vieja* and *viejo,* but was equally self-deprecating when it came to himself. The nickname El Chancho (The Pig) was a particular source of enjoyment because of the outraged reaction it elicited from his socially sensitive father.

Ernesto on a hitchhiking trip, 1948.

When Ernesto senior discovered that Carlos Figueroa was its source, he stormed at him, furious over what he perceived as a slight to the family honor. In spite of or possibly because of his father's displeasure, Ernesto kept the nickname and, in the rugby magazine *Tackle* he founded and edited for the eleven issues it survived, signed his articles Chang-Cho. (His merciless reviews of rugby matches were written in a quickly paced sportswriter's jargon, peppered with anglicizations.)

Whereas Ernesto's relationship with his father was combative, he was solicitous of his mother, who had been diagnosed with breast cancer in 1946 and had undergone a mastectomy. Their union was so special that it excluded the other children, and several friends spoke sympathetically about the effect it had on Roberto in particular. More physically fit and two years younger than Ernesto, Roberto eventually excelled at rugby, but within the family his triumphs were overshadowed by those of his older brother, who was always seen as "conquering" his asthma. It took Roberto many years to overcome the resentment he had felt toward Ernesto since childhood.

Everyone in the family simply ignored the fact that Ernesto senior and Celia no longer shared a bed. He would come home late and, oblivious of whatever else was going on around him, flop down on the sofa and go to sleep. His other eccentricities made this behavior seem natural. He could not leave the house without intentionally forgetting something, like his keys, in order to come back. It was "bad luck" if he didn't. This became an obsessive ritual. If anyone said "snake" around the family table, he would immediately say "wild boar," the "countervenom" to the bad luck the forbidden word portended.

Celia, meanwhile, continued to run her house like a salon. The dinner table was her throne. She sat there for hours playing solitaire, which—like the cigarettes she habitually smoked—she had become addicted to, but she was always ready to receive some young person for conversation or to dispense advice. As for the practicalities of everyday life, she was above the fray. On her cook's days off, she threw together meals with whatever happened to be in the refrigerator, with no notion of measurements or recipes. Visitors noted the absence of furniture, adornments, or paintings in the house, but were struck by the plethora of books, shelved and stacked everywhere. There were other peculiarities. The kitchen stove had a perennial short circuit, and the walls gave off electrical shocks to unsuspecting newcomers who leaned against them.

Just as Ernesto found the space and quiet he needed to study at Beatriz's apartment or in the university library, his father soon found some refuge in a rented studio nearby. He had a new business partner, and together they set up a combination real estate agency and contracting firm called Guevara

Lynch y Verbruch. Before long, they had found some business around the city, but, as always with Ernesto senior, it was touch and go.*

Although his studio had a bedroom, Ernesto senior had outfitted it with desks and architects' drawing tables, and he continued sleeping on the living room sofa at Calle Araoz or else at his sister Beatriz's apartment. Inevitably, however, with Calle Araoz so crowded, the studio became a spillover study for the Guevara youngsters and their friends, who came and went as they pleased. Ernesto used it to cram for exams, as did Roberto, who went to law school. Celia, Ana María, and her boyfriend, Carlos Lino, all of whom studied architecture, regularly worked on their projects there, and for a time it served as the editorial offices of the short-lived rugby review, *Tackle*.

For money, which was always short, Ernesto embarked on a series of commercial schemes that were as impractical as they were inventive. These enterprises usually involved his old friend Carlos Figueroa, who was now studying law in Buenos Aires and, like him, was forever in search of cash. Their first venture was Ernesto's inspiration. He felt that the locust insecticide Gamexane would make a good domestic roach-killer. After testing it in the neighborhood, he decided to go into industrial production. And so, together with Figueroa and a patient of Dr. Pisani's, he began packaging boxes of the stuff, mixed with talcum powder, in the garage of his home. He wanted to give it a registered trademark and came up with "Al Capone," but was advised he needed authorization by the Capone family to use the name. His next choice was "Atila," for Attila the Hun, the idea being that it would kill everything in its path, but there was already a product with this name. In the end, he decided on "Vendaval," which in Spanish means a strong southerly gale, and he acquired a patent for it. Ernesto's father offered to introduce him to potential investors but was rebuffed. Ernesto had a jaundiced view of his father's business partners.

The Vendaval factory gave off a horrible and pervasive stench. "A nauseous smell expanded throughout the house," his father recalled. "Everything we ate tasted to us like Gamexane; but Ernesto, imperturbable, continued his work." The end came soon enough, however, when first his helpers and then Ernesto himself began feeling sick, and the business was abandoned.

The next business scheme was Carlos Figueroa's brainstorm. It involved buying shoes cheaply at a wholesale auction, then selling them door-to-door at higher prices. It seemed like a good idea, but after successfully bidding

---

*Ernesto Guevara Lynch seemed especially damned when it came to choosing partners. Once their business was up and running, Verbruch succumbed to a deep, lasting depression and abandoned him. Guevara Lynch found another partner and the company survived, with ups and downs, until the right-wing military coup in 1976 forced him to flee the country.

for a lot of shoes—sight unseen—they discovered they had bought a great pile of remaindered odd and ends, many of them mismatched. When they had sold the matching pairs, they began peddling the shoes that merely *resembled* each other. Finally, they were left with a series of right- and left-footed shoes with no pairs at all. They sold a shoe to a one-legged man who lived down the street, and this gave rise to a suggestion by family and friends that they should track down as many one-legged people as they could find and sell off the rest. Memories of the episode endured because for some time afterward Ernesto himself—no doubt relishing the stares his appearance provoked—wore two of the unsold shoes, each one a different color.

Apart from his moneymaking enterprises, Ernesto began conducting medical experiments at home. For a time, he kept on his bedroom balcony caged rabbits and guinea pigs, which he injected with cancer-causing agents. He also practiced, although with less lethal ingredients, on his friends. Carlos Figueroa allowed himself to be injected by Ernesto one day, and when he swelled up in reaction to the shot, Ernesto happily exclaimed, "That was the reaction I was expecting!" and then gave him another injection to alleviate the symptoms.

A medical school classmate of Ernesto's recalled that they carried a human foot onto the Buenos Aires subway. They had cadged the foot from assistants at the anatomy theater in order to "practice" on it at home, then wrapped it clumsily in newspaper for the journey. Ernesto relished the terrified looks of commuters.

The high jinks of Ernesto's childhood were reflected in his behavior at medical school, in sports activities, and on hitchhiking trips. For a while, the new sport of gliding, which he took up on weekends at an airfield on Buenos Aires's outskirts with his free-spirited uncle, Jorge de la Serna, fulfilled the urge to test the unknown.* But it was on Ernesto's travels away from home that he experienced the most freedom. Carlos Figueroa was his companion on many of his hitchhiking jaunts. They often went back to Córdoba, a journey that was normally ten hours by car. It would take Ernesto and Carlos seventy-two, usually in the backs of trucks. They sometimes had to earn their way by unloading cargo.

Ernesto longed to extend his horizons farther. On January 1, 1950, at the end of his third year in medical school, he headed into Argentina's interior on a bicycle outfitted with a small Italian Cucchiolo engine. This was

---

*Jorge was Celia's younger brother and a colorful personality, given to wandering around the country as a kind of solitary adventurer. He was much loved by the family—and a favorite of Ernesto's—but quite mad, and had to be institutionalized at least once in a psychiatric hospital.

Ernesto setting out on his solo
motorbike trip on January 1, 1950.
This photograph was later used
as an advertisement by the
company that sold him the engine.

his first real trip alone. Before leaving, he hammed it up for a photograph.
It shows him seated on his bike, legs poised on the ground and hands gripping the handlebars as if at the starting line of a race. He wears a cap, sunglasses, and a leather bomber's jacket. A spare bicycle tire is looped over his
neck and shoulder like a *pistolero*'s bandolier. He planned to go to Córdoba
and then to San Francisco del Chañar, about ninety-five miles farther north,
where Alberto Granado was now working at a leprosarium and running a
pharmacy on the side.

Ernesto set off from home in the evening, using the little motor to get
himself quickly out of the city, and then he began pedaling. Before long, a
bicyclist caught up with him, and they cycled together until morning. Passing through Pilar, a town outside Buenos Aires that he had set as his first
goal, and which some people at home had predicted would mark the end of
his adventure, he felt "the first happiness of one who triumphs." He was on
his way.

V

Ernesto's journey broke new ground for him in terms of two activities that
were to become lifelong rituals: traveling and writing a diary. For the first

time in his life he felt inspired to keep a running account of his day-to-day life.* He was twenty-two years old.

On the second night he reached his birthplace, Rosario, and by the next evening, "forty-one hours and seventeen minutes" after setting out, he came to the Granado family's home in Córdoba. Along the way, he had adventures. First, after allowing himself to be pulled along by a car at forty miles an hour, his rear tire burst and he ended up in a roadside heap, awakening a *linyera,* or hobo, who happened to be sleeping where he fell. They struck up a conversation, and the hobo companionably prepared an infusion of *mate* "with enough sugar in it to sweeten up a spinster." (Ernesto preferred his *mate* bitter.)

Ernesto spent several days in Córdoba visiting friends, and then took off with Alberto's brothers, Tomás and Gregorio, to camp at a waterfall north of the city, where they climbed rocks, dived from great heights into shallow pools of water, and nearly got swept away by a flash flood. Tomás and Gregorio returned to Córdoba, and Ernesto went on to join Alberto at the José J. Puente leprosarium, on the outskirts of San Francisco del Chañar. With Alberto investigating the immunological susceptibilities of lepers, and Ernesto involved in allergy research at the Clínica Pisani, the two now had more in common than rugby and books. To Granado, the world of medical research "was a kind of conductive thread for us both, in what seemed at the time would be our future."

Greatly interested in Alberto's work, Ernesto followed him on his rounds. But they soon had a disagreement. It arose over Alberto's treatment of a pretty young girl named Yolanda who did not yet exhibit the symptoms of leprosy—large spots of deadened flesh—except on her back. Granado knew that every time a new doctor arrived, the girl tried to convince him of the injustice of her internment. "Ernesto was no exception to this rule, and, visibly impressed by the beauty of the girl and the pathetic presentation of her case, he came to see me," Granado recalled. "Soon an argument erupted between the two of us."

Ernesto felt that more care should be taken in the decisions leading to the internment and isolation of the sick. Alberto tried to explain that the girl's case was a desperate one, and highly contagious. He proved his point by jabbing a long hypodermic needle into the flesh of the girl's back. She didn't feel it and was unaware of what he was doing. "I looked triumphantly

*After Che's death, this diary was discovered by his father, who transcribed it and included it in his memoir, *Mi Hijo el Che* (My Son Che). Except for some illegible sections, he said, the published version was entirely faithful to the original.

at Ernesto, but the look he gave me froze the smile," Granado said. "The future Che ordered me brusquely: 'Mial, tell her to go!' And when the patient had left the room, I saw a contained rage reflected in the face of my friend. Until that moment I had never seen him like this and I had to withstand a storm of reproaches. Petiso, he said to me, 'I never thought you could lose your sensitivity to such an extent. You have fooled that young girl just to show off your knowledge!'" Finally, after more explanations by Granado, the two friends made up, and the incident was over, if never forgotten.

After several days at the leprosarium, Ernesto was anxious to be off again. By now, he had decided to extend his journey even farther, "with the pretentious intention" of reaching Argentina's remote and little-traveled northern and westernmost provinces. He persuaded Granado, who owned a motorcycle, to accompany him on the first leg of the trip.

The two friends made their departure, Granado pulling Ernesto behind his motorcycle with a rope. The rope kept breaking, and after some distance they agreed it was better if Ernesto continued on alone. Alberto turned back to San Francisco del Chañar. "We gave each other a not very effusive hug, as between two *machitos,* and I watched him disappear like a knight on his bike, saying good-bye with his hand," Ernesto wrote.

Crossing the "silver-dyed land" of the Salinas Grandes, the Argentine Sahara, without problems, Ernesto arrived in Loreto, a small town where the local police put him up for the night. Discovering that he was a medical student, they urged him to stay on and become the town's only doctor. Nothing could have been farther from his mind at that moment, and the next day he hit the road again.

In Santiago del Estero, the provincial capital, a local correspondent for a Tucumán daily interviewed him—"The first article about me in my life," Ernesto wrote exultantly—then he headed toward Tucumán, the next city north. On the way, while repairing his umpteenth tire puncture, he met another itinerant *linyera,* and they fell into conversation. "This man was coming from the cotton harvest in the Chaco and, after vagabonding awhile, thought to go to the grape harvest in San Juan. Discovering my plan to travel through several provinces and after realizing that my feat was purely recreational, he grabbed his head with a desperate air: 'Mama mía, all that effort for nothing?'"

Ernesto could not have adequately explained to the hobo what he hoped to gain from his travels, apart from repeating that he wanted to see more of his own country. But the man's remark made him reflect. In his journal, until then a rendition of facts and glib descriptions laced with anecdotes, he began examining himself and his feelings more deeply. In a forested region north of Tucumán, on the road to Salta, he halted and got off his bike to walk into the dense foliage. He experienced a kind of rapture at the natural world surrounding him there. Afterward he wrote: "I realize that something that was growing inside of me for some time . . . has matured: and it is the hate of civilization, the absurd image of people moving like *locos* to the rhythm of that tremendous noise that seems to me like the hateful antithesis of peace."

Later that same day, he met a motorcyclist riding a brand-new Harley-Davidson. The man offered to pull him on a rope, but, remembering his recent mishaps, he declined. He and the motorcyclist shared some coffee before going on their separate ways. A few hours later, arriving in the next town, he saw a truck unloading the Harley-Davidson and was informed that its driver had been killed. The incident, and his own close escape from the same fate, provoked a new bout of introspection: "The death of this motorcyclist doesn't have the impact to touch the nerve endings of the multitudes, but the knowledge that a man goes looking for danger without even the vaguest of heroic intentions that bring about a public deed, and can die at a bend in the road without witnesses, makes this unknown adventurer seem possessed of a vague suicidal 'fervor.'"

At Salta, Ernesto presented himself at the hospital as a medical student and asked for a place to sleep. Allotted the seat of a truck, he "slept like a king" until being roused by the driver early the next morning. After waiting out a torrential rain, he headed off through a beautiful green landscape of dripping wet foliage toward Jujuy, Argentina's northernmost city. When he arrived, "anxious to know the value of the province's hospitality," he made his way to the local hospital, where he once again made use of his medical "credentials" to obtain a bed. He was granted one, but only after paying his way by picking a complaining little Indian boy's head clean of lice.

It was as far north as he would go on this trip. He had wanted to go all the way to the rugged frontier with Bolivia, but, as he wrote to his father, "several flooding rivers and an active volcano are fucking up travel in the area." Also, his fourth term of medical school was due to begin in a few weeks' time.

Turning back to Salta, he reappeared at the hospital and was asked by the staff what he had seen on his journey. "In truth, what *do* I see?" he reflected. "At least I am not nourished in the same ways as the tourists, and I find it strange to find, on the tourist brochures of Jujuy, for example, the Altar of the Fatherland, the cathedral where the national ensign was blessed, the jewel of the pulpit and the miraculous little virgin of Río Blanco and Pompeii. . . . No, one doesn't come to know a country or find an interpretation of life in this way. That is a luxurious façade, while its true soul is reflected in the sick of the hospitals, the detainees in the police stations or the anxious passersby one gets to know, as the Río Grande shows the turbulence of its swollen level from underneath."

For the first time in his adult life, Ernesto had witnessed the harsh duality of his country. He had left its transported European culture, which was also *his,* and plunged into the ignored, backward, indigenous heartland. The injustice of the lives of the socially marginalized people he had befriended along his journey—lepers, hobos, detainees, hospital patients—bore witness to the submerged "turbulence" of the region that lay "underneath" the "Río Grande." This enigmatic reference to the Río Grande—not among the rivers he crossed on his journey—may be significant, for it appears to refer to the river that has long been a politically symbolic dividing line between the rich north and poor south along the U.S.-Mexican border. If so, this is an early glimmering of an idea that would come to obsess him: that the United States, as an expression of neocolonial exploitation, was ultimately to blame for perpetuating the sorry state of affairs he saw around him.

In Argentina's northern provinces, the vast uninhabited land gave way to a few old cities, still run by a handful of landowning families of immense wealth and privilege. For centuries they and the colonial structures their forefathers erected had coexisted alongside a faceless "alien" indigenous majority over which they held power. It was the region of strongmen such as Catamarca's Senator Robustiano Patrón Costas, the despotic sugar mill owner who, as the handpicked successor of President Castillo, had been prevented from taking office by the Perón-backed army coup of 1943. Justifying that coup years later, Perón accused Patrón Costas of being an "exploiter" who ran his sugar mill like a "feudal estate," the representative of an "inconceivable" system that had to be done away with if Argentina was to take its place in the modern age.

It was from such areas that the Argentine Indians, commonly referred to as *coyas,* and the mixed-blood *cabezitas negras* ("little black heads") fled in steadily increasing numbers, pouring into the cities in search of work and setting up shantytowns like the one in front of the Guevaras' home in Córdoba. From their ranks came domestic servants such as La Negra Cabrera and Sabina Portugal, and the cheap labor force for Argentina's new industries and public works projects. Theirs was the despised social class Perón had appealed to when he called upon the nation to incorporate the *descamisados,* whose noisome presence and clamor so irritated the white elites in their once-exclusive metropolitan idylls. For the first time, these people were not servants or symbols to Ernesto; he had traveled in their midst.

Ernesto returned to Buenos Aires in time for the start of the school term. In his six weeks on the road, he had traveled through twelve provinces and covered nearly 2,500 miles. He took his little bicycle engine back to the Amerimex company, where he had bought it, for an overhaul. The delighted management proposed he do an advertisement in exchange for fixing the engine free of charge. He agreed to this, writing a letter outlining his recent odyssey and lauding the company's Cucchiolo engine that had carried him: "It has functioned perfectly during my extensive tour, and I have noted only that toward the end it lost compression, the reason for which I send it to you for repair."

VI

That year, his fourth at medical school, Ernesto passed five more exams toward his degree and continued his work at the Clínica Pisani. He also kept up his rugby, and his gliding lessons with his uncle Jorge. But a hunger to explore the world had been awakened in him, and following the success of his Argentine "raid," as he called it, he began concocting new travel plans. Then, in October, just before the end of the term, something unexpected happened. For the first time in his life, he fell in love.

One of the González-Aguilar daughters, Carmen, was to be married, and the entire Guevara clan traveled to Córdoba to attend the wedding. Among the guests was a girl Ernesto had known when he lived in Córdoba. She was a child then, but now she was a beautiful sixteen-year-old. María del Carmen "Chichina" Ferreyra belonged to one of Córdoba's oldest and wealthiest families. A brunette with soft white skin and full lips, she made an impression on Ernesto that was, according to Pepe González-Aguilar, who was also at the wedding, "like a lighting bolt."

The attraction was mutual. Chichina was fascinated by Ernesto's "obstinate physique," as Dolores Moyano later phrased it, and his playful, unsolemn character. "His messiness in his dress made us laugh and was a little embarrassing at the same time," Moyano wrote. "We were so sophisticated that Ernesto seemed an opprobrium. He accepted our jokes immutably."

For Ernesto, at least, the ensuing romance was serious. By all accounts, although Chichina was very young, she was not all feminine frippery. She was extremely bright and imaginative, and Ernesto apparently became convinced she was the woman of his life. It was almost a fairytale romance. He was from a family of aristocratic paupers. She was blueblooded Argentine gentry, heiress to a lime quarry and factory complex, one of the Córdoba region's few industries at the time. The Ferreyras owned an imposing, French-built château on enclosed parklike grounds at the foot of Avenida Chacabuco in Córdoba. Chichina's grandmother, the matriarch of the Ferreyra clan, lived there. Chichina and her parents lived in another large residence nearby, only two blocks from the

Guevaras' old home. They also owned a huge *estancia,* Malagueño, where the family summered.

The *estancia,* Dolores Moyano wrote, "included two polo fields, Arabian stallions, and a feudal village of workers for the family's limestone quarries. The family visited the village church every Sunday for Mass, worshipping in a separate alcove to the right of the altar with its own separate entrance and private communion rail, away from the mass of workers. In many ways, Malagueño exemplified everything Ernesto despised. Yet, unpredictable as always, Ernesto had fallen madly in love with the princess of this little empire."*

Whatever they felt about Ernesto's suitability for their daughter, Chichina's parents didn't reject him from the outset. At first, they found him endearingly eccentric and precocious. Pepe González-Aguilar, who witnessed their courtship, remembered the Ferreyras' amusement at Ernesto's sloppy appearance and his informality, but noticed that when Ernesto talked of literature, history, or philosophy, or told anecdotes from his travels, they listened attentively.

The Ferreyras were themselves a colorful bunch. Pepe González-Aguilar described them as cultured, worldly, and sensitive. They stuck out notably in a conservative, provincial society that idolized them as much as it envied them. Chichina's father had traveled through the Amazon on a journey that even today would be dangerous. They had participated in car races when there were almost no roads and piloted the first planes under the watchful attention of the grandmother, who, according to family lore, urged them to "fly low." During World War II, as he was on his way to join the ranks of General de Gaulle, one of Chichina's uncles died on board a ship sunk by the Germans.

For Ernesto, the "Ferreyra atmosphere" must have been extremely stimulating—and challenging. He was soon making regular trips back to Córdoba to see Chichina. He became a frequent visitor to the Ferreyras' home in the city and to Malagueño, joining Chichina and her large group of friends who assembled there.

Of all her relatives, it was Chichina's eccentric uncle Martín who, according to her friends, was most drawn to Ernesto. *Tío* Martín was an elderly

*Chichina and Dolores Moyano were first cousins, and Dolores's architect father knew Ernesto Guevara Lynch through his building work. The Ferreyras also intermarried with the illustrious Roca family, whose son Gustavo was a friend of Ernesto's. His father, one of the University Reform's founders, was another eminent Córdoba architect of Guevara Lynch's acquaintance. Tatiana Quiroga, a childhood friend of both the Ferreyras and Guevaras, was dating Chichina's first cousin Jaime "Jimmy" Roca, whom she would later marry.

María del Carmen "Chichina" Ferreyra, the wealthy girl with whom Ernesto fell in love in 1950.

recluse who lived at Malagueño, where he bred Arabian horses. He never left the *estancia* grounds. He also stood out for having steadfastly supported Nazi Germany during World War II, while the rest of the clan were staunch supporters of the Allied forces. He was a night owl and an accomplished classical pianist, and he played for Ernesto, Chichina, and their friends as they talked and danced, often until dawn.

Altogether too soon, Ernesto was trying to persuade Chichina to marry him and, for their honeymoon, travel with him throughout South America in a *casa rodante,* a house trailer. "This was when the conflicts arose," said Pepe Gonzalez-Aguilar. "Chichina was only sixteen years old and she was undecided; nor did her parents view this project with kindly eyes."

After he proposed, Ernesto's presence began to take on a subversive quality among the Ferreyra clan. "Family opposition to him was fierce," Dolores Moyano recalled. "At any social gathering, the directness, the candor, the mocking quality of his opinions made his presence dangerous. When

Ernesto came to dinner at my family's, we would wait for the worst to happen with a mixture of dread and delight."

Tatiana Quiroga portrayed Ernesto as a "hippyish and sickly" figure who appeared to seat himself at formal Ferreyra family dinners—"with his asthma and his permanent inhaler . . . and wearing his horrifying dirty nylon shirt"—while his hosts watched in appalled silence. In her opinion, Ernesto was all too aware of the disapproval his appearance elicited, which provoked him to say outrageous things "so as not to feel so diminished." Tensions reached a head one night at Malagueño during a dinner at which both Dolores Moyano and Pepe González-Aguilar were present. The conversation turned to Winston Churchill. The Ferreyras were supremely Anglophilic, and in their home Churchill's name was invoked with reverence. As each elderly member of the family contributed his favorite anecdote about the man, Dolores recalled, Ernesto listened with undisguised amusement. Finally, unable to contain himself, he leaped in, bluntly dismissing the venerated figure as just another "ratpack politician." Pepe González-Aguilar remembered the uncomfortable moment: "Horacio, Chichina's father, said: 'I can't put up with this,' and left the table. I looked at Ernesto thinking to myself that if anyone had to leave, it was us, but he merely smiled like a naughty child and began eating a lemon in bites, peel and all."

Chichina continued to see Ernesto, but secretly. Once, when she and her family traveled to Rosario to watch her father play in a polo match, Chichina arranged for Ernesto to join her there, concealed in another car with her girlfriends. While her father played, the two met clandestinely.

Chichina's devoutly religious mother, Lola, was aware of her daughter's feelings and had become so alarmed at the prospect of having Ernesto Guevara as her son-in-law that, according to Tatiana Quiroga, she made a vow to Argentina's patron saint, the Virgin of Catamarca. If Chichina broke off the romance, Lola would make a pilgrimage to the Virgin's distant shrine. (In the end, she did make her pilgrimage, but it turned into such an ordeal, with a prolonged breakdown in the hot desert, albeit in a chauffeur-driven car, that the journey itself became a favorite Ferreyra family story.)

At the end of the school term in December 1950, Ernesto did not come to Córdoba to be close to Chichina as one might have expected. Instead, he obtained a male nurse's credentials from the Ministry of Public Health and applied for work as a "doctor" with the shipping line of the state petroleum company, Yacimientos Petrolíferos Fiscales. On the surface, Ernesto's wanderlust would seem to have won out over the pull of Chichina's enchantments, but more likely his shipping out was a way of earning even more "manly credit" in her eyes, perhaps an attempt to compete with the dashing exploits of her revered father and uncles.

Ernesto left for Brazil on February 9, 1951, aboard the tanker *Anna G,* and spent six weeks at sea. From then until June, when he completed his fourth and last voyage, he spent more time at sea than on dry land, traveling as far south as the Argentine port of Comodoro Rivadavia in Patagonia, and up South America's Atlantic coast to the British colony of Trinidad and Tobago, visiting Curaçao, British Guiana, Venezuela, and Brazilian ports along the way. Chichina was never far from his mind. As soon as he was back in port he would call his sister Celia to ask if there were any letters from her. "He asked me to go running to the docks, and I ran and ran like he asked and I took him the letters," she remembered years later.

To his friends and siblings, Ernesto conveyed the impression that he was living a romantic life, bringing them back exotic little souvenirs from his ports of call and spinning tales of life on the high seas. And he did have some adventures. He told Carlos Figueroa about a fight he had in a Brazilian port with an American sailor—his sister Celia recalled it as having been with an Englishman, in Trinidad—an incident that seemed to confirm his inherent animosity toward Anglo-Saxons. And he told Osvaldo Bidinost of performing an appendectomy on a sailor at sea with a kitchen knife because the ship's only scalpel had been used in a fight and was embargoed as evidence.

But the sailor's life did not live up to Ernesto's expectations. He was frustrated that the oil tankers on which he served were not in port very long, giving him little time to see anything. In May, as classes began for his fifth term at the university, he made his last voyage. When he returned to Buenos Aires, he gave his father a notebook containing an autobiographical essay dedicated to him. It was entitled "Angustia (Eso Es Cierto)"—"Anguish (That's Right)"—and was laced with quotations, beginning with one from Ibsen: "Education is the capacity to confront the situations posed by life."

Written in a enigmatic cloak of dense metaphors, "Anguish" is an introspective and existentialist exploration of the causes and nature of a depression Ernesto experienced while at sea. The narrative is built around a shore leave with some shipmates in Trinidad. It was Ernesto's first known attempt to write a short story. Although he prefaced it by stating that he had overcome his depression and could once again "smile optimistically and breathe in the air around him," he expresses deep loneliness and seems to be anguished over his relationship with Chichina, chafing against and wanting to free himself from the constraints of society.

"I fall on my knees, trying to find a solution, a truth, a motive. To think that I was born to love, that I wasn't born to sit permanently in front of a desk asking myself whether man is good, because I know man is good, since I have rubbed elbows with him in the country, in the factory, in the logging camp, in the mill, in the city. To think that he is physically healthy, that he has a spirit of cooperation, that he is young and vigorous like a billy goat but he sees himself excluded from the panorama: that is anguish. . . . To make a sterile sacrifice that does nothing to raise up a new life: that is anguish."

VII

By late June 1951, Ernesto was back in school. He was now twenty-three and still had two years to go before obtaining his medical degree, but he no longer found the routine of classes and exams stimulating. A malaise had set in: he was lovelorn and restless. His wanderlust had been whetted by his motorbike journey and the months at sea, but his hopes of marrying Chichina and carrying her off had stagnated. Now barely seventeen, Chichina was still very much her family's girl. The weighty combination of her parent's intractable opposition and her own youthful indecision had placed her relationship with Ernesto in an uneasy and unresolved holding pattern. This situation wasn't helped by the fact that they were apart.

Rescue came in the form of Alberto Granado, who had lately begun weaving grandiose plans to spend a year traveling the length of the South American continent. He had been talking about such a trip for years but had done nothing about it, and his family had long since written off "Alberto's trip" as a harmless fantasy. He was nearly thirty years old, and he realized that if he didn't take the trip now, he never would. He decided he needed a companion. Who else but Ernesto would throw everything up for a chance at an adventure like this? When Alberto asked him, Ernesto accepted on the spot.

During the October break from classes, Ernesto traveled to Córdoba to see Alberto. As he later lyrically evoked it, they sat under the grape arbor of Alberto's house, drank sweet *mate,* and fantasized about where they would go. "Along the roads of daydreams we reached remote countries, navigated on tropical seas and visited all of Asia. And suddenly . . . the question arose: And if we go to North America? To North America? How? With La Poderosa, man. And this was how the trip was decided, which forever after would be pursued along the same general lines it was planned: Improvisation."

La Poderosa (The Powerful One) was the vintage 500-cc Norton motorcycle with which Alberto had unsuccessfully tried to pull Ernesto on his visit to San Francisco del Chañar. On January 4, 1952, they set out on it, heading for the beach resort of Miramar, where Chichina was on a holiday with an aunt and some friends. Ernesto wanted to say good-bye, and, as he rode on the back of the motorcycle, he carried a gift in his arms. It was a young, wriggly puppy he had given an English name: "Come-back."

5

Escape to the North

I

Miramar, where Chichina was staying, was the final hurdle between Ernesto and Alberto and the open road. Ernesto was still in love and nagged by doubts about leaving. Was he doing the right thing? Would she wait for him? He hoped to receive her assurances and had decided that if she accepted the puppy Come-back, it would be a sign that she wanted him to return.

Alberto worried that his friend would end their journey before it had even begun. Ernesto knew this. "Alberto saw the danger and imagined himself alone on the roads of America, but he didn't raise his voice," he wrote in his journal.* "The struggle was between she and I." Their planned two-day stay "stretched like rubber into eight," as Ernesto tried to extract Chichina's promise to wait for him. Holding hands with her "in the enormous womb of a Buick," he asked for the gold bracelet she wore, as a talisman and keepsake on his journey. She refused.

In the end, Ernesto decided to go. He had received neither the keepsake nor Chichina's benediction, but she had accepted Come-back, despite her girlfriends' sneers that the dog was a mongrel rather than, as Ernesto claimed, a purebred German shepherd. And she gave him fifteen American dollars to buy her a scarf when he reached the United States. As a sign of undying affection and loyalty, it wasn't much, and it must have been

---

*Notas de Viaje, the account Ernesto wrote of his journey, which contains extracts from his journal, was transcribed and published posthumously by Che's widow, Aleida March. The published version is supposedly authentic and unabridged, although some explicit sexual references have almost certainly been expurgated. It was first published in English in 1995 as *The Motorcycle Diaries*.

with a sense of foreboding that Ernesto climbed back on La Poderosa on
January 14.

II

The road was clear to begin their great trek, and the two gypsies sped off. It
took them four more weeks, however, to leave Argentina. Before they were
halfway across the settled pampa west of Bahía Blanca, Ernesto developed
a fever and had to be hospitalized for several days. By the time they reached
the picturesque Lake District on the eastern slopes of the Andean cordillera, bordering Chile, their meager revenues had dwindled and they had
become expert freeloaders—*mangueros motorizados,* motorized scroungers,
as Ernesto wryly put it—throwing themselves on the mercy of roadside
families. They competed with each other in the art of grubbing for survival.

Sometimes they were forced to pitch their tent, but more often than
not they found floor space in garages, kitchens, barns, and frequently police stations, where they shared cells and meals with an interesting variety
of criminals. One night when they were staying in the barn of an Austrian
family, Ernesto awoke at dawn to hear scratching and growling at the barn
door and saw a pair of glowing eyes peering in. Having been warned about
a fierce puma that was in the area, he aimed the Smith and Wesson that his
father had given him and fired. But he didn't bag a puma. It was their hosts'
beloved Alsatian dog, Bobby. Ernesto and Alberto made their escape, followed by wails and imprecations.

They hiked around lakes, climbed a peak—frightening themselves by
nearly falling to their death—and used the revolver to poach a wild duck.
At one particularly scenic lakeside spot they fantasized about returning together to set up a medical research center. In the jailhouse of the ski resort
of Bariloche, Ernesto opened a letter from Chichina informing him that she
had decided *not* to wait for him. A storm raged outside. "I read and reread
the incredible letter. Just like that, all my dreams . . . came crashing
down. . . . I began to feel afraid for myself and to write a weepy letter, but
I couldn't, it was useless to try." The romance was over. Evidently she had
begun seeing someone else.

Alberto always wondered if he bore some responsibility for the
breakup. In full view of Chichina and her friends, he had taken one of the
Ferreyras' *mucamas*—who was wearing a bathing suit that belonged to
Chichina's aunt—into his tent on the beach, thus defying the unanimously
understood social convention prohibiting overt intimacy with the servant
class. "Chichina didn't like that very much," Granado recalled. "And I think
she resented me as the person who was taking Ernesto away from her."

Outwardly reconciling himself to his loss, Ernesto was determined to enjoy the rest of the journey. Writing about their crossing of the Andes to Chile, he invoked the lines of a poem that began: "And now I feel my great root floating naked and free."

Entering Chile, they obtained passage on a ferry across Lake Esmeralda by manning the bilge pumps of the leaky cargo barge it pulled in its wake. Some Chilean doctors were on board, and Ernesto and Alberto introduced themselves as "leprologists." The gullible doctors told them about Chile's only leper colony. It was on Easter Island, which was also, the Chilean doctors assured them, home to hordes of sensuous, pliant women. Ernesto and Alberto immediately resolved to add the leper colony to their ambitious itinerary, and they extracted a letter of recommendation to the Society of Friends of Easter Island in Valparaiso.

At the Pacific port of Valdivia, they paid a visit to the local newspaper, the *Correo de Valdivia,* and came away with a glowing profile of themselves, published under the headline "Two Dedicated Argentine Travelers on Motorcycle on Their Way through Valdivia." They had solemnly reinvented themselves as "leprosy experts" with "previous research in neighboring countries." They must have offered their opinions on a wide variety of topics, for the *Correo* went on to laud them for having, "during their very short stay in our country, penetrated its social, economic, and sanitary problems."

They were interviewed again in Temuco. The headline of an article published in *El Austral de Temuco* on February 19, 1952, reads, "Two Argentine Experts in Leprology Travel South America on Motorcycle." An accompanying photograph shows Ernesto and Alberto in heroic poses. Ernesto stares straight at the camera, with his thumbs locked casually in his belt. He looks dashing. Alberto leans toward him deferentially, wearing a rather impish expression. Ernesto referred to the clippings as "the condensation of our audacity."

A day later, La Poderosa took a fall. The gearbox was smashed and the steering column snapped. Repairs were made in the whistle-stop of Lautaro, where Ernesto and Alberto became instant celebrities. They managed to scrounge a few free meals and were invited to drink wine with their new friends. Ernesto found the Chilean wine delicious, so much so that by the time he and Alberto arrived at a village dance, he felt "capable of great feats." After having drunk even more, he invited a married woman to dance and began to lead her outside, even though her husband was watching them. She resisted, Ernesto kept insisting, and she fell to the floor. Both Ernesto and Alberto were chased from the hall. They left town, "fleeing a place that was no longer so hospitable to us," but a few miles down the road the motorcycle's rear brake failed on a corner, and then, as La Poderosa picked up speed downhill, the hand brake failed as well. Ernesto swerved to avoid a herd of cows that suddenly loomed in front of him, and they crashed into the road bank. Miraculously, La Poderosa was undamaged, and, finding the rear brake mysteriously working once again, they continued their trek.

"Backed up as always by our 'press' letter of recommendation, we were put up by some Germans who treated us in a very cordial manner," Ernesto wrote. "During the night I got a colic which I didn't know how to stop; I was ashamed to leave a souvenir in the chamber pot, so I climbed onto the window, and gave up all of my pain to the night and the blackness. . . . The next morning I looked out to see the effect and I saw that two meters below lay a great sheet of zinc where they were sun-drying their peaches: the added spectacle was impressive. We beat it from there."

Leaving a lengthening trail of irate hosts behind them, the two young men continued their escape to the north, but their faithful steed began to fail them. Every time they reached a hill, La Poderosa balked. It finally gave out completely. A truck deposited them and the crippled motorcycle in the next town, Los Ángeles. They found lodging in the local firehouse after chatting with the three daughters of the fire chief. Later, Ernesto paid coy homage to the uninhibited girls as "exponents of the grace of the Chilean women who, whether pretty or ugly, have a certain something of spontaneity, of freshness, that captivates immediately."

Alberto was more explicit. "After dinner we went out with the girls. Once again I noticed the different attitudes toward freedom between Chilean women and our own. . . . We returned to the firehouse lax and silent, each one ruminating on his experience. . . . Fuser made his bed, really agitated, I don't know if from asthma or the girl."

The next day they left on a truck headed for Santiago, lugging the carcass of La Poderosa with them like the body of a fallen comrade. The Chilean capital made little impression on them, and after finding a garage where they could leave the motorcycle, they were off again, on their own, still intent on reaching Easter Island.

III

In Valparaíso, they camped out at a bar, La Gioconda, where the generous owner fed and housed them free of charge. When they went down to the port, they were told that the next ship to Easter Island didn't leave for six months, but they didn't lose hope, for they had yet to call upon the Society of Friends of Easter Island. Meanwhile, their imaginations took flight. "Easter Island!" Ernesto wrote in his journal. "There, to have a white boyfriend is an honour for the female. . . . There—what a wish—the women do all the work. One eats, sleeps, and keeps them content." It was a tantalizing vision. "What would it matter to stay a year there, who cares about work, studies, family, etc."

After making abundant use of his alleged doctor's "degree," Ernesto was asked to look in on one of La Gioconda's clients, who turned out to be an elderly servant woman, prostrate with chronic asthma and a failing heart. He found her room, where he breathed in an odor "of concentrated sweat and dirty feet." She was surrounded by "the ill-concealed acrimony" of her family, who seemed to suffer her presence badly. She was dying, and there was little Ernesto could do for her. After giving her a prescription for her diet, what remained of his own supply of Dramamine tablets, and a few other medicines, he left, "followed by the praising words of the old lady and the indifferent stares of her relatives."

The encounter affected him deeply and led him to think about the heartlessness of poverty. "There, in the final moments of people whose farthest horizon is always tomorrow, one sees the tragedy that enfolds the lives of the proletariat throughout the whole world; in those dying eyes there is a submissive apology and also, frequently, a desperate plea for consolation that is lost in the void, just as their body will soon be lost in the magnitude of misery surrounding us. How long this order of things based on an absurd sense of caste will continue is not within my means to answer, but it is time that those who govern dedicate less time to propagandizing the compassion of their regimes and more money, much more money, sponsoring works of social utility."

A few days later, after the Society of Friends of Easter Island confirmed that no ships would be sailing there for many months, Ernesto and Alberto reluctantly resigned themselves to their original itinerary. After a fruitless round of the wharves asking for work on board ships, they stowed away on the *San Antonio,* a cargo ship headed to the port of Antofagasta in northern Chile. Slipping aboard at dawn with the collusion of a friendly sailor, they crept into a latrine, where they hid. Once the ship started moving, Alberto began vomiting. The stench in the latrine was terrible, but they remained where they were until they could bear it no longer. "At five in the afternoon, dead of hunger and with the coast no longer in sight, we presented ourselves to the captain."

The captain turned out to be a good sport and, after giving them a thundering scolding in front of his junior officers, ordered them to be fed and given chores to help pay their way. "We devoured our rations contentedly," Ernesto recalled. "But when I found out that I was in charge of cleaning the famous latrine, the food backed up in my throat, and when I went down protesting under my breath, followed by the joking stare of Alberto,

in charge of peeling the potatoes, I confess I felt tempted to forget everything written about the rules of comradeship and request a change of jobs.
It's just not fair! He adds his good portion to the shit that's accumulated
there and I have to clean it up!"

Once they had finished their chores, the captain treated them as honored guests, and the three of them played canasta and drank together long
into the night. The next day, as the Chilean coastline slipped by, Alberto
again did kitchen duty while Ernesto cleaned the decks with kerosene under
the watchful eye of an irascible steward. That night, after another "tiring
round of canasta," the two friends stood together at the ship's rail to look
out at the sea and sky, with the lights of Antofagasta just beginning to appear in the distance.

In Antofagosta, a second attempt at stowing away on a ship heading
farther north failed when the two young men were discovered before the
ship set sail. It was their own fault. Hidden under a tarpaulin with a load of
tasty melons, they had been devouring the fruit and heedlessly hurling the
rinds overboard. The ever-growing procession of waterborne melon rinds
eventually drew the captain to their hiding place. "A long line of melons,
perfectly peeled, floated in Indian file upon the tranquil sea. The rest was
ignominious."

Their fantasy of continuing at sea having been rudely truncated, they
hitchhiked inland. Peru was their next destination, but first they wanted to
see the huge Chuquicamata copper mine, the world's largest open-pit mine
and the primary source of Chile's wealth. Ernesto's antipathy was already
aroused. As the ultimate symbol of foreign domination, "Chuqui" was the
subject of acrid debate within Chile. It and Chile's other copper mines were
run by American mining monopolies such as Anaconda and Kennecott. The
Chilean subsidiary of Kennecott was the Braden Copper Company, which
had once been owned by the family of the American proconsul Spruille
Braden, whose meddling in Argentina's politics during Perón's rise to power
had raised so many nationalists' hackles. These companies reaped huge profits, and Chile's economy was dependent on the revenues it received from
them, which varied from year to year, depending on the fluctuating copper
market. Resentful over the terms of this unequal partnership, many Chil-
eans, particularly on the left, were lobbying for the nationalization of the
mines. In response, the United States had pressured Chile's recent governments to break up the mining unions and outlaw the Communist Party.

While waiting for a ride in the arid desert mountains halfway to the
mine, Ernesto and Alberto met a marooned couple. As hours passed and
the Andean night fell in all its harsh coldness, they talked. He was a miner,
just released from prison, where he had been held for striking. He was lucky,

he told them. Other comrades had disappeared after their arrests and had presumably been murdered. But as a member of the outlawed Chilean Communist Party, he was unable to find work, and so, with his wife, who had left their children with a charitable neighbor, he was headed for a sulfur mine deep in the mountains. There, he explained, working conditions were so bad that no questions about political allegiances were asked.

Ernesto wrote at length about this encounter. "By the light of the single candle which illuminated us . . . the contracted features of the worker gave off a mysterious and tragic air. . . . The couple, frozen stiff in the desert night, hugging one another, were a live representation of the proletariat of any part of the world. They didn't even have a miserable blanket to cover themselves, so we gave them one of ours, and with the other, Alberto and I covered ourselves as best we could. It was one of the times when I felt the most cold, but it was also the time when I felt a little more in fraternity with this, for me, strange human species."

Here were the shivering flesh-and-blood victims of capitalist exploitation. Ernesto and Alberto had momentarily shared their lives—equally cold and hungry, equally tired and stranded. Yet he and Alberto were traveling for their own pleasure, while the other two were on the road because they had been persecuted for their beliefs.

The next morning, a truck heading for Chuquicamata came by. Leaving the couple behind to their uncertain future, Ernesto and Alberto climbed on board. The visit to the Chuquicamata copper mine became a wholly political experience for Ernesto, who still had the couple's image fresh in his mind. He wrote disdainfully of the American mine administrators as "blond, efficient, and impertinent masters" who grudgingly let them see the mine quickly on the condition that they leave as soon as possible, because it wasn't a "tourist attraction."

Their appointed guide, a Chilean, but a "faithful dog of the Yankee masters," nonetheless excoriated his bosses as he led them around. He said that a miners' strike was brewing. "Imbecile gringos, they lose millions of pesos a day in a strike in order to deny a few centavos more to a poor worker."

Ernesto dedicated a special chapter in his journal to the mine, carefully detailing its production process and its political importance to Chile. In his depiction, the ore-rich mountains surrounding Chuquicamata are "exploited proletariat," too. "The hills show their gray backs prematurely aged in the struggle against the elements, with elderly wrinkles that don't correspond to their geological age. How many of these escorts of their famous brother [Chuquicamata] enclose in their heavy wombs similar riches to his, as they await the arid arms of the mechanical shovels that devour their entrails, with their obligatory condiment of human lives?"

Chile was in the midst a heated presidential campaign, and most of the working class seemed supportive of the right-wing candidate, the former dictator General Carlos Ibañez del Campo, a man with aspirations to a populist caudillismo similar to those of Perón. Ernesto called the political scene "confusing," but ventured some guesses as to the outcome of the elections. Disqualifying the leftist candidate, Salvador Allende, from any chance at the polls because of the legal prohibition against Communist voters, he predicted that Ibañez woud win on an anti-American nationalistic platform that would include nationalizing the mines and undertaking large-scale public works projects.* He concluded with a recommendation and a prescient caveat for this "potentially rich" Latin American country. "The biggest effort it should make is to shake the uncomfortable Yankee friends from its back and that task is, at least for the moment, herculean, given the quantity of dollars invested and the ease with which they can exercise efficient economic pressure the moment their interests seem threatened."

When they left Chuquicamata, Ernesto and Alberto set out for Peru, crossing the border a few days later. Riding on the backs of trucks loaded with taciturn Aymara Indians, they headed inland, climbing toward Lake Titicaca, three miles above sea level. As the land unfolded, revealing ancient Incan canals sparkling with cascading water cut into the steep mountain slopes, and higher up the snowcapped Andean peaks, Ernesto became jubilant. "There we were in a legendary valley, detained in its evolution for centuries and which is still there today for us, happy mortals, to see."

IV

Ernesto's euphoria didn't last long. Stopping in the Indian town of Tarata, he looked around for effects of the Spanish conquest and found them: "A beaten race that watches us pass through the streets of the town. Their stares are tame, almost fearful, and completely indifferent to the outside world. Some give the impression that they live because it is a habit they can't shake."

---

*As Ernesto predicted, Ibañez was elected president. Salvador Allende came in last. The mines would not be nationalized under Ibañez, who soon had to go begging to the International Monetary Fund to cover a major balance-of-payments deficit. The IMF's harsh anti-inflationary terms caused widespread unrest, further polarizing the country. The preponderant role of North America in Chile's economy continued until 1970, when Salvador Allende became the hemisphere's first popularly elected socialist president. One of Allende's first acts was to nationalize the mines. North American influence in Chile did not lessen, however. Within three years, Allende's government was overthrown in a military coup backed by the United States.

Sustained contact with the "beaten race" over the next several weeks had an impact on Ernesto as he and Alberto wandered through the Andes. The harsh historical realities of four centuries of white domination were all too evident. If indigenous people in his own country were almost completely eradicated, devoured in the melting pot of modern Argentina with its millions of European migrants, here in Peru's highlands they were still a visible majority, their culture largely intact but pathetically subjugated.

In the crowded trucks they traveled on, carrying produce and human cargo alike in squalid heaps, Ernesto and Alberto were usually invited to ride up front with the drivers. It was the *cholos,* or Indians, with their filthy ponchos, their lice and unwashed stench, who sat in the exposed open backs of the trucks. For all their lack of money and their need to scrounge their way, Ernesto and Alberto were privileged, and they knew it. As whites, professionals, and Argentinians, they were the social superiors of those around them and, as such, were able to obtain favors and concessions beyond the imagining of Peru's indigenous citizens.

For accommodation and the occasional meal, they threw themselves at the mercy of Peru's Guardia Civil, the national police force, which had posts in every town. They were almost never refused. In one town, the police chief reacted to their plight by exclaiming: "What? Two Argentine doctors are going to sleep uncomfortably for lack of money? It can't be." And he insisted on paying for them to stay in a hotel. In Juliaca, they were having drinks in a bar as guests of a drunken Guardia Civil sergeant when he decided to show off his prowess as a marksman by firing his revolver into the wall. When the bar's owner, an Indian woman, ran for help and returned with a superior officer, Ernesto and Alberto went along with their host's story that no gunshot had been fired. Alberto, they said, had set off a firecracker. After an admonishment, they were free to go. As they exited the bar, the Indian woman screamed in futile protest: "These Argentines, they think they are the owners of everything." They were white; she was Indian. They had power; she didn't.

They were repeatedly asked questions by Peruvian Indians eager to hear about the marvelous land of Perón, where the poor had the same rights as the rich. Like doctors lying to terminally ill patients, they found themselves saying what their listeners wanted to hear.

The spectacular colonial city of Cuzco, built on the ruins of the Incan capital, with its outlying temples and fortresses, inspired Ernesto to fill his journal with lyrical and studious descriptions of the area's architecture and history. He and Alberto spent hours in the city's museum and library to gain a clearer understanding of the mysterious Incan archaeology and the culture that had created it.

Their luck as expert scroungers held out in Cuzco. Alberto went to see a doctor he had once met at a medical conference. The doctor graciously put a Land Rover and driver at their disposal to visit the Valley of the Incas, and he obtained tickets for a train journey to Machu Picchu, where they spent hours prowling around the stone ruins. After joining in a soccer game and showing off what Ernesto called their "relatively stupendous skills" at the sport, they were invited to stay on by the manager of the local tourist inn. After two days and nights, however, they were asked to leave to make way for a busload of paying North American tourists.

Returning to Cuzco on the stop-and-start, narrow-gauge train through the mountains, Ernesto saw the filthy third-class wagon reserved for Indian passengers and compared it to cattle cars in Argentina. Evidently still smarting over being forced to leave Machu Picchu, he vented his spleen at North American tourists. "Naturally the tourists who travel in their comfortable buses would know nothing of the condition of these Indians. . . . The majority of the North Americans fly directly from Lima to Cuzco, visit the ruins and then return, without giving any importance to anything else."

By now, he found it hard to contain his antipathy. In his journals, he took jabs at the "blond, camera-toting, sport-shirted correspondents from another world" whose presence he found irritating and intrusive. In a chapter called "The Land of the Inca," he derided North Americans as "ignorant of the moral distance separating them from the living remnants of the fallen [Incan] people, because only the semi-indigenous spirit of the South American can appreciate these subtle differences."

Ernesto had a fraternal feeling for the conquered indigenous races through whose lands he now traveled, whose ruins he visited, whose ancestors his own forebears had helped put to the knife. The two races, the Indian and the European, had met in a vast bloodletting, and centuries of intolerance and injustice still held them apart, but it was also what joined them together. It was from this unholy union that a new race, the mestizo, had been born. As the progeny of their shared history, the mestizo was perhaps the truest Latin American of all. But together, all of them—European-blooded Creoles, mestizos, and Indians—were closer to one another than to the Anglo-Saxons from the north, strolling around Cuzco and Machu Picchu's ruins like so many "aliens." They had a common language, history, and culture, and they faced common problems.

Like the medical researcher he was on his way to becoming, Ernesto searched for a cause when he saw a symptom. And, having found what he thought was the cause, he searched for an antidote. Thus, in Ernesto's mind, the old woman dying in Valparaíso and the persecuted couple on the road to Chuquicamata were "living examples of the proletariat in the whole world," who were in misery because of an unjust social order, and whose lives would not improve until enlightened governments changed the state of things. Symptom and cause were wrapped up into one ugly package. Standing behind the local regimes and perpetuating the injustice were the North Americans and their overwhelming economic power. Ernesto's antidote in the case of Chile was to "get the uncomfortable North American friend off its back," but he warned in the same breath of the dangers and difficulties of expropriation. Ernesto didn't have a cure for all these ills, but he was searching. Perhaps the "red flame dazzling the world" was the answer, but he wasn't yet sure.

V

After a fortnight in the domain of the Inca, Ernesto and Alberto traveled on to the Andean town of Abancay, where they requested, and received, free room and board at the hospital. In return, they gave some lectures on leprosy and asthma and flirted with the nurses. Ernesto had an attack of asthma, which had hardly bothered him since leaving Argentina; it was serious, and Alberto had to inject him with adrenaline three times.

Having made so much of being "leprosy experts," they were trying to live up to the description, and they had secured a letter of recommendation from their doctor friend in Cuzco to the authorities at the remote Huambo leprosarium. They set off for Huambo, and at the village of Huancarama, with the leper colony still several miles away over the forested hills, and with Ernesto's asthma so bad he could barely stand up, they asked an official for help in obtaining horses. A little while later, a Quechua-speaking guide appeared before them with two skinny mounts.

After traveling for several hours, Ernesto and Alberto noticed that they were being pursued on foot by an Indian woman and boy. When the pair finally caught up, they explained that the horses belonged to them. The official had seized them to help out the Argentine doctors. After many apologies, Ernesto and Alberto returned the horses and continued on foot.

The Huambo leprosarium was a rudimentary compound of thatched huts with dirt floors built in a mosquito-infested jungle clearing. A small but dedicated medical staff worked there on a minuscule budget. From the doctor in charge they learned that the founder of the leprosarium, Dr. Hugo Pesce, director of Peru's leper-treatment program, was also a prominent Communist, and they resolved to look him up when they reached Lima.

They were lodged and fed at the nearby home of a wealthy *hacendado* who explained the system he used to settle his immense wilderness landholding. He invited poor *colonos,* or settlers, onto the land to clear a patch of forest and plant crops. After the first harvests came in, the settlers were moved gradually to higher and less hospitable terrain. In this fashion, the *hacendado* said, his land was cleared for free.

They spent a couple of days in Huambo, but after an onset of heavy rains and a worsening of Ernesto's asthma, they decided he needed proper hospital treatment. The *hacendado* sent one of his Indian servants with them for the trek out. "In the mentality of the rich people of the zone," Ernesto observed, "it's completely natural that the servant, although traveling on foot, should carry all the weight and discomfort." Once out of sight of the rancher, he and Alberto relieved the Indian of their bags. The *cholo*'s face "revealed nothing" about what he thought of their gesture.

In the town of Andahuaylas, Ernesto went into the hospital for two days until his asthma subsided. Then they moved to the Guardia Civil barracks to wait for a truck leaving for Lima. They had little to eat except potatoes, corncobs, and yucca. The barracks also served as the local jail, and they shared the stove of the prisoners, most of whom were not criminals but Indians who had deserted from the military during their three years of obligatory service. Ernesto and Alberto were welcome there until the day Alberto complained that one of the guards was lewdly fondling the Indian women bringing food to their detained husbands. The atmosphere cooled considerably, but, fortunately, a cattle truck was leaving Andahuaylas, and Ernesto and Alberto were able to depart before they were kicked out.

For another ten days, uncomfortable and hungry, they followed an uncertain route through the Andes toward Lima. "Our trip continued in the same fashion, eating once in a while, whenever some charitable soul took pity on our indigence," Ernesto wrote. These were the most miserable days of their entire journey, and their strategies for obtaining hospitality now verged on the desperate.

They had perfected a formula for obtaining a free meal. They would first provoke curiosity by speaking in exaggerated Argentine accents. That generally broke the ice and initiated conversation. Then, either Ernesto or Alberto would begin softly mentioning their difficulties, with his gaze lost in the distance, while the other remarked on the coincidence that today was the first anniversary of their year on the road. "Alberto, who was much more brazen than I was, would launch a terrible sigh and say, as in confidence to me, 'What a shame to be in this condition, since we can't celebrate it,'" Ernesto recalled. At this point their candidate for a handout invariably offered to stand them a round of drinks, over Ernesto's and Alberto's protests that they couldn't possibly accept, since they couldn't reciprocate, until finally they gave in. This was followed by Ernesto's coup de grâce. "After the first drink I categorically refuse to accept more booze and Alberto makes fun of me. The buyer becomes angry and insists. I refuse without giving reasons. The man insists and then I, with a great deal of shame, confess that in Argentina the custom is to drink while *eating*."

VI

On May 1, "penniless but content" after four months on the road, they arrived in Lima, at the foothills of the Andes. Founded by Francisco Pizarro in 1535 and once the acclaimed city of the Spanish viceroys, Lima was still a beautiful, but socially stratified, place in 1952. To Ernesto, it represented "a Peru which has not left the feudal state of the colonial era: it still awaits the blood of a true emancipating revolution."

After a morning spent wandering from one police barracks to another until they were finally given some rice to eat, they called on the leprologist Dr. Hugo Pesce. Pesce received them warmly and arranged for them to stay in the Hospital de Guía, a leper hospital. There, his warmhearted assistant, Zoraida Boluarte, took them in hand. Before long, Ernesto and Alberto were eating their meals and having their laundry done at the Boluarte home.

For the next three weeks they ate, rested, caught up on correspondence, and explored the city. Most important, they received some money from their families. They also attended some of Pesce's lectures and were his frequent guests for dinner, after which they talked for hours about everything from leprosy and physiology to politics and philosophy.

Alberto noted that Ernesto and the man he called respectfully *el maestro* had a special affinity. Pesce had graduated from medical school in Italy, and when he returned home he became a disciple of the the the Peruvian Marxist philosopher José Carlos Mariátegui, whose pioneering *Seven Interpretative Essays on Peruvian Reality* outlined the revolutionary potential of Latin America's disenfranchised Indians and peasantry. After Mariátegui's death in 1930, Pesce remained a prominent member of the Peruvian Communist Party while continuing his career in medicine. In addition to earning renown as a leprologist, he was a university lecturer and a researcher in tropical diseases, with several discoveries about malaria to his credit. President Odría had exiled him to the Andes for a time but eventually allowed him to return to his teaching post in Lima. He had published a book called *Latitudes del Silencio* (Latitudes of Silence) based on his experience as an exile.

Pesce was the first man of medicine Ernesto had met who was consciously dedicating his life to the common good. He must have seemed like a Peruvian Schweitzer or Gandhi, pursuing the kind of principled life Ernesto hoped to lead himself. As for Marxism-Leninism, Ernesto was interested, but he still had to acquire more knowledge before committing himself to a particular ideology. He needed to finish the journey with Alberto, return to Argentina, complete his exams to get his degree, and explore the world some more.

Pesce seems to have sensed the younger man's anxiety about finding his place, and he responded by giving Ernesto a great deal of time and encouragement. A decade later, Ernesto acknowledged Pesce's influence when he sent him a copy of his first book, *Guerrilla Warfare*. It was inscribed "To Doctor Hugo Pesce: who, without knowing it perhaps, provoked a great change in my attitude toward life and society, with the same adventurous spirit as always, but channeled toward goals more harmonious with the needs of America."

Not all of Ernesto's and Alberto's time in Lima was spent on philosophical enlightenment. They played soccer with local youths near the Guía Hospital, told jokes to the lepers, and met the Boluarte youngsters' friends. One Sunday, they went to a bullfight. It was Ernesto's first *corrida de toros,* and he recorded his impressions in laconic style. "In the third *corrida* there was a certain degree of excitement when the bull flamboyantly hooked the *torero* and sent him flying into the air, but there was no more than that. The party ended with the death of the sixth animal, without shame or glory. I don't see art in it; bravery, after a fashion; skill, very little; excitement, relative. In summary, it all depends on what there is to do on a Sunday."

Now that Ernesto's health had improved and they had some—modest—funds, they resolved to continue their journey. They had given up hope of getting to the United States but planned to reach Venezuela. First, they would travel to the San Pablo leper colony in Peru's Amazonia region, the largest of Pesce's three treatment centers. Pesce gave them some clothes to replace their soiled and patched garments. Ernesto inherited a tropical white suit of the doctor's that was far too small for him, but he wore it with pride anyway. Zoraida Boluarte gave them a jar of marmalade, and the hospital patients and staff took up a collection and presented them with 100 Peruvian *soles,* the national currency, and a portable Primus stove.

A week later, after another muddy, stop-and-start bus crossing of the Andes, they were on the Río Ucayali, installed as first-class passengers on the river launch *La Cenepa*. It was bound for the old rubber-boom capital of Iquitos. Among their fellow passengers who strung hammocks on *La Cenepa*'s gangways were rubber-tappers, lumber merchants, a few adventurers, a couple of tourists, some nuns, and a seductive-looking young prostitute. The third-class passengers traveled on a barge that was towed behind and loaded with a cargo of pigs and lumber.

The journey took seven days, which they spent in conversation with the passengers and crew, playing cards, fighting off mosquitoes, and gazing

out at the muddy current and passing jungle. They flirted with the prostitute, whose loose behavior scandalized the nuns and wreaked havoc among
the men on board. "Fuser and I are no exception to the rule," confessed
Alberto after several days on board. "Especially me, who has a very sensitive heart for tropical beauties." In spite of a recurrence of his asthma, Ernesto
was drawn by the prospect of a shipboard romp. Describing their second
day on the river, he wrote: "The day passed without novelties, except for
making friends with a girl who seemed really loose and who must have
thought we might have a few pesos, despite the tears we wept every time
she talked of money."

Not ones to be defeated by talk of money, the two young Argentines
found a way around it. "She is enthusiastic about our accounts of the things
seen and the marvels still to see," Alberto wrote. "She has resolved to become a traveller. As a result, without interfering, Fuser and I are trying to
give her the necessary tutorials. Of course, the honorariums are paid in advance and in kind." A couple of days later, he added: "The rhythm of the
days is the same as before. The girl divides her charms amongst good talkers like ourselves, and good payers like the man in charge of the card games."

The sexual encounters made Ernesto nostalgic. "A careless caress from
the little whore who sympathized with my physical condition penetrated like
a spike into the dormant memories of my pre-adventure life," he wrote. "During the night, unable to sleep for the mosquitoes, I thought of Chichina, now
converted into a distant dream, a dream which was very pleasant and whose
ending leaves more melted honey than ice in the memory. I sent her a soft
and unhurried kiss that she might take as from an old friend who knows and
understands her; and memory took the road back to Malagueño, in the great
hall of so many long nights where she must have been at that moment pronouncing some of her strange and composed phrases to her new heartthrob."

He looked into the star-filled night sky and asked himself if it was
worth it to lose Chichina for *this*. Something in the nocturnal void told him
that it was.

Arriving on June 1 in Iquitos, which was surrounded by jungle and
tinged red from the laterite mud of its streets, Ernesto and Alberto made
for the regional health service authorities with their recommendations from
Dr. Pesce. Pending the embarkation of a boat headed down the Amazon to
the San Pablo leprosarium, they bunked in the headquarters for the regional
anti–yellow-fever campaign and ate meals at the Iquitos general hospital.

Ernesto's asthma was crippling him, and he spent the six days they were
in Iquitos prostrate, giving himself injections of adrenaline and writing letters home. In a letter to his aunt Beatriz, he referred to an earlier letter about
their proposed route through the Amazon: "By the way, I have to make a

confession. What I wrote you about the head-hunters, etc. . . . was a lie," he said. "Unfortunately it seems that the Amazon is as safe as the [Argentine] Paraná." He asked her to send a new asthma inhaler and ampoules of Yanal antiasthma medicine to him in Bogotá but assured her that he was well. He underlined the words, *"I don't have asthma."* He said he wished only to be prepared for any eventuality.

On June 6 Ernesto and Alberto set out aboard the river launch *El Cisne,* arriving two days later at the San Pablo leprosarium, which was located on the banks of the Amazon near Peru's jungle frontiers with Colombia and Brazil. The leprosarium had 600 patients who lived in their own village, isolated from the facility's administrators and medical staff. Here, as at the Hospital de Guía, the two Argentinians made quite an impression on everyone. They enthusiastically joined the doctors on visits to patients, played soccer, and made friends with the lepers. Alberto spent hours looking through microscopes in the laboratory while Ernesto read poetry, played chess, or went fishing. The daredevil in him also reared its head, and one afternoon he impulsively swam across the wide Amazon, taking two hours to do so and greatly unnerving the doctors, who watched from the shore.

On June 14, Ernesto's twenty-fourth birthday, the staff threw a party that was well lubricated by *pisco,* the Peruvian national liquor. Ernesto stood up to make a speech of thanks, which he recorded in his diary under the heading "Saint Guevara's Day." After grandiloquently expressing his profound gratitude to his hosts, he finished up with a heartfelt "Latin Americanist" soliloquy: "We believe, and after this trip even more firmly than before, that [Latin] America's division into illusory and uncertain nationalities is completely fictitious. We constitute a single *mestizo* race, which from Mexico to the Straits of Magellan presents notable ethnographic similarities. For this, in an attempt to rid myself of the weight of any meager provincialism, I raise a toast for Peru and for a united America."

The party went on until three in the morning in a house on stilts where a band played Peruvian waltzes, Brazilian *shoras,* Argentine tangos, and the popular Cuban mambo. By prior arrangement, Alberto gave the tone-deaf Ernesto a poke every time a tango was played. Once, when the band struck up an agitated *shora* that had been a favorite of Chichina's, Alberto nudged Ernesto, saying, "Do you remember?" But Ernesto, with his eye on a nurse across the room, interpreted Alberto's nudge as a tango signal, and he took to the floor, doggedly dancing a slow and passionate tango while everyone around them jiggled to the *shora.* Alberto was laughing too hard to correct him.

When Ernesto and Alberto felt ready to push on, after a stay of a fortnight, the lepers and staff built them a raft they called the *Mambo-Tango.* They received presents of clothes, pineapples, fishhooks, and two live chickens. The evening before they embarked, a lepers' orchestra came by canoe to the staff compound dock and serenaded them. In a letter to his mother, Ernesto described the scene. "In reality it was one of the most interesting spectacles we've seen until now. The singer was blind and the accordionist had no fingers on the right hand and had replaced them with some sticks tied to his wrist." The other musicians were similarly deformed and appeared as "monstrous figures" in the lights of the lanterns and torches reflected on the river. The serenade was followed by good-bye speeches and shouts of "three hurrahs for the doctors." Alberto thanked them with outstretched arms and a display of rhetoric so purple, Ernesto wrote, that he seemed like "Perón's successor."

The next day, Ernesto and Alberto pushed their raft into the Amazon's current. Feeling a little more like explorers, they steered the *Mambo-Tango* downriver, entertaining the notion of traveling all the way to the city of Manaus, in Brazil. From there, they had been told, they could reach Venezuela through its back door, along the Amazon's tributaries. Three days later, however, having been swept downriver past the tiny Colombian port of Leticia, and after losing their fishhooks and their remaining chicken, they decided to give up their ambitious intentions. After persuading a riverside *colono* to row them back upriver in exchange for their raft and provisions, they made for Leticia, where a twice-monthly plane flew to the Colombian capital of Bogotá.

Scroungers again, they secured free room and board with the police as well as the promise of a 50 percent discount on the next airplane out. Argentina's reputation for having Latin America's best soccer players served them well in the interim. The local soccer team was facing a series of play-off matches, and Ernesto and Alberto were hired as coaches. They showed the players the latest Buenos Aires footwork and *were* able to improve the team's performance. Although their team didn't win the tournament, it came in a respectable second, and everyone was pleased.

On July 2, settled in comfortably with a cargo of virgin rubber, military uniforms, and mailbags, they took off from Leticia in an ancient twin-engine Catalina hydroplane that Ernesto compared to a cocktail shaker. The airplane ride marked another euphoric first for Alberto, who had never flown before, and his excitement led him to wax poetic for their fellow passengers about his vast flying experience.

VII

Ernesto and Alberto found Bogotá unfriendly and unsettling. The city was a tense island of rigidly enforced law and order with a vicious civil war swirling around it in the countryside. They were given lodging at a hospital, thanks to another letter from Dr. Pesce, and were able to eat their meals at the university, where they made friends among the students; but, as Ernesto wrote to his mother, "Of all the countries we have traveled through, this is the one in which individual guarantees are the most suppressed; the police patrol the streets with their rifles on their shoulders and constantly demand one's passport. . . . It is a tense calm that indicates an uprising before long. The plains are in open revolt and the army is impotent to repress it; the conservatives fight among themselves and can't agree on anything; and the memory of the 9th of April 1948 weighs like lead over everyone's spirit. . . . In summary, an asphyxiating climate, which the Colombians can stand if they want, but we're beating it as soon as we can."

Ernesto was referring to the April 1948 assassination of the popular Liberal Party leader Jorge Eliécer Gaitán, which had led to the violent breakdown of Colombia's political system. Suspecting the incumbent Conservative government of having ordered his death, Gaitán's supporters had taken to the streets of the capital in three days of bloody rioting that became known as "El Bogotazo." The riots occurred during a summit meeting of hemispheric foreign ministers who, under U.S. auspices, had gathered to sign the charter of the Organization of American States. At the same time, an "anti-imperialist" Latin American students' conference had been convened to protest the summit. Student leaders from all over the region had come for the event. Among them had been a twenty-one-year-old Cuban law student named Fidel Castro Ruz. He took up arms in the uprising that followed Gaitán's killing, but avoided arrest after escaping to the Cuban embassy. He had returned to Cuba, became increasingly active in politics, and was now secretly plotting an armed uprising against the recently installed regime of Fulgencio Batista.

In Colombia, the violence spawned by the Bogotazo had been polarizing. The Liberal Party had refused to participate in the 1949 presidential elections, and the ruling Conservative Party's candidate, Laureano Gómez, who was supported by the military, was elected unopposed. Many Liberals had found allies among Colombia's fledgling Communist guerrilla groups based in the countryside. As anarchy spread, the army and groups of armed peasant vigilantes led by Conservative political bosses took reprisals, and massacres became commonplace. The bloodshed was called simply "La Violencia," a euphemism for what had become a national plague, and in 1952 there was no end in sight.

Before they could get out of Bogotá, Ernesto and Alberto found themselves in trouble with the police. One day, on their way to the Argentine consulate to pick up letters from home, they were stopped, questioned, and searched by a suspicious police agent. The agent confiscated Ernesto's knife, a silver replica gaucho's dagger that had been a going-away gift from his brother Roberto. When the policeman found his asthma medicine, Ernesto tactlessly taunted him: "Be careful, it's a very dangerous poison." They were promptly arrested and hauled to several police stations until finally they were brought before a judge and accused of "making fun" of the authorities. The incident was defused after they showed identification. But for Ernesto, the matter hadn't ended. It was a question of honor for him to get back his knife, which the arresting police agent had kept for himself. The knife was finally returned to him, but he had raised the policemen's hackles. Ernesto's student friends urged him and Alberto to leave Colombia immediately. They even took up a collection of money to help them depart.

Without regrets, they left Bogotá by bus, heading to the Venezuelan border. Ernesto's asthma had not bothered him since Iquitos, but as they descended into the tropical lowlands, it returned. Alberto had to give Ernesto so many adrenaline injections that he began worrying about the effects on his friend's heart.

At a pit stop a day's journey from Caracas, they discussed their prospects. Both of them were enthusiastic about forging on to Central America and Mexico. On the other hand, they had no money to continue traveling. They reached an agreement. Ernesto's uncle Marcello, who bred horses, had a business partner in Caracas. If he would let Ernesto on the plane they used to transport the horses, he would return to Buenos Aires to finish his medical studies. Alberto would try to stay on in Venezuela, working either at a leprosarium or for one of the universities to which he carried letters of recommendation. If neither of these plans worked out, they would try to continue as far as Mexico.

The next day, July 17, they reached Caracas, a bustling city rich from the country's oil boom and swollen with migrants. Ernesto had rarely been around black people. They were a rarity in Argentina but common on South America's Caribbean coast, and after meandering through a Caracas *barrio,* he made observations that were rather stereotypical and reflected white, especially Argentine, arrogance and condescension. "The blacks, those magnificent examples of the African race who have conserved their racial purity by a lack of affinity with washing, have seen their patch invaded by a different kind of slave: the Portuguese," he wrote. "The two races now share a common experience, fraught with bickering and squabbling. Discrimination and poverty unite them in a daily battle for survival but their different attitudes to life separate them completely: the black is indolent and fanciful, he spends his money on frivolity and drink; the European comes from a tradition of working and saving which follows him to this corner of America and drives him to get ahead, even independently of his own individual aspirations."

They installed themselves in a shabby pension, but after they contacted Margarita Calvento, the aunt of a friend of Ernesto's, their lives improved. She fed them and found them lodging at a Catholic Youth hostel, and from there they set out on their respective missions: Ernesto to look for his uncle's partner, and Alberto to look for a job. With a letter of recommendation from Dr. Pesce, Alberto was offered, and accepted, a well-paying position at a leprosarium near Caracas. Ernesto was granted a seat on the next plane transporting his uncle's racehorses from Buenos Aires to Miami. When it stopped for refueling in Caracas, Ernesto would get on board, and after the cargo was unloaded in Miami, he would fly home.

The two friends' last days in Caracas together were weighed down by sadness over their impending separation. Both tried to hide their feelings by discussing the immediate future. Ernesto would get his degree and rejoin Alberto in a year's time. If all went well, he could also get work at the leprosarium, and after saving some money they would go off on new adventures together.

On July 26, Ernesto boarded the plane with its equine cargo and flew to Miami. Upon landing, however, the pilot discovered an engine fault. They would have to lay over until it was repaired. Expecting a delay of a few days, Ernesto went to stay with Chichina's cousin Jaime "Jimmy" Roca, who was in Miami finishing up at architecture school. Roca was as broke as Ernesto, but he had made a deal to eat his meals on credit at a Spanish restaurant until he sold his car. Ernesto's meals were now added to his bill.

As the repairs on Ernesto's plane dragged on, and the days turned into weeks, the two youths devoted themselves to having as good a time as possible without cash, going to the beach every day and roaming the city. A friendly Argentine waiter at the Spanish restaurant gave them extra food, and at a bar another friend of Roca's slipped them free beers and french fries. When Roca learned that Ernesto was still carrying the fifteen dollars Chichina had given him to buy her a scarf, he tried to persuade him to spend it. Ernesto refused. Chichina might have broken up with him, but he was determined to keep his promise, and despite Roca's entreaties he bought her scarf.*

Finally, Roca arranged for Ernesto to earn some pocket money cleaning the apartment of a Cuban airline stewardess he knew. This was a disaster, since Ernesto didn't have a clue how to go about his task. After his one attempt, the stewardess told Roca not to send him again. Instead of

---

*According to Pepe González-Aguilar, Ernesto did not try to see Chichina again when he returned home, but he did send her the scarf.

cleaning it, she said, Ernesto had somehow managed to leave her place dirtier than it was before. In spite of this, she had taken a liking to him and she helped him get a temporary job washing dishes at a restaurant.

Ernesto was finally in the United States, that "country to the north" whose exploitative presence in Latin America had rankled him so during his journey. What he saw there evidently confirmed his negative preconceptions, for he later told friends in Buenos Aires that he had witnessed incidents of white racism against blacks and had been questioned by American policemen about his political affiliations. Roca would recall only that Ernesto once spoke to him about the need for low-income housing for Latin America's poor. They didn't talk politics, he said, but just tried to enjoy themselves.

6

I Am Not the Person I Was Before

Ernesto returned to an Argentina that had been altered in his absence. On July 26, 1952, five days before his arrival in Buenos Aires, Evita Perón succumbed to cancer at the age of thirty-three. Her body was to lie in state for two weeks before the funeral, which was the occasion for an unprecedented public display of grief. A monument larger than the Statue of Liberty was being planned for her. Juan Domingo Perón, her grieving husband, carried on with his presidential duties while his courtiers whispered and his enemies conspired. It was politics as usual in Argentina, but to those around him, Perón seemed adrift, less whole.

Ernesto's private life had its own drama. He had to pass examinations in thirty subjects to get his medical degree; he had sixteen under his belt before taking off with Alberto Granado, but if he wanted his diploma in the coming school year, he needed to pass fourteen more by May. He had little time to waste. The first round of exams was scheduled for November. He began studying furiously, barricading himself behind his books at his aunt Beatriz's apartment and sometimes at his father's studio on Calle Paraguay, coming home only for the occasional meal. Despite the pressure, he also put in time at the allergy clinic, where Dr. Pisani was glad to have him back.

He began to take stock of the journey he had made with Alberto by expanding the material in his travel diary. He knew that the journey had changed him: "The person who wrote these notes died upon stepping once again onto Argentine soil. The person who edits and polishes them, me, is no longer. At least I am not the person I was before. The vagabonding through our 'America' has changed me more than I thought."

At home, things were much the same. His father continued to struggle with the construction and property-rental business. His mother, the distracted queen bee of Calle Araoz, played solitaire and looked after Juan Martín, who was now nine and still in grade school. Roberto had finished high school and was doing his compulsory military service, while Celia and Ana María were both studying architecture at Buenos Aires University. Celia *madre*'s salon had grown, and some new personalities had attached themselves to the Guevara clan. Ana María had formed a study-circle of student friends. Among them were Fernando Chávez and Carlos Lino, both of whom were vying for her attentions. For now, she was dating Lino, but she would eventually marry Chávez. The Guevaras were pleased that Ernesto was home, hoping he had rid himself of his wanderlust and that he would settle down in Buenos Aires as a doctor or allergy researcher.

In the midst of the first round of exams, in November, Ernesto fell seriously ill, not from his asthma this time, but from a fever contracted by exposing himself to diseased human viscera. Doctor Pisani had acquired a machine designed to grind viscera for research purposes, and, impatient to use it, Ernesto had obtained some infected human remains from the Medical Faculty and began grinding them up without using a protective shield. Afterward he felt ill and took to his bed with a high fever. His father found him there. Alarmed, and seeing him appear to worsen by the minute, Ernesto senior offered to call Dr. Pisani. Ernesto refused. Some time passed; his father waited by his side, watching his son closely. "All of a sudden he made me a sign and, when I drew near, he told me to call a hospital to bring him a cardiac stimulant immediately, and to call Dr. Pisani," Ernesto Guevara Lynch recalled.

Within minutes of Ernesto senior's call, Pisani and a nurse arrived, and Pisani took charge of the situation, staying alone with Ernesto for several hours. When he left, he told the family to buy certain medicines and ordered complete rest for the paitent. The anguished family stayed up with him the whole night. It was one of many such episodes—caused, his father thought, by Ernesto's "imprudence"—that they had suffered over the years.

"At about six in the morning," his father recalled, "Ernesto had improved, and, to our great surprise, we saw that he began to get dressed. I didn't say anything. I knew he was very stubborn, but in the end, seeing he was dressing to go outside, I asked him: 'What are you going to do?' 'I've got an exam, the examiners arrive at eight in the morning.' 'But don't be an animal,' I replied. 'Don't you see you can't do that?' All the objections I made to him at that moment were in vain. He had decided to take his exam that day and he had to do it. And that is what he did."

Ernesto passed three exams in November and ten more the next month. He had only one remaining examination to pass in April before he qualified for his medical degree and could return to Venezuela. In the meantime, he spent as much time as possible on his research at the Pisani Clinic. He was finding it exciting, for he could not only apply himself to the cases of actual patients afflicted by allergies but also attempt to isolate their causes and find antidotes in the laboratory.

Pisani encouraged him as much as possible and began giving him credit in some published findings. One, which appeared in the scientific quarterly *Alergia* for November 1951–February 1952, listed Ernesto's name along with Dr. Pisani's and several others as coauthors of a paper entitled "Sensibilization of Guinea Pigs to Pollens through Injections of Orange Extract."

On April 11, 1953, Ernesto sat for his final exam. His father remembered the occasion: "I was in my studio when the telephone rang. I picked it up and instantly recognized his voice, which said: 'Dr. Ernesto Guevara de la Serna speaking.' He put emphasis on the word Doctor."

"My happiness was great," his father wrote. "But it lasted only a short time." Ernesto would not be staying in Buenos Aires to work. He and his old friend Calica Ferrer were going to take a trip. They planned on traveling through Bolivia so that Ernesto could revisit the Incan ruins he had studied. As for their longer-range plans, Ernesto spoke of going to India, while Calica, more interested in the good life, saw himself in Paris, well dressed at cocktail parties, with pretty women on his arm. "Our goal, as I recall it," Calica said later, "was to get to Venezuela, work a little, as little as possible, and then go to Europe."

Ernesto's family knew they couldn't persuade him to stay. And they knew the trip would be physically rigorous. "He didn't even remotely consider his asthma or his state of health," his father said. But "he was no longer the child or the youth, but Dr. Ernesto Guevara de la Serna, who did whatever he wanted." When Ernesto informed Dr. Pisani that he was leaving, the doctor offered him a paying job, an apartment at the clinic, and a future at his side in allergy research. Ernesto refused. His mind was made up; he didn't want to "stagnate" like Pisani.

In June, Ernesto received a copy of his medical degree, and a few days later he celebrated his twenty-fifth birthday. He and Calica set about getting their visas and assembling funds for the trip. As Calica recalled: "First, we asked our aunts. All our aunts, grandmothers . . . , whoever we could ask for a loan. And as we went along, Ernesto and I made our calculations. 'Did you hit up so-and-so?' 'Yes, I asked her for so much.' 'My grandmother's going to give me some, and Mama is also going to give me money.'"

Soon, they had collected the equivalent of $300 each and all the visas they needed, except for the one for Venezuela. With its oil-boom economy, Venezuela had become a magnet for thousands of foreign job-seekers and had clamped down on visas. When they presented themselves at the Venezuelan consulate, they were refused visas because they didn't have return airplane tickets. Ernesto told Calica not to worry; they would get the visas in another country along the way. Meanwhile, he turned the incident into a humorous anecdote for his friends. To Tita Infante, he said it had all been a simple misunderstanding. The consul had mistaken one of his asthma attacks, which contorted his features, for anger and became frightened for his own safety.

Calica had been designated the "economist" of the trip—that is, he would carry the money. His mother made him a money belt to wear inside his underwear, and when Ernesto saw it he immediately dubbed it the "chastity belt." They bought second-class tickets for the July 7 train to Bolivia leaving from Belgrano station. They were ready to go.

A large crowd of family and friends gathered at the station to see them off. Ernesto was dressed in military fatigues, a gift from his brother Roberto. They had brought far too much baggage. Ernesto had packed more books than clothes. As they sat down on the wooden benches in a second-class compartment that was crowded with Indians and their bundles, both young men were painfully aware of the contrast between their humble fellow passengers and their own well-dressed relatives and friends. At the last minute, a plethora of gifts and packages of goodies were pressed into their hands: cakes from Calica's mother, sweets from someone else.

Watching from the platform, Ernest's mother, Celia, clutched the hand of Roberto's fiancée, Matilde, and said forlornly: "My son is leaving; I won't see him again." The conductor whistled and the train began to move out of the station. Everyone shouted good-bye and waved.

As the train pulled slowly away, a lone figure separated itself from the throng and ran alongside the compartment where Ernesto and Calica sat. It was Celia, waving a handerchief in the air. She said nothing, but tears ran down her face. She ran alongside the train until the station platform ended and she could run no more. Then the train was gone.

7

Without Knowing Which Way Is North

I

Ernesto Guevara, medical doctor and veteran road gypsy, was off again. "This time, the name of the sidekick has changed," he wrote in a new journal he entitled "Otra Vez" (Once Again).* "Now Alberto is called Calica, but the journey is the same: two disparate wills extending themselves through America without knowing precisely what they seek or which way is north."

Ernesto's train had not been gone long when his cousin Mario Saravia made a surprising discovery. Returning to the Guevara home, where he was staying, Saravia noticed that his three new silk shirts were missing. He suspected Ernesto of taking them, and he told Celia *madre* as much. She was shocked and disbelieving, but when Saravia wrote to Ernesto to ask if he had taken the shirts, Ernesto replied that he had. Not to worry, he said, the shirts had been put to good use. He had sold them and used the money to "eat and sleep for fifteen days." In revenge, Saravia wrote back to inform him, falsely, that he'd sold the prized microscope Ernesto had left with him for safekeeping, and used the money to go "on a holiday."

Ernesto and Calica languished in the dusty border post of La Quiaca for three days, recovering, and continued their journey into Bolivia by train.

---

*This journal, spanning three years of Guevara's life, was found and transcribed by his widow, Aleida March, after his death. Except for a few extracts, it had never been made public when I was in Cuba working on this book, but Aleida March made the entire text available to me. It appeared to be largely unabridged, except for several sexually graphic passages that she acknowledged having deleted in the interest of preserving the "propriety" of her late husband's image. Subsequent to the publication of my book in 1997, the journal was published in Spanish and English.

But at Calica's insistence, they now traveled in a first-class sleeping compartment. Two days later, they descended from the freezing brown altiplano
and into the great natural crater where the city of La Paz huddled like some
kind of experimental lunar colony. The setting was impressive. At the city's
far edges the clean lines of the crater broke up into eroded badlands of giant white stalagmites that jutted out like daggers. Above them, the land
climbed into a swooping rise of alpine rock and glacial ice to form the blue
and white volcano of Mount Illimani.

    Ernesto was enthralled. "La Paz is the Shanghai of the Americas," he
wrote enthusiastically in his journal. "A rich gamut of adventurers of all
the nationalities vegetate and flourish in the polychromatic and mestizo city."

    After checking into a dingy hotel, they set out to explore the steep
cobblestoned streets thronged with colorfully costumed Indians and groups
of armed vigilantes. This was revolutionary Bolivia, Latin America's most
Indian of nations and also one of its poorest, with a notorious history of
exploitation. The majority indigenous population had languished as virtual
serfs for centuries while a few ruling families were made extremely wealthy
from their tight control of the tin mines—Bolivia's prime source of income—
and the productive agricultural land. But now the long-standing state of
affairs appeared to have been overturned. Since seizing power in a popular
revolt a year earlier, the Movimiento Nacionalista Revolucionario (MNR)
had disbanded the army and nationalized the mines. A hotly debated agrarian reform law was due to come into effect in a few weeks' time.

    Bolivia remained unsettled, with many political forces still at odds and
threatening the regime's stability. In the countryside, impatient peasants
were forcing the land-reform issue by attacking private haciendas, while
miners led by the newly created independent trade union federation, the
Central Obrera Boliviana (COB), marched in displays of force to extract
further concessions from the government. Armed people's militias roamed
the streets, and rumors flew of countercoups by disgruntled elements of the
disbanded army. One conspiracy had already been quelled in January. At
the same time, right- and left-wing branches within the ruling MNR coalition pursued opposing agendas, with the Communists calling for a total
handover of power to the workers while the center-right wing, including
President Víctor Paz Estenssoro, sought to follow a middle road that isolated both the Communists and the local oligarchs.

    While prowling around town, Ernesto and Calica bumped into a
young Argentinian they had met on their train ride. He was visiting his
father, Isaías Nogues, a prominent politician and sugar-mill owner from the
province of Tucumán who was now in exile as an an opponent of Perón. It
soon emerged that Nogues was acquainted with both their families, and he

invited Calica and Ernesto to his home for an elaborate dinner, at which they met other members of La Paz's expatriate Argentine community. Ernesto described their host as a hidalgo, a nobleman. "Exiled from Argentina, he is the center of the [expatriate] colony, which sees in him a leader and a friend. His political ideas have been outdated in the world for some time now, but he maintains them independently of the proletarian hurricane that has been let loose on our bellicose sphere. He extends a friendly hand to any Argentinian without asking who he is or why he has come, and his august serenity throws over us miserable mortals his eternal, patriarchal protection."

They also met Nogues's visiting playboy brother, "Gobo," just back from the good life in Europe. A social high roller with an open wallet and a great many contacts, Gobo claimed to be a friend of the Greek shipping tycoon Aristotle Onassis. He took a liking to the young travelers and introduced them to the city's bars and restaurants. With him they discovered the Gallo de Oro, an Argentine-owned cabaret where politicians, exiles, and adventurers mingled with La Paz's fast set over drinks. The Gallo de Oro soon became one of their regular hangouts. Here they were able to see a different Bolivia from the one pullulating on the streets outside. Once, suffering from diarrhea, Ernesto made a dash to the Gallo's men's washroom, returning a few minutes later to tell Calica in a shocked tone that he had just observed two men snorting cocaine.

Another hangout was the terrace of the Hotel La Paz, where Argentine exiles dallied over drinks and coffee while discussing the politics of home and the Bolivian revolution. It was a good aerie from which to observe the daily processions of Indians marching by on their way to the presidential palace, demanding this or that from the government. One day, looking out at the crowd on the sidewalk, Calica spotted a pair of pretty girls and ventured down to see if he could pick one of them up. The girls were accompanied by an older man who turned out to be a Venezuelan general named Ramírez who was serving in "gilded exile" as his country's military attaché. Showing good grace in spite of Calica's blatant intentions, the general invited him for a drink, and before long Calica had extracted Ramírez's promise to grant his and Ernesto's previously denied Venezuelan visas.

General Ramírez not only secured visas for Ernesto and Calica. He invited them out on the town. Calica paired off with one of the girls he'd met with the general on their first encounter, and one evening Ernesto also met someone who seemed promising. "Something undulating and with a maw has crossed my path," he wrote in his diary. "We'll see." The "something undulating" turned out to be Marta Pinilla, the rich daughter of an aristocratic family whose lands extended for miles outside the capital.

On July 22, 1953, buoyed by the upturn in their fortunes, Calica wrote his mother a spirited letter. Thanks to Nogues, they had been able to move out of their hotel and were now being well looked after as paying guests in the home of an affluent Argentine family. They were living "an intense social life," he said. "The best people of La Paz invite us to lunch. . . . All the Argentines here are very united, they have behaved fantastically with us. All the time it's tea, meals in the Sucre and the Hotel La Paz, the two best ones. . . . This afternoon we're having tea with a couple of rich girls and tonight we're going to a dance."

Although Ernesto wanted to get to know the Bolivian revolution better, their social contacts gave them entrée into a La Paz elite that was the natural enemy of the changes taking place in the country. Calica recalled, for instance, that Marta's wealthy family was about to have its lands expropriated in the upcoming agrarian reform. One night, as they returned home from the Gallo de Oro, their car was stopped at gunpoint by one of the ubiquitous Indian patrols roaming the city. "They made us get out, asked us for documents, and Gobo, a bit drunk, said to one of them, '*Indio,* put away that shotgun, use it to shoot partridges,'" Calica recalled.

Calica tended to echo the racist attitudes of their rich white friends, but Ernesto reflected on what he was seeing. "The so-called *good* people, the cultured people, are astonished at the events taking place and curse the importance given to the Indian and the *cholo,* but in everyone I seem to sense a spark of nationalist enthusiasm with some of the government's actions. . . . Nobody denies the need to finish off the state of things symbolized by the power of the three tin-mine hierarchies, and the young people believe it has been a step forward in the struggle toward a greater equality in people and fortunes."

They had intended to stay only a week in La Paz, but it was hard to leave. "This is a very interesting country and it is living through a particularly effervescent moment," Ernesto wrote to his father on July 22. "On the second of August the agrarian reform goes through, and fracases and fights are expected throughout the country. We have seen incredible processions of armed people with Mausers and 'piripipí' [tommy guns], which they shoot off for the hell of it. Every day shots can be heard and there are wounded and dead from firearms.

"The government shows a near-total inability to restrain or lead the peasant masses and miners, but these respond to a certain degree and there is no doubt that in the event of an armed revolt by the Falange, the opposing party, they will be at the side of the MNR. Human life has little importance here and it is given and taken without any great to-do. All of this makes this a profoundly interesting situation to the neutral observer."

Ernesto wanted to witness the historic and possibly tumultuous event on August 2. Meanwhile, he and Calica took advantage of every dinner invitation from Nogues. Calica wrote to his mother, "Ernesto eats as if he hasn't eaten in a week. He's famous in the group." Gobo placed bets on how much Ernesto could down in one sitting and promised that if they met up in Lima, where they were all headed, he would take Ernesto and Calica to a restaurant where the food was free if the clients ate enough. It would give him great pleasure, he declared, "to show off these proud examples of the Argentine race."

It was during one of these evenings at the Nogueses' home that they met the Argentine lawyer Ricardo Rojo. A tall, beefy, balding man with a mustache, Rojo was only twenty-nine but was already a seasoned political veteran. An *antiperonista* of the opposition Unión Cívica Radical, he had recently escaped from police custody in Buenos Aires, where he had been detained on suspicion of terrorism. He had taken refuge in the Guatemalan embassy and was flown to Chile with travel documents from the leftist Guatemalan government of Jacobo Arbenz. Rojo made his way to La Paz and, like Ernesto Guevara and every other Argentinian passing through, beat a path to the home of Isaías Nogues. Proud of his recent exploit, he carried a clipping from *Life* magazine with an account of his escape and flight to safety. From Bolivia he planned to go to Peru, then to Guatemala, and eventually to the United States.

At the Nogues home, Rojo also took notice of Guevara's "savage" eating habits and was surprised to learn that he was a medical doctor, since he talked mostly about archaeology. "The first time I saw him, Guevara didn't particularly impress me," he said later. "He spoke little, preferring to listen to the conversation of others. But then, suddenly, he would cut the speaker down with a disarming smile and a razor-sharp comment." It was a trait they shared. Rojo too had a mordant wit and sharp tongue, and he enjoyed debating as much as Ernesto did. That first night, they walked back together to Ernesto's hostel, talking. According to Rojo, they "became friends, although the only thing we really had in common at the time was that we were both young university students pressed for money. I wasn't interested in archaeology, nor he in politics, at least not in the sense that politics had meaning for me then and would later have for him." Following this encounter the two arranged to meet again; in fact, Rojo would keep popping into and out of Guevara's life over the next decade.*

Ernesto wanted to be in La Paz on the second of August, but he was also eager to see the conditions in the notorious Bolivian mines for himself.

*See Notes.

Although it meant being out of town on the momentous day, with its threat of a counterrevolutionary uprising, he and Calica arranged a visit to the Bolsa Negra wolframite mine. (Wolframite is a major source of tungsten, which is traditionally used in the manufacture of munitions.) The mine's engineers showed them where striking miners and their families had been cut down by machine guns before the revolution. Now, the mine belonged to the state. Here, as at Chuquicamata, Ernesto was moved by what he saw. "The silence of the mine assails even those like us who don't know its language," he wrote.

Ernesto and Calica spent a night at Bolsa Negra, and as they prepared to go back to La Paz they saw truckloads of miners returning from the city. The miners had been demonstrating their support for the agrarian reform law and now they were firing their guns into the sky. With their "stony faces and red plastic helmets" they appeared to be "warriors from other worlds" to Ernesto, although it turned out that there had been little unrest for them to be involved in.

The visit to Bolsa Negra reinforced Ernesto's belief that real independence was impossible as long as the United States controlled export markets: "Today this is the only thing that keeps Bolivia going; it is a mineral the Americans buy and for this reason the government has ordered production increased." Bolivia's revolutionary government had already come under strong pressure from the Eisenhower administration to proceed cautiously with its reforms. And it had heeded the advice. Only the mines of the three biggest tin barons had been confiscated. Bolivia was still dependent on the United States as a buyer for its minerals and for the prices they brought.

Since Eisenhower had assumed office, the United States had embarked on an aggressive policy to contain "Soviet-Communist expansionism" abroad, and Bolivia's President Paz Estenssoro had only to look around in the summer of 1953 to see what difficulties his government might encounter should he incur Washington's wrath. Guatemala's left-leaning government was coming under mounting attack from Washington for its own agrarian reforms, which had nationalized the powerful United Fruit Company's interests there. United Fruit wanted revenge and was already showing that it had influential friends in high places.

Joseph Stalin had died in March 1953, but the Cold War continued unabated. In a bid to achieve strategic-arms parity with the United States, the U.S.S.R. was putting finishing touches on the hydrogen bomb, which it would explode on August 12. Two weeks earlier an armistice was signed in Korea, ending three years of bloodletting. The truce left the peninsula divided and in ruins. Now East and West faced each other across another hostile border, adding a new flash point to an increasingly divided world.

In Cuba, a country considered "safe" by Washington, events were taking place that would soon have a profound significance in Ernesto's life. On July 26, a group of young rebels hoping to spark off a national revolt against the military dictator Fulgencio Batista had attacked and temporarily overrun the Moncada army barracks in the city of Santiago. Only eight rebels died in the actual fighting, while nineteen government soldiers were killed, but the rebels were finally routed. Despite attempts by Batista to link the attack to "Communists," Cuba's Communist Party decried it as a bourgeois putsch and denied any involvement. Sixty-nine of the young rebels were subsequently executed or tortured to death. The survivors, including the revolt's twenty-six-year-old student leader, Fidel Castro, and his younger brother, Raúl, were taken into custody.

II

In revolutionary La Paz, Ernesto and Calica met with the head of the newly created Ministry of Peasant Affairs, Ñuflo Chávez, whose job it was to implement the agrarian reform bill. Ernesto found the ministry "a strange place, full of Indians of different groups of the altiplano waiting their turns to be received in audience. Each group had its typical costume and was led by a caudillo or indoctrinator who addressed them in their native tongue. The employees dusted them upon entering with DDT."

The spectacle made Ernesto indignant. It pointed to the cultural divide that still existed between the revolution's leaders and the common people they were supposed to represent. To Calica, the spraying with DDT seemed reasonable enough, since the Indians "were filthy and crawling with lice, and the ministry's carpets and curtains had to be protected from such vermin." Whenever they saw an Indian in the street with his hair dusted white, he and Ernesto would look at each other and remark, "Look, he's been with Ñuflo Chávez."

By now Ernesto and Calica had been in La Paz nearly a month. They had spent half of their available capital, and they had their visas for Venezuela. It was time to get back on the road, but both of them were finding it difficult to pull up roots. When they finally agreed to leave, Ernesto wrote: "Each of us had his amorous reference to leave behind. My good-bye was more in the intellectual plane, without sweetness, but I believe there is something between us, her and me." Calica, meanwhile, believed he was in love, and had made promises to return to La Paz for his new sweetheart after he had found his feet in Caracas.

After a brief trip to Lake Titicaca, Ernesto and Calica reached the Peruvian border. At the customs post in the border town of Puno, Ernesto's books provoked an incident. As he told it, "they confiscated two books: *Man in the Soviet Union* and a publication of the Ministry of Peasant Affairs, which was described as Red, Red, Red in exclamatory and recriminating tones." After a "juicy chat," however, the police chief let them go and agreed to send Ernesto's books to Lima.

They traveled from Puno to Cuzco. Ernesto was delighted to be back, but Calica was singularly unimpressed. He wrote his mother that although Cuzco was an interesting city, it was also "the dirtiest you can possibly imagine," so filthy that it "obliged one to bathe." However, he told her jokingly, in the eight days they were there, Ernesto "bathed once and by mutual agreement, for health purposes only."

After a few days, Calica's complaints about the dirt and discomfort had begun to wear on Ernesto. Writing to Celia on August 22, he vented his frustration. "Alberto threw himself on the grass to marry Incan princesses, to recuperate [lost] empires. Calica curses the filth and every time he steps into one of the innumerable turds that litter the streets, instead of looking at the sky and a cathedral framed in space, he looks at his dirty shoes. He doesn't smell the evocative mystery of Cuzco, but instead the odor of stew and dung; a question of temperaments. We've decided to leave this city rapidly in view of how little he likes it."

As for his immediate future, he told his mother, he was uncertain, because he "didn't know how things were" in Venezuela. As for the more distant future, he said he hadn't budged on his hopes to somehow earn "$10,000 U.S." Then, "with Alberto, maybe we'll take a new trip, but in a North-South direction, and maybe by helicopter. After Europe and after that, darkness." In other words, anything was possible.

After a detour to Machu Picchu, which, although still crawling with American tourists, continued to entrance Ernesto, they set out on a grueling three-day bus trip to Lima. Some comic relief came at a rest stop where he and Calica climbed down the hillside for a swim in the cold waters of the Río Abancay. Stark naked, Ernesto took a special delight in leaping up and down to wave to the shocked female passengers on the road above. Arriving exhausted in Lima, they found a hotel and slept "like dormice."

On September 4 Ernesto wrote to his father, complaining that he had expected to discover "a ton of letters" from Buenos Aires, but had found only one, from him. "I'm glad to hear the economic difficulties aren't so many that some little help from me is urgently needed. I am happy for all of you . . . but don't forget to tell me *'si las papas queman'* [if things get bad], to hurry up a bit." Although he felt under pressure to find paying work to help the family, his father's reassurances that things were all right had eased his conscience for the time being. In the same letter, he sent a barbed reproof to pass on to his mother for not writing to him. He suggested she try writing each time she sat down to play solitaire, as a cure for her addiction to the game.

In Lima, Calica was finally in his element. "I like it a lot, it's modern, clean, with all the comforts, a great city," he wrote to his mother on September 8. They were well taken care of, having met up with Ernesto's friends at the Guía leprosarium and with Dr. Pesce, who helped them find a clean pension with hot water and a university cafeteria in which to eat their meals. And they had met up again with Gobo Nogues. "Gobo has introduced us to the social life. We've eaten twice in the Country Club, really good, super-expensive. Naturally they didn't let us put our hand in our pockets, and we've been a lot to the Gran Hotel Bolívar [Lima's most expensive hotel]," Calica gushed.

Ernesto, by contrast, viewed Lima with an ascetic's critical eye. "Her churches full of magnificence inside don't achieve externally—my opinion —the display of august sobriety of Cuzco's temples. . . . The cathedral . . . seems to have been built in a period of transition when the warrior fury of Spain entered into decadence to give way to a love of luxury, of comforts." In his journal, there is a dismal mention of a party at which "I wasn't able to drink because I had asthma, but it allowed Calica to get totally smashed." As for their visit to a cinema to see a "revolutionary" new "3-D" film for the first time, he was unimpressed. "It doesn't seem to be a revolution in anything and the films are still the same."

Ernesto saw Dr. Pesce a couple of times and enjoyed "a long and amiable discussion on a wide range of topics." But afterward he and Calica were detained and interrogated, and their hostel room was turned upside down by Peruvian detectives, who apparently mistook them for a pair of "wanted kidnappers." Although the misunderstanding was cleared up, Ernesto decided to avoid further contact with Pesce in case the police still had them under scrutiny.

Ernesto wasn't entirely convinced that their brush with the police was simply a matter of mistaken identity. There had been the fuss over his "Red" literature confiscated at the border, and his and Calica's names were probably on file as suspicious characters. With Peru's dictator Manuel Odría still in power and undoubtedly worried about Bolivia's left-wing revolution "contaminating his chicken coop," as Ernesto put it to Calica, there was no point in encouraging the authorities to draw undue links between them and the Communist Dr. Pesce. Ernesto also gave up hope of retrieving his confiscated books. Pursuing the issue could only complicate their stay in Lima.

On September 17, Ernesto received a letter from his mother, who informed him that she had arranged for them to be "put up" by the president of Ecuador when they arrived there. The next day, Calica wrote to his

mother to give her the news, crowing jubilantly that he and Ernesto anticipated "a beautiful panorama in terms of room and board." They also
bumped into their exiled Argentine friend Ricardo Rojo again. He was on
his way to the Ecuadoran port city of Guayaquil, where he hoped to board
a boat for Panama, on his way to Guatemala. Rojo gave them the name of a
pension in Guayaquil where they could find him.

III

Ernesto was again suffering from asthma when they traveled by bus up the
Peruvian coast. After entering Ecuador on September 28 and waiting for
transportation in the border town of Huaquillas, he complained of "losing
a day's traveling, which Calica took advantage of by drinking beer." Another day and night of boat travel down a river, into the Gulf of Guayaquil,
and across its swampy delta brought them to the tropical city of Guayaquil
itself. They were met at the pier by Ricardo Rojo and three law-student
friends from Argentina's Universidad de La Plata who led them back to
the pension where they were staying. Rojo's companions were Eduardo
"Gualo" García, Oscar "Valdo" Valdovinos, and Andro "Petiso" Herrero.
Like Rojo, they were heading next to Guatemala, and trying to have a bit of
an adventure along the way.

The pension was a crumbling colonial mansion with a canoe dock on
the muddy banks of the Río Guayas in a run-down quarter called the Quinta
Pareja. Its large rooms were in the process of being subdivided into tiny
cubicles fashioned from wooden shipping crates. Ernesto and Calica joined
the four others in a cavernous room as the house's internal dimensions gradually shrank around them.

The pension's hard-pressed owner was a good-hearted woman named
María Luisa. Life in her rustic establishment was like being part of a large,
chaotic family going through hard times. María Luisa ran the place with
her mother, Agrippina—an ancient crone who spent her days swinging in
a hammock in the foyer, endlessly smoking cigarettes—and her husband,
Alexander. He too had been a guest, so the story went, but his debts had
grown so high he had been forced to marry María Luisa.

In the end, they didn't have to go to Quito to call upon President
Velasco Ibarra. He was visiting Guayaquil, and Ernesto and Calica got
dressed up and went to throw themselves on the mercy of his private secretary. On October 21, Ernesto wrote to his mother to tell her, mockingly, how
his interview had gone. "He told me that I couldn't see Velasco Ibarra, that
the disastrous personal economic situation I had painted for him was one of
life's low points, adding in a philosophical tone: 'For life has highs and lows,

you are in a low one, have spirit, have spirit.'" Ernesto and Calica were back where they had been, virtually broke, and so were their companions. Meanwhile, their debts with María Luisa were mounting. They pooled their funds and instituted a strict economic regimen that Ernesto enforced. Calica may have started out the trip as the wearer of the "chastity belt," but their time on the road had made it all too clear who was the better economizer. Ernesto established a system of "absolute thrift," which he himself broke only to buy the occasional banana, practically all he was eating at the time.

In mid-October, Ricardo Rojo and Oscar Valdovinos shipped out to Panama on a boat belonging to the United Fruit Company; the others were to follow on the next available ship. For now, Ernesto and Calica remained camped out with Gualo García and Andro Herrero. While they pondered their next move, enjoying the camaraderie and unwilling quite yet to depart for Venezuela, Ernesto explored Guayaquil. In the pension he played chess and conversed with his new friends. They were all a little homesick for Argentina, and they talked of their families, their past, and their hopes for the future.

A swimming break while on the road in Central America in 1953. Ernesto is in the foreground. Eduardo "Gualo" García is standing behind him. Ricardo Rojo is on the right.

8

Finding North

I

There was nothing compelling to prolong Ernesto's stay in Guayaquil. He dismissed it as "a pretend city almost without its own life, which revolves around the daily event of ships coming and going." But he didn't leave. He hung around, counting his pennies and sharing the poverty of his marooned friends. He confessed to Andro Herrero that he had never previously enjoyed the experience of unconditional comradeship, where everyone shared what they had without misgivings and faced common problems together. The closest he had come to it was when he played rugby; his fellow players were good "mates," they were fine to go out for a drink with, but none of them was really close, and off the pitch their kinship had ended. His closest friend, he said, was Alberto Granado. Calica was a good guy whom he had known since childhood, but the truth was they had little in common.

True camaraderie, Ernesto told Andro, had eluded him. It was something he had always craved but felt lacking in his own family, which was fragmented and overrun with adopted outsiders. He spoke a lot about his mother. It was obvious that they had a special relationship, but Ernesto blurted out that she had surrounded herself with poets and frivolous literary types, women who were "probably lesbians." A few years older than Ernesto, Andro understood his remarks as expressing feelings of emotional exclusion. He thought that Ernesto was lonely and in great need of affection.

"Guevara was a very particular guy," Andro recalled. "At times he seemed inexpressive, with a demeanor that was almost disagreeable. But it was because of his asthma. The effort to breathe caused him to contract, and he could appear *hard*. Afterward, he would relax and his eyes smiled; the sides of his eyes wrinkled."

The severity of Ernesto's asthma attacks had come as a shock to his
new companions, and they responded by helping him as much as they could.
"I remember waking up in the night with Guevara trying to reach his
Asmapul [medicine] but not having the strength. One of us had to get it for
him," Andro recalled.

While he reveled in this newfound fraternal atmosphere, Ernesto was
torn by conflicting feelings about what to do next. He had a path that was
laid out for him; before he had left Buenos Aires, Alberto Granado had
written to say a job awaited him at the leprosarium. If he needed money to
get there, not to worry, Alberto would lend it to him. Ernesto had some
emotionally powerful motives for going. He told Andro that he wanted to
earn enough money to send his mother to Paris for medical treatment. He
feared that she still had cancer, and he wanted her to receive the best treatment possible.

But then Gualo García threw out a casual invitation to come along with
him and Andro to Guatemala. They were going off to observe a leftist revolution that had challenged the might of the United States. Guatemala's
struggle might determine the future of Latin America. And just like that,
Ernesto accepted the invitation, abandoning his plans and throwing all his
promises out the window.

It was one thing to have decided to go to Guatemala, another to actually get there. They would need visas for Panama, which required proof of
paid arrangements to leave. Since they were broke and this was impossible,
they would have to persuade friendly ship captains to vouch for them with
the Panamanian authorities while agreeing to take them for free. It was a
tall order, and they knew it, but they doggedly began making the rounds of
the docks. Their first attempts met with failure, and the days wore on in a
penny-pinching tedium.

Ernesto made friends with the crew of an Argentine scrap vessel that
was making a port call. It brought back fond memories of one of the ships
he had worked on in 1951, and after he went on board to eat and drink red
wine a few times, he returned to the pension loaded down with American
cigarettes and *yerba mate*. An Argentine diplomat on the ship who knew
his family gave Ernesto unexpected news from home, informing him "almost in passing" of the recent death of his aunt Edelmira Moore de la Serna.
With an almost cruel bluntness that was beginning to characterize his correspondence with his family, he sent a condolence letter to his uncle and
cousins. "It is very hard to send words of hope in circumstances like these
and it is even more so for me," he wrote, "who for reasons emanating from
my position toward life, cannot even insinuate the religious consolation that
so helped Edelmira in her final years."

By now, Calica was impatient to make a move, and he decided to proceed alone as far as Quito, Ecuador's inland capital. Ernesto would wait a few more days, and if the situation didn't improve, he would send a telegram to say that he was on the way to meet Calica. A few days after Calica's departure, the captain of a small boat, the *Guayos,* vouched for their onward passage from Panama and they obtained their visas. But no sooner had Ernesto telegraphed Calica, saying *not* to wait for him, than the *Guayos*'s sailing date was postponed "indefinitely."

Ernesto had an asthma attack made worse by medicine that caused nausea and diarrhea. He and his friends had a huge unpaid bill at María Luisa's pension, and every day their debt grew larger. They discussed dodging out without paying but abandoned this plan after realizing it would impossible to get past the indomitable Agrippina in the foyer. They began to sell their possessions.

On October 22, Ernesto wrote to his mother to announce his "new position as a 100 percent adventurer." Breaking the news that he was going to Guatemala, he told her that he had sold the new suit she had given him as a farewell gift. "The pearl of your dreams died heroically in a pawnshop, and the same fate befell all the unnecessary things of my luggage." He had even decided to sell his treasured camera, but "the bourgeois remnants of my proprietorial hunger" made him balk when a buyer appeared. A few days later, Ernesto noted in his diary, with desperation, "There's practically nothing left to sell, and so our situation is really precarious: we don't have a peso on us and our debt is 500 [Ecuadorean sucres], possibly 1,000, that's the thing."

It was Andro who came up with a solution. He would stay behind as guarantor for their debts, and the others would try to send him funds so he could leave and join them. Ernesto argued against this plan, saying that after all *he* was the newcomer, and if anyone should stay behind, it was himself. But Andro was firm about it, and the matter was settled when a friend of his, a food buyer for the elegant Hotel Humboldt, agreed to pay off most of their debts if Andro went to work for him.

After further delays, the *Guayos* was ready to sail. Ernesto traded his seaman's duffel bag to Andro for a bigger suitcase in which to lug his books. On October 31, Andro saw Ernesto and Gualo off on a wharf that was piled with coconuts. Ernesto's account of their leave-taking is detached: "The instant of the farewells as usual cold, always inferior to one's hopes, finding oneself in that moment incapable of showing deep feelings." But Andro remembers the normally reserved Ernesto "crying like a child," saying how much he valued Andro's friendship. Andro was touched by this display of feeling and, overcome with emotion himself, turned away and left the dock before the *Guayos* sailed.

In the end, Andro was never able to rejoin his comrades. He remained for months in Ecuador working at a variety of odd jobs, including one as a "human cannonball" in a circus. Calica reached Caracas, contacted Alberto, and found a job. He lived in Venezuela for almost ten years before returning home. Neither he nor Andro would ever see Ernesto again.

II

As he sailed north to Central America, Ernesto knew he was about to enter a region "where the countries were not true nations, but private *estancias*" belonging to dictators. A few years earlier, his favorite poet, Pablo Neruda, had written a poem called "The United Fruit Co.," damning the company for creating a slew of subservient "banana republics" ruled by local despots. "The Tyrannical Reign of the Flies," Neruda called it. "Trujillo the fly, and Tacho the fly, the flies called Carías, Martínez, Ubico . . . the bloody domain of the flies."

Indeed, in 1953, with the sole exception of Guatemala, the backward agrarian nations on the Central American isthmus were all "banana republics" dominated by the United States. On the slender neck of land joining the North and South American continents, Panama was barely a sovereign state fifty years after its creation by Theodore Roosevelt to ensure American control of the newly built Panama Canal. Despite mounting nationalist sentiment, the United States retained jurisdiction over the Canal Zone, which bisected the country. It had its own military bases and exercised a preponderant role in Panama's economy and political life.

Nicaragua had been ruled by the corrupt General Anastasio "Tacho" Somoza García since the 1930s. Somoza's rule had been secured by treachery. He ordered the assassination of the nationalist guerrilla leader Augusto César Sandino during talks to end years of civil war and repeated incursions to "restore order" by American marines. Staunchly anticommunist, Somoza had a lot of friends in Washington, and it was on his urging that the CIA had first initiated hostilities against Guatemala's reformist revolution.

Tiny El Salvador was firmly in the hands of an oligarchy of coffee growers. A succession of military rulers had run the country ever since a Communist-inspired peasant rebellion was quelled twenty years before at the cost of 30,000 lives. The peasant majority lived in feudal conditions. Neighboring Honduras was almost roadless, undeveloped, and underpopulated, and its governments were woefully subservient to United Fruit, which had extensive plantations there and owned the country's ports and railroads.

Costa Rica also played host to United Fruit, but since a reformist revolution in 1948, led by José "Pepe" Figueres, it had extracted better trade terms for itself while managing to stay on Washington's good side. Touted as the "Switzerland of Central America," Costa Rica exuded an atmosphere of political tolerance and moderation.

The neighboring Caribbean islands, with their plantation economies and poor black populations descended from African slaves, were a soup of imperial dominions ruled by white governors appointed from London, Paris, or The Hague. These same European powers still had colonies on the mainland as well: tiny British Honduras on the Yucatán peninsula and the remote Guyanas on South America's northern cape remained in Dutch, French, and British hands. The United States had joined this imperial crowd with its virtual annexation of Puerto Rico, which it had seized from Spain half a century earlier. Puerto Rico had been made the first U.S. "commonwealth" in 1952. Only Haiti, the Dominican Republic, and Cuba were independent republics, and all remained under rule that was unstable, corrupt, or both. The egomaniacal, sinister General Rafael Trujillo had ruled and robbed the Dominican Republic since 1930. As for black Haiti, politically shaky since a coup in 1950, it would soon succumb to the terrifying rule of Dr. François "Papa Doc" Duvalier. Cuba was under the freewheeling grip of General Fulgencio Batista, who had come to power in a military coup in 1952.

III

When the *Guayos* docked in Panama, Ernesto and Gualo made their way to a cheap pension where they were allowed to sleep in the hallway for a dollar a day each. At the Argentine consulate, they discovered that Ricardo Rojo and Oscar Valdovinos had already gone on to Guatemala but had left a letter for them. It contained the names of some contacts at the Panama University students' federation, and the surprising news that Valdovinos had gotten married after a whirlwind romance to twenty-three-year-old Luzmila Oller, the daughter of a Panamanian congressman.

They met Luzmila, who had stayed behind, and learned that her sudden marriage with Valdo had caused a "revolution" in the Oller family. Her father had moved out of their home; Luzmila's mother had refused to meet Valdo. It was a real scandal, complete with accusations by the Ollers that Valdo was a rascal and a gold digger. In his journal, Ernesto disparaged Valdo for taking off to Guatemala without having "gotten a screw or, it seems, even a serious feel" with his bride. As for the new Mrs. Valdovinos, she was *"muy simpática,* seems really intelligent but is far too Catholic for my tastes."

Ernesto and Gualo began to hustle. The Argentine consul was helpful, and so were their university contacts. They quickly made friends among the students and fell in with an interesting crowd of poets, artists, and political activists who hung out at two cafés, the Iberia and the Coca-Cola. Their new friends helped them pay their pension bill and steered Ernesto toward magazine editors, to see if he could publish some travel articles, and to the university medical faculty, where it was arranged for him to give a talk on allergies.

Ernesto was paid twenty dollars for an article he wrote about the raft adventure with Alberto Granado, which was published in *Panamá América*. In his journal he remarked that an article on Machu Picchu was "being fought over" with the editors of *Siete* because of its pronounced anti-American slant. The article, "Machu Picchu, Enigma de Piedra en America," was published in *Siete* on December 12, 1953. In it, he fires both barrels at the Yankee looters of Peru's archaeological patrimony. After describing the history of the Incan empire and Hiram Bingham's discovery of Machu Picchu, he writes, "Here comes the sad part. All the ruins were cleared of overgrowth, perfectly studied and described and . . . totally robbed of every object that fell into the hands of the researchers, who triumphantly took back to their country more than two hundred boxes containing priceless archaeological treasures. . . . Where can one go to admire or study the treasures of the indigenous city? The answer is obvious: in the museums of North America." It isn't surprising that he had trouble with his editors: these were provocative words. His conclusion revealed his emerging political viewpoint. "Let's be content then, with giving the Incan city its two possible significances: for the fighter who . . . with a voice of stone shouts with continental reach, 'Citizen of Indoamerica, reconquer the past'; for others . . . a valid phrase can be found in the visitors' book of the hotel, left imprinted there by an English subject with all the bitterness of his imperial nostalgia: 'I am lucky to find a place without a Coca-Cola advertisement.'"

Panama must have seemed an appropriate place to initiate hostilities against the country Ernesto had come to see as a mortal enemy. He began listing and describing the people he met there in his journal, evaluating them according to their human qualities and, increasingly, for their political "soundness" as well. At Panama University he mentioned meeting a "Dr. Carlos Moreno, who impressed me as an intelligent demagogue, very knowledgeable of the psychology of the masses but not so much in the dialectics of history. He is very simpatico and cordial and treated us with deference. He gives the impression of knowing what he does and where he is going but he wouldn't take a revolution further than what was strictly necessary to contain the masses."

Doctor Moreno's knowledge of Marxist ideology and his potential value as a *revolutionary* were what mattered to Ernesto. One cannot help feeling that people were being marked for their use as players in a revolution that transcended national boundaries. It was as if glimmerings of his future program were already seeping into his consciousness.

While Ernesto honed his sword in Panama, his father, in Buenos Aires, was fussing over his vagabond son. He had been fuming ever since he received Ernesto's letter from Guayaquil with the account of pawning the suit. Determined that *el doctor* Guevara should be properly attired, Ernesto senior decided to have a new wardrobe—a suit, blazer, and ties—made and sent to Panama. Soon after Ernesto received them, he wrote to his father, saying, "What little value Argentine clothes have—for the whole lot I got only one hundred dollars!"

By late November, Ernesto and Gualo's economic situation was getting desperate again. A ship they had hoped to take to Guatemala had been delayed. They resolved to continue overland but faced more visa problems. "Our situation is bad," Ernesto wrote in his diary. "The Costa Rican consul is a dickhead and won't give us the visa. . . . The struggle becomes hard."

Luzmila was ready to leave and join Valdo. The situation had been smoothed over with her family, and she was hoping for a possible diplomatic post at the Panamanian embassy in Guatemala. Before she took off, she came to Ernesto and Gualo's rescue, lending them forty-five dollars. They had finally obtained their Costa Rican visas and were ready to go. With five dollars remaining in their pockets after paying debts, they were off. But they didn't get very far before things started going wrong.

Somewhere in the middle of northern Panama the truck they were riding in broke down, then later drove off the road. After two more days of cadging rides on rural trains and hiking on foot, they crossed into Costa Rica and reached the pretty Pacific port of Golfito, a banana port of the United Fruit Company, built for its "10,000 employees." Ernesto took note of the "city's division into well-defined zones with guards who impede entry. Of course, the best zone is that of the gringos. It looks something like Miami but, naturally, without poor people. The gringos are trapped behind the four walls of their homes and the narrow social group they make up." He visited the company hospital and observed critically, "The hospital is a comfortable house where correct medical attention can be given but the benefits vary according to the category of person working in the company. As always, the class spirit of the gringos can be seen."

They embarked the next day aboard a United Fruit Company ship that Ernesto nicknamed "the famous *Pachuca* (which transports *pachucos,* bums)." The ship's real name was the *Río Grande,* and it made the run to the Costa Rican port of Puntarenas. The trip started well enough, but within a few hours the sea got rough. "Almost all the passengers including Gualo started to vomit," Ernesto wrote. "I stayed outside with a *negrita,* Socorro, whom I'd picked up, more whorish than a hen with sixteen years on her back." Seasoned mariner that he was, Ernesto was unaffected by seasickness, and spent the next two days romping with the pliant Socorro. After docking at Puntarenas, he said good-bye to her, and he and Gualo headed inland for the Costa Rican capital of San José.

A tiny city perched on gently rolling green hills, San José was the new headquarters for the Caribbean Legion, a regional pro-democracy alliance that had previously been based in Havana, where it had enjoyed the patronage of Cuba's former president, Carlos Prío Socarrás. The Caribbean Legion had moved to San José following Batista's coup. Now, under the guiding hand of President Figueres, exiled political leaders from the dictatorships in Venezuela, the Dominican Republic, and Nicaragua met in San José to plot and conspire.

Pepe Figueres was a rarity—a Latin American politician whose opinion was respected in Washington by both conservative and liberal policy makers. He had achieved this feat by treading a cautious middle ground in his political reforms. He had abolished Costa Rica's army, nationalized the banks, and extended state control over the economy, but he left foreign interests untouched. He had further endeared himself by banning Costa Rica's Communist Party, while lobbying Washington to move away from its traditional reliance on dictatorships in the region and to support democratic reform.

At the time, in addition to Figueres, Latin America's leading "democratic alternatives" were Victor Raúl Haya de la Torre's Alianza Popular Revolucionaria Americana (APRA) movement in Peru, and Venezuela's Acción Democrática, led by Rómulo Betancourt, who had presided over a liberal coalition government until it was toppled by the military in favor of Marcos Pérez Jiménez. The policies they espoused were moderately "social democratic," yet firmly anticommunist, and promoted social reform and foreign investment at the same time. The Dominican Partido Democrático Revolucionario, led by the mulatto storyteller and politician Juan Bosch, represented the most left-wing of the exile parties, though it too fell short of an overtly Marxist platform.

While Haya de la Torre was in his fifth year of political asylum as a guest of the Colombian embassy in Lima, both Bosch and Betancourt were in Costa Rica, and Ernesto very much wished to hear their ideas on social and political reform. He was especially interested in their positions regarding the United States, a topic that had become his weather vane for determining political legitimacy. But he and Gualo also needed to survive, and so a new round of scrounging began as they pursued their double agenda.

They spent a day chatting with Juan Bosch and the Costa Rican Communist leader Manuel Mora Valverde. A few days later, Ernesto finally met Rómulo Betancourt. Of the three, it was the Communist Mora Valverde, "a calm man . . . with a series of movements like tics that indicate a great internal restlessness," who most impressed Ernesto. He took careful notes on Mora's analysis of Costa Rica's recent history and of Figueres's pro-American policies. "When Figueres is disabused of his faith in the compassion of the Department of State comes the *incognita:* Will he fight or submit? There is the dilemma and we will see what happens," Ernesto wrote.

Ernesto described Juan Bosch as "a literary man of clear ideas and leftist tendencies. We didn't speak of literature, simply of politics. He described Batista as a gangster surrounded by gangsters." He was scathing in his appraisal of Rómulo Betancourt. "He gives me the impresson of being a politician with some firm social ideas in his head but the rest are fluttery and twistable in the direction of the best advantages. In principle he's on the side of the United States. He went along with the [1948] Rio [Inter-American Defense] Pact and dedicated himself to speaking horrors of the Communists."

Soon afterward, Ernesto and Gualo began hitchhiking to Nicaragua, which Ernesto referred to as "Tacho's [Somoza's] *estancia*." Across the border, during a torrential downpour, Ricardo Rojo suddenly reappeared. He was traveling with two Argentine brothers, the Beverragis, who were driving their own car to South America. Feeling at loose ends after a few weeks in Guatemala, Rojo had come along for the ride. Since the road into Costa Rica was impassable, they went to the coast to see about a ferry south, while Ernesto and Gualo traveled to the Nicaraguan capital of Managua.

The parched, hot lakeside city of Managua held little interest for Ernesto, and he spent his time in "a pilgrimage to consulates with the usual imbecilities," hunting for visas. At the Honduran consulate, he ran into Rojo and his companions, who had been unable to get a ferry. On the spot, the group decided to split up: Rojo and Walter Beverragi would fly to San José; Ernesto and Gualo would drive with Domingo Beverragi to Guatemala, where Domingo would sell the car. That night, they had a long discussion about Argentina and Argentine politics, and, as Ernesto recorded it, they concluded the following about one another's political positions. "Rojo, Gualo, and Domingo were *radicales intransigentes* [a liberal wing of the Argentine Unión Cívica Radical, led by Dr. Arturo Frondizi, Rojo's mentor]; Walter was a *laborista* [of the leftist Partido Laborista] and I am a 'sniper,' at least according to El Gordo [Rojo]."

Walter Beverragi had been imprisoned and tortured in 1948 for his part in a plot to overthrow Perón. He escaped but was stripped of his citizenship while in exile in the United States.* It was a reminder of how far Perón would go to punish his opponents, and Rojo was nervous for himself because he and Valdovinos had given a press conference in Guatemala City airing their own complaints against Perón. Ernesto himself was mostly aloof from this Argentine polemic, but he *was* interested and listened intently, occasionally launching one of the barbed commentaries that had earned him the Sniper nickname.

Ernesto drove on with Gualo and Domingo Beverragi to the Honduran border. They had twenty dollars among them. Stopping only to change punctured tires, they continued their journey across an arid stretch of rural Honduras, crossed El Salvador's volcano-dominated landscape in a day, and pushed on to the green highlands of Guatemala. They paid the border tolls with coffee upon exiting El Salvador, and with a lantern upon entering Guatemala. On the morning of December 24, they arrived in Guatemala City with three dollars left.

IV

In the 1950s, Guatemala City was a small, conservative, provincial place, a privileged white and mestizo urban enclave in an overwhelmingly rural and Indian country of astonishing natural beauty. The surrounding highlands of forested volcanos, lakes, and coffee plantations—dotted with the villages of indigenous peasants—dropped away to the sugar plantations and farms of the tropical Pacific coastal lowlands.

But the picture-postcard image—colorfully clad natives working happily in harmonious communion with their habitat—presented by successive Guatemalan governments to outsiders was deceptive. Guatemala was a place where the Spanish conquest seemed fresh despite the passage of time. A white and mixed-blood Creole minority had ruled for centuries over a native majority that existed by laboring on the vast private plantations of the oligarchy, or on those of the United Fruit Company.

This state of affairs was a fact of life until the reformist "revolution" of Juan José Arévalo overturned the ruthlessly authoritarian Ubico dictatorship in the 1940s and called for democratic change. Arévalo was unable to implement all the reforms he promoted, but he was succeeded by a left-leaning Guatemalan colonel, Jacobo Arbenz, who pushed on with them. The most inflammatory was the land-reform decree Arbenz had signed into law

---

*In later years, Walter Beverragi became a prominent ultranationalist, espousing anti-Semitic views. In his book *El Dogma Nacionalista,* he attacked "democracy" and "liberalism" as twin evils of modern, decadent society.

in 1952, ending the oligarchic *latifundia* system and nationalizing the properties of United Fruit.

Arbenz had earned the undying enmity of Guatemala's conservative
elite and of United Fruit, which enjoyed extraordinarily close contacts with
the Eisenhower administration. John Foster Dules, the secretary of state,
and his brother Allen Dulles, the director of the CIA, had been associated
with United Fruit through their work with the law firm Sullivan and
Cromwell. This firm had a client, the J. Henry Schroder Banking Corporation, which acted as the financial adviser to the International Railways of
Central America (IRCA). Most of Guatemala's railways were owned by
IRCA before they were sold to United Fruit in a deal handled by John Foster Dulles. Allen Dulles had been a director of the Schroder Bank, which
was used by the CIA to launder funds for covert operations.

There were other cozy relationships with United Fruit. For instance,
the family of the assistant secretary of state for inter-American affairs, John
Moors Cabot, owned interests in United Fruit. President Eisenhower's personal secretary was the wife of the company's public relations director. With
such friends, United Fruit could afford to throw its weight around. The
company hired the tenacious Spruille Braden, Harry Truman's former top
Latin emissary, as a consultant. In March 1953, Braden gave a fiery speech
at Dartmouth College, urging the United States to intervene militarily
against the "Communists" in Guatemala. Immediately afterward, in a hint
of how far it was prepared to go, United Fruit organized an armed uprising in the provincial capital of Salamá. In the subsequent trials of some of
the captured raiders, the company's involvement in the rebellion was unmasked, but what *wasn't* known publicly yet was that the CIA was also involved and that the agency was discussing plans with United Fruit to
overthrow Guatemala's government.

By the end of 1953, the battle lines were clearly drawn between Guatemala and Washington; Guatemala's Central American neighbors, especially dictators such as Somoza, were vociferous about their concerns of a
spillover effect to their countries. Meanwhile, hundreds of Latin American
leftists had arrived in Guatemala, either as political exiles or, like Ernesto,
as sympathizers eager to see Guatemala's "socialist" experiment firsthand.
Their presence lent a combustive element to Guatemala's hothouse atmosphere as the war of words between the Arbenz government and the
Eisenhower administration escalated daily.

Although it remained mostly concealed beneath his aloof exterior, by
the time he arrived in Guatemala, Ernesto seems to have undergone a political conversion—or at least he was trying to talk himself into one. He
wouldn't act on his new beliefs for a while, but they help explain what drew

him to Guatemala. Part of the evidence for this lies in an enigmatic passage he wrote in Buenos Aires while transcribing his *Notas de Viaje.* Appropriately, he called it "Note on the Margin," for it didn't mesh with the rest of his travel narrative at all. It describes a "revelation."

Ernesto writes that he was in "a mountain village under a cold star-filled night sky." A great blackness surrounded him, and a man was there with him, lost in the darkness, visible only by the whiteness of his four front teeth. "I don't know if it was the personality of the individual or the atmosphere that prepared me to receive the revelation, but I know that I had heard the arguments many times by different people and they had never impressed me. In reality, our speaker was an interesting guy; when he was young he had fled some European country to escape the dogmatizing knife; he knew the taste of fear (one of the experiences that make you value life), and afterward, after rolling from country to country and compiling thousands of adventures, he had come to rest his bones in this remote region where he patiently awaited the coming of the great event.

"After the trivial phrases and the commonplaces with which each put forth his position, the conversation languished, and we were about to part ways. Then, with the same rascally boy's smile which always accompanied him, accentuating the disparity of his four front incisors, he let slip: 'The future belongs to the people, and little by little or in one fell swoop they will seize power, here and in the whole world. The bad thing is that they have to become civilized, and this can't happen before, but only after, taking power. They will become civilized only by learning at the cost of their own errors, which will be serious ones, and which will cost many innocent lives. Or perhaps not, perhaps they won't be innocent, because they will have committed the enormous sin *contra natura* signified by lacking the capacity to adapt.

"'All of them, all the unadaptable ones, you and I, for example, will die cursing the power they, with enormous sacrifice, helped to create. . . . In its impersonality, the revolution will take their lives, and even use their memory as an example or a domesticating instrument for the youth who will come after them. My sin is greater, because I, more subtle and with more experience, call it what you wish, will die knowing that my sacrifice is due only to an obstinacy which symbolizes the rotten civilization that is crumbling.'"

This mysterious speaker, by inference a Marxist refugee from Stalin's pogroms whose conscious sin was his "inability to adapt" to the new power wielded by the uncivilized masses, now turned his premonitory attention to Ernesto.

"'You will die with your fist clenched and jaw tense, in perfect demonstration of hate and of combat, because you are not a symbol (something inanimate taken as an example), you are an authentic member of a society which is crumbling: the spirit of the beehive speaks through your mouth and moves in your actions; you are as useful as I am, but you don't know how useful your contribution is to the society that sacrifices you.'"

Duly warned of the consequences of the revolutionary path, Ernesto acknowledges the "revelation" that came to him. "I saw his teeth and the picaresque expression with which he took a jump on history, I felt the squeeze of his hands and, like a distant murmur, the formal salute of farewell. . . . In spite of his words, I now knew . . . I will be with the people, and I know it because I see it etched in the night that I, the eclectic dissector of doctrines and psychoanalyst of dogmas, howling like one possessed, will assault the barricades or trenches, will bathe my weapon in blood and, mad with fury, will slit the throat of any enemy who falls into my hands.

"And I see, as if an enormous tiredness shoots down my recent exaltation, how I die as a sacrifice to the genuine revolution of individual will, pronouncing the exemplary *mea culpa*. I feel my nostrils dilated, tasting the acrid smell of gunpowder and of blood, of the dead enemy; now my body contorts, ready for the fight, and I prepare my being as if it were a sacred place so that in it the bestial howling of the triumphant proletariat can resonate with new vibrations and new hopes."

This passage reveals the extraordinarily passionate—and melodramatic —impulses at work in Ernesto Guevara at the age of twenty-five. Powerful and violent, uncannily precognitive of his death and the posthumous exploitation of his legacy by many so-called revolutionaries, "Note on the Margin" must be seen as a decisive personal testimonial, for the sentiments it contained would soon emerge from the penumbra of his submerged thoughts to find expression in his actions.*

V

In Guatemala City, Ernesto and his companions looked up Valdo and Luzmila and then found a pension where, as Ernesto put it, "we could get stuck and begin owing money." Ricardo Rojo arrived and soon introduced Ernesto to a woman, Hilda Gadea, who would become an important addition to his life. Hilda was an exiled leader of the youth wing of Peru's APRA and was now working with the Arbenz government. She was in her late twenties, short and plump, with Chinese-Indian features. "On our first meeting," she wrote later, "Guevara made a negative impression on me. He seemed too superficial to be an intelligent man, egotistical and conceited."

*See Notes.

Despite her initial disdain, which she admitted had been compounded by her innate "distrust" of Argentines, who are renowned among their neighbors for their snobbery and conceit, Hilda soon became infatuated with Ernesto. For the time being, however, his mind was elsewhere. He was busy meeting people to see about getting a job, and he took little notice of Hilda. She is mentioned briefly in his journal as the person who introduced him to the American Marxist professor Harold White: "I met a strange gringo who writes stupidities about Marxism and translates it to Spanish. The intermediary is Hilda Gadea, and Luzmila and I are the ones who do the work. Until now we've charged twenty-five dollars. I give English-Spanish lessons to the gringo." But this activity was just a time-filler. What Ernesto was hoping for was an interview with Guatemala's minister of public health, although all his attempts to meet with the man failed.

"My personal opinion is that Guatemala is interesting, although, like all revolutions, it loses something with intimacy," Ernesto wrote to Andro Herrero. "Revolutionary" Guatemala may not have fulfilled all of Ernesto's expectations, but then he had yet to venture into the countryside, where the land reform had taken place. The capital remained largely unchanged. Its small commercial center was noisy with street vendors and cluttered with neon signs. The wealthy residents in the outlying residential districts continued living tranquilly in their bougainvillea-shrouded walled compounds. Even so, Ernesto met compelling new people among the eclectic community of Latin American political exiles gathered there. There were *apristas* from Peru, Nicaraguan Communists, Argentine *antiperonistas,* Venezuelan social democrats, and Cuban *antibatistianos.*

After a meeting with a Honduran exile, Helena Leiva de Holst, Ernesto wrote enthusiastically, "She's close on some points to the Communists and she gave me the impression of being a very good person. In the evening I had a discussion with [Nicanor] Mujíca [an exiled Peruvian *aprista*] and Hilda, and I had a little adventure with a dirty female teacher. From now on I will try to write in my diary every day and try to get closer to the political reality of Guatemala."

Try as he did to find gainful employment in Guatemala's health ministry, Ernesto had not come this far just for a job. He was on a political quest, and if his family had been unaware of the fact previously, his letters now dispelled any other notions they may have harbored. On December 10, while still in San José, he had sent an update of his journey to his aunt Beatriz. For the first time, his ideological convictions made a marked appearance in his personal correspondence. "My life has been a sea of found resolutions until I bravely abandoned my baggage and, backpack on my shoulder, set out with *el compañero* García on the sinuous trail that has brought us here.

Along the way, I had the opportunity to pass through the dominions of the United Fruit, convincing me once again of just how terrible the capitalist octopuses are. I have sworn before a picture of the old and mourned comrade Stalin that I won't rest until I see these capitalist octopuses annihilated. In Guatemala I will perfect myself and achieve what I need to be an authentic revolutionary."

After this declamation, which must have been quite mystifying to Beatriz, Ernesto signed off with hugs and love and kisses "from your nephew of the iron constitution, the empty stomach and the shining faith in the socialist future. Chau, Chancho."

In Managua, Ernesto had checked the Argentine consulate for mail from home and found a "stupid" telegram from his father, who was anxious for news of him and had offered to wire him money if he needed it. It had infuriated Ernesto, and in his first letter from Guatemala, on December 28, he was as harsh as he could be. "I guess you now realize that even if I'm dying I'm not going to ask you for dough, and if a letter from me doesn't arrive when expected you'll just have to be patient and wait. Sometimes I don't even have stamps but I am getting along perfectly and I always manage to survive. If you ever are worried about anything, take the money that you're going to spend on a telegram, and go and drink with it or something like that, but I'm not going to answer any telegram of that type from now on."

The harsh tone seemed to be Ernesto's way of throwing up a defensive line between himself and his family. From a safe distance away, in a place where he couldn't be stopped or sidetracked by their persuasions, he was saying, "This is me, the real me, like it or not; you can't do anything about it, so you'd better get used to the idea."

Guatemala, 1954. Ernesto is standing, third from the right, next to his future wife, Hilda Gadea, who is second from the right. Ricardo Rojo is next to her in the sunglasses. Gualo García is in the foreground.

9

Days without Shame or Glory

I

For better or for worse, Ernesto had chosen Guatemala's leftist revolution as the first political cause he openly identified with. Despite its many flaws and defects, he told his family, Guatemala was the country in which one could breathe the "most democratic air" in Latin America. The skeptic, the analytical Sniper, the "eclectic dissector of doctrines and psychoanalyst of dogmas" had taken the plunge.

Finding something useful to do was the next hurdle he faced. Ironically, he never would. The next six months became a succession of "days without shame or glory, a refrain that," he wrote, "has the characteristic of repeating itself to an alarming degree." Meanwhile, however, he was meeting people. Hilda Gadea introduced him to some high-level government figures, including the aristocratic economics minister, Alfonso Bauer Paiz; and President Arbenz's secretary, Jaime Díaz Rozzoto. Ernesto grilled them about Guatemala's revolution and also attempted to secure a medical post.

Through Hilda, Ernesto met Professor Edelberto Torres, a Nicaraguan political exile and a scholar of the late poet Rubén Darío. Torres's pretty young daughter, Myrna, had just returned from a year in California studying English, and she worked with Hilda in the Instituto de Fomento a la Producción, a farm credit agency set up by the Arbenz government. Myrna's brother Edelberto Jr., who was secretary general of Guatemala's Communist Youth organization, the Juventud Democrática, had just come back from a trip to China. The congenial Torres household was a gathering point for Hilda and other exiles, and Ernesto and Gualo were welcomed into this circle.

On his first day at the Torreses' home, Ernesto met some ebullient and outspoken Cuban exiles who had been in town for several months: Antonio

"Ñico" López, Armando Arencibia, Antonio "Bigotes [Mustache]" Darío López, and Mario Dalmau. The Cubans stood out in the exile community because they alone were veterans of an armed uprising against a dictatorship. Although their effort had failed, they had shown determination and bravery, and they earned widespread admiration—and publicity—for their campaign against Batista. After participating in the attacks led by the young lawyer Fidel Castro Ruz against the Moncada and Bayamo army barracks, Ñico and his comrades had eluded capture by taking refuge in the Guatemalan embassy in Havana. Granted asylum by the Arbenz regime, the *moncadistas,* as they were called, were cooling their heels in Guatemala as guests of the government until they received further orders from their organization. Meanwhile, they were celebrities, de rigueur guests at dinner parties and picnics.

Castro had just been tried in Cuba and sentenced to fifteen years in prison. He was serving his sentence in a solitary cell on the Isle of Pines. But despite the adverse circumstances, the Cubans in Guatemala, and particularly Ñico, spoke with passionate conviction about the future of their struggle. "Ñico was sure that his stay in Guatemala would be a short one," Hilda wrote, "and that soon he would be leaving for another country to join Fidel and work for the revolution. His faith was so great that whoever listened to him was forced to believe him."

Ernesto too was impressed and quickly developed a strong liking for the warm, extroverted Ñico. They saw each other socially and became friends. To earn some pocket money, Ñico and his comrades teamed up with Ernesto selling products on commission. It was Ñico who gave Ernesto the nickname El Che Argentino. *Che* is a Guaraní word that Argentinians typically use in a locution that translates loosely as "Hey, you."

When another Cuban exile, José Manuel "Che-Che" Vega Suárez, who lived in their hostel, experienced sharp stomach pains, Ñico and Dalmau called for Ernesto's help. Ernesto examined Vega, called an ambulance, and accompanied him to the hospital, where he was treated and improved within a few days. After that experience, said Dalmau, the Cubans saw Ernesto almost every day, either in the Central Park or in the pension.

Ernesto struck out with the minister of public health, who informed him that he needed to go back to medical school for a year in order for his Argentine medical degree to be valid in Guatemala. He made light of his economic woes to his family, quipping in a letter on January 15, 1954, "I am selling a precious image of the Lord of Esquipulas, a black Christ who makes amazing miracles. . . . I have a rich list of anecdotes of the Christ's miracles and I am constantly making up new ones to see if they will sell." If his family thought he was joking, they were wrong. Ñico López had come up with what he thought was a lucrative gimmick. He placed little portraits of Guatemala's black Christ behind glass frames and rigged up a lightbulb at the base to illuminate them. Ernesto helped sell them.

Ernesto's Aunt Beatriz sent him some money in a letter that never arrived, and then sent another letter asking if he'd received it. His reply to her second letter, on February 12, was doggedly tongue-in-cheek. He told Beatriz he could only assume that a "democratic post office employee made a just distribution of the riches. Don't send me any more money, as you can't afford it and here I find dollars lying around on the ground. I should tell you that at first I got lumbago from so much bending to pick them up."

II

Myrna Torres and some of her girlfriends had begun to entertain romantic notions about Ernesto and Gualo. One night, Myrna and Blanca Mendez, the daughter of Guatemala's director of petroleum reserves, playfully tossed a coin to see which of them would get Ernesto. "Blanca won," Myrna wrote later. "Ernesto, of course, never knew anything about it." But soon enough, Myrna became aware that it was the older, plainer Hilda who most attracted Ernesto. "Little by little, my friends, too, came to realize that the Argentinians, especially Ernesto, preferred to talk with Hilda because she could discuss politics." On January 11, Myrna noted in her diary: "The Argentine boys are the strangest people: today they came through my office on their way to Hilda's, and all they said was, *'Buenos días,'* and when they came back, just *'Adiós, Myrna. . . .'* It seemed odd to me because I'm so used to the effusiveness of the Cubans. Actually they were sociable enough; but they just preferred political connections."

Hilda was well read, politically oriented, and generous with her time, her contacts, and her money, and she appeared in Ernesto's life when he was in need of all these things. Hilda later claimed to have introduced Ernesto to Mao and Walt Whitman, while he widened her knowledge of Sartre, Freud, Adler, and Jung, about whom they disagreed. Hilda rejected what she saw as the narrowness of Sartre's existentialist philosophy and Freud's sexual interpretation of life. Over time, she said, Ernesto's adherence to these points of view softened as his interpretations gradually became more and more Marxist.

Hilda's own philosophy had some Marxist influences but remained within a social democratic outlook. It was one of their main bones of contention. Ernesto pointed out that while Hilda "thought" like a Marxist, she was a member of the APRA, whose constituency was primarily the urban middle class. In conversations with other *apristas,* Ernesto had discerned that at the core of APRA's ideology lay a fundamental anticommunism. He viewed the APRA and its leader, Victor Raúl Haya de la Torre, with disdain. He resented Haya de la Torre for abandoning his original antiimperialist platform, which had called for struggle against the Yankees and the nationalization of the Panama Canal. Hilda countered that the party's guiding philosophy was still anti-imperialist and antioligarchist, that any abandonment of APRA's original principles was purely tactical, and that once power was attained, a "true social transformation'" would be carried out.

Ernesto argued back that given present circumstances in Latin America, no party that participated in elections could remain revolutionary. All such parties inevitably would be forced to compromise with the right and then seek an accommodation with the United States. For a revolution to succeed, a head-on confrontation with Yankee imperialism was unavoidable. At the same time, he was critical of the Communist parties, which he felt had moved away from the working masses by engaging in tactical alliances with the right.

Others joined in these debates. Frequently, they included the Honduran exile Helena Leiva de Holst, with whom Ernesto had developed a close rapport. She was politically active, versed in Marxism, and had traveled to the Soviet Union and China. Ricardo Rojo was also involved in the discussions, and he and Ernesto argued incessantly. "Guevara would tell about his great sympathy for the achievements of the revolution in the Soviet Union, while Rojo and I frequently interposed objections," Hilda wrote. "But I admired the [Soviet] revolution, while Rojo deprecated it with superficial arguments. Once after one of these discussions, while they were taking me home, the discussion started again and promptly became bitter. The subject was always the same. The only way, said Ernesto, was a violent revolution; the struggle had to be against Yankee imperialism and any other solutions . . . were betrayals. Rojo argued strongly that the electoral process did offer a solution. The discussion became more heated with each argument offered."

While Ernesto and his friends debated political theory, the Central Intelligence Agency was well along in its plans to bury Guatemala's brief experiment with social revolution. By January 1954 the covert program even had a code name: Operation Success. Throughout the region, friendly dictators such as Trujillo, Somoza, Pérez Jiménez, and the presidents of neighboring Honduras and El Salvador were brought in on the CIA's plans. A Guatemalan figurehead had been handpicked to lead the anti-Arbenz "Liberation Army," a former army colonel and furniture salesman named Carlos Castillo Armas. His paramilitary force was now being armed and trained in Nicaragua.

To better coordinate the operation, loyal CIA men had replaced American envoys in Costa Rica, Nicaragua, and Honduras. John Puerifoy, the flamboyant new ambassador to Guatemala, had taken up his post only two months earlier. He had been selected for the specific purpose of coordinating Operation Success and the transition of power in Guatemala.

At the end of January, the covert campaign was unmasked when correspondence between Castillo Armas, Trujillo, and Somoza detailing their machinations in alliance with a "government to the North" was leaked. The Arbenz government promptly made the news public and demanded an explanation from the "government to the North" (the United States). In a letter of February 2 to his father, Ernesto wrote, "Politically, things aren't going so well because at any moment a coup is suspected under the patronage of your friend Ike."

The State Department denied any knowledge of the plots being hatched and the CIA calmly continued with its preparations. Agents circulated throughout Guatemala and the neighboring countries with an openness that would seem buffoonish today, but the CIA counted on creating a climate of tension and uncertainty that would prompt divisions in the armed forces, weaken Arbenz's resolve, and, with luck, provoke a coup d'état.

In this unsettled atmosphere, Ernesto's habitual suspicions about Americans were sharpened. When Rojo introduced him to Robert Alexander, a professor at Rutgers University who was gathering material for a book about the Guatemalan revolution, Ernesto wondered aloud if Alexander was an FBI agent. Neither Hilda nor Rojo shared Ernesto's suspicions, but they found it difficult to convince him and had to admit that he might be right.

Ernesto thought the Arbenz government was being too complacent. "He believed it was necessary to organize a *defensa popular* [an armed people's militia] and be prepared for the worst," Alfonso Bauer Paiz, the economics minister, recalled. Interestingly, in the wake of his own recent attempt at writing slanted journalism, one of Ernesto's chief targets of scorn was the unbridled freedom of Guatemala's press. In a letter of January 5 to his aunt Beatriz, he wrote, "This is a country where one can expand one's lungs and fill them with democracy. There are dailies here run by United Fruit, and if I were Arbenz I'd close them down in five minutes, because they're shameful and yet they say whatever they want and help contribute to creating the atmosphere that North America wants, showing this as a den of thieves, Communists, traitors, etc."

In a letter to his family, he predicted, "In the [upcoming OAS] conferences in Caracas, the Yankees will set all their traps to impose sanctions on Guatemala. It is certainly true that the governments bow to them, and their battle horses are Pérez Jiménez, Odría, Trujillo, Batista, Somoza. That is to say, among the reactionary governments, the ones that are most fascist and antipopular. Bolivia was an interesting country, but Guatemala is much more so, because it has set itself against whatever comes, without having even an iota of economic independence and withstanding armed attempts of all sorts . . . yet without even going against the freedom of expression."

With storm clouds gathering menacingly on the horizon, many political exiles began leaving town. These included most of the Venezuelans and Hilda's *aprista* comrades. In early February, Oscar Valdovinos and Luzmila took off. Valdo was homesick, and Luzmila had wangled a diplomatic post in Argentina for herself. Then Ricardo Rojo and Gualo announced their intention to leave as well. Very few of the political exiles in Guatemala seemed willing to defend Guatemala's revolution. Here was a chance to fight for political freedom, just as internationalists had fought to defend the Spanish Republic in the 1930s, and yet nothing was happening.

Ernesto declared his intention to stay for the time being, come what may. "Guatemala right now is the most interesting country in America and must be defended with all possible means," he wrote to Beatriz.

III

As his quest for a job continued, Ernesto read up on medical topics that interested him, occasionally treated patients, and helped out in the lab of Dr. Peñalver, a Venezuelan specialist in malaria. He also began work on a new project that wedded his two chief interests, medicine and politics. "I am preparing a very pretentious book that I think will take me two years of work," he wrote to Beatriz. "Its title is *The Role of the Doctor in Latin America* and so far I have only the general outline and the two first chapters written. But I think that with patience and method I can say something good."

Once he had done a bit of work on the book, he showed Hilda what he had written. "It was an analysis of the lack of state protection and the scarcity of resources that the medical profession had to face, and of the tremendous problem of sanitation prevailing in our countries," she recalled. "He asked me to help him collect health statistics for each Latin American country, and I promised to do so, as I believed it a very worthwhile work. Moreover, it showed me that this was the work of a restless mind, sensitive to social problems." The proposed work was a manual for a doctor in a revolutionary society. It was not a coincidence that Ernesto planned to take two years to finish the book, the same length of time he hoped to serve as a doctor in the Guatemalan backwoods.

In his outline, Ernesto charted the history of medicine in Latin America from the colonial period to the present day, the range of clinical problems, and the geographic and economic contributing factors. His broad analysis for treatment concluded that only a preventive program of social medicine could adequately deal with the ills caused by underdevelopment. A sketch for a chapter called "The Doctor and the Environment" set forth a scenario in which the doctor would play a direct role in helping to bring about a revolutionary transformation to socialism. The doctor would have to confront the established authorities openly in order to obtain adequate medical attention for the people and wipe out pillage and profit. During the transition from "armed neutrality" to "open war," the doctor should acquaint himself intimately with the people under his care and their health conditions, and help raise their class consciousness and their awareness of the importance of good health in daily life. It was the duty of the *médico revolucionario* to fight against all the blights—social and otherwise—affecting the people, who were the "only sovereigns" he should serve.*

At that moment, Guatemala's internal situation could be described as "armed neutrality," while "open war" was threatened by the U.S.-backed Liberation Army of Castillo Armas. Ernesto still hoped that when the crisis came, the militants of the Partido Guatemalteco de los Trabajadores (PGT), the Guatemalan Communist Party, would be armed by the government to help in its defense. If this were to happen and the "people" were successful in repelling the invasion, a socialist revolution could be unequivocally established in Guatemala.

His work on the book led him to deepen his readings of Marx, Lenin, Engels, and the Peruvian José Carlos Mariátegui. Hilda joined in this reading marathon, and they spent many hours discussing the works and the points they raised. Hilda lent Ernesto a copy of Mao Tse-tung's *New China*. "It was the first work he had read on the great revolution," she wrote. "When he had read it and we talked about the book, he expressed great admiration for the long struggle of the Chinese people to take power, with the help of the Soviet Union. He also understood that their road toward socialism was somewhat different from the one followed by the Soviets and that the Chinese reality was closer to that of our Indians and peasants. Since I also admired the Chinese Revolution, we often talked about it." Ernesto talked

---

*I was not permitted to see Che's outline when I was working on this book, but the historian Maria del Carmen Ariet, who has worked in Che's personal archives for many years, described it to me in detail. In 2004, a sketch of one chapter, "El Médico y el medio," appeared in an anthology, *Latin America, el despertar de un continente* (Latin America: The Awakening of a Continent), which was published under Che's name.

about China with Helena Leiva de Holst and Edelberto Torres, who had both been there. He added China to his list of countries to visit.

Somewhat ironically, given his antipathy for and suspicion of Americans, one of the key figures in Ernesto's political education during this time was Harold White. Ernesto's initial reserve about the older man had softened, and before long he told Hilda, "This is a good gringo. He is tired of capitalism and wants to lead a new life." Ernesto, Hilda, and White now spent a lot of time together, just the three of them. Most weekends they organized a picnic in the countryside. With Ernesto's rudimentary English and White's rough Spanish, smoothed by Hilda's frequent translation, they discussed everything from current events "to Marxism, Lenin, Engels, Stalin, Freud, science in the Soviet Union, and Pavlov's conditioned reflexes."

IV

By late February, Gualo García and Ricardo Rojo had left Guatemala. Ernesto's closest remaining friend was Hilda. Already, their mutual acquaintances teased them about what they saw as a budding romance, but in fact nothing had happened between them yet.

Besides their intellectual affinities and her physical attraction to him, Hilda's infatuation with Ernesto appears to have been spurred on at least partly by maternal instincts. Soon after they met, Ernesto had told her about his asthma. "Thereafter, I always felt a special concern for him because of his condition," she wrote. For his part, Ernesto, all too aware of the effect he had on Hilda, seems to have exploited her feelings while trying to avoid committing himself to a serious relationship.

A few days after Gualo and Rojo's departure, Hilda called upon Ernesto at his boardinghouse. She found him waiting for her in the downstairs lobby, in the grip of an asthma attack. "It was the first time I had seen him or anyone else suffering from an acute attack of asthma, and I was shocked by the tremendous difficulty with which he breathed and by the deep wheeze that came from his chest. I hid my concern by insisting that he lie down; he agreed that it would be better, but he couldn't climb the stairs and refused to accept my help. He told me where his room was and asked me to go up and bring him a syringe that was ready to use. . . . I did as he said and watched him as he applied an injection of adrenaline.

"He rested a bit and began to breathe more easily. We went slowly up the stairs; we reached his room and he lay down. He told me that since the age of ten he had been able to give himself injections. It was at that moment that I came to a full realization of what his illness meant. I could not help admiring his strength of character and his self-discipline. His dinner was brought up—boiled rice and fruit. . . . Trying to conceal how much I had been touched by all this, I conversed about everything and anything, all the while thinking what a shame it was that a man of such value who could do so much for society, so intelligent and so generous, had to suffer such an affliction; if I were in his place I would shoot myself. I decided right there to stick by him without, of course, getting involved emotionally."

In her memoirs, Hilda portrays Ernesto as the one who chased her, but Ernesto's journal describes Hilda as the hunter. In late February he wrote, "I haven't budged due to the asthma, although it seemed to reach a climax with vomiting last night. . . . Hilda Gadea continues worrying a great deal about me and constantly comes by to see me and brings me things." The main contender for Ernesto's attentions in February and March 1954 was a nurse named Julia Mejía. She had arranged for a house at Lake Amatitlán where Ernesto could spend weekends; she helped him in his job search as well. Soon, they were having a casual affair.

Unaware of Ernesto's secret fling, Hilda continued using her contacts to help him find a job. She spoke to a man who worked in her office, Herbert Zeissig, a member of the youth wing of the Communist Party. Zeissig found Ernesto a job but told Hilda he would first have to join the Party. Ernesto told Hilda to tell Zeissig that when he joined the Party he would "do so on his own initiative," and refused on ethical grounds to do so for the purpose of getting a job. This principled stance made Hilda admire Ernesto even more.

Meanwhile, Ernesto's money situation remained critical. Ricardo Rojo had paid Gualo's half of their pension bill before leaving, but Ernesto was still seriously in arrears and the occasional paying work he found simply didn't bring in enough. On February 28, he wrote to his parents and asked them for the address of Ulíses Petit de Murat, an actor friend of his father's who made films in Mexico: "Just in case I beat it to there." Meanwhile, he told them, he had an offer to work in a sign-painting factory but was not inclined to take it, since it would rob him of time to look for work in the health field. He had offered his services as a doctor to a peasant cooperative and to a banana plantation, but both jobs had slipped from his grasp because he didn't belong to the "shitty" Guatemalan doctors' union.

He heard from home that his aunt Sara de la Serna, his mother's sister, was gravely ill with cancer, and, betraying his self-absorption with almost casual brutality, he wrote to Celia *madre,* "I can offer you no type of consolation, not even that of my presence which is impossible due to the economic reasons you're aware of. Just a strong embrace and look to the future, distance yourself a little from the present is my only advice. Chau."

In March, Hilda paid off part of his pension bill, and Julia Mejía got him a job interview for a medical post in the Petén jungle, the site of the

Mayan temple complex of Tikal, which briefly lifted his spirits. "I Am Optimistic," he wrote in his diary. The Petén was precisely the place he wanted to go. He wrote to his mother and father that it was "a splendid place because that is where the Mayan civilization flourished . . . and because there are more illnesses there than shit, one can really learn in style (if one wants to, of course)!" The job was tied, however, to the approval of the doctors' union, and the president of the union, with whom Ernesto had an interview, was enigmatic. "A man with hopes of conserving his job, anticommunist, an intriguer it seems to me, but he appears disposed to helping me," Ernesto wrote. "I wasn't sufficiently cautious but I didn't take too many risks either."

When Hilda heard of the possibility of a job in the Petén, she kicked up a fuss, apparently demanding some kind of commitment from him in their relationship. A few days later Ernesto wrote, "Hilda told me of a dream she had in which I was the protagonist and which clearly betrayed her sexual ambitions. Though I hadn't dreamed, I had an asthma attack. Up to what point asthma is an escape is something I would like to know. The funny thing is that self-analysis leads me honorably—as far as one can take it—to the conclusion that I don't have anything to run from. And yet . . . Hilda and I are slaves of the same boss and both of us deny it with our actions. Maybe I am more consistent but deep down it's the same."

The tentativeness he recognized in his personality extended into the political arena. "When I heard the Cubans make grandiloquent affirmations with absolute serenity I felt small," he wrote. "I can make a speech ten times more objectively. . . . I can read it better and convince an audience that I am saying something that is right but I don't convince myself, and the Cubans do. Nico left his soul in the microphone, and for that reason he inspired even a skeptic such as myself. The Petén puts me face-to-face with my asthma problem and myself, and I believe I need it. I have to triumph without help and I believe I can do it, but it also seems to me that the triumph will be more the work of my natural aptitudes—which are greater than my subconscious beliefs—than the faith I put in them." Mere identification with Guatemala's revolution wasn't enough, and Ernesto knew it. Hilda was still affiliated with APRA, and at the crucial moment Ernesto himself had abstained from joining the Communist Party. However principled his motives for doing so, the fact was that he was *still* hanging back, still the skeptical outsider; the same dispassionate Sniper as before.

The Petén was a humid jungle region that would undoubtedly be terrible for his health, yet it was also the right setting for him to implement his plan to be a revolutionary doctor. His asthma had come to symbolize the malignant shackles of heredity that he was in the process of rejecting. He wished to form a new identity, to reforge himself as a revolutionary, to vanquish once and for all the limitations he had been born with.

Ernesto's bout of self-analysis helped clear his mind a little, but his asthma persisted relentlessly. A few days later, prostrate in his bed at the pension, he wrote that "not much and a lot has happened." The job was looking likely, the union president had told him. "Hilda declared her love in epistolary and practical form. I was very sick or I might have fucked her. I warned her that all I could offer her was a casual contact, nothing definitive. She seemed very embarrassed. The little letter she left me upon leaving is very good. Too bad she is so ugly. She is twenty-seven."

By now Ernesto was telling everyone he was going to the Petén, even though he didn't have the slightest assurance that he really was. "I'm about to prepare a list of necessary things to take," he wrote. "I burn to go. Hilda has me feeling nervous, on top of the anxiety I have about becoming ever more trapped in this country."

The political pressure on Guatemala was intensifying. In March, at the Tenth Inter-American Conference of the Organization of American States held in Caracas, John Foster Dulles had twisted enough arms to obtain a majority resolution effectively justifying armed intervention in any member state that was "dominated by Communism" and that therefore constituted a "hemispheric threat." Only Mexico and Argentina withheld their votes. Guatemala, the target of the resolution, was the only state to vote against it.

The Eisenhower administration now pressed its advantage. The CIA's military training of Guatemalan exiles was well under way on one of Somoza's ranches in Nicaragua. Mercenary pilots and a couple of dozen planes had been smuggled into Nicaragua, Honduras, and the Panama Canal Zone for use in the coming attack. Psychological warfare operatives were busy preparing taped recordings for propaganda and disinformation broadcasts, printing leaflets to be air-dropped over Guatemala, and buying up Soviet-issue weapons to be planted in Guatemala at the right moment as "evidence" of Soviet involvement with Arbenz.

Myrna Torres flew to Canada, where she had a fiancé. She left behind "a balance of broken hearts," Ernesto wrote.* "But the worst of it is I don't

---

*The previous year, when Myrna was studying in California, she had become engaged to a Canadian student she met there, but, as she explained years later, after she returned to Guatemala she fell in love with the Guatemalan activist Humberto Pineda. The purpose of her trip to Canada was to tell the Canadian that she was not going to marry him after all. Ernesto's allusion to "broken hearts" was to the anxiety felt by Humberto. The only real broken heart, according to Myrna, was that of Armando Arencibia, a Cuban who had fallen in love with her.

know if I'm leaving. Always the same uncertainty . . ." A few days later, his uncertainty had deepened, after the president of the medical union seemed cool and evasive when Ernesto saw him about the job in the Petén. Ernesto consoled himself in his journal: "Only Julia responds to me." Julia aside, his mood was bitter. He now referred to the union president as an *hijo de puta,* a son of a whore. He expected "nothing" from their next meeting and complained he had had to stop writing letters because of all his running around. "Enthusiasm depends on health and circumstances. Both are failing me. The post in the Petén seems farther away all the time. . . . Everything is getting fucked up. I don't know what the shit to do. Hilda is being a pain in the neck. I feel like flying the fuck away. Maybe Venezuela."

But he couldn't leave. He had no money. To do something productive with his time, he persisted in his studies of parasitic diseases at Peñalver's lab. He paid off part of his pension bill with some of Hilda's jewelry, but he still owed several months' rent. Then his landlady extracted a promise to pay a month's worth within a few days, and when the day of reckoning came, he couldn't pay anything. "I pawned my watch, a gold chain, and a ring stone of Hilda's, and promised a gold ring—also Hilda's," he wrote. The banana plantation job, at a place called Tequisate, was still a possibility, but when he went there he had an asthma attack on the way: "a vision of what things will be like."

He heard from home that his aunt Sara had died. Taking a break from his own travails, he mulled over his feelings. "I didn't love her but her death affected me. She was a healthy person and very active and a death of this kind seemed the most unlikely, which nonetheless is a solution, since the conditions in which the illness would have left her would have been horrible for her." He wrote to his mother, with peppy brevity, "Have spirit, what happened to Sara is now over and Paris awaits."

It was now April, and his chief remaining obstacle for securing the job in Tequisate was obtaining his Guatemalan residency. He was becoming fatalistic. "The days keep passing but I could care less. Maybe one of these days I'll go stay at Helena de Holst's, maybe not, but I know one way or another matters have to fix themselves so I'm not going to overheat my brains anymore."

One weekend, returning from the countryside, Ernesto, Hilda, and Harold White witnessed a candlelit Easter procession of hooded men carrying an effigy of Christ, which gave Ernesto the chills. "There was a moment I didn't like at all, when the men with the lances passing by gave us ugly looks."

On April 9, Guatemala's Catholic Church issued a pastoral letter denouncing the presence of Communism in the country and calling on all

Guatemalans to rise up against it. The message was lost on no one. What wasn't known to the public was that the pastoral letter was the direct result of an approach to the Guatemalan archbishop Mariano Rossell Arellano by the CIA. As priests read the letter aloud in churches, thousands of leaflets bearing the message were dropped all over rural Guatemala.

Ernesto wrote his mother a long letter. In their recent correspondence she had been enthusiastic about the prospect of their meeting in Paris. He had warned her that it might be the only chance they would have to see each other in the next ten years, the period of time he planned to be exploring the world. She had evidently inquired if he was interested in becoming an anthropologist, given his interest in archaeology and the condition of Latin America's Indians, but he shot that down. "It seems a little paradoxical to make as the goal of my life the investigation of that which is irremediably dead," he wrote. He was sure of two things, he told her: first, that he would reach his "authentically creative stage at around thirty-five years of age," and would work in "nuclear physics, genetics, or some field like that"; and second, that "America will be the theater of my adventures and of a much more important nature than I had thought. I truly believe I have come to understand her and I feel [Latin] American; we possess a distinctive nature compared with any other of the world's peoples."

In the final days of April Ernesto made a "heroic and unbreakable" decision. He would leave Guatemala within fifteen days if his residency was not approved. He informed the owners of the pension of his plan and began arranging places to leave his possessions. "A kilo of adrenaline arrived, sent by Alberto from Venezuela, and a letter in which he asks me to go, or rather invites me to go," Ernesto wrote. "I don't really want to."

As Ernesto prepared to leave, Washington was taking the next step in activating its destabilization plan. With a great deal of intentional publicity, Ambassador Puerifoy had been recalled to Washington for consultations. Well-placed news leaks indicated that the purpose of his visit was to discuss U.S. measures against Arbenz in view of the recent Caracas resolution regarding Communist involvement in the hemisphere. On April 26, Eisenhower warned that "the Reds" were already in control of Guatemala and now sought to spread their "tentacles" to El Salvador and other neighbors.

By May 15, Ernesto's decision about where to go was made for him when he was told officially that he would have to leave the country to renew his visa. Just before leaving, he wrote to his brothers, whose birthdays were coming up. "Central America is *rechulo* [cute], as they say around here, no year passes without some rumpus in favor or against something or other. . . . Right now Honduras is in the midst of a fantastic strike where almost 25 percent of the country's workers are stopped and Foster Dulles, who is the lawyer of the fruit company in these parts, says that Guatemala has meddled in it. There's a clandestine radio that calls for revolt and the opposition dailies also do it so it wouldn't be strange that with the help of the U.F. [United Fruit] they send a little revolution here so as not to lose the habit. . . . I believe if the United States doesn't intervene directly (which isn't probable yet) Guatemala can withstand any attempt of this type well, and it also has its back covered, because there's a lot of people in Mexico who sympathize with the movement."

Despite Ernesto's optimistic prognosis, an incident occurred on that same day that irrevocably doomed the Arbenz regime. The Swedish freighter *Alfhem,* which had left a Polish port a month earlier secretly loaded with Czechoslovaki arms, docked in the Guatemalan port of Puerto Barrios. Tipped off in Poland about the mysterious voyage and suspicious about its cargo and final destination, the CIA had monitored the ship as it crossed the Atlantic and altered its course several times. When it reached Puerto Barrios, Washington was quickly apprised of the true nature of *Alfhem's* cargo—more than two tons of war matériel for the Arbenz regime—and went into action.

The *Alfhem* provided the United States with evidence that the Soviet bloc was involved in Guatemala. Allen Dulles convened the CIA's executive intelligence advisory board and the National Security Council and got their backing to set the Guatemalan invasion date for the next month. On May 17, the State Department issued a statement denouncing the arms delivery, and Eisenhower followed up with a public warning that the Czech arms could allow the consolidation of a "Communist dictatorship" in Central America.

Guatemala was in an unenviable position. Having arranged for the shipment secretly and been discovered in flagrante, Arbenz looked like a man with something to hide. In succeeding days, Eisenhower and Secretary Dulles told the press that the arms shipment was larger than Guatemala's military needs, and hinted that Guatemala's real intention might be to invade its neighbors to impose Communist rule and, possibly, to launch an attack on the Panama Canal. With Washington's propaganda machine in full swing, few journalists remembered that the United States had thwarted the Arbenz regime's efforts to upgrade its army's equipment, repeatedly rejecting direct appeals for American military assistance and blocking moves by other Western countries to sell Guatemala the arms it requested.

Less than a week after the *Alfhem* docked, Secretary Dulles signed a "mutual security treaty" with Honduras. It followed a similar treaty signed with Nicaragua's dictator, Somoza, only weeks earlier. Now Honduras would be defended by the United States in the event of a Guatemalan invasion. To drive the point home, U.S. military cargo planes flew to Nicaragua and Honduras, ostensibly carrying weaponry for their defense. In fact, the shipments were to be handed over to Castillo Armas's Liberation Army, which awaited its marching orders to move to the Guatemalan border.

On May 20, in a move authorized by Allen Dulles to stop the delivery of the *Alfhem*'s weapons to Guatemala City, a band of CIA saboteurs set explosives on the railroad tracks outside Puerto Barrios. The explosives did little damage, and so the CIA men opened fire as the military train passed. One Guatemalan army soldier was killed and several were wounded, but the train and its cargo reached its destination without further incident.

Against this backdrop of escalating political drama, Ernesto left his pension. He still owed about three months' rent, but the proprietors let him go in return for an IOU. He and Hilda spent the night in the village of San Juan Sacatepéquez. It was their first night alone together. A few days later, Ernesto left for El Salvador with twenty borrowed dollars in his pocket.

V

For a declared partisan in the confrontation in Guatemala, Ernesto was behaving in a remarkably carefree fashion. Once again he absented himself at a climactic moment. He couldn't have picked a worse time to be visiting Guatemala's neighbors. He carried some "questionable literature" that was confiscated at the Salvadoran border, but he bribed a policeman and was allowed to enter the country. After obtaining a new Guatemalan visa in the provincial city of Santa Ana, he continued on to the capital, San Salvador. There, he applied for a Honduran visa, thinking he might visit the Mayan ruins of Copán and also "check out" the ongoing workers' strike. Over the weekend, he took off for the Pacific coast and camped out on the beach, where he made friends with some young Salvadoran men. Writing to his mother later, he told her that when they were all a bit drunk, he engaged in a little "Guatemalanesque propaganda and recited some verses of profoundly red color. The result was that we all appeared in a police station, but they let us go right away, after a *comandante* . . . advised me to sing about roses in the afternoon and other beauties instead. I would have preferred making a sonnet with smoke [gunfire]."

Returning to San Salvador, he found that his Honduran visa had been denied. He assumed this was because he had come from Guatemala, which was almost a criminal offense in the current political climate. With Honduras no longer an option, he headed to Chalchuapa in western El Salvador to see the pre-Columbian Pipil Indian pyramid of Tazumal. He explored the ruins, making studious observations in his journal. That night he slept by the roadside outside Santa Ana, and in the morning he hitchhiked back across the Guatemalan border, heading for the ancient Indian ruins of Quiriguá. The next day he reached Jalapa, then got a train to the town of Progreso, where a woman took pity on him and gave him twenty-five cents. He set out on foot along the nearly completed new road to the now infamous port of Puerto Barrios. When he reached the ruins of Quiriguá, he noted similarities in the stone constructions to those of the Incas in Peru. But he was especially struck by the carvings' Asian features and thought that one figure on a stela was "reminiscent of Buddha," while another resembled Ho Chi Minh.

The next day he hit the road again, deciding to strike out *"a lo macho"* for Puerto Barrios. He spent his last money on the train trip. It was a gamble, but it worked out. Right away, he found a night job unloading barrels of tar on a road construction crew. "The work is twelve hours straight, from six in the evening to six in the morning and is really a killer, even for guys with more training than me. At 5:30 we were automatons or *'bolos,'* as they call drunks here." He worked a second night—"with a lot less desire than the first"—but he proudly completed his shift, despite "the mosquitoes that are a real bother and the lack of gloves."

The next morning, promised a train ticket back to Guatemala City from Puerto Barrios by one of the foremen, Ernesto relaxed at an abandoned shack at the sea's edge, exulting in his achievement. It was the first sustained stint of physical labor he had ever done. "I have turned into a perfect *chancho,* full of dust and asphalt from the head down, but really content. I got the ticket, the old woman where I ate on credit told me to pay a dollar to her son in Guatemala [City], and I demonstrated that I am capable of standing whatever comes, and if it weren't for the asthma, even more than that."

VI

"I paid back the dollar," Ernesto wrote proudly after his return to Guatemala City. Hilda was surprised and pleased to see him back, for she had feared he wouldn't return. As invasion jitters mounted, more people were leaving the country. A government official she knew had urged her to seek asylum, and Harold White had advised her to do the same.

Rumors abounded, and one of the first ones Ernesto heard had to do with himself. He learned from a Paraguayan acquaintance that he was widely believed to be a Perónist agent. Apparently, he quashed the rumor. He didn't return to the pension, probably because he couldn't repay his debt, but ate his meals at Helena Leiva de Holst's and shared a room with Ñico López and another Cuban who sang tangos. He was sneaked into and out of the room clandestinely, and since there were only two single beds, they pushed them together and slept sideways. Ñico was preparing to leave for Mexico on the orders of his organization, and spent his days "shitting with laughter but doing little else."

Despite Ernesto's expectations, life settled back into the same routine as before. The medical post beckoned like a mirage. He was told to come back for a meeting, then to wait, and, finally, to give it another week. There were few letters from home. Ñico left, and Ernesto moved into another room with a Guatemalan named Coca. Helena Leiva de Holst was also preparing to leave but promised to fix him up for meals at another woman's house and to talk one last time with the minister of public health. To top everything off, his asthma returned.

Ernesto's days of tedium were about to end, however, because of increased activity in the U.S.-Guatemala standoff. American warships had begun inspecting all suspicious shipping in the Caribbean, and Secretary Dulles was noisily preparing a document calling for sanctions against Guatemala to be ratified at the next OAS conference, slated for July. Howard Hunt (later of Watergate fame), the CIA propaganda chief of Operation Success, had organized a Congress Against Soviet Intervention in Latin America in Mexico City.

All over Latin America, the CIA was placing newspaper articles and propaganda films and handing out booklets that warned of the growing Communist threat in Guatemala. Arbenz sent his foreign minister to speak to Ambassador Puerifoy, offering conciliatory measures to begin negotiations with Washington and ward off the invasion. The overture went nowhere.

The CIA's psychological warfare campaign was paying off. On June 2, a plot against Arbenz was foiled and some arrests were made. The next day, a group of military officers asked Arbenz to dismiss Communists from government posts. He told them he had the Communists under control. But many officers remained unsettled, and on June 5 a retired air force chief defected. His voice was soon heard on broadcasts over a radio station that called itself "La Voz de Liberación." Broadcasts on the station were directed by a CIA agent named David Atlee Phillips. They exhorted Guatemalans to help the Liberation Army, giving the impression that it had thousands of fighters. The broadcasts also played on the military's fears by accusing Arbenz of planning to disband the armed forces and turn weapons over to Communist-controlled unions to form "peasant militias." On June 6, invoking the threat of invasion, Arbenz suspended constitutional guarantees for thirty days.

On June 14, Ernesto celebrated his twenty-sixth birthday. The next day, President Eisenhower called a high-level meeting to put the final touches on Operation Success. Two days later American mercenaries began flying bombing missions over Guatemala. On June 18, at the head of his paltry Liberation Army of some 400 fighters, Castillo Armas drove across the Honduran border into Guatemala. The invasion had begun.*

*See Notes for elaboration.

10

A Terrible Shower of Cold Water

I

Ernesto was thrilled at being under fire for the first time. In a letter to his mother, he confessed to "feeling a little ashamed for having as much fun as a monkey." When he watched people run in the streets during the aerial bombardments, a "magic sensation of invulnerability" made him "lick his lips with pleasure." He was awed by the violence. "Even the light bombings have their grandeur," he wrote. "I watched one go against a target relatively close to where I was. You could see the plane get bigger by the moment while from the wings intermittent little tongues of fire came out and you could hear the sound of its machine gun and the light machine guns that fired back at it. All of a sudden it stayed suspended in the air, horizontal, and then made a rapid dive, and you could feel the shaking of the earth from the bomb."

A few days later, in a more sober frame of mind, Ernesto wrote in his journal, "The latest developments belong to history. It is a quality that I believe appears for the first time in my notes. A few days ago, planes coming from Honduras crossed the frontier with Guatemala and passed over the city, machine-gunning people and military targets in the full light of day. I signed up with the health brigades to collaborate in the medical area and in the youth brigades that patrol the city at night."

A nocturnal blackout had been imposed, and one of Ernesto's duties was to ensure that nobody showed any lights that would provide bombing targets. Hilda also did her bit, attaching her name to a communiqué signed by political exiles in support of Guatemala's revolution and assembling a women's brigade at her office to take food to the men on patrol.

On June 20, Ernesto sent a birthday letter to his mother. "I imagine you've been a little worried about me," he wrote. "I'll tell you that if right now there is nothing to fear, the same can't be said for the future, although personally I have the sensation of being inviolable (inviolable isn't the word but maybe the subconscious gave me a bad turn)."

Despite the provocations of the aerial attacks and Castillo Armas's ground incursion, he told her, the Arbenz government had proceeded cautiously, allowing the mercenaries to get far enough into Guatemala to avoid any border incidents that would allow the United States and Honduras to claim Guatemalan aggression and invoke their mutual security treaty. So far, Guatemala had limited itself to a diplomatic protest against Honduras, and to a presentation of its case to the United Nations Security Council for a special hearing. "The incident has served to unite all Guatemalans under their government, and those like myself, who had been drawn to their country," Ernesto wrote. He closed with a judgment that would soon prove woefully wrong. "Without a doubt Colonel Arbenz is a guy with guts, and he is ready to die in his post if necessary."

Initially, the news from the battlefronts was encouraging. The government forces were fighting back, with some success. Castillo Armas had managed to enter the town of Esquipulas, the pilgrimage site of Guatemala's black Christ, but elsewhere his troops had bogged down in the thrusts toward their main objectives, the towns of Zacapa and Puerto Barrios. Despite the early panic they had caused, the CIA's mercenary planes had so far done relatively little damage, frequently missing their targets. Several of them had been hit by ground fire and put out of action. A Honduran ship, the *Siesta de Trujillo,* was seized at Puerto Barrios as it tried to offload a cargo of arms and munitions for the invaders. Finally, as the victim of an attack coming from outside its borders, Guatemala had a good case for requesting UN intervention on its behalf.

On the day Ernesto wrote to his mother, June 20, the American overseers of Operation Success were becoming alarmed at the likelihood that their Liberation Army was about to be routed. At Allen Dulles's request, President Eisenhower authorized the dispatch of two more fighter bombers to the field. By June 23 the new planes were in action and remained so for the next three days, strafing and bombing important targets in key Guatemalan towns, including the capital.

Simultaneously, the United States was engaged in a blocking maneuver to thwart Guatemala's request for a special session of the UN Security Council to discuss the crisis. The acting council president for June was the U.S. ambassador, Henry Cabot Lodge, who went to battle with Secretary General Dag Hammarskjöld over the affair. Lodge finally agreed to convene a session on June 25, by which time the new bombers had wreaked their havoc, allowing Castillo Armas's forces to regroup and launch new assaults.

On June 24 the invaders seized the small town of Chiquimula, and Castillo Armas proclaimed it the headquarters of his "provisional government." La Voz de Liberación beat the war drums, giving listeners the impression that the Liberation Army forces were an unstoppable military juggernaut, scoring successes left and right as government defenses crumbled.

The confidence of Arbenz and some of his top military men began to crack. Meanwhile, Ambassador Lodge was busily lobbying other council members to vote against Guatemala's request for a UN investigative team to be sent to Guatemala. Particular pressure was put on Britain and France, with Eisenhower and John Foster Dulles leaning on the visiting British prime minister, Winston Churchill, in Washington. Their message was that if London and Paris didn't go along with the Americans on Guatemala, U.S. help would not be forthcoming in Cyprus, Indochina, and the Suez. When the Security Council vote was taken on June 25, the United States scored a narrow victory, a 5–4 vote against a UN inquiry, with Britain and France abstaining. Guatemala was on her own.

II

By July 3, Operation Success had earned its name. That day, the "Liberator," Castillo Armas, flew into Guatemala City with Ambassador Puerifoy at his side. His ascension to power, brokered by the United States, followed a confusing week of power struggles between Guatemalan military leaders after they forced Arbenz's resignation on June 27.

"A terrible shower of cold water has fallen over the Guatemalan people," Ernesto observed a few days later. He wrote to Celia again, rueful over the heroic rhetoric of his last letter, explaining that he had written it "full of glorious dreams, just before going to the front I would never reach, to die if it were necessary . . .

"It's all happened like a wonderful dream which one clings to after awakening. Reality is knocking on many doors, and now the sound of gunfire can be heard, the rewards for the more ardent adherents to the ancien régime. Treason continues to be the patrimony of the army, and once more proves the aphorism that calls for the liquidation of the army as the true principle of democracy (if the aphorism doesn't exist I create it)." In Ernesto's mind, the other culpable sectors were the "reactionary" press and the Catholic Church, which had aided and abetted Arbenz's downfall, and he mentally earmarked them as problem sectors needing special attention if socialist revolutions were to succeed elsewhere in the future.

Ernesto went on to castigate Arbenz—who had immediately sought asylum in the Mexican embassy*—for buckling under to military officers. Egged on by Puerifoy, they had demanded and won his resignation. Ernesto especially resented Arbenz's reluctance to arm the people to defend the country. He was in an understandably bitter mood. In the final days of June, he had joined an armed militia organized by the Communist Youth. A Nicaraguan volunteer, Rodolfo Romero, was the "military chief" for the Augusto César Sandino Brigade at a house in northern Guatemala City. Ernesto was accepted into the brigade and remained with it several days, anxiously awaiting his chance to go to the front and do some fighting, but the public health minister appeared and transferred him to a hospital to await further orders. At this point, Romero and Ernesto lost sight of each other. (They would meet again four and a half years later, when Romero, in search of support for an anti-Somoza guerrilla war, flew into the newly liberated Cuban capital of Havana at the invitation of Comandante Ernesto "Che" Guevara.) At the hospital, Ernesto once again offered to go to the front, but, as he noted in frustration, "They haven't paid me any mind." He waited for another visit by the health minister, but on Saturday, June 26, the day before Arbenz's resignation, he lost his last chance when the minister came and left while he was out visiting Hilda.

During the tense buildup to Arbenz's downfall, Hilda recalled Ernesto desperately seeking to forestall the collapse, trying to get a message to Arbenz that he should turn his back on his military advisers and arm the people so that they could fight a guerrilla war in the mountains. (In fact, two days before his ouster, Arbenz had tried to distribute arms to the militias like the one Ernesto had joined, but the army had refused.) Now, from his post in the hospital, Ernesto watched with increasing anxiety and frustration as one capitulation after another led to the consolidation of Castillo Armas's triumph and the ignominious demise of the Guatemalan revolution. Martial law was declared, the Communist Party was banned, and the embassies began filling with fearful asylum seekers. Ernesto predicted his own expulsion from the hospital, since he was seen as a "Red," and Hilda took precautions by moving into new lodgings.

On the day of Castillo Armas's entry into the city, Ernesto observed that "the people really applauded him." His army of swaggering, submachine-gun-toting paramilitaries roamed around, savoring their status as the country's liberators and looking for trouble. Ernesto was anxious about rumors that

*In August, Castillo Armas finally allowed Arbenz to leave for Mexico, but reserved a special humiliation for him at the airport, where he was jeered and then, at customs, forced to strip off his clothing in public.

Edelberto Torres had been arrested for being a Communist, and he worried about the fate of Torres's father, the Rubén Darío scholar. (In fact, Edelberto junior was in hiding, but Ernesto's fears for his father turned out to be well founded. The scholar was soon detained and imprisoned.) Ernesto's own situation was tenuous, and after being kicked out of the hospital, as he had predicted he would be, he found refuge in the home of two Salvadoran women who had already sought asylum.

Amid the political upheaval, he and Hilda continued their cat-and-mouse romance. She sent him some verses she'd written in which she spoke "stupidities," as he called them. "What is happening to her," he wrote in his diary, "is a mixture of calculation to win me over, fictive imagination, and the sense of honor of a free woman affronted by my indifference. I sent her a little animaloid verse:

> *Surrender yourself like the birds do,*
> *I'll take you like the bears do,*
> *and, maybe, I'll kiss you slowly*
> *So I can feel like a man, I who am a dove.*

"I gave her a new ultimatum, but the abundance of these meant that it didn't have much effect. What *did* affect her was that I confessed about the fuck with the nurse. She still has hopes of marrying me."

By mid-July, the new regime's witch hunt had begun in earnest. Everyone connected with the Arbenz regime or suspected of being a Communist was threatened with arrest. Those who had not already fled Guatemala were attempting to do so. Ernesto lost his refuge when his Salvadoran hosts arranged to leave the country. Their house was to be closed, and Ernesto had to find a new hiding place. Helena Leiva de Holst had been arrested, but her aunt took him in. He spent his days going back and forth to the Argentine embassy. According to Hilda, he took advantage of his access to the embassy and the confusion in Guatemala City "to carry out errands for those in asylum at the embassy, to collect some arms, and to arrange asylum for those in difficult positions or those who wished to leave the country."

Ernesto continued his activities unscathed for a few more days, but then Hilda was arrested. Before she was taken away, the police questioned her about him. It was a warning Ernesto couldn't ignore, and he too now requested and was granted asylum at the Argentine embassy. "My plans are very fluid," he wrote, "although most probably I'll go to Mexico. . . . Far or near, I don't know why but I'm in one of those moments in which a slight pressure from one side could twist my destiny around completely."

III

Ernesto joined a large group of people who were already installed inside the walled compound of the embassy. Once there, he quickly became restless and began to fret. "One can't call asylum boring, but sterile, yes," he wrote. "One can't do what one wants, because of all the people there."

His asthma had worsened. Hilda had been released after several days in custody, as he learned from the newspapers, when she had gone on a hunger strike. He didn't understand why she hadn't come to see him, and wondered whether it was "ignorance about where I am or whether she doesn't know she can visit me."

Ernesto now seemed intent upon a particular destination. Mexico City was the place where Arbenz and most of his allies who had escaped arrest— as well as many of the Latin American political exiles in Guatemala—were heading. Several of them had taken refuge in the Mexican embassy and hoped to travel as soon as the new Guatemalan regime provided them with *salvocondúctos*. Since Mexico's own "anti-imperialist" revolution only four decades earlier, the politically tolerant and culturally dynamic Mexican capital had become a sanctuary for thousands of left-wing political exiles from around the world, including significant numbers of European Jews and Spanish Republicans fleeing Fascism in the 1930s and 1940s.

Ernesto considered the possibility that his request for a Mexican visa might be denied, but the prospect did not seem to overly concern him. For now, he stayed put. To pass the time, he began recording his impressions of his companions. The first to catch his interest was the renowned Communist peasant leader Carlos Manuel Pellecer. Ernesto described Pellecer as "an intelligent man and, it seems, brave. He seems to have great influence over the other asylum seekers, an influence that emanates I'm not sure whether from his own personality or because of the fact that he is the maximum leader of the party. . . . But he is somewhat effeminate in his gestures, and he wrote a book of verse in earlier years, a sickness very common in these parts. His Marxist formation doesn't have the solidity of other figures I have known and he hides it behind a certain petulance. The impression he gives me is of an individual who is sincere but overexcited, one of those ambitious persons who might stumble and renounce their faith violently, but are yet capable of carrying out the highest sacrifices at a determined moment."*

Of his Cuban acquaintance José Manuel "Che-Che" Vega Suárez, he wrote: "He is as dumb as a piece of rubble and lies like an Andalusian. Of

---

*Ernesto's appraisal was prescient. Pellecer found asylum in Mexico, where he repudiated his earlier beliefs and wrote anticommunist pamphlets under CIA sponsorship.

his previous life in Cuba there is nothing certain except for indications that he was what is called a *jodedor* [carouser], to whom Batista's police gave a royal beating. . . . His behavior before taking asylum was cowardly. Here he is entertaining with his unmalicious exaggerations. He is a big boy, selfish and spoiled, who believes that everyone else should put up with his caprices. He eats like a pig."

Suffering from asthma and "deeply bored," Ernesto spent his days in "meaningless arguments and every other possible way of wasting time." On August 2, there was a revolt by army cadets who had been humiliated at the hands of Castillo Armas's undisciplined Liberation Army. The revolt ended after Ambassador Puerifoy sent word that the United States expected the Guatemalan military to stand solidly behind Castillo Armas. The situation of the people packed into the embassies, hoping they would be able to get out of the country, was much more tenuous than they realized. Anxious to consolidate the victory over Communism in this first important Cold War skirmish in Washington's backyard, the CIA had dispatched teams of agents to Guatemala to collect—and, in some cases, to plant—evidence of the pro-Soviet nature of the Arbenz government. The Dulles brothers were also demanding that Castillo Armas arrest suspected Communists and their suspected sympathizers who remained in the country.

Castillo Armas was a willing partner in this campaign and had already carried out the first of a series of repressive measures to shore up his power while rolling back the revolution's reforms. He had created a National Committee for Defense Against Communism and decreed a Preventive Penal Law against Communism that imposed the death penalty for a wide range of crimes, including "political sabotage." The committee had broad powers to arrest and detain anyone suspected of being a Communist. Illiterate citizens were banned from voting, which instantly disenfranchised the vast majority of Guatemala's population. The agrarian reform laws were overturned and all political parties, labor unions, and peasant organizations were outlawed. Books considered subversive were confiscated and burned. The blacklist included novels by Victor Hugo and Dostoevsky, and those by Guatemala's noted (and future Nobel prize–winning) writer Miguel Angel Asturias, who would even be stripped of his citizenship.*

Secretary Dulles insisted that Castillo Armas go after the estimated 700 asylum seekers in the foreign embassies. "Dulles feared that they might 'recirculate' throughout the hemisphere if they were allowed to leave

---

*Asturias's son was to become a top guerrilla leader under the nom de guerre Gaspar Ilom, which he adopted from an Indian character in one of his father's novels.

Guatemala," wrote the authors of *Bitter Fruit,* the authoritative account of the overthrow of Arbenz. "His fear soon became an obsession. . . . Early in July, he told Puerifoy to instruct the new regime to bring 'criminal charges' against 'Communist' refugees as a way of preventing them from leaving the country." Dulles went so far as to propose a plan in which Castillo Armas would grant safe-conduct to Communists on the condition they be sent directly to Moscow. Castillo Armas resisted, apparently feeling that such a breach of international norms would be going too far, even for him. In early August he began approving safe-conduct visas for most of the refugees at the embassies.

By mid-August, the first few safe-conduct passes had arrived, but for Ernesto life was unchanged. He spent his time playing chess, sending notes to Hilda, and writing psycho-political profiles of his companions. He turned his attention to the Guatemalans. Roberto Castañeda, a photographer and dancer, had traveled "behind the Iron Curtain and is a sincere admirer of all of that but won't enter the Party. He lacks theoretical knowledge of Marxism, and maybe he wouldn't be a good militant for what we could call these bourgeois defects, but it is sure that in the moment of action he would be up to the task. . . . He has practically none of the effeminate mannerisms of a dancer." Of another, Arana, he wrote, "He is weak and without an ideological base but he is loyal to the Party. Of medium intelligence, he is nonetheless able to realize that the only ideal path for the working class is Communism."

Hilda twice visited the embassy, which was now under heavy guard, but was prevented from entering. Ernesto's asthma continued to plague him. He resolved to fast for a day and see if that would help "purge" his system. Hilda sent him a bottle of honey and a letter.

The days dragged on. Ernesto helped out in the kitchen but complained that the effort was tiring. The weariness of his muscles showed how out of shape he was. His descriptions of the other inhabitants of the embassy had become more caustic. He was especially critical of the large number of young Guatemalan leftists who also claimed to be poets. The verse of the eighteen-year-old student Marco Antonio Sandoval—an "energetic admirer of himself"—was "plagued with meditations upon death." When the poet Hugo Blanco escaped from the embassy by leaping over the fence, Ernesto wrote that he was "a bad poet. I don't even think he is an intelligent person. The inclination that seems to accompany them all is compassion. The good boy's smile accompanies the poet."

Safe-conduct passes continued to trickle in, and news came that Perón had agreed to grant asylum in Argentina to those in the embassy, along with their families. For those he respected, Ernesto issued some informal *salvoconductos* of his own, in the form of notes addressed to his family and friends.

The fugitive Communist leader Víctor Manuel Gutiérrez sneaked into the embassy one night by climbing over a wall. Gutiérrez was high on Castillo Armas's wanted list, and the situation caused a clash between the Argentine ambassador and Guatemalan officials, but Gutiérrez was granted asylum and placed in a room with his comrade Pellecer. Soon afterward, Ernesto was confined in the embassy garage along with twelve others who were viewed as troublesome Communists. They became known as the "Group of Thirteen." According to Ernesto's less than explicit notes, the extreme measure was taken after Humberto Pineda, Myrna Torres's boyfriend, had created a disturbance. They were threatened with force if they did not cooperate, and were prohibited from talking with the other asylum seekers. In the Group of Thirteen's first night in detention, however, Humberto Pineda and his brother Luis Arturo both escaped to join in the underground resistance activities being planned by the Communist Party against the new regime. In her memoirs, Hilda says that they took their action at Ernesto's urging. In his diary, Ernesto simply lauds the two as having "a lot of balls."

He was now focusing his descriptive profiles on the men in the garage. "Ricardo Ramírez is perhaps one of the most capable leaders of the youth movement," he wrote. "His general level of culture is high and his manner of facing problems is much less dogmatic than that of other comrades."*

August was coming to an end, and everyone's patience was wearing thin. The group in the garage was placed under even stricter confinement after Che-Che Vega "raised a ruckus with a whore who is a *mucama,* a cleaning girl." Tensions eased somewhat when 118 of the asylum seekers at the Argentine embassy—including Pellecer and Gutiérrez—were evacuated on five planes sent from Buenos Aires. Ernesto was offered passage home, but, adamant about going to Mexico, he declined. Since the ambassador could not force anyone to seek repatriation, he reluctantly allowed Ernesto to leave the embassy grounds.

A friend of Gualo García's had come in on one of the evacuation flights, bringing Ernesto $150 sent by his family, as well as "two suits, four kilos of *yerba,* and a mountain of stupid little things." He wrote to thank them for their gifts but said that he was forging on to Mexico and

---

*Then only twenty-three years old, Ricardo Ramírez would go on to become "Rolando Morán," leader of the Ejército Guerrillero de los Pobres, the strongest of several Marxist guerrilla forces that emerged in the early 1960s and fought successive Guatemalan governments for nearly four decades.

might not take along the clothes. "My slogan is little baggage, strong legs, and a fakir's stomach."

IV

When Ernesto left the embassy, the first thing he did was to look for Hilda. Since her release from prison on July 26, she had been living in limbo, lonely and frightened, having been refused a passport at the Peruvian embassy. She was now awaiting clearance from Lima. In a bizarre audience with Castillo Armas at the presidential palace, to which she had been summoned at his request, Hilda had been assured she would not be rearrested. Since then she had lived quietly in a rented apartment in the center of town, waiting anxiously for Ernesto.

They met in a restaurant where she usually took her meals. "He appeared there one day while I was having lunch," Hilda recalled. "Everyone in the restaurant studiously ignored him, except for my good friend the proprietress, who invited him to come and eat anything he wished. And when we walked through the downtown streets after lunch, everyone who knew us looked at us in surprise and were afraid to speak with us; they wouldn't even wave. They doubtless thought we were being watched by the police."

Deciding that there was nothing concrete that could be held against him, Ernesto turned his passport in to the immigration authorities so that he could get an exit permit, the first step toward receiving a Mexican visa. While he waited, he went to Lake Atitlán and the Guatemalan highlands. Within a few days, he returned to Guatemala City, picked up his passport, and finally obtained the Mexican visa.

His relationship with Hilda had reached a crossroads. Ernesto was ready for a new adventure in Mexico, while Hilda expected to head home to Peru. According to Hilda, Ernesto seemed unconcerned about their separation and made cavalier assurances that they would eventually meet up in Mexico and marry, while she sadly contemplated the prospect of losing him forever. The air was thick between them. They took a good-bye excursion together to their old picnic haunt of San Juan Sacatepéquez and had what Ernesto described as "a profusion of fondles and a superficial screw."

In fact, marriage with Hilda was the farthest thing from Ernesto's mind. On the same day as their final tryst, he wrote: "I believe I'll take advantage of the fact that she can't leave yet to split definitively. Tomorrow I will say good-bye to all the people I want to and on Tuesday morning I'll begin the great adventure to Mexico."

In mid-September, Ernesto crossed the border with a young Guatemalan student, Julio Roberto "El Patojo" Cáceres, whom he had met on the road, and headed for Mexico City. (The two men became close friends, and years later, Ernesto wrote a story in honor of Cáceres called simply "El Patojo.") Although Ernesto had some small doubts about his safety, their journey passed uneventfully.*

In the end, John Foster Dulles's instincts about the political exiles would prove correct. Besides Ernesto "Che" Guevara, a host of future revolutionaries had escaped his grasp in Guatemala. In Mexico and elsewhere, they *would* regroup and, from the ashes of the Arbenz debacle, eventually emerge—often with Guevara's help—as the Marxist guerrillas who would haunt American policy makers for the next forty years.

*In fact, Ernesto's position was more precarious than he realized, since the CIA had already begun a file on him. As Peter Grose, the author of a courteous biography of the CIA director Allen Dulles (*Gentleman Spy: The Life of Allen Dulles,* Houghton Mifflin, 1994), wrote: "Sorting through the files of the fallen Arbenz regime in Guatemala a few weeks after the coup, David Atlee Phillips came across a single sheet of paper about a twenty-five-year-old Argentine physician who had arrived in town the previous January to study medical care amid social revolution. 'Should we start a file on this one?' his assistant asked. The young doctor, it seemed, had tried to organize a last-ditch resistance by Arbenz loyalists; then he had sought refuge in the Argentine Embassy, eventually moving on to Mexico. 'I guess we'd better have a file on him,' Phillips replied. Over the coming years the file for Ernesto Guevara, known as 'Che,' became one of the thickest in the CIA's global records."

II

My Proletarian Life

I

Mexico City in the 1950s was far from the smog-shrouded megalopolis it has become. You could still see the snowcapped volcanoes Popocatépetl and Ixtacihuatl towering on the horizon. Apart from its historic labyrinthine downtown—the old Spanish colonial city built on the ruins of the Aztec capital—it was a place of serene, village-like neighborhoods and tree-lined boulevards. It was not uncommon to see men dressed as *charros*—Mexico's cowboy-dandies—promenading on horseback down the Paseo de la Reforma on Sunday afternoons. But the city was also cosmopolitan and sophisticated. It retained some of the political and artistic effervescence that had peaked in the 1930s and 1940s when artists such as Diego Rivera, José Clemente Orozco, David Alfaro Siqueiros, Frida Kahlo, and Tina Modotti were doing the work that made them famous. The influx of thousands of exiles fleeing Fascism in Europe had helped spark a cultural renaissance. Writers, artists, and political figures mingled at night in a thriving cabaret scene that featured the great stars of the Mexican bolero; a booming movie industry spawned cinema legends such as the director Emilio "El Indio" Fernández, the comic actor Cantinflas, and the screen idols Dolores del Río and María Félix. From the French writers Antonin Artaud and André Breton to the Beat poets and writers Jack Kerouac and William S. Burroughs, foreigners flocked to seek nourishment in Mexico.

The political and the creative worlds had always intermingled in Mexico City, which had been the site of some infamous assassinations—of the Cuban Communist leader Julio Antonio Mella in 1929 and of Leon Trotsky in 1940. Modotti was Mella's lover. Kahlo had had an affair with Trotsky. The muralist Siqueiros had led an attack with machine guns against Trotsky's home before the Stalinist agent Ramón Mercader achieved grisly success with an ice pick. Since the postrevolutionary consolidation of power by the ruling Partido Revolucionario Institucional (PRI),* Mexico had earned widespread popularity among anti-imperialist Latin American nationalists and a grudging respect from Washington. In the 1930s, President Lázaro Cárdenas had nationalized Mexico's oilfields and pushed through a sweeping program of agrarian reform. Espousing a foreign policy fiercely independent of Washington, Mexico was a highly politicized environment, full of intrigue, where both the United States and the Soviet Union had important embassies and intelligence operations, and where exiles, spies, and wanderers mingled and conspired.

There is no single defining moment for the eclipse of Mexico's "romantic" era, but few events are more emblematic of its passage than the last public appearance made by Frida Kahlo, on July 2, 1954. It was a cold, damp day, and the pneumonia-stricken artist left her bed to join a protest against the overthrow of Arbenz by the CIA. Kahlo's husband, Diego Rivera, pushed her wheelchair through the streets to the rally, which was held outside the pantheon of Mexican culture, the Palacio de Bellas Artes. There, for four long hours, Kahlo joined in the crowd's cries of *"Gringos Asesinos, fuera!"* and held aloft her glittering, ring-festooned hands. In her left hand was a banner depicting a dove of peace. Her clenched right fist was raised in defiance. Eleven days later, at the age of forty-seven, she died.

II

The first letter Ernesto wrote home from Mexico, on September 30, 1954, was to his aunt Beatriz. "Mexico, the city, or better said the country, of the *mordidas* [bribes], has received me with all the indifference of a big animal, neither caressing me nor showing me its teeth." His immediate plans were to find work and make enough money to survive, then to travel around Mexico and "ask for a visa from the Titan of the North [the United States]." If successful, he would visit his aunt Ercilia in New York, "and if not, to Paris."

Guessing that his money would hold out at most two months, Ernesto immediately began looking up people who might help him. One was Ulíses Petit de Murat, a friend of his father's who now worked as a screenwriter. Before leaving Guatemala, Ernesto had mentioned Petit to Hilda and had said that there might be an opportunity for him to work as a film extra in

*After several name changes following its creation in 1929, Mexico's long-ruling party adopted its present name in 1946.

Mexico. He could try out his "unrealized artistic ambitions of becoming an actor." Hilda called this a frivolous scheme and begged him not to waste his talents. According to Hilda, a somewhat chastened Ernesto had defended the idea, saying that he had merely thought of it as a means of making ends meet, but finally agreed with her and promised not to be sidetracked.

Now he needed work, and Petit de Murat was one of the few contacts Ernesto had in Mexico. Their meeting went well enough. "He took me out to show me around and we argued about politics," Ernesto reported in his diary. "He has a nice daughter, but she comes from a typical clericaloid bourgeois education." Petit and his daughter Marta took Ernesto to see the Aztec pyramids of Teotihuacán on the outskirts of the city. Using Marta as a model, Ernesto tried out a new toy he had bought purchased with half of his remaining funds—a 35mm Zeiss camera.

Petit invited Ernesto to stay at his house and offered help in getting some kind of study grant, but Ernesto declined the offer. In a letter to his father on September 30, he wrote, without apparent irony, that he had "decided to maintain a certain degree of independence as long as the pesos you sent hold out." Certainly, he and Petit were not a good match politically. "We locked horns over the same argument you and I always had about liberty, etc., and he is as blind as you are, with the aggravating element that it's easy to see that deep down what has happened in Guatemala makes him happy."

Several "zero days" followed, in which Ernesto explored the city, visited museums, and looked up friends. He tracked down Helena Leiva de Holst, who had also left Guatemala for exile in Mexico. Afterward he wrote in his diary that there seemed to be "something weird" going on between her and Hilda. Helena had spoken of Hilda in a "very disparaging manner." Whatever Helena told him must have been convincing, for he wrote in his diary, "I believe I must cut off this unsustainable situation with Hilda."

From home, he heard that most of the "Guatemalan lefties" who had been evacuated to Argentina had been imprisoned. A letter to his mother is full of recriminations about why his family hadn't done more for the comrades he had sent their way. In an aside, he shared with Celia his frustration over what had occurred in Guatemala and confessed to feeling torn about what to do with himself. In light of events, he declared himself "completely convinced that [political] halfway measures can mean nothing other than the antechamber to treason. The bad thing is that at the same time I haven't taken the decisive attitude that I should have taken a long time ago, because deep down (and on the surface) I am a complete bum and I don't feel like having my career interrupted by an iron discipline."

Ernesto was still digesting his Guatemalan experience, and in his letters he carried on a kind of extended postmortem. He wanted everyone to understand what he thought was the "truth" about what had happened there. To his friend Tita Infante, whose last letter to him in Guatemala he thought had betrayed a concern that went beyond the platonic, he wrote, "Today, with the distance—material and spiritual—that separates me from Guatemala, I reread your last letter and it seemed strange. I found in it a special warmth, in your desperation over not being able to do anything, that really moves me." Like the Spanish Republic, he said, Guatemala had been betrayed "inside and out," but it had not fallen with the same nobility. What sickened him most of all was the revisionist picture of the Arbenz government. "Falsehoods" were being printed in newspapers all over the Americas. For one thing, he told her, "there were no murders or anything like it. There *should* have been a few firing squads early on, which is different; if those shootings had taken place the government would have retained the possibility of fighting back."

Ernesto was convinced that the American intervention in Guatemala was merely the first skirmish in what would be a global confrontation between the United States and Communism, and he brought up this terrifying prospect rather inopportunely in a letter to his sister Celia. He had learned she was engaged to the young architect and Guevara family friend Luis Rodríguez Argañaraz. She had evidently inquired about job prospects in Mexico, for he wrote, "Stay there without thinking nonsense about other countries, because the storm is coming, and although it might not be atomic it'll be the other, that of hunger, and Argentina will be one of the less affected because it depends less on the friend to the north."

He repeated these dire predictions to his father. A world war was inevitable, he announced in a letter sent a few months later. The risks had grown "gigantically" in the wake of the shake-up in the Kremlin since Stalin's death. "Argentina is the oasis of America, and we have to give Perón all possible support to avoid entering into a war that promises to be terrible—whether you like it or not, that's the way it is. Nixon is traveling through all these countries, apparently to set the quotas of men and cheap primary resources (paid with expensive and old machinery) with which each of the poor states of America will contribute to the new Koreas."

Ernesto continued to look for work. He tried to arrange interviews for hospital jobs but made little headway. For the time being, he used his new camera to earn money, taking people's portraits in the city's parks and plazas. Over the coming months, he would work as a night watchman, a photographer for the Argentine news agency Agencia Latina, and an allergist and researcher at both the General Hospital and the Pediatric Hospital.

Hilda Gadea reentered his life. Just after Ernesto's departure from Guatemala, Hilda had been rearrested, jailed overnight, and sent under escort to the Mexican border. After a few days, she had been smuggled into Mexico by her own guards, for a fee. After being stranded in the border town of Tapachula for eight days, waiting to be granted political asylum by the Mexican government, she made her way to Mexico City and to Ernesto.

Ernesto's thoughts and actions since their parting had not been those of a concerned lover. Upon hearing that she was marooned at the border, he commented laconically in his diary, "Hilda is in Mexico in Tapachula and it isn't known in what condition."

As usual, Ernesto and Hilda's accounts about their on-again, off-again relationship don't dovetail with regard to events in Mexico City. Following their first meeting, Ernesto wrote, "With Hilda it seems we've reached a status quo, we'll see." Hilda's version reasserted her position that things were more intense: "Again Ernesto spoke of the possibility of getting married. I said we should wait. . . . I had the feeling that my ambiguous response had created a certain tenseness, because he then said that we would just be friends. I was a little surprised: I was only asking him to wait. But I accepted his decision. I had just arrived and here we were already quarreling." They continued to see each other, occasionally going out for a meal together or to the cinema, and Hilda soon moved into a boardinghouse with an exiled Venezuelan poet, Lucila Velásquez, in the affluent Condesa neighborhood. She too began looking for work.

A happier development was Ernesto's accidental reunion with the Cubans he had met in Guatemala, notably his friend Ñico López, who showed up one day at the General Hospital, where Ernesto was volunteering. Ñico was seeking treatment for a comrade who was suffering from allergies. As Hilda told it, Ernesto and Ñico immediately rekindled their friendship. Ñico was buoyant about the future, telling Ernesto confidently that he expected Fidel Castro, his younger brother Raúl, and the other imprisoned comrades to be released from prison before too long.

Castro's exiled Cuban followers had been trickling into Mexico City from around the hemisphere since early 1954. They had established an informal headquarters at the apartment of María Antonia González, a Cuban woman married to a Mexican professional wrestler named Dick Medrano. Castro had become a cause célèbre in Cuba. Batista had called for elections to legitimize his de facto rule, and now there was mounting public pressure on him to release Castro and the other imprisoned *moncadistas* in an amnesty. Once Castro was free, Ñico told Ernesto, Mexico was to be the base for his grand scheme, to organize and train an armed insurrectionary movement that would return to Cuba and fight a guerrilla war to topple Batista.

Ernesto responded to a letter in which his mother had criticized the behavior of the Guatemalan Communist exiles he had sent to their house: "The Communists don't have the same sense of friendship that you have, but among themselves they possess it equally, or better than your own. I saw it clearly in the hecatomb that Guatemala became after the fall, where everyone thought only of saving themselves. The Communists maintained their faith and comradeship intact, and were the only group which continued to work there. . . . I believe they are worthy of respect and that sooner or later I will join the Party; more than anything else what impedes me from doing it now is that I still have a fantastic urge to travel through Europe, and I couldn't do that submitted to an iron discipline."

A month later, in December, he wrote to his mother again, apparently in response to her alarm over his declaration of intent to eventually join the Communist Party. "That which you so fear is reached by two roads: positively, by being directly convinced, or negatively, after disenchantment with everything," he wrote. "I reached it by the second route only to immediately become convinced that one has to follow the first. The way in which the gringos treat America had been provoking a growing indignation in me, but at the same time I studied the theory behind the reasons for their actions and I found it scientific. Afterward came Guatemala."

What he had seen in Guatemala had added weight to his convictions, he wrote, and at some moment he had begun to *believe*. "At what moment I left the path of reason and took on something akin to faith, I can't tell you even approximately because the path was very long and with a lot of backward steps." There it was. If his family hadn't had enough prior warning, Ernesto had now declared himself and described his conversion. He was a Communist.

III

For the moment, Ernesto remained simply a young Argentine vagabond—who just happened to have a medical degree—scrabbling for work in a foreign country. His relationship with Hilda had had its ups and downs but reached a comfortable plateau early in 1955. This appears to have had less to do with any reconciliation over their basic differences than the fact that Ernesto needed her for the occasional loan and, as he wrote in his diary, to satisfy his "urgent need for a woman who will fuck." By now, he knew her well enough to realize she was always available for both.

In mid-January, he had brought her a belated New Year's present: a miniature copy of the Argentine classic *Martín Fierro* by José Hernández, bound in green leather. It was one of Ernesto's favorite books. He inscribed it with what must have seemed a maddeningly ambiguous message: "To

Hilda, so that on the day of our parting, you retain a sense of my ambitions for new horizons and my militant fatalism. Ernesto 20-1-55."

Hilda was still jobless but sustained by funds from home, and she had found ways to keep herself busy. She had signed up for a two-month course on the Mexican revolution at the Autonomous University, and she discussed what she was learning with Ernesto. They read relevant books, including John Reed's *Insurgent Mexico* and Pancho Villa's memoirs.

By now, there were a dozen or so Cuban *moncadistas* in Mexico City. Several were installed in a rooming house on Calle Gutenberg, and Ñico López and Calixto García were housed separately in the Hotel Galveston, downtown. They kept in close contact with the movement's unofficial co-ordinator, María Antonia González, at her apartment in an ugly modern pink building at 49 Calle Emparán in the city center. Since his chance encounter with Ñico López at the hospital, Ernesto had stayed in intermittent contact with him and his comrades, gradually meeting more of the new arrivals. In March, he hired two of them, Severino "El Guajiro" Rossell and Fernando Margolles, to develop photographs he took for Agencia Latina of the second Pan American Games. José Ángel Sánchez Pérez, a *moncadista* just in from Costa Rica, came to live in Ernesto's pension on Calle Tígres. A couple of months earlier, Sánchez Pérez had joined in the fighting in Costa Rica to defend President Figueres from an invasion backed by Somoza.

Just before the Pan American games began, Sánchez Pérez introduced Ernesto to María Antonia. According to Heberto Norman Acosta, a researcher at the Cuban Council of State and the son-in-law of one of Castro's rebel expeditionaries—who spent many years researching the "exile" period prior to the Cuban revolution—Ernesto was taken in as a trusted friend by María Antonia on the basis of his contacts with Ñico López, Calixto García, and the other Cubans. He also hit it off right away with María's husband, the wrestler Dick Medrano.

Meanwhile, Hilda was anxious to renew her affair with Ernesto, which he had interrupted after a recent argument. "I decided that, since I missed Ernesto and wanted to make up," she wrote, "I should take the initiative." Hilda's opportunity came with the arrival from Canada of Myrna Torres; she had decided to marry her boyfriend, Humberto Pineda, who was now in Mexico after months on the run in Guatemala. "Taking advantage of her friendship, I asked her to accompany me to visit the house of the Cubans; I knew that Ernesto was frequently there developing pictures," Hilda recalled. The visit gave Hilda the opening she wanted. They resumed their affair.

Agencia Latina folded that spring. Perón's bid to create an international news agency had not paid off, and with its demise went Ernesto's main source of income. He calculated that the agency owed him 5,000 pesos. "It's an amount that I could really use," he wrote. "With it, I could pay off some debts, travel around Mexico, and beat it to hell." Ernesto waited anxiously for the money, but, just in case, he made off with one of the agency's cameras.

On the "scientific" side of things, he was starting to make some headway. He had turned down a tempting offer to work in Nuevo Laredo, on the Mexican border with the United States, unwilling to commit himself to a two-year contract. He also self-righteously rejected his aunt Beatriz's offer to use her contacts to get him a job in a pharmaceutical laboratory. "In spite of my vagabonding, my repeated informality and other defects, I have deep and well-defined convictions," he wrote to Beatriz. "These convictions prevent me from taking a job of the type you describe, because these places are dens of thieves of the worst type, who traffic with human health that is supposed to be under my qualified custody. . . . I am poor but honest." In case Beatriz harbored any doubts about where he was coming from, he signed the letter "Stalin II."

In April, Ernesto traveled to León in the state of Guanajuato to attend a conference on allergies and present a paper, "Cutaneous Investigations with Semidigested Food Antigens." It received what he described as a "discreet reception" but was commented upon favorably by Dr. Mario Salazar Mallén, his boss at Mexico City's General Hospital, and was due to be published in the next issue of the journal *Alergia*. Afterward, Salazar Mallén, "the *capo* of Mexican allergy," according to Ernesto, offered him an internship at the General Hospital and a small sinecure to carry out new allergy research. Ernesto began the internship in May. He received a minuscule salary of 150 pesos a month, with free lodging, board, and laundry. For now, at least, the job covered his basic needs. In a letter to his mother, he wrote, "If it weren't for the charity of friends I would have gone on the police blotter as a death by starvation." As for wages, he was indifferent: "Money is an interesting luxury but nothing more."

Hilda offered to marry and support him. "I said no," he wrote in his diary. "We should stay as little lovers until I beat it to hell, and I don't know when that'll be." But when, soon afterward, Hilda invited Ernesto to move into the apartment she shared with Lucila Velásquez, he accepted. The two women had recently gotten a new place on Calle Rhin, and Hilda had found a temporary job at the UN's Economic Commission for Latin America and the Caribbean. The arrangement not only solved the question of food for Ernesto—and offered a more comfortable lodging than the hospital bed he had been granted—but also enriched his circle of contacts. Hilda knew a great many people among Mexico's flourishing expatriate community. They included the prominent Cuban exile Raúl Roa, an editor of the magazine *Humanismo,* and his coeditor, the Puerto Rican exile Juan Juarbe y Juarbe. Others in the group were the young Peruvian lawyer Luis de la Puente

Uceda,* leader of a leftist youth wing of APRA; and Laura Meneses, the Peruvian wife of Pedro Albizu Campos, the Puerto Rican independence fighter imprisoned in the United States for leading an attack on the governor's palace in San Juan in 1950. Ernesto got along especially well with the Puerto Ricans, and he and Hilda began visiting them to discuss Latin American politics, particularly the issue of Puerto Rican independence, a cause he had come to sympathize with strongly.

Ernesto's life with Hilda slipped into an unexciting, but not unhappy, routine of work, study, and domesticity. They met with friends, went to the occasional movie, and cooked dinners at home. Many nights, Lucila came back to the apartment to find the two of them deeply absorbed in study, usually of books on economics. On such occasions she didn't speak, but tip-toed past them to her bedroom and retired for the night. In the middle of May, Ernesto and Hilda consecrated their union with a weekend tryst at the popular retreat of Cuernavaca and began exploring other sites within easy reach of the capital. His life, as he told his mother in a letter sent in mid-June, had acquired a "monotonous Sunday-style rhythm."

In Cuba, the pace of events had begun to quicken. In November 1954, running unopposed, Fulgencio Batista was elected president, and in January, Vice President Richard Nixon made a congratulatory visit from the United States. Then, in April, over the Easter weekend, the CIA's director, Allen Dulles, visited Havana and met with Batista. Dulles successfully urged Batista to open a special police intelligence bureau to deal with Communist encroachment in the hemisphere. The result, largely funded and advised by the CIA, was the Buro de Represión a las Actividades Comunistas (BRAC). Soon enough, its activities were to earn it a sinister reputation.

Ironically, neither Dulles nor the CIA's station chief in Havana had Fidel Castro in mind when they proposed the creation of BRAC. In May, Fidel, his brother Raúl, and the eighteen other *moncadistas* incarcerated with them on the Isle of Pines were granted their freedom. Batista described his ill-advised amnesty as a goodwill gesture in honor of Mother's Day.

IV

Batista was not the worst of Latin America's dictators at the time. Rafael Leonidas Trujillo had ruled over the Dominican Republic as absolute

---

*Ernesto and Luis de la Puente Uceda did not meet at this time. Uceda had already left for Peru when Hilda and Ernesto patched things up. But he and Ernesto would meet a few years later, in Cuba, when Uceda was organizing a Peruvian guerrilla movement.

dictator since the 1930s, thanks to the ruthless efficiency of his secret police. Trujillo imposed an official cult of personality that was unparalleled in the western hemisphere. The capital of the Dominican Republic, Santo Domingo, had been renamed Ciudad Trujillo. Signs bearing Orwellian-sounding messages like "God Is in Heaven—Trujillo Is on Earth" and "We Live in Happiness, Thanks to Trujillo" were ubiquitous.

Compared with the flamboyant despotism of his Dominican colleague, Batista was a political choirboy. A mulatto army officer, he had left the barracks to be Cuba's president once before, in the 1940s. That time, he had achieved office through elections generally considered fair, and he ruled over a coalition government with the Partido Socialista Popular, the Communists. The uninspired, graft-ridden presidencies of Grau San Martín and his protégé, Carlos Prío Socarrás, followed. (Grau founded the Partido Revolucionario Cubano Auténtico in the 1930s. Its followers were known forever after as *auténticos*.) Batista put an end to Prío Socarrás's presidency in the coup of 1952, and although he may have legitimized his rule in Washington's eyes—with elections and by turning against his old Communist allies—to Cuba's disenfranchised political parties, the students, and the urban middle-class intelligentsia, he was a dictator who had usurped power and sabotaged their hopes for a constitutional reform to bring about social change and a genuine Cuban democracy.

Since the Moncada assault, Batista had shown that he was not averse to resolving challenges to his rule through police death-squad tactics, and official graft and bribery flourished as never before. By the mid-1950s, Cuba was earning a reputation as the whorehouse of the Caribbean, where weekending Americans came to gamble, drink, and carouse with Havana's many prostitutes. A notorious character named Schwartzmann ran a theater featuring hard-core "blue" films and live sex performances, and the American crime syndicates were moving in as well, opening nightclubs and gambling casinos.

Cuban aristocrats despised Batista, perceiving him as a half-caste gangster. He was put in his place when as president he applied for membership in one of Havana's most exclusive whites-only country clubs and was summarily rejected. To Cuba's new generation of nationalist idealists, exemplified by Fidel Castro, he was little more than a pimp, selling off their country to degenerate foreigners. His behavior compounded the resentment they already felt over such issues as the continued U.S. naval presence at Guantánamo Bay, a legacy of the ignominious days earlier in the twentieth century when (after the United States had won the Spanish-American War and ousted the Spaniards from Cuba) Washington had governed Cuba like a vassal state.

Fidel Castro wanted to change his country, and his time in prison had only toughened his resolve. When he emerged from the gates of the Modelo prison on May 15, to media fanfare, he was in an ungrateful, scrappy mood. He vowed to continue the struggle against Batista's "despotism."

At this point, Castro's movement had a fairly hard inner core of mostly middle-class, reform-minded Cuban professionals who were united by their hatred of Batista. Only a few *moncadistas* were Communists. Most of them were activists from the youth wing of the opposition Ortodoxo Party. Castro had emerged as their most charismatic leader in the vacuum left by the suicide in 1951 of the party's leader, Eduardo Chibás. Castro was a Young Turk who, since Moncada, had shown he was not just full of bombast. His followers were nationalists, imbued with the romantic rhetoric of José Martí, the apostle of Cuban independence who was shot off his horse in 1895 during a reckless charge against Spanish colonial troops.

Among this group were a few tactfully undeclared Marxists such as Ñico López, Calixto García, and Fidel's brother Raúl. Fidel's own ideology was publicly anticommunist, although he was already showing signs of the wily political opportunism he was to become famous for, gathering useful people from all political stripes to help implement his goals. The reckonings would come later. For now there was an uphill battle to be waged, and he needed all the help he could get. The movement's actual philosophy could be ironed out over time; what held them all together for now was their attraction to Fidel Castro.

Castro's organization had acquired a name—the July 26 Movement—but so far, it remained a secret known only to his closest followers. Publicly, Castro denied any intention of forming his own political party and strenuously reavowed his loyalty to the Ortodoxo Party. In truth, Castro's plan was to build up his base of support in Cuba before going to Mexico and preparing for the next phase of the struggle, the guerrilla war that would oust Batista and bring his own party to power.

Taking advantage of Batista's amnesty, Ñico López and Calixto García returned to Havana to meet with their leader and help him coordinate strategy. Two days before they left Mexico, on May 27, Ernesto wrote an intriguing letter to his father. Opening with a description of his allergy research, he began to ramble on about his future travel plans, enigmatically letting slip the possibility that he "might go to Cuba." He was involved in two separate "collaborations," he wrote: one involving allergy research, and the other—in an allusion that must have mystified his father—with a "good chemist" in Mexico "about a problem of which I have only an intuition, but I believe something very important is going to come out. . . . I hope for a recommendation to the places where the dawn is ripening, as they say. . . . Havana in particular attracts me as a place to fill my heart with landscape, well mixed with quotes from Lenin."

Yet when he heard of a ship sailing for Spain in early July, he was prepared to abandon all his plans and go on it. He was told he could attend the upcoming Communist Youth Congress in China if he could pay for part of his travel costs, but as tempting as it was to see the "land of Mao," the pull of Europe was stronger, "almost a biological necessity," as he wrote to his mother a few days later.

V

Eager for some excitement, Ernesto joined an "improvised" attempt to scale Mount Popocatépetl, one of two majestic volcanos towering over Mexico City. Although he and his companions reached only the lower lip of the summit's crater, he did get to "peer into the entrails of Mother Earth."

He was following the news from Argentina with mounting anxiety. On June 16, the Argentine navy launched a bloody attempt to topple Perón. Hundreds of civilians died in a messy aerial bombardment of the presidential palace. The attempt failed, but Perón was shaken, and an atmosphere of tense uncertainty lingered as his regime teetered on the brink of collapse. Ernesto wrote to his mother, asking for news because he didn't trust the reports being published in Mexico: "I hope the thing isn't as bad as they paint it, and that there's none of ours stuck in a dispute where there's nothing to be gained." Aware of his family's strong *antiperonista* sentiments, Ernesto was concerned that some of them, especially his brother Roberto, who worked for the navy, might be at risk. Moving on to his own news, Ernesto told Celia that he was now spending much of his free time imparting the "doctrine of San Carlos," a euphemism for Karl Marx, to "a bunch of sixth-grade kids"—presumably his less worldly exile friends.

The political climate in Havana had deteriorated rapidly. Since his release, Fidel had been busy recruiting new members to his organization and denouncing Batista to the press. On the night of June 12, in a secret meeting in Old Havana, the July 26 Movement was formally founded with an eleven-member National Directorate, headed by Fidel. Political violence committed by the police, students, and Fidel's party militants resumed with a vengeance. An exile who had returned to the city was murdered; a wave of bombs ripped through Havana. Fidel accused the government of unleashing the violence, while the authorities accused Raúl of placing one of the bombs and issued an arrest warrant for him. Fidel publicly accused the regime of plotting to kill him and his brother. On June 16, having already

Climbing Mt. Popocatépetl,
Mexico.

banned him from making radio broadcasts, the police closed down his chief
remaining media outlet, the tabloid daily *La Calle*.

Realizing he had little time left in which to act, Fidel ordered Raúl to
flee to Mexico and prepare the way for his own arrival. After seeking asylum in the Mexican embassy in Cuba and spending a week holed up there,
Raúl flew to Mexico City on June 24. He went straight to María Antonia's
house. Among those waiting to meet him was Ernesto Guevara.

By all accounts, the two hit it off immediately. First of all, they shared
an ideological affinity. Raúl, Fidel's younger brother by five years, had joined
the Cuban Communist Party's youth wing at Havana University, helped
edit its publication *Saeta,* and in May 1953 attended the World Youth Festival in Bucharest, Romania. No doubt Raúl had already heard about Ernesto
from Ñico López, who had stayed with him and Fidel after returning to
Havana.

Soon after Raúl's arrival, Ernesto invited him to Hilda and Lucila's
apartment for dinner. Ernesto didn't mention the event in his diary, but in
her memoirs, Hilda said she had liked Raúl immediately. "In spite of his
youth," Hilda recalled, "twenty-three or twenty-four years, and his even
younger appearance, blond and beardless and looking like a university

student, his ideas were very clear as to how the revolution was to be made and, more important, for what purpose and for whom."

Raúl spoke of his faith in his older brother and of his personal belief, echoing Ernesto's views, that in Cuba and the rest of the region power could be gained not through elections, but only through war. With popular support, one could gain power and then transform society from capitalism to socialism. "He promised to bring Fidel to our house as soon as the latter arrived in Mexico," Hilda wrote. "From then on he visited at least once a week, and Ernesto saw him almost every day."

A mystery that has endured over the years is the question of *when* the Soviets became involved with the Cuban revolution. Although "involvement" is probably too strong a term to use, the earliest contacts between Fidel Castro's revolutionaries and Soviet officials took place in Mexico City during the summer of 1955.

Coincidentally, a twenty-seven-year-old official in the Soviet foreign ministry whom Raúl knew was also in Mexico City in 1955. His name was Nikolai Leonov. They had met two years earlier, on the monthlong voyage that brought Raúl back from the European youth festival, and had become friends. The last they had seen of each other was when Raúl disembarked in Havana. Within a few weeks, Raúl had joined in the Moncada assault and gone to prison, while Leonov had traveled on to Mexico to take up his junior post at the Soviet embassy and attend a Spanish-language course at the Autonomous University. Now chance had brought Nikolai Leonov and Raúl Castro together again.

According to Leonov (who retired from the KGB in 1992 as deputy chief of its First Chief Directorate, covering the United States and Latin America), he happened to bump into Raúl in the street one day while shopping. Delighted to see him again, Raúl gave Leonov the address of María Antonia's house and invited him to drop by. Prohibited from initiating any social contacts without the prior knowledge of the embassy, Leonov nonetheless violated this rule and made his way to 49 Calle Emparán. There, he met Ernesto Guevara.

"He was acting as a doctor, treating Raúl, who was suffering from flu," Leonov recalled. "My first impression was of a happy man, a joker; practically all he did to treat Raúl was to cheer him up, telling him anecdotes, jokes." After the introductions were made, Ernesto and Leonov began to talk. Leonov says that Ernesto was full of questions about Soviet life and pumped him about everything from Soviet literature to "the concept of Soviet man—'How do they think? How do they live?'" Leonov offered to give him some books to read; if he still had questions, they could talk some more. Ernesto requested *A Man Complete,* about a Soviet aviation hero in World War II, and two novels set during the Russian civil war of 1918–1922—*Chapaev,* by Dmitri Furmanov; and *How the Steel Was Tempered,* by Nikolai Ostrovsky. A few days later, Ernesto showed up at the embassy to get the books and they talked again, "but this time, as friends," as Leonov put it. They agreed to keep in touch, and Leonov gave Ernesto his embassy card. That, said Leonov, was the last they saw of each other in Mexico.

12

God and His New Right Hand

I

In the summer of 1955, Ernesto noted an event in his diary: "A political occurrence is having met Fidel Castro, the Cuban revolutionary, a young man, intelligent, very sure of himself and of extraordinary audacity; I think there is a mutual sympathy between us."

Their encounter took place a few days after Castro's arrival in Mexico on July 7. Ernesto met him at María Antonia's apartment at 49 Calle Emparán. After talking for a while, Ernesto, Fidel, and Raúl went to dinner together at a restaurant down the block. Several hours later, Fidel invited Ernesto to join his guerrilla movement. Ernesto accepted on the spot.

Che, as the Cubans had begun calling him, was to be their doctor. It was the early days—Fidel was a long way from putting together his ambitious scheme—but it was the cause Ernesto had been searching for.

II

Ernesto Guevara and Fidel Castro were natural opposites.

At twenty-eight, Castro was a consummate political animal, overflowing with self-confidence. He was one of nine children from a landowning family in eastern Cuba's Mayarí province. His father, Ángel Castro, was an illiterate Galician immigrant who arrived in Cuba penniless and made a modest fortune in land, sugar, lumber, and cattle. Presiding over a large *finca,* Manacas, with its own store, slaughterhouse, and bakery, Castro was a rural patriarch who ruled the destiny of 300 workers and their families.

Ángel Castro gave his bright, rebellious third son (the offspring of his second marriage, to Lina Ruz, the family's cook) the best education money could buy. He went to the Marist-run Dolores primary school in Santiago,

On Sunday, May 15, 1955, Fidel Castro, in the dark suit, was freed
from prison on Cuba's Isle of Pines. He had spent nearly two years
there after being convicted of leading an attack on the Moncada
army garrison in Santiago. Castro had received a sentence of
fifteen years but had been amnestied. With him are, from left
front, his brother Raúl, Juan Almeida, and Ciro Redondo.

was a boarder at Havana's exclusive Jesuit Colegio Belén high school, and
attended law school at Havana University. Intensely competitive and hot-
tempered, Fidel acquired a reputation as a gun-toting rabble-rouser on the
volatile university campus. Even before the attack on the Moncada barracks
he had been linked to two shootings—one of a policeman—but had successfully avoided arrest in both cases.

Castro came of age during the presidencies of Grau San Martín and
Prío Socarrás, which were marked by corruption, gangsterism, and police brutality. He immersed himself in student politics, invoking the pur-
ist rhetoric of Cuba's national hero, José Martí, in his calls for clean
government, students' rights, and social equality. When the vociferous
Senator Eduardo Chibás formed the Ortodoxo Party to run for president
against Grau San Martín in 1947, Castro joined the new party's youth
wing. Before long, he was seen by many as Chibás's successor. The fact

that he had friends in the Communist Party and sided with them on certain issues did not prevent him from campaigning with Catholic factions against them in student elections.

Fidel was also strongly anti-imperialist and joined several student associations propounding such views, including one promoting independence for Puerto Rico. He was all too aware of Cuba's status as a neocolony of the United States after the Spanish-American War and the subsequent U.S. military occupation. Cuba's putative independence had been won at the cost of the ignominious 1901 Platt Amendment, which granted Washington the right to intervene in Cuba's "defense" at will and ceded Guantánamo Bay to the United States as a naval base on open-ended terms. By the time Fidel was in high school, the Platt Amendment had been abrogated, but the Americans retained Guantánamo Bay, had large stakes in Cuba's sugar-based economy, and took a proconsular role in its political life. In 1949, after American sailors urinated on the statue of José Martí in Old Havana's Parque Central, Fidel helped organize a protest in front of the U.S. embassy and was beaten by Cuban police. In 1951, both he and his brother Raúl had vocally opposed the Prío government's intention of sending Cuban troops to fight in the "American war" in Korea.

Fidel Castro felt a deep antipathy toward the Yankees who had turned independent Cuba into a pseudo-republic and allowed venal dictatorships to take root there. His native Mayarí province was a virtual vassal state of the United Fruit Company, which owned gigantic tracts of land and most of the sugar mills. American and privileged Cuban employees enjoyed an exclusive life on the company's housing estates, which had shops, hospitals, sports facilities, and private schools. Fidel's father depended on "the Company." Having leased much of his land from it, he was required to sell his sugarcane to United Fruit's mills.

Fidel had probably always thought of himself as Cuba's future leader. At school, he fought to become the undisputed leader of his peers, whether by coming in first in a poetry competition in grade school, becoming captain of the basketball team at Colegio Belén, or winning recognition in student politics at Havana University. At the age of twelve, he sent a letter to Franklin Delano Roosevelt to congratulate him on his third inauguration as president and to ask him for a dollar. While José Martí remained his lifelong inspiration, he came to admire powerful historical figures such as Julius Caesar, Robespierre, and Napoleon. He seemed to possess an innate knack for the horse-trading and cunning that make for success in politics, and he knew how to dissemble artfully.

These traits pointed up a major distinction between him and the man who would later stand at his right side. For Ernesto Guevara, politics represented a mechanism for social change, and it was social change, not power itself, that impelled him. If he had insecurities, they were not social. He lacked the chip on his shoulder that Castro wore and had converted into a source of strength. His own family were blue bloods, however bankrupt, and he had grown up with the social confidence and sense of privilege that come from knowing one's heritage. The Guevaras may have been black sheep within Argentine society, but they were still *society*. However much Ernesto sought to reject his birthright and to sever his family links, he was indelibly imprinted by them.

Although Ernesto certainly had a robust ego, it did not compare to that of Fidel Castro. In large groups, where Ernesto tended to hang back, observe, and listen, Castro was compelled to take over and be recognized as the authority on whatever topic was under discussion, from history and politics to animal husbandry.

Because of his asthma, Guevara was all too aware of his physical short-comings, whereas the burly Castro recognized none in himself. He was not a natural athlete but felt he could excel in anything if he set his mind to it, and he very often did. Castro had an urge to *win*. It had been an achievement for Ernesto just to be able to *play* rugby and the other sports of his youth, to be accepted as a team member. It was camaraderie, not leadership, that he craved.

Taller than average, with Brylcreemed hair and a small mustache that didn't suit him, Fidel had the well-fed look of a man used to pampering himself. And he was. He loved food and liked to cook. When he was in prison he wrote letters to friends describing in detail and with relish the meals he had whipped up. Ernesto, who was two years younger, was both shorter and slighter, with the pallor and dark dramatic eyes associated with a stage actor or poet. In many ways, their physiques reflected their personality differences. Fidel was unconsciously self-indulgent. Ernesto was a creature of the self-discipline imposed upon him by asthma.

Despite their many differences, Ernesto and Fidel shared some traits. Both were favored boys from large families, extremely spoiled, careless about their appearance, and sexually voracious. For both of them, relationships came in second to personal goals. Both were imbued with Latin machismo. They believed in the innate weakness of women, were contemptuous of homosexuals, and admired brave men of action. Both possessed an iron will and a larger-than-life sense of purpose. And finally, both wanted to carry out a revolution. By the time they met, they had tried to play direct roles in historic events of their time, only to be thwarted. And they identified a common enemy—the United States.

In 1947, while still at the university, Fidel had joined a group of Cubans and Dominicans undergoing military training on a remote Cuban key with the intention of invading the Dominican Republic to overthrow General Trujillo. The expedition was aborted at the last minute by Cuban troops, after President Grau San Martín had been alerted by Washington. As a delegate to the "anti-imperialist" youth congress organized in Bogotá by Perón in 1948, Fidel had joined in the rioting that took place after the Liberal Party opposition leader Eliécer Gaitán was assassinated. He tried to organize a popular resistance against the Conservative government. Then came Batista's coup, Moncada, and prison.

Fidel had followed the events in Guatemala with interest when he was in prison and had sympathized with the battle of the beleaguered Arbenz government against that familiar specter, the United Fruit Company. The fall of Arbenz was instructive. It taught Fidel that if his revolution for Cuba was to be successful, he would have to proceed cautiously and to acquire a strong foothold of power before antagonizing American interests. It was just as obvious to him that if he was to rule Cuba with a free hand, foreign companies such as United Fruit would have to be nationalized. The trick, Fidel knew, was to proceed with tact and guile.

It was apparent to Ernesto, as it was to most people who met him, that Fidel's rare personality was enhanced by the utter conviction that he would ultimately succeed. And if Fidel was not yet as convinced as Ernesto that socialism was the correct course to follow, he exhibited sympathy for the same goals. It would be up to those close to him, including Ernesto Guevara, to ensure that Fidel Castro's revolution followed a socialist course.

"Ñico was right in Guatemala when he told us that if Cuba had produced anything good since Martí it was Fidel Castro," Ernesto told Hilda not long after meeting Fidel. "He will make the revolution. We are in complete accord. . . . It's only someone like him I could go all out for." He admitted that Fidel's scheme of landing a boatful of guerrillas on Cuba's well-defended coasts was a "crazy idea," but he felt compelled to support him anyway.

On July 20, Ernesto wrote to his aunt Beatriz, telling her enigmatically: "Time has provoked a sifting out of the torrent of projects I was doing and now . . . I can be certain of finishing only one, which . . . will be exported to the next country I visit, the name of which no one knows but God and his new right hand."

In honor of his new friend and comrade, Ernesto asked Hilda and Lucila to prepare a dinner for Fidel, and to invite Laura de Albizu Campos and Juan Juarbe as well. That night, Castro displayed three of the traits he was to become famous for: his propensity to keep others waiting interminably, his tremendous personal charisma, and his ability to pontificate for hours on end. Lucila took offense at the long delay and went to her room, but Hilda waited patiently and was suitably impressed. "He was young, . . . light of complexion, and tall, about six feet two inches, and solidly built," she wrote. "He could very well have been a handsome bourgeois tourist. When he talked, however, his eyes shone with passion and revolutionary zeal, and one could see why he could command the attention of listeners. He had the charm and personality of a great leader, and at the same time an admirable simplicity and naturalness."

After dinner, Hilda overcame her awe and asked Castro why he was in Mexico if his struggle lay in Cuba. "He answered: 'Very good question. I'll explain.'" Fidel's answer lasted four hours.

A few days later, Ernesto told Hilda that he intended to join the rebels' invasion of Cuba. Soon afterward, Hilda informed him that she was pregnant.

III

On July 26, to commemorate the second anniversary of the Moncada assault, Fidel organized a ceremony—complete with speeches given by himself and other Latin American exiles—in Chapultepec Park. Afterward, everyone gathered at a home where Fidel prepared one of his favorite dishes, *spaghetti alle vongole*.

At dinner, Ernesto sat quietly without saying much. Noticing his reserve, Fidel called out: "Hey Che! You're very quiet. Is it because your controller's here now?" It was a reference to Hilda. "Obviously Fidel knew we were planning to get married; hence the joke," she wrote. "I then realized that they did a great deal of talking together. I knew very well that when Ernesto felt at ease he was talkative; he loved discussions. But when there were many people around he would remain withdrawn."

Hilda interpreted Ernesto's silence as a meditation on the momentousness of the enterprise he was involved in, but this has the unmistakable ring of after-the-fact mythologizing. It seems much more likely that he was pondering the dilemma he faced with her. He had decided to marry her—it was, after all, the honorable thing to do—but he wrote in his journal, "For another guy it would be transcendental; for me it is an uncomfortable episode. I am going to have a child and I will marry Hilda in a few days. The thing had dramatic moments for her and heavy ones for me. In the end, she gets her way—the way I see it, for a short while, although she hopes it will be lifelong."

Marriage could not have come at a worse moment for a man who had always resisted domesticity and who had just found a cause and a leader to follow. Nonetheless, Ernesto went through with it, and on August 18, he and Hilda were married at the civil registrar's office in the little town of Tepozotlán on the capital's outskirts. Their witnesses were Lucila Velásquez; Jesús Montané Oropesa, a short, flap-eared public accountant (and a member of the Movement's freshly formed National Directorate) who had just arrived from Havana as Fidel's treasurer; and two of Ernesto's colleagues from the General Hospital. Raúl Castro went along for the occasion but, on Fidel's orders to keep a low profile, didn't sign the ledger. Fidel, who suspected that his actions were being monitored by Batista's secret police and the American FBI, did not attend, for security reasons, although he showed up at the party Ernesto and Hilda gave afterward, at which Ernesto prepared an *asado,* Argentine-style.

Ernesto and Hilda moved out of the apartment with Lucila into their own flat, in a five-story apartment building on Calle Nápoles in Colonia Juárez. Then they broke the news to their parents. "My parents sent back a letter scolding us for not telling them in advance, so they could come for the wedding," Hilda recalled. "They also sent us a bank draft for five

Ernesto and Hilda on their honeymoon in the Yucatán, 1955.

hundred dollars as a present, asked us to send photographs, and Mother asked for a church wedding and said we should send her the exact date so she could have the announcements made for our friends back home."

Ernesto wrote back to his new in-laws, employing a mixture of candor and light ribaldry that must have raised some eyebrows in the middle-class Gadea household. "Dear Parents: I can imagine your surprise at receiving our bombshell of news, and can understand the flood of questions it must have provoked. You're of course correct in scolding us for not having informed you of our marriage. We thought it wiser to do it this way, in view of the numerous difficulties that we encountered, not foreseeing that we would have a child so soon. . . . We are very grateful for the expressions of affection you've given us, I know they're sincere: I've known Hilda long enough to feel that I know her family. I shall try to show that I deserve her at all times. I am also grateful for the 'small gift': You've done more than enough. Don't worry about us. It is true that we're not wealthy, but Hilda and I earn enough to keep up a home properly. . . .

"I believe this adequately answers your affectionate letter, but I should add something about our future plans. First we wait for 'Don Ernesto.' (If it's not a boy, there's going to be trouble.) Then we'll consider a couple of firm propositions I have, one in Cuba, the other a fellowship in France, depending on Hilda's ability to move around. Our wandering life isn't over yet and before we definitely settle in Peru, a country that I admire in many ways, or in Argentina, we want to see a bit of Europe and two fascinating countries, India and China. I am particularly interested in the New China because it accords with my own political ideals. I hope that soon, or if not soon someday, after knowing these and other really democratic countries, Hilda will think like me.

"Our married life probably won't be like yours. Hilda works eight hours a day and I, somewhat irregularly, around twelve. I'm in research, the toughest branch (and poorest paid). But we've fitted our routines together harmoniously and have turned our home into a free association between two equals. (Of course, Sra. Gadea, Hilda's kitchen is the worst aspect of the house—in order, cleanliness, or food. . . .) I can only say that this is the way I've lived all my life, my mother having the same weakness. So a sloppy house, mediocre food, and a salty mate, if she's a true companion, is all I want from life.

"I hope to be received into the family as a brother who has long been traveling the same path toward an equal destiny, or at least that my peculiarities of character (which are many) will be overlooked in view of the unqualified affection of Hilda for me, the same as I have for her. With an *abrazo* for the family from this new son and brother—Ernesto."

To his own family, Ernesto downplayed the news of his marriage and impending fatherhood, placing it at the end of a letter sent September 24 to his mother. The letter dwelled overwhelmingly on his reaction to the military coup d'état that had finally toppled Perón four days earlier. "I will confess with all sincerity that the fall of Perón deeply embittered me," he wrote. "Not for him, but for what it means for all of America, because as much as you hate to admit it, and in spite of the enforced renunciation of recent times,* Argentina was the Paladin of all those who think the enemy is in the North."

After predicting further social divisions and political violence for his homeland, he got around to his own news, writing: "Who knows in the meantime what will come of your wandering son. Maybe he will have decided to return and settle his bones in the homeland . . . or begin a period of real struggle. . . . Maybe a bullet of those so profuse in the Caribbean will end my existence (this isn't a boast or a concrete possibility, it's just that the bullets really do wander around a lot in this latitude) . . . or I'll just simply carry on vagabonding for as long as necessary to finish off a solid training and to satisfy the desires I reserved for myself within my life's program, before dedicating myself seriously to the pursuit of my ideal. Things are moving with tremendous speed and no one can know or predict where or for what reason one will be next year."

Almost as a postscript, he added: "I don't know if you've received the formal news of my marriage and of the coming of the heir. . . . If not, I communicate the news officially, so that you share it out among the people; I married Hilda Gadea and we shall have a child."

Around this same time, the health of María, an elderly patient Ernesto had been treating over the previous year, suddenly deteriorated. Despite all his efforts, she died, asphyxiated by her asthma. He was at her bedside when she took her last gasp. The experience drove him to write a poem in which he poured out his anger over the social neglect he felt had driven her to death. In "Old María, You're Going to Die," she personifies all the wasted, poor lives of Latin America. To Ernesto, she had become the old woman in Valparaíso, the fugitive couple in Chuquicamata, and the browbeaten Indians of Peru.

*A reference to Perón's recent rapprochement with American financial interests and his controversial attempt to push through a bill allowing Standard Oil to undertake explorations in the Patagonian oilfields.

Poor old María . . .
don't pray to the inclement god that denied your hopes
your whole life
don't ask for clemency from death,
your life was horribly dressed with hunger,
and ends dressed by asthma.
But I want to announce to you,
in a low voice virile with hopes,
the most red and virile of vengeances
I want to swear it on the exact
dimension of my ideals.
Take this hand of a man which seems like a boy's
between yours polished by yellow soap,
Scrub the hard calluses and the pure knots
in the smooth vengeance of my doctor's hands.
Rest in peace, old María,
rest in peace, old fighter,
your grandchildren will all live to see the dawn.

IV

For now, the world of "red vengeance" was forced to boil away in Ernesto's imagination. He could channel his indignation only in his writing, the occasional political discussion, and his growing hopes for Fidel Castro's revolutionary project.

That project was moving slowly forward. Fidel, who had turned twenty-nine in August, was in regular contact, through couriers, with members of the Movement still in Cuba and was busy planning, plotting, reading, writing, issuing orders, and, above all, talking, always talking. As he had done in Cuba, Fidel took over the lives of whoever in Mexico proved susceptible to his varied charms and powers of persuasion. Arzacio Vanegas Arroyo, a short, Indian-faced printer and wrestler ("Kid Vanegas"), a friend of María Antonia and her husband, was drafted to print 2,000 copies of Fidel's "Manifesto No. 1 to the Cuban People." Fidel then had another friend smuggle copies back to Cuba, with orders to distribute them at Eduardo Chibás's grave site on August 16, the fourth anniversary of his late mentor's death. The manifesto revealed the formation of the July 26 Movement as a revolutionary organization seeking the restoration of democracy and justice in Cuba. Point by point, it outlined Fidel's call for reforms: elimination of the feudal landowning oligarchy, or *latifundia,* and distribution of the lands to peasants; the nationalization of public services; a mandatory rent decrease; an ambitious housing, education, industrialization, and rural electrification program; and so on, encompassing virtually every aspect of Cuban life. In essence, it was a call for the imposition of radical measures to turn Cuba into a modern, more humane society.

Fidel's plans had progressed beyond pamphleteering and veered into military strategy. He had decided to land his invasion force along an isolated stretch of Cuba's southeastern coast where the land rises up to form the Sierra Maestra mountain range. Fidel would launch his guerrilla war in the mountains of the Oriente region. It was not only where Fidel came from but also where Cuba's nineteenth-century patriots, including José Martí, had launched their invasions to fight against the Spanish.

Beyond symbolism, there was a sound strategic reason for his choice: the sierra's close proximity to Cuba's second-largest city, Santiago. Here, Fidel counted on the able offices of his underground coordinator, a twenty-year-old student named Frank País. Once his men had landed and were in the mountains, Santiago would provide a pool of funds, intelligence, weapons, and recruits to fuel the war.

Celia Sánchez, a plantation doctor's daughter and a recent convert to the Movement, had procured the coastal charts Fidel needed and had handed them over to Pedro Miret, an old university friend who was responsible for coordinating the invasion plans. Miret had gone over the area personally to pick possible landing sites; in September he came to Mexico to give the charts to Fidel and discuss strategy. Meanwhile, the Movement's cells were screening their members for future fighters. It was Miret's job to get the chosen ones to Mexico to undergo military training.

Fidel had already approached a man about training his force: the one-eyed, Cuban-born military adventurer General Alberto Bayo. Bayo had been a career officer in the Spanish army, fighting in the colonial campaign against the Moroccan guerrilla leader Abd-El-Krim and then with the Republican forces against Franco. Later, he had advised and trained men for several wars around the Caribbean and Central America and had written a book, *Storm in the Caribbean,* about these experiences. Now retired from the military, Bayo worked as a university lecturer and ran a furniture factory in Mexico. He seemed to be just the man Fidel needed.

Fidel began preparing for a speaking and fund-raising tour among the Cuban émigré communities of Florida, New York, Philadelphia, and New Jersey. For this effort he was to be joined by his friend Juan Manuel Márquez, an Ortodoxo Party leader with good contacts in the United States. In the meantime, he kept up a continuous stream of messages to the members of his National Directorate in Cuba, instructing them to raise funds there as well, and outlining new rules governing the duties and obligations of Movement members.

By now, his Cuban comrades were getting to know the man they called Che well enough to recognize his idiosyncrasies, and one of the personality traits that rubbed many of them the wrong way, at first, was his self-righteousness. When Jesús Montané's new wife, the Moncada veteran Melba Hernández, arrived from Havana, he took her to meet Che at the General Hospital. Che took one look at Melba, just off the plane and still dressed up, and told her bluntly that she couldn't possibly be a revolutionary with so much jewelry on. "Real revolutionaries adorn themselves on the inside, not on the surface," he declared. Hernández's first impression of Che was understandably negative, but when she got to know him better she realized, as others did, that although he was judgmental and even rude, he was equally tough on himself. Eventually, Hernández said, she mulled over Che's remark, decided he was right, and thereafter wore less jewelry.

Ernesto had continued with his physical conditioning, and in the second week of October he scaled Popocatépetl again. On this, his third try, he finally reached the volcano's true summit, after six and a half hours, placing an Argentine flag there on the occasion of National Flag Day.

In a mordant letter to Beatriz, Ernesto joked about the name he planned for his son (Vladimiro Ernesto) and about the "new Argentina" since Perón's ouster. "Now the people of class can put the common scum back in their proper place, the Americans will invest great and beneficent quantities of capital in the country, in sum, [it will be] a paradise." He mockingly lamented the rejection of his offer of services to the Mexican government in the wake of the "aptly named" Hurricane Hilda, denying him the opportunity of seeing the catastrophe up close. "Part of the city was flooded and the people were left in the street but it doesn't matter because no people of class live there, they're all pure Indians." Characteristically, he signed off by begging her to send him more *yerba mate*.

In mid-November, Ernesto and a visibly swelling Hilda took off for Chiapas and the Yucatán peninsula to see the Mayan ruins. The high point of their five-day stay in Veracruz was finding an Argentine ship in port. Ernesto managed to cadge a few kilos of *yerba*. "One can imagine Ernesto's joy," Hilda wrote. "*Mate* of course was an inveterate habit with him; he was never without his equipment, the *bombilla, boquilla,* and a two-liter thermos for hot water. Studying, conversing, he always drank *mate*; it was the first thing he did when he got up and the last thing he did before going to sleep."

As they traveled south to the Mayan temples at Palenque in the tropical swelter of Chiapas, Ernesto's asthma—which had all but vanished in the high altitude of Mexico City—suddenly returned. Hilda's offer to give him an injection brought on what she called the "first spat" of their trip. "He violently refused," she wrote. "I realized that it was that he did not want to feel protected, to be helped when he was sick. I kept quiet in the face of his brusqueness, but I was hurt."

Ernesto was entranced with Palenque's temple pyramids and their carved bas-reliefs. He scribbled page after page in his journal on Palenque and the Mayan sites of Chichén Itzá and Uxmal, combining elaborately detailed physical descriptions of the ruins with histories of the ancient civilizations that had built them. He ran around the ruins excitedly, dragging a weary Hilda along behind him. "Ernesto joyfully wanted to climb every temple," she wrote. "I gave out on the last one, the tallest. I stopped halfway up, partly because I was very tired, and partly because I was worrying about my pregnancy. He kept urging me not to play coy and join him."

Finally, feeling "tired, impatient, and thoroughly cross," Hilda refused to budge another step. Undeterred, Ernesto asked someone to snap their picture. In the photograph, a dowdy-looking Hilda glares angrily out from under a Mexican sombrero. At her side, wearing a dark short-sleeved shirt and a Panama hat, Ernesto looks slim, youthful, and thoroughly preoccupied.

After visiting Uxmal, they sailed back to Veracruz on a small coastal freighter, the *Ana Graciela*. Hilda was reluctant to go to sea, but Ernesto was teasingly reassuring, telling her that at least they'd die together. The voyage began peacefully enough, but on their second day out a strong northerly blew, and Ernesto wrote gleefully that it gave them "a good dance." Hilda's own rendition was more sour: "Almost all of the passengers were seasick. I didn't exactly feel great either. But Ernesto was like a boy. Wearing swimming shorts, he was all over the decks, jumping from one side to the other, calculating the roll of the boat to keep his balance, taking pictures and laughing at the discomfiture of the others."

Hilda's implication was obvious: Ernesto had been inconsiderate and irresponsible, and she didn't appreciate it one bit. Pleading the safety of her unborn child, she took to her bunk for the rest of the trip, plied by a rueful Ernesto with mugs of hot tea and lemon. But afterward, Hilda romanticized the experience. "They had been fifteen days of unforgettable travel, with the immense satisfaction of being in one another's company at all times, alone in the midst of all that beauty." By contrast, in his own account of the trip, Ernesto never once mentioned Hilda.

Fidel returned to Mexico before Christmas. His fund-raising and organizing trip to the United States had been a great success. He had traveled up and down the East Coast for two months speaking, convincing, and

promising. He had invoked Chibás and Martí and made grandiose vows
such as: "In 1956 we shall be free or we will be martyrs"; in return, he had
been applauded and given money, enough to begin organizing his rebel
army. July 26 Movement chapters and "Patriotic Clubs" had been opened
in several of the cities he had visited. His media profile had grown even more
prominent, and in Cuba his widely publicized intention to launch a revolution had spurred a mood of mounting expectation. Back in Mexico, Fidel
Castro was invigorated, on a roll, ready for war. On Christmas Eve he
cooked a traditional Cuban dinner of roast pork, beans, rice, and yucca. Che
and Hilda were there, and Fidel expounded his plans for Cuba's future with
"such certainty," said Hilda, that she imagined for a moment that the war
had already been fought and won.

V

On his own word, 1956 was to be the decisive year for Fidel Castro's revolution. To be in shape, Ernesto had kept up his mountain climbing. He now
threw himself at Ixtacihuatl, the smaller but more difficult volcano next to
Popocatépetl, making several abortive attempts to reach the summit.

During January and February, Fidel's future fighters began arriving
in Mexico City from Cuba, and half a dozen safe houses were rented around
the city to house them. By mid-February, there were twenty or so future
expeditionaries in place. Strict codes of discipline and secrecy were imposed
on them as their training began. At first, the training consisted of marathon
walks around the city. Then, led by Arzacio Vanegas, the men went on
conditioning and endurance hikes on hills around the capital's outskirts.
Vanegas made them climb backward and sideways to strengthen their legs
and teach them balance. On one outing, he found Che gasping for breath
and struggling with his asthma inhaler. Later, when Che had recovered, he
asked Vanegas not to tell anyone, even Fidel, what he had seen. He was
clearly worried about being dropped from the force because of his affliction and was under the illusion that his comrades didn't know about it.

At the Calle Bucarelli gymnasium, which was owned by friends,
Vanegas gave the men exercise and personal defense classes. "I was very
brusque with them," Vanegas recalled. "I told them they were not señoritas,
and had to become tough if they wanted to make war." He showed Che and
the others "how to hit people to cause maximum pain, to kick them in the
balls, to grab their clothes and throw them on the ground."

Alberto Bayo started giving classes in guerrilla warfare theory to the
men in the safe houses, and in February a select group including Che began
going to a firing range, Los Gamitos, to practice their shooting skills. By an

arrangement between Fidel and its owner, Los Gamitos was closed on certain days so the men could shoot in privacy, with live turkeys sometimes provided so they could practice on moving targets.

VI

Ernesto and Hilda spent Valentine's Day moving into a larger apartment on a different floor of the same building on Calle Nápoles. That night, Hilda went into labor. She gave birth the next day.

"A lot of time has passed and many new developments have declared themselves," Ernesto wrote soon afterward. "I'll only note the most important: as of the 15th of February 1956 I am a father; Hilda Beatriz is the firstborn. . . . My projects for the future are nebulous but I hope to finish a couple of research projects. This year could be important for my future. I have left the hospitals. I will write with more details."

But he never did. Those were the last lines Ernesto wrote in the journal he had begun nearly three years before, after passing his medical exams and taking to the road with Calica Ferrer. He had set out intending to rejoin his friend Alberto Granado at the leprosarium in Venezuela. Instead, he had veered off in an altogether different direction, on the road to revolution.

Ernesto Guevara's mug shot, taken on June 24, 1956,
when he was arrested in Mexico.

13

The Sacred Flame within Me

I

Like a marooned sailor who has finally seen the hope of rescue on the horizon, Ernesto threw his energies into the Cuban revolutionary enterprise. To keep his weight down, he cut out his usual steak for breakfast and went on a diet consisting of meat, salad, and fruit for supper. In the afternoons, he went straight to the gymnasium. Already looking ahead to the day when the revolution would triumph, he embarked on a cram course on the work of Adam Smith, John Maynard Keynes, and other economists; boned up on Mao and Soviet texts borrowed from the Instituto Cultural Ruso-Mexicano; and discreetly sat in on meetings of the Mexican Communist Party. Most evenings, he joined the Cubans at the safe houses for discussions on the situation in Cuba and other Latin American countries.

His knowledge of Marxism was maturing. Using his old philosophical notebooks as a base, he streamlined them into a single volume. This final *cuaderno filosófico,* totaling more than 300 typewritten pages, reflects the narrowing of his interests and shows a deepening understanding of the works of Marx, Engels, and Lenin. The last entry in the index, on the concept of "I" (*yo* in Spanish), is attributed to Freud: "There, where love awakens, dies the I, dark despot."

He had begun to live a double life, withdrawing from contact with everyone he did not completely trust. He repeatedly warned Hilda to be cautious with her friends so as not to disclose his involvement with Fidel. Finally, he asked her to stop meeting her Peruvian *aprista* acquaintances—whom he especially distrusted—altogether. Apart from the Cubans, he saw very few people now.

Ernesto spent his spare moments with the baby. He was delighted with her. On February 25, when she was ten days old, he had written to his mother to announce her birth: "Little Grandmother: The two of us are a little older, or if you consider fruit, a little more mature. The offspring is really ugly, and one doesn't have to do more than look at her to realize she is no different from all the other children of her age. She cries when she is hungry, pees with frequency. . . . the light bothers her and she sleeps all the time; even so, there is one thing that differentiates her immediately from any other baby: her papa is named Ernesto Guevara."

Meanwhile, in his other identity—as Che the apprentice guerrilla—he was turning out to be a very good marksman. On March 17, Miguel "El Coreano" Sánchez—a U.S. Army veteran of the Korean War who had been enlisted by Fidel in Miami to become the force's shooting instructor—summed up Guevara's performance on the firing range. "Ernesto Guevara attended 20 regular shooting lessons, an excellent shooter with approximately 650 bullets [fired]. Excellent discipline, excellent leadership abilities, physical endurance excellent. Some disciplinary press-ups for small errors at interpreting orders and faint smiles."*

Che already stood out from the crowd. His strong personality, closeness to Fidel and Raúl, and rapid rise to preeminence within the group doubtless aggravated the early resentment felt by some of the Cuban trainees toward this "foreigner" in their midst. Most of the Cubans referred to him as El Argentino. Only those who knew him best called him Che.

Fidel later recalled "a small, disagreeable incident" that took place after he appointed Che—"because of his seriousness, his intelligence, and his character"—as leader of one of the safe houses in Mexico City. "There were about twenty or thirty Cubans there in all," Fidel said, "and some of them . . . challenged Che's leadership because he was an Argentinian, because he was not a Cuban. We of course criticized this attitude . . . this ingratitude toward someone who, although not born in our land, was ready to shed his blood for it. And I remember the incident hurt me a great deal. I think it hurt him as well."

In fact, Che was not the only foreigner in the group. Guillén Zelaya, a nineteen-year-old Mexican whom he had met briefly months earlier through Helena Leiva de Holst at a meeting of Honduran exiles, had run away from home to join up with Fidel and had been accepted. In time there would be others, including a Dominican exile and an Italian merchant marine, but that was where Fidel drew the line, explaining he didn't want a "mosaic of nationalities."

In his letters home, the preeminence of revolutionary thought in Ernesto's life became more manifest, even when he was being whimsical.

*See Notes section.

Writing to Celia about his infant daughter, he gave a new twist to a father's pride. "My Communist soul expands plethorically," he said. "She has come out exactly like Mao Tse-tung. Even now, the incipient bald spot in the middle of the head can be noted, the compassionate eyes of the boss and his protuberant jowls; for now she weighs less than the leader, five kilos, but with time this will even out."

His irritation with Hilda, held in abeyance during her pregnancy, grew more evident. Returning to the familiar theme of Argentina in his correspondence, he badgered his mother about the capitulation of Argentina's new regime to U.S. corporate interests and then went out of his way to take a swipe at Hilda: "It consoles me to think that the aid of our great neighbor isn't confined only to this region. . . . It now seems that it has lent its help to APRA and soon everyone will be back in Peru and Hilda can go there in tranquillity. Big pity that her intemperate marriage to this fervent slave of the red plague will rob her of the enjoyment of a well-remunerated salary as deputy in the next parliament."

Ernesto told Hilda that the revolution was a cause for which they both had to make sacrifices, the first of which would be their prolonged separation. Although she claimed to feel both pain and pride at the idea of his going off to war, Hilda was most likely deeply unhappy about the turn of events. Having espoused a certain revolutionary commitment herself, however, she could not very well hold him back. If she tried, he would have cited it as proof that she was hopelessly tied to her middle-of-the-road *aprista* political philosophy.

Money had begun to trickle in from Fidel's supporters in the United States and Cuba, and he now had some guns and was acquiring more through Antonio del Conde, a Mexican arms trafficker he nicknamed El Cuate (The Pal). El Cuate was sent on an arms-buying trip to the United States and asked to look for a suitable boat for Castro's "army" to sail on to Cuba when the time came. Meanwhile, Fidel was searching for a place outside Mexico City where his men could complete their field training in greater secrecy.

Fidel was evidently hoping to time his invasion to coincide with the third anniversary of Moncada, on July 26. Not only had he made a public vow to launch the revolution in 1956, but recent events had shown that if he wanted to play the revolutionary trump card, he needed to act soon. He was facing increasingly serious competition from several quarters. Among his potential rivals was former president Carlos Prío Socarrás. After first testing the insurrectionary waters by assisting the recently formed Directorio Revolucionario, a militant underground student group, in an abortive plan to assassinate Batista, Prío had taken advantage of the general amnesty that had freed Fidel and had returned to Cuba. Publicly renouncing the use of violence, he was trying to extend his base of support by declaring his intention of opposing Batista through legal, democratic means.

The autumn of 1955 had been fractious in Cuba, with civic unrest countered by police brutality, and some armed attacks against the police by the Directorio. At the year's end, a broad spectrum of opposition groups, including Fidel's July 26 Movement, backed a sugar workers' strike, and more street riots ensued. Although an atmosphere of rebellion was spreading, there was still little organization or unity in opposition circles, and for now Batista retained the upper hand.

When that balance shifted, Fidel planned to be at the fore. In March 1956, he publicly broke with the Ortodoxo Party, accusing its leaders of not supporting the "revolutionary will" of its rank and file. This was a clever move, for it left him a free hand to proceed with his revolution without feigning loyalty to a political party he hoped to supersede. Now everyone in Cuba's various *antibatistiano* camps would have to choose a side, and Fidel would be able to see more clearly who his friends and enemies were.

Fidel was vigilant about the danger of betrayal and had already taken precautionary measures, creating a cell structure for his men in Mexico. They had been separated into groups, met up only during training sessions, and were forbidden to inquire about one another. Only Fidel and Bayo knew the location of all of the safe houses. Finally, Fidel had drawn up a list of punishments for infractions. The Movement now lived according to the rules of war, and the punishment for the crime of betrayal was death.

Fidel had good reason to be security conscious. He knew that if Batista wanted to have him killed, there were ways and means to do it, even in Mexico. He didn't have to wait long to confirm that he was indeed an assassination target. In early 1956, Batista's Servicio de Inteligencia Militar (SIM) denounced Castro's conspiracy and conducted a wave of arrests of his followers in Cuba. Shortly after the SIM investigations chief arrived in Mexico, Fidel got wind of a plan to assassinate him. When he let it be known that he was aware of the plot, the scheme was aborted, but Cuban government agents and Mexicans on their payroll remained active, tracking his movements and reporting back to Batista.

The political climate within Cuba continued to heat up. In April, the police uncovered a plot by army officers to overthrow Batista. When a Directorio squad tried to take over a Havana radio station, one of its members was gunned down. Days later, in emulation of Castro's Moncada assault, a militant group of Prío's *auténticos* attacked some provincial army barracks in a bid to force their leader out of his public posture of peaceful opposition. They were massacred for their efforts. Afterward the regime unleashed a massive crackdown on Prío's party, and he fled back into exile in Miami.

In Mexico, the number of Cubans with Fidel had grown to about forty. Ernesto's tireless distinction in the training exercises had become obvious to Fidel, and one day he used the Argentine as an example to the others and as a reproof of their own flagging efforts. In May, the trainees were asked to evaluate the performances of their comrades, and Ernesto was unanimously judged by his mates to be qualified for a "leadership or chief of staff position." It was an important threshold. Ernesto had won the respect he so craved from his new peers.

II

Ernesto was able finally to fulfill his old urge to try out his acting skills. Bayo and Ciro Redondo, one of Fidel's key men, had found a ranch for sale at Chalco, about thirty-five miles east of the city. The Rancho San Miguel was huge. Encompassing both rangeland and rough hills, it was perfect terrain for guerrilla training. The main house itself was not large, but the grounds were surrounded by a high fortress like stone wall, complete with crenellated sentry's turrets at the corners. There was one problem: its price was almost $250,000. The ranch's owner, Erasmo Rivera, had a colorful personal history, having fought alongside Pancho Villa in his youth, but being a revolutionary veteran had apparently not made him impervious to greed.

In his negotiations with Rivera, Bayo claimed to be the front man for a wealthy Salvadoran colonel interested in the purchase of a large ranch outside his native country. Rivera fell for the story, whereupon Bayo introduced the foreign-sounding Guevara as the colonel. Rivera either couldn't tell the difference between a Salvadoran and an Argentine accent or decided against asking any questions that might offend his rich client. In any case, the con job worked. Rivera agreed to a token rent of eight dollars per month while certain necessary "repairs" to the main house were made to bring the place up to the colonel's specifications. After that the sale would go through. The repairs meanwhile would be undertaken by several dozen "Salvadoran laborers" to be brought in for the purpose.

As soon as the deal was struck, Fidel ordered Bayo to select a group of fighters to go to the ranch. Bayo thought highly of Ernesto—he later called him "the best guerrilla of them all"—and named him "chief of personnel." In late May, they departed for the ranch with a first group of trainees. Ernesto said good-bye to Hilda, telling her he might not be back. Fidel had located a military-surplus American PT boat for sale in Delaware and hoped to buy it and have it brought to Mexico in time to sail for Cuba in July. If everything worked out, they would finish their training at the ranch and go directly from there to the boat, and on to Cuba.

The training was tough. The walled compound at Rancho San Miguel was their headquarters, but the men spent most of their time on forays out from two rudimentary camps in the adjacent parched, brushy hills. Food and water were in short supply, and Bayo and Che led them on endurance hikes and night marches lasting from dusk to dawn. When they weren't slogging through the bush, they engaged in simulated combat and stood guard. This was the first time Che had shared life on a sustained daily basis with the Cubans. Some of them still resented his presence, regarding him as an interloping foreigner, and now they had him as their direct jefe. They found him to be a rigid disciplinarian, but one who also joined in the marches and exercises, on top of his doctor's duties.

It must have been a shock to the Cubans to find that this well-educated, wellborn Argentine doctor was something of a slob, even though the shabby brown suit he wore in the city had already established him as an oddball. His appearance didn't jibe with the Cubans' image of how a "professional" should look. In the socially stratified Latin America of the 1950s, being well groomed and formally attired was the norm for any self-respecting urban male. Now, out in the field, they discovered that Che didn't like to wash, either. According to Hilda, "Ernesto used to be amused at the Cubans' mania for cleanliness. When the daily work was done, they all took baths and changed their clothes. 'That's fine,' he said, 'but what will they do in the hills? I doubt we'll ever be able to take a bath or change clothes.'"

One of the rebels, the mulatto songwriter Juan Almeida, wrote later about Che's rigidity. He described an episode in which one of the men refused to walk any farther, protesting about the long marches, the excessive discipline, and the lack of food. Almeida wrote that the disgruntled man "sat down on the trail in frank protest against the Spanish [Bayo] and Argentine [Guevara] leadership."

Che ordered the men back to camp. Insubordination was a severe breach of discipline that called for a death sentence. Fidel and Raúl were immediately notified of the incident and came quickly from Mexico City to hold a court-martial. In keeping with the Cuban revolution's tradition of glossing over such unpleasant episodes, Almeida omitted the name of the rebellious trainee, but in his memoirs Alberto Bayo recounted the dramatic trial of the man whom he identified as Calixto Morales. In Bayo's account, the Castro brothers called for the death sentence, comparing Morales to a "contagious disease" that had to be "exterminated" before he infected his comrades. Despite a plea by Bayo to spare his life, Morales was sentenced to death, but Fidel later pardoned him, and Morales went on to win favor during the guerrilla war. According to the Cuban historian María del Carmen Ariet, even though Che had called for Morales's court-martial, he argued against execution.

Universo Sánchez, Fidel's aide responsible for counterintelligence at the time, was to have been Morales's executioner. In an interview with Tad Szulc, the author of the most complete biography of Fidel Castro, Sánchez divulged that other trials took place and that at least one of them, of a spy unmasked in their midst, ended in execution. Szulc wrote that "the man, whose identity is unknown, was sentenced by a safe house court-martial and executed on Universo's instructions by one of the rebels. 'He was shot and buried there in a field,' he says." Locals living in the vicinity of Rancho San Miguel still speak of three bodies that lie buried within the compound's sturdy walls. But for Universo Sánchez's admission, such rumors could be dismissed easily as folklore. In Cuba, any mention of these events is taboo, and they remain officially unclarified and ignored.

By early June, Almeida's group had returned to the city, and a second group arrived at the ranch for training. On June 14, Che celebrated his twenty-eighth birthday. Everything seemed to be progressing nicely when, on June 20, Fidel and two companions were arrested on a street in downtown Mexico City. Within days, virtually all the Movement's members in the city had been rounded up. Safe houses were raided; documents and arms caches were seized. Bayo and Raúl were alerted and went into hiding. Before she too was arrested, Hilda—whose address was used by Fidel as a secret letter-drop—managed to hide Fidel's correspondence and Ernesto's more inflammatory political writings. She was interrogated repeatedly about the activities of Ernesto and Fidel and spent a night in custody, with the baby, before being released.

Fidel and his comrades were accused of plotting Batista's assassination in collusion with Cuban and Mexican Communists, and Havana had demanded their extradition. On June 22, Fidel was allowed to issue a carefully worded public denial of his alleged Communist affiliations, pointing out his signal relationship with the late anticommunist Ortodoxo leader Eduardo Chibás. Meanwhile, still at large, Raúl and other comrades scrambled to assemble his legal defense team.

Out at the ranch, Che prepared for the inevitable police raid. After moving most of the weaponry to new hiding places, he and twelve comrades were waiting when the police arrived on June 24. Anxious to avoid a confrontation, Fidel went along to instruct Che to surrender himself and his men. Che obeyed and was taken away to join his comrades in the Interior Ministry's prison on Calle Miguel Schultz.

III

The Mexican police mug shots of Ernesto show a determined-looking young man, clean-shaven but with unkempt hair. In the frontal shot, he stares straight into the camera. In the profile shot, his prominent forehead is plainly visible, his mouth is set, and his expression is thoughtful. The rap sheet beneath the photograph gives his name, the date and place of his birth, his local address, his physical characteristics, and the offense he was charged with—overstaying his visa. Beneath is a one-line declaration: "He says he is a tourist."

On June 26, two days after the mug shot was taken, Ernesto made his first statements to the police. He admitted only as much as they already knew about him. Explaining the circumstances of his arrival from Guatemala, he admitted having been a sympathizer of Arbenz's and having served in his administration. Once in Mexico, someone whose name he couldn't remember had introduced him to María Antonia González. Later, he became aware that her house was a hub for Cubans "discontented" with their country's political regime. Eventually he had met Fidel Castro Ruz, their leader. When, about a month and a half before, he learned that the Cubans were undergoing training to direct a revolutionary movement against Batista, he had offered his services as a doctor and was accepted. At Castro's request, he had also served as his intermediary for the lease of the Chalco ranch. He dissembled about the quantity of men and guns at the ranch, saying they had only two rifles, which they had used for target practice and small-game hunting, as well as a .38 revolver for "personal defense."

That same day, Mexico's broadsheet pro-government daily *Excelsior* ran the story of the arrests across its front page under a banner headline: "Mexico Breaks Up the Revolt against Cuba and Arrests 20 Ringleaders." The next day, a follow-up story quoting Mexican federal police sources revealed "More Apprehensions of Cuban Plotters Who It Is Said Had Help of Communists."

The chief culprit, according to Dirección Federal de Seguridad (DFS) sources, was none other than "the Argentine doctor Ernesto Guevara Serna . . . the principal link between the Cuban plotters and certain Communist organizations of an international nature. . . . Doctor Guevara, who has also figured in other political movements of an international nature in the Dominican Republic and Panama, was identified by the DFS as an 'active member of the Instituto Intercambio Cultural Mexicano-Ruso.'" In the caption to a group photograph taken of the detained rebels, he was singled out as the man whose "intimate links with Communism have led to suspicions that the movement against Fulgencio Batista was cosponsored by Red organizations."

The first known photograph of Che Guevara and Fidel Castro together. They are in prison in Mexico in the summer of 1956.

While the media flurry continued, Fidel's people worked hard to free him. His lawyer friend Juan Manuel Márquez flew in from the United States and hired two defense attorneys. A sympathetic judge issued Fidel's release order on July 2, but the interior ministry blocked it. Despite this setback, the judge managed to stay the deportation order. Trying other routes, Fidel reportedly authorized Universo Sánchez to try to bribe a high-level government official, but the attempt failed. The men went on a hunger strike, and on July 9 twenty-one of the Cubans were released; several more were freed a few days later. Fidel, Che, and Calixto García remained behind bars.

Che wrote to his parents on July 6, informing them of his predicament and finally coming clean about his activities. "Some time ago, quite a while now, a young Cuban leader invited me to join his movement, a movement for the armed liberation of his country, and I, of course, accepted." As for the future, he told them, "My future is linked with that of the Cuban Revolution. I either triumph with it or die there. . . . If for any reason that I can't foresee, I can't write anymore, and later it is my luck to lose, regard these lines as a farewell, not very eloquent but sincere.

Throughout life I have looked for my truth by trial and error, and now, on the right road, and with a daughter who will survive me, I have closed the cycle. From now on I wouldn't consider my death a frustration, only, like Hikmet [the Turkish poet]: 'I will take to the grave only the sorrow of an unfinished song.'"

Despite all the police leaks and sensational headlines regarding their revolutionary conspiracy, they were still officially detained only on charges of violating Mexico's immigration laws. Meanwhile, behind the scenes, Mexican and Cuban officials were wrangling over what should be done with them. At the same time, the police were trying to find out more about Ernesto Guevara. In the first week of July, he was interrogated at least twice more. Inexplicably, he now spoke freely and at length. These declarations to the police were kept classified in Mexico, but copies were obtained by Heberto Norman Acosta, the historian of the Cuban Council of State. A perusal of the carefully guarded papers reveals that Ernesto Guevara openly admitted his Communism and declared his belief in the need for armed revolutionary struggle, not only in Cuba but throughout Latin America.

Over the years, Fidel occasionally alluded to Che's declarations to the Mexican police in a tone of fond admonishment, citing them as an example of how his late comrade was "honest to a fault." At the time, however, Fidel was understandably furious. While Che prattled on about his Marxist convictions, here *he* was, billing himself as a patriotic reformer in the best Western nationalistic and *democratic* tradition. Since the one thing certain to mobilize increased support for Batista's regime from the Eisenhower administration was a Communist threat, any evidence that Fidel or his followers contemplated turning Cuba into a Communist state would doom the revolution before it began. In this context, Che's remarks were extraordinarily reckless, providing Castro's enemies with just the kind of ammunition they needed.

In a second public statement on July 15, Castro accused the American embassy of pressuring the Mexican authorities to thwart his release. Where he got his information is unclear, but he was right. The Americans *had* asked the Mexicans to hold up his release. But Washington's move had less to do with feelings of disquiet about Fidel Castro than with placating Batista for the sake of its own interests. The Cuban leader had threatened to boycott the July 22 summit of American presidents held in Panama if Castro was freed; the Americans wanted to make sure everyone attended.

Fidel was taking no chances, and he went even farther than before in distancing himself from Communism. He said that allegations that he was a Communist were "absurd," and he pointed to Batista's past alliance with

Cuba's Partido Socialista Popular. He named Captain Gutiérrez Barrios of Mexico's Dirección Federal de Seguridad, the number three man in Mexico's secret police hierarchy, as a witness to his being cleared of any links to "Communist organizations."

Fidel's mention of the twenty-seven-year-old Fernando Gutiérrez Barrios was revealing. He had struck some kind of a deal with Gutiérrez Barrios, and although neither of them ever gave details of their pact, the Mexican's help was a key factor in Castro's eventual liberation. In an interview years later, Gutiérrez Barrios admitted to having "sympathized" with Castro from the outset. "First, because we were of the same generation, and second, for his ideals and his sense of conviction. He has always been a charismatic leader. And at that time it was obvious that there were no alternatives for him other than to triumph in his revolutionary movement or die. . . . These reasons explain why there was a cordial relationship from the beginning. . . . I never considered him to be a criminal, but a man with ideals who sought to overthrow a dictatorship and whose crime was to violate the [immigration] laws of my country." Mexican nationalists (whose own revolution had occurred only four decades before) had little love for their meddlesome American neighbors, and a certain stick-it-in-your-eye attitude very likely played a part in Gutiérrez Barrios's gesture. Indeed, later on, during his long career—more than thirty years—as chief of Mexico's secret police, Gutiérrez Barrios granted protection to many other Latin American revolutionary exiles, including several on Washington's wanted list.

On the day of Fidel's second public statement, July 15, Ernesto responded defiantly to a remonstrative letter from Celia. Judging from his tone, she had questioned his motives for being involved with Fidel Castro in the first place, and wondered pointedly why he hadn't been freed along with the others after their hunger strike. He told her he and Calixto would probably remain in prison even after Fidel's release. Their immigration papers were not in order. But as soon as he was freed, he would leave Mexico for a nearby country and await Fidel's orders, to be "at the ready whenever my services are necessary."

"I am not Christ or a philanthropist, old lady. I am all the contrary of a Christ," he wrote to his mother. "I fight for the things I believe in, with all the weapons at my disposal and try to leave the other man *dead* so that I don't get nailed to a cross or any other place. . . . What really terrifies me is your lack of comprehension of all this and your advice about moderation, egoism, etc., . . . that is to say, all of the most execrable qualities an individual can have. Not only am I not moderate, I shall try not ever to be, and when I recognize that the sacred flame within me has given way to a timid votive light, the least I could do is to vomit over my own shit. As to your call to moderate self-interest, that is to say, to rampant and fearful individualism . . . I must tell you I have done a lot to eliminate these. . . .

"In these days of prison and the previous ones of training I identified totally with my comrades in the cause. . . . The concept of 'I' disappeared totally to give place to the concept 'us.' It was a Communist morale and naturally it may seem a doctrinaire exaggeration, but really it was (and is) beautiful to be able to feel that removal of I." Breaking the severe tone, he wisecracked: "The stains [on the stationery] aren't bloodstains, but tomato juice. . . ." Then he went on: "It is a profound error on your part to believe that it is out of 'moderation' or 'moderate self-interest' that great inventions or artful masterpieces come about. For all great tasks, passion is needed, and for the revolution, passion and audacity are needed in large doses, things we have as a human group."

He ended with a soliloquy on their changed personal relationship: "Above all, it seems to me that that pain—pain of a mother who is growing old and who wants her son alive—is respectable, something I have an obligation to attend to, and which I *want* to attend to. I would like to see you not only to console you, but to console myself for my sporadic and unconfessable pinings." He signed the letter with his new identity: "Your son, El Che."

What Che didn't tell his mother was that he was primarily responsible for his prolonged detention. In the end, he cared less about this than about the future of the Cuban revolutionary enterprise. The most important thing at the moment was for Fidel to be freed so that the struggle could go forward.

Batista attended the Panama summit, and on July 22 a joint declaration committing the hemisphere to a pro-Western course of political and economic development was signed. While Eisenhower was rubbing shoulders with military dictators, Fidel's lawyers went to see Lázaro Cárdenas—Mexico's former president and the architect of its land reform. Cárdenas agreed to use his influence with President Adolfo Ruíz Cortines on Fidel's behalf. It worked, and Fidel was finally released on July 24, on the condition he leave the country within two weeks.

Only Che and Calixto García were left in prison, for the official reason that their immigration status was more "complicated." In Che's case, his Communist affiliations undoubtedly had a lot to do with it. García was apparently held because he had stayed illegally in Mexico for the longest period, since March of 1954. Meanwhile, even as the threat of extradition continued to hang over both their heads, Che refused offers made by his Guatemalan friend Alfonso Bauer Paiz and Ulíses Petit de Murat to pull diplomatic strings on his behalf. An uncle of Che's happened to be the Argentine ambassador to Havana, and Hilda was pushing the idea of using him to secure Che's release. "Fidel approved, but when we explained the idea to Ernesto, he said: By no means! I want the same treatment as the Cubans," Hilda wrote.

While Che balked, Fidel was under pressure to get moving. Mexico was no longer a safe place; he was vulnerable to both the Mexican police and Batista's agents. As a precaution, he had dispersed his men, sending most of them to await developments in remote areas far from Mexico City. Che told him to proceed without him, but Fidel swore he would not abandon him. It was a magnanimous gesture that Che never forgot. "Precious time and money had to be diverted to get us out of the Mexican jail," he wrote later. "That personal attitude of Fidel's toward people whom he holds in esteem is the key to the fanatical loyalty he inspires."

Around this time. Che wrote a poem that he called "Ode to Fidel." He showed it to Hilda and told her he planned to give it to Castro when they were at sea, on their way to Cuba. Though sophomoric and purple, the poem reveals the depth of Ernesto's feelings toward Fidel.

> *Let's go, ardent prophet of the dawn,*
> *along remote and unmarked paths*
> *to liberate the green caiman you so love . . .**
> *When the first shot sounds*
> *and in virginal surprise the entire jungle awakens,*
> *there, at your side, serene combatants*
> *you'll have us.*
> *When your voice pours out to the four winds*
> *agrarian reform, justice, bread and liberty,*
> *there, at your side, with identical accent,*
> *you'll have us.*
> *And when the end of the battle for*
> *the cleansing operation against the tyrant comes,*
> *there, at your side, ready for the last battle,*
> *you'll have us . . .*
> *And if our path is blocked by iron,*
> *we ask for a shroud of Cuban tears*
> *to cover the guerrilla bones*
> *in transit to American history.*
> *Nothing more.*

---

*"Green caiman" was a metaphor for the reptile-shaped island of Cuba. It was coined by Cuba's Communist poet Nicolás Guillén.

IV

In mid-August 1956, after having been incarcerated for fifty-seven days, Che and Calixto García were freed, apparently because Fidel had bribed someone. Che hinted as much to Hilda, and he later wrote that Fidel had done "some things for the sake of friendship which, we could almost say, compromised his revolutionary attitude."

Like their comrades before them, Che and Calixto were freed on the condition that they leave Mexico within a few days. And, also like the others, they went underground. But first, Che went home for three days to sort out his affairs and to see the baby. Hilda said that he spent hours sitting by Hildita's crib, reciting poetry aloud to her or simply watching her in silence. Then he was gone again.

On Fidel's orders, Che and Calixto went to the weekend retreat of Ixtapan de la Sal. They registered in a hotel there under false names. During this underground period, which lasted three months, Che returned discreetly to the city a couple of times, but mostly Hilda traveled to see him. Che's absorption with Marxism and revolution now dominated his life. Even at home on visits, he was unrelenting, either delivering sermons to Hilda on "revolutionary discipline" or burying himself in dense books on political economy. He was even ideological with the baby. He recited the Spanish Civil War poem by Antonio Machado in honor of General Lister to her, and he regularly referred to her as "my little Mao."

Once, Hilda watched as Ernesto picked up their daughter and told her in a serious voice: "My dear little daughter, my little Mao, you don't know what a difficult world you're going to have to live in. When you grow up this whole continent, and maybe the whole world, will be fighting against the great enemy, Yankee imperialism. You too will have to fight. I may not be here anymore, but the struggle will inflame the continent."

In early September, after suffering a recurrence of his asthma, Ernesto moved with Calixto from Ixtapan de la Sal to Toluca, where the climate was drier. Then Fidel called for them to join some of the other expeditionaries for a meeting in Veracruz. Afterward, they returned to the capital, where they lived for several months in one of the safe houses in the Casa de Cuco, near the shrine to the Virgin of Guadalupe in the northern suburb of Linda Vista. Fidel was desperately trying to get things ready for their departure, and the men were asked to provide information about next of kin. Che recalled this later as a significant moment for him and his comrades. They realized that they might soon die.

Fidel was keeping up a frenetic pace. Besides moving his men around to avoid surveillance, he sought to shore up a political alliance with the increasingly competitive Directorio Revolucionario, whose leader, José Antonio

Che with his first child, Hilda Beatriz. He called her "my little Mao."

Echeverría, had flown to Mexico to meet him at the end of August. They had signed a document called the Carta de Mexico, voicing their shared commitment to the struggle against Batista. It fell short of an actual partnership, but the two groups agreed to advise each other in advance of any actions, and to coordinate their efforts once Castro and his rebels landed in Cuba.

A few weeks later, forty new recruits for the war arrived from Cuba and the United States. With the loss of the Rancho San Miguel, they had to be trained at far-flung bases—one in Tamaulipas just south of the U.S.-Mexican border, and another at Veracruz. By now, most of Fidel's general staff had joined him in Mexico City, leaving regional chiefs behind to coordinate activities on the island. But his coffers were nearly empty and he still had no vessel to carry his men to Cuba. The hoped-for purchase of the PT boat had fallen through, as had a short-lived scheme to buy a vintage Catalina flying boat.

In September, Fidel made a secret trip across the U.S. border to Texas, where he met with his erstwhile enemy, the former president, Carlos Prío

Socarrás. Since his ouster, Prío had been linked to several anti-Batista conspiracies, and the latest reports had him plotting an invasion of Cuba together with the Dominican dictator, Trujillo, but now he agreed to bankroll
Fidel. Perhaps he believed that Castro would do the heavy lifting that could
sweep him—Prío—back into power, or perhaps he simply saw Fidel as a
useful diversion in his own campaign against Batista. Whatever Prío's motivations were, Castro came away from the meeting with at least $50,000—
with more to be handed over later—according to those involved in arranging
the encounter. Fidel took a political risk by accepting money from the man
he had so vociferously accused of corruption while president, but right now
he had little choice.

According to Yuri Paporov, the KGB official who bankrolled the
Instituto Cultural Ruso-Mexicano at the time, the money Fidel received was
not Prío's at all, but the CIA's. He did not specify his sources for that asser-
tion, but, if true, it would lend weight to reports that the CIA had tried early
to win over Castro, just in case he succeeded in his war against the increasingly embattled Batista. According to Tad Szulc, the CIA *did* funnel money
to his July 26 Movement, but later on, during a period in 1957 and 1958, via
an agent attached to the American consul's office in Santiago, Cuba.

Whatever the provenance of Fidel's money, he continued to act as his
own man. He may have made a pact with the devil in the form of Prío, but
no evidence has emerged that he ever delivered his end of the deal—if indeed there were strings attached. Any funding he received from Prío—or,
unwittingly, from the CIA—certainly had no negative repercussions on his
quest for power.

Fidel still needed a boat. In late September he found a battered thirty-
eight-foot motor yacht owned by Robert Erickson, an American expatriate. Erickson was willing to sell it if Fidel also bought his riverside house in
the Gulf port town of Tuxpan. He asked for $40,000 for everything. The
boat—the *Granma*—was neither seaworthy nor nearly large enough for his
needs, but Fidel was desperate and agreed to Erickson's terms. After making a partial down payment, he assigned several men to live in the house
and oversee the *Granma*'s overhaul.

In late October, Che and Calixto moved to a more centrally located
safe house in Colonia Roma. Che continued seeing Hilda on the weekends,
but each time he left she knew he might not return. This uncertainty and
the stress of his impending departure wore down her nerves, and she became increasingly anxious. To lift her spirits, Che told her he would try to
take her to Acapulco for a short holiday.

"I had begun to be hopeful about the Acapulco trip, if only for a weekend," wrote Hilda. "Then came the news . . . that the police had broken into

the house of a Cuban woman in Lomas de Chapultepec, where Pedro Miret was staying, and that they had confiscated some weapons and arrested him. On Saturday, when Ernesto came, I told him about it. He reacted very calmly, saying only that precautions had to be doubled because the police might be watching. Early Sunday, Guajiro came. I knew right away he was nervous from the way in which he asked: 'Where's Che?' I told him that Ernesto was taking a bath, whereupon he marched right into the bathroom. When Ernesto came out, still combing his hair, he said calmly: 'It seems that the police are on the hunt, so we have to be cautious. We're going to the interior and I probably won't be back next weekend. Sorry, but we'll have to leave our Acapulco trip until later.'"

Hilda became upset. She asked Ernesto if there was anything imminent about to happen. "'No, just precautions . . . ,' he answered, gathering his things and not looking at me. When he finished, as he was always accustomed to doing before leaving, he went to the crib and caressed Hildita, then he turned, held me, and kissed me. Without knowing why, I trembled and drew closer to him. . . . He left that weekend and did not come back."

The discovery of Miret's safe house meant that the organization had a traitor in its ranks. Suspicions focused on Rafael Del Pino, one of Castro's closest friends and confidants. Of late, Del Pino had been entrusted with helping El Cuate procure and smuggle arms. But he had recently vanished and was the only person unaccounted for who had known where Miret was staying. (Subsequent Cuban investigations unearthed evidence that Del Pino had been an informant for the FBI for several years. If he didn't do more damage, it was possibly because he had been holding out on his American handlers in exchange for more money.)

Fidel sent the men in Mexico City into new safe houses and ordered the repairs on the *Granma* to be sped up. Che and Calixto hid in a little servant's room in the apartment where Alfonso "Poncho" Bauer Paiz lived with his family. The first night they spent there, they came dangerously close to being rearrested when a robbery in a neighbor's apartment resulted in a door-to-door police search. Alerted beforehand, Che hid Calixto (who was black and therefore attracted attention in Mexico) underneath the mattress of the bed in their room. When the police arrived, he went out to stall them. The tactic worked, and the police left the flat without searching his room. They were safe for the moment, but the next day Calixto went off to a new hiding place, leaving Ernesto alone at Bauer Paiz's house. He was to stay there until it was time to leave.

Fidel, meanwhile, was dealing with a number of last-minute hurdles. In recent weeks, both friends and rivals had tried to persuade him to postpone the invasion. His coordinator in Oriente, Frank País, came twice to see him—in August and October. País was in charge of sparking off armed uprisings throughout eastern Cuba to coincide with the *Granma*'s landing, but he argued that his people weren't ready to undertake such a grand plan. Fidel was insistent, however, and País agreed to try to do what he could. Fidel said he would send a coded message with his expedition's landing time just before leaving Mexico.

In October, the Cuban Communist Party, the PSP, sent emissaries to meet with Fidel. Their urgent message was that conditions weren't right for an armed struggle in Cuba, and they tried to win Fidel's agreement to join forces in a gradual campaign of civil dissent leading up to an armed insurrection in which the PSP would also participate. He refused and told them he would go ahead with his plans but hoped the Party and its militants would support him nonetheless by carrying out uprisings when his army arrived in Cuba.

At this point, Fidel's relations with the Cuban Communists were cordial but strained. Despite his public repudiation of any such links, he still had some close friends in the PSP, and he had allowed Marxists such as Raúl and Che into his inner circle. He discreetly maintained open lines of communication with the Party but kept a critical distance—not only to avoid negative publicity but to avoid political compromises until he was in a position of strength. Meanwhile, there was unease at the Soviet embassy resulting from the unwelcome publicity over the links between members of Castro's group and the Instituto Cultural Ruso-Mexicano. In early November, Nikolai Leonov was recalled to Moscow, as punishment, he says, for initiating contact with the Cuban revolutionaries without prior approval.

The Communists were not alone in trying to find a place at Cuba's insurrectionary table. As Fidel prepared to leave Mexico, a game of brinksmanship ensued with the Directorio, which jostled to take the revolutionary trump card. In spite of the fraternal document signed by José Antonio Echeverría in August, the Directorio had persisted in carrying out violent actions on its own. Shortly after a second meeting between Fidel and Echeverría in October, Directorio gunmen had murdered Colonel Manuel Blanco Rico, who was in charge of Batista's Military Intelligence Service. Remarkably, for someone about to launch an invasion, Fidel publicly condemned the killing as "unwarranted and arbitrary." His insinuation to Cuba's opposition-minded citizens was obvious. *He* was the responsible revolutionary, whereas Echeverría was a loose cannon, a terrorist whose activities could reap only more violence. Within days, Fidel's words acquired a retrospective halo of prescience when policemen hunting for the colonel's assassins murdered ten hapless young asylum seekers inside the Haitian embassy.

On November 23, the moment for which Che had prepared for so long had finally come. Fidel had decided it was time to go. He ordered the rebels in Mexico City, Veracruz, and Tamaulipas to converge the next day in Pozo Rico, an oil town just south of Tuxpan. Without any notice, Che had been picked up by the Cubans and driven to the Gulf coast. That night, November 24, they would load up the yacht and depart.

The irony in all this cloak-and-dagger activity was that Fidel Castro's planned invasion of Cuba had become public knowledge. Everyone in Cuba knew he was going to do it. The only question was exactly where and when he planned to land his rebel force. Indeed, a few days earlier, Batista's chief of staff had held a press conference in Havana to discuss—and deride—Fidel's possibilities of success, while beefing up military land and sea patrols along the island's Caribbean coast.

Fidel was gambling on the support of the July 26 Movement in Oriente under Frank País, and on keeping the exact date and place of the *Granma*'s landing secret until the last minute. He had estimated that their voyage would take five days, and so, just before leaving Mexico City, he dispatched a coded message to País that the *Granma* would arrive November 30 at a deserted beach in Oriente called Playa las Coloradas.

In the predawn darkness of November 25, Che was among the throng of men scrambling to board the *Granma*. The final hours of Fidel Castro's rebel army on Mexican soil were jittery and confusing. Not everyone had arrived, and some of those who had come were left behind at the last minute for lack of space. Now, for better or worse, they were off. The *Granma*, crammed with eighty-two men and a heap of guns and equipment, pushed off from the Tuxpan riverbank and slipped downriver toward the Gulf of Mexico and Cuba.

Ernesto left behind a letter to be forwarded to his mother. He wrote that, "to avoid premortem patheticisms," it would not be sent until "the potatoes are really on the fire and then you will know that your son, in a sunstruck American country, will be cursing himself for not having studied more of surgery to attend to a wounded man. . . .

"And now comes the tough part, old lady; that from which I have never run away and which I have always liked. The skies have not turned black, the constellations have not come out of their orbits nor have there been floods or overly insolent hurricanes; the signs are good. They signal victory. But if they are mistaken, and in the end even the gods make mistakes, then I believe I can say like a poet whom you don't know: 'I will only take to my grave / the nightmare of an unfinished song.' I kiss you again, with all the love of a good-bye that resists being total. Your son."

Part Two

Becoming Che

Che, seated in the foreground, with some comrades in the Sierra Maestra, Cuba, early in 1957.

14

A Disastrous Beginning

I

Ernesto's words in his last, melodramatic letter home were as prescient about the danger he faced as they were mistaken about his own reactions to it. When the potatoes were really "on the fire," in the form of an army ambush that caught the rebels by surprise a few days after the *Granma* landed, the last thing on Ernesto's mind was his inexperience with field surgery.

In the panicked melee that followed, as some men were shot down and others fled in all directions, Ernesto faced a split-second decision over whether to rescue a first aid kit or a box of ammunition. He chose the latter. If there was ever a decisive moment in Ernesto Guevara's life, that was it. He may have possessed a medical degree, but his true instincts were those of a fighter.

Moments later, hit in the neck by a ricocheting bullet and believing himself to be mortally wounded, he went into shock. After firing his rifle once into the bushes, he lay still and in a reverie began pondering the best way to die. The image that came to him was from Jack London's story "To Build a Fire," about a man in Alaska who, unable to light a fire, sits against a tree to freeze to death with dignity.

Ernesto had envisioned himself fighting back tenaciously to the shout of *"victoria o muerte,"* but in the shock of the ambush and his own wounding, he momentarily gave up hope. In contrast to many of his comrades—who either lost their nerve completely or responded as soldiers, firing at the enemy while moving toward cover—Ernesto lay back, coolly meditating on the prospect of his imminent death.

If reaching for ammunition rather than a medical kit in his first taste of combat revealed something fundamental about Ernesto Guevara, so did being wounded: a fatalism about death. Over the next two years of war, this trait became manifest as he developed into a combat-seasoned guerrilla with a distinct taste for battle and a notorious disregard for his own safety. In war, Celia's errant son finally found his true métier.

II

The voyage of the *Granma* across the choppy Gulf of Mexico and into the Caribbean had been an unmitigated disaster. Instead of the expected five days, the journey took seven. Then, weakened from seasickness, the rebels landed at the wrong spot on the Cuban coast. Their arrival was to have coincided with an uprising in Santiago led by Frank País, and a reception party awaited them at the Cabo Cruz lighthouse, with trucks and 100 men. The two forces were to have attacked the nearby town of Niquero together, then hit the city of Manzanillo before escaping into the Sierra Maestra. But the revolt in Santiago took place while Fidel was at sea, and any element of surprise was irrevocably gone. Batista rushed reinforcements to the Oriente province and dispatched naval and air force patrols to intercept Fidel's landing party.

The *Granma* approached the Playa las Coloradas before dawn on the morning of December 2, 1956. As the men on board anxiously strained to spot the Cabo Cruz lighthouse, the navigator fell overboard. Rapidly using up the precious remaining minutes of darkness, the boat circled until his cries were heard and he was rescued. Then, after Fidel ordered the pilot to aim for the nearest point of land, the *Granma* struck a sandbar, turning their arrival in Cuba into more of a shipwreck than a landing. Leaving most of their ammunition, food, and medicines behind, the rebels waded ashore in the broad daylight of mid-morning.

They didn't know it yet, but they had been spotted by a Cuban coast guard cutter, which in turn had alerted the armed forces. They had also landed more than a mile short of their intended rendezvous point, and be-tween them and dry land lay a mangrove swamp. In any case, their recep-tion party, after waiting in vain for two days, had withdrawn the night before. They were on their own.

Split into two groups after reaching dry land, the exhausted rebels floundered on through the bush, jettisoning more equipment as they went. As Che described them later, they were "disoriented and walking in circles, an army of shadows, of phantoms walking as if moved by some obscure psychic mechanism." Government planes flew continuously overhead look-ing for them, machine-gunning the bush for good measure. Two days went by before the two groups found each other and, with the guidance of a local peasant, trekked inland, moving eastward toward the Sierra Maestra.

Just after midnight on the morning of December 5, the column halted to rest in a sugarcane field, where the men devoured stalks of cane—carelessly leaving traces of their presence—before marching on until daybreak to a place called Alegría de Pío. Their guide then left them, making tracks to the nearest detachment of soldiers to turn them in. The rebels passed the day bivouacked in a glade at the edge of the cane field, totally unaware of what awaited them.

At 4:30 that afternoon, the army attacked. Caught by surprise, the rebels panicked and milled around as volleys of bullets flew into their midst. Fidel and his closest companions ran from the cane field into the forest, ordering the others to follow. In their effort to do so, men abandoned their equipment and ran off in headlong flight. Others, paralyzed by shock or terror, stayed where they were. That was when Che tried to rescue the box of bullets: as he did, a burst of gunfire hit a man next to him in the chest and Che in the neck. "The bullet hit the box first and threw me on the ground," Che recorded cryptically in his field diary. "I lost hope for a couple of minutes."*

Surrounded by wounded and frightened men screaming to surrender, and believing himself to be dying, Che slipped into his reverie. Juan Almeida snapped him out of it, telling him to get up and run. Che, Almeida, and three other men fled into the jungle with the sound of the cane field roaring in flames behind them.

Che had been lucky. His neck wound was only superficial. Although some of his comrades escaped with their lives, over the coming days Batista's troops summarily executed many of the men they captured, including the wounded and even some of those who had surrendered. The survivors tried desperately to gain refuge in the mountains and, somehow, to find one another. Of the eighty-two men who came ashore from the *Granma,* only twenty-two ultimately regrouped in the sierra.[†]

*Che's private wartime journal, "Diario de un Combatiente" (A Fighter's Diary), was the source for his book *Pasajes de la Guerra Revolucionaria* (Episodes [or Reminiscences] of the Cuban Revolutionary War), first published in Havana in 1963. When I was writing this book, the journal itself had not been published, except for a few carefully vetted excerpts about Che's first three months in Cuba. I worked from a complete text of the journal, which was shown to me by Che's widow, Aleida March. The unexpurgated version of events, from Guevara himself, provides raw and revealing glimpses of his life during the guerrilla war. See the Sources section for more information.

†The exact figure of the *Granma*'s survivors has remained imprecise. Official accounts have always referred to the number who survived and regrouped to form the core of the rebel army as twelve. This figure, with its unabashed Apostolic symbolism, was consecrated by the revolutionary Cuban journalist and official historian Carlos Franqui in his book *Los Doce* (The Twelve). Like many other early supporters, Franqui later went into exile as an opponent of Castro.

Che and his comrades stumbled on through the night. At dawn, they hid in a cave and made a portentous pledge to fight to the death if they were encircled. In his diary, Che wrote, "We had a tin of milk and approximately one liter of water. We heard the noise of combat nearby. The planes machine-gunned. We came out at night, guiding ourselves with the moon and North Star until they disappeared and [then] we slept." They knew they had to keep heading east to reach the sierra, and the "North Star" was Che's discovery, but his recollection of astronomy was less complete than he thought. Much later, he realized that they had actually followed a different star, and it had been sheer luck that they marched in the right direction.

Desperate from thirst, the five fugitives hiked through the forest. They had almost no water by then, and their only tin of milk had been accidentally spilled. They ate nothing that day. The next day, December 8, they came within sight of the coast and spotted a pond of what appeared to be fresh water below. But dense forest and 150-foot cliffs lay between them and it, and before they could find a way down, airplanes appeared overhead and once again they had to take cover, waiting out the daylight hours with only a liter of water between them. By nightfall, desperate from hunger and thirst, they gorged themselves on the only thing they could find, prickly pears. Moving through the night, they came across a hut where they found three more comrades from the *Granma*. Now they were eight, but they had no idea who else had survived. All they knew was that their best chance of finding any others was by heading east, into the Sierra Maestra.

The following days were an ordeal of survival as the little band hunted for food and water, dodging army airplanes and enemy foot patrols. Once, from a cave overlooking a coastal bay, they watched as a naval landing party disembarked on the beach to join the hunt for rebel stragglers. That day, unable to move, Che and his friends shared water, drinking from the eyepieces of their binoculars. "The situation was not good," Che wrote later. "If we were discovered, not the slightest chance of escape; we would have no alternative but to fight it out on the spot to the end." After dark they moved off again, determined to leave a place where they felt like "rats in a trap."

On December 12, they found a peasant's hut. Music was playing, and as they were about to enter the hut they overheard a voice inside make a toast: "To my comrades in arms." Assuming the voice to be a soldier's, they ran off. They marched along a streambed until midnight, when, reeling from exhaustion, they could go no farther.

After another day spent hiding without food or water, they took up the march again, but morale was low and many of the weary men balked, saying they no longer wanted to continue. The mood changed late that night when they reached a farmer's home, and, despite Che's wariness, they knocked at the door and were received warmly. Their host turned out to be a Seventh-Day Adventist pastor and a member of the fledgling July 26 peasant network in the region.

"They received us very well and gave us food," Che wrote in his field diary. "The men got sick from eating so much." When he recalled the experience later, in *Pasajes de la Guerra Revolucionaria,* Che rendered the experience with dark humor: "The little house that sheltered us turned into an inferno. Almeida was the first to be overcome by diarrhea; and, in a flash, eight unappreciative intestines gave evidence of the blackest ingratitude."

They spent the next day recovering from their gluttony and receiving an endless succession of curious Adventists from the surrounding community. The rebel landing was big news, and, thanks to a flourishing bush telegraph, the locals were surprisingly well informed about what had taken place. Che and his companions learned that sixteen of the *Granma's* men were known to be dead, murdered immediately after surrendering. Five more were believed to have been taken prisoner alive, and an unknown number had, like themselves, managed to escape into the mountains. It wasn't known whether Fidel had survived.

They decided to spread themselves out, staying in different homes in the area. They took other security precautions as well, shedding their uniforms and dressing up as peasants, and hiding their weapons and ammunition. Only Che and Almeida, acting jointly as the unofficial leaders of the group, each kept a pistol. Too sick to move, one of the men was left behind. But as they moved out, they learned that news of their presence had reached the army's ears. Only hours after they left the house they had been staying in, soldiers arrived, found their weapons cache, and took their sick comrade away as a prisoner. Someone had squealed, and now the soldiers were hot on their trail.

Fortunately, help arrived quickly. Alerted to their presence, Guillermo García, a key member of the July 26 peasant network, came to guide them out of harm's way. From him they learned that Fidel, or "Alejandro"*— his nom de guerre—was still alive; he and two companions had made contact with the rebel movement's collaborators and he had sent García out to look for survivors.

Several days of marching lay between them and Fidel's refuge deeper in the mountains, but thanks to García, Che and his comrades were aided by friendly peasants along the way. Finally, at dawn on December 21, they

*Castro's full name is Fidel Alejandro Castro Ruz.

reached the coffee *finca* where Fidel awaited them. There they found that
Raúl Castro too had survived, arriving separately with four companions after
his own grueling odyssey.

Despite the catastrophic setback to his plans, Fidel was already organizing things. Peasants had been enlisted to help find survivors from the
Granma still on the run, and a courier had been dispatched to Santiago and
Manzanillo to seek help from Frank País and Celia Sánchez, the woman
who had set up the July 26 peasant network in the sierra. Still, the outlook
was grim. Of the eighty-two men who had come ashore from the *Granma,*
only fifteen had reassembled, with nine weapons left between them. Almost
three weeks had passed, and the possibility of finding more stragglers grew
slimmer by the day. With Che's arrival came word of Jesús Montané's capture and the death of Fidel's friend Juan Manuel Márquez and two others.
By now, Che also knew that his friend Ñico López had been killed. Over
the coming days, five more expeditionaries would trickle in, including Che's
old prison mate Calixto García, but Fidel's rebel army was a mere shell. It
would have to rely upon local peasants to rebuild.

The reunion with Fidel was not a happy one for Che and his companions. Fidel was furious with them for having lost their arms. "You have not
paid for the error you committed," he told them. "Because the price to pay
for the abandonment of your weapons under such circumstances is your life.
The one and only hope of survival that you would have had, in the event of
a head-on encounter with the army, was your guns. To abandon them was
both criminal and stupid." That night, Che suffered an asthma attack, very
possibly caused by the emotional upset of Fidel's disapproval. Several years
later, he admitted that Fidel's "bitter reproach" had remained "engraved
on his mind for the duration of the campaign, and even today."

Fidel certainly had a valid point, but his tirade was somewhat gratu-
itous, for by then his courier had returned from Manzanillo with Celia
Sánchez's promise of new weapons. Indeed, the day after Che arrived, so
did the new guns, which included some carbines and four submachine guns.
Che's asthma vanished, but the arms delivery didn't cheer him up much,
for there was important symbolism in the way Fidel distributed the weapons. Taking away Che's pistol—a symbol of his status—Fidel gave it to the
leader of the peasant network, a wily strongman named Crescencio Pérez.
In its place, Che was given what he sourly called a "bad rifle."

It was a firsthand lesson in Fidel's masterful ability to manipulate
the feelings of those around him by bestowing or withdrawing his favors
at a moment's notice. Che was extremely sensitive to Fidel's approval and
anxious to retain his status as a member of his inner circle; it had been only
a few months since he had written his "Ode to Fidel," swearing his undy-

ing loyalty and describing Fidel as an "ardent prophet of the dawn." Perhaps aware of Che's wounded feelings, Fidel gave him a chance to redeem
himself the next day. Deciding suddenly to carry out a surprise test of
combat readiness among the men, he selected Che to pass on his orders to
prepare for battle. Che responded with alacrity. In his diary, he wrote, "I
came running to give the news. The men responded well with a good fighting spirit."

That day Celia's couriers arrived from Manzanillo with more arms,
bringing 300 rifle bullets, forty-five more for their Thompson submachine
gun, and nine sticks of dynamite. Che was overjoyed when the expedition's
only other doctor, Faustino Pérez, who had been dispatched to Havana to
assume duties there as Fidel's point man, gave him his own brand-new rifle
with a telescopic scope—"a jewel"—Che wrote elatedly in his diary.

Things had righted themselves again. Fidel's ire abated as he turned
his mind to the exigencies of organizing for war. But the upbraiding must
have been galling. Fidel may have hung on to *his* weapon in flight, but his
judgment had led them into catastrophe in the first place, beginning with
the *Granma*'s grounding offshore. And after the ambush at Alegría de Pío,
in the absence of any contingency plans, it had been a matter of *sálvase quien
puede*—every man for himself. Che's group had done the best it could, and
had survived.

If Che harbored resentment, he didn't dwell on it, but over the next
several days a certain impatience with Fidel's style of command began to
creep into his diary. On December 22, Che observed that it had been "a day
of almost total inactivity." The next day, they were "still in the same place."
And on Christmas Eve, in "a wait that seems useless to me," they remained
rooted, awaiting more arms and ammunition. He described Christmas Day
with fine irony: "At last, after a sumptuous feast of pork we began the march
toward Los Negros. The march began very slowly, breaking fences with
which [our] visiting card was left. We carried out an exercise of assaulting
a house, and as we did the owner, Hermes, appeared. We [then] lost two
hours between coffee and conversation. At last we resolved to take to the
road and advanced some more but the noise [we made] betrayed our presence to any hut along the way, and they abound. At dawn we reached our
destination."

Che wanted to see more organization, discipline, and action. He
wanted the war to begin. One item that did cheer him up a bit during this
period was a report in a Cuban newspaper about a loathsome personality in
Fidel's expeditionary force, "an Argentine Communist with terrible ante-
cedents, expelled from his country." Wrote Che, "The surname, of course:
Guevara."

III

In Mexico, as elsewhere, the news of the debacle at Alegría de Pío had been front-page news. The American UPI correspondent in Havana had fallen for the Batista government's claim of a total victory and sent it out on the wires as a news scoop. Many papers had picked it up. Along with Fidel and Raúl Castro, Ernesto Guevara was listed among the dead.

Hilda heard the news at her office. "When I arrived at work I found everyone with solemn looks: there was an embarrassed silence, and I wondered what was happening. Then I became conscious that everyone was looking at me. A fellow coworker handed me a newspaper and said: 'We are very sorry—about the news.'"

Devastated, Hilda was given leave to go home. Over the following days, her friends, including Myrna Torres, Laura de Albizu Campos, and General Bayo, rallied around her. Trying to comfort her, Bayo reminded her that the report had not yet been confirmed and insisted that he for one didn't believe it. She anxiously waited for more news, but little appeared in the press to confirm or deny the initial reports.

The Guevara family was equally distraught by the news reports. The first to hear, Ernesto senior, rushed to the newsroom of *La Prensa* to ask for confirmation but was told all he could do was wait. Celia called the Associated Press and received the same reply.

As Christmas approached, the Guevara household remained plunged in gloom. Many days had gone by and there was still no word. Then a letter with a Mexican postmark arrived. It was the letter Ernesto had left with Hilda to be mailed after his departure on the *Granma,* in which he talked to his mother of death and glory. She had sent it on, and now, with incredibly bad timing, it had reached its destination. "For our family it was simply horrifying," recalled Che's father. "My wife read it aloud to all of us without shedding a tear. I gritted my teeth and could not understand why Ernesto had to get involved in a revolution that had nothing to do with his homeland."

Some days later, Ernesto senior was summoned to the Argentine foreign ministry, where a cable had just come in from his cousin, the ambassador in Havana. It seemed that Ernesto was not among the dead and wounded rebels, or among the prisoners held by the Batista regime. This was good enough for Che's father, who ran home excitedly to give the news. "That afternoon everything changed," he wrote. "A little halo of optimism enveloped us all, and my house once again became a noisy and happy place."

Ernesto's father telephoned Hilda with the news, and she heard other rumors that renewed her hope that Ernesto was still alive. "I lived on that hope," she recalled years later. Meanwhile, she went ahead with her plans to go home to Peru and spend Christmas with her family. But as she prepared to leave, Hilda was still very distraught. "The last few days in Mexico I was so upset and worried by the lack of news clarifying Ernesto's situation that I was unable to take care of our belongings. I gave away most things or just abandoned them."* On December 17, she and ten-month-old Hilda Beatriz left Mexico for Lima.

While they awaited proof that Ernesto was alive, the Guevaras based their faith on the promising report from the Argentine embassy in Havana. Christmas came and went. Then, at around 10 P.M. on December 31, the family was preparing to celebrate the New Year when an airmail letter was pushed under the front door. It was addressed to Celia and postmarked Manzanillo, Cuba. Inside, on a single sheet of notepaper, in Ernesto's unmistakable hand, was the following message: "Dear old folks: I am perfectly fine. I spent two and I have five left. I am still doing the same work, news is sporadic and will continue to be, but have faith that God is an Argentine. A big hug to you all, Teté."

Teté had been Ernesto's nickname when he was a toddler. He was letting them know that, like a cat, he had used up only two of his seven lives.† The champagne was uncorked and the toasts began. Then, just before midnight struck, another envelope was pushed under the door. This too was addressed to Celia. Inside was a card with a red rose printed on it and a note: "Happy New Year. TT is perfectly well."

"This surpassed all our expectations," Ernesto senior recalled. "The bells of the New Year rang out and all the people who had come to my house began to show their happiness. Ernesto was safe, at least for now."

IV

Spreading along most of Cuba's anvil-shaped southeastern tip for a hundred miles, the Sierra Maestra range rises sharply from the Caribbean coastal shelf, forming a rugged natural barrier between it and the fertile lowlands that spread from its opposite flanks, thirty miles inland. The sierra is dominated by Cuba's highest mountain, the 6,500-foot Pico Turquino, and in the late 1950s was also home to one of the island's few remaining wildernesses. An indigenous rain forest, too inaccessible to be cut down, still survived.

*Presumably, this is how Hilda lost many of the letters, poems, and other writings Ernesto had left in her care.

†Che apparently believed cats had seven, not nine, lives.

With only a few small towns and villages, the sierra was sparsely inhabited by 60,000 or so hardscrabble *guajiros:* the poor, illiterate black, white,
and mulatto peasants whose beaten-up straw hats, gnarled bare feet, and
unintelligible, devoweled, rapid-fire Spanish vernacular had made them a
butt of derisory jokes among Cuba's urban middle class. *Guajiro* meant
someone stupid, a half-witted hillbilly. Some of the *guajiros* were tenant
farmers, but many were illegal squatters, or *precaristas,* who had built their
own dirt-floor huts, cleared a patch of land, and scratched out a living as
subsistence farmers, honey collectors, or charcoal burners. Like the rest of
Cuba's rural peasantry, the *guajiros* earned cash by working as sugarcane
cutters on the llano during the *zafra,* or harvest season, or as cowboys on the
cattle ranches. Some enterprising souls grew marijuana illegally and used a
series of smuggling trails to evade the *guardia* and get it to market. A few
logging companies had concessions to extract timber from the forests, and
there were some coffee plantations, but for the most part the sierra offered
little gainful employment and had virtually no roads or schools, and practically no modern amenities. News of the outside world came by transistor
radio or more commonly through a flourishing "bush telegraph" system
known as "Radio Bemba."

The starkness of the lives of the Sierra Maestra's *guajiros* contrasted
sharply with those of its landowners and, for that matter, with most of the
people living in Oriente's towns and cities: Santiago, Manzanillo, Bayamo,
and Holguín. The best land in the sierra, and in the llano below, was privately owned, often by absentee landlords living in Cuba's cities, and was
administered by armed foremen called *mayorales,* whose job it was to chase
off the persistent *precaristas.* These freewheeling, sometimes brutal men
carried real weight in the area, and acted as a virtual second police force to
the ill-trained, underpaid *guardia rurales* units based in outposts and garrisons throughout the region. Because of its remoteness and ruggedness, the
Sierra Maestra was also a traditional redoubt for criminals escaping the law,
and in lieu of an effective governmental writ, blood feuds and acts of vengeance were settled in the hills by machete and revolver. Exploiting the
guajiros' poverty and fear of authority, the *guardia* used *chivatos,* or informers, to keep abreast of occurrences and to investigate crimes. In the hunt for
Fidel and his men in the days immediately after the *Granma* landing, they
had already deployed their *chivato* network, with devastating success.

Not surprisingly, violence frequently broke out between the *precaristas*
and the *mayorales.* "Each side had its known leaders and gangs of followers," the historian Hugh Thomas wrote. Crescencio Pérez worked as a truck
driver for the sugar tycoon Julio Lobo but was also a *precarista* boss rumored
to have killed several men and to have fathered eighty children. Pérez had

a huge extended family, numerous contacts, and quite a few men at his beck and call. It was to him that Celia Sánchez had gone to prepare for a civilian rebel support network in the sierra. With no love for the authorities, Pérez had placed himself, his family, and relatives such as Guillermo García—his nephew—as well as some of his workers at Fidel's disposal.

If Fidel had any qualms about working with such a man, he didn't show it. Restructuring his "general staff" the day after Christmas 1956, he promoted Crescencio Pérez and one of his sons to a new five-man *estado mayor*, presided over by himself as *comandante;* his bodyguard, Universo Sánchez; and Che. His brother Raúl and Juan Almeida, having shown their mettle by leading their groups out of Alegría de Pío, were made platoon leaders commanding five men each. As advance scouts, he named Ramiro Valdés, a Moncada veteran and one of Fidel's early adherents; the newly resurrected Calixto Morales; and another man, Armando Rodríguez.

Given the recent debacle and the actual size of his force—not to mention his dubious prospects for success—Fidel's grandiloquent handout of an officer's rank to seven of the fifteen men with him might seem almost comic, but it was born of Fidel's boundless faith in himself. He had lost more than two-thirds of his force and practically all his armaments and supplies, but he had reached the sierra, he had renewed his lifelines to the July 26 underground in the cities, and he now had Crescencio Pérez at his side to help familiarize him with the new terrain and to rebuild his army. He placed his new *guajiro* officer in charge of all peasant recruits, with his nephew Guillermo García as his deputy.

Indeed, Fidel was already behaving as if he were Cuba's commander in chief. He had established a rigid hierarchy for the army he intended to lead to power, with himself situated firmly at the top. The autocratic nature he would become famous for was already visible as he fired off messages to the llano, demanding weapons and supplies from the hard-pressed urban underground while simultaneously turning his attention to bringing the sierra and its inhabitants under his domain.

For all the post-triumph revolutionary lyricism about the "noble peasantry" of the Sierra Maestra, in these early times Fidel and his men were very much on alien ground. They neither knew nor understood the hearts and minds of the locals, and they relied on Crescencio and his men to negotiate for them, often with disastrous results. In many of his early contacts with the area's peasants, Fidel passed himself off as an army officer, gingerly feeling out where their true sympathies might lie.

Che, who worried about the danger of being trapped by the army if they remained too long in one spot, bristled at Fidel's decision to linger. As they waited for some volunteers who were being sent by Celia Sánchez, he

wrote in his journal, "It doesn't seem wise to me but Fidel insists on it."
Couriers came and went from Manzanillo, bringing hand grenades, dynamite, and machine-gun ammo, along with three books Che had requested:
"Algebra, and a basic history of Cuba, and a basic Cuba geography." The
volunteers didn't appear, but half a dozen new *guajiro* recruits trickled into
camp, and the rebel army began to grow. The fact that *locals* were volunteering was a triumph. Finally, on December 30, Fidel decided to wait no
longer and to head deeper into the mountains toward a new sanctuary.

   Che's diary entries acquired a more reassured, secure tone. Late on
New Year's Eve, a courier brought the news that an army battalion was
preparing to come into the sierra after them. Che wrote, "The last day of
the year was spent in instruction of the new recruits, reading some, and doing
the small things of war."

V

New Year's Day 1957 brought rain and new details of the enemy's plans.
Four hundred soldiers were on their way into the mountains, and all the
local garrisons had been reinforced. Guided by a local *guajiro,* the rebels
continued their exhausting trek. The night of January 2 was an ordeal recorded by Che as "a slow and fatiguing march, through muddy trails, with
many of the men suffering from diarrhea," but the next day his diary had a
tone of grim satisfaction: "The good news was received that Nene Jérez was
badly wounded and is dying. Nene Jérez was the one who guided the soldiers to the place we were [ambushed] in la Alegría [de Pío]." By January 5
they could see the 4,000-foot-high Pico Caracas, the first of the series of
jungle-covered mountains crowning the Sierra Maestra's central spine. "The
perspectives are good, because from here to La Plata is all steep and forested,
ideal for defense," Che observed.

   Nine of the promised volunteers arrived from Manzanillo, and they
camped in the Mulato valley on the flanks of Pico Caracas, awaiting updates
on the army's movements. Contradictory reports were coming in from their
guajiro couriers. One said there were no soldiers in the vicinity, but another
gave the alarming news that a *chivato* had gone to report their presence to a
nearby garrison. On January 9, they decided to move off again, and by the
next afternoon, from a new bivouac with a good vantage point, they saw
that the report about the *chivatazo* had been accurate: eighteen naval marines appeared walking along the road leading from the Macías garrison,
apparently heedless of any danger. But the rebels didn't attack. They were
waiting for Guillermo García—returning from a fruitless final mission to
look for survivors from the *Granma*—and a food delivery, and Fidel wanted

to be well prepared before engaging the enemy in battle. Che rued the lost opportunity. "It would have been an easy target," he wrote in his journal.

To counter government claims of their defeat and build up civilians' confidence in their fighting capabilities—as well as to boost their own morale —the rebels needed to prove they were a force to be reckoned with. This meant launching an attack, preferably against a remote and ill-defended garrison where they could retain the element of surprise. La Plata, some small coastal barracks with reportedly few *guardias,* seemed to offer the perfect opportunity to Fidel. Che had different ideas, and he wrote in his diary on January 10, "Fidel's plan is to carry out an ambush and escape to the forests with enough food for several days. It doesn't seem bad to me but it's a lot of weight [to carry]. My plan was to form a [central] camp with abundant food and [from there] send out assault troops."

Che was also concerned about the men who could be counted on in the event of combat. "Together with the temporary casualty of Ramiro [Valdés, who had hurt his knee in a fall], there are one or two definitive casualties among the *manzanilleros.*" One had already been told he could leave after announcing—"suspiciously," it seemed to Che—that he had tuberculosis, and a couple of the others seemed indecisive. He was also worried about the menace posed by *chivatos,* and in his journal he vowed to deal with this threat: "A lesson must be given."

The next day, as Che had predicted, five of the *manzanilleros* opted to leave the field, but Fidel decided to press on. Their presence in the area had become too well known for them to stay put. A first goal was to kill three local *mayorales,* or plantation foremen, who, Che wrote, "were the terror of the peasants." The three overseers worked for the Nuñez-Beattie timber and sugar company and had earned notoriety among the *guajiros* for their brutality. Killing them would earn the rebels popularity among the locals.

The incapacitated Ramiro was left at the home of a friendly peasant, with a pistol to defend himself, and the rest of the men headed off for La Plata. Guillermo García had shown up with some new peasant recruits— the rebel "army" had now swelled to thirty-two men—but they were still short of arms, with only twenty-three weapons and a few sticks of dynamite and hand grenades among them. They hiked into the night, their path laid out for them by a collaborator who had cut marks into the trees with a machete, and escorted by Eutimio Guerra, a well-known local *precarista* leader who had volunteered himself and a neighbor to be their guides.

On January 15, with a hostage in tow—a local teenager they had found collecting honey and decided to keep with them in case he was tempted to spread the alarm—the rebels reached a point overlooking the mouth of the Río de la Plata, about half a mile away from the army encampment. Using their telescopic sights, they could see the target, a half-built barracks sitting in the middle of a clearing between the riverbank and the beach. A group of casually uniformed men were doing domestic chores. Just beyond lay the home of one of the *mayorales* they had vowed to execute. At dusk a coast guard patrol boat loaded with soldiers appeared and apparently signaled to the men on shore. Uncertain what this meant, the rebels decided to stay hidden and delay their attack until the following day.

At dawn on January 16, they posted lookouts to observe the barracks. The patrol boat had vanished and no soldiers could be seen. This unnerved them, but by mid-afternoon they decided to make their approach. The whole group forded the river and took up positions alongside the trail leading to the barracks. A little after nightfall, two men and two boys appeared on the trail, and the rebels seized them. One was a suspected *chivato*. To extract information, he was "squeezed a little," as Che worded it euphemistically in his diary. The man told them that there were ten soldiers in the barracks and that Chicho Osorio, one of the most notorious of the three *mayorales* on their hit list, was headed in their direction and could be expected any minute.

Osorio appeared, mounted on a mule and escorted by a young black boy on foot. The rebels decided to trick him, and shouted out, "Halt, the rural guard!" Osorio shouted back, "Mosquito!"—the soldiers' code word—and then his name. The rebels moved in, confiscating Osorio's revolver and a knife found on the boy before leading them over to where Fidel waited.

What happened next has become Cuban revolutionary folklore. As Che told it later in his published account of the episode, "[Fidel] made him think he was a colonel of the *guardia rural* who was investigating some ir-regularities. Osorio, who was drunk, then gave an account of all the enemies of the regime who in his words 'should have their balls cut off.' There was the confirmation of who were our friends and who weren't." With each word he spoke, the unsuspecting Osorio dug his own grave a little deeper. "Colonel" Fidel asked him what he knew about Eutimio Guerra, their guide, and Osorio replied that it was known that Guerra had hidden Fidel Castro. In fact, Osorio said, he had been looking for Guerra, and if he found him, he would kill him. Giving the inebriated *mayoral* even more rope, Fidel opined that if "Fidel" were found, he should also be killed. Osorio agreed enthusiastically and added that Crescencio Pérez too should die. Really into his stride now, Osorio went on to brag about men he had killed and mis-treated and, as evidence of his prowess, pointed to his feet. "'Look,' he said," Che wrote afterward, "pointing to the Mexican-made boots he wore (and which we wore also), 'I got them off one of those sons . . . [of whores] we killed.' There, without knowing it, Chicho Osorio had signed his own death sentence."

Then, either so drunk or so naive as to believe that Fidel was indeed a *guardia* officer, and anxious to win his favor, Osorio offered to guide them to the barracks to point out the weakness in its security defenses, and even allowed himself to be tied up as a mock prisoner to play his role in the "inspector's" charade. As they advanced on the barracks, Osorio explained where the sentry stood watch and where the guards slept. One of the rebels was sent ahead to check and returned to report that Osorio's information was accurate. The rebels finally made ready for the attack, leaving Osorio behind in the custody of two men. "Their orders were to kill him the minute the shooting started," Che wrote matter-of-factly, "something they obeyed with strictness."

It was now 2:40 in the morning. The rebels fanned out into three groups. Their targets were the zinc-roofed barracks and the rustic house next to it, which was owned by the second of their targeted *mayorales*. When they were about 130 feet away, Fidel fired two bursts from his machine gun. Then all the others opened fire. They shouted for the soldiers to surrender but were answered with gunfire. Che and a comrade from the *Granma,* Luis Crespo, threw their grenades, but neither exploded. Raúl threw a burning stick of dynamite, but nothing happened then either. Fidel ordered them to set fire to the overseer's house. Two initial attempts were repelled by gunfire, but a third try by Che and Crespo was successful, except that it was not the overseer's house but a storehouse next to it, full of coconuts, that caught fire.

The soldiers inside the barracks, evidently fearing they were going to be burned alive, began fleeing. One practically ran into Crespo, who shot him in the chest. Che fired at another man and, although it was dark, believed he had hit him. Bullets flew back and forth for a few minutes, and then the firefight abated. The soldiers in the barracks surrendered, and an inspection of the overseer's house showed it to be full of wounded men. The fight was over. Che took a tally in his diary: "The result of the combat was 8 Springfields, one machine gun and about a thousand rounds [captured]. We had spent approximately 500 [rounds]. Also [we got] cartridge belts, helmets, canned food, knives, clothes and even rum."

The *guardia* had been hit badly, and the barracks had been so riddled with bullets it looked like "a sieve." Two soldiers lay dead and five were wounded, three mortally. Three others were taken prisoner. There were no rebel casualties. Before they withdrew, they set the buildings on fire. Che personally set fire to the house of the overseer, who, along with the barracks' commander, a sergeant, had managed to escape.

Back in the hills, the rebels freed their prisoners and their civilian hostages, after issuing a warning to the suspected *chivato*. Overriding Che's opposition, Fidel gave all their medicine to the soldiers to treat the wounded men who remained in the ravaged clearing below. The rebels' enthusiasm was dampened slightly when realized that their first hostage, the teenage boy, had run away during the fracas, along with a scout. Worse, they had taken with them two weapons—a shotgun and the late Chicho Osorio's confiscated revolver.

It was still only 4:30 A.M. Taking advantage of the remaining darkness, they fled east toward Palma Mocha, a farming community named for the river entering the sea about two miles away. They arrived in time to witness what Che described as a "pitiful spectacle"—families fleeing with their belongings after being warned that the air force was going to bomb the area. "The maneuver was obvious," Che wrote in his diary. "To evict all the peasants and later the [Nuñez-Beattie] company would take over the abandoned lands."

Having seen firsthand the fallout from their action, the rebels moved on, looking for a place to ambush the soldiers they knew would be coming in after them. The men were keyed up and tired when, at a pit stop in the march, Fidel ordered a review of their ammunition. Each man was supposed to have forty rounds. When Sergio Acuña, one of the new *guajiro* recruits, was found with 100 rounds, Fidel asked him to give up the excess, and he refused. Fidel ordered him arrested, and Acuña cocked his rifle threateningly. The incident was defused when Raúl and Crescencio persuaded Acuña to hand over his weapon and ammunition, telling him that his infraction would be ignored if he made a "formal request" to stay with the rebels. Che was displeased with this solution but wrote in his journal, "Fidel agreed, creating a really negative antecedent that would later rear its head, because Acuña was seen to have gotten away with imposing his will."

The rebels marched on and reached a peasant's home in a clearing, surrounded by a forested rise of land on three sides, and near a creek that Che christened "Arroyo del Infierno" (Hell's Creek). The site offered both water and an escape route, and was a perfect place to lay an ambush. As they arrived, the owner was preparing to join the exodus to the coast, leaving the place to the rebels, and over the next few days they organized themselves, setting out an ambush position in the forest with good views of the house and the dirt track leading into the clearing.

The men were jumpy, though, and one morning as he and Fidel inspected the fighters' position, Che was almost shot when a fighter saw him coming from a distance and fired off a round at him. It was partly Che's fault. He was wearing an army corporal's cap he had taken as a trophy at La Plata. Even more alarming was the reaction of the other rebels, who, instead of scrambling into defensive positions at the sound of the gunshot, immediately ran off into the bush. In his later published account, Che told of being shot at but omitted any mention of the men's running away. Instead, he used the anecdote as a parable to exalt the condition of men at war. "This incident was symptomatic of the state of high tensions that prevailed as we waited for the relief the battle would bring. At such times, even those with nerves of steel feel a certain trembling in the knees and each man longs for the arrival of that luminous moment of battle."

All was quiet for a few more days. Fidel ordered provisions from some of the few peasants who had remained in the area, and he repaid a farmer who showed up looking for a lost pig, one that Fidel had shot for food on their first day in camp. They began hearing rumors that the army was inflicting reprisals on local peasants for the La Plata attack. Their new guide, Eutimio Guerra, took off for his home, carrying some messages for Fidel and orders to find out about the army's movements. The rebels anxiously listened to their radio, but no news of the army's activity was broadcast.

Before dawn on January 22, they heard gunshots in the distance and they readied themselves for battle, but the morning dragged by and no soldiers appeared. Then, at noon, a figure appeared in the clearing. Calixto García, seated next to Che, spotted him first. They looked through their telescopic sights. It was a soldier. As they watched, a total of nine figures came into view and gathered around the huts. Then the shooting began. Che recorded it in his field diary: "Fidel opened fire and the man fell immediately shouting '*Ay mi madre*'; his two companions fell immediately [as well]. All of a sudden I realized there was a soldier hidden in the second house barely twenty meters from my position; I could see only his feet so I fired in his direction. At the second shot he fell. Luis [Crespo] brought me a grenade sent by Fidel because they had told him there were more people in the house. Luis covered me and I entered but fortunately there was nothing else."

Che recovered the rifle and cartridge belt of the soldier he had hit, then inspected the body. "He had a bullet under the heart with exit on the right side, he was dead." To his certain knowledge, Che had killed his first man.

VI

While Che was proving himself in combat, Hilda and the baby were visiting with the Guevara family in Argentina. On New Year's, Ernesto senior had called Hilda with the news of his son's first message and sent her a ticket to fly to Buenos Aires. On January 6, after three weeks at home with her own family in Lima, she flew to Buenos Aires with the baby to meet her in-laws for the first time. They bombarded her with questions. Why had their Ernesto gone into harm's way for a foreign cause? Who was Fidel Castro, anyway? It was quickly apparent to Hilda that Ernesto, or "Ernestito" as his aunts still called him, was the family's favorite son. "Because of their deep affection for Ernesto," she wrote, "his parents found it hard to adjust to the idea of his being in danger. They kept coming back to the feeling that it would be better if he were in Argentina." She did her best to explain what she knew of Ernesto's political evolution, but she was merely repeating things he had already told them in his letters, which they had obvious difficulty in accepting. Celia was most in need of reassurance. "I told Doña Celia, my mother-in-law, of the deep tenderness that Ernesto felt for her," Hilda wrote. "This was not exaggeration for the sake of comforting her. I knew what she meant to him."

Hilda and the baby stayed a month with the Guevaras. When they returned to Lima she found a letter from Ernesto waiting for her. It was dated January 28, 1957. "*Querida vieja:* Here in the Cuban jungle, alive and thirsting for blood, I'm writing these inflamed, Martí-inspired lines. As if I really were a soldier (I'm dirty and ragged at least), I am writing this letter over a tin plate with a gun at my side and something new, a cigar in my mouth." In the same boasting, hearty tone, he breezily recapped everything that had happened since the *Granma*'s "now famous" landing, emphasizing the dangers faced and hardships overcome: "Our misfortunes continued. . . . [W]e were surprised in the also now famous Alegría, and scattered like pigeons. . . . I was wounded in the neck, and I'm still alive only due to my cat's lives. . . . [F]or a few days I walked through those hills thinking I was seriously wounded . . . we got reorganized and rearmed and attacked a troop barracks, killing five soldiers. . . . [They] sent select troops after us. We fought these off and this time it cost them three dead and two wounded. . . . Soon after we captured three guards and took their guns.

"Add to all this the fact that we had no losses and that the mountains are ours and you'll get an idea of the demoralization of the enemy. We slip through their hands like soap just when they think they have us trapped. Naturally the fight isn't all won, there'll be many more battles. But so far it's going our way, and each time will do so more."

He signed the letter "Chancho" and sent a *gran abrazo* to her, as well as hugs and kisses for the baby, and told her that in his rush to leave he had left behind the snapshots he had of them in Mexico City. Could she send them? He gave her the address of a mail drop in Mexico where letters would be forwarded to him eventually.

Hilda couldn't have been very pleased by the letter, which she reproduced without comment in her memoirs. While she, the despondent wife and mother, had done little but worry about him, he was having a rousing adventure, thoroughly enjoying life as an unwashed, cigar-smoking, "bloodthirsty" guerrilla. When he had finally written, he hadn't even inquired or expressed concern for her own possible travails.

VII

Over the next three weeks, the rebels roamed across the Sierra Maestra, picking up a few new volunteers, but dogged by desertions and *chivatazos*. On January 30, the air force bombed the place they had chosen for a base camp, on the slopes of Pico Caracas. Although the raid caused no casualties, it sent the rebels on a panicked exodus through the forest. Meanwhile, their pursuers, led by a notoriously brutal officer—Major Joaquín Casillas, who was said to possess a private collection of human ears shorn from previous victims—sent out spies disguised as civilians to follow them. His soldiers left in their wake a trail of burned huts and murdered peasants accused of collaborating with the rebels.

Che was now emerging as an audacious, even reckless guerrilla fighter. Evidently eager to prove himself and to make up for his sorely felt error of losing his rifle en route from Alegría de Pío, he routinely volunteered for the most dangerous tasks. During the aerial bombardment on Pico Caracas, when everyone else—including Fidel—ran away, Che stayed behind to pick up stragglers and retrieve abandoned belongings, including weapons and Fidel's *comandante* cap.

Other strong traits were emerging. He had begun to show a prosecutorial severity with guerrilla newcomers, especially those from the city, usually distrusting their personal valor, fortitude, and commitment to the struggle. No less mistrustful of the peasants they met, he often described them in his diary as "charlatans, fast talkers," or "nervous." He was also developing a deep hatred of cowards, an obsession that was soon to be one of his most renowned and feared wartime traits. He disliked one member of the band in particular, "El Gallego" José Morán, a veteran from the *Granma* whom he suspected of cowardice and viewed as a potential deserter.

Che sought opportunities to mete out punishment as an example to others. When three army spies were detained by the rebels and confessed their true identities, Che was among those who called for their deaths. Fidel chose to show mercy by sending them back to their barracks with a warning and a personal letter from him to their commander. Keen to see the guerrillas tempered into a tough, disciplined fighting force and worried about Fidel's toleration of malingerers and insubordinates, Che was gratified when Fidel finally laid down the law at the end of January. From that moment on, Fidel told his men, three crimes would be punishable by death: "desertion, insubordination, and defeatism." When one deserter, Sergio Acuña, met a grisly end at the hands of army captors—Acuña was tortured, shot four times, then hanged by the neck—Che termed the incident "sad but instructive."

By the end of January, there were signs that Fidel's little band was having an effect throughout Cuba. Word arrived from Havana that Faustino Pérez, Fidel's man there, had raised $30,000 for the rebels; that the July 26 urban cells were carrying out sabotage in the cities; and that there was simmering discontent in army ranks over the embarrassing rebel attacks. Batista was said to be about to fire the army chief of staff, but he and his generals persisted in claiming that the rebels had been virtually exterminated, were on the run, and posed no threat to the army. This propaganda campaign greatly irked Fidel, and he ordered Faustino Pérez to arrange an interview for him with a credible journalist who could come to the sierra and verify his existence to the world at large. He also wanted to hold a meeting with his National Directorate to coordinate strategy, and sent word to Frank País and Celia Sánchez to organize a conference.

In early February the rebels spent a few days resting up, enduring torrential rains and aimless daily bombing runs by the air force. In the comparative lull, Che began giving French lessons to Raúl. These were interrupted when they set out again and Che was weakened by diarrhea and a crippling but short bout of malaria. In an army ambush on a hill called Los Altos de Espinosa, Julio Zenon Acosta—an illiterate black *guajiro* to whom Che had recently begun teaching the alphabet—was killed. It was the rebels' first combat death since the *Granma*'s landing. Later, Che would exalt Zenon Acosta, whom he called "my first pupil," as the kind of "noble peasant" who made up the heart and soul of the revolution.

As time had worn on, Che and Fidel had begun to suspect that their peasant guide Eutimio Guerra—who came and went, and whose absences always coincided with the army's attacks—was a traitor. After the ambush on Los Altos de Espinosa, they learned from knowledgeable peasants that their suspicions were correct. On one of his outings, Guerra had been captured by the army and promised a reward if he betrayed Fidel. Both the aerial bombardment on Pico Caracas and the latest ambush had been carried out with his collusion. But by the time they learned this, Guerra had vanished, followed by El Gallego Morán.

By mid-February a number of men were sick and demoralized, and Fidel decided to conduct a purge. They would be given "convalescent leave" at a *guajiro*'s farm under Crescencio Pérez's care. At the same time, couriers brought word that the members of the July 26 National Directorate were on their way to Oriente, and that Herbert Matthews, a prominent *New York Times* journalist, was arriving to interview Fidel at a farmhouse on the sierra's northern flanks. It was to be a fateful meeting.

15

Days of Water and Bombs

I

Che Guevara was now at war, trying to create a revolution. He had made a conscious leap of faith and entered a domain where lives could be taken for an ideal and where the end *did* justify the means. People were no longer simply people; each person represented a place within the overall scheme of things and could be viewed, for the most part, as either a friend or an enemy. Those in between were distrusted, as they had to be. His goal was to help Fidel Castro take power, and he awoke each day with the prospect of killing and dying.

Just as Che's worldview had been expanded by leaving home, it had contracted when his quest to decide what he believed in was resolved in Marxism. Reality was now a matter of black and white. At the same time, Che believed that the faith he had chosen was limitless. What he was doing had a historic imperative.

II

As the rebels sat down to eat a goat stew cooked for them by a friendly black family on the second day of their trek to the farmhouse where the National Directorate meeting would be held, El Gallego Morán suddenly reappeared. He told an unconvincing tale to explain his disappearance. He had gone out hunting for food and spotted the traitor Eutimio Guerra. When he lost him, he was unable to find his way back to camp. Che remarked in his diary, "The truth of El Gallego's behavior is very difficult to know, but to me it is simply a matter of a frustrated desertion. . . . I advised killing him there and then, but Fidel blew off the matter."

Heading on, they reached a rural store owned by a friend of Eutimio Guerra's. The friend was gone, so they broke down the door and discovered

Fidel and Che, lighting a
cigar, in the Sierra Maestra.

"a true paradise of canned goods," which they proceeded to devour. After
laying a false trail to throw off pursuers, they marched through the night
and, at dawn on February 16, reached the farm of a peasant collaborator
named Epifanio Díaz. The meeting was to take place there.

The members of the National Directorate had already started to arrive. Frank País and Celia Sánchez were there; next came Faustino Pérez
and Vílma Espín, a new female Movement activist from Santiago; then
Haydée Santamaría and her fiancé, Armando Hart. This was the active inner
core of the July 26 steering group that Fidel had assembled in the summer
of 1955 after his release from prison on the Isle of Pines.

At twenty-three, Frank País was the youngest of the Directorate's
members, but he had already chalked up an impressive career as a political activist in Oriente, where he was vice president of the student federation. Since the creation of the July 26 Movement, he had thrown in his lot
with Fidel as coordinator of rebel activities in Oriente. Celia Sánchez,
thirty-seven, had been active in the campaign to free the Moncada prisoners and, from her home base in Manzanillo, had collaborated with Fidel
since the Movement's founding. It was she who had recruited Crescencio
Pérez and organized the reception party that had awaited the *Granma*'s
arrival. Like Fidel, the thirty-seven-year-old doctor Faustino Pérez—
unrelated to Crescencio—had come out of Havana University and had
been a student leader in opposition to Batista after the 1952 coup. Joining

forces with Fidel, he had gone to Mexico and been aboard the *Granma*. Armando Hart, a twenty-seven-year-old law student who was the son of a prominent judge, had come out of the Ortodoxo Youth movement. Hart joined Faustino Pérez in organizing student opposition to Batista and helped found Fidel's movement. His twenty-five-year-old fiancée, Haydée Santamaría, had joined the Moncada assault and been jailed for seven months afterward; she too was a July 26 founder and had joined in the November 1956 uprising in Oriente led by Frank País. Her family had already paid dearly for their involvement with Fidel. Her brother Abel, an Ortodoxo Youth militant, had been Fidel's deputy until his death by torture at Moncada, and her brother Aldo was in prison for Movement activities. The newest face, Vílma Espín, was the twenty-seven-year-old, MIT-educated daughter of an affluent Santiago family, a member of Frank País's student group, which had fused with the July 26 Movement and had participated in the November 1956 uprising. These young, mostly upper-middle-class urbanites were in charge of the Movement's entire national underground structure, responsible for everything including recruiting new members, obtaining and smuggling arms and volunteers into the sierra, raising cash and supplies, disseminating propaganda, conducting foreign relations, undertaking urban sabotage, and continuing the effort to come up with a political platform.

It was a historic day. Fidel was meeting Celia Sánchez—soon to become his closest confidante and lover—for the first time. Raúl met the woman who would become his future wife: Vílma Espín. For Che, it was his first look at the men and women who formed the elite backbone of Fidel's revolutionary movement.

In general, Che viewed Fidel's middle-class, well-educated colleagues as hopelessly bound to timid notions of what their struggle should achieve, and he was correct in thinking that they held views very divergent from his own. Lacking his Marxist conception of a radical social transformation, most saw themselves as fighting to oust a corrupt dictatorship and to replace it with a conventional Western democracy. Che's initial encounter with the urban leaders reinforced his negative assumptions. "Through isolated conversations," he wrote in his diary, "I discovered the evident anticommunist inclinations of most of them, above all Hart." By the next day, however, his analysis had modified slightly. "Of the women, Haydée seems the best oriented politically, Vílma the most interesting. Celia Sánchez is very active but politically strangled. Armando Hart [is] permeable to the new ideas."*

---

*See the Notes for elaboration.

Over the next couple of days, one thing became clear: Fidel wanted to make his rebel army the absolute priority of the Movement. The National Directorate had come with their own ideas about what the Movement's strategy should be, but Fidel told them that their efforts should be directed toward sustaining and strengthening his guerrillas. He sidestepped Faustino's proposal to open a second front nearer Havana in the Escambray mountains of Villa Clara province, and Frank País's argument that he leave the sierra to give speeches and raise funds abroad. In the end, the others were overwhelmed by Fidel's arguments and agreed to begin organizing a national "civic resistance" support network. Frank País promised to send him a contingent of new fighters from Santiago within a fortnight. Epifanio Díaz's farm, which in the future would serve as their secret gateway to the sierra, was to be the meeting place.

Che was not a member of the National Directorate and, careful not to overstep his authority at this early stage, did not attend their meetings. But he was privy to all that happened in them, and, as his diary reveals, signs of the future rift that would develop between the armed fighters in the sierra and their urban counterparts in the llano were already in evidence. For now, Fidel was able to plead his case for the sierra's priority as an undeniable issue of survival. But as the war expanded, the rift would break into the open as an ideological dispute between left and right, and as a struggle for control between the llano leaders and Fidel.

Herbert Matthews—the senior correspondent for *The New York Times* and a press veteran of the Spanish Civil War, Mussolini's Abyssinian campaign, and World War II—arrived in camp early on the morning of February 17. Che wasn't present for Matthews's three-hour interview with Fidel, but Fidel briefed him afterward, and in his diary Che noted the points of most significance to him. Fidel had complained about the military aid lent to Batista by the United States, and, when Matthews had asked if he was anti-imperialist, Fidel had responded carefully that he was if this meant a desire to rid his country of its economic chains. This did not imply, Fidel hastened to add, that he felt hatred for the United States or its people. "The gringo," Fidel told Che, "had shown friendliness and didn't ask any trick questions."

Fidel had engaged in a little trickery of his own, however, by arranging for a fighter to burst in sweatily, bearing "a message from the Second Column." Fidel hoped to make Matthews believe he had a sizable number of fighters, when in fact his rebel army at this point numbered fewer than twenty armed men. When the interview was over, Matthews was driven back to Manzanillo, where he would go on to Santiago, fly to Havana, and board another plane for New York; he knew he had a major scoop on his hands and wanted to publish it as quickly as possible.

"The gringo left early," Che wrote in his diary. "And I was on guard when they came to tell me to redouble the vigilance because Eutimio was at Epifanio's house." Juan Almeida led a patrol to seize Eutimio, who, unaware that his treason had been discovered, was taken prisoner, disarmed, and brought before Fidel. By now, an army safe-conduct pass bearing Eutimio's name and proving his collaboration with the enemy had fallen into the rebels' hands. Fidel showed it to him.

"Eutimio got down on his knees, asking that he be shot to have it over with," Che wrote. "Fidel tried to trick him, making him believe he would pardon him, but Eutimio remembered the scene with Chicho Osorio and didn't allow himself to be deceived. Then Fidel announced he would be executed and Ciro Frías inflicted a heartfelt sermon on him in the tone of an old friend. The man awaited death in silence and a certain dignity. A tremendous downpour began and everything turned black."

Precisely what happened next remained a carefully guarded Cuban state secret for decades. None of the eyewitnesses to Eutimio Guerra's execution— the first traitor executed by the Cuban rebels—has ever said publicly who fired the fatal shot. It is easy to see why. The answer is to be found in Che's private diary, in a passage that is unlikely ever to be officially published.

"The situation was uncomfortable for the people and for [Eutimio]," Che wrote, "so I ended the problem giving him a shot with a .32 [-caliber] pistol in the right side of the brain, with exit orifice in the right temporal [lobe]. He gasped a little while and was dead. Upon proceeding to remove his belongings I couldn't get off the watch that was tied by a chain to his belt, and then he told me in a steady voice farther away than fear: 'Yank it off, boy, what does it matter. . . .' I did so and his possessions were now mine. We slept badly, wet and I with something of asthma."

Che's narrative is as chilling as it is revealing about his personality. His matter-of-factness in describing the execution, his scientific notations on the bullet's entry and exit wounds, suggest a remarkable detachment from violence. To Che, the decision to execute Eutimio himself was, in his own words, simply a way to end an uncomfortable situation. As for his recollection of Eutimio's posthumous last words, it is simply inexplicable and lends a surreal dimension to the grim scene.

It is also in stark contrast to Che's published account of the event. In the chapter "Death of a Traitor" in *Pasajes,* he rendered the scene with literary aplomb and turned it into a dark revolutionary parable about redemption through sacrifice. Describing the moment when Eutimio fell on his knees in front of Fidel, he wrote: "At that moment he seemed to have aged; on his temple were a good many gray hairs we had never noticed before."

Of Ciro's "lecture," in which he upbraided Eutimio for causing the deaths and suffering of many of their friends and neighbors, Che wrote: "It was a long and moving speech, which Eutimio listened to in silence, his head bent. We asked him if he wanted anything and he answered yes, that he wanted the Revolution, or rather us, to take care of his children." The revolution had kept its promise to Eutimio, Che wrote, but his name had "already been forgotten, perhaps even by his children," who bore new names and were attending Cuba's state schools, receiving the same treatment as other children and preparing themselves for a better life.

"But one day," he added, "they will have to know that their father was executed by the revolutionary power because of his treachery. It is also just that they be told how their father—a peasant who had allowed himself to be tempted by corruption and had tried to commit a grave crime, moved by the desire for glory and wealth—had nevertheless recognized his error, and had not even hinted at a desire for clemency, which he knew he did not deserve. Finally, they should also know that in his last moments he remembered his children and asked that they be treated well."

Che completed his parable with a description of the final moment of Eutimio's life that was heavily imbued with religious symbolism. "Just then a heavy storm broke and the sky darkened; in the midst of a deluge, the sky crossed by lightning and the noise of thunder, as one of these strokes of lightning burst and was closely followed by a thunderbolt, Eutimio Guerra's life was ended and even those comrades standing near him did not hear the shot."

This incident was seminal in the growth of Che's mystique among the guerrillas and the peasants of the Sierra Maestra. He had acquired a reputation for a cold-blooded willingness to take direct action against transgressors of the revolutionary code. In fact, according to Cuban sources who prefer anonymity, Che stepped forward to kill Eutimio only when it had become clear that nobody else wanted to take the initiative. Presumably, this included Fidel, who, having given the order for Eutimio's death without selecting someone to carry it out, simply moved away to shelter himself from the rain.

One of the *guajiros* wanted to place a wooden cross on Eutimio's grave, but Che forbade it on the grounds that it could compromise the family on whose land they were camped. Instead, a cross was carved into a nearby tree.

If Che was bothered by the execution, there seemed little sign of it by the next day. In his journal, commenting on the arrival of a pretty July 26 activist at the farm, he wrote: "[She is a] great admirer of the Movement who seems to me to want to fuck more than anything else."

III

On February 18, the summit meeting of the July 26 leaders was over and Fidel spent the morning writing a manifesto for his urban comrades to take with them and disseminate throughout the island. Fidel's "Appeal to the Cuban People" contained combative language close to Che's heart, and he applauded it in his diary as "really revolutionary."

The manifesto led off with a brief account of the war, delivered in rhetoric that was suitably overblown for the occasion. Not only had the rebels not been exterminated, he said; they had "bravely resisted" the modern weapons and vastly superior forces of the enemy in eighty days of fighting, and their ranks had been "steadily reinforced by the peasants of the Sierra Maestra."

Fidel ended with a six-point "guideline to the country," calling for stepped-up economic sabotage against the sugar harvest, public utilities, transportation, and communications systems; and for "the summary and immediate executions of the henchmen who torture and kill revolutionaries, the regime's politicians whose stubbornness and inflexibility have brought the country to this situation, and all those who stand in the way of the Movement's success." He also called for the organization of a "civic resistance" throughout Cuba; an increase in money-raising efforts "to cover the rising costs of the Movement," and a "general revolutionary strike" to bring the struggle against Batista to a climax.

Defending his decree to burn sugarcane, Fidel wrote: "To those who invoke the workers' livelihoods to combat this measure, we ask: Why don't they defend the workers when . . . they suck dry their salaries, when they swindle their retirement pensions, when they pay them in bonds and they kill them from hunger during eight months?* Why are we spilling our blood if not for the poor of Cuba? What does a little hunger today matter if we can win the bread and liberty of tomorrow?"

Fidel's manifesto was based on more than a little deception. Just as he had tricked Herbert Matthews into believing he had many more troops than he did, he now declared that his army's ranks were "steadily increasing" because of "peasant support." That support was largely fictitious at this point. Other than Crescencio's loyalty, which Che still had doubts about in those days, the rebels' peasant support was still very tenuous. The rebel band had nearly been annihilated through the betrayal of a peasant, Eutimio Guerra. Many more peasants had heeded the army's advice and fled the sierra after

---

*Most Cuban sugarcane workers were hired only for the four months of *zafra,* harvest season. They survived the *tiempo muerto,* or "dead time," by wandering the country as itinerant laborers or as pickers of other crops, such as coffee and tobacco.

the attack on La Plata. Although there were some notable exceptions, many of the peasants whom the rebels relied on, either as paid smugglers or as providers of food and other supplies, had their own self-interest at heart. Certainly Fidel's continuing practice of passing himself off as a *guardia* with unfamiliar peasants showed that he was well aware of the precarious nature of his hold on them.

Heading back into the mountains from the Díaz farm, Fidel confronted a peasant who had been detained. He told the man that he and his men were *guardias rurales* looking for information about the "revolutionaries." The frightened man denied all knowledge of the rebels, and when Fidel insisted, he promised that if he saw anyone suspicious he would report them to the nearest garrison. As Che rendered it in his diary, "Fidel [finally] told him we were revolutionaries and that we defended the poor man's cause, but since he had shown willingness to help the *guardia* he would be hanged. The reaction of the man, Pedro Ponce, was extraordinary, he arose sweating and trembling. 'No, how can it be, come to my house to eat chicken with rice.' After a philippic from Fidel complaining about the lack of help from the peasants we took him up on his offer of food."

This episode was left out of Che's published accounts of the war, no doubt because it showed that Fidel sometimes took his penchant for deception a little too far. Still, Fidel was probably wise to take such precautions. Some *guajiros* proved sympathetic without prodding, but to many more the rebels were a nettlesome presence that had brought death and destruction to the Sierra Maestra. The army was still the preponderant force. It controlled the towns and roads and it could win over individuals, as it had done with Eutimio Guerra, through a combination of material incentives and terror. Until Fidel became the dominant military force, he would have to use trickery, bribery, and selective terror to neutralize potential traitors or spies.

It was now common knowledge among the *guajiros* that whoever helped the rebels would be likely to suffer for it. Civilians were caught in a vicious trap between the army's brutality on the one hand and the rebels' reprisals against informers on the other. By executing Eutimio Guerra, Che had come to the fore of the rebel army's new policy of "swift revolutionary justice."

A new incident underscored that on February 18. Just as the members of the Directorate were preparing to leave the Díaz farm, a pistol shot rang out nearby and everyone grabbed weapons. But it was a false alarm. Che recorded, "Right away we heard a shout of 'It's nothing, it's nothing,' and El Gallego Morán appeared, wounded by a .45 bullet in one leg. . . . I gave him emergency treatment, dosing him with penicillin, and left the leg stretched out with a splint. . . . Fidel and Raúl accused him of doing it on purpose. I'm not sure of one thing or the other." Once again, firm evidence of Morán's true motivations eluded them, but the timing of his "accident," coming only a day after Eutimio's execution and just prior to the departure of their last visitors—permitting him to be evacuated from the field—made it look suspicious.

Morán knew that "desertion, insubordination, and defeatism" were capital offenses, and he was openly suspected of wanting to desert. Che was his likely nemesis, observing him constantly, and just days earlier had argued for his execution. Morán must have thought his days were numbered, and he was probably right.

Later on, Che wrote an epitaph for Morán, who defected to the Batista forces. "Morán's subsequent history, his treachery and his death at the hands of revolutionaries in Guantánamo, seems to establish that he [had] shot himself intentionally." This brief conclusion to his narrative about Morán resembles many of his portraits of men who took part in the war; conscious of his role as an architect of Cuba's new official history, Che gave each individual symbolic significance as a representative of values to be cherished or vilified in the "new" Cuba. Eutimio Guerra was a peasant whose soul had been corrupted, whose name had become synonymous with treachery, and whose errors should never be repeated. By contrast, the guajiro Julio Zenon Acosta became in his prose a revolutionary martyr, an exemplary archetype for workers and peasants to imitate. El Gallego Morán was a deserter, and then a traitor, and that he eventually paid the ultimate price for his treachery was a fate Che endorsed for enemies of the revolution. Its formal enemies were the army troops and the secret police, to be sure, but as great a danger was posed by the enemy *within*. Che had embraced revolution as the ultimate embodiment of history's lessons and the correct path to the future. Now, convinced he was right, he looked around with an inquisitor's eye for those who might endanger its survival.

IV

As they moved off into the hills, having decided to stay in the vicinity to await the promised arrival of Frank País's volunteers on March 5, Che's asthma returned, bringing on what he later called "for me personally the most bitter days of the war." Che would periodically succumb to debilitating bouts of his chronic condition, leading sturdier comrades to marvel at his willpower as he struggled to keep up on their marathon marches. But many would also have to help Che, at times to physically carry him, when his asthma left him incapacitated. It was ironic that a severe asthmatic such as Che should have ended up in humid, subtropical Cuba, a country with a disproportionately high per capita asthma rate, possibly the highest of any country in the Western Hemisphere.

It is hard to escape the sense that Che's deeply felt desire to rid himself of his "I" and to become part of a group derived from the inherent isolation imposed by his asthma. Happily for him, he had found that fraternity he sought. He no longer had to endure it alone. Indeed, in the Sierra Maestra, there were times when he was completely helpless, and his dependence on the support of his comrades became quite literally a matter of life or death. But no one suffered alone in the guerrilla community. One day, it was Che who needed help; it would be another man's turn the next day. Quite possibly, it was this sense of sharing, more than any other factor, that gave rise to his intense personal reverence for the ethos of guerrilla life.

On February 25—"a day of water and bombs," as he termed it—Che and his comrades awoke to the sound of mortar blasts and machine-gun and rifle fire that gradually drew nearer to them. Suspecting that the army was combing the area, they moved camp after dark, but they were in bad shape. Their food was practically finished and they were surviving on chocolate and condensed milk. Che had felt the stirrings of a "dangerous asthma attack" for several days and it now struck him with full force, worsening to the point where sleep was impossible. Then, after a peasant collaborator fed them pork, which made most of them ill, Che was weakened still further by two days of vomiting. Following a rain-sodden march, his wheezing became constant. They were in a zone where the peasants wanted nothing to do with them, they were out of food, and their latest guide had abruptly disappeared. Fidel ordered the men to withdraw into the hills, but by now Che was so weak that he could no longer walk. As the others waited, he injected one of the last two adrenaline ampoules he had with him, and it gave him just enough strength to get back on his feet.

Reaching the crest of a hill, they spotted a column of enemy troops climbing up to occupy the ridge, and they broke into a run to get there first. When a mortar shell exploded, the rebels realized the soldiers were on to them; as Che later acknowledged, he almost didn't make it. "I couldn't keep up the pace of the march, and I was constantly lagging behind." His faithful sidekick, Luis Crespo, helped Che by alternately carrying him and his backpack, and threatening to hit him with his rifle butt, calling him an "Argentine son of a whore."

They escaped the troops, but Che was drenched in another heavy rain and, barely able to breathe, had to be carried the final part of their trek. They found sanctuary in a place appropriately called Purgatorio, where Fidel reached a decision. He paid a peasant to make a quick trip to Manzanillo for asthma medicine and left Che with a *guajiro* escort. He and the others went on. The plan was that as soon as Che was better, he should return to the Díaz farm to meet the new rebel volunteers and then lead them into the sierra and rejoin Fidel.

The man delegated to remain behind with Che was called El Maestro (the Teacher), a recent volunteer who claimed falsely to be a Moncada veteran but whom they had accepted into their ranks anyway. As Che described him later, he was "a man of doubtful repute but great strength." After Fidel's departure, he and El Maestro concealed themselves in the forest to await the return of the peasant with the medicine. They spent two days of "hope and fear" there. Che's asthma rose and abated and kept him from sleeping. They could hear the machine guns and mortars of the army troops that were searching for them. The courier arrived with a bottle of asthma medicine, but it only partially relieved Che's symptoms. That night he still couldn't walk. On March 3, he made a supreme effort to get moving, but it took him five hours to climb a hill that normally would have taken one. He wrote that it had been a "day marked by a spiritual victory and a corporeal defeat."

It took Che a week to reach the Díaz farm. He was five days late. He had received little help from El Maestro and still less from local peasants. A normally friendly peasant farmer became so nervous upon seeing him that, Che wrote witheringly, "His fear is such that it looks like it might break *shitometers*."

It didn't matter much that Che was late, since the new troops hadn't arrived yet. But Epifanio Díaz had news for him, and it wasn't good. A few days earlier, Fidel's column had been surprised by enemy troops at a place called Los Altos de Merino and had split into two groups. There was no word of Fidel's fate.

V

In one of the many ironies that would mark the Cuban revolution, the most desperate days of the rebel band in the Sierra Maestra coincided with one of the most devastating blows to the Batista regime. In late February, the news of Fidel's defiant interview with Herbert Matthews had hit Cuba like a bombshell. "The interview of Matthews with Fidel has surpassed all expectations," Che noted euphorically. Batista's defense minister denounced Matthews's article as a hoax and challenged him to produce a photograph of himself and Fidel, but this would quickly turn out to be only one of the public relations blunders made by the government.

The first part of Matthew's three-part series was published in *The New York Times* on February 24. Batista lifted press censorship the following day, and the article was immediately translated and reprinted in newspapers, sparking comments and debate on the airwaves throughout Cuba. The interview proved that Fidel was still alive and well, despite the government's claims to the contrary, and was powerful in terms of international publicity. Matthews sympathized with Fidel's cause. "Fidel Castro, the rebel leader of Cuba's youth," he wrote, "is alive and fighting hard and successfully in the rugged, almost impenetrable vastness of the Sierra Maestra, at the southern tip of the island. . . . [T]housands of men and women are heart and soul with Fidel Castro and the new deal for which they think he stands. . . . Hundreds of highly respected citizens are helping Señor Castro . . . [and] a fierce Government counterterrorism [policy] has aroused the people even more against General Batista. . . . From the look of things, General Batista cannot possibly hope to suppress the Castro revolt."

Matthews portrayed an admirable and virile figure, and he had been taken in by Fidel's deceptions as to the real size of his force: "This was quite a man—a powerful six-footer, olive-skinned, full-faced, with a straggly beard. He was dressed in an olive-gray fatigue uniform and carried a rifle with a telescopic sight, of which he was very proud. It seems his men have something more than fifty of these and he said the soldiers feared them. 'We can pick them off at a thousand yards with these guns,' he said. . . . The personality of the man is overpowering. It was easy to see that his men adored him and also to see why he has caught the imagination of the youth of Cuba all over the island. Here was an educated, dedicated fanatic, a man of ideals, of courage and of remarkable qualities of leadership."

Matthews's description of Fidel's politics made him sound almost like a follower of FDR: "It is a revolutionary movement that calls itself socialistic. It is also nationalistic, which generally in Latin America means anti-Yankee. The program is vague and couched in generalities, but it amounts to a new deal for Cuba, radical, democratic and therefore anti-Communist. The real core of its strength is that it is fighting against the military dictatorship of President Batista. . . . [Castro] has strong ideas of liberty, democracy, social justice, the need to restore the Constitution, to hold elections."

The media battle, which continued to rage over the next few days, was followed with relish by the rebels on their radio. It reached a head on February 28 when *The New York Times* published a photo of Matthews with Fidel, dramatically crushing the regime's incautious claims that the journalist had dreamed up the entire encounter. Further boasts by the Oriente military commander that "the zone where the imaginary interview took place is physically impossible to enter" merely lent weight to Fidel's claims of being invincible and impossible to catch.

On the heels of Fidel's interview, however, came the bad news that Frank País and Armando Hart had been arrested. Then, on March 13, as Che awaited the new rebel volunteers at the Díaz farm, radio reports began broadcasting the first details of an attempt on Batista's life in Havana. Armed groups belonging to the Directorio Revolucionario led by José Antonio Echeverría, together with some of Carlos Prío's *auténticos,* had launched an audacious daylight assault on the presidential palace and temporarily seized the twenty-four-hour Radio Reloj station in Havana. But the assaults failed, and in the shoot-outs that ensued, at least forty people had died. The dead included Echeverría and more than thirty of his followers, five palace guards, and an American tourist who happened to be in the wrong place at the wrong time. Batista himself, who was, ironically, reading a book about Lincoln's assassination when the attack came, survived unscathed.

In his private notes Che routinely referred to the Directorio as *"el grupo terrorista."* Fidel and Echeverría may have signed a pact in Mexico City, but in reality the two leaders were bitter rivals. The failed assassination attempt left little doubt that Echeverría had hoped to deliver a fait accompli in Havana, displacing Fidel and his Movement in the struggle for power. With the death of its leader, the Directorio had suffered a heavy blow, but, as events would prove, it was not yet eliminated from the scene; it would continue to pose challenges to Fidel's hegemony right up to the end. For now, the July 26 cells in Havana came to the rescue, helping to tend the wounded and hide men in their own safe houses, and, opportunistically, taking possession of a Directorio weapons cache.

For Batista, the attempt on his life brought some short-term positive results. The conservative business community rallied around him, and he came out of the affair looking strong and in control, a caudillo who offered the last line of defense between traditional Cuban society and anarchy. In succeeding days the police carried out numerous arrests and gunned down several fugitive survivors of the assault. They murdered Pelayo Cuervo Navarro, a prominent former senator and the acting Ortodoxo Party leader, whom they suspected of having links to the assassination attempt.

In spite of a few mishaps, fifty recruits from Santiago and a handful of new weapons arrived at the Díaz farm on March 17. Che's biggest problem was to find sufficient food to feed so many men, and then to move them through the hills to rejoin Fidel at their previously arranged rendezvous, a spot not far from Los Altos de Espinosa. As they marched out, Che observed that the new troops from Santiago had all of the same flaws the men from the *Granma* had at the beginning—little sense of military discipline and less physical endurance. They complained about the food, and some could barely make it up the first hill they climbed. Once they had scaled it, Che let them rest for an entire day to recuperate from what for them, as he ironically put it in his diary, "had been the greatest achievement of the revolution so far."

Sending for some *guajiros* to come and help, Che began slowly moving the new men into the sierra, and after eight days of painful hiking they met up with Fidel and the others—who had, after all, survived the recent ambush. For the moment they were safe; Che had accomplished his mission, and the Rebel Army was no longer only eighteen men, but now seventy.

16

Lean Cows and Horsemeat

I

After a weeklong climb into the Sierra Maestra with his army of blistered, complaining greenhorns, Che rejoined Fidel at the remote hillside community of La Derecha. Once again Che was scolded, this time for not having sufficiently imposed his authority over Jorge Sotús, the leader of the new volunteers. The newcomer's arrogance had irritated Che and brought angry protests from many of his men en route, but Che had limited himself to giving Sotús a sermon about the need for discipline, evidently preferring to let Fidel deal with him.

As Fidel saw it, Che had not taken command, and his displeasure was reflected in a reorganization of the general staff. He handed out promotions and divided the troops into three expanded platoons led by Raúl, Juan Almeida, and Jorge Sotús. Che was confirmed in his humble capacity as general-staff doctor. In his diary, Che noted, "Raúl tried to argue that I be made political commissar as well, but Fidel was opposed."

This incident, which went unmentioned in Che's published accounts of the war, reveals not only Raúl's regard for Che but Fidel's political acumen. Batista was already accusing Fidel of being a Communist, a charge Fidel was vigorously denying, and to appoint an unabashed Marxist such as Che as his political commissar would have played into Batista's hands and alienated many of the July 26 rank and file, who were overwhelmingly anticommunist.

Fidel then held a conclave with his eight top men, including Che, to decide on their immediate war plans. Che argued that they should immediately engage the army, to give the new men their first test of fire, but Fidel and most of the others preferred to break them in gradually. "[It was] resolved," wrote Che in his diary, "that we would walk through the bush toward [Pico] Turquino, trying to avoid battle."

On March 25, a courier brought a message smuggled out of Frank País's jail cell in Santiago. According to his sources, País wrote, Crescencio Pérez had struck a deal with Major Joaquín Casillas to betray their location to the army at a time when all the rebels were in one place and could be wiped out. In his diary, Che seemed to give credence to País's information, for he already had reason to doubt Crescencio's loyalty. The *guajiro* leader had been away for some time, entrusted with the mission of recruiting peasant fighters, and he had recently sent a message claiming to have enlisted 140 armed men. En route from the Díaz farm, however, Che had stopped in to see him and found only four men with him—the remnants of the convalescing fighters—and no new recruits. He had also found Crescencio confused and upset over Fidel's decree to burn sugarcane. This disagreement underscored a gulf of incomprehension between the rebel leadership and its foremost peasant ally over revolutionary strategy at a crucial moment. The leaders could not be sure whether this had escalated to treason, but they could not take any chances. Fidel summoned his small group of most trusted men and told them they would mobilize.

Raúl Castro and Che, the two radicals in the Rebel Army.

The first trek of the revamped Rebel Army looked like an episode in a Keystone Cops movie. Climbing up the first large hill, one of their most exotic new volunteers—one of three teenage American runaways from the U.S. naval base at Guantánamo Bay—fainted from exhaustion. On the descent, two men from the advance squad became lost, promptly followed by the entire second platoon. Then Sotús's platoon and the rear guard unit got lost as well. "Fidel threw a terrible tantrum," Che wrote. "But in the end, we all reached the agreed-upon house."

After a day spent resting and devouring yucca and plaintains raided from a farmer's field, they made what Che called "another pathetic ascent" up Los Altos de Espinosa, the hill where they had been ambushed. They held a brief ceremony in honor of Jorge Zenon Acosta at the spot where he was buried. Che found the blanket he had lost caught in a bramble nearby, a reminder of his "speedy strategic retreat," and he vowed to himself that he would never again lose equipment in that manner. A new man—"a mulatto named Paulino"—was named to the general staff to help carry Che's heavy load of medicine, for the strain of carrying it had already begun to aggravate his asthma.

This was to be the pattern of the rebels' existence for the next few weeks. Fidel had intended to use their break from combat to build up reserves of food, arms, and ammunition, and to expand his peasant support network, but first they had to find enough food just to get them from one day to the next. As they moved around the sierra, he made deals with peasants to reserve a portion of their future harvests for him, but things remained extremely tight—and since there were now over eighty men, they could no longer arrive en masse at a peasant's home and expect to be fed. Meat had become a rarity. Their diet often consisted of plantains, yucca, and *malanga,* the starchy, purple-colored tuber that is a staple of Cuba's peasants. For Fidel, who enjoyed a good meal, this period of *vacas flacas,* or "lean cows," was particularly disagreeable and put him in a bad mood. On April 8, after Fidel had left camp on a short mission and missed the evening meal, Che saw his temper flare. "Fidel returned late, pissed off because we had eaten rice and because things hadn't worked out the way he had hoped."

The lack of food soon led them to carry out more desperate actions, including some that bordered on simple banditry. One night some men were sent to plunder a general store, while another group was dispatched to give a reputed *chivato* named Popa a scare and confiscate one of his cows. When the second squad returned, Che noted, "They struck a good blow and took a horse from Popa, but have come away with the impression that he isn't a *chivato* after all. He wasn't paid for the horse, but was promised he would be if he behaved himself." The horse went into the cooking pot, but at first the *guajiros,* outraged that a useful working animal had been killed for food, refused to eat it. Leftovers were then salted to be made into *tasajo,* a kind of jerky. Fidel delayed his plans to move camp while it was being prepared. As Che observed drily, "The consideration for the *tasajo* made Fidel change his mind."

Outside the Sierra Maestra, the political climate had become volatile. In the face of increasing violence, there were demands for new elections. A few politicians called for talks with the rebels, which suggested that they were being taken more seriously, but then Batista declared that such talks were unnecessary because there were no rebels. Nevertheless, he promoted Major Barrera Pérez, the "pacifier" of Santiago's November uprising, to colonel and gave him 1,500 soldiers to clean up the Sierra Maestra.

Fidel received a garbled message from Crescencio Pérez in which the *guajiro* leader admitted that he didn't have the number of men he had previously claimed—nor were his men armed—but that he had gathered some volunteers together, and he asked if Fidel could come and pick them up. He couldn't bring them himself, he said, because he had a "bad leg." Che's notes are cryptic: "Fidel answered that all offers that were serious were accepted, and that he should come later with the armed men." Fidel was being cagey, avoiding a situation that might be a trap in case the *guajiro* was attempting a double cross.

By necessity, the rebels began making a stronger effort to establish their relationship with the sierra's inhabitants. Che even began holding open-air medical *consultorias.* "It was monotonous," he recalled. "I had few medicines to offer and the clinical cases in the sierra were all more or less the same: prematurely aged and toothless women, children with distended bellies, parasitism, rickets, general vitamin deficiency." He blamed the condition of the peasants on overwork and a meager diet. "We began to feel in our flesh and blood the need for a definitive change in the life of the people," he wrote. "The idea of agrarian reform became clear, and oneness with the people ceased being theory and was converted into a fundamental part of our being." Perhaps without realizing it, Che had evolved into the revolutionary doctor he had once dreamed of becoming.

II

While the rebels adapted to life in the sierra, the Movement leaders in the llano were working hard to build them a lifeline in the "Resistencia Cívica" underground support network. Frank País had recruited Raúl Chibás, president of the Ortodoxo Party and brother of the late senator Eduardo Chibás, to head the Havana branch. The economist Felipe Pazos, the former president of the Cuban National Bank and father of Javier Pazos—who had helped arrange the Herbert Matthews interview—joined as well. In Santiago, the network was headed by a well-known physician, Dr. Angel Santos Buch.

Coordination efforts had been dealt a blow with the recent captures of key members of the National Directorate. Faustino Pérez and the journalist Carlos Franqui, the underground propagandist of the July 26 Movement, had been arrested on suspicion of having links to the assault on the palace. They joined Armando Hart in Havana's El Príncipe prison, while Frank País remained in custody in Santiago. Contact was maintained by means of smuggled letters. Virtually alone among the Movement leadership, Celia Sánchez remained at large. She had become Fidel's principal contact with the outside world. He constantly sent her letters, alternately cajoling and irate, asking for more funds and supplies for his growing army.

By April 15 the rebels were back in Arroyo del Infierno, where Che had killed his first man. A squad sent out to find food and collect intelligence from the locals learned that there was a *chivato* nearby. His name was Filiberto Mora. Fidel fretted. The news of the *chivato* had coincided with an overflight by a government plane, and he was anxious to move camp again. As they prepared to head out, one of the new squad leaders, Guillermo García, showed up with the alleged squealer. García had impersonated an army officer to trick him into coming. "The man, Filiberto, had been deceived," Che wrote in his journal, "but the minute he saw Fidel he realized what was happening and started to apologize." Terrified, he confessed all his past crimes, including his role in guiding troops to the ambush at Arroyo del Infierno. Even more alarming, it emerged that one of Mora's companions had gone off to inform the army of the rebels' current location. "The *chivato* was executed," Che wrote. "Ten minutes after giving him the shot in the head I declared him dead."

As they decamped, a runner arrived with a letter from Celia and $500. She wrote that more money would be coming soon and, in response to Fidel's request for more journalists, promised to find some and bring them into the sierra herself. A letter also came from Armando Hart, smuggled out of his jail cell. Che was displeased and suspicious with whatever Hart wrote. He remarked in his journal, "In it he shows himself to be positively anticommunist and he even insinuates a certain kind of deal with the Yankee embassy."*

---

*This particular letter has disappeared from the official record of Cuba's revolutionary history, as have any on-the-record admissions about the secret contacts made during the guerrilla campaign between the July 26 underground and the U.S. government, but such contacts evidently did take place. Previous accounts have speculated that the contacts began in the summer of 1957. Che's remark suggests that U.S. government officials were making overtures to some of Fidel's comrades as early as March.

By the end of April, more peasants had joined up, and the rebels' supply system had begun to work more effectively. Men and mules now arrived daily with foodstuffs. Word came that two gringos, Robert Taber and Wendell Hoffman from the American CBS network, would be arriving to meet with Fidel, accompanied by Celia Sánchez and Haydée Santamaría. Herbert Matthews's articles in *The New York Times* on Fidel and the rebellion in Cuba had sparked widespread interest in the American press. Taber was to file for CBS radio, and he and his cameraman also planned to make a television documentary about the rebels. Fidel moved his *estado mayor* above the main rebel camp onto the summit of a hill, both for increased protection and, as Che noted, "to impress the journalists."

The journalists were suitably impressed and began working right away, spending their first day interviewing the three American runaways, who had become famous in the United States. For his own interview, Fidel had another spectacular media coup in mind. He wanted to climb Cuba's highest mountain, Pico Turquino, and give a press conference at the summit. On April 28, almost everyone made the climb to the top—about 6,500 feet, according to Fidel's handy altimeter. There, at Cuba's highest point, Fidel gave his filmed interview to Taber and Hoffman, and everyone fired off weapons. Wheezing from asthma, Che was the last man up, but felt immensely pleased with himself for having made it.

After descending from Pico Turquino, Che observed with relief that his asthma had begun to clear, but, even so, Fidel assigned him to the rear guard to assist Victor Buehlman, one of the three American runaways, who complained that he had a stomachache and was unable to carry his backpack. Che helped him, grudgingly, and grumbled in his journal that he suspected the young American of suffering more from homesickness than anything else.

The ascent of Pico Turquino coincided with the influx of a type of volunteer the rebels had not seen before: youths romantically attracted to the cause. One boy who showed up said he had been trying to track them for two months. Che initially dismissed two other adolescents, from central Cuba's Camagüey province, as "a couple of adventurers," but the Rebel Army could not afford to be too choosy, and they were accepted. One of them, Roberto Rodríguez, eventually became one of the "most likable and best-loved figures of our revolutionary war, 'Vaquerito' [Little Cowboy]," Che noted later. Vaquerito's exploits would earn him a hallowed place in Cuba's pantheon of revolutionary heroes. "Vaquerito did not have a political idea in his head, nor did he seem to be anything other than a happy, healthy boy, who saw all of this as a marvelous adventure," Che wrote. "He came barefoot and Celia lent him an extra pair of shoes, which were made of leather and were the type worn in Mexico; this was the only pair that fit him, since his feet were so small. With the new shoes and a great palm leaf hat, Vaquerito looked like a Mexican cowboy, or vaquero, which is how he got his name."

Another new volunteer was a *guajiro* named Julio Guerrero, one of the late Eutimio Guerra's neighbors in the valley of El Mulato. The army had suspected him of having links to the rebels and his home had been burned down. Guerrero said that he had been offered a bounty to kill Fidel, but a much more modest one than the reputed $10,000 that Eutimio had been promised: a mere $300 and a pregnant cow.

Just as the rebels could not afford to turn away prospective fighters whose political mettle was unproved, neither could they be overly selective about their civilian allies. When a July 26 man brought news that weapons rescued from the Directorio's failed assault on the palace had been smuggled to Santiago, Fidel sent him back to retrieve some with a local guide who, as Che noted in his journal, knew the sierra well "thanks to his profession of marijuana distributor."

To Che's surprise, El Gallego Morán reappeared. Still limping from his wounded leg, Morán was brimming over with excitement about a "super-secret plan" he wished to propose. Che was chagrined to learn that Fidel had agreed to send El Gallego to Mexico to bring back the July 26 Movement members who had been left there and to go to the United States to raise funds. "Everything I said to him about how dangerous it was to send a man like El Gallego, a confessed deserter, with low morals, a charlatan, an intriguer and liar to the maximum . . . was useless," Che wrote. "He argues that it is better to send El Gallego to do something, and not let him go to the U.S. feeling resentful."

Word arrived that another American reporter was on his way to meet Fidel. Taber's cameraman had already left, with the film smuggled out separately, but Taber was staying on to do a story for *Life* magazine. When he heard about the new reporter, Taber asked Fidel to stall him until he had finished, so he could be sure of having an exclusive. Fidel agreed and ordered the other reporter detained en route for several days.

Their *marijuanero* guide returned, bringing supplies, money, and the news that a rendezvous point for the arrival of the new weapons had been arranged in an area several days' march northeast of Pico Turquino. As they prepared to move out, Che carried the message from Fidel to where most of the rebels were camped, but it was after dark and he became lost. He spent the next three days on his own, alternately hiding and wandering around in the bush until he found his way back to his comrades. When he finally reached the rearguard camp, where the new journalist, a Hungarian-

American freelancer named Andrew St. George, was still being detained, he was welcomed with spontaneous applause. "The reception from everyone was affectionate," he wrote. But he was disturbed to learn that a "people's trial" had been held in the camp. "They told me that they had liquidated a *chivato* named Napoles and freed two others who weren't so guilty. The men are doing whatever they please."

The two groups of rebels were reunited and went together to where the weapons were to be delivered, but no one came to the rendezvous, and they withdrew uncertainly back into the hills, where they met up with Crescencio Pérez. He had finally arrived with his long-promised band of peasant volunteers, twenty-four poorly armed men. They had stumbled onto an army patrol, attacked it, and escaped, but a young rebel had been taken prisoner, shot, and bayoneted to death, his body dumped in the road. Most of the rebels, including Che, demanded that revenge be exacted by killing an army corporal they had just taken prisoner, but Fidel insisted on releasing him unharmed. (Any lingering doubts over Crescencio's loyalties either had been forgotten or were ironed out in secrecy, for Che never mentioned them again in his diary; nor has the episode in which he was under suspicion ever been referred to in other published accounts of the war.)

As the rebels awaited word about the new time and place for the weapons drop, the radio carried news that the trial in Santiago of a large number of July 26 Movement members, including survivors from the *Granma,* was over. As expected, the accused were sentenced to prison terms, but over the dissenting votes of the prosecutor and the tribunal president, Manuel Urrutia, who had bravely declared that because of the "abnormal situation" in the country, the defendants were within their constitutional rights to take up arms. An added bonus was the release of Frank País from custody, indicating that the authorities were still unaware of his true status in the rebel movement. These positive developments were followed by a quick visit of two July 26 men, who came to arrange the new weapons drop and revealed that they now had even more arms to deliver—"a total of about fifty irons," Che noted gleefully.

Fidel was not cheered up by the good news. He was in a foul mood and was pointedly ignoring Andrew St. George, who had already spent two weeks with the rebels and was anxious to complete his assignment. (Bob Taber had left, taking with him two of the three American boys, who had decided to return to their homes.) St. George was planning a radio interview and had already submitted a questionnaire that Che had translated into Spanish. Since no one in the camp spoke English, and both he and St. George spoke French, Che had become his escort and interpreter, but Che was finding his role as intermediary with Fidel increasingly embarrassing. "His behavior is really rude," Che wrote in his journal. "During the photo session he didn't move from his hammock, where he lay reading *Bohemia*"—a popular illustrated weekly magazine—"with an air of offended majesty, and finally he threw out all the members of the general staff." Fidel kept postponing the interview with St. George for reasons that were hard to support —for instance, that the stream they were camped next to made too much noise. He finally did do the interview, but the next day it was reported on the radio that Taber's film, *The Story of Cuba's Jungle Fighters,* was to be broadcast throughout the United States, as was his radio interview with Fidel. Andrew St. George left the camp without saying good-bye.

The rebels faced a mass defection that began when one of the youngest recruits, a boy of fifteen, asked permission to leave on health grounds. Another man asked to go with him; then a sixteen-year-old joined in, and finally another man, who claimed "weakness." Fidel ordered the older men in the group detained but let the youths go. Che disapproved, noting that if the boys were captured they might reveal where the weapons were to be delivered. But the weapons arrived the next day and were collected: three machine-gun tripods, three Madsen machine guns, nine M-1 carbines, ten Johnson repeaters, and 6,000 bullets. Che was ecstatic to learn that one of the Madsens would go to the *estado mayor,* and that he was to be in charge of it. "In this way," he wrote later, "I made my debut as a full-time combatant, for until then I had been a part-time combatant and my main responsibility had been as the troop's doctor. I had entered a new stage."

III

With their new weapons, the rebels were ready to attack. The "new" troops were no longer new—after two months of steady hiking and foraging in the Sierra Maestra, they were tougher and leaner—but they were still not combat-tested, and it was time for their baptism of fire. The area they were in, Pino del Agua, was a timber extraction zone, dotted with sawmills and crisscrossed by roads frequently patrolled by the army. Che was eager to ambush some army troop trucks, but Fidel claimed he had a better plan: to attack the coastal army garrison at El Uvero. It was farther to the east than they had ever operated and, with sixty soldiers, would be the biggest target they had yet attacked; success would have a tremendous moral and political impact.

Fidel was able to count on the help of a childhood friend, Enrique López, who worked near El Uvero as the manager of a sawmill owned by the Lebanese-Cuban Babún brothers. The Babúns themselves—cement manufacturers, shipbuilders, and landowners with extensive lumber

interests in Oriente—had already secretly lent their cooperation to the
rebels, helping to transport the latest cache of weapons on one of their
company's boats from Santiago, and then allowing their land to be used
as the weapons drop. Enrique López had begun buying food and other
supplies for the rebels, disguised within the purchases he made for his own
employees.

As they began to mobilize, Fidel made some adjustments in the troops.
Che was assigned a new squad of four youths to help carry and operate his
Madsen machine gun. They were two brothers, Pepe and Pestan Beatón, a
young man named Oñate—soon changed to "Cantinflas," after the Mexican comic actor—and fifteen-year-old Joel Iglesias. Like El Vaquerito, Joel
would go on to become one of Che's devoted companions.*

On the eve of battle, Fidel gave anyone who wanted to go a final opportunity to do so. Nine men went, leaving 127 to move out, heading deeper
into the hills. They were camped in the mountains when they heard a star-
tling report on the radio: an armed rebel expeditionary force had landed on
the northern Oriente coast at Mayarí and run into an army patrol. Of the
twenty-seven men on board, five had, reportedly, been captured. The
Fidelistas didn't know it yet, but this was the *Corynthia,* a boat that had left
Miami days before under the command of a U.S. army veteran named
Calixto Sánchez who was also one of Carlos Prío's *auténticos.* The expedition, made up of *auténticos* and some Directorio men, was armed and paid
for by Prío, who was apparently eager to field a force of his own to compete
with Fidel. (The initial reports were misleading: twenty-three of the
Corynthia's men, including Sánchez, were captured, and then executed after
a few days. A few months later, one of the three survivors reached the sierra
and joined Fidel's forces.)

Meanwhile, word came from Enrique López, the sawmill manager,
that three *guardias* in civilian clothes were sniffing around, and Fidel sent
some men to capture them. One of the *guardias* had fled by the time Fidel's
men arrived, but two of them—a black man and a white man—were
brought back to the camp, where they confessed to being spies. "They inspired not pity, but repugnance for their cowardice," Che wrote. They were
both shot as the last order of business before the rebels set off for combat.
"The pit was dug for the two *chivato* guards and the marching orders were
given," Che noted in his diary. "The rear guard executed them."

*After the war, the Beatón brothers became outlaws, murdering a revolutionary commander
and taking up arms against the revolution before they were caught and executed. Joel Iglesias
became an army commander and leader of the Juventud Rebelde (Rebel Youth) organization. Cantinflas remained in the army with the rank of lieutenant.

They marched all night to reach El Uvero. As they neared the sawmill, they were met by another friendly employee of the Babún Company, Gilberto Cardero, who had been sent ahead to warn the sawmill administrator to evacuate his wife and children. Cardero reported that the family didn't want to do anything that would attract suspicion, and they had refused to leave. Fidel said they would take precautions to avoid harming the civilians, but the attack would take place anyway, at dawn.

The rebels took their positions, but in the early morning light they realized that most of them couldn't see the garrison clearly. Che had a clear view, although he was more than a quarter of a mile from the target. It was too late for changes, however, and the attack began with a shot from Fidel. "The machine guns began to rattle," Che wrote. "The garrison returned fire with a great deal of effectiveness, as I realized later. Almeida's people advanced in the open impelled by his fearless example. I could see Camilo advancing with his cap adorned with the July 26 armband. I advanced along the left with two helpers carrying clips and Beatón with the short machine gun."

Che's group was joined by several more men. They were within 200 feet of the enemy position now and continued to advance behind tree cover. Reaching open ground, they began to crawl, and a man at Che's side, Mario Leal, was shot. After giving Leal mouth-to-mouth resuscitation, Che covered his wound with the only bandage he could find, a piece of paper, and left him in the care of young Joel. He went back to his Madsen, firing at the garrison. Moments later another man, Manuel Acuña, fell wounded, hit in the right hand and arm. Then, just as the rebels were mustering their courage for a frontal assault, the garrison surrendered.

The Fidelistas had their victory, but it came at a high cost. They had lost six men, among them one of their original *guajiro* guides, Eligio Mendoza. He had flung himself into battle with abandon, claiming he had a saint who protected him, but within minutes he had been shot. Also dead was Julito Díaz, a veteran from the *Granma,* hit in the head at Fidel's side soon after the fighting began. Mario Leal, shot in the head, and another man, Silleros, with a lung wound, were in critical condition. Seven others were wounded as well, including Juan Almeida, who had been hit in the right shoulder and leg. But they had killed fourteen soldiers, wounded nineteen more, and taken fourteen prisoners; only six soldiers had escaped. Remarkably, given the intense gunfire, none of the civilians in the area, including the administrator's family, had been harmed.

Che was overwhelmed by the needs of the wounded—soldiers as well as rebels. "My knowledge of medicine had never been very extensive," he wrote. "The number of wounded was enormous and my vocation at the

moment was not centered on health care." He asked the garrison doctor for
help, but despite his advanced age the man claimed he had little experience.
"Once more I had to change from soldier to doctor, which in fact involved
little more than washing my hands," Che wrote. He saw to as many men as
he could. "My first patient was Comrade Silleros. . . . His condition was
critical, and I was able only to give him a sedative and bind his chest tightly
so he could breathe more easily. We tried to save him in the only way possible at that time. We took the fourteen prisoners with us and left our two
[most] wounded men, Leal and Silleros, with the enemy, having received
the doctor's word of honor that they would be cared for. When I told this
to Silleros, mouthing the usual words of comfort, he answered me with a
sad smile that said more than any words could have, expressing his conviction that it was all over for him." (In fact, the Cuban army treated the two
wounded rebels with decency, but Silleros died before he reached a hospital. Mario Leal miraculously survived his head wound and spent the rest of
the war in the Isle of Pines prison.)

Using the Babúns' trucks, the rebels withdrew from El Uvero, carrying their dead and the men whose wounds were not critical and as much
equipment as they could plunder from the garrison. Che collected medical
supplies and was the last to leave. That evening he treated the wounded and
was present for the burial of his six dead comrades at a bend in the road.
Knowing that the army would soon be coming after them, it was agreed
that Che would stay behind with the wounded men while the main column
made its escape. Fidel's friend Enrique López would be Che's liaison, helping him with transportation and a hiding place for seven wounded men, a
guide, and Che's two faithful assistants, Joel and Cantinflas. Juan Vitalio
"Vilo" Acuña, another of the sierra war veterans whose fate would forever
be linked to Che's own, also stayed behind to help his wounded uncle,
Manuel Acuña.

After the war, Che credited the bloody action at El Uvero with having been a turning point for the rebel army. "If one considers that we had
about 80 men and they had 53, for a total of 133 men, of whom 38—that is
to say more than a quarter—were put out of action in a little over two and
a half hours of fighting, one can see what kind of battle it was. It was an
assault by men who had advanced bare-chested against an enemy protected
by very poor defenses. Great courage was shown on both sides. For us this
was the victory that marked our coming-of-age. From this battle on, our
morale grew tremendously; our decisiveness and our hopes for triumph
increased also."

El Uvero had indeed caught the Batista regime off guard. During the
long period of inactivity by Fidel's rebels, the government had become over-

confident. Colonel Barrera Pérez had stayed in the sierra only a short while after taking over antiguerrilla operations in March. He had launched a "psyops" campaign to win over the sierra peasants with free food and medical services and then returned to Havana. Now he was now ordered back into the field. He set up a new command center at the Estrada Palma sugar mill, just north of the sierra foothills, and his hearts-and-minds campaign was shelved in favor of a tough new antiguerrilla strategy. His boss, the Oriente commander Díaz Tamayo, was replaced by a new officer, Pedro Rodríguez Ávila, with orders from Batista's armed forces chief of staff, General Francisco Tabernilla, to crush the rebels by any means necessary. The new policy called for the forced evacuation of civilians from rebel areas, to create free-fire zones where the air force could conduct a massive aerial bombardment campaign. The action at El Uvero had showed the army that it couldn't defend small garrisons in remote areas, so they were abandoned, leaving the territory open to the rebels.

After Fidel's departure, Che confronted the nightmarish prospect of moving his wounded charges to safety in the face of an imminent army incursion. He had the added burden of the weapons captured from the garrison, too many for his fighters to carry. He was dependent on Enrique López for his escape; when López didn't show up with a promised truck, Che had no choice but to conceal most of the arms temporarily and move out on foot. Most of the men were able to walk, although a man who had been shot in the lungs and another man with infected wounds were carried on improvised stretchers.

Over the coming days, as they moved from one farm to another in search of food, rest, and sanctuary, Che had to make all the major decisions. Juan Almeida was theoretically Che's senior in the field, but he was in no shape to take charge. One of Che's biggest headaches was finding men to carry the wounded. On the third day out, they came across some unarmed soldiers wandering through the bush—the prisoners from El Uvero whom Fidel had set free. After letting them go on their way, Che gleefully congratulated himself in his diary for giving the soldiers the false impression that the rebels "controlled" the countryside. But he also worried that they would soon relay word of his group's presence in the area.

Help came from what seemed to Che an unlikely source. David Gómez, the *mayoral* on the Peladero estate, which belonged to a lawyer in Havana, offered his services. Che's first impression of Gómez was not good, but it was tempered by his group's desperate situation. "D. is an individual of the old *auténtico* type, Catholic and racist, with a servile loyalty toward the *patron* who only believes in electoral ends and in saving for his master all his ill-gotten lands in this region," he wrote. "I also suspect him of having participated in the dispossession of the peasants. But, leaving that aside, he is a good informant and he is ready to help."

In fact, Gómez was already helping. The cows they had been eating were his bosses' property, killed with his connivance. And Gómez offered to do more. As an initial test, Che gave Gómez a list of purchases to make in Santiago and, craving information from the outside world, included a special request for the latest editions of *Bohemia*. Che's relationship with the overseer showed that he was becoming more like his *jefe*. Fidel had always understood that one of the keys to success in a struggle for power was to make short-term, tactical alliances, even with one's ideological foes. Now, as the leader of a group of hunted men in alien territory, Che found he had needs that only Gómez could satisfy, and he was able to swallow his distaste and be pragmatic.

Indeed, his time in Cuba had already shown Che that the revolution was not going to be won by a fraternity of high-minded souls. Among the rebel ranks were any number of scoundrels: former rustlers, fugitive murderers, juvenile delinquents. The corrupt Carlos Prío himself had helped pay for the *Granma,* and the battle of El Uvero had been a success in large measure thanks to the aid of the wealthy and duplicitous Babún brothers, who, though friends of Batista, probably hoped to protect their interests in Oriente by helping the rebels.

When David Gómez arrived back from Santiago with the promised supplies, a more trusting Che sent him on a new mission, this time with messages for the National Directorate. By now, three weeks after the battle at El Uvero, most of the men had recovered from their wounds, and all of them could walk. Thirteen new volunteers had shown up, although only one had a weapon—a .22-caliber automatic pistol. On June 21, Che took stock of his growing force. "The army ascends to: 5 recovered wounded, 5 healthies who accompany the wounded, 10 men from Bayamo, 2 more just joined up and 4 men of the area, total 26 but deficient in armaments."

A few days later, after beginning a slow march into the mountains, Che observed that his army now consisted of "36 terrible soldiers." The next day, he gave all those who wanted to leave their chance. Three took up his offer, including one who had joined the previous day. In the succeeding days, more men joined and others left, either deserting or sent packing by Che. But as "terrible" as most of them were, they were the core of a new guerrilla force growing spontaneously under his direction. By the end of June, Che's small army was functioning autonomously, with its own system of couriers, informants, suppliers, and scouts.

July 1 was a bad day for Che personally—he awoke with asthma and spent the day lying in his hammock—but an interesting one in terms of news, for the radio reported rebel actions taking place all over Cuba. "In Camagüey they are patrolling in the streets," Che noted in his diary. "In Guantánamo, some tobacco deposits were burned, and they tried burning the sugar warehouses of a strong American company. In Santiago itself they killed two soldiers and wounded a corporal. Our casualties were 4 men, among them, a brother of Frank País called Josué."

July 2 marked the seven-month anniversary of the *Granma*'s landing. Che spent it leading his weary men up a large mountain. During the day two men deserted, and by the time they pitched camp that evening, three more asked permission to leave. To forestall any more desertions, Che gave anyone who wanted to leave another chance to do so. Two men accepted the offer, but by that afternoon three new men had arrived, each with a weapon. Two were former army sergeants from Havana, and Che didn't trust them. "According to them they are instructors," he wrote in his diary that night, "but to me they're a couple of shit eaters who are trying to accommodate themselves." Despite his suspicions, he let them stay.

The next addition to Che's band was none other than Fidel's friend at the Babún Company, Enrique López, who decided to join the armed struggle himself. Another man showed up, telling Che he had a "fantastic plan" to attack a guard post where he said there were forty soldiers without a commanding officer. He also asked for two men to go and "skin a *chivato*." Che turned him down: "I told him to stop fucking around . . . to kill the *chivato* with his own people and then send them here."

In order to meet up with Fidel, who had returned to their old haunts around Palma Mocha and El Infierno, Che was moving his force westward across the sierra toward Pico Turquino. His runners brought word of a large troop presence in the direction they were heading and of heavy combat near the army base at Estrada Palma, and a report that Raúl Castro had been wounded—a rumor that later proved unfounded—but Che decided to forge on, taking a tougher route over the mountains to avoid the enemy.

On July 12, Che's guide, Sinecio Torres, and another rebel, René Cuervo, deserted with their weapons. After a fruitless chase, Che learned new details about the two men. Both, it was now revealed, were *bandoleros*, fugitive outlaws, and they had probably gone off to raid the marijuana plantation owned by two other newcomers to his force, Israel Pardo and Teodoro Bandera. Suspecting that the two *marijuaneros* would desert next to defend their interests, Che decided to get rid of them by ordering them to go in pursuit of the deserters; he didn't expect them back. The next day brought a new problem, when Che learned of a mass-desertion plot being hatched among a small group of men. Their alleged plan was to escape with their weapons, rob and kill a *chivato* they knew, then form an outlaw gang to carry

out more assaults and robberies. Che spoke with several of the men implicated in the plot, each of whom denied his role and blamed a man called El
Mexicano. When El Mexicano realized that his plan had been discovered,
he came voluntarily before Che to profess his innocence. Che found his
explanations wanting, but wrote: "We let it pass as if it were the truth so as
to avoid more complications."*

During their trek, Che also made his debut as a dentist. He used what
he called "psychological anesthesia," which consisted of cursing at his patients if they complained too much. His treatment succeeded with Israel
Pardo, but not Joel Iglesias. Che wrote later that a stick of dynamite would
have been needed to extract Joel's rotten molar, which remained in his
mouth, broken in several places, until the end of the war. Although Che
suffered from a toothache himself, he wisely left his own teeth alone.

By July 16, they were back in familiar terrain on the western flanks of
Pico Turquino and reached Fidel's camp the next day. Che saw that the rebel
army had matured in the past month and a half. There were now some 200
well-disciplined and confident men. And there were new weapons. Most
important of all, they now possessed their own "liberated territory."

The reunion was dampened for Che when he learned that Fidel had
just signed a pact with two representatives of the bourgeois political
opposition—Raúl Chibás and Felipe Pazos—both of whom were staying
in Fidel's camp at that moment. Their pact, "The Manifesto of the Sierra
Maestra," was dated July 12 and had already been sent out for publication
in *Bohemia*. The "Sierra Pact" was Fidel's cleverly timed repudiation of
Batista's schemes to stay in power. A reform bill had been passed that provided for presidential elections on June 1, 1958. Despite Batista's avowal
not to stand as a candidate himself, widespread skepticism persisted as to
his true intentions; most observers suspected him of intending to manipulate the elections on his behalf or that of a handpicked successor. The election initiative was repudiated by Carlos Prío's Auténtico Party and
Chibás's Ortodoxo Party, but breakaway factions from both formed a
coalition with a grouping of smaller parties and announced their intention to run.

---

*Israel Pardo and Teodoro Bandera returned without finding René Cuervo or Sinecio Torres,
but Cuervo was later caught and executed by a revolutionary firing squad. Sinecio Torres's
fate is unknown. Bandera later died in battle. Pardo survived and remained in the revolutionary army after the war, attaining the rank of captain. El Mexicano rose to a captain's rank
in the Rebel Army, but when one of the men who had informed on him was killed during a
battle, there was a suspicion that El Mexicano may have murdered him. As of 1962, according to Che, he was living in Miami, "a traitor to the Revolution."

By allying himself with Chibás and Pazos, two respected Ortodoxos, Fidel hoped to obtain a moral high ground and secure a broader base of support among Cuban moderates with nowhere else to turn. Writing in his diary on July 17, Che was circumspect, but it clearly didn't please him to find Pazos and Chibás wielding influence over Fidel. "Fidel was telling me projects and realities; a text has already been sent out that calls for Batista's immediate resignation, rejects the Military Junta, and proposes a member of the civic institutions as a candidate for the transition, which should last no more than one year, and elections [should be] called within that time. It also includes a miminal program in which the foundations of the Agrarian Reform are outlined." Then he added, "Fidel didn't say so but it seems to me that Pazos and Chibás have polished his declarations a great deal." The truth, of course, was more complex. Fidel had *sought* the support of Chibás and Pazos, and if he signed a manifesto less radical than his true aspirations, it could only help him in the short term. This pact, like so many others Fidel was to sign in his life, was merely one more tactical alliance—to be broken at the first opportunity.

If he thought any more about the Sierra Pact at the time, Che didn't make note of it in his diary. His chief concern was a new command, which Fidel had bestowed upon him on July 17, the day Che arrived in camp. He had been promoted to captain and he was to head a group of seventy-five men. In addition to the men he had arrived with, he was to take command of the platoons led by comrades from the *Granma,* Ramiro Valdés and Ciro Redondo; and another led by Lalo Sardiñas, a sierra merchant who had recently joined up after killing a stranger at his house. Lalo Sardiñas was also to be his deputy. They were to hunt down Captain Angel Sánchez Mosquera and his men.

Che's new position represented Fidel's seal of approval. Che had fought hard to obtain recognition for his abilities, and the process had matured him. He had been given a difficult mission to accomplish on his own—bringing the wounded men to safety—and he had succeeded. He had fulfilled his doctor's duties by returning the men to health while managing to avoid battle and the risk of new casualties, had added to the strength of the Rebel Army by building up a new column, and had made invaluable contacts among the civilian population at the same time. He had shown himself to be a strict taskmaster, harsh with slackers and cheats, and to be scrupulously honest himself. Above all, Che had shown he could be a leader of men.

Che went to work immediately, leaving the next morning to take up a position on a hill between two rivers, the Palma Mocha and La Plata. It happened to be the same place where the executed *chivato* Filiberto Mora was buried, and he named it after him: "the summit of Filiberto." The next three days were spent preparing ambushes and sending scouts out to look for soldiers. On the morning of July 22, a rebel accidentally fired his gun and was brought before Fidel, who was in a newly hardened, unforgiving mood, and he summarily ordered the man to be shot. "Lalo, Crescencio, and I had to intercede with him to reduce the sanction," wrote Che, "because the unfortunate didn't deserve a punishment as drastic as that."

Later that morning, all the rebel officers signed a letter being sent to Frank País, expressing their condolences for the recent death of his brother. Without any advance notice, Fidel chose that moment to give Che another promotion. When his turn came to sign the letter, Fidel told him to put down *comandante* as his rank. "Thus, in a most informal manner, almost in passing, I was promoted to commander of the second column of the guerrilla army, which would later become known as Column No. 4," Che wrote.* "My insignia, a small star, was given to me by Celia. The award was accompanied by a gift: one of the wristwatches ordered from Manzanillo." It was a great honor. *Comandante* was the highest rank in the Rebel Army. The only other *comandante* was Fidel.

"There is a bit of vanity hiding somewhere within every one of us," Che wrote afterward. "It made me feel like the proudest man on earth that day." From then on, to all but his closest friends, he was Comandante Che Guevara.

---

*Che's command was called the "Fourth Column" in order to confuse the enemy as to the Rebel Army's real troop strength. Cuban historians often cite Che's promotion as evidence of the high regard Fidel felt for him, pointing out that he had been favored over Fidel's brother, without offering any explanation as to why Raúl hadn't earned the honor. But Che's laconic diary entry for that fateful day may hold part of the answer. "There were several promotions. I [now] had the rank of *comandante*. The *guajiro* Luis [Crespo] was given the rank of lieutenant, Ciro [Redondo] captain, and Raúl Castro, who had been stripped of rank for an insubordination of his entire platoon, was named lieutenant." Exactly *what* happened between Raúl and his men was left out of Che's later public writings and all official histories of the Cuban revolution. Today, despite an increasing openness about some aspects of revolutionary history, Cuba's historians would probably still have a hard time dredging up such details.

17

Enemies of All Kinds

I

Che's orders were to pursue Sánchez Mosquera, but he soon learned that his prey had already left the mountains. As he pondered his options, he set about imposing control over his unruly and heterogeneous fighters. He instituted a hierarchy. Novices were *descamisados*—shirtless ones, named after Juan Perón's working-class supporters—who did grunt work before earning recognition as *combatientes*. Many of the men in his troop were *descamisados*. Almost immediately, he was plagued by desertions, and he responded with severity. When he sent two fighters to track down a fugitive, he gave them orders to kill him if they found him. His wariness about newcomers increased when he received a message from his overseer ally David Gómez warning of the army's plans to send *chivato* assassins to infiltrate the guerrillas.

Che decided to strike at the army on the other side of Pico Turquino to distract attention from Fidel's group. As his troops started moving in that direction, one of the men Che had sent after the deserter returned on his own, claiming that his companion had also tried to desert and that he had killed him and left his body unburied. "I gathered the troop together on the hill facing the spot where this grim event had taken place," Che wrote later. "I explained to our guerrillas what they were going to see and what it meant. I explained once again why desertion was punishable by death and why anyone who betrayed the revolution must be condemned. We passed silently, in single file, before the body of the man who had tried to abandon his post. Many of the men had never seen death before and were perhaps moved more by personal feelings for the dead man and by political weakness natural at that period than by any disloyalty to the revolution. These were difficult times, and we used this man as an example."

In his diary at the time, however, Che expressed misgivings. "I am not
very convinced of the legality of the death," he wrote, "although I used it as
an example. . . . The body was on its stomach, showing at a glance that it
had a bullet hole in the left lung and had its hands together and the fingers
folded as if they were tied."

Che had decided to hit the army garrison of Bueycito, a day's march
away. The attack took place on the night of July 31, but did not go according to plan. When some of his units didn't show up on time, Che began the
attack on his own, walking straight up to the barracks and coming face-to-
face with the sentry. Che aimed his Thompson submachine gun and shouted
"Halt!" but the sentry moved. Che pulled the trigger, aiming at the soldier's
chest. Nothing happened. A young rebel who was with Che then tried to
shoot the sentry, but his rifle didn't fire, either. At that point, Che's survival
instincts took over, and he ran away under a hail of bullets. By the time he
repaired his tommy gun, the garrison had surrendered. Ramiro Valdés's men
had broken in from the rear and taken the twelve soldiers inside prisoner.
Six soldiers were wounded, two fatally, and the rebels had lost one man.
After looting the garrison, they set it on fire and left Bueycito in trucks, taking as prisoners the sergeant in charge of the post and a *chivato* named Orán.

They entered the village of Las Minas to cheers, and Che indulged in
some street theater with an Arab merchant. "A Moor *who is one of ours*
improvised a speech asking that we set free the two prisoners. I explained
to him that we had taken them to prevent [the army from] taking reprisals
against the people but if that was the will of the inhabitants, I had nothing
more to say." After freeing the prisoners, the rebels went on their way, stopping only to bury their dead man in the local cemetery.

II

Antigovernment actions in Santiago had been stepped up to commemorate
July 26, and police repression had also escalated. Arrests and killings of rebel
suspects became commonplace; tortured bodies were found hanging from
trees or dumped at roadsides. Frank País, the Movement coordinator for
Oriente, had been in hiding in Santiago since his release from jail, moving
from one safe house to the other, but in recent letters to Fidel he had expressed doubts about how much longer he could avoid detection. On July
30, his luck ran out. He and a companion were executed on the street, in
broad daylight. País was twenty-three.

Frank País's killing caused a huge outcry, with noisy antigovernment
demonstrations. Strikes spread across the entire island, and Batista reim-
posed a state of siege and media censorship. Unfortunately for him, the

events in Santiago coincided with a visit there by the new American ambassador, Earl Smith, who was on a get-acquainted tour.

By mid-1957, few officials in the State Department retained any illusions about Batista. His increasingly repressive and corrupt regime was becoming an embarrassment. In general, U.S. policy toward Cuba was aimed at protecting the sizable American economic interests there, and unrest was not good for business. The prevailing opinion in Washington was that the best method of defusing the violence would be to encourage Batista to "democratize" Cuba by holding elections—after which, it was hoped, one of the traditional parties would assume office. But Fidel's persistence had thrown a wild card into the equation, and the State Department, CIA, and Department of Defense were divided over how best to deal with him. As a consequence, throughout 1957 and into 1958, various U.S. government agencies pursued their own, not always compatible, Cuban agendas.

Earl Smith had come away with the definite impression that the State Department wanted to see Batista out, and that it was actively, if covertly, supporting Castro's bid for power. Roy Rubottom, the assistant secretary for Latin American affairs, and William Wieland, the newly appointed head of the Caribbean desk, both opposed Batista, as did the CIA's Cuban specialist, J. C. King. When Smith got to Cuba, he found the CIA men there to be anti-Batista as well. The officers in the American military mission, on the other hand, continued to enjoy a close relationship with their Cuban counterparts. The anticommunist police bureau, BRAC, functioned with American support, and, more controversially, Batista's military was using American war matériel that had been assigned to Cuba for "hemispheric defense" in its antiguerrilla campaign.

Opinion was divided as to Castro's political orientation, but few policy makers credited Batista's repeated denunciations of him as a Communist. At his first press conference, Smith had trod a careful line by praising Cuba's efforts in the common struggle against Communism, while saying he did not believe Castro was pro-Communist. But in Santiago, after witnessing the police turn their batons and water hoses on a crowd of demonstrating women, Smith publicly deplored the rough police tactics and, before leaving, laid a wreath at País's tomb. This gesture gave Cubans hope of a policy shift in Washington, for it stood out in sharp contrast to the pro-Batista attitudes of Smith's predecessor, Arthur Gardner. The unpopular Gardner had never said anything publicly to criticize Batista's excesses and privately had gone so far as to suggest that he send an assassin into the sierra to kill Fidel.

After Smith's remarks about police brutality in Santiago, the debate over Castro began to heat up, with Batista's officials and American ultraconservatives accusing Washington of going soft on Communism. In August, the ubiquitous Spruille Braden, who had served as U.S. ambassador during Batista's first elected term as president during World War II, threw down the gauntlet, denouncing Castro as a Communist "fellow traveler."

The CIA was, in fact, already pursuing contacts with the Movement through officials stationed in Santiago and Havana. The first inkling of such contacts is revealed in Che's scathing reference to Armando Hart's letter "suggesting a deal with the Yankee embassy" in April 1957. The next reference is in a letter of July 5 sent by Frank País to Fidel, saying that he had managed to get an American visa for Lester "El Gordito" Rodríguez, a July 26 member who was to help coordinate U.S. fund-raising and arms purchases for the rebels. "The very meritorious and valuable American embassy came to us and offered any kind of help in exchange for our ceasing to loot arms from their [Guantánamo] base,"* País wrote to Fidel. "We promised this in exchange for a two-year visa for El Gordito and for them to get him out of the country. Today they fulfilled their promise: the consul took him out personally, and the papers, letters, and the maps that he needed were taken out in the diplomatic pouch. Good service."

On July 11, País wrote to Fidel again: "María A. told me very urgently at noon today that the American vice consul wanted to talk with you, in the presence of some other man, but she didn't know who. . . . I'm sick and tired of so much backing and forthing and conversations from the embassy, and I think it would be to our advantage to close ranks a bit more, without losing contact with them, but not giving them as much importance as we now do; I see that they are maneuvering but I can't see clearly what their real goals are."

In his biography of Castro, Tad Szulc wrote that between autumn 1957 and mid-1958 the CIA paid out at least $50,000 to various July 26 agents. Szulc named Robert Wiecha as the man who disbursed the funds.

In an undated reply to Frank País, Fidel agreed to the meeting with the vice-consul. "I don't see why we should raise the slightest objection to the U.S. diplomat's visit," he wrote. "We can receive any U.S. diplomat here, just as we would any Mexican diplomat or a diplomat from any country." He then continued with the kind of bombast that seems to indicate he expected the letter to be passed on to the Americans. "If they wish to have closer ties of friendship with the triumphant democracy of Cuba? Magnificent! This is a sign they acknowledge the final outcome of this battle. If they propose friendly mediation? We'll tell them no honorable mediation, no patriotic mediation—no mediation is possible in this battle."

*The July 26 Movement had a flourishing underground operating among the Cuban employees at the Guantánamo base and had been stealing weapons and ammunition from its stores since before the *Granma* expedition. Like most of the wartime rebel correspondence quoted here, this comes from Carlos Franqui's *Diary of the Cuban Revolution*.

The meeting between Fidel and the CIA men seems never to have come about. Possibly it was postponed because of País's death and then dropped when the CIA's policy shifted. But the agency's contacts with the National Directorate's llano officials continued for some time, and evidently paid off in funding and possibly other forms of aid to the Movement. It is worth noting that the CIA's overtures coincided with País's meetings with representatives of a group of reformist officers at Cuba's Cienfuegos naval base who were plotting an uprising against Batista. William Williamson, the CIA's number two man in Havana, had told the naval conspirators that if they were successful, they could count on U.S. recognition. By July, the group had made contact with Faustino Pérez in Havana and País in Santiago to propose an alliance of forces. After hearing them out, País had strongly endorsed the plan and passed it along to Fidel.

It was a tempting proposition. The officers were planning not a mere barracks coup but a full-scale uprising to oust Batista, assisted by dissident factions within the air force and army, with simultaneous uprisings in Cienfuegos, Santiago, and Havana. Despite his public opposition to any kind of post-Batista military junta that could preempt his own bid for power, Fidel was not one to miss an opportunity and had little to lose by supporting the Cienfuegos plotters. First, it would be the Movement's llano people, not his men from the sierra, who would take part, giving him some deniability if the plot was discovered. Second, if he opposed the plan and the conspirators were successful, he would have alienated them and would still be trapped in the mountains. Of course, if he *did* help, there was the risk he could be outmaneuvered, but he could then continue to fight from the hills, as he had promised in the manifesto. For the time being, Fidel's position was good. The Americans and, now, Cuban military mutineers were coming to *him*. He had become a power broker, and he could afford to remain circumspect about the deals on offer while continuing to fight his war in the sierra.

In the meantime, he faced other problems. País's murder came at a time of mounting tension between Fidel and the National Directorate in the llano over the control and direction of the July 26 Movement. Since their meeting at Epifanio Díaz's farm in February, País and Faustino Pérez had continued to lobby Fidel to permit the establishment of a "second front." They had a double agenda. A second guerrilla front would not only ease matters for Fidel's rebels by helping to divert the attention of the army but also offset Fidel's maneuverings to exercise total control of the armed struggle. Fidel was just as adamant that the Movement make the support of *his* fighters in the sierra its priority; until his forces were secure, he argued, no arms should be diverted elsewhere.

During their time in prison together, Carlos Franqui, Faustino Pérez, and Armando Hart had talked at length with jailed representatives of most of the other Cuban opposition parties. They had concluded that insurmountable differences of ideology prevented a July 26 alliance of forces with the Partido Socialista Popular, Cuba's Communist Party, which remained critical of Fidel's "putschist" strategy for taking power. There seemed to be genuine possibilities, however, of a pact with the Directorio, although so far a working alliance had been thwarted, owing primarily to the Directorio's fears about Fidel's perceived caudillismo tendencies. The llano officials themselves had begun to resent Fidel's autocratic demands and ceaseless complaints. His letters show that he regarded them more as his suppliers than as equal partners in a common struggle involving both rural and urban guerrilla warfare. He seemed oblivious of the precarious existence they led in the cities, exposed to the constant dangers of arrest, torture, and execution.

In addition to their efforts to broaden the Movement's links with other groups, the llano people oversaw the campaign of urban bombings, sabotage, and assassination as well as counterintelligence operations within the armed forces. They also operated clandestine safe houses, clinics, and arms-smuggling rings. Now they had the added duty of implementing the campaign of rural and industrial sabotage as decreed by Fidel in his February "Appeal": the formation of a national workers' front to compete with the labor union movement controlled by Batista, organizing a general strike, and, last but not least, the unceasing program to supply Fidel with money and weapons through the Resistencia Cívica network.

The prospect of opening new guerrilla fronts became feasible only after the Movement seized the weapons left over from the Directorio's assault on the presidential palace. Some of these had been sent to Fidel just before El Uvero, but Frank País had used the rest of the weapons to establish a new rebel group led by a former law student, René Ramos Latour, aka "Daniel." Daniel's group had based itself in Oriente's small but strategic Sierra Cristal mountain range—east of the Sierra Maestra, with Santiago on one side and Guantánamo on the other. Its first action in June against an army garrison had failed and resulted in the loss of many arms and several men. Frank País had rescued some weapons and hidden Daniel and twenty of his men at safe houses in Santiago. País had then come up with an audacious new plan: to explode a bomb at a pro-Batista rally being held by the political gangster Rolando Masferrer, who was the leader of a paramilitary force called Los Tigres. The bomb had failed to go off, and, soon after, the final blow to País's bid to assert himself had come when his own brother, Josué, and two comrades were killed.

Following these failures, País had begun lobbying Fidel to widen his political appeal by forging links with mainstream political figures, including encouraging the visit of Raúl Chibás and Felipe Pazos to the sierra. He had also outlined a plan with Armando Hart—who coincidentally had just escaped from police custody—to revamp the entire structure of the Movement by putting decision making in the hands of a new executive body, while six provincial leaders would form a new National Directorate. The plan implied a vast curtailment of Fidel's powers. He would be reduced to being one of the six provincial leaders. "If you have any suggestions or tasks to be done," País wrote Fidel, "tell me so. In any case, when the draft of the program is complete, I will send it for you to look over and give your opinion."

Fidel's response came in the form of his Sierra Maestra Manifesto, effectively quashing País's curtailment efforts. Writing to him afterward, Fidel deftly avoided mentioning País's proposal, saying ambiguously, "I'm very happy—and I congratulate you—that you so clearly saw the necessity of formulating working plans on a national and systematic scale. We'll keep fighting here as long as it is necessary. And we'll finish this battle with either the death or triumph of the *real* Revolution."

A couple of weeks later, Frank País was dead, and Fidel made haste to fill the breach. The day after his murder, on July 31, Fidel wrote to Celia Sánchez expressing his sorrow and outrage over the loss and asking her to assume "a good portion of Frank's work." Meanwhile, to replace País on the National Directorate, he proposed Faustino Pérez, and urged her to bring him up to date on País's duties. On this matter, however, the National Directorate won a rare victory over Fidel, choosing not Pérez but Daniel— René Ramos Latour—as País's replacement.

Lately, to implement his wishes, Fidel had begun to rely more and more heavily on Celia Sánchez, whom he regularly bombarded with letters, telling her she was indispensable to his survival and complaining bitterly about the lack of support of the llano. Indeed, ever since their first meeting in February, Celia had become Fidel's primary confidante in the llano, and now her authority increased. The other July 26 officials quickly comprehended Celia's new status, and began dealing with her as their principal intermediary with Fidel.

As Daniel tried to carry on País's effort to assert more control over Fidel and his rebels, he singled out Che in particular as someone who needed to be reined in, complaining to Fidel that Che had not even contacted him since he had replaced País, and was causing problems by making his own supply arrangements with people not authorized by the Directorate. Fidel's

response was to ignore Daniel while sending increasingly bitter letters to
Celia about the llano's "abandonment" of the sierra.

III

As Che prepared for another attack against the forces of Major Joaquín
Casillas, he found himself dealing with the usual problems of green recruits,
deserters, and *chivatos*. A group of new volunteers from Las Minas joined
him, among them his first female volunteer, a seventeen-year-old girl named
Oniria Gutiérrez. In the usual pattern, though, he let several of them go a
few days later when they began showing signs of *cofard,* the French word
he used to describe cowardice.

David Gómez, his overseer collaborator, apparently had been arrested,
tortured, and murdered. The army had then occupied the Peladero estate
where Gómez worked and had pressured one of the workers into telling
them everything he knew about the rebels' local ties. "The result was that
they killed 10 people, including two of David's muleteers, took all the merchandise, burned down all the houses in the area, and beat several of the
neighbors badly, some of whom later died and others, like Israel's father,
who suffered broken bones," Che wrote in his diary. "According to the reports, there were three *chivatos,* and I asked for volunteers to kill them.
Several offered themselves but I chose Israel, his brother Samuel, Manolito,
and Rodolfo. They left early with some little signs that read: *Executed for
being a traitor to the people M-26-7.*"

The execution team returned a week later, having tracked down and
killed one of the *chivatos*. The reports of David Gómez's death turned out
to be inaccurate; he later came personally to tell Che that although he had
been arrested and brutally tortured, he had not opened his mouth.

By late August, Che's column was camped in the valley of El
Hombrito. Despite his efforts to seek out the enemy, his men had seen no
combat since Bueycito nearly a month before. On August 29, a peasant
warned Che of a large column of enemy soldiers approaching, then led him
to where the soldiers were camped. Che decided to attack immediately,
before the enemy advanced farther. That night he positioned his fighters
along both sides of a trail leading from the soldiers' bivouac, up which they
would march the following day. His plan was to allow the first ten or twelve
soldiers to pass, then ambush the middle of the column, dividing the soldiers into two groups that could be easily surrounded and picked off.

At first light, the soldiers roused themselves and began climbing the hill
toward them. Che felt restless, anxious about the coming battle and eager to
test his new Browning for the first time. As the soldiers drew near, Che began

counting. But one of the men shouted, and Che reacted reflexively, opening fire and shooting the sixth man in line. At his second shot, and before his own men had reacted, the first five soldiers vanished from sight. Che ordered his units to attack; as they did, the enemy column recovered from its surprise and opened fire with bazookas. Che ordered a retreat to a fallback position, and learned that Hermes Leyva, Joel Iglesias's cousin, had been killed. From their new vantage point, a little over half a mile away, they watched as the soldiers advanced, stopped, and then, in full view of them, desecrated Leyva's body by burning it. "In our impotent rage," recalled Che, "we were limited to long-range firing, which they answered with bazookas."

They exchanged fire all day, and by nightfall the enemy column had retreated. To Che, the action constituted a "great triumph," despite the fact that he had lost a valuable man and captured only one enemy weapon. With their handful of arms, his men had fought off 140 soldiers armed with bazookas, halting their advance. But a few days later, Che learned that the company had murdered several peasants and burned down their homes in reprisal for their suspected complicity with his forces, a chastening reminder of the price paid by unprotected civilians after rebel attacks in their areas. Che resolved to evacuate civilians in advance of attacks to prevent more such atrocities.

After the battle, Che met up again with Fidel, who had just attacked an army encampment near Las Cuevas; he had lost four men but inflicted casualties and forced the army to retreat. Deciding to press their advantage, Fidel and Che planned a coordinated attack on Pino del Agua, where there was a small army garrison. If they found troops, they would attack; if not, they would advertise their presence and draw the army into the hills. Fidel's column would be the bait, while Che would lay an ambush. With the plan worked out, the two columns headed toward the target area.

But in Che's column, things were not going well. There were several more desertions, and then a young rebel, disarmed after being insubordinate with his lieutenant, borrowed a revolver and shot himself in the head before his shocked comrades. When he was buried, a disagreement ensued between Che and some of his men over whether or not the dead youth should be given military honors. Che was opposed. "I argued that committing suicide under such conditions should be repudiated, whatever good qualities the man may have possessed. After a few stirrings of insubordination by some of the men, we wound up holding a wake, without rendering him honors."

The discontent among his men spurred Che to take strict new measures, and he named a young rebel to head up a new disciplinary commission. It was a decision that caused bad blood among the fighters. Enrique Acevedo, a fifteen-year-old runaway who had recently joined the column as a *descamisado* with his older brother, Rogelio, recalled the disciplinary commission as being like a small military police unit. "Among other things,"Acevedo said, "it was supposed to make sure that nobody talked in loud voices, didn't light fires before nightfall, to ensure that there were buckets of water next to fires in case an airplane appeared . . . , to check up on those doing guard duty, and to prevent anyone from keeping a diary. They made sure that we felt the severity of the new disciplinary measures. It became a nightmare for all of us."

Che's penchant for strict discipline was notorious among the rebels, and there were those who asked to be transferred out of his column. Young Acevedo, who had been allowed to stay on despite Che's initial rejection— *"What do you think this is, an orphanage or a crèche?"*—continued to observe Che with great caution. In his own "illegal" diary, he wrote: "Everyone treats him with great respect. He is hard, dry, and at times ironic with some men. His manners are smooth. When he gives an order you can see he really commands respect. It is obeyed at once."

A few days later, the brothers witnessed an example of Che's summary justice. Enrique Acevedo recorded the moment vividly: "At dawn they bring in a big man dressed in green, head shaved like the military, with big mustaches: it's [René] Cuervo, who is stirring up trouble in the zone of San Pablo de Yao and Vega la Yua. He has committed abuses under the flag of the July 26. . . . Che receives him in his hammock. The prisoner tries to give him his hand, but doesn't find a response. What is said doesn't reach our ears, even though their words are strong. It seems to be a summary trial. At the end [Che] sends him away with a contemptuous gesture of his hand. They take him to a ravine and they execute him with a .22 rifle, because of which they have to give him three shots. [Finally] Che jumps out of his hammock and shouts: 'Enough!'"

Che was unapologetic about his decision to kill Cuervo. "Using the pretext of fighting for the revolutionary cause and executing spies, he simply victimized an entire section of the population of the sierra, perhaps in collusion with the army," he wrote. "In view of his status as a deserter, the trial was speedy, then proceeding to his physical elimination. The execution of antisocial individuals who took advantage of the prevailing atmosphere in the area to commit crimes was, unfortunately, not infrequent in the Sierra Maestra."

A few weeks later, a more merciful side of Che was revealed. After ambushing a truckload of soldiers near Pino del Agua, Che approached to inspect the damage. "In capturing the first truck, we found two dead and one wounded soldier, who was still going through the motions of fighting as he lay dying," he wrote. "One of our fighters finished the man off without giving him an opportunity to surrender—which he was unable to do, being only half-conscious. The combatant responsible for this barbaric act had seen his family wiped out by Batista's army. I reproached him violently, unaware that my remarks were overheard by another wounded soldier, concealed and motionless under some tarpaulins on the truck bed. Emboldened by my words and by the apology of our comrade, the enemy soldier made his presence known and begged us not to kill him. He had a fractured leg and remained at the side of the road while the battle went on elsewhere. Every time a fighter passed near him he would shout, 'Don't kill me! Don't kill me! Che says not to kill prisoners!' When the battle was over we transported him to the sawmill and gave him first aid."

IV

As they made their way through the hills during that first week of September, the rebels heard that the national uprising had finally taken place. On September 5, rebels had attacked and seized the naval base and police headquarters in the city of Cienfuegos. Along with the naval mutineers and a smattering of men from other groups, including Prío's *auténticos,* a large number of July 26 fighters had participated. But things hadn't gone as planned. At the last minute, the rebel's coconspirators in Havana and Santiago had stalled, and the Cienfuegos uprising had gone off alone.

The rebels held the city that morning, but by afternoon the regime had sent in tanks from the large Santa Clara garrison and dispatched American-made B-26 bombers to hit them from the air. The rebels committed the fatal mistake of making a stand in the city instead of escaping to the nearby Escambray mountains, and they were slaughtered. The three July 26 officials involved—Javier Pazos, acting head of the Havana underground; Julio Camacho, action chief for Las Villas province; and Emilio Aragonés, the July 26 leader for Cienfuegos—managed to flee, but as many as 300 of the estimated 400 men involved from various organizations were killed, many of them by being shot after surrendering. The revenge taken against the rebels was barbaric. Reports emerged of wounded men being buried alive, and the captured ringleader, the former naval lieutenant Dionisio San Román, was tortured for months before being killed.

It had been the biggest and bloodiest action so far in the Cuban conflict, and there was plenty of fallout. Fidel was accused of treachery by Justo Carrillo, a former cabinet minister under Prío and leader of his own "Montecristi" anti-Batista group, who had been in league with one of the military factions involved in the conspiracy. Previously, Carrillo had provided money to the July 26 Movement; he flirted with—but declined—Fidel's invitation for an

alliance at the time of the Sierra Pact. Now, Carrillo accused Fidel of per-
fidy for allegedly giving his go-ahead to the Cienfuegos revolt, knowing it
would fail and result in the deaths of the military men whom he saw as rivals for power. Indirectly answering this charge later, Che wrote, "The July
26 Movement, participating as an unarmed ally, could not have changed the
course of events, even if its leaders had seen the outcome clearly, which they
did not. The lesson for the future is: he who has the strength dictates the
strategy."

But Batista would also face repercussions from Cienfuegos. His use of
U.S.-supplied firepower in quelling the revolt was a blatant breach of U.S.
defense treaties with Cuba; the tanks and B-26 bombers had been supplied
for Cuba's hemispheric defense, not to suppress internal uprisings. The
Americans asked for explanations, and when these weren't forthcoming,
they began considering the suspension of arms shipments to the regime.

Meanwhile, in the Sierra Maestra, Che and Fidel had drawn close to
their next military target. On September 10, the two columns reached Pino
del Agua. Fidel made sure the locals knew where he was headed, expecting
someone to leak it to the army, and then he marched his column off. That
night Che surreptitiously set up his ambushes along the roads and trails
where the enemy forces were expected to arrive. If their plan worked, they
hoped to hit a motorized army convoy and capture several trucks. After a
week of waiting in a forest on a cliff overlooking one of the main roads, Che
finally heard the sounds of truck engines. The enemy had seized the bait.

As battles went, it was a decidedly small-scale affair. Once the ambush
began, two truckloads of soldiers were able to escape, but the rebels captured
the three remaining trucks—which they burned—as well as some valuable
new weapons and ammunition. They had also killed three soldiers and taken
one prisoner, a corporal who ended up joining them and becoming their
cook. But to their great sadness, they lost "Crucito," a *guajiro* poet who had
entertained the fighters in poetic dueling sessions with the other rebel lyri-
cist, Calixto Morales. Crucito had nicknamed himself "the nightingale of
the Maestra" and dubbed his rival "the buzzard of the plains."

V

Che moved his men toward Peladero, where Fidel's column had headed.
Along the way, he confiscated a mule owned by a merchant who was believed to be pro-Batista and friendly with the large landowners. "Juan
Balansa had a mule, celebrated in the vicinity for its staying power, and as a
kind of war tax, we made off with it," Che wrote. The mule showed itself
to be surefooted and agile, and Che took it as his own personal mount and

kept it until it was "recaptured" by Captain Angel Sánchez Mosquera, the officer who was becoming his bête noire, later in the war.

The Sierra Maestra was now crawling with armed men, and a kind of anarchy reigned as deserters, freelance outlaw groups, and some of the rebels themselves committed abuses, using their weapons and the absence of government control to rob, rape, and commit murder. The rigid code of conduct for rebel behavior, meanwhile, was causing resentment, particularly in Che's column, where tension was running high over the zeal displayed by his newly appointed "disciplinary commission." The situation now reached a bloody climax.

A couple of days after his column had arrived at Peladero, Che went off to meet Fidel, who was camped nearby. Not long after he and Fidel had begun talking, Ramiro Valdés came to interrupt them. Something very bad had happened. "Lalo Sardiñas, in an impulsive act of punishment toward an undisciplined comrade, had held his pistol to the man's head as if to shoot him," Che wrote later. "The gun went off unintentionally and the man was killed on the spot. There were stirrings of a riot among the troops." Che found himself facing a full-scale mutiny over Lalo's action, with many of the men demanding a summary trial and execution. He began to take evidence from the men, some of whom said Lalo had carried out an act of premeditated murder, though others said it was an accident. A trial was held to determine Lalo's fate. He was not only an officer but a good and brave fighter, and both Che and Fidel wished to spare his life, but the other fighters had to be consulted, and their speeches made it obvious that most of them wanted the death penalty. Che finally spoke out: "I tried to explain that the comrade's death had to be ascribed to the conditions of the struggle," he recounted later, "to the very fact that we were at war, and that it was after all the dictator Batista who was guilty. My words, however, were not convincing to this hostile audience."

Fidel's turn came next. According to Che's account, he spoke at length in Lalo's defense. "He explained that, in the end, this reprehensible act had been committed in defense of the concept of discipline and that we should keep that fact in mind." Many of the men were swayed by what Che termed Fidel's "enormous powers of persuasion," but many still disagreed. Finally, it was determined that a vote would be held to put the matter to rest: Lalo would be either shot to death or demoted. The majority would decide. Che tallied up the votes in a notebook. In the end, of the 146 fighters, seventy voted for death, seventy-six for demotion.

Lalo's life was spared. He was stripped of his rank and ordered to win his rehabilitation by fighting as a common soldier. But the matter hadn't ended. A large group of fighters remained unhappy over the decision, and the next day they threw down their weapons and demanded to leave. Curiously, among them were the head of Che's disciplinary commission and several of its members. As was his custom when writing about this incident later on, Che made sure to point out that among those who left, some went on to betray the revolution. "These men, who had not respected the majority and abandoned the struggle, subsequently put themselves at the service of the enemy, and it was as traitors that they returned to fight on our soil."

In spite of Che's best efforts at ascribing treasonous motivations to the men who left, the incident is less convincing as a moral tale than as a glimpse into Che's hardened personality. His trail through the Sierra Maestra was littered with the bodies of *chivatos,* deserters, and delinquents, men whose killings he had ordered and in some cases carried out himself. The code of discipline he had imposed within and without his growing family of fighters had created an atmosphere in which acts such as Lalo's could easily occur. The leader sets the example. Che's underlings were merely imitating his behavior in their own crude way.

After the mutiny, Fidel transferred some fighters to Che's command to replace those who had left and named a substitute for Lalo: Camilo Cienfuegos. The handsome, blond, extroverted former baseball player now became the captain of Che's vanguard platoon. It was a good move, for Camilo's devil-may-care personality helped offset Che's strictness. The two men were mutually respectful, and Che allowed Camilo a degree of intimacy that he permitted no one else. Their dialogues were ribald banter laced with friendly put-downs and goads.

Camilo's first mission was to hunt down a group of "bandits" who were committing their crimes under the banner of the revolution. While he went off in their pursuit, Che returned to the area that was becoming his own headquarters—the valley of El Hombrito. Since his ambush there in August the army had not returned, and Che had begun to establish the rudiments of a permanent base. He had left a *guajiro* named Aristidio in charge of a halfway house for new volunteers in the valley and had even built an oven for baking bread. The area was calm, but it was assumed that Sánchez Mosquera, who had established a base in Minas de Bueycito, would launch a raid into the mountains soon. Aristidio was evidently not immune to the general sense of alarm, for in Che's absence he had sold his revolver and imprudently told people he planned to make contact with the army before it arrived. "These were difficult moments for the revolution," Che recalled. "In my capacity as chief of the sector, we conducted a very summary investigation, and Aristidio was executed."

The adolescent Enrique Acevedo watched as Aristidio was brought in. "By our side passes a barefoot prisoner, they have him tied. It's Aristidio.

Nothing remains of his chieftain's façade. Later a shot can be heard. When we get to the place they are throwing the dirt on top of him. At dawn, after an exhausting day, he [Che] explains to us that Aristidio was executed for misusing the funds and resources of the guerrillas."

Che later sounded almost apologetic about Aristidio's fate. "Aristidio was a typical example of a peasant who joined the ranks of the revolution without having any clear understanding of its significance. . . . Today we may ask ourselves whether he was really guilty enough to deserve death, and if it might not have been possible to save a life that could have been put to use by the revolution in its constructive phase. War is harsh, and at a time when the enemy was intensifying its aggressiveness, one could not tolerate even the suspicion of treason. It might have been possible to spare him months earlier, when the guerrilla movement was much weaker, or months later, when we were far stronger."

After executing Aristidio, Che moved off toward Pico Caracas to help Camilo hunt down an armed gang led by "Chino Chang," a Chinese-Cuban bandit who had robbed and killed peasants in the vicinity. Camilo had already captured some of the culprits and was holding them pending their trial before a revolutionary tribunal. For the first time, the rebels had a real lawyer on hand to implement their system of justice: Humberto Sorí-Marín, a well-known attorney and July 26 man from Havana. Most of the members of the Chino Chang gang were acquitted, but Chang himself and a peasant who had raped a girl were sentenced to death. As usual, Che observed their last moments with a keen eye, noting whether they displayed courage or cowardice as they met death: "First we executed Chino Chang and the peasant rapist. They were tied to a tree in the forest, both of them calm. The peasant died without a blindfold, his eyes facing the guns, shouting 'Long live the revolution!' Chang met death with absolute serenity but asked for the last rites to be administered by Father Sardiñas"—a priest from Santiago who had joined the rebels but who wasn't then in the camp. "Since we were unable to grant this request, Chang said he wanted it known he had asked for a priest, as if this public testimony would serve as an extenuating circumstance in the hereafter."

The rebels decided to teach three young members of the gang a lesson by conducting a mock execution. The boys went through the experience of being sentenced to death and, after witnessing Chang's and the rapist's executions, awaited their own. "They had been deeply involved in Chang's outrages," Che explained, "but Fidel felt they should be given another chance. We blindfolded them and subjected them to the anguish of a simulated firing squad. After shots were fired in the air, the boys realized they were still very much alive. One of them threw himself on me, and, in a spontaneous gesture of joy and gratitude, gave me a big noisy kiss, as if I were his father." As Che told it later, the decision to spare their lives proved worthwhile; the three stayed in the Rebel Army, one of them in Che's column, and earned their redemption by becoming "good fighters for the revolution."

The journalist Andrew St. George had reappeared and was present for the executions—both simulated and real—and took photographs of the events as they unfolded. His photographs and accompanying article were published in *Look* magazine, and he also apparently filed reports to American intelligence. (St. George never refuted allegations that he used his visits to gather information on Fidel and the Movement for the U.S. government.)

A few days later, more transgressors were caught. Among them was Dionisio Oliva, a peasant who had been instrumental in unmasking Eutimio Guerra; in the intervening months he and his brother-in-law had stolen provisions intended for the rebels and become cattle rustlers. Dionisio had also commandeered private homes in which he maintained two mistresses. Captured along with them were several others, including a youth named Echeverría. Several of Echeverría's brothers were rebels, and one had even been aboard the *Granma,* but this boy had joined a freelance armed gang. Still, as Che admitted, his case was "poignant." Echevarría begged to be allowed to die in battle—he did not want to disgrace his family by dying in front of a revolutionary firing squad—but the tribunal's decision was firm. Before he was shot, Che said, Echeverría wrote a letter to his mother, "explaining the justice of his punishment and asking her to remain faithful to the revolution."

The last man to die was none other than El Maestro, Che's skittish companion during his asthma-plagued trek to meet the new volunteers from Santiago. Claiming illness, El Maestro had since left the guerrillas and "dedicated himself to a life of immoralities." His real crime was passing himself off as Che "the doctor" and attempting to rape a peasant girl who came to him as a patient.

Fidel later talked about these executions with the July 26 journalist Carlos Franqui. He was dishonest in his account of the number of executions he had authorized during the war but became downright voluble in the case of El Maestro. "We lined up very few people before firing squads, very few indeed. During the entire war we did not shoot more than ten guys in twenty-five months," Fidel said. But as for El Maestro, "He was an orangutan; he grew a huge beard. He was also a born clown and carried loads as though he were Hercules, but he was a bad soldier. . . . What stupidity to pretend he was Che, in that area, where we had spent a long time, where everyone knew all of us. . . . And now, with the new beard, El Maestro was passing himself off as Che: *'Bring me women. I'm going to examine them all!'* Did you ever hear of anything so outrageous? We shot him."

VI

After the wave of executions, Che and his men headed back to El Hombrito. It was now late October 1957, and Che wanted to begin building an "industrial" infrastructure to sustain a permanent guerrilla presence there. His ambitions were given a boost by the arrival of a couple of former students from Havana University who were put to work building a dam to produce hydroelectric energy from the Río Hombrito. Their other task was to help start a guerrilla newspaper, *El Cubano Libre* (The Free Cuban). By early November, they had printed the first issue, run off on a vintage 1903 mimeograph machine.

Che began writing a series of columns titled "The Wild Shot" under his old nickname, the Sniper. In his first article, "The Beginning of the End," he took aim at the issue of American military aid to Batista, deftly pegging it to the recent protests by animal lovers outside the UN building in New York over the Soviet decision to send a dog named Laika into space aboard Sputnik II. (The month before, the Soviets had launched Sputnik I, the world's first satellite, into orbit around the earth.) "Compassion fills our soul at the thought of the poor animal that will die gloriously to further a cause that it doesn't understand," Che wrote. "But we haven't heard of any philanthropic American society parading in front of the noble edifice asking clemency for our *guajiros,* and they die in good numbers, machine-gunned by the P-47 and B-26 airplanes . . . or riddled by the troops' competent M-1s. Or is it that within the context of political convenience a Siberian dog is worth more than a thousand Cuban *guajiros?*"

Che had visions of a proper social infrastructure for El Hombrito. He built a rudimentary hospital and had plans for another. Soon, in addition to his bread oven, there was an embryonic pig and poultry farm as well as a shoemaking and saddler's workshop, and his "armory" was going full tilt. Work had begun to produce some primitive land mines and rifle-launched grenades, dubbed "Sputniks" in honor of the new Soviet satellites. Once they had obtained the right materials, the next project was to make mortars. To crown these achievements, Che commissioned the sewing of a huge July 26 flag emblazoned with *"Feliz Año 1958!"* to be placed at the summit of El Hombrito mountain. Che felt proud that he was establishing a "real authority" in the area, and, mindful of the marauding troops of Captain Sánchez Mosquera, he had his men construct antiaircraft shelters and defensive fortifications along the routes leading into their little fiefdom. "We intend to stand fast here," he wrote to Fidel on November 24, "and not give this place up for anything."

Reports had come in that Sánchez Mosquera's troops were on the march up the adjacent valley of Mar Verde, burning peasants' homes as they went. Che dispatched Camilo Cienfuegos to ambush the troops. He followed, intending to hit the enemy column from behind. He and his men stuck to the flanking forested hills of the valley, trying to catch up with the soldiers without being seen. When they discovered that their new mascot, a puppy, was trailing them, Che ordered the fighter who was looking after the puppy, a man named Félix, to make it go back, but the little dog continued trotting loyally behind. They reached an arroyo where they rested, and the puppy inexplicably began howling. The men tried to hush it with comforting words, but the little dog didn't stop. Che ordered it killed. "Félix looked at me with eyes that said nothing," Che wrote later. "Very slowly he took out a rope, wrapped it around the animal's neck, and began to tighten it. The cute little movements of the dog's tail suddenly became convulsive, before gradually dying out, accompanied by a steady moan that escaped from its throat, despite the firm grasp. I don't know how long it took for the end to come, but to all of us it seemed like forever. With one last nervous twitch, the puppy stopped moving. There it lay, sprawled out, its little head spread over the twigs."

The band of men moved on without speaking. The enemy was now well beyond them. Hearing distant gunshots, they knew Camilo had struck, but when Che sent scouts ahead to check, they found nothing except a freshly dug grave. Che ordered it dug up, and they found the body of an enemy soldier. Whatever clash had taken place was over, and both the enemy troops and Camilo's squad were gone. Disappointed at having missed the action, they walked back down the valley, reaching the hamlet of Mar Verde after nightfall. All its inhabitants had fled, leaving their possessions behind. The rebels cooked a pig and some yucca, and one of the men began singing along to a guitar.

"I don't know whether it was the sentimental tune, or the darkness of night, or just plain exhaustion," Che wrote. "What happened though, is that Félix, while eating seated on the floor, dropped a bone, and a dog came up meekly and grabbed it. Félix patted its head, and the dog looked at him. Félix returned the glance, and then he and I exchanged a guilty look. Suddenly everyone fell silent. An imperceptible stirring came over us. The dog's meek yet roguish gaze seemed to contain a hint of reproach. There in our presence, although observing us through the eyes of another dog, was the murdered puppy."

They were still in Mar Verde the next day when scouts brought word that Sánchez Mosquera's troops were camped a little over a mile away. Camilo's force had taken up a position nearby and was waiting for Che's column before attacking. Che quickly moved his men to the spot. By dawn the next morning, November 29, the rebels were in ambush positions along the Río Turquino, covering all of Sánchez Mosquera's possible escape routes. Che chose a particularly vulnerable spot for himself and his own unit; they would have to fire at point-blank range on any soldiers who came their way.

Che and two or three others were concealed behind trees when a small group of soldiers passed directly before them. Armed with only a Luger pistol, Che nervously rushed his first shot and missed. The firefight began, and in the confusion the soldiers escaped into the bush. Simultaneously, the other units opened up on the farmhouse where most of the enemy soldiers were positioned. During a lull in the firing, Joel Iglesias was hit by six bullets as he searched for the soldiers who had escaped. Che found him covered with blood but still alive. After evacuating the boy to his field hospital at El Hombrito, Che rejoined the fray, but Sánchez Mosquera's troops were well entrenched and kept up a heavy return fire, making any rush on their position extremely dangerous. When army reinforcements began arriving, Che sent patrols to stop them while he kept Sánchez Mosquera pinned down. In an attempt to move in closer, Che's friend Ciro Redondo, a fellow veteran of the *Granma,* was killed by a bullet in the head.

By mid-afternoon it was over. The enemy reinforcements had fought their way past Che's positions, and he had finally ordered his men to retreat. It had been a bloody day. In addition to Ciro, they had lost another man when he was taken prisoner and then murdered; five more, including Joel, had been wounded. Expecting a pursuit by the army, they rushed back to El Hombrito to prepare themselves for the next showdown.

After a few feverish days preparing their defenses, the alert sounded: Sánchez Mosquera's troops were on their way. Che had evacuated his wounded fighters and reserve stocks to a fallback position at La Mesa. To stop the enemy advance into El Hombrito, Che invested high hopes in his armory's new land mines, which were placed along the approach road. When the soldiers did come, however, the mines didn't explode, and Che's forward ambush units had to retreat quickly; the enemy now had a clear path into El Hombrito. With little time to lose, Che and his men withdrew from the valley along a road leading up a hill they called Los Altos de Conrado, for a Communist peasant who lived there and had helped them. It was a steep climb to his abandoned house, the spot Che thought best to lie in wait for the enemy, and they found an ambush site behind a boulder overlooking the road. They were to wait there for the next three days.

This time, Che's plan was modest but risky. Hidden behind a large tree next to the track, Camilo Cienfuegos would try to kill the first soldier who appeared, shooting at point-blank range. Sharpshooters flanking the road would then open fire while others began shooting from the front. Che and a couple of men were situated in a reserve position twenty yards away, but Che was only partially concealed behind a tree, and the men near him were in similarly exposed positions. He had ordered that no one was to peer out—they would know the soldiers had arrived only upon hearing the first shot—but Che broke his own rule to sneak a look.

"I could at that moment sense the tension prior to combat," he wrote later. "I saw the first soldier appear. He looked around suspiciously and advanced slowly. . . . I hid my head, waiting for the battle to begin. There was the crack of gunfire and then shooting became generalized." The forest filled with the roar of combat as the two sides blasted away at each other at close quarters. The army hastily fired mortars, but they landed well beyond the rebels, and then Che was hit. "Suddenly I felt a disagreeable sensation, similar to a burn or the tingling of numbness. I had been shot in the left foot, which had not been protected by the tree trunk."

Che heard some men moving through the brush in his direction and realized he was now defenseless. He had emptied his rifle clip and hadn't had time to reload; his pistol had fallen on the ground and lay beneath him, but he couldn't lift himself up to get it for fear of showing himself to the enemy. He rolled over in desperation and managed to grab the pistol just as he saw one of his own men, Cantinflas, coming toward him. Cantinflas had come to say that his own gun was jammed and that he was retreating. Che snatched the gun, adjusted the clip, and sent the youth off with an insult. In a display of courage, Cantinflas left the tree cover to fire upon the enemy, only to be hit by a bullet that entered his left arm and exited through his shoulder blade.

Both Che and Cantinflas were now wounded, with no idea where their comrades were, but they managed to crawl to help. Cantinflas was put in a hammock-stretcher, and Che, his adrenaline still pumping, walked the first part of the trip to a peasant collaborator's house a mile or so away. Finally, the pain from his wound overcame him and he had to be lifted onto a horse.

On December 9, Che sent a letter to Fidel asking for more weapons and apologizing for having put himself in the line of fire. After sending the letter, he found that their situation wasn't as bad as he had feared. The enemy troops had completely withdrawn from the area. There was other good news. Young Joel Iglesias would recover. In their new refuge, a doctor who had recently joined the rebels "operated" on Che, using a razor blade to extract the bullet from his foot, and he was able to start walking again. When he returned to El Hombrito, however, he found devastation. "Our oven had been painstakingly destroyed; in the midst of the smoking ruins we found nothing but some cats and a pig; they had escaped the destructive fury of the invading army only to wind up in our mouths." They would have to start all over again, but not in El Hombrito. As his first year of war came to an end, and 1958 began, Che set about erecting a new base at La Mesa.

VII

In his letter of December 9 to Fidel, Che addressed a problem that went far beyond his immediate military situation. It concerned a growing dispute with the July 26 National Directorate in the llano. Che had never liked the llano people—nor had they, evidently, liked him—but now the relationship had reached the point of open acrimony.

The problem was formally over supply arrangements. Since becoming a *comandante,* Che had ignored Frank País's successor, Daniel, as the rebel army's Oriente coordinator and had made independent deals with suppliers. But that was only the surface problem. Che was now known within the National Directorate as a "radical" Marxist. To the growing alarm of Armando Hart and Daniel, who were both manifestly anticommunist, Che headed his own column with almost total autonomy and clearly enjoyed influence with Fidel, while their own rapport with Fidel had weakened. Che's refusal to contact Daniel or use his organization in Santiago was undercutting the llano's authority.

To resolve the growing rift, Daniel and Celia Sánchez had journeyed into the Sierra Maestra to see Fidel in late October. The visit coincided with new political developments. Armando Hart, as chief of the July 26 "general organization" in the llano, reported potentially positive moves made by the opposition parties to form a revolutionary government in exile, in which the July 26 Movement and Prío's *auténticos* would predominate. At the same time, he wrote to Fidel in October, "cordial relations with certain diplomatic circles" were continuing, and he had learned that people "close to the [U.S.] embassy" had been talking with the ambassador on their behalf. "I think this is the best policy," Hart concluded, "since we are kept up to date on everything happening there and of all the possible U.S. plans, and at the same time the Movement does not officially commit itself."

In the wake of the failed Cienfuegos uprising, which had been endorsed covertly by the CIA, the Americans were probably hedging their bets, fishing around for an alternative means to see Batista out of office. A broad-based coalition of Cuba's acceptable political groups—including a reined-in July 26 Movement—must have seemed like an ideal solution. The Cuban conflict was getting out of hand, the army had proved itself utterly incapable of dealing the rebels a decisive blow, and Batista's solution had been to unleash his dogs. Murders of rebel suspects by the police were now routine, and periodic massacres of peasants by the army in Oriente exacerbated the atmosphere of growing anarchy. An army colonel, Alberto del Río Chaviano, who was notorious for his role in the torture and murders of the Moncada rebels, had been promoted to take over the antiguerrilla campaign in the Sierra Maestra, and a $100,000 reward had been placed on Castro's head.

Batista's enemies were also stepping up the violence. In October and November, the July 26 Movement went after spies and traitors in the cities, finally putting an end to the life of El Gallego Morán, who had caused havoc after going to work for Batista's military intelligence service. The brutal army commander of Holguín, Colonel Fermín Cowley, who was responsible for the massacre of the *Corynthia* men and numerous other murders, was assassinated. The rebels also stepped up their economic sabotage, burning cane fields on a much larger scale than before. To show he meant business, Fidel promised to burn his family's own sizable cane fields in Birán.

Paradoxically, Cuba's economy was booming in spite of the conflict, thanks to improved sugar prices and increased foreign investment, most of it from the United States. The American-owned nickel concerns in Oriente had recently announced expansion plans, and in Havana port facilities were being expanded to cope with the increasing maritime trade. Tourists continued to flood into Havana, and new luxury hotels were being built. The latest sugar harvest had been one of Cuba's best, bringing several hundred million dollars in extra revenues to the state.

Uncertain about Batista's ability to hold things together, Washington continued to give mixed signals to his regime. Despite increased dissatisfaction with Batista in the State Department and the CIA, the U.S. military was strongly supportive of him. Batista's air force chief, Colonel Carlos Tabernilla, was awarded the U.S. Legion of Merit in November, and Batista himself was toasted as "a great general and a great president" in a speech by General Lemuel Sheperd of the Marine Corps. After a few months in his new post, Ambassador Earl Smith had heard more about the rebels' "Communist influences" and was increasingly skeptical regarding Castro. He cabled CIA director Allen Dulles to suggest sending a spy into the Sierra Maestra to determine the "extent of Communist control" in the Movement.

Fidel was walking a tightrope in his quest to emerge as the de facto leader of Cuba's political opposition. To be successful, he had to acquire military muscle by expanding the war, but he also needed more political and economic support, and to obtain that he had to present a suitably moderate, nonthreatening front.

After receiving Armando Hart's letter telling of the impending unity pact, Fidel shot off a letter to his representative in the United States, urging him to lead a delegation to the planned November 1 meeting. Fidel also sent a list of his nominees for key posts in the proposed alliance. No doubt confident that his wishes would be met, Fidel went back to the business of directing the guerrilla war. An evidently chastened Daniel returned to Santiago after meeting with Fidel and was soon working hard to get him the ammunition and other supplies he said he needed. Celia Sánchez remained behind in the Sierra Maestra. Fidel had told her he wanted her "feminine presence" at his side for some time.

On November 1, in Miami, a "Cuban Liberation Junta" was formed, with representatives signing on behalf of most of Cuba's main opposition groups. The Communists had been excluded, but the July 26 Movement dominated the new junta's national committee. Without Fidel's consent, Felipe Pazos had acted as the official July 26 representative, and Fidel saw this as a bid to upstage him. Apart from the standard calls for Batista's resignation, fair elections, and a return to constitutionality, the pact had pandered openly to Washington. There was no statement opposing foreign intervention or the idea of a military junta succeeding Batista—something Fidel greatly feared. The pact called for a "post-victory" incorporation of Fidel's guerrillas into the Cuban armed forces, thereby ensuring the Rebel Army's dissolution. The issue of economic injustice was similarly passed over with a tepid clause promising to create more jobs and raise living standards. In sum, it was a political manifesto designed to warm Washington's heart.

Armando Hart and Daniel claimed to be upset with the terms of the pact, but they intimated that they could live with it. Raúl was livid, accusing Felipe Pazos of outright treachery, and proposing that he be shot. Fidel let it be known that he was unhappy, but as the llano officials scrambled to clarify their positions, he maintained an enigmatic silence. Immersed in the war, Che kept quiet but anxiously awaited clarification from Fidel. On December 1, after the battle of Mar Verde, Che had diplomatically urged Fidel to issue a statement he could print in *El Cubano Libre*. Then came Che's retreat from El Hombrito and his injury at Altos de Conrado. It was in the December 9 letter from La Mesa that Che finally threw down the gauntlet to Fidel. Invoking his suspicions of the National Directorate and accusing it of intentionally "sabotaging" him, he demanded to be allowed to take

unspecified "stern measures" to remedy the situation, or else he would resign. However diplomatically couched, it was an ultimatum to the *jefe*.* Not
only Che's future relationship with Fidel Castro hinged on the reply but, in
fact, the political course of Cuba's revolutionary struggle.

The contents of Fidel's letter of reply to Che have never been revealed,
but whatever he said, Che experienced a reaffirmation of faith. On December 15, he wrote to Fidel, "At this very moment, a messenger arrived with
your note of the thirteenth. I confess that it . . . filled me with peace and
happiness. Not for any personal reason, but rather for what this step means
for the Revolution. You know well that I didn't trust the people on the
National Directorate at all—neither as leaders nor as revolutionaries. But I
didn't think they'd go to the extreme of betraying you so openly."

Che went on to say that Fidel's continued silence was "inadvisable";
the Americans were obviously "pulling the wires behind the scenes," and it
was time to take the gloves off. "We unfortunately have to face Uncle Sam
before the time is ripe." He again urged Fidel to sign a document denouncing the Miami Pact; he would run off 10,000 copies and distribute them all
over Oriente and Havana—the whole island if he could. "Later, if it becomes more complicated, with Celia's help, we can fire the entire National
Directorate."

Fidel *did* break his silence. On the day of his letter to Che, he issued a
statement condemning the Miami Pact and sent it to Che, to the National
Directorate, and to each of the pact's signatories, accusing them of showing
"lukewarm patriotism and cowardice." He was very clear. "The leadership
of the struggle against the tyranny is, and will continue to be, in Cuba and
in the hands of revolutionary fighters." As for the post-victory future of his
guerrilla forces, "The July 26 Movement claims for itself the role of maintaining public order and reorganizing the armed forces of the republic."
Finally, to sabotage what he perceived to be Felipe Pazos's attempt to secure for himself the presidency of a future transition government, Fidel
designated his own candidate: the elderly Santiago jurist Manuel Urrutia.
Fidel completed his tour de force by declaring, "These are our conditions.
. . . If they are rejected, then we will continue the struggle on our own. . . . To
die with dignity does not require company."

---

*Che acknowledged his period of doubt—in which this episode was an important milestone—
in his farewell letter to Fidel, written as he left for the Congo in 1965. "Reviewing my past
life, I believe I have worked with sufficient integrity and dedication to consolidate the revolutionary triumph. My only serious failing was not having had more confidence in you from
the first moments in the Sierra Maestra, and not having understood quickly enough your
qualities as a leader and a revolutionary."

It was a powerful indictment, and it effectively destroyed the newly created junta. The Ortodoxos withdrew from the pact; Pazos resigned from the July 26 Movement; and Faure Chomón, the new leader of the Directorio, began planning his own invasion of Cuba. Fidel still faced a showdown with his llano Directorate; that would come in a few months' time. Meanwhile, Che and Daniel crossed swords in a bitter exchange of letters. Defiantly proclaiming his Marxist beliefs and his restored faith in Fidel "as an authentic leader of the leftist bourgeoisie," Che castigated Daniel and the Directorate's "rightists" for having shamefully allowing the Movement's "ass to be buggered" in Miami. Daniel vigorously denied Che's charges and accused him of thinking Cuba would be better off under future "Soviet domination." He and his llano comrades also had their reservations about the Miami Pact, Daniel insisted, but they believed that before breaking with it, the July 26 Movement should decide, "once and for all," what it stood for and where it was headed.*

More than any other documents, those of the epistolary war between Daniel and Che reveal the depth of the ideological divisions within the Movement. Daniel wrote his rebuttal letter to Che before knowing of Fidel's break with the Miami Pact, but the die had already been cast—Cuba's other opposition groups were being informed they could have a role in the Cuban revolution only after acknowledging Fidel as its paramount leader, and on his conditions. And soon, the news of Fidel's rupture was all over Cuba. As promised, Che ran Fidel's letter off on his mimeograph machine, and on February 2, *Bohemia* reproduced it in a special press run of 500,000 copies. On January 6, as he was having it printed, Che wrote Fidel to praise him for the "historic" document. "Lenin already said it, the policy of principle is the best policy. The end result will be magnificent. . . . Now you are on the great path as one of the two or three [leaders] of America who will get to power by a multitudinous armed struggle."

At the time, only a few people besides Che were aware of the momentous step Fidel had actually taken, one that would eventually affect the lives of millions of people in Cuba and beyond. His public break with the Miami Pact was the visible tip of a much greater political decision that, for now, was to remain a carefully guarded secret.

VIII

Fidel had always known that one day he was going to have to confront the United States, but he had hoped to avoid doing so until after he seized

*See Notes for elaboration.

power. The tentacles of the United States in his homeland went too far
for half measures, and if he was ever to govern as he saw fit and achieve a
genuine national liberation for Cuba, he was going to have to sever them
completely. As Che understood it, this meant carrying out a socialist revolution, although Fidel had carefully refrained from mentioning the
dreaded word in public.

Until now, Fidel had kept the Communist Party of Cuba, the Partido
Socialista Popular, at arm's length. He had shaped his political message to
appeal to a broad-based political alliance and to avoid antagonizing the
Americans. But the unmistakable signs of U.S. influence in the Miami Pact
and on some of the July 26 people in the llano had shown Fidel that the days
of temporizing were over.

On the eve of the *Granma*'s sailing, the PSP had made clear to Fidel
that it supported his goal of ousting Batista but disagreed with his tactics.
As time went on, the Party was forced to consider increasing its involvement in the armed struggle. Despite continued discomfort with Fidel's war
strategy, it made sense for the Communists to come to terms with him. If
the Party wanted a say in the country's political future, there would have to
be some sort of alliance. Under pressure from the United States, Batista had
begun to persecute Party members ruthlessly, using them as scapegoats for
the political violence. In view of Che Guevara's known political affinities
and his close relationship with Fidel, he was the obvious rebel leader for the
Party to approach as it pursued the goal of closer links with Castro. These
overtures came early in the struggle. On Party orders to assist him, a young
Communist, Pablo Ribalta, had traveled from Havana to join Che in the
summer of 1957.

Ribalta, a black Cuban, had studied at Prague's International Union
of Students and graduated from the Communist Party's elite school for
political cadres. At the time of his trip, he was a member of the National
Secretariat of the Communist Youth. Ribalta has confirmed that he was
selected by the Party in mid-1957 to join Che in the sierra for the specific
mission of carrying out political indoctrination among the rebel troops. "Che
had asked for a person with my characteristics: a teacher, with a good level
of political education and some experience in political work."

Ribalta entered the sierra from Bayamo and arrived at La Mesa at a
time when Che was on the move. In his absence, Ribalta organized the incorporation of local Communists into the guerrilla forces and set up a political indoctrination school. When Che finally returned, he sat Ribalta down
and questioned him. Apparently satisfied, Che ordered Ribalta to undergo
a period of guerrilla training. A few months later, Che sent him to Minas
del Frío, where he had established a permanent rearguard base with a school

for recruits, a prison, and other facilities. Ribalta was to be an instructor, and his task was to produce 'integrally educated' fighters. "I had precise instructions not to say that I was a member of the PSP," Ribalta said, "although a group of leaders, including Fidel, knew it; but at that moment it could have created divisions, and I complied to the letter of the law."

The Party had also maintained discreet contacts with Fidel and other Directorate officials, culminating in a meeting in October 1957 between Fidel and Ursino Rojas, a PSP official and former leader of the Sugar Workers' Union. According to Rojas, they discussed the possibility of forging a coalition between their organizations and also explored the main obstacles to such a plan—the rampant anticommunism of some of the Movement's llano leaders, and within the new July 26 labor front group, the Frente Obrero Nacional. For Fidel, some sort of an alliance with the PSP made good practical sense. Whatever his differences with the Party, it had the best political organization in the country, with long-standing ties to organized labor, making its active participation in the upcoming general strike vital. Until Fidel was able to impose his leadership over the entire July 26 Movement, however, any closer links with the PSP would have to be both gradual and discreet.

Feeling more secure about the political direction of the revolution, and with the renewal of his faith in Fidel, Che became more open about his Marxist convictions. He even indulged in some discreet proselytizing among his fighters, most of whom were not only politically ignorant but viscerally anticommunist, much like their American neighbors during the Cold War. Communism was widely perceived as the "Red threat," a kind of insidious foreign infection to be both feared and resisted. How Che dealt with this mentality among his own men is interesting.

Enrique Acevedo, the fifteen-year-old runaway who had joined up with his older brother and been assigned to Che's *descamisados*, later recalled that once when Che was away, some of his men were arguing over whether their *jefe* was a Communist. One of them who insisted that Che was a *ñangaro*—a "Red"—challenged the others. "Haven't you noticed that in the commander's squad there is a great mystery surrounding his books, and they read them at night in a closed circle? That's how he works: first he recruits those closest to him, and later they go filtering it throughout the troops."

Acevedo was too much in awe of Che to approach him personally on the topic, but gradually he and the other fighters in Che's column came to realize that their *comandante* believed in socialism. The first to know it were the rebels attached to his general staff. One of them was Ramón "Guile" Pardo, a teenager who had joined the column in August 1957, following in his older brother Israel's footsteps. Over the course of several months, the

Che with the men of Column No. 4 in El Hombrito, in front of a banner proclaiming "Happy 1958."

younger Pardo became one of Che's group of devoted mascots, mostly teenage boys who served as his couriers and personal bodyguards.

"When we were in El Hombrito," Pardo recalled, "I heard it said that there were some peasants who belonged to the PSP. . . . On our trips, Che visited them and I noticed that he had an affinity with them. He also argued politics a lot with Father Sardiñas, who stayed awhile in our column. Che had a blue book, which was one of the selected works of Lenin, and he studied it frequently. I was curious and wanted to know who Lenin was and I asked him. He explained: 'You know of José Martí, Antonio Maceo and Máximo Gómez'"—Cuba's late-nineteenth-century national independence war heroes—"'Lenin was like them. He fought for his people.' It was the first time someone spoke to me of Lenin."

The young fighters were blank slates upon whom Che made a lasting imprint. He personally taught Israel Pardo and Joel Iglesias, who were illiterate, how to read and write. And for Guile and some of the others, who had more education, he initiated daily study circles. The study material gradually evolved from Cuban history and military doctrine to politics and Marxism. When Joel had finally learned to read, Che gave him a biography of Lenin to study.

Just as he was circumspect about his political role during the war, Che made only oblique references to the early PSP–July 26 links in his later published writings. He sought to depict the revolution as evolving *naturally* toward socialism, an organic result of the Rebel Army's life among the neglected peasants of the Sierra Maestra. "The guerrillas and the peasantry began to merge into a single mass, without our being able to say at what precise moment on the long revolutionary road this happened, or at which moment the words became profoundly real and we became a part of the peasantry," he wrote in an article published in *Lunes de Revolución,* the literary supplement of *Revolución,* a newspaper founded during the guerrilla war and run by Carlos Franqui.* When he described the peasantry's gradual acceptance of the revolution, Che employed religious symbolism, rendering their travails as a kind of Pilgrim's Progress in which individuals found redemption through sacrifice, attaining final enlightenment by learning to live for the common good. "It is a new miracle of the revolution that— under the imperative of war—the staunchest individualist, who zealously protected the boundaries of his property and his own rights, joined the great common effort of the struggle. But there is an even greater miracle: the rediscovery by the Cuban peasant of his own happiness, within the liberated zones. Whoever witnessed the apprehensive murmurs with which our forces were formerly received in each peasant household notes with pride the carefree clamor, the happy, hearty laughter of the new Sierra inhabitant. That is a reflection of the self-confidence that the awareness of his own strength gave to the inhabitant of our liberated area."

Che wrote this article, "War and the Peasantry," only seven months after the war had ended. However consciously he had idealized life in the sierra for public consumption, his evocation of a pastoral utopia wrought through armed struggle was a vision he sought to replicate on an international scale. Most important of all, he identified war as the ideal circumstance in which to achieve a socialist consciousness. In essence, socialism was the natural order of mankind, and guerrilla war the chrysalis from which it would emerge.

*See Notes section.

18

Extending the War

I

By December 1957, Fidel had brought the war down from the Sierra Maestra. Rebel squads began trickling into the llano to launch harassment attacks, firing on garrisoned soldiers as far away as Manzanillo and burning cane trucks and passenger buses on the highway. The strategy expanded the war and diverted attention from the Sierra Maestra, where the rebels had consolidated their control. An uneasy standoff persisted into the new year, with the army mounting no new incursions and the rebels refraining from large-scale assaults.

In the relative calm, no one was more active than Che Guevara. At his new base of operations at La Mesa, facilities were built to replace those destroyed at El Hombrito, among them a butcher shop, a leather workshop, and even a cigar factory. (Che had become addicted to Cuban tobacco and, like Fidel, smoked cigars whenever they were available.) The leather workshop was to provide the troops with shoes, knapsacks, and cartridge belts. The first military cap produced was presented to Fidel and was greeted with raucous laughter. Unwittingly, Che had produced a cap almost identical to those worn by Cuban bus drivers. "The only one showing me any mercy was a municipal councillor from Manzanillo who was visiting . . . and who took it back with him as a souvenir," Che recalled.

Che gave top priority to the Rebel Army's media projects. *El Cubano Libre* was now being printed on a new mimeograph machine, and a small radio transmitter had been installed. By February, Radio Rebelde was making its first broadcasts. He also put great effort into improving the quality and output of war matériel. Che was especially enthusiastic about the small M-26 "Sputnik" bombs. The first ones had been catapulted from the elastic bands of underwater spearguns. Later they were launched from rifles, but the early models were little more than explosive slingshots—a bit of gun-powder packed into condensed milk tins. They made a huge and frighten-ing noise but inflicted little damage, and before long the enemy learned to put up anti-Sputnik nets of wire mesh around their camps. In early 1958 the bombs had not yet been tested in battle, and Che had high hopes for their performance.

Meanwhile, Fidel made a curious overture to Batista. If the army was withdrawn from Oriente, Fidel told a go-between, he would agree to inter-nationally supervised elections. His proposal coincided with an upsurge in public concern over sabotage by the rebels and atrocities by the police in the cities, and Fidel apparently wanted to give the impression that he too wanted peace. The would-be mediator duly carried the proposal to Havana, where the offer was so vehemently rejected that the messenger fled into exile.

The international press was beating a path to Fidel's door. Cuba had become a big story, scrutinized in regular editorials by *The New York Times* and covered by the *Chicago Tribune*'s Latin American correspondent, Jules Dubois. In January and February, numerous reporters, including correspon-dents from *Paris Match* and various Latin American dailies, climbed to the sierra for interviews. Andrew St. George came back, and Fidel made suit-ably friendly declarations to him for his American audience. Fidel even wrote an article for *Coronet,* one of St. George's media outlets, avowing that he was in favor of free enterprise and foreign investment, and against na-tionalization. The provisional government he envisioned as replacing Batista would be composed of Rotary Club members and other solidly middle-class professionals.

In January, the Movement suffered a potentially disastrous setback when Armando Hart and two other July 26 men were arrested after visit-ing Fidel. By all accounts, their captors were planning to execute them, but the American vice-consul (and CIA agent) in Santiago, Robert Wiecha, came to their rescue by getting Ambassador Smith to inquire about their fates. Unfortunately, Hart had been carrying a rather incriminating document when he was captured—a critical salvo he had written to Che in response to Che's fiery missive to Daniel. He had addressed the issue of Che's and Raúl's Marxism as well as the dispute between the llano and the sierra. Fidel had seen the letter and ordered Hart not to send it, fearing that if the epistolary war continued, a letter would eventually fall into enemy hands and give Batista a new propaganda weapon to use against him. These fears had now been realized. Within days of Hart's arrest, Rafael Díaz-Balart, Fidel's former brother-in-law—who despised him passionately—cited the letter on a radio broadcast as evidence of Communist influence in Fidel's organization.

The anti-Fidel propaganda campaign was squandered a few days later, however, when the army took twenty-three rebel suspects from the prison in Santiago to the sierra foothills and murdered them, then reported that they had been killed in battle, with no army casualties. Che wrote a scathing response in his column "Wild Shot" in *Cubano Libre*. After listing a number of other revolutionary wars occurring around the world, Che noted:

> All of them have common characteristics: (A) The governing power "has inflicted numerous casualties on the rebels." (B) There are no prisoners. (C) "Nothing new" [to report] by the governing power. (D) All the revolutionaries, whatever the name of the country or region, are receiving "surreptitious help from the Communists."
> How Cuban the world seems to us! Everything is the same. A group of patriots are murdered, whether or not they have arms, whether or not they are rebels, always after "a fierce fight" . . . , they kill all the witnesses, that is why there are no prisoners. The government never suffers a casualty, which at times is true, because killing defenseless human beings is not very dangerous, but at times it is also a great lie; the Sierra Maestra is our unimpeachable witness.
> And, finally, the same handy accusation as always: "Communists." Communists are always those who pick up their arms tired of so much misery, wherever in the world the action takes place; democrats those who kill the indignant people, whether they be men, women, or children. How Cuban the world is! But everywhere, as in Cuba, the people will have the last word, that of victory, against brute force and injustice.

The slaughter of the Santiago prisoners caught the attention of the Cuban public but did not divert the scrutiny of Fidel by the United States. The revelations in Hart's letter lent further credence to Ambassador Smith's mounting suspicions about "Red" infiltration of the July 26 Movement. In January, Smith made a trip to Washington to make a case for keeping up arms deliveries to Batista, who had promised to restore constitutional guarantees and go through with the June elections if the United States didn't cut him off. As for Castro, Smith told reporters, he did not trust him, and did not think the U.S. government was able to do business with him.

By early February, Che's armory was racing to put the finishing touches on the Sputniks in preparation for the first major military action of the year. Fidel had decided to attack the sawmill community of Pino del Agua again. An army company had established a permanent presence there.

Batista had just lifted censorship everywhere except Oriente, and Fidel wanted to "strike a resounding blow" to earn some headlines.

II

The attack began at dawn on February 16. Fidel's plan was to surround the army camp, destroy its guard posts, and then ambush reinforcements when they came. Che's men brought along six Sputniks, to be fired at the beginning of the attack. Another of his armory's creations, a land mine made from unexploded airplane bombs, was also given its first test. Mines were placed in a road that the army was expected to use. The Sputniks fired successfully but did little damage, and the land mines produced what Che called a "lamentable result." Their first victim was a civilian truck driver who happened along at just the wrong moment.

The attack started well enough. The first wave of fighters overran the guard posts, killing half a dozen sentries and taking three prisoners, but the main body of soldiers quickly rallied, effectively stopping the rebels' advance. Within minutes, four rebels were killed and two more were mortally wounded. Camilo Cienfuegos was wounded twice trying to rescue an abandoned machine gun.

The rebels had better luck against the army reinforcements. The first patrol walked directly into an ambush and was wiped out. But Che wanted to inflict a total defeat and begged Fidel to attack the entrenched enemy camp again, to completely overrun it this time. At his insistence, Fidel sent a couple of platoons to make another try, but they too were repelled under heavy fire. Che then asked Fidel for command of a new assault force; he would try to rout the soldiers by torching their camp. Grudgingly, Fidel let him go but warned him to take great care.

Just as he was preparing the advance, Che received a note from Fidel: "February 16, 1958. CHE: If everything depends on the attack from this side, without support from Camilo and Guillermo [García], I do not think anything suicidal should be done, because there is a risk of many casualties and failure to achieve the objective. I seriously urge you to be careful. You yourself are not to take part in the fighting. That is a strict order. Take charge of leading the men well; that is the most important thing right now. Fidel."

Fidel knew that Che would probably not go forward with his plan if he couldn't take part in the fighting himself—and he was right. "With all this responsibility weighing on my shoulders," Che wrote later, "it was too much, and, crestfallen, I took the same path as my predecessor." He ordered his men to withdraw. Later, speaking about Che's recklessness in battle, Fidel mused that "In a way, he even violated the rules of combat—that is, the ideal norms, the most perfect methods—risking his life in battle because of that character, tenacity, and spirit of his. . . . Therefore, we had to lay down certain rules and guidelines for him to follow."

The next morning, while government planes circled overhead, the rebels retreated into the hills, with five prisoners and forty new weapons. After they withdrew, the army apparently murdered thirteen peasants found hiding near the rebel positions. Denouncing this atrocity in *El Cubano Libre,* Che calculated the enemy losses at eighteen to twenty-two dead, but the army produced different statistics. An official dispatch claimed that "sixteen insurgents and five soldiers" had died in the battle but could not confirm reports that "the well-known Argentine Communist Che Guevara was wounded." A paper in Havana reported that the attack had been led by "the international Communist agent known as 'Che' Guevara."

The weeks following the battle at Pino del Agua saw increased rebel attacks throughout the country. On February 23, in one of the most spectacular publicity coups carried out by the Movement so far, a July 26 unit kidnapped Juan Manuel Fangio, a world-famous Argentine race-car driver who was in Havana to compete in an international championship. Later released unharmed, Fangio declared that his kidnapping had been "friendly," his treatment "warm and cordial."

The Directorio, virtually crippled after its disastrous attack on the presidential palace the previous year, was becoming more active as well. A tiny Directorio breakaway group had been operating in the central Escambray mountains near Cienfuegos for several months. It was led by Eloy Gutiérrez Menoyo, whose brother had died leading the palace assault, and was aided by an American military veteran named William Morgan. In February, their efforts were bolstered with the arrival of a fifteen-man armed Directorio expeditionary force from Miami led by Faure Chomón. Temporarily joining ranks, they carried out a few hit-and-run attacks, then issued a somewhat grandiose proclamation calling for a Cuba with ample employment and educational opportunities, and appealing for the formation of a Bolivarian-style "confederation of American republics." Fidel played the magnanimous elder statesman, sending a note to welcome the Directorio's guerrillas to the "common struggle" and offering them his assistance.

Fidel took new steps to extend his own theater of operations. On February 27, he named his three principal lieutenants—his brother Raúl, Juan Almeida, and Camilo Cienfuegos—as *comandantes* of their own columns. In keeping with his custom of exaggerating his force's size, Fidel called Raúl's "Frank País" unit Column Six and Almeida's "Santiago de Cuba" unit Column Three. Raúl was to open up a Second Eastern Front in the Sierra Cristal in northeastern Oriente, adjacent to the American naval base at Guantánamo Bay, while Almeida was to start up the Third Eastern Front, covering the area from the eastern Sierra Maestra to the city of Santiago. Camilo's theater of operations would be determined once he recovered from the wounds he suffered at Pino del Agua.

Fidel also set about consolidating his power within the *territorio libre* of the Sierra Maestra. Humberto Sorí-Marín, the lawyer who had assisted in the "bandit trials" in October, drafted legislation that imposed revolutionary authority over the inhabitants of rebel-held territory. Sorí-Marín also prepared an agrarian reform law that gave "legal" backing to the wholesale rustling of cattle from landowners and their distribution among Fidel's fighters and the peasants of the region.* In March, impetus was given to another project, the creation of a training school for recruits and officers at Minas del Frío. It was to be run under Che's direction, with day-to-day administration handled by a new convert named Evelio Lafferte.

Just a month earlier, Lafferte had been a twenty-six-year-old army lieutenant fighting against the rebels at Pino del Agua. The rebel leader he most feared was Che Guevara. "The propaganda against him was massive," Lafferte recalled. "They said that he was a murderer for hire, a pathological criminal . . . a mercenary who lent his services to international Communism, that he used terrorist methods and that he *socialized* [brainwashed] the women and took away their sons. . . . [It was said] that any soldier he took prisoner he tied to a tree and opened up his guts with a bayonet."

Immediately after the ambush in which Lafferte was captured and many of his fellow soldiers were killed, he was led before the feared Argentine. "He told me: 'So you are one of the little officers who come to finish off the Rebel Army, huh?' He repeated that 'little officer' and this angered me," Lafferte said. "It was in an ironic tone and it seemed to be a hint of worse to come." Lafferte was convinced that the rebels meant to kill him, but he was taken instead to an improvised prison at Che's La Mesa camp. The rebels realized they had a potentially valuable man on their hands. Lafferte was a bright and distinguished young officer, the best of his class at Cuba's military academy, and was beset by doubts about the army's brutal conduct of the war. Fidel personally urged Lafferte to join his side. After a month of preferential treatment, he accepted Fidel's offer and was immediately made a captain and sent to run Che's training school in Minas del Frío.

---

*By the end of the war, an estimated 10,000 head of cattle had been "liberated" in this fashion by the rebels in Oriente. Because many peasants became the owners of livestock for the first time in their lives, it was one of the Rebel Army's most popular measures and won the support of numerous *guajiros*.

Che was careful in his dealings with Lafferte. He spent time with the
young officer, talking about his family and about literature and poetry, a
love they shared. Lafferte showed Che some poems he had written, and Che
gave him a copy of a book by Pablo Neruda. He listened to Lafferte's suggestions for running the school at Minas del Frío and accepted those he found
convincing. One he did not accept was Lafferte's idea that recruits should
"swear by God" in their oath of allegiance. "When the comrades come to
the Sierra," Che told him, "we don't take into account whether they believe
in God or not, so we can't oblige them to swear by God. For example, I don't
believe, and I am a fighter of the Rebel Army. . . . Do you think it's right to
force me to swear an oath to something I don't believe in?" Lafferte was
convinced by Che's argument: "I was Catholic," he said, "but I understood
the correctness of what he was proposing, and I took God out of the oath."

Once the school was up and running, Che brought Pablo Ribalta, the
Communist Youth leader, to take charge of the ideological orientation of
the recruits. Ribalta concealed his identity under the pseudonym Moisés
Pérez. So as not to scare off his pupils with Marxist texts, he used the expe-
riences of the sierra war, Cuban history, and the writings and speeches of
Fidel and other guerrilla leaders to drive his points home. One of the other
guerrilla leaders was Mao Tse-tung. "For Che, the guerrilla war wasn't just
a military proving ground, but also a cultural and educational one," recalled
Harry Villegas Tamayo, who was sixteen when he was at Minas del Frío.
"He was concerned with forming the future cadres of the Revolution."

III

Some of the reporters who met Che in the Sierra Maestra came away as
admirers and disciples.* One of these was the Uruguayan Carlos María
Gutiérrez, who met Che immediately after the battle of Pino del Agua. Che
had pumped Gutiérrez for information about his photographic equipment.
What light meters did he use? How long did he expose his film? And—a
question Che was to repeat to every visitor from the *mate*-drinking countries of Uruguay and Argentina—had he brought some *yerba mate* with

---

*Bob Taber, the CBS journalist, would eventually cross the line altogether, helping to found
the Fair Play for Cuba Committee and lobbying in the United States on behalf of the Castro
government. Herbert Matthews's early romantic boosterism of Fidel Castro undermined his
journalistic credibility and ultimately damaged his career at *The New York Times*. The young
Ecuadorean journalist Carlos Bastidas, who came to the sierra in early 1958, was determined to
take up the Movement's cause with the Organization of American States in Washington. Before
he could leave the country, however, Bastidas was murdered by Batista's intelligence police.

him? Over the next few days, as he was shown around the base hospital and the shoe factory, Gutiérrez took note of the unusual warmth and camaraderie among Che's men. "There were no orders given, nor permissions granted, nor military protocol," he said. "The guerrillas of La Mesa reflected a discipline that was more intimate, derived from the men's confidence in their leaders. Fidel, Che, and the others lived in the same places, ate the same, and at the hour of combat fired from the same line as they did. Guevara didn't have to abandon his *porteño*'s brusqueness to show that he loved them, and they paid him back with the same virile reticence, with an adherence that went deeper than mere obedience."

Among the visitors to the sierra in the spring of 1958 was the young Argentine journalist Jorge Ricardo Masetti. Like some of his predecessors, Masetti, who had a background in an ultraright Perónist youth group, would find his life irrevocably changed by the experience. By coincidence, Masetti came with a letter of introduction from Ernesto Guevara's old acquaintance Ricardo Rojo, who had returned to Argentina in 1955 after the right-wing military coup that toppled Perón.* In late 1957, Masetti tracked down Rojo at the Café La Paz, a literary and theater hangout in central Buenos Aires, and asked for help in meeting the Sierra Maestra rebels. Rojo jotted off a quick note to Che: "Dear Chancho: The bearer is a newspaperman and friend who wants to do a news program for El Mundo radio station in Buenos Aires. Please take good care of him, he's a good man." Rojo signed it "The Sniper," the nickname he and Che had traded back and forth in their Central American days, little knowing that his friend had once again appropriated it for himself.

Masetti was the first Argentine visitor to the mountains, and some of the young rebels asked excitedly if he was Che's brother. Masetti seemed determined not to feel impressed at their first meeting: "From his chin sprouted a few hairs that wanted to be a beard. . . . The famous Che Guevara seemed to me to be a typical middle-class Argentine boy." Over a shared breakfast, Masetti prodded Che on why he was fighting in a land that was not his own. Che puffed on a pipe as he spoke, and Masetti thought his accent sounded no longer Argentine but a mixture of Cuban and Mexican. "In the first place," Che told Masetti, "I consider my fatherland to be not

---

*Rojo had gone to work for his political mentor, Arturo Frondízi, who in 1956 formed the liberal Radical Party breakaway, the Union Cívica Radical Intransigente. When General Aramburu acceded to elections, Rojo was instrumental in setting up talks between Frondízi's party and Perón—still powerful in exile—for the purpose of winning Frondízi the crucial *peronista* vote. The bid was successful: Frondízi won the presidential elections held in February 1958 and Rojo was repaid for his efforts with a diplomatic post in Bonn.

Che with the Argentine journalist Jorge Ricardo Masetti
in the spring of 1958. Masetti's taped interviews with Che
were broadcast internationally.

only Argentina, but all of America. I have predecessors as glorious as Martí
and it is precisely in his land where I am adhering to his doctrine. What is
more, I cannot conceive that it can be called interference to give myself personally, to give myself completely, to offer my blood for a cause I consider
just and popular, to help a people liberate themselves from tyranny. . . . No
country until now has denounced the American interference in Cuban
affairs nor has a single daily newspaper accused the Yankees of helping
Batista massacre his people. But many are concerned about me. I am the
meddling foreigner who helps the rebels with his flesh and blood. Those
who provide the arms for a civil war aren't meddlers. I am."

As Che talked, it struck Masetti that he spoke in a completely impersonal fashion, although a smile seemed constantly to play on his lips. Masetti
asked about Fidel Castro's Communism. At this, Che smiled broadly but
answered with the same detachment as before. "Fidel isn't a Communist. If
he was, we would at least have more arms. But this revolution is exclusively
Cuban. Or better said, Latin American. Politically, Fidel and his movement
can be said to be 'revolutionary nationalist.' Of course it is anti-Yankee, in
the way that the Yankees are antirevolutionaries. But in reality we don't put
preach anti-Yankism. We are against the United States because the United

States is against our people. The person most attacked with the label of Communism is myself."

As for his reasons for joining the Cuban force in Mexico, Che saw a strong connection to his years of travel. "The truth is that after the experiences of my wanderings across all of Latin America and, to top it off, in Guatemala, it didn't take much to incite me to join any revolution against a tyrant, but Fidel impressed me as an extraordinary man. He faced and overcame the most impossible things. He had an exceptional faith that once he left for Cuba, he would arrive. And that once he arrived, he would fight. And that fighting, he would win. I shared his optimism. . . . It was time to stop crying and fight."

Masetti returned to Argentina with his scoop. He had interviewed Fidel and Che—who had spoken for the first time to an international broadcast audience. He also returned with a recorded greeting from Che to the Guevara family. During the past year, letters from Ernesto had been rare. More often than not, the family learned about him through magazines and newspapers. They were delighted by the photograph accompanying Herbert Matthews's famous interview with Fidel in *The New York Times,* in which Ernesto appeared holding a gun and sporting a scraggly beard. Matthews's articles had also calmed the Guevaras' anxieties about their son's adopted cause. "Now we knew," his father wrote, "that Ernesto was fighting for a cause recognized as just." In the spring of 1958, Che's father saw an article about Che written by Bob Taber: "Will Che Be Able to Change the Destiny of America?" To the elder Guevara, it proved his son was *someone.* "I confess that what Taber wrote impressed the whole family," he recalled. "Ernesto was not just another guerrilla, but was mentioned as a future leader of countries."

Other news came from Dolores Moyano, Ernesto's childhood friend, who now lived in New York and who sent the Guevaras clippings from the Miami-based *Diario de las Americas.* The July 26 committee in New York sent them copies of rebel army communiqués. And soon Ernesto senior was getting regular briefings from the *Chicago Tribune*'s Latin American correspondent, Jules Dubois, who looked him up on a visit to Buenos Aires. They would meet for a chat over whiskey whenever Dubois was in town. In exchange for details of Che's latest exploits, Dubois pumped the elder Guevara about the young Che. Ernesto senior became suspicious when Dubois asked him to write down a summary of what he knew about Fidel Castro. He claimed that his suspicions that Dubois was actually a CIA official were confirmed by a "very good source." (True or not, this charge became official dogma in Cuba, where the elder Guevara was living when he wrote his memoir.)

When Carlos María Gutiérrez returned from Cuba, brimming with admiration for the revolution and for Che, he too looked up Che's family in Buenos Aires. "When he talked to us about Ernesto," Che's father recalled, "his words didn't entirely convince us, because he spoke of a romantic and bohemian hero." Also a very busy one. According to Gutiérrez, Che "had laid the bases for agrarian reform in the Sierra; built an arms factory; invented a bazooka rifle; inaugurated the first bread factory in the mountains; built and equipped a hospital . . . created the first school and . . . installed a radio transmitter called Radio Rebelde . . . and he still had time left to found a small newspaper for the rebel troops."

Masetti's visit increased the Guevara family's feeling of vicarious celebrity. They listened to the recording their son's latest admirer had brought them, and the broadcasts of Che's interviews on Radio El Mundo. After their first visits, Masetti and Gutiérrez became frequent visitors and family friends, and, infected by their enthusiasm, Ernesto senior embraced the Cuban revolution with fervor. "The defense of the Cuban Revolution entrapped us all," he wrote. "My house on Calle Araoz turned into a revolutionary center." He rented another studio near his office and turned it into a branch of the local July 26 support committee and, in a move reminiscent of his work during the Spanish Civil War and World War II, founded a "Comité de Ayuda a Cuba," which held dances and sold bonds to raise funds.

Hilda had become the official representative of the July 26 Movement in Peru. July 26 chapters had been set up throughout Latin America and the United States, raising funds, advertising the aims of the Movement, and disseminating information to the press. "I worked, complying with instructions sent me by the committee, on propaganda and money collection," Hilda wrote. With some members from the leftist wing of APRA, which she had rejoined, she founded a support group to help Cuban exiles seeking refuge in Peru. Yet, for all her political activity, Hilda's reminiscences of the period have a certain scolding quality. "Letters came from time to time from Ernesto. Only a few of mine managed to reach him, however, although I followed his instructions. . . . When Hildita was two years old, February 15, 1958, I wrote Ernesto and asked him to authorize my coming to the mountains of Cuba, to be with him and help; the child was then old enough to be cared for either by my family or his. His reply took four or five months to arrive. He said I couldn't come yet; the fight was at a dangerous stage, and an offensive would begin in which he himself would not remain in any one place."

There was another reason why Hilda's presence in the Sierra Maestra would not be opportune. In the spring of 1958, Che had taken a lover, a young *guajira* named Zoila Rodríguez. Che's adolescent protégé, Joel

Iglesias, observed the lightning courtship. "In Las Vegas de Jibacoa, Che met a black girl, or better said a *mulata,* with a really beautiful body, called Zoila, and he liked her a lot," Iglesias said. "A lot of women went crazy over him, but he was always very strict and respectful in that sense . . . but he liked *that* girl. They hooked up and were together for a time."

Zoila was a single mother of eighteen and still living on her father's farm when she met Che. "It was about four in the afternoon of a date I can't remember," she reminisced years later. "I was corralling some cows when he came. He was mounted on a mule. . . . He was dressed in a strange green uniform, with a black beret." He had come to see if her father, a rebel collaborator, could shoe his mule; with her father away, Zoila offered to do it for him. "As I shoed the mule, I looked at him sideways and I realized he was observing me, but he was looking at me in the way boys look at girls and I got really nervous. When I went to the box of irons to choose a rasp, he asked me what I was going to do and I explained that I had cut the hooves and now I had to level them off to mount the shoes. Guevara said was it really necessary to make them so beautiful. I said that's the way it had to be. He kept looking at me in that way . . . a stare a little bit naughty, like he wanted to scold me for something I hadn't done."

When Zoila had finished shoeing the mule she offered Che coffee. As he drank it he asked Zoila about herself. Where had she learned how to shoe mules? Was she married or single? "He impressed me a lot," Zoila recalled. "The truth is that, and I can't deny it, as a woman I liked him very much, above all his stare, he had such beautiful eyes, a smile so calm that it would move any heart, it could move any woman."

When Zoila's father returned home, he explained to her in admiring tones that Guevara was an extraordinary man who had come to lift them from their misery and disgrace. Soon afterward, Zoila began to carry out small errands for the rebels, meeting Che occasionally, until one day he asked her to stay on permanently at Minas del Frío. She helped out in the kitchen and in the hospital, and she worked hard. "He told me he admired me for that and he admired the peasants for the difficult work we had to do," Zoila recalled. "He asked me many things about the Sierra Maestra, how the plants were called, what were they good for, especially the medicinal ones. . . . He wanted to know all about the animals and the birds of the bush. A great and beautiful love arose in me and I committed myself to him, not just as a fighter but as a woman."

For the next several months, Zoila stayed by Che's side. Interestingly, he doesn't appear to have tried to educate her politically. Zoila remembered one day when she saw one of his books and was amazed at the sight of its golden letters. "I asked him if they were made of gold. He thought the question was

funny. He laughed, and he said: 'That book is about Communism.' I was
too shy to ask him what Communism meant, because I had never heard that
word before."

IV

In March 1958, Fidel Castro faced a potential new roadblock in his path to
power: a peace initiative. The Catholic Church had called for an end to rebel
violence and the creation of a national unity government. A "harmony commission" made up of conservative politicians, businessmen, and a priest was
created to mediate. Batista went through the motions of seeming receptive,
but Fidel rejected the commission as overly pro-Batista. This was risky, since
there was growing public support for a negotiated settlement, and Fidel
could be viewed as an impediment. But at a crucial moment, Batista gave
him a way out.

The catalyst was provided when a judge in Havana indicted two of
Batista's most notorious henchmen for murder. Batista responded by again
suspending constitutional guarantees and throwing out the indictment. The
offending judge fled the country and the United States suspended arms
shipments to Cuba. In the face of Washington's disapproval, increased rebel
sabotage, and mounting calls for his resignation by Cuban civic institutions,
Batista compounded his problems by postponing the scheduled June elections until November. Fidel—whose firepower had been reinforced by a
planeload of weapons flown directly on a C-47 transport from Costa Rica
to a rendezvous point near Estrada Palma—met with his National Directorate (minus Armando Hart, who was imprisoned on the Isle of Pines and
would remain there until the rebels' victory).* On March 12, they signed a
manifesto calling for preparations to begin for the long-planned general
strike and for "total war" against the regime.

The goal was nothing less than a complete paralysis of the nation. As
of April 1, no taxes were to be paid; by April 5, anyone remaining in the

---

*With the arms shipment came Pedro Miret, who had been in prison in Mexico at the time
of the *Granma*'s sailing; he now rejoined Fidel as a member of his general staff. Accompanying him was Huber Matos, a Manzanillo schoolteacher and rice grower who had gone into
exile after helping transport the first rebel reinforcements to the sierra the year before. Fidel
made Matos an officer, and he would later become *comandante* of Column Nine. The pilot
of the plane—which the rebels burned after unloading its cargo—was Pedro Luis Díaz Lanz,
a defector from Batista's air force. Before the war was over, Díaz Lanz would make a number of arms deliveries to the rebels and would be named the revolution's air force chief; later,
he would become one of the Castro regime's most dangerous enemies.

executive branch of government would be considered a traitor, and those joining the armed forces were to be considered criminals. Judges should resign their offices. When the strike call was announced over the radio, the rebels would launch armed attacks in Havana and throughout the country. While Faustino Pérez, who had recently been released from prison, organized the strikes in Havana, Fidel would prepare his army for what he hoped would be a full-scale insurrection.

Eager to be involved, the Communist Party of Cuba, the PSP, ordered its own militants to begin organizing for action, but once again the conservative llano leaders of the National Directorate blocked their involvement. Even after the PSP had sent an emissary to Fidel to plead its case, and Fidel responded by ordering the movement to allow "all Cuban workers, no matter what their political or revolutionary affiliations," to participate in the strike committees, the llano leaders studiously excluded the Communists.

The strike call came on April 9, and it was a catastrophe. The Confederación de Trabajadores Cubanos, which was controlled by Batista, and the disenfranchised PSP ignored it. Most shops and factories in Havana remained open, and the key sectors of electricity and transport were unaffected. The strike also fizzled in Santiago, and by the end of the day as many as thirty people lay dead at the hands of police and Rolando Masferrer's death squads. As for the other decrees for resignations and nonpayment of taxes, they were scarcely heeded. Nonethless, Fidel put a brave face on things, and in a broadcast on April 10 thundered, "All Cuba burns and erupts in an explosion of anger against the assassins, the bandits and gangsters, the informers and strikebreakers, the thugs and military still loyal to Batista."

But for all of Fidel's face-saving rhetoric, the failure of the strike had been a severe blow to the rebel cause. "The strike experience involved a great moral rout for the Movement," Fidel wrote to Celia Sánchez on April 16, "but I hope that we'll be able to regain the people's faith in us. The Revolution is once again in danger and its salvation rests in our hands." If Fidel's pride had been hurt, his ego was essentially undamaged. "We cannot continue to disappoint the nation. There are many things we must do, do them well and on a grand scale; and I will do them. Time will justify me one day."

Fidel blamed the llano leadership for the failure of the strike, and the Communists blamed the July 26 Movement generally for "adventurism." The fiasco was a boon for Batista. His old enemy in the Dominican Republic, Rafael Trujillo, sent him five planeloads of war matériel; and with a notable drop-off in rebel activity after the strike, Batista began drawing up ambitious plans to launch a summer offensive for liquidating Fidel's insurgency once and for all.

Fidel's ill-disguised appeal for "workers' unity" was fresh evidence that
the Communists and Castro were getting cozy. Indeed, the PSP had suddenly become rather public in its support of the rebel movement. In February, the National Committee of the PSP had issued a document stating that
"in spite of the radical discrepancies it has with the tactics of the '26 de Julio'
in the rest of the territory of the country, [the Party] justifies and compre-
hends the guerrilla action in the Sierra Maestra." On March 12, an article
titled "Why Our Party Supports the Sierra Maestra" was published in the
Party's weekly bulletin, Carta Semanal. "We don't limit ourselves to view
with sympathy the activity of the forces in arms commanded by Fidel Castro,
'Che' Guevara, and others," the article asserted. "We adopt the position of
supporting actively, in all of the guerrilla zone, the troops who fight against
the [Batista] tyranny. . . . In addition to trying to aid the activities of the
patriotic forces that operate in the Sierra Maestra, we are trying to push
forward the links between the guerrilla action and the class struggle in all
the neighboring zone."

Even today, most surviving former Soviet officials of the period ad-
here to the official dogma that Soviet leaders were largely ignorant of events
in Cuba and that the rebel victory in January 1959 caught them by surprise,
but such claims fly in the face of an abundance of contrary evidence. For a
start, the Soviets had already had direct contacts with Che and Raúl Castro
in Mexico, where the Soviet Union maintained an important embassy, and
where its officials kept in touch with leaders of the region's Communist
parties, including the Cuban PSP. And while old Latin American Communists bristle at the notion that they were minions of Moscow, the fact is that
most of the regional Communist parties of the day depended on Moscow
for subsidies as well as policy directives. It would appear unlikely almost to
the point of absurdity that the Soviets remained unaware of the Cuban
Party's moves toward an alliance with Fidel Castro's revolution in the spring
of 1958. What is certain is that by early 1958, more Communists had begun
joining the Rebel Army, in particular Che's and Raúl's columns.

Meanwhile, Fidel was preparing to deal a masterstroke against the
Movement in the llano. The failure of the general strike had painfully borne
out the leadership's weaknesses, and it gave Fidel a new position of strength
from which to assert direct control over the entire Movement. He told Celia
Sánchez at the time, "No one will ever be able to make me trust the organization again. . . . I am the supposed leader of this Movement, and in the eyes
of history I must take the responsibility for the stupidity of others. . . . With
the excuse of fighting caudillismo, each one attempts to do more and more
what he feels like doing. I am not such a fool that I don't realize this, nor
am I a man given to seeing visions and phantoms."

On April 16, after Camilo Cienfuego's column had returned to the sierra from a brief foray onto the plains, Fidel named him military chief of the triangle of land between Bayamo, Manzanillo, and Las Tunas, with orders to coordinate all guerrilla activities in the region. He was to take over command of sabotage and supply in those cities, to carry out agrarian reform, and "to modify the civil code"—extending Fidel's revolutionary writ from the Sierra Maestra to the llano. Fidel's rebels could now, theoretically, strike anywhere in Oriente, but before he could give real teeth to his new plan, Fidel realized he was going to have to dig in and defend the Sierra Maestra. It was clear that Batista planned to launch a major army offensive.

In mid-April, Fidel and Che moved from their bases at La Plata and La Mesa to the northeast foothills. Fidel set up his command headquarters at El Jíbaro, while Che's unit was a day's march away, near the village of Minas de Bueycito, where Sánchez Mosquera had quartered his troops. Che's mission was to hold the rebel front line against army penetration, and he based himself in a commandeered landowner's house in a place called La Otilia, a little over a mile from the enemy base. Neither side seemed eager to risk a decisive battle. At night the rebels fired their M-26 bombs, and their patrols routinely skirmished with the army, but Sánchez Mosquera's main activity took the form of reprisals against civilians in the area, burning and looting homes and killing people suspected of collaborating with the rebels. For some reason, La Otilia was not attacked.

"I have never been able to find out why Sánchez Mosquera allowed us to be comfortably settled in a house," Che wrote later, "in a relatively flat area with little vegetation, without calling the enemy air force to attack us. Our guess was that he was not interested in fighting and that he did not want to let the air force see how close his troops were, because he would then have to explain why he did not attack."

La Otilia may have remained unscathed, but its approaches were a dangerous free-fire zone. One night, returning to base from a visit with Fidel, Che and his guide came upon a chilling scene. "In this last leg of the trip, already near the house, a strange spectacle presented itself by the light of a full moon that clearly illuminated the surroundings: in one of those rolling fields, with scattered palm trees, there appeared a row of dead mules, some with their harnesses on. When we got down from our horses to examine the first mule and saw the bullet holes, the guide's expression as he looked at me was an image out of a cowboy movie. The hero of the film arrives with his partner and sees a horse killed by an arrow. He says something like, 'The Sioux,' and makes a special face for the occasion. That's what the man's face was like and perhaps my own as well, although I did not bother to look at myself. A few meters farther on was the second, then the third, then the fourth or fifth dead mule. It had been a convoy of supplies for us, captured by one of Sánchez Mosquera's expeditions. I seem to recall that a civilian was also murdered. The guide refused to follow me. He claimed he did not know the terrain and simply got on his mount. We separated amicably."

Within a few weeks of setting up camp at La Otilia, Che received new orders. In preparation for the army invasion, which appeared more imminent by the day, Fidel wanted Che to take direct charge of the recruit training school at Minas del Frío; a large number of new volunteers had assembled there, and they were to provide the backbone of a new command that was to undertake a risky crossing of the island as soon as they were ready and conditions were right. Taking charge of Che's column in the line against Sánchez Mosquera would be his deputy, Ramiro Valdés.

As a safeguard, Fidel also wanted to consolidate the Rebel Army's infrastructure. Radio Rebelde and *El Cubano Libre* were moved from La Mesa to his command base at La Plata. With its hospitals, electric generators, and munition stores, La Plata was a vital nerve center the rebels could not afford to lose, and it was to be the last line of defense. Food and medicine had to be brought and stockpiled for what could be a long siege.

Feeling fretful, Che set off to assume his new duties accompanied by a small handpicked group of fighters. His diary reflected his dampened mood: "We left at dawn, me with low spirits, for having to abandon a zone that I had under my control for nearly a year, and in really critical moments, because Sánchez Mosquera's troops are coming up with more enthusiasm."

Fidel's new orders had also dashed Che's hopes of joining Camilo Cienfuegos on the expanded war front of the llano. When Camilo learned of Che's reassignment, he wrote a note to console him: "Che. Soul brother: I see Fidel has put you in charge of the Military School, which makes me very happy because now we can count on having first-class soldiers in the future. . . . You've played a very principal role in this showdown and if we need you in this insurrectional stage, Cuba needs you even more when the war ends, so the Giant [Fidel] does a good thing in looking after you. I would like to be always at your side, you were my chief for a long time and you will always continue to be. Thanks to you I now have the opportunity to be more useful. I'll do the unspeakable to not make you look bad. Your eternal *chicharrón,* Camilo."

V

For the rest of April, Che was constantly on the move. Together with some pilots now working for the rebels, he searched for a good site to build an airstrip and found one near La Plata. He left men in charge of clearing the brush and digging a tunnel in which to hide the planes from view. He inspected the work under way at the unfinished recruits' school at Minas del Frío and met every few days with Fidel.

As Batista's grip weakened, the Byzantine jockeying of the opposition increased. Given Fidel's prominence and moral authority, a succession of groups attempted to curry favor with him while simultaneously trying to undermine his position. Justo Carrillo, the exiled leader of a failed 1956 military uprising, who still had deep connections in the Cuban army, offered Fidel military support in return for a manifesto "eulogizing" the armed forces. Although Fidel was interested in winning over sectors of the armed forces, he also saw the danger of being outfoxed. A coup organized by Carrillo, together with his imprisoned coconspirator, Colonel Ramón Barquín, would probably appeal to the Cuban business community, traditional political parties, and Washington. Carrillo could then simply turn against Fidel.

Perhaps the greatest threat to Fidel's power, however, was to be found within his own July 26 Movement. With the embarrassing failure of the general strike, Fidel had the ammunition he needed to move against the National Directorate leaders, and he summoned them to Altos de Mompié. Che played a principal role in a dramatic showdown on May 3. "I made a small analysis of the situation," Che wrote in his diary, "setting forth the reality of two antagonistic policies, that of the Sierra and that of the Llano, the validity of the Sierra's policies and our correctness in fearing for the success of the strike." He blamed the llano leaders' "sectarianism" in blocking the PSP's involvement, which had doomed the strike before it even started. "I gave my opinion that the greatest responsibility fell upon the chief of the workers, on the top leader of the llano militia brigades and on the chief for Havana, that is to say Mario [David Salvador], Daniel, and Faustino. So they should resign."

After a heated debate that lasted into the evening, Fidel put Che's proposals to a vote, and the measures passed. The result was a total revamping of the llano leadership, with Faustino, Daniel, and David Salvador dismissed from their posts and transferred to the Sierra Maestra. The most important change of all was that the National Directorate itself would be moved to the Sierra Maestra. Fidel was now the general secretary, with sole authority over foreign affairs and arms supply, as well as commander in chief of the Movement's nationwide network of underground militias. A five-member secretariat would serve under him, dealing with finances, political affairs, and workers' issues; and the July 26 office in Santiago, once the Oriente headquarters, would now be a mere outpost, a "delegation" answerable to the general secretary.

In "A Decisive Meeting," which Che wrote for the armed forces magazine *Verde Olivo* in late 1964, he summed up the achievements of that fateful day: "At this meeting decisions were taken that confirmed Fidel's moral
authority, his indisputable stature, and the conviction among the majority
of revolutionaries present that errors of judgment had been committed. . . .
But most important, the meeting discussed and passed judgment on two
conceptions that had clashed with one another throughout the whole previous stage of directing the war. The guerrilla conception would emerge
triumphant from that meeting. Fidel's standing and authority were
consolidated. . . . There now arose only one authoritative leadership, the
Sierra, and concretely one single leader, one commander in chief, Fidel
Castro."*

If others had been concerned about Fidel's caudillismo, it was now a
moot point. It had never been a problem for Che. He had always thought
ahead to the day when the *true* revolution would be built, and he believed
that only a strongman could do it. From now on, the road forward was clear.

Che had little time to savor the victory. Already, the army had begun
to make moves in its summer offensive, positioning troops along the flanks
of the mountains and reinforcing the garrisons along the coast. Ambush
positions had to be selected, trenches dug, and supply and fallback routes
worked out, all within a coordinated plan of action. To the west, in the hills
around Pico Caracas, Crescencio Pérez would have to hold the line with
his "small and poorly armed groups," while Ramiro Valdés was to hold the
land around La Botella and La Mesa to the east. A huge responsibility was
resting on Che's shoulders, and he kept up a frenetic pace of activity to meet
it. "This small territory had to be defended, with not much more than two
hundred functioning rifles, when a few days later Batista's army began its
'encirclement and annihilation' offensive."

VI

An air of crisis pervaded the sierra, with daily reports and rumors of enemy
troops closing in. On May 6, the army occupied two rice farms at the edge
of the sierra and took a rebel prisoner. On May 8, more troops disembarked
at two points along the coast. On May 10, La Plata was bombed from the air
and from the sea. Che rushed from one place to the other, moving or reinforcing rebel positions according to the latest intelligence. He also carried
out nonmilitary missions. He pushed the agrarian reform program forward

*See Notes for elaboration.

and attempted to collect taxes from Oriente landowners and planters. Fidel wanted to get in as much money as he could to help sustain the Rebel Army during the offensive, but Che found the plantation owners recalcitrant. "Later," he wrote in his diary, "when our strength was solid, we got even."

With recruits from the school at Minas del Frío, Che formed a new column, Number Eight, named in honor of his late comrade Ciro Redondo. The recruits had been trained by a volunteer weapons instructor, an American Korean War veteran named Herman Marks. Fidel, meanwhile, was quite clearly alarmed about the ability of his forces to withstand the invasion, and had begun hatching schemes that verged on the apocalyptic. On April 26, he had written to Celia Sánchez: "I need *cyanide*. Do you know any way to obtain it in some quantity? But we also need *strychnine*—as much of it as possible. We must get these very circumspectly, for if word leaks out, it will be of no use. I have some surprises in store for the time the offensive hits us." Whether or not Fidel obtained the poisons, or what he planned to do with them, is unknown. Presumably he planned to poison the water supplies in his camps if they were overrun. In the grip of this bunker mentality, he sent an urgent note to Che, who was inspecting the frontline defenses, and ordered him back to headquarters.

Che drove back in a jeep with Oscar "Oscarito" Fernández Mell, a twenty-five-year-old doctor who had just left Havana to join the rebels. With Che in the driver's seat, they traveled at breakneck speeds along a narrow dirt road that skirted steep precipices. Oscarito was visibly nervous, and Che told him not to worry, adding, "When we get to where we're going, I want to tell you something." Oscarito was later duly informed that Che had never driven before. With his old sidekick, Alberto Granado, he had learned to drive a motorbike, but he had never sat behind the wheel of a car.

While Che waited for Fidel to return from an inspection of the coastal front, his most trusted courier, Lidia Doce Sánchez, went on a mission to make contact with "friends" in Havana, Camagüey, and Manzanillo. Lidia was a woman in her mid-forties who had left her bakery in San Pedro de Yao to accompany the rebel force after her only son joined up. She carried the most compromising rebel communiqués and documents into and out of the Sierra Maestra and to Havana and Santiago. These were highly dangerous assignments that involved repeatedly crossing enemy lines and would have meant torture and almost certain death if she were caught. On this mission, she would have to exit the sierra at a place where there was a *guardia* presence.

Lidia was to become one of Che's most exalted revolutionary personalities, an examplar of self-sacrifice, honesty, and bravery. Che repaid her loyalty by leaving her in command of an auxiliary camp situated close to enemy lines. The camp became increasingly dangerous, and several times he had tried to pull her out, but Lidia refused to leave. Che wrote that she led the camp "with spirit and a touch of high-handedness, causing a certain resentment among the Cuban men under her command, who were not accustomed to taking orders from a woman." Only when Che was transferred did she agree to leave the camp, in order to follow him.

Che waited for Fidel to return to headquarters for several days, from May 15 to May 18. During this time, he played host to a number of visitors. His journal entries are vague but they indicate that he was fielding overtures from a number of political groups, including the Communist Party. The most significant visit was from someone he described only as "Rafael, an old acquaintance," and a PSP man named Lino. By May 19, the other visitors had left, but the PSP men stayed on to meet with Fidel. Then the journalist José Ricardo Masetti unexpectedly reappeared in camp, having come back to the sierra for another interview with Fidel. His arrival meant a further delay in Fidel's meeting with the Communists, for, as Che noted in his diary, "it isn't convenient that he [Masetti] hears anything."

On May 22, with Masetti finally gone, the summit between the PSP and Fidel got under way. Rafael and Lino carried a proposal for a united front of revolutionary forces but also conveyed the Party's enduring doubts over the "negative attitude" of the National Directorate. Fidel accepted the idea of a union "in principle," Che wrote, "but he put up some reservations about the forms without ending the discussion." The paramount item on Fidel's agenda was to beat back the unfolding enemy offensive, and although a unity of forces on the llano was desirable, it was not essential at the moment. He hoped to avoid a protracted and bloody showdown with the armed forces, and the way to do that was by breaking their morale in the sierra; then he would sweep down onto the llano, and political alliances would be his for the asking. As always, Fidel's fear of American intervention on Batista's behalf dictated that he continue his go-slow policy with the Communist Party.

There were certainly signs that this fear was not misplaced. In spite of the State Department's suspension of arms shipments to Batista, the Defense Department had just delivered 300 rockets to the Cuban air force from its stocks at the American base at Guantánamo. Fueling Fidel's suspicions that Trujillo and Somoza were working as U.S. proxies to provide Batista with war matériel, a ship from Nicaragua had arrived with thirty tanks in early May.

If anything, U.S. concern about Fidel's true political sentiments had grown over the past few months. In May, Jules Dubois, the *Chicago Tribune*'s correspondent, used Radio Rebelde's newly boosted transmitter links with the outside world to conduct an interview with Fidel from Caracas; his main line of inquiry centered on charges linking Fidel to the Communists. Fidel accused Batista of spreading the rumor in order to obtain U.S. arms, and denied any intention of nationalizing industry or the private business sector. He had no presidential aspirations of his own, Fidel explained. But the July 26 Movement would become a political party after the revolution, to "fight with the arms of the Constitution and of the law."

There was a growing gulf between Fidel's public reassurances and his private thoughts. On June 5, shortly after the first American-supplied rockets were used by Batista's air force in the Sierra Maestra, hitting a civilian's home, he wrote to Celia Sánchez, "When I saw the rockets that they fired on Mario's house, I swore that the Americans are going to pay dearly for what they're doing. When this war is over, I'll start a much longer and bigger war of my own: the war I'm going to fight against them. I realize that will be my true destiny."

In the short term, Fidel waged a campaign to win over key military officers, writing a flattering note to General Eulogio Cantillo, the commander of the Havana military headquarters. At the same time, he was trying to undermine the confidence of the army troops massed in the sierra. "The armed forces are now facing a very difficult task," he claimed in a statement to the Venezuelan press. "Every entrance to the Sierra Maestra is like the pass at Thermopylae, and every narrow passage becomes a death trap. The Cuban army has lately begun to realize that it has been led into a real war, an absurd war, a meaningless war, which can cost it thousands of lives, a war that is not theirs, because after all, we are not at war against the armed forces but against the dictatorship. These circumstances always have led inevitably to a military rebellion."

Fidel's daily activities had become increasingly administrative and sedentary. "I'm tired of the role of overseer and going back and forth without a minute's rest, to have to attend to the most insignificant details, just because someone forgot this or overlooked that," he wrote to Celia. "I miss those early days when I was really a soldier, and I felt much happier than I do now. This struggle becomes a miserable, petty bureaucratic task for me." But, for all his complaints, it was Fidel's nature to take control. He both plotted the overall strategy of the war and obsessed over the tiniest and most mundane details. In between the orders for blasting caps and rifle grease, he hounded Celia to provide him with personal comforts he missed. "I need a fountain pen," he wrote one day. "I hate being without one." On May 8, he had carped, "I'm eating hideously. No care is paid to preparing my food. . . . I'm in a terrible mood." By May 17, the list of complaints had expanded: "I have no tobacco, I have no wine, I have nothing. A bottle of rosé wine, sweet and Spanish, was left in Bismarck's house, in the refrigerator. Where is it?"

Fidel lacked faith in the judgment and decision-making of virtually all his subordinates except Che, who had become his chief confidant as well as his de facto military chief of staff. When they were apart, he kept up a constant stream of notes to Che, confiding military plans, financial matters, and political machinations, and, like an enthusiastic youth, recounting experiments with new weapons from the armory. "It's been too many days since we've talked," he had written to Che in early May, "and that's a matter of necessity between us. I miss the old comrades here. Yesterday I carried out an experiment with a tin grenade that produced terrific results. I hung it from a tree branch about 6 feet from the ground and set it off. It showered lethal fragments in all directions. It sends fragments downward and on all sides, as if it were a sprinkler. I think that in open terrain it could kill you at 50 yards."

During the third week of May, the government troops began their initial probes of rebel territory. General Cantillo had a total of fourteen battalions for his assault on the sierra, in addition to the support of the air force, and artillery and tank regiments. Cantillo's plan was to drive into the sierra from several points, gradually surrounding the rebels and reducing their territory until he could attack and destroy Fidel at his La Plata *comandancia* on the central ridge of the Sierra Maestra.

To the south, the coastal garrisons had been reinforced, and naval frigates stood ready to provide artillery support and seal off escape in that direction. To the north, flanking the western and eastern limits of rebel territory, Cantillo had deployed two army units composed of two battalions each. A few miles north of Las Mercedes, which was held by Crescencio's column, an army company led by Major Raúl Corzo Izaguirre had assembled at the sugar *central* of Estrada Palma. To the east, at Bueycito, a company under Sánchez Mosquera, who was now a lieutenant colonel, was prepared to enter the hills that were held by Che's old column, led by Ramiro Valdés. If Cantillo had one weakness, it was the unreadiness of his men: of 10,000 troops, only a third were experienced soldiers; the rest were conscripts recently called up for the occasion. But if all went according to plan, the rebels would simply be squeezed into an ever-tightening circle.

This circle was never that wide to begin with. The entire rebel stronghold, with its precious installations at La Plata, Las Vegas de Jibacoa, Mompié, and Minas del Frío, was actually only a tiny area of a few square miles. The distance between Fidel's *comandancia* and the northern frontline village of Las Mercedes was a little over seven miles, and the recruits' school at Minas del Frío sat halfway between them. To the south, less than five miles from rebel headquarters, lay the coast. Fidel counted on about 280 armed fighters, with approximately fifty bullets apiece, to defend his mountain fastness.

On May 19, after an aerial barrage to soften up the rebel defenses, Corzo Izaguirre's troops tried to march on Las Mercedes, but Crescencio's units held the line just beyond its outskirts. The battle lines were drawn, with the two sides facing off at a distance of less than a quarter mile. But even as his communiqués trumpeted the "stout resistance" displayed by his fighters and a brief quiet settled on the battlefront, Fidel was privately worried about Crescencio's abilities as a leader; a few days later, he asked Che to go to Las Mercedes and assume command.

Before leaving, Che attended an almost surreal assembly called by Humberto Sorí-Marín with the area's peasants to discuss how to carry out the coffee harvest. Surprisingly, 350 farmers showed up. Although it passed completely unnoticed by the outside world, it was an important moment. This was the first practical step in the agrarian reform process undertaken by the Cuban revolution. Che watched the proceedings with keen interest. He wrote that "the steering committee, which included Fidel, proposed that the following measures be adopted: to create a type of Sierra currency to pay the workers, to bring the straw and sacking for the packing, to create a work and consumer cooperative, to create a commission to supervise the work and provide troops to help in the coffee picking. Everything was approved, but when Fidel was going to close the ceremony with his speech the planes started to machine-gun in the zone of Las Mercedes and the people lost interest." It was May 25. The enemy offensive had begun in earnest. Che rushed to Las Mercedes, and for the next three months, he was rarely still as he rallied rebel defenses to resist the overwhelming firepower and troop strength of Batista's invading army. When his courier Lidia arrived and informed him that Faustino Pérez, who was in Havana with orders to hand over his post, was balking, Che observed in his diary that "the thing looks worse all the time." But he could do no more than register the news.

As always, there were disciplinary problems with recruits trying to escape the tightening army net. Once when Fidel was visiting Las Mercedes, a recruit who had escaped was captured and brought in. "Fidel wanted to shoot him immediately," Che noted in his journal, "but I opposed it and in the end the thesis of condemning him to indefinite reclusion at [the rebel prison of] Puerto Malanga triumphed." A few days later, in a demonstration of the often arbitrary nature of Fidel's application of revolutionary justice, he absolved a deserter.

For all of Fidel's rhetoric about turning the mountain passes into death traps for the army, Che's diary reveals just how undermanned the rebels really were, and how tenuous their morale was.* With enemy troops disembarking on the coast, Fidel took charge of the defense of Las Vegas and sent Che to put order into Crescencio Pérez's command, where one of the officers was reportedly acting abusively toward his men. Before leaving, Che held a summary trial for a rebel officer accused of murder and sentenced him to death. Che spent his thirtieth birthday sitting in judgment of Crescencio's officer, whom he decided to strip of his command. Returning to the front, he found it in disarray, with army troops advancing on all fronts. Fidel had moved on to Mompié; Las Vegas had been overrun. Minas del Frío was now threatened, and Che spent several days shoring up Fidel's front with his own men, building new defensive lines, stripping another officer of his command, and disarming others who had been insubordinate.

On June 26, he met up with Fidel again at Mompié, and Fidel ordered him to stay with him for the moment. The outlook was grim; the rebels were ceding ground everywhere. Fidel had ordered Camilo and Almeida to bring their columns back to the sierra to help out, but a defeatist attitude had begun to permeate the rebel ranks. "In the night there were three escapes," Che wrote the next day. "One of them was double; Rosabal, condemned to death for being a *chivato*, Pedro Guerra from Sori's squad, and two military prisoners. Pedro Guerra was captured; he had stolen a revolver for the escape. He was executed immediately."

By the end of June, the rebels had their first clear victory. An army company under Sánchez Mosquera had been turned back, and the rebels captured twenty-two soldiers and fifty or sixty weapons. But elsewhere the army was on the move, with reports flowing in of enemy advances on La Maestra and other hills in the area. The second wave of the offensive had begun. Hearing of soldiers advancing to take the heights of Altos de Merino, Che rushed over there on the morning of July 3. "Upon arriving I found that the guards were already advancing. A little combat broke out in which we retreated very quickly. The position was bad and they were

*On June 8, amid the general chaos, a strange American visitor showed up at the rebel camp. Che wrote that he was "a suspicious gringo with messages from people in Miami and some eccentric plans." The man wanted to see Fidel, but he was kept where he was. The next morning, after an intense aerial bombardment in the eastern part of the front around the village of Santo Domingo, Che found Fidel and told him about the visitor. "Fidel had received word that the gringo was either FBI or hired to kill him." According to Pedro Álvarez Tabío, the director of the Cuban government's historical archives, the visitor was probably Frank Fiorini, a gunrunner. Later, under the alias "Frank Sturgis," Fiorini went to work for the CIA in its anti-Castro operations, and in the 1970s earned notoriety as one of the Watergate burglars.

encircling us, but we put up little resistance. Personally I noted something I had never felt before: the need to live. That had better be corrected in the next opportunity."

It is hard to imagine many other men in the same situation making this sort of critical self-judgment, but this was how Ernesto Guevara, in his new identity as Che, now confronted life. It was one of the facets of his character that set him apart from the vast majority of his guerrilla comrades, who, even as they fought, still hoped to survive the experience. Indeed, most of the problems he encountered on a daily basis with his men pointed up this fundamental difference between them. Their nervousness, their lack of "combativity," the desertions, not being where they should on the front line—all the complaints and observations that peppered his daily journal came down to the same complaint: they felt "*the need to live.*"

VII

On the eve of battle, Che had used the new radio-communication links from the Sierra Maestra to call his mother, and she wrote back to wish him a happy thirtieth birthday.

Dear Teté:

I was so overcome to hear your voice after so much time. I didn't recognize it—you seemed to be another person. Maybe the line was bad or maybe you have changed. Only when you said "old lady" did it seem like the voice of old. What wonderful news you gave me. What a pity the communication was cut before I could give you mine. And there is a lot to tell. Ana [María, Che's youngest sister] was married on April 2 to Petít [Fernando Chávez] and they went to Vienna. . . . What a thing all of my children leaving! She left behind a very big emptiness in the house. . . . Roberto has two beautiful blond daughters who will be two and one on the first of July, and the [male] heir is expected in August. He is working hard and well to maintain his numerous family. . . .

Celia has just won an important [architectural] prize together with Luis [Argañaraz, her fiancé] and Petít. Between the three of them they get 2 and ½ million pesos. I am so proud of having such capable children that I don't fit in my clothes. Juan Martín, of course, [now] fits into your clothes. It isn't that he's tall. He's as puny as his brothers and sisters were and he is still an enchanting child. Life is not going to knock this one around.

María Luisa [Che's aunt] is the same as before. Physically and
emotionally incapacitated and very sad. It seems a characteristic
of her illness. She always asks about you. . . . I too am the same.
With a few years more and a sadness that is no longer so sharp. It
has turned into a chronic sadness, blended once in a while with
great satisfactions. The prize won by Celia was one of them, the
return of the Little One will be another, hearing your voice was a
very big one. I have become very solitary. I don't know how to
write you, or even what to say to you: I have lost the measure.

The housework tires me out a lot. For a long time now I have
been my own cook and you know how I detest the chores of the
home. The kitchen is my headquarters and there I spend most of
my time. There was a big blowup with the old man [Che's father]
and he no longer comes around. My companions are Celia, Luis,
and Juan Martín. So many things I wanted to say, my dear. I am
afraid to let them out. I leave them to your imagination.

A hug and a long kiss of years, with all my love, Celia.

One wonders how Che reacted to this poignant letter. Did he read it
with emotional detachment or suffer pangs of yearning for the normal life
that continued in his absence: brothers and sisters growing up, getting married, leaving home and having children; his parents growing older? And
what of his own family—his wife, Hilda, and their daughter, Hildita? But
more than Teté's voice had changed. He had made a conscious choice to
divorce himself from his "outside" life. He seldom wrote to Hilda or his
parents, although he had opportunities to do so. In late April, Fidel had told
him that someone in Peru, presumably Hilda, had tried to call him on the
radio; evidently Che did not phone back, for Hilda makes no mention of it
in her memoirs. Indeed, one of the most remarkable aspects of his diary of
the time is the almost total lack of personal details or introspection, especially compared with the self-absorption of the vagabond Ernesto just a few
short years before.

VIII

The Cuban army had not taken fully into account the topography of their
battlefield. Army units quickly bogged down or lost contact with one another in the Sierra Maestra's thick forests and deep ravines. The rebels gave
ground when necessary and then encircled isolated army units. It was soon
the rebels who were on the offensive.

To press their advantage, Che and Fidel split their forces again. Fidel set off to attack the army troops at Jigüe, while Che stayed to defend Mompié and command the resistance at Minas del Frío. As Che arrived in Mompié on July 11, the Cuban air force launched a ferocious aerial bombardment of the place, this time dropping napalm as well as bombs. Then came unsettling news. Fidel's brother Raúl, leading rebel forces in the Sierra Cristal, had just taken forty-nine Americans hostage. Che noted that Raúl had "written a manifesto made out to the entire world and signed by him. It was too strong and together with the arrest of the 49 Americans it seemed a note of dangerous 'extremism.'"

In the four months since his move to the Sierra Cristal, Raúl had rapidly built up his fighting strength and made his presence felt throughout eastern Oriente. By July, he had more than 200 men under arms and had built up a guerrilla infrastructure complete with an armory, hospitals, schools, a road-building unit, an intelligence service, and a revolutionary judicial system. But all of that was now under threat. Although he was not facing the same kind of full-scale ground assault as his brother in the Sierra Maestra, Raúl's forces were being pounded by Batista's planes. In late June, with his forces dangerously low on ammunition, he decided to take drastic action by ordering the seizure of all Americans found within his territory.

On June 26, Raúl's fighters attacked the American-owned Moa Bay Mining Company and made off with twelve American and Canadian employees. Another dozen North Americans were grabbed at the Nicaro nickel mine and the United Fruit Company's sugar mill at Guaro. Twenty-four American sailors and marines were then abducted from a bus on the outskirts of the Guantánamo naval base. In a statement sent to the press, Raúl claimed he had taken the action to protest the delivery of rockets and napalm to Batista by the United States, and the secret refueling and loading of bombs onto Cuban warplanes at Guantánamo. The action sparked outrage in Washington, with several senators demanding American military intervention. Park Wollam, the American consul in Santiago, journeyed to meet with Raúl, and negotiations began.

Upon learning of the crisis, Fidel had gone on Radio Rebelde and ordered Raúl to release the hostages. He carefully balanced his public statements by declaring that hostage-taking was not the Movement's policy, but that such actions were comprehensible in light of the delivery of rockets to Batista. Then he sent Raúl a private note in which he appeared to be warning his brother not to take any drastic steps with the hostages that might endanger the rebels' image in the United States.*

---

*See the Notes.

Raúl's dramatic show of force brought him some immediate dividends, however. The air attacks against his forces in the Sierra Cristal suddenly ceased, proving the extent of American influence over Batista after all. Raúl didn't release all the hostages immediately, but drew the process out and used the lull to resupply his forces. It was July 18 before he freed the last hostages, after which the attacks resumed, but by then his Second Front was resupplied, able to defend itself, and ready for action. The hostage crisis had highlighted a facet of Raúl's character that was worrying to some of his comrades. Without strict controls, Raúl was something of a loose cannon, and other widely publicized excesses would earn him a reputation as a violent man who would stop at nothing.

Che was losing comrades on a daily basis. Geonel Rodríguez, who had helped him found *El Cubano Libre* back in the days when El Hombrito was the first "free territory" of the Sierra Maestra, was mortally wounded in a mortar blast. "He was one of our most loved collaborators, a true revolutionary," Che wrote in his journal. That night, word came of the death of Carlitos Más, whom Che described as an "old-young fighter who died from the burns and breaks he suffered together with Geonel." Perhaps most frustrating of all, the deaths could not be translated into advances on the battlefield, at least not in Che's sector. He continued to hold the line at Minas del Frío, but a stalemate had settled in, with the enemy soldiers digging trenches instead of advancing or falling back. The aerial bombardments continued. On July 17, the hospital at Mompié was hit, and Che oversaw the evacuation of its patients. The next day, he wrote, "Nothing new in the zone. The only pastime of the guards is killing the pigs we left around."

As Che tried to rally his perimeter defenses around Minas del Frío, Fidel was beginning to wear down the enemy in his siege at Jigüe. In two days in early July, he took nineteen prisoners and captured eighteen weapons, including bazooka grenades, and he thought the enemy force, now without food supplies, would surrender within forty-eight hours. Discovering that the enemy commander, Major José Quevedo, was an old law school classmate of his, he wrote him a curious note on July 10: "I have often remembered that group of young officers who attracted my attention and awakened my sympathies because of their great longing for culture and the efforts they made to pursue their studies. . . . What a surprise to know that you are around here! And however difficult the circumstances, I am always happy to hear from one of you, and I write these lines on the spur of the moment, without telling you or asking you for anything, only to greet you and to wish you, very sincerely, good luck."

If Fidel had hoped to weaken Quevedo's resolve, it didn't work. He then used loudspeakers to barrage the besieged troops with propaganda broadcasts, hoping to wear down their morale. On July 15 he wrote again to Quevedo, this time directly appealing to him to surrender: "It will not be a surrender to an enemy of the fatherland but to a sincere revolutionary, to a fighter who struggles for the good of all Cubans."

Still Quevedo held out. But after one of Fidel's men masqueraded as an army communications technician and sent word to the air force that the rebels had taken the camp, planes attacked Quevedo's force, spreading panic among his troops. By July 18, Fidel had forty-two prisoners, a booty of sixty-six weapons, and 18,000 rounds of ammunition. "The encircled troops are on the verge of collapse," he told Che.

The fall of Jigüe finally came on the evening of July 20. Quevedo walked out of the camp to surrender, with 146 soldiers following behind him. This was a watershed victory for the rebels. The army's offensive had been effectively routed, and now it would be their turn to press their advantage.* That same day, the "Caracas Pact" was announced over Radio Rebelde. Previously signed by Fidel on behalf of the July 26 Movement, it brought together eight opposition groups, including Carlos Prío's *auténticos,* the Directorio Revolucionario, the so-called "Barquínista" military faction, and Justo Carrillo's Montecristi movement. They were committed to a common strategy of overthrowing Batista through armed insurrection and the formation of a brief provisional government. Most important, the "Unity Manifesto of the Sierra Maestra" acknowledged Fidel Castro's authority as "commander in chief of revolutionary forces." As in all the previous pacts, the most notable Cuban opposition group not invited to sign was the PSP; and Che, who evidently thought it would be, remarked in his journal, "The unity seems to be going well on the outside but in the announcement the Partido Socialista is not included, which seems strange to me." (It would appear that on the issue of links between the PSP and July 26, Fidel was momentarily keeping his counsel. To avoid provoking controversy, their ongoing high-level talks remained a secret.)

A two-day truce was finally arranged through the Red Cross, and on July 23 and 24 a total of 253 famished, exhausted army prisoners, including fifty-seven wounded, were handed over. They left behind a total of 161 weapons in rebel hands, including two mortars, a bazooka, and two heavy machine guns. Two hours before the cease-fire ended, Che mobilized his men; some of them were to hold the pass at La Maestra, while all the others would lay siege to the troops in Las Vegas. Within a day, they had the camp

---

*Fidel persuaded Quevedo to join the Rebel Army. He was one of several army officers to do so in the course of the war.

encircled, and, following Fidel's example in Jigüe, Che urged the soldiers there to surrender. On the morning of July 28, he met with two army officers who offered a deal. If Che let the army troops withdraw, they would leave all their food behind but take their arms with them. Che told them this was impossible, and returned to his own lines. Soon a sentinel warned him that the army was beating a retreat, driving away in trucks flying a white flag and a Red Cross flag. The meeting had been a diversionary tactic. Che ordered his men to open fire while he led units in pursuit.

"A desolate spectacle could be seen," he wrote. "Backpacks and helmets thrown around along the road, bags with bullets and all kinds of belongings, even a jeep and a tank that was still intact . . . Later the first prisoners started falling, among them the company doctor." As Che's units pressed the advance, however, they increasingly came under "friendly fire" from rebels hidden in the surrounding hills; one of Che's prisoners was killed and a rebel officer badly wounded. "I had the uncomfortable situation of being besieged by our forces, who opened fire every time they saw a helmet. I sent a soldier to stop the fire with his hands up and in one place it gave results but in the other they continued firing for a while, wounding two more soldiers."

When the situation was finally normalized and the scores of captured *guardias* were being led back to Las Vegas, an urgent message from Fidel reached Che as he was inspecting the captured tank. The army had also retreated from the sector of Santo Domingo that day, but it had been a ruse. As the rebels chased after the fleeing troops, Sánchez Mosquera took the Arroyones hilltop near Las Mercedes and outflanked them. One of the two rebel captains commanding the fighters there had been killed, while the other—Che's former llano rival René Ramos Latour (Daniel)—had survived and was fighting back, but the battle was fierce. By the afternoon of the following day, Daniel was dead from a mortar wound in the stomach. "Profound ideological discrepancies separated me from René Ramos," Che wrote in his journal that evening, "and we were political enemies, but he knew how to die fulfilling his duty, on the front line. Whoever dies like that does so because he feels an interior impulse [the existence of] which I had denied him and which I rectify at this time."

The army tank Che had captured at Las Mercedes now became an almost comic focus of the fighting. It was a grand prize in this essentially small-scale war, and Fidel wanted to preserve it at all costs. The enemy just as desperately sought its destruction. While the rebels tried to extract it from where it sat, stuck fast in the mud, planes tried to hit it with bombs. But the exertions of both sides proved fruitless. On August 5, Fidel commissioned a peasant with a team of oxen to drag it free, and in the process its steering wheel was broken. There was little hope of repairing it. "Hopes dashed," Fidel wrote Che that night. "It has been a long time since I've had such great pipe dreams."

Two days later, shielded by a withering cover fire, the army began to move out en masse from its last besieged position in the Sierra Maestra. Batista's vaunted offensive was over—but not the dying. On August 9, Beto Pesant, a veteran of the first group of volunteers from Manzanillo, was killed when an antiaircraft shell he was handling exploded. Che's lover, Zoila Rodríguez, was at the scene. "Comandante Guevara, other rebels, and myself were carrying out a mission when Beto Pesant died," she recalled. "When I heard an explosion, I saw that Guevara's mule, called Armando, was injured and had thrown him [Che] into the air, I ran to his side but he was already getting up. I looked over at Pesant and saw that he was missing an arm, his head was destroyed and his chest was open. . . . I began to scream: 'Beto, don't die, don't die.' They attended to him quickly. The *comandante* told me: 'Zoila, he's dead.'" Che ordered the dead man's wife in Manzanillo to be contacted, and when she arrived, Zoila recalled: "She began to weep at his tomb, and we all cried and when I looked at Guevara he had tears in his eyes."

In the wake of the army's withdrawal, Fidel held another 160 soldiers, including some who were wounded, and he was eager to be rid of them. After much back-and-forth negotiating, a meeting was arranged on the morning of August 11 among him, Che, the army commanders, and Red Cross representatives. They talked amiably while having coffee. Over the next two days, a truce held in the Sierra Maestra as the wounded men and their able-bodied comrades were released. At one point, Che and Fidel even went on a short helicopter ride with their enemy counterparts. The truce also allowed the rebels to pause for judicial proceedings. Che recorded, "An army deserter who had tried to rape a girl was executed."

In the lull, a high-level army emissary whom the rebels believed to be Batista's personal representative urged Fidel to enter into negotiations with the regime. "He indirectly proposed his [Batista's] replacement with a magistrate of the Supreme [Court] (the oldest one) and a peaceful solution," Che observed. "[But] nothing concrete was reached." Fidel saw no reason to rush into negotiations. He was planning to extend the war across the island and still had hopes of wooing General Cantillo, whose offensive he had just defeated. Che concluded later, "Batista's army came out of that last offensive in the Sierra Maestra with its spine broken, but it had not yet been defeated. The struggle would go on." Indeed, on August 14, after a rare act of civility in which the army airlifted some blood plasma to the rebels, the bombing and strafing attacks resumed.

Meanwhile, unnoticed by either the enemy or Fidel's putative allies in the Caracas Pact, an important visitor to the Sierra Maestra took his leave from rebel territory. An official of the Communist Party Central Committee, Carlos Rafael Rodríguez, had held secret talks with Fidel, after first visiting Raúl's Second Front in the Sierra Cristal. Che recorded Rodríguez's visit circumspectly, mentioning it in his journal only upon the PSP official's departure: "Carlos Rafael left for the free zone. His impression is positive despite all the internal and external intrigues."*

Rodríguez's visit is still clouded by secrecy, but he evidently received Fidel's go-ahead to pursue a merger between the PSP and the July 26 Movement in a reconstituted labor front. Another signal of cooperation was Fidel's authorization for the Party to send a permanent representative to the sierra. Only three weeks after Rodríguez left, Luis Más Martín, a veteran PSP official and an old friend of Castro's, arrived, and in September Rodríguez himself returned, staying with Fidel until the end of the war.

Raúl Castro and the PSP had forged much more than an "understanding" in the Sierra Cristal. Around the time Raúl left the Sierra Maestra to open his new front, José "Pepe" Ramírez, chief of the National Association of Small Farmers, which was controlled by the PSP, was ordered by the Party to make his way to the Sierra Cristal and "report to Raúl." When Ramírez arrived, Raúl gave him the job of organizing the peasants living within his territory and preparing a Peasant Congress to be held in the autumn. That work was now well under way, as was the formation of a Communist-run troop instructors' school, complete with Marxist political orientation.

Curiously, Raúl also enjoyed the support of a considerable number of militant Catholics from the city of Santiago. But it was the Communist influence that was the salient characteristic of Raúl's Second Front. Indeed, it was the spawning ground for many of Cuba's future Communist Party officials. Although he had not been formally a Party member since his ouster from the Socialist Youth after his role in Fidel's "putschist" adventure at Moncada, Raúl had remained faithful and, with a wink and a nod from Fidel, proceeded to cement his ties.

---

*Rodríguez, who died in 1997, never said much about this trip, except that in Raúl's zone he had found "nothing but understanding for the Communists, but when I got to Fidel in the Sierra Maestra, the understanding had turned to suspicion." Rodríguez was undoubtedly referring to the antagonism his presence had provoked in Carlos Franqui, Faustino Pérez, and other llano men who were now in the sierra. Che seemed to have been alluding to this when he noted, a few days after Rodríguez's departure, "the formation of an opposition directed by Faustino and composed also of Franqui and Aldo Santamaría [brother of Haydée and the late Abel Santamaría] in the Sierra Maestra."

These developments could not have been very comforting to the Americans, but for now there was little they could do to assuage their growing fears about the true goals of the increasingly powerful Cuban Rebel Army. Right now, those goals called for an ambitious expansion of the war. Che and Camilo Cienfuegos were to leave the Sierra Maestra and take the war to central and western Cuba. Che's Ciro Redondo column was to assume revolutionary authority in the Escambray mountains of central Las Villas province, "strike relentlessly at the enemy," and cut the island in half. Meanwhile, Camilo was to replicate the feat of his column's illustrious nineteenth-century namesake, Antonio Maceo, a hero of the Cuban war of independence, by marching all the way to the westernmost province of Pinar del Río.

Che was anxious to get going, but on August 15 he complained, "I haven't been able to organize the column yet because of a cumulus of contradictory orders as to its composition." It was a matter of finding the men to go with him, and so far only a tiny trickle of volunteers had filtered in from different squads. Che himself didn't help matters by telling the fighters that probably only half of those who came with him would survive the mission, and that they should be prepared to do battle continuously and go hungry most of the time. Che's mission was not for everybody. Fidel summoned him to Mompié. He had organized one squad for him, led by El Vaquerito, and told Che to recruit any other men he needed from the platoons on hand. Che's political commissar at Minas del Frío, Pablo Ribalta, began selecting men from the school.

Over the next fortnight, under incessant aerial bombardments, Che painstakingly pieced together his expeditionary force: a column of 148 men, with half a dozen jeeps and pickup trucks. Camilo's smaller force of eighty-two men was also assembled and ready to go. Then, on the night of August 29—as he prepared for a dawn departure by loading some jeeps with ammunition just flown in from Miami—the army captured two of his pickups loaded with supplies, and all his gasoline for the journey. His remaining vehicles now useless, he resolved to set out on foot.

On August 31, as Che finally prepared to leave, Zoila asked to accompany him. He said no. They bade each other farewell in the village of El Jíbaro. It was the last time they would be together as lovers. "He left me in charge of his mule Armando," Zoila recalled. "I cared for him as if he were a real Christian."

Che and Camilo Cienfuegos, his swashbuckling friend and a hero of the revolution.

19

The Final Push

For six weeks, from early September into October 1958, in the unceasing downpours of the Cuban rainy season, Che and Camilo's troops waded through the rice fields and swamps of the llano, forded swollen rivers, dodged the army, and came under frequent aerial attacks. The exhausting marches through stinking swamps and along devilish trails, Che wrote, became "truly horrible." They had been detected by the enemy early on, and after firefights on September 9 and 14, the army had tracked their movements closely.

"Hunger, thirst, weariness, the feeling of impotence against the enemy forces that were increasingly closing in on us, and above all, the terrible foot disease that the peasants call *mazamorra*—which turned each step our soldiers took into an intolerable torment—had made us an army of shadows," Che wrote. "It was difficult to advance, very difficult. The troops' physical condition worsened day by day, and meals—today yes, tomorrow no, the next day maybe—in no way helped to alleviate the level of misery we were suffering."

Several men were killed in firefights, others deserted, and Che allowed a few more demoralized or frightened men to leave. As always, *chivatos* were a problem. Che reported to Fidel that "the social consciousness of the Camagüeyan peasantry is minimal, and we had to face the consequences of numerous informers." In the meantime, propaganda reports about Che's Communism had intensified. On September 20, Batista's chief of staff, General Francisco Tabernilla, reported that army troops had destroyed a 100-man column led by Che Guevara, and had captured evidence that his rebels were "being trained through Communist methods."

"What happened," Che explained to Fidel later, "was that in one of the knapsacks [left behind after a firefight] they found a notebook that listed the name, address, weapon, and ammunition of the entire column, member by member. In addition, one member of this column, who is also a member of the PSP [Pablo Ribalta] left his knapsack containing documents from that organization." The army exploited the "Communist evidence" to instill fear and hatred of the rebels. In a cable dated September 21 that was sent to the army units stationed along Che's route to the Escambray, Lieutenant Colonel Suárez Suquet exhorted his officers to use all available resources and "muster courage" to stop the "guerrilla enemy" that was "murdering men no matter what their beliefs are." Suárez pointed out that "the recent capture of Communist documentation from the foreigner known as 'Che Guevara' and his henchmen, who have always lived beyond the law . . . , [shows they are] all paid by the Kremlin. . . . Onward Cuban Soldier: we will not permit these rats who have penetrated surreptitiously in this province to leave again."

As Che approached the Escambray, he knew he was heading into a hornets' nest of rivalries and intrigues. Various armed groups were operating in the area, virtually all of them were competing for influence and territorial control, and some were little more than rustling marauders, or *comevacas* (cow-eaters). Che wrote in his diary, "From here I get the impression there are a lot of dirty rags to wash on all sides." Fidel had ordered him to unify the various factions and bring them under his control, but he wasn't counting on much help from the July 26 Movement. His experience on the llano so far had shown him that his natural ally was the PSP.

Che's arrival provided the PSP with a golden opportunity to acquire a central role in the armed struggle, something the other factions in the area had consistently denied it. In rural Yaguajay, in northern Las Villas, the PSP now had its own rebel front, the Máximo Gómez, with sixty-five armed men led by Félix Torres, who had been refused cooperation by both the local chapter of the July 26 Movement and Eloy Gutíerrez Menoyo's "Second National Front of the Escambray," a Directorio splinter group. The Party sent emissaries to greet Che in early October, as he approached the Escambray. They offered him guides and money, and promised a radio transmitter and mimeograph machine for his propaganda efforts. Che accepted, gratefully, and asked for a direct connection with the PSP leadership in Las Villas.

After another miserable week of slogging through mud and swamps and being harassed by warplanes, Che and his men reached a farm in the foothills of the Escambray. They had crossed more than half the length of Cuba, a distance of more than 350 miles, mostly on foot, and they were hungry, sick, and exhausted. Twenty-six-year-old Ovidio Díaz Rodríguez, the secretary of the Communist Party's Juventud Socialista for Las Villas province, met them on horseback. The government's incessant propaganda about the "Argentine Communist" had fueled his awe of Che, and, as he neared their rendezvous, he was overwhelmed with emotion. "I wanted to hug him when I met him," he recalled, but he shyly shook Che's hand. "I saw he was very thin and I imagined all the suffering he had surely gone through since leaving the Sierra Maestra. I was struck by his personality and the respect everyone showed him. My admiration grew."

Che, with characteristic bluntness, chastised Díaz for being incautious in approaching his camp head-on. "You should have followed my tracks," he said, before inviting Díaz to sit down and talk. "He asked me to summarize everything I knew about the situation in the Escambray," Díaz said— "the armed groups, the situation of the Party in the province and in the mountains, the support it had, whether the socialist bases were strong. He spoke to me with respect and in an affable way." Che noted in his diary on October 15 that he had met with "a representative of the PSP," who told him that the Party was "at his disposition" if he could forge a unity deal with the various armed groups. It was a good start.

Camilo had also made contact with the PSP. His column had veered north, to Yaguajay, where Félix Torres's column was located, and on October 8 the two men had met in the field. Torres happily placed himself and his men under Camilo's command. The two groups maintained separate camps but coordinated their actions. Fidel was so pleased with the arrangement that he ordered Camilo to stay on in Las Villas and act as a bolster to Che's operations instead of pushing on to Pinar del Río.

Over the next couple of days, as Che and his men moved into the Escambray proper, Díaz visited him. Each time, he came away more impressed with Che's leadership abilities. "He knew his men well," Díaz said— "who had come from the different revolutionary organizations, who had risen up as workers or peasants, who were anticommunists due to a lack of culture. He measured his men for their fighting spirit but he knew how to distinguish perfectly between those of left or right."

It was a heterogeneous group. In addition to the relatively inexperienced graduates of Minas del Frío, Che had brought along his protégés. Besides the Communists, Ribalta and Acosta, there was Ramiro Valdés, his trusted deputy, who now sported a sinister-looking goatee that Che liked to say made him resemble Feliks Dzerzhinsky, the founder of the KGB. The young doctor Oscarito Fernández Mell, whose company Che enjoyed, and whom he liked to tease as a "petite bourgeoisie," was with them, as were the loyal youngsters Joel Iglesias, Guile Pardo, El Vaquerito—who led his own daredevil "Suicide Squad"—and the Acevedo brothers. And there were exotic characters such as "El Negro" Lázaro, a huge, brave black man with

an equally grand sense of humor who dragged a saddle with him throughout the invasion, saying he wanted it for the day when he found a horse to
ride—a day, of course, that never came. Finally, there was a group of young
men whose destinies were to become permanently linked to Che's, many of
whom stayed with him after the war as his personal bodyguards. Most of
them had few political notions but were eager for adventure, and Che was
their key to glorious future lives, in which they too would become modern-
day "liberation heroes."*

What was it about Che that so magnetized these men? He could not
have been more different from most of them. He was a foreigner, an intellectual, a professional. He read books they did not understand. As their
leader, he was demanding, strict, and notoriously severe in his punishments—especially with those he had selected to become "true revolutionaries." When young Harry Villegas and a few other youths went on a hunger
strike at Minas del Frío over the bad quality of the food, Che threatened to
shoot them. In the end, after conferring with Fidel, he softened, making
them go without food for five days, "so they could know what real hunger
was." There were many more times when they suffered Che's severity for
mistakes that other commanders might have passed over or even committed themselves.

Each sanction Che meted out came with an explanation, a sermon
about the importance of self-sacrifice, personal example, and social conscience. He wanted the men to know why they were being punished, and
how they could redeem themselves. Naturally, Che's unit was not for everyone. Many fell by the wayside, unable to take the hardship and his rigorous
demands, but for those who stuck it out, being "with Che" became a source
of pride. He earned their respect and devotion because he lived as they did,
refusing extra luxuries due to his rank, taking the same risks as they did in
battle. He was a role model for these youths, about half of whom were black,
many of them from poor farming families.†

Although he was careful to conceal it, Che was paying a personal price
for the austere revolutionary image he had constructed for himself. His

*See Notes.

†Che had many good men with him on his long march to the Escambray, but some began to
suffer from what he called *apendijitis,* or yellowitis. "In an attempt to clean out the scum of
the column," he told Fidel, he had cashiered seven men on October 7. The next night, the
American volunteer Herman Marks, who had a captain's rank, left as well. Although Marks,
who was a Korean War veteran, had been an excellent instructor of Che's fighters and had
proved himself repeatedly in battle, Che wasn't sorry to see him go, and in his journal he
wrote, "He was wounded and ill, but fundamentally, he didn't fit into the troop." Enrique

relationship with Zoila, his attachment to his mules, his habit of keeping pets, all could be taken as signs that he craved tenderness and solace to ease the harsh life he had adopted. When he arrived in the Escambray, he was expecting his personal messenger, Lidia, to join him. She was to be his courier to Fidel and Havana, and she had promised to bring him a puppy to replace Hombrito, a little dog named after the valley he'd fought over, which he'd had to leave behind in the Sierra Maestra. But Lidia never made it. She and her companion, twenty-one-year-old Clodomira Acosta Ferrals, were betrayed, captured, and then "disappeared" by Batista's agents. Che felt her loss deeply. As he wrote a few months after her murder, "[For] me personally —Lidia occupies a special place. That is why I offer today these reminiscences in homage to her—a modest flower laid on the mass grave that this once happy island became."

During the trek across Camagüey, Che lost the military cap that had belonged to his friend Ciro Redondo. He had worn it ever since Ciro's death. Oscarito Fernández Mell had rarely seen Che as upset as he was that day. "That cap was a disaster," Oscarito recalled. "The visor was broken, it was dirty and shitty, but because it had belonged to Ciro, it was what he wanted to wear. Che was a man who was both hard and extraordinarily sentimental." The cap was replaced by the black beret that would soon become Che's trademark.

II

The *barbudos*—as Fidel's bearded, long-haired rebels were now known— were seen by a growing segment of the public as holding the keys to Cuba's political future. Fidel thus expected popular support for an island-wide offensive, which was to be launched by sabotaging the elections scheduled for November 3. He decreed a traffic ban, a consumer boycott of the lottery, and a halt to purchases of newspapers and attendance at parties or festivities of any kind. Citizens should buy only the bare essentials so as to deny the regime revenue. In case anyone harbored doubts about his opposition to the elections, Fidel threatened all candidates with prison or death.

The limited field of candidates was a study in out-of-touch politics. Running against Prime Minister Andrés Rivero Agüero, who had been

---

Acevedo explained in more detail: the American was "brave and crazy in combat, tyrannical and arbitrary in the peace of camp." In particular, according to Enrique Acevedo, he had displayed a disquieting predilection for executing condemned men, often volunteering for the task with an enthusiasm that was unseemly.

chosen by Batista as his successor, were the Ortodoxo splinter politician Carlos Márquez Sterling and Ramón Grau San Martín, the discredited former president who now headed a faction of the Auténtico Party. Not surprisingly, there was little enthusiasm among the citizens, and voter turnout was expected to be minimal.

To enforce his decrees, Fidel sent out new columns to operate on the llano of Oriente and Camagüey, and he gave Juan Almeida orders to begin encircling the city of Santiago. He also took the urban action groups off their tether, and in September they carried out some spectacular assaults in Havana, destroying the transmitting facilities of two government radio stations and setting fire to Rancho Boyeros, the country's main airport.

Political repression by the regime continued unabated. Several gruesome police murders of civilians, including those of two young sisters in Havana, outraged and sickened the public. The routine torture of people detained by the Buró de Represión a las Actividades Comunistas (BRAC), which was funded by the CIA, had become so notorious that the CIA's own inspector general complained. In September, one of Che's columns in Camagüey fell into an ambush. Eighteen rebels were killed, and the eleven captured survivors, including wounded men, were summarily executed.

The revolution in Cuba was also drawing in players far from its shore. With the U.S. State Department still blocking new arms shipments to the Cuban regime, Batista had begun turning to alternative arms suppliers. Fidel's intermediaries appealed to Prime Minister Harold Macmillan to halt the sale of fifteen British Sea Fury warplanes to Cuba, but the intermediaries were snubbed. Fidel responded by decreeing the confiscation of all British-owned property in Cuba and called for a boycott of British goods.

In a dress rehearsal for their future showdown, Fidel and Washington had begun a war of words. The White House rebuffed the rebels' appeal to withdraw the U.S. military mission from Cuba, and a more hostile State Department hinted it might take action after rebels briefly seized two employees of American Texaco in an ambush. In late October, Batista withdrew his soldiers guarding the American nickel mine of Nicaro. When Raúl's forces moved in to occupy the mine, the U.S. Navy sent a transport ship, backed up by an aircraft carrier, to evacuate the fifty-five American civilians there. The State Department issued a veiled threat of retaliatory action if American hostages were taken again. Fidel warned that if the State Department made the error of "leading its country into an act of aggression against our sovereignty, be certain that we will know how to defend it honorably."

There were increasing reports of discontent brewing within the armed forces, and Fidel used every opportunity to urge military men to reconsider their service at the hands of "the tyranny" rather than to "the fatherland," which *he* represented. Officers or soldiers who defected to the rebels' "Free Territory" were welcome as long as they brought their weapons with them; their current salaries would continue to be paid, and they were promised free room and board through the end of the war. Fidel wrote again to General Cantillo, urging him to lead a revolt against Batista, but Cantillo remained noncommittal. At the same time, one of Fidel's agents was trying to persuade some dissident officers to defect and form a Rebel Army column of their own.

As Fidel plotted and schemed, a stream of visitors and emissaries came and went from the Sierra Maestra. Some, such as the PSP official Carlos Rafael Rodríguez, stayed on as permanent guests. Thanks to a new cook brought up especially from a restaurant on the llano, Fidel was eating well again and had even gained weight. He had his own jeep and permanent electric power from a generator. He had time to read books and listen to music. He could speak by telephone to the outside world when he wanted to. Celia Sánchez was sharing his double bed. Life was good.

Fidel was confident, but not complacent, about the future. In Oriente, the Rebel Army now numbered more than 800 men. Arms and ammunition were no longer in short supply, thanks to the matériel captured in the summer offensive and to continuing arms-supply flights from abroad. He was also successfully filling his war chest. He had imposed a fifteen-cent tax on each 250-pound bag of sugar harvested, and the sugar mills of Oriente, including those owned by the United States, were paying up. He even had his own modest rebel air force under the command of Pedro Luis Díaz Lanz.

Fidel announced his long-planned agrarian reform bill, called "Law One of the Sierra Maestra." It promised to distribute state land and any land owned by Batista to landless peasants, guaranteed the continued ownership of land not exceeding 150 acres, and promised that if land was confiscated from those with large "idle" landholdings, they would be compensated. Most significantly, at least in terms of the future, Fidel was edging ever closer to an overt alliance with the Communist Party. By late October, the formation of a new labor organization, the Frente Obrera Nacional de Unidad, which included the PSP, was announced.

Fidel was operating on several levels. While he pacified his anticommunist allies with a middle-of-the-road agrarian reform bill, he was shoring up a working alliance with the Communists that went far beyond the labor unity deal. The practical groundwork was already being carried out by Che, Raúl, and Camilo. In Raúl's Second Front, a political-military alliance between the PSP and July 26 was up and running. The Peasant Congress that Pepe Ramírez had organized was held in September, presided over by Raúl. Immediately after arriving in Las Villas, Camilo set in motion plans

for a National Conference of Sugar Workers. This was one of the first steps
in the gradual merger of the July 26 Movement and the PSP that eventually
culminated in the creation of a new Cuban Communist Party, headed by
Fidel.

Che marched through Oriente and Camagüey with agrarian reform
in mind, but he had been too busy trying to survive to do very much about
it. A week after setting out, in the rice-growing region of eastern Camagüey,
he had urged workers at a large private farm to form a union and had gotten an enthusiastic reaction. "One person with a social consciousness could
work wonders in this area," he told Fidel later. "There is plenty of vegetation to hide in." Three weeks later, in western Camagüey, finding himself
on a large rice farm owned by an associate of Batista, Che stopped to talk
with its American manager. He noted in his journal, "I spoke to the administrator to explain the essence of our economic concepts and our assurances
for the protection of the rice industry so that he could transmit it to his boss."

Joel Iglesias recalled the encounter in more detail. "When we left there,
[Che] asked me: 'What did you think of him?' I replied that I didn't like
those guys. He told me: 'Me neither, [and] in the end we'll have to fight
against them,' and added: 'I would die with a smile on my lips, on the crest
of a hill, behind a rock, fighting against these people.'"

But before he fought the Yankees, Che had to deal with problems closer
to home. He entered the Escambray proper on October 16 and was engulfed
in the intrigues there. Eloy Gutiérrez Menoyo, the leader of the Second
National Front of the Escambray, had briefly seized the July 26 commander
operating in Las Villas, Víctor Bordón Machado. He was also at odds with
the official Directorio Revolucionario armed group, led by Faure Chomón.
A delegation representing the Las Villas July 26 complained about Bordón,
who they said had become "aggressive" and was acting on his own. Hoping
to settle things, Che called for a council to be held at the Directorio's base
camp. Meanwhile, he tried to convince the July 26 men of the need for a
local unity agreement, and proposed a strategy for joint urban uprisings and
guerrilla attacks in Las Villas's cities during the elections. "I didn't find much
enthusiasm for the idea," he noted.

Che had just established a provisional camp at a place called Los
Gavilanes when he was approached by an officer of Gutiérrez Menoyo's
Second Front. Despite the front's anticommunist ethos and its reputation
for banditry, Che was anxious to see if some form of anti-Batista coalition
could be forged. In mid-October, he and his men set out for the camp of
one of the most notorious Second Front warlords, Comandante Jesús
Carreras. When they got there, after a two-day hike, they found Carreras
gone, but he had left behind a threatening notice. As Che recounted in

his diary, the notice warned that "no troops could pass through this territory, that they would be warned the first time but the second, expelled or exterminated."

When Carreras returned, Che saw that "he had already drunk half a bottle of liquor, which was approximately half his daily quota." When Che announced he could not permit Carreras's use of the word "warning," Carreras quickly backed down, explaining that the threat had been intended only for marauding fighters from the Directorio faction. Che left believing he had handled things diplomatically, but he also knew that Carreras was "an enemy."*

At the Directorio headquarters at Los Arroyos, Che met with Faure Chomón and Rolando Cubela. They were open to the idea of cooperation with the July 26 Movement but rejected any talks with the Second Front or the Communists, and stressed their unwillingness to cede their independent status in a unity pact with Che. As an alternative, Che proposed that they work out "measures to partition territory and zones of influence where the forces of other organizations could operate freely." Setting aside the fine points, he suggested launching a joint attack against Güinía de Miranda, a town with an army garrison at the base of the Escambray, after which the Directorio force and his would split any weapons captured. "They accepted in principle but without enthusiasm," he noted in his diary.

Enrique "Sierra" Oltuski, the Las Villas coordinator of the July 26 Movement, arrived in Che's camp one pitch-black night. Men were milling around a bonfire, and Oltuski approached them, trying to make out faces. "I had in my mind the image of Che that I had seen published in the newspapers," he recalled. "None of these faces was that face. But there was a man, of regular build, who was wearing a beret over very long hair. The beard was not very thick. He was dressed in a black cape with his shirt open. The flames of the bonfire and the mustache, which fell over either side of the mouth, gave him a Chinese aspect. I thought of Genghis Khan."

Their first meeting did not go well. The Havana-born son of Polish emigrants, Oltuski was trained as an engineer but had put aside his career for the revolution. He had helped to organize the Civic Resistance, and was a member of the July 26 National Directorate. He was also an anticommunist. He and Che immediately locked horns, their first clash coming over Che's proposal to carry out bank robberies in Las Villas to acquire funds.

---

*After the revolution, Carreras returned to the Escambray with other disgruntled former rebels and took up arms in a guerrilla war against the revolution. He was captured and executed in 1961.

Oltuski and his llano comrades were vehemently opposed. Che wrote contemptuously in his diary, "When I told him to give us a report of all the banks in the towns, to attack them and take their money, they threw themselves on the ground in anguish. [And] with their silence they opposed the free distribution of land and demonstrated their subordination to the great capital interests, most of all Sierra [Oltuski]."

Oltuski reconstructed his own version of their argument over land reform in a memoir:

> *Guevara:* When we have broadened and consolidated our territory we will implement an agrarian reform. We will divide the land among those who work it. What do you think of the agrarian reform?
>
> *Oltuski:* It is indispensable. [*Che's eyes lit up*] Without agrarian reform economic progress is not possible.
>
> *Guevara:* Or social progress.
>
> *Oltuski:* Yes social progress, of course. I have written an agrarian thesis for the Movement.
>
> *Guevara:* Really? What did it say?
>
> *Oltuski:* That all idle land should be given to the peasants and that large landowners should be pressured to let them purchase the land with their own money. Then the land would be sold to the peasants at cost, with payment terms and credits to produce.
>
> *Guevara:* That is a reactionary thesis! [*Che boiled over with indignation*] How are we going to charge those who work the land? You're just like all the other Llano people.
>
> *Oltuski:* [*I saw red*] Damnit, and what do you think we should do?! Just give it to them? So they can destroy it as in Mexico? A man should feel that what he owns has cost him effort.
>
> *Guevara:* Goddamnit, listen to what you're saying! [*Che shouted and the veins on his neck bulged*]
>
> *Oltuski:* In addition, one must disguise things. Don't think that the Americans are going to sit idly by and watch us do things so openly. It is necessary to be more discreet.
>
> *Guevara:* So you're one of those who believes we can make a revolution behind the backs of the Americans. What a shiteater you are! The revolution must be carried out in a life-and-death struggle against imperialism from the very first moment. A true revolution cannot be disguised.

On October 22, with the issues between Che and his local July 26 colleagues unresolved, a new problem arose with the Second Front. Che was visited by a Commander Peña, "famous in the region for rustling the peasants' cattle." In his diary, Che wrote, "He began by being very friendly but later showed his true colors. We parted cordially, but as declared enemies." Peña had warned Che not to attack Güinía de Miranda, which lay within *his* territory. "Naturally," Che, wrote, "we paid no attention." But before Che could go ahead with the attack, his men, whose boots were rotting on their feet after their long trek, needed new footwear. He was enraged to learn that a shipment of forty boots sent to him by the July 26 Movement had been "appropriated" by the Second Front. For Che, it was nearly the last straw. "A storm was brewing."

Amid this crisis, Víctor "Diego" Paneque, the July 26 action chief for Las Villas, arrived, bringing 5,000 pesos and an old letter from Fidel, both forwarded by Oltuski. Che gave Diego his orders for the upcoming offensive: "to burn the voting centers in two or three important cities on the llano and to give Camilo the order to attack Caibarién, Remedios, Yaguajay, and Zulueta [towns in northern Las Villas]." Che had yet to work out exactly what his own plan of attack would be. Everything depended on the cooperation he got from the other rebel forces.

On October 25, Víctor Bordón, the local July 26 guerrilla chief, finally came to see Che and was immediately humbled. Among other things, Che found Bordón guilty of overstepping his authority and of having lied about a meeting with Fidel that had never taken place. He demoted Bordón to captain and ordered Bordón's 200 men to bring their weapons and place themselves under Che's command. Those not in agreement were told to leave the mountains.

That night, the Directorio leaders came to tell Che they were "not in a condition" to join his attack against Güinía de Miranda, which was planned for the next day. Che had suspected as much and told them he would go ahead without them. The following night, he and his men hiked down to Güinía de Miranda and opened fire on the barracks with a bazooka. Its first shot missed the target, however, and the soldiers returned fire. A fierce firefight ensued, punctuated by three more wild shots from the bazooka. Rebels began to drop. In desperation, Che grabbed the weapon himself and hit the barracks on his first shot. The fourteen soldiers inside surrendered immediately.

Che was far from pleased with the results. "We captured very few bullets and [only] eight rifles. Our loss, because of the amount of ammunition wasted and grenades used." Two rebels had died and seven were injured. By dawn the attackers were safely back in the hills. Che pointedly left a stolen jeep near the Directorio camp as a "gift" from the battle in which its members had not participated.

Che decided to keep up pressure on the army, with or without help from the other factions. The next night he set off to attack the Jíquima garrison, which was defended by fifty soldiers. He was more cautious this time, and suspended the attack just before daylight when Fonso, his bazooka man, said he couldn't find a good firing position. Back in the sierra on October 30, Che received visits from the July 26 action chiefs from Sancti Spíritus, Cabaiguán, Fomento, and Placetas; all of them endorsed his plans to attack their towns during the coming days. "They were also in agreement with the bank robberies," Che noted, "and promised their help."

After a few more days of skirmishing, Che set about organizing his men for the series of attacks that would be carried out on November 3, Election Day, in concert with the urban action groups. On the eve of battle, however, he was visited by the very anxious action chief for Sancti Spíritus. The city coordinator for Sancti Spíritus had learned of the bank robbery scheme, the action chief explained, and had refused to help. He had even made threats. A short time later, Che received a threatening letter from "Sierra" Oltuski, the July 26 coordinator for Las Villas, ordering him to abort the robbery plan. Che fired back a withering letter:

> You say that not even Fidel himself did this when he had nothing to eat. That is true. But when he had nothing to eat he was also not strong enough to carry out an action of this type. . . . According to the person who brought me the letter, the local leaderships in the towns are threatening to resign. I agree that they should do so. Even more, I demand it now, since it is impermissible to have a deliberate boycott of a measure that would be so beneficial to the interests of the revolution.
>
> I find myself faced with the sad necessity of reminding you that I have been named commander in chief, precisely to provide the Movement with unity of command and to improve things. . . . Whether they resign or don't resign, I intend to sweep away, with the authority vested in me, all the weaklings from the villages surrounding the mountains. I never imagined things would come to a boycott by my own comrades.
>
> Now I realize that the old antagonism we thought had been overcome is resurrected with the word *Llano*. You have leaders divorced from the masses stating what they think the people believe. I could ask you: Why is it that no peasant disagrees with our thesis that the land belongs to those who work it, while the landlords do?

Is this unrelated to the fact that the mass of combatants are in favor of the assault on the banks when they are all penniless? Have you never considered the economic reasons for this respect toward the most arbitrary of financial institutions? Those who make their money loaning out other people's money and speculating with it have no right to special consideration. . . . Meanwhile, the suffering people are shedding their blood in the mountains and on the plains, and suffering on a daily basis from betrayal by their false leaders.

You warn me that I bear total responsibility for the destruction of the organization. I accept this responsibility, and I am prepared to render an account of my behavior before any revolutionary tribunal, at any moment decided by the National Directorate of the Movement. I will give an accounting of every last cent provided to the combatants of the Sierra, however it was obtained. But I will also ask for an accounting of each of the fifty thousand pesos you mention.*

You asked me for a signed receipt, something I am not accustomed to doing among comrades. . . . My word is worth more than all the signatures in the world. . . . I will end by sending you revolutionary greetings, and I await your arrival together with Diego.†

Once again, Che's plans had been foiled by the llano. On the very day they were supposed to be waging war together against the regime, his city-based comrades had done nothing, choosing to attack him instead.

Still determined to do something, Che ordered a three-pronged attack on the town of Cabaiguán. It was to begin with a bazooka blast, but at around four in the morning, his captain, Angel Frías, reported that he couldn't fire "because there were too many guards." Furious, Che wrote in his diary, "The indecision of this captain has cost us much prestige, because everyone knew we were going to attack Cabaiguán and we had to retreat without firing a shot." Arriving back in the Escambray the next morning, Che ordered a new

---

*Oltuski had said this amount had been collected by the llano, and that part of it would be given to Che to show him they had enough support to make robbing banks unnecessary.

†Oltuski had told Che that Víctor Paneque—Diego—the action chief for Las Villas, also opposed the bank robberies. Later, in his memoir of the episode, Oltuski wrote that Diego had reacted with shock when he heard of Che's plans and said it was "craziness," that it would alienate July 26 supporters, and that he was "sure" that Fidel wouldn't approve such actions.

attack on Jíquima that night, but this too was aborted when Angel Frías couldn't find a "good firing position."

Che's disappointment over these poor showings was offset by good news coming in from around the province. The combination of his actions and Camilo's attacks in the north had brought most traffic in Las Villas to a standstill on Election Day, with voter abstention very high. In the rest of the country, the results were similar, and in Oriente the rebels had compounded the paralysis by launching multiple attacks. Nationwide, the rebel strategy had been a tremendous success, with perhaps less than 30 percent of the eligible voters showing up at the polls. As expected, Rivero Agüero had won, thanks to massive voting fraud carried out with the assistance of the armed forces, and he was to assume the presidency on February 24. The rebels were determined to see that the inauguration never took place.

For a few days, Che stayed in the hills to oversee construction work at Caballete de Casas, which was to be his permanent rearguard base. The work was proceeding well, and several adobe houses were already finished, but to accelerate the work Che organized the nearly 200 men he had assembled into crews. He set up a recruits' school, modeled on Minas del Frío, which he named the Ñico López in honor of his late comrade, and, once again, the Communist Party official Pablo Ribalta was appointed political commissar. Within a few days, a field-radio system was installed, courtesy of the PSP. The mimeograph machine also arrived, and by mid-November Che had founded a newspaper called *El Miliciano* (The Militiaman). Soon, there would be an electrical plant, a hospital, a tobacco factory, leather and metals workshops, and an armory.

Several people who were to become closely linked to Che now joined him in the Escambray. The movement in Santa Clara sent a smart, serious young accountancy student named Orlando Borrego. In time they would become best friends, but at their first meeting Che greeted him imperiously. "He was very rough, very cold, and was contemptuous of students," Borrego recalled. Borrego was one of seven children raised on a hardscrabble farm in Holguín, Oriente. His father was a farm foreman turned taxi driver, and his mother was a rural schoolteacher. Money had always been a struggle, and Borrego had gone to work at fourteen to help his family. Since then, he had learned what he knew from night classes, and now he had run away to join the rebels.

One of Che's bodyguards, Orlando "Olo" Pantoja, intervened with Che on Borrega's behalf, suggesting that Che take him on to help manage his funds. Che agreed to let Borrego stay on as his treasurer, but ordered him to first undergo a military training course at Caballete de Casas. It was there that Borrego made friends with a lively young July 26 guerrilla named

Jesús "El Rubio" Suárez Gayol. A former student leader from Camagüey, he had abandoned his architectural studies to join a July 26 expedition that had landed in Pinar del Río in April. When Borrego met him, he was recovering from wounds suffered during an attack on a radio station in Pinar del Río. He had rushed into the office of the station in broad daylight, carrying a stick of dynamite in one hand and a pistol in the other. After removing the fuse, he somehow caught on fire. Stripped to his underpants, with severe burns on his legs, he rushed out into the street—just as the building blew—to come face-to-face with a policeman. Luckily for him, the shocked policeman ran away. Then, still waving his pistol, Suárez Gayol ran down the street and leaped into an old woman's house. Fortunately the woman was a rebel sympathizer, and she hid him and treated his wounds until he could be smuggled out of the province and into the Escambray. When the war was over, Suárez Gayol and Borrego remained close friends and became two of Che's most trusted disciples.

A young lawyer from a patrician Havana family also arrived at the Escambray camp in early November. Miguel Ángel Duque de Estrada was not a Marxist, but he admired Che and had closely followed the reports of the march across Cuba. He asked to be sent to Che's Escambray unit. Che needed someone qualified to enforce the guerrilla legal code in rebel territory, and the young lawyer filled the bill; he made Duque de Estrada his *auditor revolucionario,* or judge. "He had a clear political strategy worked out in his mind," Duque de Estrada recalled. "He told me prisoners were to be kept alive. There were to be no firing squads. This would change later, but for now he didn't want executions to put off men who might surrender to his forces." Like Borrego and Suárez Gayol, Duque de Estrada would become one of Che's select cadres after the war.

Che was assembling a brain trust of aides and advisers to help in the postwar battle: the political and economic revolution that would be necessary to build socialism in Cuba and free the country from U.S. domination. He wasn't concerned with their political ideology. If they had a progressive outlook, he could eventually make them believe in socialism. And, indeed, most of his guerrilla protégés were not Marxists at first but ended up adopting Che's ideology as their own.

By the time he reached the Escambray, Che was actively planning a central role for himself in the postwar transformation of Cuba's economy. Whether this was the result of an understanding worked out between Fidel and the PSP is a point that has been left intentionally unclarified in Cuba, but there is strong evidence to suggest that it was. Che had been studying political economy ever since his days in Mexico. At Fidel's behest, he had helped set the agrarian reform process in motion in the Sierra Maestra, had been a key participant in the delicate talks with the PSP, and was now empowered to carry out land reform in Las Villas. But it was not a one-man show. For both his present and his future projects, Che was relying on the PSP. Besides the Communists already working with him in the Escambray, there was a small, well-placed group of Party militants at his service in Havana. One of them was thirty-seven-year-old Alfredo Menéndez, a sugar expert employed at the Instituto Cubano de Estabilización del Azúcar (Cuban Institute for the Stabilization of Sugar), the sugar-industry syndicate headquarters in Havana. A veteran Communist, Menéndez had for years used his strategic position to feed economic intelligence to the PSP Politburo, and—with the aid of a colleague, Juan Borroto, and two July 26 men at the institute—he now did the same for Che.

No matter how much Che depended on the PSP, he wanted to avoid the appearance that he was in their pocket. Ovidio Díaz Rodríguez, the Socialist Youth leader who helped coordinate Che's agrarian reform efforts in Las Villas, was present when a Party man came to a meeting carrying a present for Che. "It was a tin of Argentine *mate* and in front of everyone he said: 'Look, Commander, this is a gift from the Party Directorate.' Che accepted it without saying anything, but afterward he told me: 'Tell the Party not to send me such indiscreet comrades.'"

III

Simply because he had launched attacks—as few of the other groups had done—Che became the de facto authority in the Escambray, and people began arriving to pay him their respects. On November 8, two dairy company inspectors visited to ask if they could continue to collect milk in the area; their dairy business was almost paralyzed because of the rebels' activities. "I told them yes, but that we would charge an extraordinary war tax, with which they agreed." A transport union leader from Santa Clara came proposing joint actions in the city. Che said he was willing if the man could organize a union meeting and if all the leaders requested it. A delegation from Placetas brought Che diagrams of the town and offered him support if he attacked.

Clearly put out by Che's seizure of the limelight in "their" zone of influence, the warlords of the Second Front were making increasingly bellicose noises. Che received notes from William Morgan, the American military veteran helping Gutiérrez Menoyo, ordering him to return the weapons that Bordón's men had brought with them when they joined Che. Entirely ignoring Morgan, Che wrote a strongly worded letter to Gutiérrez Menoyo and ordered his men "not to hand over a single weapon and to repel any

Che speaking to the citizens of Cabaiguán during the final push to victory in
December 1958.

attack." Che also wrote to the Directorio leader Faure Chomón to inform
him of the "delicate situation" with the Second Front. The situation was of
"crisis proportions," he said, "making it impossible to reach an agreement
with this organization." He also urged Chomón to consider including the
PSP in a proposed alliance. "In official talks with members of the Popular
Socialist Party, they have openly expressed a pro-unity stance and have
placed their organization in the towns and their guerrillas on the Yaguajay
front at the disposal of this unity."

Che heard that soldiers loyal to Commander Peña of the Second Front
were extorting money from local civilians, and he sent out men to detain
the culprits. Within a few days, two complete Second Front columns were
brought in. Che warned them that they could no longer operate in the zone,
much less use their arms for extortion. One of the columns asked to join
him, and Che accepted. Before letting the rest go, he confiscated the
"war taxes" they had extorted—a total of 3,000 pesos—and sent a note to
Commander Peña. In this "Military Order No. 1," Che's first decree as

"commander in chief of the Las Villas region for the July 26 Movement,"
he made it clear that life in the area was about to change. After outlining
the terms for agrarian reform, he turned, obliquely, to his competitors in the
Second Front: "Any member of a revolutionary organization other than the
July 26 Movement may pass through, live, and operate military in this territory. The only requirement shall be to abide by the military orders that
have been or will be promulgated.

"No one who is not the member of a revolutionary organization has
the right to bear arms in this territory. No member of any revolutionary body
is permitted to drink alcoholic beverages in public establishments. . . . Any
shedding of blood due to violation of this order will fall under the Penal
Code of the revolutionary army. . . .

"All military or civil crimes committed within the borders of the administrative territory encompassed by this order will fall under the jurisdiction of our appropriate regulations."

Perhaps because they were intimidated, the Directorio faction accepted
unification with Che's group and agreed to impose a single tax in the area
and to divide the proceeds equally between their two organizations. As a
practical first step for their new alliance, they planned to begin launching
joint attacks. The one area of disagreement that remained was Chomón's
refusal to widen the alliance to include the PSP. Che let the matter rest, but
on December 3, less than three weeks after the unity agreement between
the Directorio and the July 26 Movement, he and the PSP leader Rolando
Cubela signed the "Pedrero Pact," declaring their alliance in the struggle as
"brothers."

The quarrels within the July 26 Movement continued. Enrique
Oltuski, together with Marcelo Fernández, the new July 26 Havana chief,
and three officials from the Las Villas directorate, called on Che in late
November for another round of talks. Che found Fernández "full of airs
about himself," and he prepared for battle. "We argued all night. . . . We
accused each other mutually. They accused me of being a Communist and
I accused them of being imperialists. I told them the facts on which I based
myself to give such an opinion and they did the same to me. When the argument ended we were more apart than when we began."

As Oltuski recalled, Che was away when they arrived, and they were
received by one of his young bodyguards, Olo Pantoja. As an act of courtesy, Pantoja offered them some goat meat, which they noticed was already
green with rot. So as not to offend, they each tried a bite, a decision Oltuski
immediately regretted: overcome by nausea, he discreetly went outside and
spat out his mouthful. When Che returned at midnight and settled down
before the meal, Oltuski watched with horrified fascination.

"As he spoke," Oltuski wrote, "he took the pieces of meat with dirty fingers. Judging from the relish with which he ate, it tasted gloriously to him. He finished eating and we went outside. . . . Che handed out cigars. They were rough, no doubt made in the zone by some *guajiro*. I inhaled the bitter and strong smoke: I felt a warmth in my body and a light dizziness. To my side, Che smoked and coughed, a damp cough, as if he was all wet inside. He smelled bad. He stank of decomposed sweat. It was a penetrating odor and I fought it with the tobacco smoke. . . . Che and Marcelo had some verbal wrangles. Among other things, they argued over the program of the 26 of July. . . .

"When we were on our way back, Marcelo asked me: 'What do you think?'

"'In spite of everything, one can't help admiring him. He knows what he wants better than we do. And he lives entirely for it.'"

IV

Aleida March met Che in late November. Her first impression was that he looked old, not to mention skinny and dirty. He didn't seem like much of a romantic prospect.* Aleida had traveled to Che's base from Santa Clara on behalf of Diego, her boss in the Las Villas rebel underground, who entrusted her with his most delicate missions. In the dossiers of Batista's secret police, she appeared as "Cara Cortada" (Scarface) and "Teta Manchada" (Stained Tit). Aleida's unlovely nicknames had been coined from the descriptions of *chivatos,* who told the police about the small scar on her right cheek, from a childhood dog bite, and the large pink birthmark that spread from her left breast to above her collarbone. But the police intelligence sheets were misleading. In spite of her scars, Aleida March was a pretty blond woman of twenty-four.

The youngest of six children, Aleida had been raised on a fifty-acre tenant farm in the hilly agricultural country south of Santa Clara. Her mother was tiny, barely five feet, while her father was tall, with blond hair and blue eyes. Both were from formerly affluent Spanish émigré families who had lost their wealth, but Aleida liked to say that her family was "middle class" because their home had a concrete floor. Their neighbors' homes and the one-room grammar school she attended until the sixth grade had dirt floors.

---

*Aleida March published her memoir, *Evocación: mi vida al lado del Che* (Evocation: My Life at Che's Side), in 2008. The book contains some previously unpublished poems Che wrote for her, as well as several of his letters to her.

Their two-bedroom house was much like everyone else's, with a palm-thatched roof and whitewashed mud walls, a family room with a kitchen, and a front room for receiving visitors. The ceiling was yellow from all the rice bags Aleida's father stored in the attic. A vertical wood strut rising from the floor between the living room and the kitchen held up the roof, and in the evenings her father leaned his back against it to read her stories. At night, Aleida could hear her mother singing to her father in their bedroom, next to hers. A river ran across their land; this was where her mother washed their clothes, and where Aleida and her sisters bathed.

Their part of Las Villas was populated by people much like themselves —poor white farmers, the descendants of immigrants from impoverished parts of Spain—Galicians, Andalusians, and *isleños* (Canary Islanders). In the socially and racially stratified pecking order of the region, as in much of Cuba, such families remained at the bottom rung of white society, but they were still head and shoulders above the mulattos and blacks. Only three generations out of slavery, *los negros* were the dirt-poor laborers, the despised effluvia of Cuban society. In 1958, Santa Clara's central park was still off-limits to blacks; there was a fence around it, and blacks could congregate around its edges, but not go inside.

Like many poor whites, Aleida's mother, Eudoxia de la Torre, was both a racist and a snob. She liked to brag about the illustrious lineage of Aleida's father, Juan March, whose Catalan ancestors had supposedly been noblemen. When she was small, mimicking her mother, Aleida used to tell people she was related to the "dukes of Catalunya." Whether her father was of direct noble lineage or an illegitimate offspring, Aleida never knew, but it *was* true that both her parents' families had once possessed land and money. Her father's family had owned a sugar plantation but had lost their land years before, and the land her father now sharecropped had belonged to Aleida's maternal grandparents, before they lost it in the hard times of the 1920s. When her parents married, they had rented the land and settled in as tenant farmers. The last remaining legacy of their comfortable past, an antique crystal *bonbonnière,* stood prominently displayed on an old wooden bureau in the front room, where guests were received.

The family's status was further bolstered by the fact that the local schoolteacher lodged with them throughout Aleida's childhood. They had the only home in the area "decent" enough for her. But the Marches also had their blemishes. Her mother, a devout churchgoing Presbyterian, had caused a local scandal by giving birth to Aleida at the age of forty-two, well past the "appropriate" childbearing years. This was a source of perpetual mortification for Aleida's sisters—the next closest in age was fifteen years older—and they used to tell people that Aleida was not their sister at all, but the daughter of the much younger schoolteacher.

The nearest community was Seibabo, a hamlet with a few houses in it, and once a month her father saddled up his horse and rode into the city of Santa Clara to buy provisions on credit from the Chinese bodegas. He had fruit orchards, grew vegetables, and owned a couple of dairy cows, but he still had to go into debt to feed his family. When the crops didn't give him enough to pay off the landlord, he had to sell things.

When Aleida reached the sixth grade, she went to live with a married sister in Santa Clara and attended high school there. She decided to become a teacher and, when she finished high school, went on to Santa Clara University to earn a degree in education. While she was there, Fidel carried out his Moncada assault. The event and its violent aftermath awakened her politically, as they did many other young Cubans of her generation. By the time the *Granma* landed, she had graduated from college and was an active member of the local July 26 underground.

Until she reached her early twenties, Santa Clara was the biggest city Aleida had ever been in. She first saw four-lane roads when she made a trip to Havana on a mission for the July 26 Movement. She first heard Che Guevara's name when an Italian merchant marine, Gino Donne, mentioned it to her. Donne had been on the *Granma,* become separated from his comrades at Alegría del Pío, and eventually, after many misadventures, made it to Santa Clara. Covered with blisters, famished, and with a pounding toothache, he was given refuge at the house of María Dolores "Lolita" Rossell, a pretty, dark-haired mother of four who was a kindergarten teacher. Lolita's brother Allan Rossell was the July 26 coordinator for Las Villas, and her house functioned as a way station on the rebels' underground railroad.

It was because of Donne's arrival that Lolita and Aleida met, and they soon became close friends. By then, Aleida was chief liaison for the July 26 action chief in Villa Clara and was earning a reputation as extremely audacious, smuggling weapons and bombs around the province under her full-length skirts. "She wasn't afraid of anything," Lolita recalled. "She was totally dedicated, very serious, had stayed single, and wasn't one for parties and that kind of thing." Aleida came to Lolita's house to plan sabotage attacks with Donne, and for a time the two carried out missions around the city. But Donne didn't stay long; disillusioned by the festive mood he saw in Santa Clara that first Christmas—which he perceived as revealing a lack of insurrectionary spirit—he found a ship leaving Cuba and went with it.

Aleida participated in the September 1957 uprising in Cienfuegos, and in armed actions during the April 1958 general strike in Las Villas. During

the security crackdown that followed the strike, the Las Villas directorate
organized a guerrilla force to operate in the rural areas of the province.
Aleida helped: sneaking fugitives into the countryside; smuggling food,
weapons, and ammunition, and messages to them. After Che's arrival,
Aleida made repeated trips to and from the sierra, taking visitors and carrying correspondence and money to him. By November, an effective, if not
acrimony-free partnership between the llano and sierra July 26 factions had
been secured in the Escambray, and Aleida, as the principal courier, was
becoming a familiar face at Che's encampment. One day, Che told her he
had decided to impose a war tax on sugar-mill owners, and asked her help
in collecting it. It was after returning from such a mission in late November that she found out that her cover had been blown and that the police
had raided her home. Returning to Santa Clara was now out of the question, but when she went to ask Che's permission to remain in the guerrilla
zone, he was not pleased; as a rule, women were not permitted to live in the
guerrilla camps. Given Aleida's situation, however, the *comandante* relented.

Like most of her llano comrades, Aleida had a poor opinion of the
Cuban Communist Party. Her antipathy stemmed from her university days,
when she had a Communist professor who was vociferously opposed to
insurrectional activity. Now, however, the war was at a critical stage, and
Che's unifying efforts had helped to defuse the sectarian rivalries and galvanized Las Villas's opposition groups into action. And if she initially distrusted *el comunista* Che, she put aside her feelings, for very soon she found
herself falling in love with him. (Eventually, because of Che, Aleida would
alter her negative opinion of "socialists," but she would never lose her distrust of the "old Communists" of the PSP.)

By late November, the air force was pounding Che's front in daily
bombardments, and the army had begun moving several companies of
heavily armed troops and tanks toward Pedrero in a three-pronged offensive. Camilo Cienfuegos came with some of his units to help out, and for six
days the two sides battled. By December 4, the army's offensive was shattered. The guerrillas had stopped the advance on all fronts, then chased the
soldiers all the way to Fomento in the west and to the village of Santa Lucia
in the east. They also captured a healthy supply of war matériel, including
a tank equipped with a 37mm cannon. One of Che's squads destroyed two
strategic bridges, isolating the army garrisons in Cabaiguán, Sancti Spíritus,
and Trinidad, and opening up a large new swath of territory to the rebel
forces. Now, it was Che's turn to go on the offensive.

Before Camilo Cienfuegos returned to his main forces at Yaguajay,
he and Che mapped out a strategy for a province-wide offensive. Like an
enthusiastic surgeon especially deft at amputations, Che set about system-

atically severing road and railway bridges, isolating the province's towns and garrisons and cutting them off from reinforcements. On December 16, his men blew up the principal Central Highway bridge and railway link leading east from Santa Clara, effectively separating Havana and Santa Clara from central and eastern Cuba and cutting the nation in half. These actions, together with the offensive taking place in Oriente, where llano garrisons had begun falling like dominoes to the guerrillas, made it clear the Batista regime had little time left.

For the last two weeks of December 1958, Che moved around the province attacking and capturing one garrison after the other. First, he laid siege to the strategic town of Fomento, with its military garrison, and, despite a sustained enemy air assault, secured its surrender after two days of fighting. He immediately moved on to the towns of Guayos and Cabaiguán. Guayos surrendered on December 21, Cabaiguán two days later. In Cabaiguán, Che fell off a wall and fractured his right elbow. Doctor Fernández Mell made him a splint and cast, and he carried on. His next target was Placetas, where his troops fought together with the Directorio for the first time. After a single day's fighting, Placetas surrendered on December 23. That same day, Sancti Spíritus surrendered to Captain Armando Acosta. Meanwhile, the Second Front had finally moved into action, joining Directorio forces in a siege of Trinidad and other garrisons in the south. To the north, Camilo's forces were closing in on the main garrison town of Yaguajay.

At some point amid the chaos and euphoria of battle, Che and Aleida became lovers. Perhaps the first to take note of the romance was Oscarito Fernández Mell, although even he could not remember when or where. "Suddenly, Aleida was with Che wherever he went, in combat, everywhere. . . . They went around in the jeep together. She carried his papers for him, she washed his clothes."

A less observant graduate of Minas del Frío, Alberto Castellanos, nearly put his foot in it. A cocksure twenty-four-year-old, Alberto had already been reprimanded by Che for prankish behavior but had nonetheless endeared himself to the *jefe*, who made him a general staff orderly. Alberto considered himself quite a lad with the ladies, and when Aleida showed up she caught his eye. Deciding to try his luck, he walked over to her and delivered a saucy *piropo*, or come-on line. Che was watching, and as soon as Castellanos had uttered the words, he realized Aleida was definitely *not* available. "From the way Che looked at me, I said to myself: 'Beat it, Alberto, there's nothing for you here.'"

Aleida herself recalled how it all began. One night, unable to sleep, she left her room and went outside to sit by the road. It was three or four in the morning, and the offensive was in full swing. Suddenly a jeep raced up in the dark and came to a halt next to her. Che was at the wheel. "What are you doing here?" he asked her. "I couldn't sleep," she replied. "I'm going to attack Cabaiguán," he said. "Do you want to come along?" "Sure," she replied, and hopped into the jeep next to him. "And from that moment on," recalled Aleida with a playful smile, "I never left his side—*or* let him out of my sight."

V

Che and Aleida made an unlikely couple. Aleida came from the faction within the Cuban revolution most despised by Che. She was from the llano, she was anticommunist, and she retained many of the social prejudices she had been brought up with. Although it wasn't a factor in these early days, things such as dress were important to her, and she shared her mother's racial disdains. Che was a radical Communist, the archenemy of most of her colleagues. He was also famously careless about his appearance and personal hygiene and had surrounded himself with blacks and uneducated *guajiros*.

But when it came to women, especially attractive women, Che tended to put his political philosophy on hold—and Aleida March was very attractive. She was also worthy of respect. She was undeniably brave, having proved repeatedly that she knew how to face death. She also had a paradoxical personality that clearly appealed to Che. She was very shy but had an acute and earthy sense of humor. When she did speak out, she was tactlessly sincere, much like Che himself.

After fracturing his arm, Che had made Alberto Castellanos his driver. With Alberto at the wheel, Che and Aleida roared around the province in his jeep, accompanied by his young bodyguards—Harry Villegas, Jesús "Parrita" Parra, José Argudín, and Hermes Peña. Soon, a rumor spread that Che was traveling with "three women: a blond, a black, and a *jabao*"—the last a Cuban term for a white mulatto. Aleida was obviously the blond, but sixteen-year-old Villegas, who was black and beardless, and Parrita, a white man with wild blond hair, were mortified to realize that they had been misidentified as girls. The erroneous gossip aside, what Che had created was not a harem but his own little guerrilla family. Che and Aleida played the roles of the parents, and the young guerrillas were their wayward children.

"Che knew us like parents know their children," Villegas recalled. "He knew when we had done something naughty, when we hid something from him, when we did something wrong by accident or through mischief. And he had strict rules, which at the beginning we didn't fully understand. For example . . . he didn't want anyone to have special privileges. If he saw I had extra food he would call me to find out where I had gotten it from or

Che with Aleida March. They became lovers during the last weeks of the war.

where it came from—why I had accepted it—and he called Aleida over and made her responsible to see that it didn't happen again. Aleida helped us a lot. You could say she was like our godmother, because we were mischievous, and Che was strict, and she was the intermediary on many occasions when she evaluated the situation differently from him, and made him see he was being too severe with us."

Following the surrender of Placetas, Che moved north, and on Christmas Day he attacked Remedios and the port of Caibarién; both fell the next day. Villa Clara had become a chaos of defeated army troops, cheering civilians, and long-haired guerrillas racing around, while government planes kept up their strafing and bombing. By December 27 only one garrison, in the town of Camajuaní, remained between Che's forces and Santa Clara, the capital of Las Villas and the fourth-largest city in Cuba. When the army troops fled Camajuaní without a fight, the way was clear.

The fighters were euphoric. They knew now that they were on the verge of winning the war, and maintaining troop discipline and establishing a semblance of order were among Che's top priorities. To prevent anarchy, he had named provisional revolutionary authorities in each town he liberated and set down rules of behavior for his men. Bars and bordellos were strictly off-limits, but for many of the young guerrillas, suddenly finding themselves in towns and cities as conquering heroes after months of abstinence in the bush, the temptation to indulge themselves was too much. For the most part, they were remarkably well behaved, but invariably some succumbed to the delights on offer. On the day Remedios fell, Enrique Acevedo almost lost control of his men when a bordello owner delivered a truckload of prostitutes and a case of rum as an expression of his "admiration."

"I watched our ambush disintegrate as furtive couples began heading to the bushes. Without thinking I yelled at the guy: 'If you've done this to affect our ambush you'll pay for it. Pick up the wagonload of whores you've dumped here immediately!'" Afterward Acevedo took stock and realized he had reacted just in time. "Not everyone had sinned, but maintaining order in the face of such temptation was a titanic effort."

As Che plotted his next move, Fidel wrote him a letter by flashlight from outside the army garrison of Maffo, which his forces had been besieging for six days: "The war is won, the enemy is collapsing with a resounding crash, we have ten thousand soldiers bottled up in Oriente. Those in Camagüey have no way of escaping. All this is the result of one thing: our determined effort. . . . It's essential for you to realize that the political aspect of the battle at Las Villas [province] is fundamental.

"For the moment, it is supremely important that the advance toward Matanzas and Havana be carried out exclusively by the 26th of July forces.

Camilo's column should be in the lead, the vanguard, to take over Havana when the dictatorship falls, if we don't want the weapons from Camp Columbia [military headquarters] to be distributed among all the various groups, which would present a very serious problem in the future."

Fidel was determined to prevent rivals from snatching the political spoils at the last moment. In Washington, past differences between the State Department and the CIA had been put aside, and there was now a broad consensus that Castro was too slippery to be allowed to take power. With the events of recent weeks, however, any hopes entertained by the Eisenhower administration that the November 3 elections might somehow ameliorate the Cuban crisis had vanished. Che and Camilo's offensive moved forward in Las Villas; rebel columns were roaming throughout Oriente and Camagüey; numerous garrisons had surrendered to Raúl's forces; Holguín's water and electricity supply had been blown up; Santiago was under mounting pressure as rebel units probed its outskirts. At the end of November, after a bloody siege, Fidel's forces had taken the major garrison of Guisa, and he too had moved from the mountains onto the llano.

Ambassador Smith had dutifully shuttled to Washington to seek support for President-Elect Rivero Agüero, but in vain. It was clear to all that the military situation was deteriorating rapidly, and fears were growing that Batista might not even last until the handover of power in February. Smith was instructed to tell Batista that a Rivero Agüero government could not expect Washington's support and that he should resign immediately in favor of a civilian-military junta acceptable to the United States. Batista refused, evidently still believing he could somehow hold things together. In early December, he had rebuffed a similar petition by the CIA's station chief in Havana and by William Pawley, a former ambassador to Cuba and founder of the national airline, Cubana de Aviación.

Then the port of Nicaro fell to Raúl, and the La Maya barracks in Guantánamo fell when a rebel pilot dropped a napalm bomb on the compound. Raúl had also captured vast quantities of weapons and was holding more than 500 prisoners. As Fidel laid siege to Maffo in mid-December, his forces controlled most of the Central Highway through Oriente and seemed to have the army pinned down everywhere.

The CIA had begun exploring the possibility of backing a preemptive military coup, and agents were fishing around for suitable candidates for a junta. Once again, Justo Carrillo proposed Colonel Barquín, who was still imprisoned on the Isle of Pines. Barquín inspired strong loyalties within the armed forces and was on most people's lists of a candidate to assume military control once Batista was gone. This time, the CIA gave its go-ahead, and Carrillo received money to bribe prison officials to spring Barquín.

Simultaneously, sensing an opening for themselves, Batista's coterie of top officers began hatching coup plots. General Francisco Tabernilla, the army chief of staff, told General Cantillo, the commander of Oriente province, to open negotiations with Fidel by proposing an alliance between the military and the rebels for the final push against Batista. A junta would include Cantillo, another officer to be decided upon, the president-in-waiting Manuel Urrutia, and two civilians selected by Fidel. The unofficial slogan of all these last-ditch efforts was, of course, "Stop Castro," and Fidel saw little reason to accommodate them. He rejected the putschists' proposal and sent word to Cantillo that he wanted a face-to-face meeting to give *his* proposals.

Across the country, towns and cities were being occupied by the rebels. They were greeted by enthusiastic civilians, many of whom—genuine supporters or not—wore the red-and-black July 26 armband. By Christmas, Che's and Camilo's forces had taken most of the major towns and cities in Las Villas except for Santa Clara, Cienfuegos, Trinidad, and Yaguajay. Víctor Bordón had taken a string of towns to the west, cutting off Santa Clara from potential reinforcement from Cienfuegos or Havana. In Oriente, meanwhile, the major garrisons at Caimanera and Sagua de Támano fell; and a naval vessel, the *Máximo Gómez,* stood off Santiago awaiting the rebels' orders to defect. After a quick Christmas visit with his mother in Birán, Fidel prepared for his meeting with Cantillo. He still had plenty of worries, but on the night of December 26 he felt confident enough to give Che the orders all in the rebel movement had dreamed of for a very long time: preparations for the assault on Havana itself.

Fidel had been correct in his end-game analysis that the battle for Las Villas was crucial. The city of Santa Clara had become the last cornerstone in Batista's defensive strategy. As the major transportation and communications hub of central Cuba, with a population of 150,000, it was the one remaining obstacle to a rebel assault on the capital. If Santa Clara fell, only the port of Matanzas lay between the rebels and Havana. Batista beefed up the Santa Clara garrison with more than 2,000 new soldiers to bring its troop strength to 3,500. He sent his ablest soldier, Joaquín Casillas, now a colonel, to take over its defense. To support Casillas, he had dispatched an armored train, loaded with weapons, ammunition, and communications equipment; it was to serve as a reserve arsenal and mobile communications link with military headquarters at Camp Columbia.

Batista knew he had little time left. He was aware of Tabernilla's schemes against him and had chosen to side with General Cantillo, saying he would hand over power to a junta headed by Cantillo in late January. But Batista wasn't taking any chances; over Christmas he arranged for several airplanes to stand ready to evacuate him and a short list of handpicked officers and friends with their families. A few days later, he sent his children to the United States for safety.

Meanwhile, Che was getting ready to attack Santa Clara. On December 27, he was joined in newly liberated Placetas by Antonio Nuñez Jiménez, a young geography professor from Santa Clara University who brought maps and diagrams to help plan Che's approach to the city. With Ramiro Valdés, they plotted a route over back roads leading to the university, on the northeastern outskirts of the city. They set out that night, with a disparity in numbers similar to those that had marked nearly every engagement between the rebels and the Cuban army. With eight of his own platoons, and a 100-man Directorio column led by Rolando Cubela, Che had 340 fighters to tackle an enemy force ten times larger and supported by tanks and air power.

Che's convoy arrived at the university at dawn the next day. Aleida's friend Lolita Rossell was on hand to meet them. She was shocked by how "dirty and messed-up" the guerrillas looked. Her father, who was standing next to her, muttered incredulously: "*These* guys are planning to take Santa Clara?" Then Lolita spotted Che, and she was struck both by how young he looked and by his air of authority. This impression was bolstered when one of his men, his face a battle-weary mask, asked her how many soldiers were in the city. When she told him "about five thousand," he nodded and said, "Good, with our *jefe* that's no problem."

After setting up a provisional *comandancia* at the university in Aleida's old stomping ground, the Pedagogical Faculty, Che and his men set out for the city itself, walking in irrigation ditches along the way. Stopping at the CMQ radio station, Che went on the air to appeal to civilians for support. Shortly afterward, B-26 bombers and new British-made Sea Furies strafed and bombed the outskirts of town, looking for his fighters.

The enemy had occupied a series of well-fortified positions around the city, but Che's first priority was the armored train, which was stationed at the entrance to the Camajuaní road leading to the university. At the eastern edge of the city, the army had occupied the strategic Capiro Hills that overlooked both the university road and the road and rail line leading out to Placetas. More than 1,000 soldiers were holed up in the Leoncio Vidal garrison in the northwestern suburbs, and nearby was police headquarters, with 400 defenders. In the city center, the courthouse, provincial government building, and jail had all been made redoubts; and to the south, the No. 31 and Los Caballitos garrisons guarded the road to Manicaragua. With most of the province now in rebel hands, Che's chief concern was to prevent enemy reinforcements from coming by the western Havana-Matanzas road, but Víctor Bordón's force had already cut the highway at several points and seized the key town of Santo Domingo.

Over that night and into the morning of December 29, Che moved his forces from the university into the city, targeting all the enemy positions but concentrating on the armored train. He moved his *comandancia* to a public-works building half a mile from town and had a section of rail track pulled up with tractors. Then his men attacked, going against the police station, the Capiro Hills, and the train. At the same time, Cubela's Directorio column, which had entered from the south the day before, laid siege to the No. 31 and Caballitos garrisons.

Over the next three days, Santa Clara became a bloody battleground as rebels slowly advanced into the city. In some places, fighters moved forward by punching holes in the interior walls of houses while others fought pitched battles in the streets outside. Numerous civilians heeded Che's call to arms, making Molotov cocktails, providing refuge and food, and barricading their streets. As tanks fired shells and airplanes continued to bomb and rocket, both civilian and guerrilla casualties piled up in the hospitals. Che was visiting one of the hospitals when a dying man touched his arm and said to him: "Do you remember me, Commander? In Remedios you sent me to find a weapon . . . and I earned it here." Che recognized him. It was a young fighter he had disarmed days earlier for accidentally firing his rifle. Che also recalled what

On December 29, 1958, Che and his fighters derailed an armored government train in Santa Clara. It was the death knell for Batista's regime.

he had told him at the time. "I had responded with my customary dryness," he wrote in his memoirs. "'Go get yourself another rifle by going to the front line unarmed . . . if you're up to it.'" The man had been up to it, with fatal consequences. "He died a few minutes later, and I think he was content for having proved his courage. Such was our Rebel Army."

The tide turned inexorably on the afternoon of December 29. After El Vaquerito's squad took the train station and other rebels stormed the Capiro Hills, soldiers fled for the protection of the armored train, which had twenty-two cars. The train moved out at speed. When it reached the missing track, the engine and the first three cars derailed in a spectacular cataclysm of twisted metal and screaming men. "A very interesting battle began," Che wrote, "in which the men were forced out of the train by our Molotov cocktails. . . . The train became, thanks to the armored plating, a veritable oven for the soldiers. In a few hours, the whole complement surrendered with its twenty-two cars, its antiaircraft guns, its machine guns . . . its fabulous quantity of ammunition (fabulous, of course, compared with our meager supply)."

With battles still raging around the city, the international wires carried the false news that evening that Che had been killed. Early the next day, Radio Rebelde went on the air, trumpeting the news of the capture of the armored train and denying Che's death: "For the tranquillity of the relatives in South America and the Cuban population, we assure you that Ernesto Che Guevara is alive and on the firing line, and . . . very soon, he will take the city of Santa Clara."

All too soon, however, Che had to go on the air himself, confirming the death of one of his most beloved men, Roberto Rodríguez—El Vaquerito, the leader of the Suicide Squad. It lent a sad note to a broadcast made to announce the imminent fall of the city. That afternoon, he had been hit by a bullet in the head while attacking the police station. Vaquerito's loss was especially painful to Che, for the youth had been a living personification of what he sought in his fighters. "Suicide Squad" had been Vaquerito's choice of names, but it was an elite attack squad made up of those fighters who aspired to Che's highest measure.

"The Suicide Squad was an example of revolutionary morale," Che wrote, "and only selected volunteers joined it. But whenever a man died— and it happened in every battle—when the new candidate was named, those not chosen would be grief-stricken and even cry. How curious to see those seasoned and noble warriors showing their youth by their tears of despair, because they did not have the honor of being in the front line of combat and death."

Surrounded by death, it is a normal human reaction to reach out for life, and even Che was not immune to this instinct. So it happened that in the midst of the battle for Santa Clara, he realized he was in love with Aleida. As he told her privately later, the realization occurred when she left his side to dart across a street under fire. For the few instants she was out of sight, he was in agony, not knowing if she had made it across safely. As for Aleida, she had known what she felt since the sleepless night a few weeks before when his jeep had stopped for her and she had climbed in.

On December 30, the Los Caballitos garrison surrendered to the Directorio, and some soldiers barricaded in a church also gave themselves up. Santo Domingo, which had been lost to an army counteroffensive, was recaptured by Bordón's forces, effectively sealing the western approaches to Santa Clara. To the south, the city of Trinidad fell to the forces led by Faure Chomón. Realizing he had not completely secured Las Villas in the east, Che had dispatched Ramiro Valdés to take the town of Jatiboníco on the Central Highway, where a column of army reinforcements was attempting to break through.

With this deployment of forces and the capture of the armored train, Santa Clara was completely isolated, and an air of desperation now seized the soldiers and policemen holding out. The military high command in Havana ordered more air attacks on the city; resistance remained fierce at the garrisons and the police station; a group of men had dug in on the tenth floor of the Gran Hotel and were directing sniper fire at the rebels. But Che now had considerable extra firepower and fresh troops at his disposal. The arms seized from the armored train had truly been a bonanza: 600 rifles, 1 million bullets, scores of machine guns, a 20mm cannon, and some precious mortars and bazookas. Throughout New Year's Eve day, one redoubt after the other fell to the rebels: first the police station, then the provincial government headquarters, followed by the courthouse and the jail, where escaping prisoners added to the confusion in the city. By the end of the day, only the No. 31 garrison, the Gran Hotel, and the main Leoncio Vidal garrison still held out.

In Oriente, Maffo had finally surrendered to Fidel's rebels after a ten-day siege, and Fidel had immediately set his sights on Santiago. On December 28, he and General Cantillo met at the Oriente sugar mill near Palma Soriano and reached an agreement: Fidel would halt his offensive for three days, allowing Cantillo time to return to Havana and organize a military rebellion for December 31. That day, he was to arrest Batista and place the army at Fidel's disposal.

As it turned out, Cantillo was intent on a double cross. He returned to Havana, told Batista of the plot, and gave him until January 6 to leave the country. He then sent a message to Fidel, asking for a delay until January 6 before launching the revolt. Fidel was wary, but by then events had begun to move so fast that neither he nor Cantillo could foresee what would happen next.

VI

Che's seizure of the armored train had sent alarm bells ringing loudly at Camp Columbia, the military headquarters in Havana, and the subsequent rapid-fire succession of army surrenders around the nation had accelerated Batista's plans for departure. By the afternoon of December 31, his last hope for buying time rested on the ability of Colonel Casillas to hold out in Santa Clara. At nine o'clock that evening Casillas called to say he couldn't resist much longer without reinforcements. When, an hour later, Cantillo warned that Santiago was also about to fall, Batista knew it was time to go.

At a New Year's party for his top officers and their families at Camp Columbia, Batista led his generals into a room adjoining the one where most of his guests were gathered and revealed that he would hand over the armed forces to Cantillo. Then, rejoining the party in the other room, he announced his decision to give up the presidency. He named Carlos Manuel Piedra, the oldest supreme court judge, as the new president; after formally swearing in Cantillo as the new armed forces chief, Batista and his wife and a coterie of officials and their families drove to the nearby military airstrip and boarded a waiting plane. By three o'clock in the predawn darkness of January 1, 1959, Batista was in the air, en route to the Dominican Republic with forty of his closest cronies, among them the "president-elect," Andrés Rivero Agüero. Before dawn broke, another plane had taken off carrying Batista's brother, the mayor of Havana, and several dozen more government and police officials. Separately, two other notorious characters also made their escape that day: the paramilitary chieftain Rolando Masferrer and the American mobster Meyer Lansky.

When, sometime that night, Colonel Casillas and his deputy, Colonel Fernández Suero, heard the news in Santa Clara, they made haste to save themselves. After concocting a flimsy excuse for their underling, the blissfully uninformed Colonel Cándido Hernández, they disguised themselves in civilian clothes and beat an escape.

As daylight broke in Santa Clara, the first rumors of Batista's flight were beginning to circulate. The No. 31 garrison surrendered; the final redoubts—the Gran Hotel and the Leoncio Vidal garrison—were surrounded; and by mid-morning Colonel Hernández asked for a truce. Che said he could accept nothing less than an unconditional surrender and sent Nuñez Jiménez and Rodríguez de la Vega in to negotiate with Hernández.

"The news reports were contradictory and extraordinary," Che wrote afterward. "Batista had fled that day, leaving the armed forces high command a shambles. Our two delegates [meeting with Hernández] established radio contact with Cantillo, telling him of the surrender offer. But he refused to go along because this constituted an ultimatum, and he claimed he had taken over command of the army in strict accordance with instructions from the leader Fidel Castro. We immediately contacted Fidel, telling him the news, but giving our opinion of Cantillo's treachery, an opinion he absolutely agreed with."

After the conversation with Cantillo, Hernández was understandably confused, but Che stood firm, insisting he surrender. At 11:30 A.M. their negotiations were interrupted by a broadcast address from Fidel over Radio Rebelde. Repudiating Cantillo's notion of a "military junta" or any understanding between them, he called for an immediate general strike and a mobilization of rebel forces toward Santiago and Havana. He gave Santiago's defenders until six that evening to surrender or be attacked, and he ended with a slogan: *Revolución Sí, Golpe Militar No!*

The panorama was clearer now, and Che gave Hernández an hour to make up his mind; if he didn't surrender by 12:30, he would be attacked and would be held responsible for the bloodshed that would follow. Hernández returned to the garrison, and the waiting began.

While Che had been negotiating with Hernández, his men had finally managed to dislodge the snipers from the Gran Hotel. The previous day, Enrique Acevedo had resorted to driving cars at high speed in front of the hotel to try to pinpoint the sniper fire, but he abandoned the tactic after one of his men was shot in the leg. That morning, however, with their comrades surrendering all around them and their own ammunition almost exhausted, the snipers gave in. Acevedo watched them come out with their hands up. They turned out to be a group of five *chivatos* and four policemen, some, in Acevedo's words, with "debts to pay to revolutionary justice." Those debts were soon paid; at 2 P.M., after a brief summary trial, the five *chivatos* were executed by a firing squad.

Colonel Casillas had not gotten very far in his civilian disguise. Victor Bordón's fighters, west of the city, had been ordered to halt any soldiers fleeing toward Havana, and Casillas, wearing a straw hat and a July 26 armband, soon fell into their hands. He immediately began trying to woo Bordón, praising him as a "great strategist." Bordón recalled that Casillas told him that "the only thing he felt bad about was not being able to stay longer with me, because he had to carry on to the capital to participate in the military

The victorious Rebel Army drives through Santa Clara toward Havana.

junta, which was going to 'resolve this business among Cubans.'" Bordón
cut him short. "I told him to stop flattering me, that we didn't need any junta,
because it would be Fidel Castro who resolved life for Cubans from then
on. And that he was going with me to Santa Clara, so that Che could see
him. That's where he changed color and asked me if I couldn't take him to
another *jefe*. I remember that when Che saw him, he told him: 'Ah! So you
are the murderer of Jesús Menéndez.'"*

Casillas did not live out the day. The official version is that he was shot
dead trying to escape while en route to see Che, but this, quite obviously,
doesn't mesh with Bordón's own account. Given Casillas's gruesome history of past atrocities and Che's record for applying revolutionary justice, it
is probable that Casillas's failed "escape attempt" took place in front of a
hastily assembled firing squad.

With ten minutes to go before Che's deadline, Colonel Hernández
agreed to surrender his garrison. His troops dropped their weapons and went
out onto the streets, joining the rebels. A cheer went up around the city: Santa
Clara had fallen. But Che was not celebrating yet. Order had to be restored,

---

*The Communist sugar-union leader murdered by Casillas in 1948.

there were henchmen and *chivatos* to be tried, and he needed to assemble his forces and give them their instructions.*

Cantillo's tenure as armed forces chief did not last long. Colonel Barquín, sprung that day from the Isle of Pines, was flown to Havana along with Armando Hart, and by early afternoon Barquín had arrived at Camp Columbia, where an outmaneuvered Cantillo promptly handed over his command. In Oriente, Santiago surrendered, and Fidel prepared to march into the city that night.

The next morning, January 2, 1959, Che and Camilo Cienfuegos were ordered to proceed to Havana. Camilo was to take over Camp Columbia, while Che was to occupy La Cabaña, the colonial-era fortress overlooking Havana at the mouth of the port. Camilo's column moved out first, since Che still had mopping-up duties to attend to, including executing some *chivatos* and appointing Calixto Morales as the military governor of Las Villas. Afterward, Che addressed the people of Santa Clara, thanking them for their help in the "revolutionary cause." He and his men were leaving, he said, "with the feeling of leaving a beloved place. I ask you to maintain the same revolutionary spirit, so that in the gigantic task of reconstruction ahead, Las Villas may continue to be in the vanguard of the revolution."

At around three in the afternoon, with Aleida at his side, Che and his men set out on the drive to Havana. Most of his comrades were jubilant at the prospect of liberating the Cuban capital, but to Che it was just the first step in the greater struggle that loomed ahead.

*One of those shot, according to the historian Hugh Thomas, was Colonel Cornelio Rojas, the police commander. At the moment of his execution, Rojas asked to be allowed to give the firing order, and his request was granted.

Part Three
Making the New Man

Havana, New Year's Day, 1959.

20

The Supreme Prosecutor

It is impossible for revolutionary laws to be executed unless the government itself is truly revolutionary.

LOUIS-ANTOINE-LÉON DE SAINT-JUST
1793, during the "Terror" of the French Revolution

The executions by firing squads are not only a necessity for the people of Cuba, but also an imposition by the people.

CHE GUEVARA
February 5, 1959

I

The Guevara family was celebrating the New Year in Buenos Aires when word came of Batista's flight. Rebel columns led by Che Guevara and Camilo Cienfuegos were said to be advancing on Havana. But the family's jubilation lasted for only a moment. "We had not put down the drinks toasting the fall of Batista when some terrible news came," Che's father recalled. "Ernesto had been fatally wounded." Two agonizing hours went by before the July 26 representative in Buenos Aires called to say the report was false. "We celebrated the New Year that night with the happiness that Ernesto lived," his father wrote, "and that he was in charge of the La Cabaña garrison in Havana."

When Che's entourage arrived at the huge Spanish colonial fortress overlooking the city in the predawn darkness of January 3, 1959, a regiment of 3,000 troops had already surrendered and stood in formation. Che addressed them patronizingly as a "neocolonial army." They could teach his rebel troops how to march, he said, but the guerrillas could teach them how to fight. Then he and Aleida installed themselves in the *comandante*'s house.

The day before, Camilo had shown up at Camp Columbia, on the other side of the city, and had taken over its command from Colonel Ramón Barquín. General Cantillo was arrested. Fidel had made his triumphal entry into Santiago and—speaking before cheering crowds—declared the city the provisional capital of Cuba. Manuel Urrutia flew in from Venezuela and Fidel proclaimed him the new president.

Carlos Franqui, who was with Fidel, couldn't understand why Che had been relegated to La Cabaña. "I remember pondering at length the reasons for Fidel's order," he said. "Camp Columbia was the heart and soul of the tyranny and of military power. . . . Che had taken the armored train and the city of Santa Clara; he was the second most important figure of the revolution. What reasons did Fidel have for sending him to La Cabaña?"

Most probably, Fidel had chosen the less visible position because he wanted Che out of the limelight. To the defeated regime, its adherents, and Washington, Che was the dreaded international Communist, and it was only asking for trouble to give him a preeminent role so early on. By contrast, the handsome, Stetson-wearing, baseball-playing, womanizing, humorous Camilo was Cuban, was not known to be a Communist, and had already become a popular folk hero. *He* could take center stage. Fidel needed Che for the indispensable job of purging the old army and of consolidating victory by exacting revolutionary justice against traitors, *chivatos,* and Batista's war criminals. Just as his brother Raúl, the other radical, was to be in Oriente—where Fidel had left him behind as military governor—Che was essential to the success of this task in Havana.

II

From the green rolling head of land where La Cabaña and its adjacent fortress, El Morro, sprawled, guarding Havana harbor, Che's view in January 1959 would have been much like that evoked in Graham Greene's *Our Man in Havana,* which had been published just months earlier: "The long city lay spread along the open Atlantic; waves broke over the Avenida de Maceo and misted the windscreens of cars. The pink, grey, yellow pillars of what had once been the aristocratic quarter were eroded like rocks; an ancient coats of arms, smudged and featureless, was set over the doorway of a shabby hotel, and the shutters of a night club were varnished in bright crude colors to protect them from the wet and salt of the sea. In the west the steel skyscrapers of the new town rose higher than lighthouses."

Closer up, Havana was a seamy city, booming with casinos, nightclubs, and whorehouses. The live sex show in Chinatown's Shanghai Theatre featured a performer called Superman, for his manly endowment. Marijuana and cocaine were available to those who wanted them. The sleaziness had attracted Greene, who made several visits to Cuba. "In Batista's day I liked the idea that one could obtain anything at will, whether drugs, women, or goats," he wrote. Greene's fictional British vacuum cleaner salesman, Wormold, walked the streets of Old Havana, taking it all in. "At every corner there were men who called 'Taxi' at him as though he were a stranger, and all down the Paseo, at intervals of a few yards, the pimps accosted him automatically without any real hope. 'Can I be of service, sir?' 'I know all the pretty girls.' 'You desire a beautiful woman?' 'Postcards?' 'You want to see a dirty movie?'"

This was the raucous milieu into which Che and his men were plunged after two largely abstinent years in the mountains, with fairly predictable results. Che tried to keep his bodyguards under strict control, but the temptation was too much for Alberto Castellanos. "I had never been in the capital before and I was in shock," he said. "Because Che kept me working with him until dawn, I didn't have time to see anything. Some nights I escaped into the city, especially to the cabarets. It fascinated me to see so many beautiful women."

Sex was heavy in the air. The guerrillas slipped out of La Cabaña for trysts with girls in the bushes under the huge white statue of Christ that looms over the harbor. It was a chaotic situation and had to be taken in hand. Che soon organized a mass wedding for all those fighters with lovers whose unions had not been made "official." The wayward Castellanos, who had a fiancée in Oriente, was one of those whose wings were clipped, in a ceremony at La Cabaña presided over by Che himself.

The war had captivated public interest, and hordes of foreign journalists descended on Havana to cover the installation of the new regime. "In Buenos Aires it was the only thing people talked about," Che's father wrote. But even in Cuba, few people understood what it all meant. While still in Santiago, Fidel had taken pains to give the new regime a moderate front, although he had also set the pattern for his future relationship with President Urrutia by allowing Urrutia to name but one appointee, the justice minister. Fidel named the rest, and Urrutia did not put up a fight. Even so, only a few July 26 men, most of them from the llano, were included in the initial cabinet roster.

From Santiago, Fidel began making his way slowly overland toward Havana, savoring his victory before adoring crowds. Reporters caught up with his caravan and followed its progress, filing dispatches to the outside world. Fidel repeated again and again that he had no political ambitions. He took orders from President Urrutia, he said. The revolution would obey the "will of the people." He had, however, accepted Urrutia's request that he serve as commander in chief of the armed forces.

Throngs of civilians cheered the ragged guerrillas wherever they appeared. A young rebel from Holguín, Reinaldo Arenas, recalled the atmosphere. "We came down from the hills and received a heroes' welcome," he wrote. "In my neighborhood in Holguín I was given a flag of the 26th of July Movement and for a whole block I walked holding that flag. I felt a little ridiculous, but there was a great euphoria, with hymns and anthems ringing out, and the whole town in the streets. The rebels kept coming, with crucifixes hanging from chains made of seeds; these were the heroes. Some, in fact, had joined the rebels only four or five months earlier, but most of the women, and also many of the men in the city, went wild over these hairy fellows; everybody wanted to take one of the bearded men home. I did not yet have a beard because I was only fifteen."*

The atmosphere in Havana was a mix of festive anarchy and uncertainty. Hundreds of armed rebels were camped out in hotel lobbies, treating them like a guerrilla bivouac in the countryside. Most government troops had surrendered after Batista's flight and had remained in their barracks, but here and there a few snipers held out, and manhunts were on for fugitive police agents, corrupt politicians, and war criminals. In a few places, mobs had attacked casinos, parking meters, and other symbols of Batista's corruption, but they had been brought under control quickly when the July 26 militias came out onto the streets. Boy Scouts acted as ad hoc policemen. Meanwhile, the embassies were filling up with military officers, policemen, and government officials who had been left in the lurch by Batista's sudden flight.

On January 4, Carlos Franqui left Fidel's rolling caravan in Camagüey and flew ahead to Havana. He found the capital transformed. "The gloomy Camp Columbia, mother of the tyranny and of crime, which I had known as a prisoner, was now almost a picturesque theater, impossible to imagine," he wrote. "On the one hand, the bearded rebels with Camilo, no more than five hundred of them, and on the other hand, twenty thousand army soldiers —generals, colonels, majors, captains, corporals, sergeants, and privates. When they saw us walk by, they stood at attention. It was enough to make you burst out laughing. In the *comandante*'s office was Camilo, with his romantic beard, looking like Christ on a spree, his boots thrown on the floor and his feet up on the table, as he received his excellency the ambassador of the United States."

Then Che arrived. There were difficulties at the presidential palace. The Directorio had installed themselves there and appeared to have no plans to give it up. Che tried to talk with the leaders, but they had refused to see him. "Camilo, half joking and half serious, said a couple of cannonballs should be fired off as a warning," Franqui recalled. "As I was not an admirer of the palace, I said it seemed like a good idea, but Che, with his sense of responsibility, told us it wasn't the right time to waste cannonballs, and

---

*Arenas described this secene in his memoir, *Before Night Falls*. He became a well-known writer but suffered because of his homosexuality. Years later, he fled Cuba for New York, where he lived until his death from AIDS in 1990.

he patiently returned to the palace, met Faure Chomón, and matters were straightened out. Camilo aways listened to Che."

By the time Fidel arrived on January 8, Urrutia was installed in the palace and a semblance of governmental authority had been restored. Public buildings, police stations, and newspaper and trade union offices had been taken over. The Communist Party had come out of the woodwork to call for mass demonstrations in support of the victorious rebels. Exiled Party leaders began returning, and the Party's banned newspaper, *Hoy,* began publishing again. Even Carlos Prío, the former president, arrived back from Miami. Abroad, the major Cuban embassies were occupied by July 26 representatives. Venezuela had recognized the new government, and so had the United States. The Soviet Union followed suit on January 10.

Cuba's civic and business institutions declared their support for the revolution with hyperbolic expressions of gratitude and fealty. The "nightmare" of Batista was over; the Fidelista honeymoon had begun. The business community bent over backward to pay tribute, volunteering to pay back taxes. Some major corporations announced new investments while declaring their optimism about Cuba's brave new future.

The media lionized Fidel and his heroic *barbudos*. The magazine *Bohemia* became an unabashed revolutionary fanzine, printing obsequious homages to Fidel. In one illustration he was rendered with a Christlike countenance, complete with halo. Even the ad pages were tailored to suit the moment. The Polar beer brewery emblazoned a page with a graphic of a sturdy peasant cutting cane and the words, "Yes! IT IS TIME TO GET TO WORK. With the happiness of being free once more and feeling ourselves prouder than ever to be Cubans, we must blaze a trail of work: constructive and intense work to meet the demands of the Fatherland. . . . And after working, IT IS TIME FOR POLAR! There is nothing like a really cold Polar to complete the satisfaction of a duty fulfilled."

In the once clandestine July 26 newspaper, *Revolución,* Carlos Franqui added to the flood of tributes by lauding Fidel as Cuba's "Hero-Guide." Grateful citizens hastily commissioned a bronze bust of Fidel that was erected on a marble plinth at an intersection near Havana's military complex, with an engraved inscription honoring the man who had "broken the chains of the dictatorship with the flame of liberty."

Che too came in for his share of lyrical tributes. Cuba's foremost living poet, the Communist Nicolás Guillén, was in exile in Buenos Aires when the triumph came, and at the request of a weekly newspaper editor there he wrote a poem in Che's honor.

CHE GUEVARA

As if San Martín's pure hand,
Were extended to his brother, Martí,
And the plant-banked Plata streamed through the sea,
To join the Cauto's love-swept overture.

Thus, Guevara, strong-voiced gaucho, moved to assure
His guerrilla blood to Fidel
And his broad hand was most comradely
When our night was blackest, most obscure.

Death retreated. Of its shadows impure,
Of the dagger, poison, and of beasts,
Only savage memories endure.

Fused from two, a single soul shines,
As if San Martín's pure hand,
Were extended to his brother, Martí.

If Che was already a well-known figure to readers abroad, his literary consecration by Guillén—a peer of Federico García Lorca, Pablo Neruda, and Rafael Alberti—brought him into the pantheon of Latin America's most venerated historical heroes. Here he was, at the age of thirty, being compared to the "Liberator," José de San Martín. The hyperbole had a resounding effect on Cuba's hero-hungry public. When, a few days after his arrival, Che sent for Juan Borroto, the sugar expert who had smuggled him economic intelligence reports while he was in the Escambray, Borroto was awed. "He was already a legend," Borroto recalled. "To actually see him for many Cubans was like a vision; you rubbed your eyes. He was physically imposing, too, with very white skin and chestnut-colored hair. He was attractive."

To the American embassy officials in Havana, however, Che was already the fearsome Rasputin of the new regime. The influence of his ideology on Fidel and his new role behind the forbidding walls of La Cabaña were topics of much worried speculation.

III

Fidel made his triumphal entry into Havana like a grand showman, riding at the head of a noisy calvacade on top of a captured tank. After paying his respects to Urrutia in the palace, he hopped aboard the *Granma,* which had been brought to Havana and was now moored in the harbor. Then, accompanied by Camilo and Raúl—while Che stayed discreetly out of sight in La Cabaña—he proceeded to Camp Columbia through streets lined with thousands of ecstatic, flag-waving *habaneros*.

That night, Fidel gave a long speech, broadcast live on television, stressing the need for law and order and revolutionary unity. In the new Cuba, there was room for only one revolutionary force; there could be no private armies. His words were a warning to the Directorio, whose fighters had vacated the palace but still occupied the grounds of the university and were reported to be stockpiling arms. Adding to the ominous signs that a confrontation was in the offing, Faure Chomón had publicly voiced the Directorio's concerns about being shut out of power. But before Fidel had finished speaking, the Directorio relayed word that it would hand over its weapons. Fidel's display of force majeure had won out.

Fidel also used his presence to reinforce the nationalistic nature of the new regime. Asked by a reporter what he thought of the rumored offer by the U.S. government to withdraw its military mission, he replied quickly, "It *has* to withdraw it. In the first place, the government of the United States has no right to have a permanent mission here. In other words, it's not a prerogative of the Department of State, but of the revolutionary government of Cuba." If Washington wanted good relations, Fidel was saying, it had some fence-mending to do, and the first step was to deal with Cuba as an equal. Meanwhile, he told the nation, the army would be reorganized. Henceforth it would be made up of men loyal to the revolution who would defend it if the occasion arose. He warned that victory was not yet secure. Batista had fled to the Dominican Republic with his stolen millions and sought the protection of that other reviled dictator, General Trujillo. It was always possible the two of them might counterattack.

Fidel had deftly prepared Cubans for things to come, but what most people remembered from that night was the moment when white doves flew out of the audience to alight on his shoulder. To many, it was a mystical epiphany that validated Fidel's standing as the charismatic *maximo lider* of the revolution; to others it was a masterful example of Fidel's ability to put forward an awe-inspiring public image at exactly the right moment.

In the blur of rapid-fire events that followed, contradictory signals about the direction of the revolution kept observers off balance. By quickly recognizing the new regime, Washington had tried to appear conciliatory. In a second gesture of appeasement, Earl Smith resigned as ambassador and left the country. A chargé d'affaires remained in his place. The Eisenhower administration could hardly complain about the makeup of the new regime. Urrutia's cabinet was stacked with politically safe Cuban political veterans and aspirants, virtually all of them solidly middle-class, pro-business anticommunists, including many of Fidel's former rivals. By giving them posts with apparent authority in the new government, Fidel had placated the conservative political and business community and co-opted potential sources of opposition.

The biggest surprise was his appointment of Dr. José Miró Cardona, an eminent lawyer and secretary of the Civic Opposition Front, as the new prime minister. "Miró Cardona's designation was a bombshell," Franqui wrote later. "He was president of the Havana Bar Association, the representative of great capitalistic enterprises, and one of Cuba's most pro–North American politicians. Years before, he had defended the biggest thief among Cuban presidents, Grau San Martín, who had stolen 84 million pesos. He had defended Captain Casillas, the murderer of the black sugar workers' leader, Jesús Menéndez. We did not understand Fidel's choice but it was understood by those whom Fidel wanted to understand. It was actually an intelligent move, which confused the Americans, the bourgeoisie, and the politicians."

Bouncing back from the ill-fated Miami Pact, the redoubtable Felipe Pazos was made president of the National Bank; Justo Carrillo became president of the Development Bank; and the Harvard-educated economist Regino Boti returned from the United States to become minister of the economy. Rufo López Fresquet, an economist and analyst for the influential conservative newspaper *Diario de la Marina,* was named minister of finance. Foreign affairs went to the Ortodoxo politician Roberto Agramonte. Others, such as Faustino Pérez, who was appointed to head the newly created Ministry for the Recovery of Illegally Acquired Property, came from the July 26 Movement's right wing. The Education Ministry went to Armando Hart, while Che's wartime antagonist Enrique Oltuski became minister of communications. Fidel's old publisher friend, Luis Orlando Rodríguez, who had helped set up Radio Rebelde and *El Cubano Libre,* was made interior minister. Another new post, minister for revolutionary laws, was given to Osvaldo Dorticós Torrado, a lawyer in Cienfuegos with discreet PSP links. His appointment seemed innocuous enough at the time, but Torrado was to play a key role in Fidel's future plans.

The cabinet got to work, holding marathon sessions to reform the constitution, rebuild damaged infrastructure, and clean up Cuba's debauched society. At the top of Urrutia's agenda was a bill to ban gambling and prostitution. Simultaneously, the new ministers began housecleaning, firing employees who had been receiving secret sinecures, or *botellas,* from the Batista regime. Their initial decrees were of a similar purging nature. Political parties were temporarily banned. Batista's properties, as well as those of his ministers and of politicians who had participated in the last two Batista-era elections, were confiscated.

Fidel began speaking before large crowds in an ingenious exercise he called "direct democracy." He would take soundings of the crowd, spontaneous referendums on revolutionary policy. The forums were employed to test, mold, and radicalize the public mood and, ultimately, to pressure the government. Fidel repeated over and over that it was the duty of the new government to obey the will of the people, because the revolution had been fought by the people.

He also began to reform the army, his true power base. The ranks of the "old" army and police forces were weeded out, their officers either sidelined or purged. Colonel Ramón Barquín was made chief of the military academies; Major Quevedo, one of several career officers who had defected to the rebels after the failed summer offensive, became head of army logistics. Others were shipped off to gilded exile as military attachés in foreign countries. The new military elite was made up of loyal rebels. Camilo, already the military governor of Havana province, became the army chief of staff. Augusto Martínez Sánchez, a lawyer who had served as the judge with Raúl's Second Front, was named minister of defense. Efigenio Ameijeiras, the head of Raúl's elite "Mau-Mau" guerrilla strike force, became chief of police. The pilot Pedro Díaz Lanz, Fidel's rebel air force commander, was now given that title officially. Perhaps most telling, loyal July 26 men had been installed as military governors in all of Cuba's provinces.

It was soon evident that the real seat of revolutionary power lay not in the ornate presidential palace in Old Havana but wherever Fidel happened to be at the time. And Fidel seemed to be everywhere. His base camp was a penthouse suite on the twenty-third floor of the new Havana Hilton in downtown Vedado, but he also slept and worked at Celia Sánchez's apartment nearby and in a villa in the fishing village of Cojímar, about thirty minutes east of Havana. It was in this villa, rather than at the presidential palace, that the future of Cuba was being decided. Over the coming months it became the setting for nightly meetings between Fidel, his closest comrades, and Communist Party leaders. The purpose of the meetings was to secretly meld the PSP and the July 26 Movement into a single revolutionary party. Fidel, Che, Raúl, Ramiro, and Camilo represented the guerrillas. Carlos Rafael Rodríguez, Aníbal Escalante, and Blas Roca, the Party's secretary-general, led discussions for the Communists.

IV

On the surface, Che and Raúl were the odd men out in the distribution of plum appointments. Raúl was military governor of Oriente and Che had the minor title of commander of La Cabaña. But the job descriptions were misleading. While Fidel concentrated on presenting a moderate front for the revolution and avoiding a premature confrontation with the United States, Raúl and Che worked secretly to cement ties with the PSP and to shore up Fidel's power base in the armed forces.

Che kept up a formidable pace of activity. On January 13, he inaugurated a military cultural academy in La Cabaña. Classes were given in civics, history, geography, the Cuban economy, "the economic and social characteristics of the Latin American republics," and current affairs. Che sought to reform his charges. He banned cockfighting and organized chess classes, an equestrian team, sports events, art exhibits, concerts, and theater productions. Movies were shown nightly in the fortresses' several cinemas. He founded a regimental newspaper, *La Cabaña Libre,* and soon helped kick off *Verde Olivo,* a newspaper for the Revolutionary Armed Forces. Che quietly placed the academy under the supervision of PSP men. Armando Acosta, his commissar in the Escambray, became the academy administrator.

By the end of January, Che had an additional title—chief of the Department of Training of the Revolutionary Armed Forces—but it did not give a full picture of his activities, either. On Fidel's instructions, he was secretly meeting with Raúl, who shuttled between Havana and his Santiago post; Camilo; Ramiro Valdés, Che's wartime deputy; and the PSP's Víctor Pina to create a new state security and intelligence apparatus. The agency, Seguridad del Estado, or G-2, was placed in Valdés's able hands. Osvaldo Sánchez, a PSP Politburo member and head of its Military Committee, was his second in command.

Meanwhile, Cuban exiles were arriving home from all over the hemisphere. An airplane was sent to Buenos Aires to bring back the exiles living there, and the Guevara family was invited to board it. Che's parents; his sister Celia; her husband, Luis Argañaraz; and Juan Martín, now a teenager of fourteen, accepted the offer. (Family and work obligations kept Roberto and Ana María at home, and it would be another two and a half years before they saw their famous brother.) They arrived in Havana on January 9. Ernesto senior kissed the tarmac at Havana's Rancho Boyeros airport. "We were immediately surrounded by bearded soldiers wearing really dirty uniforms and armed with rifles or machine guns," he wrote. "Then came the obligatory salutes and, in a rush, they led us into the interior of the terminal, where Ernesto awaited us. I understand that they had wanted to surprise him and that he became aware of our arrival only minutes before. My wife ran to his arms and could not contain her tears. A mountain of photographers and television cameras recorded the scene. Soon afterward I hugged my son. It had been six years since I had last seen him."

La Cabaña, the colonial-era fortress and army garrison that overlooks the harbor and city of Havana. Che assumed command of the bastion on January 3, 1959.

Che with his parents at the Havana airport on January 9, 1959.

One of the photographs taken that day shows Che in fatigues and beret and sparse beard, flanked by his mother and father, amid a tumult of curious onlookers. A submachine gun pokes up into view behind Che's back. What is truly memorable, though, is the look of deep, passionate pride on Celia's face, and on Che's. His conservatively dressed father stands beside them, smiling and looking bemused.

The Guevaras were installed as guests of the revolution in a suite at the Hilton. The hotel's swank lobby was by now a rowdy meeting place for disheveled armed guerrillas, aggressive journalists, favor-seekers, and perplexed-looking American tourists whose holidays had been interrupted by events. When they got to their rooms, just a few floors below where Fidel was staying, Ernesto senior produced some bottles of Argentine wine that had been his son's favorite back home. "Their sight surely brought back to him pleasant memories of other happy times, when the whole family lived together in Buenos Aires," he wrote. As they celebrated, Ernesto senior thought he saw "in his physique, in his expressions, in his happiness, the same boy who had left Buenos Aires one cold July afternoon more than six years before."

Ernesto senior's observation contained a fair degree of wishful thinking. His son had become Che, the man he wanted to be. And if Che was pleased to see his family, the truth was they couldn't have arrived at a more inconvenient time. Even as they settled into the Hilton, he had to rush back to La Cabaña. There were revolutionary tribunals to be overseen.

Throughout January, suspected war criminals were being captured and brought to La Cabaña daily. For the most part, they were not the top henchmen of the ancien régime; most of those had escaped or remained holed up in embassies. The ones left behind were deputies or rank-and-file *chivatos* and police torturers. Nevertheless, the old walls of the fort rang out nightly with the fusillades of the firing squads. "There were over a thousand prisoners of war," explained Miguel Ángel Duque de Estrada, who had been put in charge of the Cleansing Commission. "Many didn't have dossiers. We didn't even know all of their names. But we had a job to do, which was to cleanse the defeated army."

The trials began at eight or nine in the evening, and, more often than not, a verdict was reached by two or three in the morning. Duque de Estrada gathered evidence, took testimony, and prepared the trials. He also sat with Che, the "supreme prosecutor," on the appellate bench, where Che made the final decision on men's fates. "Che consulted with me," Duque said, "but he was in charge, and as military commander his word was final. We were in agreement on almost 100 percent of the decisions. In about a hundred days we carried out perhaps fifty-five executions by firing squad, and we got a lot of flak for it, but we gave each case due and fair consideration and we didn't come to our decisions lightly."

The twenty-one-year-old accountant Orlando Borrego, who administered La Cabaña's finances, was also a tribunal president. "It was very difficult because most of us had no judicial training," Borrego recalled. "Our paramount concern was to ensure that revolutionary morality and justice prevailed. Che was very careful. Nobody was shot for hitting a prisoner, but if there was extreme torture and killings and deaths, then yes—they were condemned to death. . . . The whole case was analyzed, all the witnesses seen, and the relatives of the dead or tortured person came, or the tortured person himself."

Che told some hostile Cuban television interviewers that he never attended the trials or met with defendants himself. He went over the cases with the judges and reached his final verdicts coldly and neutrally, on the basis of the evidence alone. According to Borrego, Che took great care in selecting judges and prosecutors. For instance, rebels who had been mistreated were not allowed to pass judgment on their former torturers. "There were sometimes prosecutors who were on the extreme left," Borrego explained. "One had to moderate those who always asked for the death sentence." When it came to the executions themselves, however, Che evidently overcame his earlier reservations about the American volunteer Herman Marks, who had been a problem in Camagüey. Marks reappeared at La Cabaña, where he took an active role in the firing squads.*

Over the next months, several hundred people were officially tried and executed by firing squads in Cuba. Most were sentenced in conditions like those described by Borrego. They were aboveboard, if summary, affairs, with defense lawyers, witnesses, prosecutors, and an attending public. But there were also a number of arbitrary executions. The most notorious incident occurred when, soon after occupying Santiago, Raúl Castro directed a mass execution of more than seventy captured soldiers. A trench was bulldozed and the condemned men were lined up in front of it and mowed down with machine guns. Raúl's reputation for ruthlessness was confirmed.

There was little overt public opposition to the workings of revolutionary justice. On the contrary. Batista's thugs had committed some sickening crimes and the Cuban public was in a lynching mood. Newspapers were full of morbid revelations and gruesome photographs of the horrors and

---

*Borrego, who got to know Marks at La Cabaña, described him as a strange, aloof man, who was "sadistic" and who liked to participate in the firing squads. He was about forty years old, spoke little Spanish, and was rumored to be on the run from U.S. justice. After several months, he disappeared from Cuba.

brutalities that had taken place under Batista. *Bohemia* published snide interviews with suspects awaiting trial and provided sanctimonious captions to pictures of the executions. In its February 8, 1959, issue, the culminating moment of the trial of two gunmen responsible for several murders in Manzanillo, the Nicolardes Rojas brothers, was described.

> The Prosecutor, Dr. Fernando Aragoneses Cruz: "Do the Nicolardes brothers deserve freedom?"
> Noooo! was the thundering shout of the enormous multitude.
> "Do they deserve prison with the hope that one day they can be useful to Society?"
> Noooo!
> "Should they be shot, as exemplary punishment to all future generations?"
> Yeeees!
> The Prosecutor . . . glanced over at the infuriated multitude. And, in the face of their unanimous opinion, he expressed himself calmly, while directing a look that was part anger and part pity to those who had been condemned by the People.
> "That is, ladies and gentlemen, the petition of the citizenry, whom I represent in this session."

The Nicolardes brothers were immediately taken out and shot.

The account in *Bohemia* seems to be a fairly accurate depiction of the atmosphere prevailing in Cuba's revolutionary courtrooms. Orlando Borrego recalled that he felt under great pressure from his civilian audiences to be severe. "They often thought the sentencing was too benign," he said. "Sometimes one asked for a sentence of ten years and the people wanted it to be twenty." The tribunals were attracting mounting criticism abroad, with American congressmen decrying them as a bloodbath. Indignant over the accusations, in late January Fidel had decided to hold some high-profile public trials—of Major Sosa Blanca and several other ranking officers accused of multiple acts of murder and torture—in Havana's sports stadium. The plan backfired, however. Attending foreign reporters were nauseated by the spectacle of jeering crowds and hysterical cries for blood. The sympathetic Herbert Matthews tried to rationalize the trials from the "Cuban's perspective" in an editorial that *The New York Times*'s editor in chief refused to print.

Che warned his judges to be scrupulous about weighing the evidence in each case so as not to give the revolution's enemies additional ammunition, but the trials had to continue if Cuba's revolution was to be secure. He never tired of telling his Cuban comrades that Arbenz had fallen in Guatemala because he had not purged his armed forces of disloyal elements. Cuba could not afford to repeat Arbenz's mistake.

In his memoirs, Ernesto senior avoided the issue of Che's leading role in the tribunals, but he alluded to his shock at discovering his son's transformation into a hard man. He recalled asking Che what he planned to do about his medical career. Che smiled and replied that, since they had the same name, his father could substitute for him if he wanted. He could hang up a doctor's shingle "and begin killing people without any risk." Che laughed at his own joke, but his father insisted that he give a more serious reply. "As for my medical career, I can tell you that I deserted it a long time ago," Che said. "Now I am a fighter who is working for the consolidation of a government. What will become of me? I don't even know in which land I will leave my bones." Che's father didn't understand the significance of the remark until much later. "It was hard for me to recognize the Ernesto of my home, the normal Ernesto," he wrote. "He had been transformed into a man whose faith in the triumph of his ideals reached mystical proportions."

His father's befuddlement was shared by some of Che's old friends and acquaintances. Tatiana Quiroga and Chichina's cousin Jimmy Roca, who had been Che's roommate in Miami, were married and living in Los Angeles in January 1959. "I sent a telegram to La Cabaña and it cost me five dollars," Tatiana recalled. "I still remember because, as a student, it was a lot of money for me, but I spent the five dollars to congratulate him. Then came the killings of La Cabaña, and I'll tell you I have never felt so horrible as to have spent five dollars on that telegram. I wanted to die."

V

The revolutionary tribunals did much to polarize the political climate between Havana and Washington. Fidel was incensed by the criticism. How could the country that had bombed Hiroshima brand what he was doing a bloodbath? Why hadn't his critics spoken out when Batista's murderers were committing their atrocities? The criticism, he said, was tantamount to intervention, and he warned that if the gringos tried to invade Cuba, the price would be 200,000 dead Americans. There were rumors of an assassination threat against him, but if *he* was killed, he said, the revolution would survive. Behind him stood other comrades who were prepared to lead it, men who were more radical than he was. If anyone had any doubts about to whom he was alluding, Fidel dispelled them in the next breath, announcing that his brother Raúl was his chosen successor. In fact, although Raúl's official appointment as minister of the Revolutionary Armed Forces did not come until October 1959, he was already the Cuban military's de facto chief of staff. And where did that leave Che? The U.S. embassy was monitoring his activities and speeches closely, with a growing sense of disquiet.

On January 27, at a forum in Havana sponsored by the PSP, Che gave a speech titled "Social Ideals of the Rebel Army." He left little doubt as to where he stood, and he hinted that the revolution had radical ambitions far beyond those so far acknowledged by Fidel. To anyone who grasped its significance, it was perhaps the most important speech delivered by any of the revolutionary leaders, including Fidel, since they had come to power. Quite simply, Che was outlining the future.

One of the rebels' "ideals"—an armed democracy—had already been achieved, he said, but much more needed to be done. The revolutionary agrarian reform decree issued two months earlier in the Sierra Maestra wasn't enough to right Cuba's wrongs. The revolution had a debt to repay to the campesinos, on whose backs the war had been fought. The landowning system itself had to be reformed, as Cuba's constitution of 1940 stated it would be. "It is the job of the organized peasant masses to demand a law that proscribes the *latifundia,*" Che said. What's more, the constitutional requirement for prior compensation to owners of expropriated land should be waived. It was an impediment to the goal of "a true and ample agrarian reform." A process of rapid industrialization must also take place to free Cuba from the sugar-export economy. Only then could the country liberate itself from U.S. capitalist domination. "We have to increase the industrialization of the country, without ignoring the many problems that this process brings with it," Che said. "But a policy of industrial growth demands certain tariff measures that protect the nascent industries and an internal market capable of absorbing the new products. We cannot expand this market unless we give access to the great peasant masses, the *guajiros,* who don't have acquisitive power today but do have needs to fulfill."

Che warned that the United States was not going to take kindly to what he was proposing. "We must be prepared for the reaction of those who today dominate 75 percent of our commercial trade and our market. To confront this danger we must apply countermeasures, among which stand out tariffs and the diversification of markets abroad." To industrialize, Cuba must first rescue its natural resources, which had been given over to "foreign consortiums by the Batista dictatorship." The nation's mineral wealth and electricity should be in Cuban hands, and the state telephone company, a subsidiary of ITT, should be nationalized.

"What resources do we have for a program like this?" Che asked. "We have the Rebel Army and this should be our primary instrument for the struggle, the most positive and vigorous weapon. We should destroy all that remains of Batista's army. Understand well that this liquidation is not done out of vengeance or even merely a spirit of justice, but because of the need to ensure that all the people's goals can be achieved in the least amount of time."

Che said that he expected resistance from many quarters: "National recovery will have to destroy many privileges and because of that we have to be ready to defend the nation from its declared and its disguised enemies." Alluding to the rumors of invasion plans being hatched in the Dominican Republic, Che invoked the menacing specter of the United States. "We know that if we are attacked by a small island, it would be with the help of a power that is practically a continent; and we would have to withstand an aggression of immense proportions on our soil. For this reason we must be forewarned and prepare our vanguard with a guerrilla spirit and strategy. . . . The entire Cuban nation should become a guerrilla army, because the Rebel Army is a growing body whose capacity is limited only by the number of 6 million Cubans. Each Cuban should learn how to use weapons and when to use them in the defense of the nation."

Most dramatically of all, Che bared his evolving vision of a continental revolution, not only challenging the conventional Communist theory of Party-led mass struggle, but throwing down the gauntlet of violent confrontation throughout the hemisphere. "The example of our revolution and the lessons it implies for Latin America have destroyed all the coffeehouse theories: we have demonstrated that a small group of men supported by the people and without fear of dying were it necessary can overcome a disciplined regular army and defeat it. This is the fundamental lesson. There is another for our brothers in the Americas who are in the same agrarian category we are, and that is to make agrarian revolutions, to fight in the fields, in the mountains, and from there to the cities. . . . Our future is intimately linked to all the underdeveloped countries of Latin America. The revolution is not limited to the Cuban nation, because it has touched the conscience of Latin America and alerted the enemies of our peoples. . . . The Revolution has put the Latin American tyrants on guard. They, like the foreign monopolies, are the enemies of popular regimes."

The revolution had enemies, but it also had friends. Che ended with a call for a "spiritual union between all the people of the Americas, a union that goes beyond demagoguery and bureaucracy to effective assistance, lending our brothers the benefits of our experience. Today, all the people of Cuba are on a war footing and should remain so. Their victory against dictatorship is not transitory but rather the first step in Latin America's victory."

Che's speech was nothing less than a siren call to the hemisphere's would-be revolutionaries and an implicit declaration of war against the interests of the United States.

VI

On February 2, Daniel Braddock, the American deputy chief of mission in Havana, sent a classified dispatch to the State Department, the CIA, the Army, the Navy, the Air Force, and the U.S. embassies in Ciudad Trujillo and in Managua. It carried the heading "Cuba as a Base for Revolutionary Operations against Other Latin American Governments," and it spelled out a specific warning: "A number of leaders of the successful revolutionary movement in Cuba consider that efforts should now be undertaken to 'free' the people of some other Latin American nations from their 'dictatorial' governments," Braddock wrote. "While Ernesto 'Che' Guevara Serna is generally regarded as the principal force behind such thinking, and is indeed active in the planning, he is far from alone. Fidel Castro has reportedly made remarks along such lines, particularly during his recent visit to Venezuela."*

For once, the U.S. intelligence appraisal was on target. With Fidel's backing, Che had summoned prospective revolutionaries from around the hemisphere seeking Cuban sponsorship for their own *Granma*-style armed expeditions. During the war against Batista, a number of anti-Somoza Nicaraguans, including a group of students led by Carlos Fonseca, a Marxist intellectual, had supported the Cuban revolutionary cause in acts of homage and rhetoric. Now Che offered the Nicaraguans help in organizing a guerrilla army, and a revolutionary party to lead it. But the Nicaraguans were not the only revolutionaries being encouraged, as Braddock's cable noted:

> The countries most frequently mentioned [as candidates for Cuban-sponsored guerrilla invasions] are the Dominican Republic, Nicaragua, Paraguay, and Haiti. Paraguay appears to be too far away for direct Cuban interference, but there is a great deal of preliminary talk and planning taking place about the other three countries. A number of Dominican exiles are in Cuba, including "General" Miguel Ángel RAMÍREZ. The revolutionary leaders, as

*In late January, Fidel had gone to Venezuela to thank the outgoing Larrazábal regime, which had sent him arms during the war. While there, he made remarks that were interpreted as an implicit threat toward Nicaragua's dictator, Anastasio Somoza. He also met with the president-elect of Venezuela, Rómulo Betancourt—the politician Che had so distrusted upon meeting him in Costa Rica. As Betancourt would later reveal, Fidel asked if he could count on Venezuela to supply Cuba with oil, since he was planning "a game with the Americans." The solidly pro-American Betancourt told Fidel curtly that he could buy oil like any other customer, cash on the barrelhead.

distinct from the officers of the provisional Government, seem to feel that they have a piece of unfinished business to take care of in connection with the Dominican Republic, in the form of the abortive Cayo Confítes expedition of 1947, in which a number of the revolutionary leaders, including Fidel Castro, were involved.

Louis DEJOIE is now in Habana, hoping to be able to organize and obtain support for a movement to overthrow the "fraudulent" [Haitian] government of DUVALIER. He is being assisted by Pierre ARMAND, self-styled "President of the Haitian Revolutionary Front in Habana." It appears that the Cuban revolutionaries are mainly interested in the Haitian plans as a means of getting a base from which to attack TRUJILLO. They would support Dejoie, in return for his permitting an expedition against Trujillo to be based in Haiti.

A number of Nicaraguan exiles are in town, including Manuel GÓMEZ Flores. The Embassy has today received a report from a fairly reliable source that the Nicaraguan group feels that they will be the first to attack. . . . This report mentions Guevara specifically as actively participating in the plotting, and as training some of the participants. It was indicated that they hoped to be able to launch an invasion within two months.

Braddock's cable ended with an uncannily prescient forecast. "The planning for these various adventures appears to be preliminary and unrealistic at this stage, and the groups disunited. However, in view of the background of many of the principal Cuban revolutionary leaders, and the support their own movement received from abroad, it can be expected that Cuba will be a center of revolutionary scheming and activities for some time, with consequent concern and difficulties for various governments including our own."

Among Che's men at La Cabaña, it was no secret that he was meeting with revolutionaries from other countries, and rumors of conspiracies of the kind detected by the U.S. embassy were circulating throughout Cuba. Schoolboys too young to have participated in the fight against Batista wrote to Che, asking to be allowed to go fight against Trujillo. On February 5, Che posted polite refusals to three young volunteers who had offered their services. To Juan Hehong Quintana, in Cárdenas, he wrote: "I appreciate your gesture. It is always good when the youth are willing to sacrifice themselves for a cause as noble as giving freedom to Santo Domingo, but I feel that in these moments our combat post is here, in Cuba, where there are enormous difficulties to overcome. For now, dedicate yourself to working enthusiastically for our revolution, which will be the best help we can offer to the Dominican people, that is to say, the example of our complete triumph."

In fact, Che was helping to lay the foundations for a secret agency within Ramiro Valdés's state security apparatus that would organize, train, and assist foreign guerrilla ventures. (The clandestine unit would become known as the Liberation Department within the Dirección General de Inteligencia.) The man who would eventually lead the agency, Manuel Piñeiro Losada, was a former Columbia University student and the son of Galician émigrés who owned a wine-import firm and beer distributorship in Matanzas. Piñeiro, who had been one of Raúl's former Second Front aides, said that the first guerrilla expeditions sponsored by Cuba were very "artisanal" and, in the case of the Nicaraguans and Guatemalans, relied on personal relationships Che had developed in Central America and Mexico. As of early 1959, Piñeiro said, there was still no "structured policy" regarding these missions on the part of the Cuban government.

That would soon change, however. Osvaldo de Cárdenas, a mulatto high school student from Matanzas, was only sixteen years old in January 1959, but within a year Piñeiro had recruited him as an intelligence operative specializing in assisting foreign guerrillas. Cárdenas recalled that he and his young comrades were convinced that the Cuban revolution was the beginning of other changes in Latin America, and that they were imminent. "And so, to work! We were all imbued with this spirit," Cárdenas said. "Everyone wanted to join a guerrilla army somewhere. There were plans to go to Paraguay. I don't know how we thought we were going to get there, but there were plans to go to overthrow Stroessner. There were plans to fight against Trujillo. Some went, some with authorization and others without it. There were plans to topple Somoza. Wherever there was a tyrant, a Latin American dictator, he was automatically our enemy."

Orlando Borrego, Che's hardworking young protégé, became infected by the liberation fever. In February or March 1959, a rumor spread among La Cabaña's officers that an expeditionary force of Cuban revolutionaries was being organized to support the fledgling Nicaraguan guerrillas. "Several of us tried to enlist to go to Nicaragua," Borrego recalled. "There was an officer who seemed to be at the center of the organization, but as it turned out, it was, as they say, 'freelance.' It wasn't authorized by Che or coordinated by him. And I remember that Che summoned this group and he chastised them sternly—because they were gathering weapons and planning this movement without permission—and it was stopped. But from that moment on it was pretty clear that such things were being planned."

Indeed they were, although the more serious guerrilla conspiracies were kept under tighter wraps than the plot Borrego had tried to join. In March, following an unimpressive initial meeting with a group of Nicaraguan leftists from the Partido Socialista Nicaragüense (PSN), Che saw the Nicaraguan militant Rodolfo Romero, whom he had invited to Havana. During the Castillo Armas invasion of Guatemala in 1954, when they were both hoping to actively fight in defense of President Arbenz, Romero had shown Che how to use an automatic weapon. Now their roles were reversed. After the debacle in Guatemala, Romero had gone underground. He was eventually arrested and deported to Nicaragua, but he was freed following a short stint in jail and joined forces with Carlos Fonseca's anti-Somoza student group. Che asked Romero to give him an appraisal of the Nicaraguan situation and suggest what should be done to undermine the regime there. Explaining that the PSN was politically "prostrate," Romero replied that there was only one road left, "the road of Cuba." Che then asked him if he wanted to join the Nicaraguan guerrilla column that was being trained on the island under the command of a former Nicaraguan National Guard officer named Rafael Somarriba. Romero said yes.

VII

On February 7, Urrutia's government had approved the new Cuban constitution. It contained a clause designed especially for Che, conferring Cuban citizenship on any foreigner who had fought in the war against Batista for two or more years and who had held the rank of *comandante* for a year. A few days later, Che was officially made a Cuban citizen "by birth." The occasion coincided with the new government's first internal crisis. Fidel had been at loggerheads with Urrutia's cabinet over the banning of the national lottery and the refusal to reopen the brothels and casinos that had been closed following the seizure of power. Unemployed workers were demonstrating against the closings, and the last thing Fidel wanted was to alienate his constituency. The tawdry "entertainment sector" that was a visible part of Cuban life would cetainly have to be reformed, but gradually, with retraining and new jobs offered to those whose professions were to be purged. Fidel insisted that the cabinet reverse its decisions, and he threatened to find his own solution to the impasse if it didn't. Realizing Fidel was planning to run things his way whether the cabinet liked it or not, Prime Minister Miró Cardona resigned. His replacement would be none other than Fidel Castro.

To "accept" his post, Fidel insisted that Urrutia give him special powers to direct government policy. A law was issued lowering the minimum age for holding high public office from thirty-five to thirty. Now, both Che and Fidel, who were thirty and thirty-two, respectively, were eligible for ministerial posts. On February 16, Fidel was sworn in as Cuba's new prime minister. In his acceptance speech, he promised Cubans "change." By the end of February, President Urrutia was, to all intents and purposes, a figurehead. Fidel was indisputably the *real* Cuban leader.

Che was more specific about what "change" meant. In an article in *Revolución* titled "What Is a Guerrilla?" and published three days after Fidel's inauguration, he argued that the Rebel Army had the right to determine Cuba's political future. Che exalted the guerrilla as "the people's choice, the people's vanguard fighter in their struggle for liberation," someone whose sense of discipline comes not out of blind obedience to a military hierarchy but because of the "deep conviction of the individual." The guerrilla was "mentally and physically agile." He was "nocturnal." In other words, now, as during the war, the guerrillas were waiting in the shadows, vigilant and ready to strike. And their mission was not over. "Why does the guerrilla fight? . . . The guerrilla is a social reformer. The guerrilla takes up arms in angry protest against the social system that keeps his unarmed brothers in opprobrium and misery."

The guerrilla had certain tactical needs, Che wrote. He needed places where he could maneuver, hide, escape, and also count on the people's support. This meant the countryside, where, coincidentally, the main social problem was land tenure. "The guerrilla is, fundamentally and before anything else, an agrarian revolutionary. He interprets the desires of the great peasant masses to be owners of land, owners of their own means of production, of their livestock, of all that for which they have fought for years, for that which constitutes their life and will also be their cemetery." For this reason, Che said, the battle standard of the new army born in the Cuban backwoods was agrarian reform. This reform, which "began timidly in the Sierra Maestra," had been transferred to the Escambray and, after recently being "forgotten in ministerial cabinets," would now go forward because of the "firm decision of Fidel Castro, who, and it is worthwhile repeating, will be the one who gives the 'July 26' its historic definition. This Movement didn't invent Agrarian Reform but it will carry it out. It will carry it out comprehensively until there is no peasant without land, nor land left untilled. At that moment, perhaps, the Movement itself may cease to have a reason to exist, but it will have accomplished its historic mission. Our task is to get to that point, and the future will tell if there is more work to do."

Che's closing comment was an early warning to the July 26 Movement that it might eventually be done away with in favor of "unity" with the Communist Party. "Unity" had become a code word for a merger of the PSP and the Rebel Army. The merger was already being implemented, primarily under the auspices of Che and Raúl in the revolutionary camp and Carlos

Rafael Rodríguez in the PSP, although things were not yet running smoothly. Opinion about Fidel was divided within the PSP. Carlos Rafael had been an early and ardent enthusiast, whereas the Party's general secretary, Blas Roca, evidently was not. Aníbal Escalante ultimately proved vital in the fence-mending process, but among the "old Communists," reservations about Fidel's leadership persisted for years.

For all his overt sympathies, the freethinking Che Guevara also provoked some disquiet for the orthodox, Moscow-line Party men. Che's argument for a vanguard role for the Rebel Army—which seemed to ignore urban workers and the traditional Communist Party organization—was theoretical blasphemy, while his forceful advocacy of rural guerrilla warfare and agrarian revolution betrayed deviant Maoist influences. Yet, despite these heretical symptoms, Che was obviously a friend and ally, and the PSP was indebted to him for providing a political opening to Fidel that the Party might otherwise not have had. His ideological kinks would, no doubt, be ironed out.

Early symptoms of a power struggle between the Communists and the July 26 Movement were visible in an incident that went almost unnoticed in Cuba at large. In its February 8 issue, *Bohemia* ran a small article reporting the "first internal crisis" since "the Day of Liberty": the abrupt resignation of Calixto Morales, who had been appointed military governor of Las Villas. Morales "had been displaying a close link with the Communist factors." The root of the problem was a resurgence of the feud between Las Villas's conservative July 26 organization and the local Communist Party organization. But racism reportedly played a part as well. Morales was a radical who was offended by Santa Clara's racial caste system, and, feeling his power, he had gone too far too fast. One of his first actions was to climb aboard a bulldozer and personally tear down the fencing around the city's whites-only central plaza. Before long he was openly feuding with the local and regional July 26 authorities. Félix Torres, the PSP chief in Las Villas, came to his aid, and—according to Aleida March's friend Lolita Rossell— Calixto soon fell under Torres's influence. Before the situation got any worse, Fidel removed Calixto from his post.

Torres's aggressive politicking on behalf of the Communist Party ultimately paid off when the PSP gained the upper hand in Las Villas, but he had alienated a great many *villaclareños* and fueled widespread antigovernment sentiment. Aleida March herself, who still despised the Communists in Las Villas, privately blamed Che for having created the mess in the first place, beginning with Morales's appointment. Before long, disgruntled July 26 men would take up arms in the Escambray in a counterrevolutionary insurgency that would receive assistance from the CIA and spread to other regions. The Castro government's campaign to quell it would become officially known as the "Lucha Contra Bandidos" (Struggle against Bandits). It would persist until 1966, when Fidel's troops finally eradicated the last rebels and, following Stalin's successful counterinsurgency tactics, forcibly evacuated the Escambray's suspected civilian collaborators to several specially built "strategic hamlets" in distant Pinar del Río.

VIII

Che's personal life during this period was both complex and crowded. Despite the fact that he had little time alone with Aleida, he made room for an old Guatemalan friend, Julio "Patojo" (The Kid) Cáceres, when Cáceres showed up in Havana. Patojo had worked with Che during his itinerant-photographer period in Mexico City and had lived with him and Hilda off and on. He shared Che's dreams of revolution and had wanted to come along on the *Granma,* but Fidel had turned him down as one foreigner too many. Now that Patojo was in Cuba, Che moved him into his house without a second thought.

Che also had to face Hilda, who arrived in late January from Peru with three-year-old Hildita in tow. The fearless Che of combat was somewhat less bold in matters of matrimony; rather than go to the airport himself, he sent his friend Dr. Oscar Fernández Mell to greet his wife and child. Hoping for a reconciliation, Hilda was to be sadly disappointed. She recorded the breakup scene:

> With the candor that always characterized him, Ernesto forthrightly told me that he had another woman, whom he had met in the campaign of Santa Clara. The pain was deep in me, but, following our convictions, we agreed on a divorce.
>
> I am still affected by the memory of the moment when, realizing my hurt, he said: "Better I had died in combat."
>
> For an instant I looked at him without saying anything. Though I was losing so much at that time, I thought of the fact that there were so many more important tasks to be done, for which he was so vital: he *had* to have remained alive. He had to build a new society. He had to work hard to help Cuba avoid the errors of Guatemala; he had to give his whole effort to the struggle for the liberation of America. No, I was happy that he had not died in combat, sincerely happy, and I tried to explain it to him this way, ending with: "Because of all this, I want you always."
>
> Moved, he said: "If that's how it is, then it's all right . . . friends, and comrades?"
>
> "Yes," I said.

Whether Hilda did, in fact, let Che off the hook so easily might be debated, but the estranged couple reached a quick and fairly amicable settlement. Hilda would stay on in Cuba and be given a useful job just as soon as things were organized. She and Che would get a divorce, and then he and Aleida would be married.

Che made a special effort to establish a fatherly role with the dark-haired little girl he knew only from photographs. Evidently trying to avoid direct contact with Hilda for Aleida's sake—the two women had despised each other on sight—Che frequently sent for Hildita to be brought to him at La Cabaña. His men often saw them together, walking around the fortress hand in hand. She would play in his office while he went through papers. On February 15, he attended her third birthday party. In a photograph taken of the occasion, a smiling Hilda sits at the head of the table, holding Hildita close to her. Che sits hunched over on the other side of the table. He is wearing his beret, a leather jacket, and a sharp, self-contained look, as though he wished he were elsewhere.

On February 15, 1959, Che attended his daughter Hildita's third birthday party. Hildita's mother, Hilda Gadea, is holding her.

Che also had his family—who stayed in Havana for a month—to deal with. In the early days, their short visits and Che's hectic schedule kept things pleasant enough, but tensions simmered between Che and his father. Quite apart from their divergent political views, Che had never forgiven his father's treatment of his mother. As he explained to close friends, his father had "spent all the old lady's money and then ditched her." Things finally came to a head when Ernesto senior went to the home of a ham radio enthusiast to speak with friends in Buenos Aires. His "Cuba support committee" in Argentina had acquired a shortwave radio transmitter to communicate with Radio Rebelde—too late to ever be used for that purpose—and he wanted to finally test it out, so he spent an afternoon on the air. That evening, he was reprimanded by his son. "Old man, you are very imprudent," Che remonstrated. "You have been speaking by shortwave to Buenos Aires in the home of a radio *aficionado* who is a counterrevolutionary." His father made his excuses, insisting he had said nothing of political interest, and the matter was dropped, but later he reflected: "It was evident that the information services of the incipient revolutionary government were already working."

The Guevaras were moved from the Hilton to the seaside Hotel Comodoro in the exclusive suburb of Miramar, presumably to make it harder for Ernesto senior to drop in on his son at La Cabaña at inconvenient times, as he was in the habit of doing. From then on, Che visited them by helicopter, alighting on the hotel's lawn. "He descended," Guevara Lynch wrote, "chatted for a while with his mother, Celia, and left again." Celia herself, by all accounts, was enthralled by Cuba, caught up by her maternal pride and the euphoria of her son's triumph. She more or less uncritically tried to share the victory he had helped bring about.

Taking a brief break from his revolutionary duties, Che escorted his family on a sightseeing trip, showing them Santa Clara and his old haunts in the Escambray, visiting the house of Aleida's family and the sites of battles he had led. At Pedrero, he left them to return to Havana, and two soldiers were delegated to guide them on horseback into the hills to see his former *comandancia*. His father provoked a new incident there when, out of curiosity, he picked up the field telephone in the old general staff headquarters. His guides told him that it had been used to communicate with the nearby radio transmitter but was now disconnected, and he got a shock when he heard a man's voice come on the line. "Who are you?" Ernesto senior asked. "And who are *you*?" came the retort. "I am Che's father," he replied. The man on the other end sputtered in disbelief, insulted him in a threatening manner, and hung up.

The soldiers escorting the family became alarmed. They tried to make contact on the radio themselves, but there was no reply, and they went into the woods to investigate. In their absence, Che's father's vivid imagination got the best of him. "I began to get worried," he recalled. "Who were the people on the other side? If they were counterrevolutionaries, they could catch us easily, because we had only two soldiers as escorts and we were armed only with pistols. It would have been a magnificent blow for the counterrevolutionaries to take Che's father, mother, and brother and sister as prisoners."

Guevara Lynch ushered his wife, daughter, and youngest son into a fortified cave. "If any strangers approached, my son-in-law Luis and I resolved to defend the entrance together by shooting." But a short time later, their escorts returned, smiling. At the radio installation, they had found some militiamen who had been disassembling the transmitter at the very moment of the call. They too had become frightened, thinking counterrevolutionaries were about to attack them, and had taken up defensive positions. Che guffawed with laughter when Celia told him the story later.

The family's visit was awkward for Che. Compared with many of his comrades, he was almost obsessively concerned about the image he presented to the public. He didn't want to appear to be abusing his power by dispensing government favors to family and friends. Camilo had arranged the Guevaras' free flight as a surprise. If Che had known about it, he probably would have forbidden it. As it was, the Guevara family experienced Che's austerity measures firsthand. They were given a car and driver for trips around Havana, but they had to pay for gas. When his father said that he wished to explore the battlefields of the Sierra Maestra, Che said he would provide a jeep and a veteran soldier to guide them, but Ernesto senior would have to pay for gas *and* meals. Guevara Lynch had not brought enough money, and abandoned his plan.

The family's final departure was abrupt. As Guevara Lynch recalled it: "My duties in Buenos Aires demanded my attention. Suddenly I decided to travel. I told Ernesto on the telephone that I was leaving that night. He went to say good-bye to me at the airport in the company of Raúl Castro."

As they chatted at the departure gate, a man came over and spoke to Che in a thick *porteño* accent. He was a fellow Argentine, he said, and wished to shake his hand. Che assented wordlessly, but when the man dug out a notebook and pen and asked for an autograph, Che turned his back. "I am not a movie star," he said.

Che and his father made a symbolic peace at the last minute. When their flight was announced, Guevara Lynch removed from his wrist the old gold watch he wore, an heirloom that had belonged to Che's beloved grandmother, Ana Isabel Lynch, and gave it to his son. Che took it, slipped off the watch he was wearing, and handed it to his father. It was, he said, the watch Fidel had given him when he was promoted to *comandante*.

IX

Che had not been looking or feeling well for some time. He was gaunt and his eyes were sunken. Ill health was one of the reasons he hadn't accompanied Fidel to Venezuela, where he had been invited to speak by a medical society, but it wasn't until March 4 that he took a break in his schedule and allowed doctors to X-ray him. He was diagnosed with a pulmonary infection and told that he had to convalesce. He was also told to stop smoking cigars. Che, who had became addicted to tobacco during the war, persuaded the doctors to allow him one *tabaco* a day. The patient interpreted this rule liberally, as Antonio Nuñez Jiménez, now a factotum for Fidel, discovered when he went to Che's house one morning. "I found him smoking a cigar about a foot and a half long," Nuñez Jiménez recalled. "He explained with a naughty smile: 'Don't worry about the doctors, I am being good to my word—one cigar a day, and not one more.'"

Che and Aleida had been moved, on doctor's orders, to a requisitioned villa at the nearby beach community of Tarará. The new location made it possible for Che to conduct his revolutionary work with more secrecy. By now he was deeply involved in preparing Cuba's agrarian reform law and designing the agency that would implement it. The agency was given an innocuous-sounding name—Instituto Nacional de Reforma Agraria (INRA)—but in essence, it was to be the genesis of the *real* Cuban revolution. An amalgamation of the July 26 Movement's left wing, the former Rebel Army, and the Cuban Communist Party, INRA was to gradually assume the functions of the regime headed by Manuel Urrutia.

Immediately after arriving at La Cabaña, Che had summoned his new group of unofficial advisers at the sugar institute, including Juan Borroto and the PSP man Alfredo Menéndez, for talks. The 1959 sugar harvest season had begun, and Che suggested reducing the working day from eight to six hours to create more jobs. Menéndez pointed out that this would set off a wave of similar work-reduction demands throughout the Cuban labor market, increase the cost of sugar production, and affect Cuba's profits on the world market.

"You may be right," Che replied. "But, look, the first mission of the revolution is to resolve the unemployment problem in Cuba. If we don't resolve it, we won't be able to stay in power." He insisted that Menéndez give him a proposal on reducing the workday, but in the end Fidel quashed the idea. It would have created too many problems. Besides, the sugar industry was still in the hands of powerful private capital interests, both Cuban and American, and he couldn't afford to antagonize them just yet. "Fidel's vision was longer-range," Menéndez observed. "He was telling the workers that they shouldn't fight for crumbs, but for power. He was already planning to nationalize the industry."

By February, the pace of consultations had increased, and Menéndez joined a high-level Communist Party group, the "Economic Commission," that met in secret every night at a house in Cojímar, conveniently close to La Cabaña. The house was rented in the name of Francisco "Pancho" García Vals, a bright young Communist Party member who spoke both English and French. Although García Vals hadn't participated in the war, Che had taken to him and made him a lieutenant and his executive assistant. García Vals's unearned military rank and new duties may have seemed inexplicable to outsiders, but he served a vital function for Che. The nightly meetings at his house were convened for the purpose of working on a draft proposal for the agrarian reform law.

Che was in the habit of dropping by the house in Cojímar in the afternoons. While García Vals and Menéndez worked away on economic affairs, Che dictated his thoughts on guerrilla warfare into a tape recorder. His new personal secretary, José Manuel Manresa, a former Batista desk sergeant he had kept on at La Cabaña, transcribed the tapes. Occasionally Che would call Menéndez over and ask him to read a section. The resulting book, *La Guerra de Guerrillas* (Guerrilla Warfare), was a how-to manual intended to adapt the lessons learned in Cuba to other Latin American nations.

Once Che was ensconced in Tarará, the work on INRA intensified. Fidel, who moved into his Cojímar villa around the same time, named Antonio Nuñez Jiménez as chairman of an agrarian reform task force that included Che, Fidel's old Communist friend Alfredo Guevara, Pedro Miret, Vílma Espín—whom Raúl had married in January—and two senior PSP advisers. The group met every night at the house in Tarará to discuss changes and additions to the proposals drafted by the PSP team at García Vals's house. Alfredo Guevara told Tad Szulc, Fidel's biographer, that they usually worked until dawn, at which point "Fidel would come and change everything." But gradually, the project began to take shape. All the while, absolute secrecy was maintained from the ministers in Urrutia's government; certainly, the putative agriculture minister, Humberto Sorí-Marín, was not invited to attend. At the same time, Che was attending the long-range unity talks between the Rebel Army and the PSP at Fidel's house.

The group's need to maintain a low profile helps explain Che's reaction to a magazine article mentioning that he was now living in a luxurious confiscated villa. He responded vehemently in *Revolución*:

I must clarify to the readers of *Revolución* that I am ill, that I did not contract my sickness in gambling dens or staying up all night in cabarets, but working more than my body could withstand, for the revolution.

The doctors recommended a house in a quiet place away from daily visits. . . . I was forced to live in a house that belonged to representatives of the old regime because my salary of $125.00 as an officer of the Rebel Army does not permit me to rent one sufficiently large to house the people who accompany me.

The fact that it is the home of an old *batistiano* means that it is luxurious; I chose the simplest, but at any rate it is still an insult to popular sentiments.

Two months later, when his health was better and the agrarian reform law had been completed, Che moved to a much humbler house in the countryside near the inland village of Santiago de las Vegas, on the other side of Havana.

The secret conclaves had coincided with the arrival of the new American ambassador, Philip Bonsal, who made the optimistic appraisal that Castro "could be handled." The military-intelligence establishment thought otherwise, and on March 10, Eisenhower's National Security Council discussed the possibility of "bringing another government to power in Cuba."

Whether or not Fidel was a Communist, most American political analysts now felt he was a loose cannon who had to be reined in before he could do real damage in Cuba and the region. Some politically moderate Latin American leaders who had previously supported him lent their voices to this growing consensus; both José Figueres, the Costa Rican president, and Rómulo Betancourt, in Venezuela, confided their suspicions to the Americans that the Communists already had a firm grip in most of the vital areas in Cuba. All the while, however, Fidel continued his vigorous public denials of Communist inclinations. He invited hundreds of reporters to Havana in a lavish public relations campaign dubbed Operation Truth, which was aimed at countering negative publicity.

There was a lot of negative publicity to counter. Fidel had recently "intervened" with the Cuban branch of the International Telephone and Telegraph Company in order to "investigate irregularities in its operations," as Che had urged in his speech in January. He had publicly excoriated the visiting President Figueres, a wartime ally, for suggesting that Cuba should side with the United States in the "Cold War confrontation," accusing him of "imperialistic tendencies." He had made wild-sounding predictions about the Cuban economy, going so far as to claim that within a few years, Cuba's standard of living would surpass that of the United States. The revolutionary tribunals had continued unabated, and he had caused an international scandal by ordering the retrial of forty-four Batista airmen who had been acquitted of bombing civilians. The tribunals were alienating the influential Cuban Catholic community, and Catholic militants who had been active supporters of the bid to oust Batista were becoming nervous about the revolution's leftward slide. The universities were alarmed about Fidel's apparent lack of regard for the hallowed tradition of academic autonomy, and a crackdown on press freedoms seemed likely.

Plans were under way to create a "revolutionary" press that would cast Fidel's actions in a more favorble light. Jorge Ricardo Masetti, the Argentine journalist who had become so enamored of Cuba's revolution, was back in Havana, along with his Uruguayan counterpart, Carlos María Gutiérrez.* Both men held talks with Che over the creation of an "independent" international Cuban news agency, to be modeled on Perón's ill-fated Agencia Latina. Che's objective, like Perón's, was to break free of such "Yankee capitalist" news monopolies as the AP and UPI. In a few months' time—with $100,000 from unused July 26 bonds collected during the war—Cuba's own Prensa Latina was founded. Masetti became the first editor in chief, and an impressive roster of correspondents around the world was assembled. Within a few months, another sierra convert, the American journalist Robert Taber, was also helping out the revolution's propaganda effort through the Fair Play for Cuba Committee, a pro-Castro U.S. lobbying group that was supported by liberal-left intellectuals such as Carleton Beals, C. Wright Mills, I. F. Stone, and Allen Ginsberg.

Along with his practical—and, at times, Machiavellian—approach to problem solving, Fidel had begun to exhibit an unsettling penchant for embracing bizarre economic schemes that would "solve" Cuba's problems. He had dreamed up a project to drain the Ciénaga de Zapáta, a vast swamp delta on the southern coast, and open it to rice farming. More important, his impolitic remarks about increasing Cuba's sugar harvest as a way to boost employment had already contributed to a fall in world sugar prices as futures investors bet on an impending market glut. In fact, the 1959 harvest, or *zafra,* was larger than usual, producing 5.8 million tons.

Some of Fidel's more outlandish proposals may have been born of simple desperation. Batista-era corruption, last-minute theft, and capital flight had stripped Cuba's treasury, leaving little more than $1 million in

---

*Upon his return to Buenos Aires, Masetti had published *Los Que Luchan y los Que Lloran* (Those Who Fight and Those Who Cry), about his time in the Sierra Maestra, lauding the Cuban revolution and its leaders.

reserves, a public debt of $1.2 billion, and a budgetary deficit of $800 million. The million-member-strong Cuban labor union, the Confederación de Trabajadores Cubanos (CTC), once a major Communist bastion, had been co-opted by Batista, but Fidel was beginning to engineer a purge under the newly appointed union leader, David Salvador. The constant reminders of imminent agrarian reform were making landowners and agricultural investors nervous, and capital investment began grinding to a halt. In March, Fidel pushed through a bill that lowered rents by 50 percent and expropriated vacant land. Tariffs were imposed on a range of imported luxury goods; laid-off workers began striking for reinstatement, and other workers demanded pay raises. Increasingly uncertain about the future, a growing stream of affluent and middle-class Cubans began packing up to leave for new lives abroad. Most of them went to that venerable haven of Cuban exiles only ninety miles away, Miami.

On April 14, the American deputy chief of mission in Havana, Daniel Braddock, sent to Washington a new confidential "action copy" dispatch, "Growth of Communism in Cuba." He warned that since the fall of Batista, the PSP had "emerged from hiding to achieve a semi-legal status which will probably become fully legal as soon as political parties register. The Party has increased its membership during these past three months by at least 3,000 and is still growing. Offices have been opened in every section of Habana and in most of the towns in the interior." The cable went on to warn that the Cuban armed forces were a primary target of the Communist infiltration:

> La Cabaña appears to be the main Communist center, and its Commander, Che GUEVARA, is the most important figure whose name is linked to Communism. Guevara is definitely a Marxist if not a Communist. Political indoctrination courses have been instituted among the soldiers under his command at La Cabaña. Material used in these courses, some of which the Embassy has seen, definitely follows the Communist line. Guevara enjoys great influence with Fidel CASTRO and even more with the Commander in chief of the Armed Forces, Commander Raúl CASTRO, who is believed to share the same political views as Che Guevara.

Orlando Borrego recalled that he was typical of many of the men at La Cabaña at the time, young former rebels with little ideological education. "From the political perspective," Borrego said, "during those first months we were very confused. The rumors had begun that the revolution was going to be socialist. This was discussed among the troops and I was one of those who said, 'No, it can't be.' And what *was* socialism, anyway? I didn't understand. The widespread impression was that Communism was bad. We wanted a revolution that was just, that was honorable, that would serve the interests of the nation and all of that, but would have nothing to do with Communism. But we also said, 'Well, if Che and Fidel are Communists, then we are too,' but it was out of a sense of devotion to them, not because of any ideological position."

Borrego served as a judge in the trial of a former police chief, General Hernando Hernández. During the trial, the defendant gave him a copy of Boris Pasternak's book *Doctor Zhivago*. Borrego had no idea who Pasternak was, and, in all innocence, he showed the book to Che. "Che looked at it and 'Ha!' he began to laugh," Borrego recalled. "'What an ignoramus you are,' he said. He explained to me who Pasternak was and what he revealed about the Stalin era. That man had made me the gift intentionally, to see if I would comprehend all that was negative about the Soviet Union."

"Until that time Che had undertaken little direct political orientation—in the sense of the socialist idea—with us," Borrego said. "But around February or March, he began to have meetings with us, the officers, in a little hall there in La Cabaña. They were political orientation talks. He didn't call them that, but that's what they were." Che placed special emphasis on the idea that the seizure of power was not the most important revolutionary goal. "He told us that the most difficult and complex task was beginning at that moment," Borrego said. "It was the stage where a distinct society would be built. He didn't speak of Communism, or of socialism, but he began to introduce, from a historical perspective, revolutionary ideas on an international scale. One day, in front of a map, he explained about the Soviet Union, the countries of the socialist bloc, what role Lenin had played, and he began to transmit to us Lenin's ideas, saying that there were valuable lessons to be learned." Borrego said that he and his comrades left the seminar that day saying to one another, "This reeks of Communism." But by now, they were more intrigued than frightened by the new ideas.

Once Che had broken the ice among his junior officers, Armando Acosta, his regimental deputy, took over the job of indocrination. "He was very clever, very intelligent in the way he explained things to us," Borrego recalled. "He clarified things in revolutionary terminology without talking about Communism, stressing above all the need for unity between revolutionaries, that there could be no political divisions." Acosta's talks and Borrego's close daily working contact with Che soon gave him "an ideology." The real moment of truth for him came in April, when a wealthy Cuban businessman, his employer before he had joined the war, offered him a well-paying job in Guatemala. Tempted, Borrego told Che about the offer and asked his advice. Che told Borrego to think seriously about his priorities because he was playing a vital role in the revolution. He should mull the offer over for a few days and then come back when he had made up his mind. Borrego did as he was told and decided to stay in Cuba. "Che had established a great deal of influence over me very quickly," Borrego said.

Orlando Borrego would become one of Che's most trusted personal friends and protégés. He was part of a loyal coterie of disciples who were followers of "Che" rather than of any political credo. By the spring of 1959, Che had begun to gather several such men around him. Yet, far from being sectarian, he dealt respectfully with many of the defeated former army officers at La Cabaña during the transition to the Rebel Army's control—even as he sent others to die before the firing squad. That Che, an ideologically committed man so close to Fidel, inspired such an unusual degree of loyalty among his soldiers was troubling to the Americans. He was a dangerous foe indeed. And, as the cables from the embassy in Havana show, they knew this very early in 1959.

X

Che Guevara had emerged as a figure of special attention in Moscow also. In January 1959, the Central Committee of the Communist Party of the U.S.S.R. sent an undercover agent to Havana to take soundings and explore the possibility of establishing relations with the new regime. His first point of contact, it was agreed, should be with Che.

The agent's name was Alexandr Alexiev. Tall, bespectacled, and gregarious, with a strong, angular face, Alexiev was a forty-five-year-old KGB agent working under diplomatic cover at the Soviet embassy in Buenos Aires when he was recalled to Moscow in August 1958. Early in his intelligence career he had served in the Spanish Civil War and in the Great Patriotic War of 1941–1945. He specialized in Latin America.

In 1957, when he was still in Argentina, Alexiev had begun hearing about Che from friends at Buenos Aires University. "They were revolutionaries," he recalled, "and were always talking about Che with pride. Their compatriot was fighting with Fidel." Alexiev was suspicious about Fidel's true political inclinations and, he admitted later, had not given Cuba his full attention. "I didn't think much about the Cuban revolution. I thought it would be like any other [bourgeois] Latin American revolution. I wasn't sure it was a very serious thing."

Once he was back in Moscow, Alexiev was named head of the Latin America Department of the Committee for Cultural Relations with Foreign Countries. He took up his post in December 1958. Within weeks of the Cuban revolutionary victory and Moscow's recognition of the new regime, his boss, Yuri Zhukov, who was in direct contact with Premier Nikita Khrushchev, came to see him. "Alexandr, I think you should travel and see what kind of revolution this is," Zhukov said. "It seems to be anti-American and it seems worthwhile that one of you go there. You are the best candidate because you know Spanish. You were in Argentina, Che is Argentine, and there are ways to establish contacts."

Yuri Paporov, who had been working in the same department as Alexiev since his own recall from Mexico a year earlier, remembered his colleague's reaction: "He didn't want to go. He said he didn't want to talk to those bourgeois revolutionaries." Paporov advised Alexiev to put aside his reservations because it would be "good for his career," an argument that Alexiev found convincing. A request for a visa was channeled through the Cuban embassy in Mexico City. It was a journalistic visa, since no actual diplomatic links had been established between Cuba and the Soviet Union.

In late January, some high-ranking Cuban PSP officials arrived in Moscow. The delegates, headed by Juan Marinello and Severo Aguirre, had officially come for a Communist Party congress, but their journey had another purpose as well. They were to try to convince the Kremlin that Cuba's revolution was an opportunity not to be missed. Their praise left Alexiev unmoved, however. He attributed it to the euphoria they felt after years of oppression under Batista.

As he waited for his visa, Alexiev spent his time monitoring Cuban news reports and, to bolster his false résumé, making favorable broadcasts about Cuba's revolution over Radio Moscow's Spanish-language Latin America service. As time passed, his cynicism evaporated, and he began to experience some of the enthusiasm he had felt as an eighteen-year-old in the embattled Spanish Republic twenty years earlier. Still his Cuban visa didn't come. The months dragged by: spring turned into summer, and Alexiev was still waiting.

Giorgi Kornienko, a high-ranking Soviet official who worked in the Central Committee's Information Department at the time, also recalled that the Soviets became enthusiastic about Cuba only *after* Castro's victory. "I remember in January 1959, when Castro proclaimed a new regime," Kornienko said. "Khrushchev asked the department: 'What kind of guys are these? Who are they?' Nobody knew how to answer his question . . . not the Intelligence Services, not the Foreign Relations Ministry, not the International Department of the Central Committee. We didn't know who these guys in Havana were. We sent a telegram to our office abroad, later to Intelligence and others. A few days later, we received a telegram from one of the Latin American capitals—I think Mexico—with some information about Castro and his people. And there was information to the effect that, if not Fidel himself, maybe Raúl . . . very possibly Che . . . and some other people close to Fidel had Marxist points of view. I was present when this information was given to Khrushchev. 'If it's really like this,' he said, 'if these Cubans are Marxists and if they develop some sort of socialist movement there in Cuba, it would be fantastic! It would be the first place in the Western Hemisphere with a socialist or prosocialist government. That would be very good, very good for the socialist cause!'"

But other evidence indicates that the Kremlin did not suddenly "discover" Cuba after reading news reports of the revolution. Contacts between the exiled PSP leadership and the Kremlin had been maintained throughout the two-year civil war, and a Soviet journalist and a trade union delegation had visited Havana in January 1959. Moscow's quick decision to recognize the new regime; the arrival of high-level PSP officials in Moscow so soon after Batista's downfall; the contacts between Cuban Communist officials and Fidel, Raúl, and Che in the sierra—not to mention their prior contacts in Mexico with Soviet officials such as Yuri Paporov and Nikolai Leonov, both of whom would soon reemerge as Soviet emissaries to Cuba— all suggest a Soviet interest in Cuba's revolution *prior to* the rebel victory. The Kremlin's policy on Cuba seem to have been ratcheted up sometime in mid-1958, after the defeat of the army offensive in the Sierra Maestra had increased the rebels' prospects of victory.

That said, there was certainly lingering skepticism about Castro's revolution in the Kremlin, for what had happened in Cuba was not in the Soviet playbook. The revolution was not the result of PSP strategy; the Party was not in control; Fidel Castro was still an unknown quantity. Even if signs were promising—Fidel had allowed the Party to play a role, and the men closest to him (Che and Raúl) were Marxists—the jury was still out.

Meanwhile, there were good reasons for the foot-dragging in Havana over Alexiev's visa. It was not an opportune time to authorize an eyebrow-raising "journalist's" visa to a known Soviet intelligence official. More to the point, the Cuban chancellery was still (although not for much longer) in the hands of Roberto Agramonte, an anticommunist *ortodoxo*, who would hardly have viewed such a request with equanimity. An abrupt loss of faith in Fidel's political allegiances by his allies, many of whom still believed he was merely biding his time before moving against the scheming, opportunistic Reds, might provoke a violent schism he could not contain.

Even more important, Fidel needed breathing space from the potentially most dangerous quarter of all—the United States. Of necessity, his first foreign-policy objective had to be to secure some sort of modus vivendi with Washington. Che, by contrast, wanted nothing to do with the United States and had already begun to prepare for what he saw as an inevitable show-down with Washington. In this he was seconded by Raúl. Both favored a sharp radicalization in revolutionary policy, a final consolidation of power, and a break with the West.

On April 15, Fidel flew to Washington to serve as the keynote speaker at the annual convention of the American Society of Newspaper Editors. He was accompanied by a large entourage that included his most conservative, pro-American government economic ministers and financial advisers. The radicals, Che and Raúl, were left behind. In spite of Fidel's repeated insistence that he was not going to ask Washington for economic aid in the time-honored tradition of new Latin heads of state, his traveling companions believed it was one of the primary motives of his trip. "Let *them* bring it up," Fidel said, "and then we'll see."

Dressed in his *guerrillero*'s fatigues, Fidel gave a well-received speech at the National Press Club in Washington and had an amicable lunch with the acting secretary of state, Christian Herter. (John Foster Dulles, who had been diagnosed with cancer, resigned the day Fidel arrived.) He spoke before the Senate Foreign Relations Committee, appeared on *Meet the Press*, and paid homage at the Lincoln and Jefferson Memorials.

Fidel was on his best behavior and bent over backward to dispel Americans' fears, reaffirming his commitment to foreign investment in Cuba and insisting that his agrarian reform law would affect only neglected or unused lands. He urged more American tourism and expressed his hope that the United States, the biggest buyer of Cuba's sugar, would increase the sugar quota—the amount of sugar Cuba was legally permitted to export to the United States in any given year. Cuba would, of course, honor its mutual defense treaty with the United States and continue to allow the U.S. Navy to use the Guantánamo base—and while it might come as a surprise to those in the know back in Havana, he was also opposed to Communism and in favor of a free press.*

Everywhere he went, Fidel was followed by reporters. With his beard and uniform, he was an exotic departure from the politicos of the day, and his habit of going on spontaneous walkabouts to meet with ordinary citizens added to his charisma. He loved the attention, although in private meetings his ego took a bruising. The powerful figures he met with were patronizing, brimming with unwanted advice and stern warnings, as if he were an intemperate adolescent who, by dint of luck, had found himself in

---

*Much has been made by historians of Fidel's pacifying remarks, carrying the suggestion that the Eisenhower administration "lost" Cuba by treating him insensitively; but subsequent events bolster the theory that Fidel was simply saying what his audience wanted to hear.

a position of power better suited to someone older and wiser. Repeatedly he found himself besieged by questions about his "purge trials" and executions, and probed about a timetable for elections. On both of these issues, he stood firm. The "people," he said, demanded the tribunals and punishment of war criminals. As for elections, he thought that more time, perhaps four years, would be needed before Cuba was ready.

President Eisenhower arranged to be out of town during Fidel's stay, going off to Georgia for a golfing holiday and leaving Vice President Richard Nixon to stand in for him. They had a private talk in the Capitol building that lasted two and a half hours. Afterward, both men were polite in public; but the talk had not gone well, and each emerged with a negative impression of the other. As Nixon later told Eisenhower, Castro either was a Communist himself or he was a dupe, "incredibly naive" about the Communist influence in his government, an appraisal that was to have serious consequences for U.S.-Cuban relations.

If Fidel had hoped for some sign of a more enlightened American policy toward Cuba, he was disappointed. If he had entertained genuine hopes of being offered some American economic aid, Nixon had dashed them by announcing that none would be forthcoming. Tactlessly, he had advised Fidel to apply the policies of Puerto Rico's governor, who had encouraged private investment in his territory to improve economic conditions there. The notion that Cuba might benefit from the lessons of Puerto Rico, a small and heavily subsidized U.S. territory, was insulting, and Fidel had reacted by telling Nixon that the days of the Platt Amendment, when the United States had the right to intervene in Cuba, were over. Fidel must have come away from the meeting convinced that the Americans would be satisfied only if he toed their line, at the expense of Cuba's sovereignty.

On April 21, after giving a talk at Princeton, Fidel agreed to a meeting with a CIA official in New York who had asked Rufo López Fresquet to act as go-between. They spoke in private for more than three hours. The CIA man, Gerry Droller, a German-American émigré who used the alias Frank Bender, told López Fresquet afterward that he was convinced Castro was an anticommunist and that they had agreed to exchange information about Communist activities in Cuba. López Fresquet was to be their liaison.*

---

*Back in Havana a month after the visit, López Fresquet was contacted by an American official with a message from "Mr. Bender" for Fidel. "I gave Castro the intelligence," López Fresquet recalled. "He didn't answer me, and he never gave me any information to pass on to Mr. Bender." In any event, within a year, the Urrutia government would be consigned to history, overtaken by Fidel and his radical comrades, and López Fresquet, the would-be liaison, would resign his post and go into exile.

Most likely, Fidel used the meeting to give the CIA and his traveling companions the impression that he was biding his time until the Communists stuck their heads out far enough to be lopped off. Indeed, he spoke to one of his aides of the need to stop the executions and the Communist infiltration of the government, and to another of his plans to send Che on a long trip abroad.

In Boston, a few days after the meeting with "Mr. Bender," López Fresquet was present when Fidel received a phone call from Raúl, who told his brother there was talk back home that he was selling out to the Yankees. Fidel reacted indignantly, and, if one considers the battering he was taking in defending himself to a skeptical American audience, Raúl's words must have added insult to injury. Their exchange was followed by a strange encounter between the brothers a few days later. Fidel had accepted an invitation to visit with President Kubitschek of Brazil on his way to attend an economic conference in Buenos Aires sponsored by the OAS. On April 27, en route to Brazil, Fidel's plane made a refueling stop in Houston, where Raúl and some aides met him. After a brief closed-door meeting at the airport, Raúl flew back to Havana, while Fidel proceeded on his journey south.

A number of possible reasons for the meeting have been put forward. "It has been said that the beardless commander of the army, Raúl, adjured his elder brother to maintain his revolutionary integrity," Hugh Thomas wrote. "It seems equally probable that the main discussion was about the theme of the speeches that Raúl Castro and Guevara would make on May 1 in Cuba." Castro's biographer, Tad Szulc, on the other hand, linked the meeting to some embarrassing incidents that appeared to verify the American intelligence analysts' early warnings about official complicity in armed plots against Cuba's neighbors. On April 18, the military commander of Pinar del Río, where most of the foreign revolutionaries were being trained, had made a display of rounding up more than 100 Nicaraguan guerrilla trainees and seizing their arms. He then made a statement saying that Fidel had forbidden such expeditions from Cuban soil. That same day in Havana, a Panamanian named Ruben Miro announced that *his* group planned to invade Panama within a month. A few days later, while Fidel was in Boston, Panamanian authorities captured three armed rebels on the coast, two of whom were Cuban. According to Manuel Piñeiro, this expedition was *por la libre,* a freelance venture that did not have prior government approval. But, approved or not, these events seriously threatened Fidel's efforts to construct a new public image in the United States. Immediately after his stop in Houston, while flying over Cuba's airspace, he made a radio broadcast condemning the Cubans involved as "irresponsible" and repeating that his government did not "export revolution."

Away from the island, Fidel could deny activity against other governments and attribute the involvement of Cubans to the revolutionary euphoria of the time. In fact, the dragnet of the Nicaraguans seems to have been a diversionary maneuver aimed at creating the impression that, far from supporting such activities, Cuba was taking steps to prevent them. But, in addition to the Nicaraguans, an anti-Trujillo Dominican rebel group was being trained in Cuba, as were some Haitians and several other nationalities.

The day after Raúl and Fidel met in Houston, even Che delivered a disclaimer about the Panamanian excursion. "The revolution must be honest at all costs," he said in a televised interview on the evening of April 28, "and I must regretfully admit that Cubans participated in it. What we have to say is that those Cubans left without our permission, without our authorization, without our auspices. . . . We are exporters of the revolutionary idea, but we do not try to be exporters of revolutions. The revolution will be fought by the people in the place where the [offending] government presides, with the people who must suffer that government. We are only the example, the rest is the work of the people."

As usual, Che's words were carefully scrutinized by the political officers at the American embassy. And, as usual, although Che tried to be tactful, his honesty came through in the ways he dodged the tougher questions, most of which probed the issue of his political beliefs. To the first question— was he a Communist?—Che replied that he "didn't feel such a question had to be answered directly" by someone who was in public life. "The facts speak for themselves," he said. "Our way of thinking is clear, our behavior is transparent. The fact that I am not a Communist affiliated with the Communist Party, as I am not, has no importance. We are accused of being Communists for what we do, not for what we are or what we say. . . . If you believe that what we do is Communism, then we are Communists. If you ask me if I am affiliated with the Communist Party or the Popular Socialist Party, as it is called here, then I have to say that I am not."

Not surprisingly, the embassy's conclusions, sent to Washington in a confidential dispatch on May 5, were: "Statements by Ernesto 'Che' GUEVARA in Television Appearance Show Communist Orientation, anti-Americanism."

Immediately after his TV interview, Che rushed off for a meeting with Raúl, who had just returned from Houston. In view of what happened next, it seems clear that one of the main discussion points of the Castro brothers had been a decision by Fidel to halt the firing squads. Since January, an estimated 550 executions had taken place in Cuba, and the issue had been a major source of irritation for Fidel during his trip to the United States. He felt he needed to make a gesture of appeasement and earn some credit from the Americans for doing so. Che strongly opposed the decision but obeyed Fidel's order.

"Che wasn't in agreement," Orlando Borrego said, "but when Fidel explained the measure, demonstrating the advantages and disadvantages, that it was more favorable to the revolution to halt the process, Che accepted it. He accepted it, but it bothered him as much as it did the rest of us, because there were cases we were in the middle of processing."

Stopping the executions ultimately earned Fidel little credit in Washington. By now, the Americans' paramount concerns were the Communist infiltration of his government, the extent of his still-to-be announced agrarian reform bill, and mounting evidence that the Cubans were trying to subvert their neighbors. To Whiting Willauer, the U.S. ambassador to Costa Rica, Cuba's disclaimers in the Panama affair were just smoke and mirrors.

Willauer—a veteran Cold Warrior and, as ambassador to Honduras, a key player in the 1954 operation against Arbenz in Guatemala— cited the Panamanian incident as proof that the Cubans were up to no good. On April 30, while Fidel was still en route to Buenos Aires, Willauer sent a seven-page, single-spaced typed letter labeled "Secret" to Roy Rubottom, the assistant secretary of state for Latin American affairs. It was the latest in an exchange of letters between them over Cuba, and Willauer made little effort to conceal his contempt for Rubottom's dovish position. He argued for a preemptive strike against Castro. "Unless there is some excellent explanation to the contrary I find it difficult to believe that this [Panamanian incident] could have happened without the connivance, to say the very least, of high officials in the Cuban Government, particularly in the army," Willauer wrote. "This conclusion seems even more plausible in view of the fact that it is known that the army is riddled with Communists and that it is generally believed that 'Che' Guevara, among others, holds a very strong position of control."

To Willauer, "the Castro visit to the United States was very probably one of the most blatant soft-soap jobs in recent Communist history." He would be prepared to believe Castro's denials of Communist links "when and only when 'Che' Guevarra [sic] and the other top Communists are given a one way ticket out of the country. . . . In short, while you state in your letter that 'considerable progress is being made in calming down this phase of Caribbean tensions,' I unfortunately find myself in complete disagreement. I feel that the situation in the Caribbean today is worse than it has ever been and that it is going to get much worse very rapidly unless the Communist beachhead in Cuba is liquidated." Willauer wrote that "the guts of the situation" was the growing body of evidence that "the Communists have a very strong position of command and control in the army. This they never achieved in any effective manner in the Guatemalan situation."

Willauer was right. Ernesto Guevara had watched and learned from the mistakes made by Guatemala's would-be socialist "revolution," and five years later, he was able to apply preventive medicine before Washington could act. The Cubans were one step ahead of the Americans. Che's many reminders to Fidel of the causes for Arbenz's failure had paid off: the old army was being thoroughly purged, and the "new army" was being staffed with trustworthy men whose loyalties and political orientation were beyond doubt. As for the rank and file, they were being politically "reeducated." Arms and training would be given to "the people," and a nationwide citizens' militia would be organized to bolster the regular army. By the time Washington could muster its forces, as Che knew it must, Cuba would be armed, ready, and waiting.

XI

Perhaps even more than Fidel himself, Che was well on his way to becoming Washington's number one concern in Latin America. On May 4, J. L. Topping, the political affairs officer at the American embassy in Havana, sent a confidential cable to Washington detailing his debriefing on April 29 of Dr. Napoleón Padilla, a Cuban tobacco industry expert. Padilla had recently been in meetings with Che as a member of El Forum Tabacalera, a committee set up to explore the possibilities of increasing tobacco production and employment. He was described as a "liberal, nationalistic, Catholic" and a past supporter of the revolution against Batista. "I felt that he was deeply worried, and sincere in his remarks," Topping noted.

> Padilla says Guevara is a "stupid international Communist"—not even a bright one. (The word in Spanish is "vulgar.") He believes Raúl Castro is even worse. He says Guevara is violently and unreasoningly anti-American and bitterly opposed to the sale of American products, even if made in Cuba. He mentioned Coca-Cola and Keds, as well as American cigarettes. He feels that Guevara and Raúl Castro want to establish a "Soviet" system in Cuba, and that they will soon show their hands. Guevara talks frequently about how he controls Fidel Castro.
>
> Guevara describes the new Army as a "people's Army," the "defender of the proletariat," as the "principal political arm" of the "people's Revolution." He also says that the new Army will be a principal source of "indoctrination" for the Cuban people, and that

it will engage in "useful works"—apparently meaning construction, harvesting, and so on—but will always be ready to spring to arms in defense of the revolution, which will inevitably be attacked by the United States. . . .

Padilla said that Guevara talked frequently about the "Guatemalan incident." Guevara had said that freedom of the press was dangerous. He had pointed out that the freedom of the press in Guatemala under Arbenz had been one of the causes for the fall of the regime. He had said that freedom should be restricted in Cuba.

Che was not usually described as "vulgar," but most of Padilla's other observations have the ring of truth if we assume Che had spoken out intentionally to provoke Padilla. He had never lost his predilection for shocking people whom he sensed were shockable. Che's alleged bragging about "controlling Fidel," on the other hand, smacks of eager-to-please speculation by Padilla, for Che was never anything but respectful of Fidel outside conversations with his closest friends.

But evidently something *did* happen during Fidel's trip abroad to cause Che to lose patience with the pace of events. According to one report, Che gathered his group of young bodyguards and told them: "*Yo sigo viaje*" ("I'm off"). Their assumption, in view of all the rumors, was that he was planning to lead an imminent guerrilla expedition against Trujillo in the Dominican Republic. If this was a possibility being considered by Che, he had a change of heart. To judge from the events that followed, his decision to stay was due to a clear signal from Fidel that he was ready to accelerate moves to build a socialist society in Cuba.

Fidel's days of temporizing were coming to an end. At the economic conference in Buenos Aires, he made new headlines and disturbed his Latin American colleagues by calling on Washington to finance a "MacArthur-style Plan" to right Latin America's economic and social ills. The price tag he came up with was $30 billion in development aid over the next decade. The United States had no intention of supporting such a scheme, and the Latin American ministers quickly fell into line with Washington. Ironically, a version of Fidel's idea would be launched two years later by a new U.S. president, John F. Kennedy: a $20 billion program called the "Alliance for Progress." Kennedy's plan, of course, was intended to prevent more Cuban-style revolutions in the hemisphere.

Within days of his return to Havana on May 7, Fidel signed the agrarian reform bill into law, and INRA became a reality. The agriculture minister, Humberto Sorí-Marín, who had been sidelined throughout the discussions of reforms, promptly resigned. Next, Fidel officially confirmed

Che's status as a *comandante* of the Revolutionary Armed Forces before dispatching him on an extended "goodwill" tour abroad. Officially, Che's mission was to increase diplomatic and commercial ties for Cuba with emerging industrial nations such as Japan and with the new nonaligned states of Africa, Asia, and Europe—most important, India, Egypt, and Yugoslavia. Unofficially, of course, Che's temporary removal from Havana helped Fidel create the impression that he was, as he had hinted in the United States, "casting off" the Argentine Communist whom the Americans and his own July 26 aides found so troublesome.

Che's trip had been on the drawing board for some time. Alfredo Menéndez first learned of Che's interest in the so-called "third-position countries" or "Bandung Pact" states—the core of the future nonaligned movement—during their collaboration on the agrarian reform law at Cojímar, when Che had asked for an economic analysis of Egypt, India, Indonesia, and Japan. "He wanted to know what commercial relations existed between Cuba and these countries, what did we import, what we exported, and what possibilities we had to increase our trade with those countries."

Menéndez finished the study and gave it to Che, but he learned about the trip only when he was introduced to Fidel as "our sugar man" on the

Che and Aleida March were married on June 2, 1959, at the La Cabaña home of his bodyguard, Alberto Castellanos. From Left, Raúl Castro, Vílma Espín, Che, Aleida, and Castellanos.

Che and Aldeida on their wedding day, with Harry "Pombo" Villegas and his wife, Cristina.

day of the signing of the agrarian reform law. With characteristic panache Fidel had made the entire cabinet travel to his old guerrilla base at La Plata for the ceremony. After asking Menéndez a few questions, Fidel suddenly said: "Get yourself ready—you're going on a trip with Che." The purpose of their mission was described to Menéndez when he returned to Havana. "Things had begun to chill [with the United States], the American pressure was getting greater and Cuba wanted to open up breathing space," he recalled. "The strategy of the revolution was to open relations with the greatest possible number of countries. That was the objective of the trip. It had a political and an economic objective, that is to say, to not let the revolution become isolated. This was a constant of Che's. . . . He always told me that Arbenz fell because he had allowed himself to become isolated, and that the [Cuban] revolution had to go out fighting in the international arena."

Before leaving, Che put his house in order. On May 22, he obtained a divorce from Hilda. On June 2, in a small civil ceremony, he and Aleida were married. There was a party at the La Cabaña home of his most rambunctious bodyguard, Alberto Castellanos. Efigenio Ameijeiras, the new police chief of Havana, was there, and so were Harry Villegas, Celia Sánchez, and Raúl and his new wife, Vilma Espín. Camilo barged in with good-natured shouts, brandishing bottles of rum. Aleida looked pretty in a new white dress, while Che wore, as always, his olive green uniform and black beret.

T wo weeks earlier, he had written to his old friend Julio "El Gaucho" Castro in Buenos Aires, inviting him to come to Cuba:

> *Gaucho,*
> This experience of ours is really worth taking a couple of bullets for. [If you *do* come,] don't think of returning, the revolution won't wait. A strong hug from the one who is called and whom history will call. . . .
>
> *Che.*

21

My Historic Duty

I

On June 12, 1959, Che flew to Madrid en route to Cairo. Fidel had urged him to take Aleida along and make it a honeymoon, but he left her behind. According to Aleida, this was because of his insistence on the need for revolutionary leaders to show austerity in their personal lives. "That was how he was," she said.

Che's new assignment was perceived by his men in La Cabaña as a *tronazo,* or demotion, especially since it came on the heels of Fidel's order to halt the firing squads. "We were really upset when we heard he was going away," Orlando Borrego recalled. "We had the impression that they had stripped him as commander of the regiment." Borrego and a few others went to see Camilo Cienfuegos to complain, but Cienfuegos was unsympathetic. He said that they were soldiers and had to obey orders, and that Che would not approve of their behavior. Chastised but unmollified, they returned to La Cabaña. Then, apparently confirming their worst fears, they were told that the La Cabaña regiment was to be demobilized and sent to Las Villas. "It was like the house falling down," Borrego said.

Che's "delegation" on his trip was both tiny and eclectic. With him were his adolescent bodyguard, Lieutenant José Argudín; his PSP aide, "Pancho" García Vals; the sugar economist Alfredo Menéndez; and a Rebel Army captain, Omar Fernández. Fifty-year-old Dr. Salvador Vilaseca, a mathematics professor from Havana University who was now on the executive board of Cuba's National Agricultural Development Bank (Banfaic), was the oldest member of the group. Their main destinations were Egypt, India, Indonesia, and Ceylon—the key Bandung Pact states with which Cuba wanted to establish diplomatic relations and, most important, trade ties. Japan, an important sugar importer and a heavily industrialized country, was also a

high priority on the itinerary, as was Yugoslavia. The agricultural reform
bill would be issued soon, and both Fidel and Che knew it was going to cause
a heavy fallout with Cuba's landowners and the Americans; alternative
markets had to be found for Cuba's sugar.

A few weeks into the trip, at Fidel's insistence, José Pardo Llada, a
right-wing political pundit and radio commentator, joined the group. Fidel's
decision to add Pardo Llada to Che's traveling caravan was curious. He had
met Che only once before, in January, when he went to La Cabaña to inquire about the fate of Ernesto De la Fé, Batista's former information minister and a personal friend. Che had told Pardo Llada flatly that there was
nothing he could do for him; the case of De la Fé was in the hands of the
revolutionary tribunals, and there was plenty of evidence against him. According to Pardo Llada, Che told him, "To be frank, if it were up to me, I'd
have him shot tomorrrow." De la Fé's case had dragged on and become
something of an issue in the Cuban media. Che had been questioned about
it during his TV appearance on April 28, and had used the occasion to damn
De la Fé further, pointing out that when arrested the former minister had
in his possession copies of files compiled by BRAC, the notorious anticommunist police bureau created by the CIA. Orlando Borrego said that Che's
inability to "conclude" the De la Fé case was one of the things that had most
frustrated him when Fidel ordered an end to the revolutionary tribunals.

Pardo Llada himself told Fidel he saw little reason why he should go
off on a trade mission. He was a journalist and he knew nothing about commerce. "Che doesn't know anything about it, either," Fidel replied. "It's all
a matter of common sense. What do you think I know about governing?"
Pardo Llada's inclusion in Che's entourage fit the pattern set by Fidel on
his trip to the United States, when he had surrounded himself with a "bourgeois right wing." It could do no harm to have an influential anticommunist along with Che to convey the impression that the mission was tame.

Fidel had another motive as well. Pardo Llado was bright, well respected
both as a journalist and as a former opposition politician, and his daily radio
program commanded a huge audience in Cuba; in other words, in the inevitable break that was coming, Pardo Llada was going to be a problem, and it
behooved Fidel to find a place where he would not be a threat. Pardo Llada
suspected that both he and Che were being put out to pasture, and he said as
much to Che, who did little to disabuse him of the notion. But it was Pardo,
not Che, whom Fidel hoped to tempt into exile. He joined the group in New
Delhi, and on his second day there, Che sounded out the idea—proposed, he
said, by Fidel—of Pardo's staying on in India as ambassador. Pardo flatly
refused to even consider the offer, and Che dropped the subject.

Pardo Llada traveled grudgingly with Che's mission for several weeks, through the visits to Indonesia and Japan, and as far as he could see, there were no benefits being gained. No Cuban sugar had been sold, nothing had been purchased. In early August, as the delegation turned westward, heading for Ceylon and on to Yugoslavia, Pardo Llada decided he'd had enough and told Che he was going home. "Might it not be that you don't want to compromise yourself by visiting a Communist country like Yugoslavia?" Che asked. Pardo denied the suggestion and repeated his suspicion that Fidel had sent them both on a kind of exiles' walking tour. Che was an army officer and had no choice but to follow orders; *he* was a private citizen and free to make his own decisions, and his decision was to quit.

Pardo Llada left the group in Singapore, agreeing to hand-deliver letters Che had written to Aleida and Fidel. He dropped Aleida's letter off at the Guevara's home in the countryside outside Havana, then went to Fidel's office in the new INRA building. Fidel asked a few questions about the trip and Che's health, then opened Che's two-page letter and read it slowly. When he had finished, he wordlessly handed Pardo one of the pages, pointing with his finger to a paragraph. Pardo Llada read it, and then reread it in order to memorize Che's words.

> Fidel,
> ... I'm taking advantage of the quick and unexpected return of your friend Pardito to send you this. Speaking of Pardo, as you'll see he didn't want to accept the Embassy [post] in India. And now it seems he isn't eager to follow us to Yugoslavia. He must have his motives. I have argued a lot during these two months with him, and I can assure you that Pardito isn't one of us. . . .

Pardo thought that Fidel showed a "perverse satisfaction" in letting him read the passage. When he handed back the letter, Fidel's only comment was, "So. It seems like Che isn't very fond of you."

Pardo Llada would meet Che several more times, and he would have to intervene for another friend in trouble with the revolution. But that problem—and Pardo Llada's own crisis—lay ahead, and for now he resumed his activities as a radio commentator, increasingly worried about Cuba's political direction. Che's "commercial mission," meanwhile, continued its apparently fruitless perambulations across Asia and North Africa to Europe.

II

Despite its apparent aimlessness, Che's trip had an important subtext. Fidel wanted to sell sugar to the Soviets as a prelude to establishing trade relations with Moscow and the Communist bloc. In and of itself, such a trade deal shouldn't have raised eyebrows. The U.S.S.R. had been a traditional, if minor, purchaser of Cuban sugar, averaging 500,000 tons annually even after Batista had severed relations with the Soviets in 1952. But, according to Alfredo Menéndez, the PSP sugar expert who traveled with Che, the last sugar sale to Moscow, in 1956, had been permitted only after Washington gave the go-ahead. If that was true, it underscored the cruel reality of Cuba's role as a virtual economic vassal state to the North Americans. Since the United States was the world's largest sugar consumer, it had enormous leverage over not just the Cuban economy but its politics and foreign policy as well. Given U.S. suspicions about the political direction of the Cuban revolution, it was important to keep any negotiations with the Soviets as discreet as possible.

Menéndez was to be the point man in negotiations that he hoped would fulfill what he called "an old aspiration of the Popular Socialist Party," to break free of Cuba's dependency on the United States once and for all. "In 1959," he said, "Cuba had the capacity to produce 7 million tons of sugar. The U.S. bought a little under 3 million tons, although it had the capacity to buy more. . . . And so we wanted to change the market. The first objective, that of selling sugar to the Soviet Union, was with a view to expanding our markets. Not only with the Soviet Union, but with the rest of the socialist countries. It was a strategy."

To pursue that strategy, Fidel first cleverly covered his bases. On June 13, the day after Che's mission left Havana, Fidel called on the United States to increase the quota for imports of Cuban sugar from 3 million to 8 million tons. The offer to buy *all* of Cuba's sugar was immediately turned down, as Fidel no doubt anticipated, but it put the rest of the world on notice that Cuba was looking for customers. (And indeed, a year later, when Nikita Khrushchev agreed to buy almost all of Cuba's sugar at above world prices, Fidel could maintain he had offered it first to the Yankees.)

Che's initial contacts with the Soviets were made in Cairo, before Pardo Llada joined the group. Che was in charge of making the approach to sell the sugar, while Menéndez handled the details. Those details were hammered out in secret over the next month of travel, with Menéndez making two trips back to Havana to consult with Fidel. By late July, the Soviets had agreed to buy 500,000 tons of Cuban sugar, to be negotiated at a neutral site— London, where the Soviets had a big trade mission and the deal could be done under the auspices of an international sugar brokerage firm. By doing it in London, Menéndez explained, "it could go through without being noticed and we didn't give it any political connotation."

While the sugar sale itself later became public, the complex prior negotiations between Che and the Soviets never appeared in the official chronology of Che's 1959 "goodwill mission." The reason for the omission is fairly obvious. The sugar negotiations were an important first step in the secret talks leading up to Cuba's alliance with the Soviet Union and are very much at odds with official Cuban history, which maintains that the Castro regime was pushed into the Soviet camp because of the United States' hostility and aggression.

The visa of Alexandr Alexiev, the KGB man who had been cooling his heels in Moscow since January, was now suddenly approved. "The Cubans put 'TASS correspondent' in my passport," Alexiev said. "They told me they had done it because they were still afraid to invite an official of the Soviet Union." Alexiev left for Cuba in September, taking a circuitous route via Italy and Venezuela, and finally arriving in Havana on October 1. The tempo of the delicate dance between the Cubans and Soviets would now pick up.

III

Che had returned to Cuba only three weeks earlier. His trip had lasted almost three months and taken him to fourteen countries. He had met and conversed with heads of state—Gamal Abdel Nasser in Egypt, Sukarno in Indonesia, Tito in Yugoslavia, and Jawaharlal Nehru in India. He had been cheered by crowds in Gaza and Pakistan, toured factories and cooperative farms, and witnessed for himself the conditions of life in a part of the world where the old colonial empires were disintegrating. His mission, he told the press, had been a success, for he had seen for himself that the Cuban revolution was respected and admired by people around the world. Diplomatic and trade relations had been established with a number of countries, and he was confident that Cubans would soon see their benefits.

Che followed up his public statements with a series of short, informative articles published in *Verde Olivo*. Occasional traces of irony and lyricism filter through, but for the most part Che's travel accounts are dry. His companions, however, had florid tales to tell of their iconoclastic *jefe*, most of them featuring his disrespect for protocol. Some of the memorable vignettes were later written up by Pardo Llada.

In New Delhi, Che's meeting with his old hero Nehru took place over a sumptuous luncheon at the government palace. As Pardo retold it, Che was on his best behavior, wearing a gabardine dress uniform for the occasion instead of his usual olive green fatigues. He quipped irreverently to his companions as he entered the palace, "I think I'm pretty elegant—enough, anyway, to dine with the gentleman Prime Minister of the most underdeveloped country on Earth."

Nehru, his daughter Indira, and her young sons, Sanjay and Rajiv, were all in attendance. Che smiled politely while the venerable Indian prime minister described each exotic dish being served. The banquet went on in this banal fashion for more than two hours, and finally Che could stand it no longer. "Mr. Prime Minister," he said, "what is your opinion of Communist China?" Nehru looked at him absently and replied, "Mr. Comandante, have you tasted one of these delicious apples?" "Mr. Prime Minister: Have you read Mao Tse-tung?" "Ah, Mr. Comandante, how pleased I am that you have liked the apples."

Che later wrote that Nehru displayed "the amiable familiarity of a patriarchal grandfather" and "a noble interest in the struggles and vicissitudes of the Cuban people," but, in fact, Che felt that there was little to be learned from the founding fathers of modern India. The Nehru government was unwilling to embark on a radical agrarian reform program or to break the powers of the religious and feudal institutions that Che felt kept India's people mired in poverty.

In Djakarta, Che fell in with a congenial compatriot, the Argentine ambassador, who regaled him with stories about Sukarno's sybaritic lifestyle: how he lived like a monarch and maintained a harem of women of different nationalities. His current favorite, Che was told, was a Russian woman, a "gift" from Nikita Khrushchev. When Che went to Sukarno's palace for a meeting, the Argentine envoy went along as his interpreter. Sukarno insisted on showing off his private collection of paintings, and the tour went on and on. Pardo could tell that Che was getting restless. Finally, Che broke his silence: "Well, Mr. Sukarno, in this entire tour we still haven't seen the little Russian girl, who they say is the best thing in your collection." Fortunately, Sukarno didn't understand Spanish. The Argentine ambassador nearly fainted with shock and disbelief, but recovered in time to invent a question about the Indonesian economy.

Alfredo Menéndez recalled Che's reaction when he was told by the Cuban ambassador in Tokyo that he was expected to go the next day to lay a wreath at Japan's Tomb of the Unknown Soldier, commemorating the men lost in World War II. Che reacted violently. "No way I'll go! That was an imperialist army that killed millions of Asians. . . . Where I will go is to Hiroshima, where the Americans killed 100,000 Japanese." The diplomat spluttered and told him it was impossible, that it had already been arranged with the Japanese chancellor. Che was adamant. "It's your problem, not mine," he said. "You made the arrangements without my authorization, and now you can go and undo it!"

Japan was one of the most important stops. Che spent much of his time there touring the factories of electronics companies such as Mitsubishi and Toshiba. The Japanese bought a million tons of sugar on the world market, a third of it from Cuba, and Che hoped to raise the Cuban share. His idea was to propose that the Japanese could pay for anything over their present quota in yen; the money would remain in Japan and be spent by Cuba on Japanese products. Che asked for a meeting to be arranged with the Japanese foreign trade minister. "Che made the proposal," Menéndez recalled, "but the man said he couldn't agree to it, that their economy was open; they would continue to buy sugar, but without any obligations. 'You're under pressure from the fair-haired Northerners, aren't you?' Che said. And the Japanese said: 'It's true,' at which Che told him there was no problem. He understood."

Che's personal security was a matter of concern to his companions. Before leaving Havana, Carlos Rafael Rodríguez, the PSP leader, had told Alfredo Menéndez that he was worried because Che was not taking many bodyguards; the only military men going along were José Argudín and Omar Fernández, and they were traveling unarmed. "We don't have any intelligence that there are plans to shoot him," Rodríguez said, "but you guys with him should take precautions. Don't leave him alone for a minute. And pick up some weapons in Europe on your way."

Menéndez bought two Colt pistols in Madrid. Argudín, who never strayed from Che's side, carried the pistols throughout the trip—no difficulty in those pre-hijacking days—and as an additional security measure, one of the men, usually Pancho García Vals, always shared Che's bedroom. The arrangements worked well enough until Che and Dr. Vilaseca were invited to a diplomatic reception in Tokyo that Argudín could not attend. The venerable professor was pressed into duty. Both pistols were stuck into his belt under his formal jacket.

Che's companions found his austerity at times stifling. In Osaka, Pardo recalled, they were invited by the Cuban consul to make a nocturnal visit to a famous cabaret, the Metropole, which was said to employ 600 women. Che said he was not interested, and he ordered the uniformed men to stay behind. Only the civilians—Pardo and Vilaseca—could go, if they wanted, and risk "having a *Time* photographer take their picture and create a scandal, showing how the members of the Cuban delegation spend the people's money partying and getting drunk with whores."

Another evening, Che found that part of his entourage had vanished. When asked where the men were, Menéndez told Che he didn't know.

"They're out whoring, aren't they?" Che said. Menéndez insisted he really didn't know, and Che seemed to relent. "I know what it's like to *putear*," he said. "I whored round in my youth, too."

Occasionally, Che loosened up in a more public fashion. He drank a lot of sake in a traditional Japanese geisha house and even went so far as to playfully mimic the geishas' dance steps. In the living room of the Chilean ambassador's residence in Delhi, he surprised his host by abruptly standing on his head to demonstrate his knowledge of yoga. But the pressure of having to maintain a rigid public posture gradually wore him down. During a flight over India, Che wrote to his mother about his frustration with the official straitjacket.

> Dear *vieja:*
>
> My old dream to visit these countries takes place now in a way that inhibits all my happiness. Speaking of political and economic problems, giving parties where the only thing missing is for me to put on a tuxedo, and putting aside my purest pleasures, which would be to go and dream in the shade of a pyramid or over Tutankhamen's sarcophagus. On top of that, I am without Aleida whom I couldn't bring because of one of those complicated mental complexes I have.
>
> Egypt was a diplomatic success of the first magnitude; the embassies of all the countries of the world came to the farewell reception we gave and I saw firsthand how complicated diplomacy can be when the Papal Nuncio shook hands with the Russian attaché with a smile that was really beatific.
>
> Now India, where new protocolar complications produce in me the same infantile panic [in deciding how to respond to greetings].

Then, as always with his mother, he became introspective.

> Something which has really developed in me is the sense of the collective in counterposition to the personal; I am still the same loner that I used to be, looking for my path without personal help, but now I have a sense of my historic duty. I have no home, no woman, no children, nor parents, nor brothers and sisters, my friends are my friends as long as they think politically like I do and yet I am content, I feel something in life, not just a powerful internal strength, which I always felt, but also the

power to influence others, and an absolutely fatalistic sense of my mission, which strips me of all fear.

No one has ever defined the essence of what made Che Guevara unique better than he did himself in this rare, private moment of truth. But then, as usual, he defensively pulled back from his reverie.

I don't know why I am writing you this, maybe it is merely longing for Aleida. Take it as it is, a letter written one stormy night in the skies of India, far from my fatherland and loved ones.

A hug for everyone, Ernesto.

Che may have longed for Aleida, but he resisted his desire to be with her. His tendency toward self-denial baffled and intrigued Fidel, who kept trying to moderate it. Aleida recalled that while Che was in Japan, Fidel summoned her to his office. He had arranged a long-distance telephone call with Che, and he suggested again that Aleida join him. Che refused again. Fidel tried later, when Che was in Morocco, to no avail.

One night in Tokyo, Che and the others gathered in a hotel room to talk, tell stories, and philosophize. According to Alfredo Menéndez, Che veered the conversation onto an odd topic, the significance of which Menéndez realized only much later. "Che started talking about his projects, but I never associated it with a real plan. He said: 'There's an *altiplano* in South America—in Bolivia, in Paraguay, an area bordering Brazil, Uruguay, Peru, and Argentina—where, if we inserted a guerrilla force, we could spread the revolution all over South America."

IV

A great many changes had occurred in Cuba in Che's absence. Fidel now had more political power, but the atmosphere was tenser and more polarized than ever. The agrarian reform law had begun to have heavy repercussions. The first seizures of land had been made, and the government was hedging on compensation, offering low-interest "bonds" to affected landowners instead of ready cash. The United States had issued a note of warning—so far left unanswered by Fidel—that it expected all American landowners to be compensated promptly. The wealthy cattlemen of Camagüey who were affected mounted a campaign against the land interventions, and the province's popular military commander, Huber Matos, joined them. He denounced the Communist encroachment in the armed

forces and INRA. Matos was emerging as the chief spokesman for the July 26
Movement's anticommunist wing as the dispute with the ascendant PSP
became increasingly acrimonious.

Following the resignation of the agriculture minister, Sorí-Marín,
Fidel had continued to clean house. Political moderates in the cabinet had
been getting the shove, and loyal Fidelistas were taking their places. Even
Fidel's old friend Luis Orlando Rodríguez, who had helped found Radio
Rebelde in the Sierra Maestra, was dropped as interior minister. Foreign
Minister Roberto Agramonte was fired and replaced by Raúl Roa, the OAS
ambassador and former dean of Havana University's Social Sciences Faculty. The sphinxlike Roa had broken with the Party in his youth, but now
he became both an unswerving Fidelista and a brilliant diplomat.

In mid-June, a Cuban-Dominican guerrilla expedition of some 200
fighters led by Delio Gómez Ochoa, a former July 26 commander, had
landed in the Dominican Republic. The group was wiped out by Trujillo's
forces. Many of the rebels were killed or imprisoned, and the survivors became fugitives. They were pursued by an anti-Castro army calling itself the
Anticommunist Legion of the Caribbean. This army, which was composed
of 350-odd fighters—150 Spaniards, 100 Cubans, and an array of right-wing
foreign mercenaries, including Croatians, Germans, and Greeks—had been
trained at a Dominican air force base. Among the Cubans in the legion were
Che's old antagonist Ángel Sánchez Mosquera, former police officials from
Havana, and Batista's personal pilot. Trujillo had offered to pay farmers a
bounty of $1,000 per head for each rebel caught, and soon peasants, taking
the generalissimo quite literally, began appearing at Dominican army posts
with burlap bags containing decapitated bearded heads and claiming the
reward. The anticommunist legionnaires complained jokingly that the peasants, who eventually turned in more heads than there had been invaders,
were not leaving them any Cubans to fight against.

Two weeks after the fiasco of the rebel incursion in the Dominican
Republic, Fidel's air force chief, Pedro Luis Díaz Lanz, defected. On July
14, he appeared before a Senate committee in Washington and denounced
Communist infiltration of the Cuban armed forces. President Urrutia appeared on television to rebut Díaz Lanz's charges and, in an obvious bid to
get Fidel to declare himself, stated his own firm opposition to Communism.

Fidel dealt an unexpected counterblow, denouncing Urrutia for attempting to break "revolutionary unity" and insinuating that Urrutia was
in league with the traitor Díaz Lanz. Then, as thousands of Fidelistas were
trucked into Havana to celebrate July 26, Fidel resigned as prime minister
and let the crowds do their work. The popular clamor for his reinstatement
grew. Belatedly realizing that he had created a trap for himself, Urrutia

resigned and sought asylum in the Venezuelan embassy. On July 26, Fidel reappeared in front of the crowds and assented to "the people's demand" that he resume his duties as prime minister. In place of the recalcitrant Urrutia, Fidel named Osvaldo Dorticós, his docile revolutionary laws minister, as the new Cuban president.

"Counterrevolution" became a catchphrase for the activities of those who, like Urrutia, had sought to "sabotage" revolutionary "unity." In fact, the first threats of counterrevolutionary activity *had* begun to appear. In addition to the force being trained in the Dominican Republic, exile groups were openly organizing paramilitary forces in Miami. After several bombs exploded and an assassination plot was uncovered in Havana, Fidel pushed through a constitutional amendment making counterrevolution a crime subject to the death penalty.

In August, Trujillo's Anticommunist Legion was finally mobilized for an invasion of Cuba, but Fidel had prepared a surprise for them. He orchestrated a ruse with the complicity of the former Second Front commanders Eloy Gutiérrez Menoyo and the American William Morgan, who tricked Trujillo into believing they were ready to lead an anti-Castro uprising (before too long, they would be doing precisely that, but for now they were cooperating with Fidel). Gutiérrez Menoyo and Morgan radioed the Dominican Republic to say their forces had seized the Cuban city of Trinidad, which was the signal for the Anticommunist Legion to invade. When their transport plane, flown by Batista's pilot, touched down in the countryside near Trinidad, Fidel and his soldiers were ready and waiting.

Quite a few of the anti-Castro legion's fighters had been left behind in the Dominican Republic, including one who would later have a profound effect on events in Latin America: an eighteen-year-old military cadet named Felix Rodríguez. Rodríguez's uncle had been Batista's minister of public works, and when Castro seized power his whole family fled into exile. Embittered by their misfortune, Rodríguez had left his military school in Perkiomen, Pennsylvania, and joined Trujillo's legion. He felt intense frustration about the defeat of his comrades, and when he returned to Perkiomen to finish his studies, he resolved to dedicate himself to destroying the Cuban revolution. Most of his attempts were to prove unsuccessful, but in the course of his career he would deal some heavy blows.

V

By the end of September 1959, Fidel faced a showdown with Huber Matos, the military commander in Camagüey, who was making no secret of his disaffection with the radically leftward turn of the revolution. Matos had urged Fidel to call a meeting of the July 26 National Directorate to discuss "Communist infiltration" in the army and INRA. Situated as he was in the wealthy, conservative Cuban heartland, Matos posed a real threat.

When Alexandr Alexiev arrived in Havana on October 1, he was met by reporters from the Communist daily, *Hoy,* and taken to the inexpensive, low-profile Hotel Sevilla in Old Havana. The next day, he met with two PSP officials—Carlos Rafael Rodríguez and Raúl Valdés Vivo, who briefed him on the volatile political situation. They offered to introduce him to Blas Roca and other Politburo members, but he declined; instead, Alexiev called Violeta Casals.

Casals was a well-known actress, a Communist, and a loyal Fidelista, having worked as one of Radio Rebelde's announcers in the Sierra Maestra. Alexiev had met her in Moscow during the summer, and he asked for her help in contacting Che. Casals agreed to arrange the meeting. While he waited, Alexiev lay low, sending off a few TASS dispatches for appearances' sake.

Che was now working in an unfinished fourteen-story building that had been erected by Batista to house Havana's future municipal headquarters. It overlooked the large civic square dominated by a huge white obelisk and statue of José Martí that had been renamed the Plaza de la Revolución. He was there to start up the Industrialization Department of INRA. Fidel was the president of INRA. Nuñez Jiménez was executive director. From these offices the *true* Cuban revolution was being launched. The official announcement of Che's new post would not come until October 8, but rumors had already begun to spread and were duly picked up by the American embassy. In a September 16 dispatch to Washington, the embassy had reported: "Rumors are circulating that he [Che] is slated for an important position in the government. Most frequently mentioned are the directorship of an industrial development institute or the Minister of Commerce."

In late September, Che had traveled to Santa Clara to see his old La Cabaña regiment. He gathered his officers at Víctor Bordón's home and told them of his new responsibilities; it was not what they had expected or hoped to hear. Orlando Borrego sat in the front row. "Che told us that Fidel and the revolutionary leadership had decided to create an Industrialization Department to develop the country. He explained to us the importance of this for the economy, and that he had been named to lead the development. This surprised us because we thought Che would once again take charge of the regiment. . . . That he was going to the civil sector was a real blow."

It sounded to Borrego as if all the rumors he had been hearing for months about Che's demotion were true. "It seemed to us that Che, who had been commander of La Cabaña, the chief of a regiment, was more important than this job he was telling us about. . . . But he explained it to us with enthusiasm; he said it was a really wonderful job that he wanted to do."

Suddenly, Che addressed him directly: "Borrego, do you want to come and work with me on this project?" Borrego replied that he was a soldier, and would do whatever Che asked of him. Looking pleased, Che told him, "Good, be at my house in Havana first thing in the morning."

The next morning, he and Che toured the INRA building's eighth floor. Nuñez Jiménez had already installed his offices on the fourth floor, and Fidel, as INRA's president, was at the top, on the fourteenth floor. So far, the vaunted Industrialization Department was only Che, his twenty-one-year-old accountant, Orlando Borrego, and the bare concrete walls. "Well," said Che, looking around, "the first thing we have to do is finish the construction. . . . Then, I want you to take over the administration of the department."

Fidel's choice of Che for the industry job was actually not so surprising. In the Sierra Maestra, Che had been the leading proponent of self-sufficient industries, beginning with his modest bread ovens, shoe repair shops, and rustic bomb factories in El Hombrito and La Mesa. Now he wanted to extrapolate the lessons of the guerrilla experience to Cuba as a whole and, if possible, throughout Latin America. Since the rebels' victory, he had been steadily advocating the industrialization of the country and, with it, the mass militarization of its society. He expected the Americans to invade, and if that happened, the entire Cuban population would have to leave the cities and fight as a guerrilla army. Even if it didn't happen, industrialization would end Cuba's dependency on agricultural exports that were controlled by the capitalist markets, and in particular by the meddlesome United States.

When Fidel made Che's INRA appointment official, he also announced that Che would be retaining his military rank and responsibilities. Orlando Borrego said that Che was excited about his new post, but there are reports that Che had hoped Fidel would appoint him to the job that went to his brother Raúl: minister of the Revolutionary Armed Forces. If Che was disappointed, he concealed his feelings.

Che's hopes that Cuba's support for armed revolution elsewhere in the hemisphere would bring early results were taking a beating. Not only had the expedition to the Dominican Republic been crushed, but the Nicaraguan force he had sponsored had also failed the test miserably. This group of fifty-four Cubans and Nicaraguans, led by Rafael Somarriba, the former Nicaraguan National Guard officer handpicked by Che, included Rodolfo Romero. Beginning in early June, the group's members had begun leaving Cuba, traveling separately to Honduras, where they linked up on a farm near the Nicaraguan border. The night of June 12–13—while Che was traveling to Spain, on the first leg of his diplomatic trip abroad, Che's personal pilot, Eliseo de la Campa, had flown in a planeload of weapons for them. Three weeks later they struck out for the border, but there must have been a *chivatazo,* for they were ambushed by a joint Honduran-Nicaraguan military force. Nine of the expeditionaries, including a Cuban, had been killed. Carlos Fonseca, the anti-Somoza intellectual leader, who had joined the group in Honduras, was badly wounded. The survivors were rounded up and put into a Honduran prison. Within a few weeks, however, they were released. According to Romero, this was because the Honduran president, Ramón Villeda Morales, was an admirer of Che, and his security chief, whose wife was Nicaraguan, was himself a fervent *antisomocista*. Romero went back to Havana.

Shortly after he returned from his long foreign mission, Che summoned Romero for a private meeting. "He was really angry," Romero recalled. "Especially when I told him how they had fucked us." Romero blamed the fiasco on the "stupidity" of Somarriba, who had led them into a ravine where they were easily attacked. "The truth is all these career military guys are shit," Che commented. He asked Romero to draw diagrams of the ambush site to show him exactly what had happened. "You're only alive by a miracle," he said.

Romero's subsequent contacts with Che were sporadic. It was decided that the Nicaraguans needed more training and field experience before they attempted another guerrilla expedition, and Romero and his comrades were subsumed into the new military counterintelligence apparatus run by Ramiro Valdés and his deputy, "Barbarroja," the red-bearded Manuel Piñeiro Losada. Given the early setbacks, it was clear that Cuba's guerrilla-support program would have to be operated in a more structured fashion.

For now, Che got on with the INRA job. First, his office was built, with spaces for Aleida and for his private secretary, José Manresa. Then an office was built for Borrego, who still didn't have a clue what he was to be doing. Their ranks were bolstered by César Rodríguez, an engineeer, and the PSP official Pancho García Vals. The Industrialization Department became a formal reality, but not even Che had a grasp of exactly how to proceed.

Che hadn't been in his new office many days when Violeta Casals called him. A TASS correspondent was in town, she explained, and wished to meet him. Che agreed to receive the Soviet "journalist," and Alexandr Alexiev was told to be at Che's office at two o'clock in the morning on October 13. Arriving at the appointed hour, he found the office dark except for two lamps, one on Che's desk and one on a nearby desk where a pretty blond woman worked in silence.

"We started to talk," Alexiev recalled. "He was very happy when he heard I had been in Argentina just a few months before. Since I knew he was Red, I talked openly, because I could see *he* was very open. . . . I had a carton of cigarettes that I had brought from Argentina, and I gave him three or four packets. They were called Tejas [for "Texas"]. I said: 'Che, I'd like to give you something that will bring back memories.' Error! He was furious. 'What are you giving me?' he said. 'Tejas, do you know what that is? It's the half of Mexico that the Yankee bandits robbed!'" Che was so angry, Alexiev said, that he didn't know what to do. "I said, 'Che, I'm sorry for giving you such a strange gift, but I'm pleased that now I know how you feel about the common enemy.' And we laughed together."

After that initial "delicate" moment had passed, Alexiev said, their conversation continued amiably, and quite soon they began using the informal *tú* to address each other. Che called him Alejandro, and he no longer addressed his host as *comandante,* but called him Che.

Noticing the late hour and that the woman he assumed was Che's secretary was still working, Alexiev joked: "'Che, you are such a fighter against exploitation, but I see that you exploit your secretary.' He said: 'Ah yes! It's true, but she's not just my secretary, she's my wife as well.'" It was Aleida.

Their talk went until almost dawn, and toward the end Che told Alexiev, "Our revolution is truly progressive, anti-imperialistic and anti-American, made by the people. . . . But we cannot conquer and maintain it without the aid of the global revolutionary movement, and above all, from the socialist bloc and the Soviet Union." Che emphasized to Alexiev that this was *his own* personal viewpoint.

Alexiev said that he was eager to learn what the other revolutionary leaders thought; could Che arrange a meeting with Fidel? "The problem is that Fidel doesn't like to talk to journalists," Che said. Alexiev assured him that a talk with Fidel would not be for the press, and three days later, on the afternoon of October 16, he received a telephone call at his room in the Hotel Sevilla. "Mr. Alejandro Alexiev," a voice said, "what are you doing at this moment?" "Nothing," he replied. "Good. You asked for an interview with Comandante Fidel Castro. If you are available, he will see you right now; we are coming to pick you up."

Alexiev got ready as quickly as he could. "I put on a dark suit, white shirt, gray tie, to present a diplomatic image." He took some Soviet vodka and caviar he had brought as gifts for the occasion and went down to await his escorts. Two bearded boys with machine guns approached him in the foyer and took him to the same INRA building where he had met with Che, but this time he took the elevator to the top floor. When he stepped out, two more bearded men in uniform were waiting for him: Fidel Castro and Nuñez Jiménez. They ushered him into Fidel's office, where they sat around a large round wooden table and began to talk. After a few minutes of polite chitchat, Fidel asked what was in the package he had brought. Alexiev pulled out the caviar and vodka and Fidel suggested they sample them. Moments later, as they sat drinking the vodka and eating the caviar with biscuits, Fidel, obviously enjoying himself, turned to Nuñez Jiménez and, as if the idea had just occurred to him, said, "The Soviet merchandise is great, isn't it? I never tried it before. It seems to me it would be worthwhile reestablishing commercial relations with the Soviet Union."

Alexiev immediately said: "Very well, Fidel—it is as good as done. But I am also interested in cultural relations and, even more importantly, diplomatic relations." According to Alexiev, Fidel quickly responded: "No, I don't think so, not *yet*. Formalities aren't important; I'm against formalisms. You have arrived, you're an emissary of the Kremlin, and we can say that we now have relations. But we can't tell this yet to the [Cuban] people. The people aren't ready, they have been poisoned by the bourgeois American propaganda to be against Communism."

Fidel cited Lenin on the revolutionary strategy of "preparing the masses"—telling Alexiev he was going to heed the dictum; he would eradicate the anticommunist press campaign and, gradually, the people's prejudices, but he needed time. Until then, Alexiev had harbored a skeptical view of Fidel, but the evidence that he had read Lenin ("not too deep but pretty good") impressed him. Still, he was a bit suspicious. He stared pointedly at the gold medallion of the Virgen del Cobre, Cuba's Catholic patron saint, hanging prominently on Fidel's chest. "Alejandro," Fidel said. "Don't pay it any mind. My mother sent it to me when I was in the sierra."

Alexiev understood that there was more to it than that. There was a strong Catholic movement in Cuba, and it did Fidel little harm to keep up appearances by wearing a medallion on his chest.

Despite himself, Alexiev found himself warming to Fidel and pointed out that they had several things in common. His first name, in Spanish, was the same as Fidel's second name—Alejandro. They were also joined by the number thirteen. Fidel was born on August 13, and Alexiev was thirteen years older than he. In addition, Alexiev was born on August 1, so their birthdays were thirteen days apart. Fidel, known for his fascination with numerology, was delighted by Alexiev's attempt to find their affinities.

Alexiev continued probing to ascertain how much Fidel's conception of his revolution matched or differed from Che's. "It's a true revolution," Fidel told him, "made by the people and for the people. We want to build a just society without man exploiting his fellow man, and with an armed people to defend their victories. If Marx were to arise now he would be pleased to see me giving arms to the people." Although Alexiev noted that

Fidel avoided using the word "socialism," whereas Che *had* used it, Fidel "made it understood" that they shared the same philosophy.

By the time their meeting ended, Alexiev had been given a mission to fulfill. It came about in the same seemingly spontaneous fashion as Fidel's decision to renew Soviet-Cuban commercial relations while sipping Alexiev's vodka. As Alexiev told it, after Fidel's explanation about the need to "go slow" with Cubans because of their rampant anticommunism, Nuñez Jiménez cut in, suggesting to Fidel that it might be a good idea to have Alexiev ask his government to bring the Soviet trade exposition, which was then in Mexico, to Havana. The exposition had been in New York in July, and Nuñez Jiménez had visited it there and had been impressed. "It's worthwhile, really!" Alexiev recalled Nuñez Jiménez saying to Fidel. "It would open the eyes of the Cuban people about the Soviet Union by showing that the American propaganda about its backwardness is untrue."

Fidel asked Alexiev his own opinion. Was it really good, this exposition? Alexiev said yes, he thought it was, but believed it would be hard to arrange. The itinerary for the exposition was already scheduled, Cuba was not on the list of countries to be visited, and, in view of the grinding Soviet bureaucracy, it would be hard to alter the plan.

But already, Fidel had made Nuñez Jiménez's idea his own and refused to take no for an answer. "It *has* to come!" he told Alexiev emphatically. The Soviet deputy premier, Anastas Mikoyan, had inaugurated the exposition in New York and was now with it in Mexico. "Mikoyan has to come here and open it," Fidel said. "Sure, it's all been planned but it *has* to come! We are revolutionaries! Go to Mexico and tell Mikoyan what kind of revolution this is—that it's worth him coming." Alexiev agreed to try but warned Fidel that he couldn't travel very freely on his Soviet passport. "Don't worry," Fidel told him. "Our ambassador in Mexico will fix everything."

Within days, Alexiev was on a plane to meet Mikoyan in Mexico City. So far, his mission to Havana was paying off. With Che's nudge, followed by Fidel's approval, the wheels of political destiny leading Cuba into the Soviet orbit had begun to turn.

22

We Are the Future and We Know It

I

When Deputy Premier Anastas Mikoyan arrived in Havana on February 4, 1960, he brought along his thirty-year-old son, Sergo; the Soviet ambassador to Mexico; a personal assistant; and, as his bodyguard and interpreter, a young KGB officer, Nikolai Leonov. Mikoyan asked Leonov, as Leonov recalled many years later, to deliver gifts to "the principal leaders of the revolution." The task gave him an opportunity to see his old acquaintances from Mexico privately, and the first person he went to see was Che Guevara.

A little over three years had passed since Leonov had given some Soviet books to the young Argentine doctor in Mexico City who was so eager to learn about socialism, but already his intemperate early contacts with Castro's rebel group had been vindicated. Here he was, in Cuba, escorting an important Soviet official. As for Guevara and the Castro brothers, they were no longer political exiles espousing a wild scheme but the undisputed leaders of a new revolutionary Cuba, evidently prepared to "go socialist" and forge an alliance with his country at the risk of war with the United States. Now, "on behalf of the Soviet people," Leonov carried as a gift for Che a Soviet-made precision marksman's pistol in a beautiful holster, with a good supply of ammunition.

Leonov recalled that in November 1956—around the time the *Granma* took off for Cuba—he had been told to return to Moscow and had been discharged from the foreign service. He decided to pursue a career as a historian of Latin America and went to work as a translator for the official Soviet Spanish-language publishing house, Editorial Progreso. In the late summer of 1958, he said, he was invited to join the KGB, and he accepted.

That fall, Leonov began a two-year intelligence training course that he didn't complete "because of the Cuban revolution."*

In October 1959, Leonov's KGB superiors ordered him to leave his studies and escort Mikoyan on his trip to Mexico to open the trade exposition. Because Mikoyan had been invited not by the Mexican government but by the Soviet ambassador, he could not travel with the usual phalanx of aides; as someone who had previously lived in Mexico, Leonov could play the roles of bodyguard, Spanish-Russian interpreter, and "adviser."

Leonov was with Mikoyan in Mexico when Alexandr Alexiev arrived on his secret mission from Cuba. As Alexiev recalled it, he went straight to see Mikoyan. "I spoke of Fidel, of Che, of Raúl, of the revolution, and he listened with great interest. Since Mikoyan had been in the [Bolshevik] revolution in his youth, it reminded him of his youthful days, of the revolutionary romanticism of that time." Alexiev told Mikoyan of Fidel's overture. "They don't want *just* the exhibition. *Fidel wants to talk*." After hearing him out, Mikoyan remarked that he too—like Fidel—was against "formalities," but as the Soviet deputy premier, he couldn't travel to a country with which Moscow had no diplomatic ties. He sent off a cable to the Kremlin and dispatched Alexiev to Moscow to explain things. "Moscow agreed to move the exhibition from Mexico to Cuba," Alexiev said, "because Khrushchev had by now also fallen in love with the Cuban revolution. I don't know exactly why, but I think he was happy to have another pawn against the Americans." The date originally set for the opening of the exhibit was November 28, 1959, but it coincided with a Catholic congress being held in Havana. Fidel saw little reason to rile conservatives, so he postponed it until the following February.

By the time Leonov arrived in Havana with Mikoyan, Che and Aleida had moved from their remote country house into the more secure confines

---

*A credible-sounding alternative version of Leonov's story was offered by Anastas Mikoyan's son, Sergo, who accompanied his father and Leonov on the trip to Cuba. In 1994, Sergo Mikoyan told me that he had known Leonov for years before the trip. They were about the same age and had gone to school together. To Mikoyan's knowledge, Leonov was sent to Mexico in the mid-1950s by the KGB. His cover was that he was working for an official Soviet publishing house. Leonov was assigned to Mexico at the same time another friend of Mikoyan's went in a similar capacity to the United States. That friend, Mikoyan said, "was certainly KGB." Leonov's first contact with Raúl Castro *was* casual, Mikoyan agreed, but his subsequent meetings in Mexico were intentional. "Ironically, he was told by the KGB to halt these contacts." Mikoyan's belief is that this order was due to pressure from the Cuban Communists, who still didn't approve of Fidel Castro, believing him and his movement to be "bourgeois and putschist."

of Ciudad Libertad, the sprawling former military headquarters on Havana's western edge. They now lived in one of the homes that formerly housed Batista's officers, next to the military airstrip. When Leonov's car pulled up in in front of the house it was almost noon, but Che was still asleep. "He was exhausted," Leonov said, "but he got up and was really excited to see me. *'Hombre!* What a miracle, it's like you dropped in from heaven!'" Over coffee, Leonov handed him the marksman's pistol, which pleased Che immensely.

Leonov congratulated Che on the rebels' victory, and then, reminding him of their past conversations and the Soviet books Che had been so avid to read in Mexico, asked, "So, it's true, you are really serious about building socialism?" "Yes," Che replied, "I'm going to devote my life to it. That's why I was reading first, to build later."

II

If Leonov was curious to know why Che was still asleep so late in the day, he soon learned the answer. Along with his job at INRA, Che had become president of Cuba's National Bank. He had an extremely heavy workload, and his unusual working hours had become legendary. Stories abounded in Havana of foreign dignitaries who showed up at his offices at 3:00 P.M. for an appointment only to be informed by José Manuel Manresa that the appointment was for 3:00 A.M. The after-midnight meeting Alexiev had with Che in October was now the rule, not the exception.

In a Christmas letter to his parents, Che had tried to give them a sense of his strange new life.

Dear *viejos:*

You know how hard it is for me to write. I am taking a pause at 6:30 in the morning, not at the beginning but at the end of the day, to wish you all that is wishable. Cuba is experiencing a moment that is decisive for the Americas. At one time I wanted to be one of Pizarro's soldiers, but that is no longer necessary to fulfill my desire for adventure and my yearning to be an eyewitness to history. Today it is all here, and with an ideal to fight for, together with the responsibility of creating a legacy. We are not men, but working machines, fighting against time in the midst of difficult and luminous circumstances.

The Industrial Department was my own creation; I half-relinquished it, with the pain of a worn-out father, to plunge myself into my apparently God-given gift for finance. I also have

the job of Chief of Training of the E. Rebelde and the direct command of a regiment in Oriente. We walk over pure history of the
highest American variety; we are the future and we know it, we
build with happiness although we have forgotten individual affections. Receive an affectionate embrace from this machine dispensing calculating love to 160 million Americans, and sometimes,
the prodigal son who returns in the memory.

Che.

Aleida saw Che at work, as his secretary, but they had little privacy
during his hours at home. His Guatemalan friend Patojo had lived with
them off and on since early 1959, and Oscar Fernández Mell moved into
their spare bedroom at the front of the house in Ciudad Libertad; he worked
nearby, in Batista's old naval headquarters, as chief of medical services of
the new army. Aleida took all of this in stride, but something *did* bother her,
and that was the unflagging presence of Hilda Gadea on the scene. Che's
ex-wife worked on another floor of INRA in an office set up to help peasant farmers whose homes had been destroyed during the war. Aleida
thought that Hilda had not given up hope of winning Che back. She seemed
to make her presence felt at every opportunity, dropping her daughter
Hildita off to play in Che's office or taking her there to eat her lunch. Che
didn't mind: his feelings for his only daughter were complex, paternal love
mixed with guilt for the broken marriage and his long absence, and he tried
to make up for it by having her with him as much as possible. When Hilda
permitted it, the little girl stayed at his home on the weekends.

Aleida put up with Hildita for Che's sake, but when the office visits
became too frequent, with Hilda seeming to use them to dally and engage
Che in conversation, she simmered with fury. Che kept his own temper in
check to avoid making a scene. One day, however, he stormed out of his
office, shouting loud enough to be heard by a young secretary: "I might as
well not have gotten divorced."

Hilda often spoke to the secretary to confide her feelings and to
bad-mouth Aleida. Aleida, in turn, fumed to the secretary about her talks
with Hilda. She demanded to know what they discussed. Finally, after a
few months, the secretary could no longer stand feeling like "a pig in the
middle," as she recalled, and asked to be transferred out of the department.

The country itself was in an increasingly divisive mood as Fidel forced
through more and more radical policies. Che was urging him along, using
cajolery in private and applause in public. Observers began to take note of a
pattern. What started out as "radical-sounding" proposals from Che were
actually important early-warning signals, for almost invariably Fidel soon

made them official policy. In January 1959, and again in April, Che had talked about Cuba's need to nationalize its oil and mineral wealth. In September 1959, Fidel said this was an issue that needed to be "carefully studied." Nine months later, he would seize the refineries owned by Texaco, Esso, and British Shell.

In November 1959, the U.S. embassy noted a recent interview with Che in *Revolución,* which made plain that "regardless of what the Agrarian Reform Law may say about making the peasants small property owners, as far as Guevara is concerned, reform will be aimed more in the direction of cooperatives or communes [*sic*]." Three months after the interview, in January 1960, Fidel issued a decree seizing all sugar plantations and large cattle ranches and making them state-run cooperatives. As for the issue that was becoming Washington's greatest grievance, the "nonpayment and illegal seizures" of American-owned properties in violation of both Cuba's 1940 constitution and the 1959 agrarian reform law, in the very first weeks of the revolution's triumph, Che had given an early warning, publicly calling for the constitution's compensation clause to be waived.

October 1959 had been a particularly crucial time. By the end of the month, the stage had been set for what Hugh Thomas has called the "eclipse of the liberals" and the final ascendancy of the anti-American, "radical" wing of the revolution. The course long advocated by Che was now being steered, more and more openly, by Fidel himself.

Employing the heavily loaded argument for "revolutionary unity," Fidel had successfully orchestrated the takeover of Havana University's student union by Rolando Cubela, the former Directorio commander who had recently returned from a few months in Prague as Fidel's military attaché. Cubela's election victory was a de facto government takeover of a campus that had traditionally been both autonomous and a hotbed of antigovernment plotting. Fidel knew this only too well, since that is where he had begun his own political career.

Che carried the same message to Cuba's second university, in Santiago, where he bluntly announced that university autonomy was over. Henceforth the state would design the curriculum. Central planning was necessary, Cuba was going to industrialize, and it needed qualified technicians— agronomists, agricultural teachers, and chemical engineers—not a new crop of lawyers. "Who has the right to say that only 10 lawyers should graduate per year and that 100 industrial chemists should graduate?" Che asked. "Some would say that that is dictatorship, and all right: it is dictatorship." Students should join the "great army of those who *do,* leaving by the wayside that small patrol of those who simply talk." (Two months later, in December, while accepting an honorary teacher's degree at the University of Las Villas, Che told the gathered faculty and students that the days when education was a privilege of the white middle class had ended. "The University, he said, "must *paint* itself black, mulatto, worker and peasant." If it didn't, he warned, the people would break down its doors "and paint the University the colors they like.")

Che spoke in a tense climate caused by the first outbreaks of counter-revolutionary activity. In Pinar del Río, a sugar mill had been bombed by an unidentified plane and a group of suspected rebels that included two Americans had been captured. At the same time, the long-simmering Huber Matos affair was finally about to blow up. On October 20, following Raúl's promotion to minister of the armed forces, Matos wrote to Fidel from Camagüey, tendering his resignation, urging him to alter his present course, and accusing him of "burying the revolution." Some fifteen of Matos's officers planned to resign with him. Fidel immediately repudiated Matos's claims and accused him of disloyalty and "ambition," among other offenses. He ordered Camilo to fly to Camagüey and arrest Matos and the other dissident officers. Fidel then flew to Camagüey himself to make a speech accusing Matos of planning an armed revolt—treason. Matos and the officers were taken to Havana and imprisoned in La Cabaña.

As Fidel, also back in Havana, prepared to address a convention of more than 2,000 American travel agents to encourage the expansion of U.S. tourism to Cuba, the defector Pedro Luis Díaz Lanz appeared overhead, piloting a B-26 bomber. He dropped leaflets calling on Fidel to purge the Communists in his regime. Cuban air force planes scrambled to intercept him, and army personnel at La Cabaña opened fire with antiaircraft batteries, but Díaz Lanz flew away unscathed.

At the INRA building on the Plaza de la Revolución, Che and José Manuel Manresa and a secretary named Cristína stood by a window watching Díaz Lanz loop down low and buzz the building, flying so close they could see him inside the pilot's cabin. Che said nothing, but he was icy with rage and frustration. Che's *escolta* asked for permission to go up to the roof and shoot down the plane, but Che told them no—they were bound to do more damage than the plane could. The incident ended on a humorous note. One of the secretaries, a plump, nervous girl, had hidden under a desk when the plane appeared. She got stuck, and everyone laughed as several of the *escolta* finally pulled her free.

Díaz Lanz's "bombing attack" was a public relations disaster for Fidel. The visiting travel agents began leaving town in alarm as he was denouncing it. At least two civilians had been killed and several were injured. Safely back in the United States, Díaz Lanz acknowledged making the flight but denied dropping anything but leaflets over Havana. If there were casualties, they had probably been the result of the Cuban soldiers' random shooting or fallout from antiaircraft fire. Nevertheless, the story that he had launched an aerial attack was officially adopted. The next day, large crowds demonstrated in front of the American embassy, and Fidel appeared on television, accusing Matos of plotting a military revolt in Camagüey, in complicity with Díaz Lanz. (There had also been an attack by an unidentified plane that dropped bombs on a sugar mill in Camagüey.) The United States, Fidel charged, harbored "war criminals" and had supplied Díaz Lanz with the plane.

On October 26, at a rally in the Plaza de la Revolución attended by an estimated 500,000 Cubans, Fidel repeated his charges and vowed that Cuba would defend itself. The people would be trained and armed, and Cuba would get the planes and other weapons it needed. The next day, the U.S. ambassador, Philip Bonsal, delivered a note of protest to Foreign Minister Roa. Fidel's cabinet voted to reinstate the revolutionary tribunals.

On October 28, after reorganizing the military command in Camagüey, Camilo Cienfuegos boarded his Cessna airplane for the return to Havana. He never arrived. Fidel and Che joined a three-day search for the missing plane, but no wreckage was found. What had happened? Camilo's pilot was experienced, and the weather that day had been fine. Many conspiracy theories sprang up. One was that Fidel had done away with Camilo, either because he was in cahoots with Matos, or because he was becoming too popular. Another theory was that a Cuban air force fighter plane shot him down, mistaking his aircraft for a hostile intruder. In any case, his plane had vanished forever beneath the blue Caribbean waters that lay under his flight path. The revolution had lost one of its most charismatic and popular figures.*

In November, Fidel continued to consolidate his power base. He succeeded in cobbling together "unity" in the CTC labor confederation at the expense of the July 26 anticommunists by imposing his own executive committee and ending the members' right to vote for delegates, paving the way for the CTC's gradual takeover by the Cuban Communist Party. The creation of "National Revolutionary Militias" was announced, the first step in the realization of Che's dream to convert Cuba into a "guerrilla society." Foreign Minister Roa rebutted an article by Carlos Franqui in *Revolución*

---

*The truth of what happened to Camilo Cienfuegos may never be known, but it is clear that Che never suspected Fidel of having anything to do with his disappearance. Che had a deep affection for Camilo; not only did he name his firstborn son after him, but the only picture hanging on the wall of his private study was a portrait of Camilo. If Che had suspected Fidel of complicity in Camilo's death, it seems highly improbable that he would have remained loyally at his side.

indicating that the Soviet deputy premier, Mikoyan, had been invited to Cuba, as, of ourse, he had been.

It was just as well that Mikoyan's November visit had been postponed, for when the Catholic laymen's congress took place, it became an open demonstration of clerical opposition to Communism. Although the ecclesiastical hierarchy had so far maintained a public "wait and see" posture, the Church was increasingly alarmed about the direction of the revolution, and its youthful militants had no patience for keeping quiet. Already, a few priests had begun to flee, reappearing amid great waves of publicity in Miami, where they echoed Díaz Lanz's claims that Cuba was going "Red." In Washington, meanwhile, the Central Intelligence Agency had quietly begun to study ways and means of getting rid of Fidel Castro.

III

In late 1959, most of Cuba's industry, both small and large, was still in private hands. The only industrial possessions of INRA were a few small factories either abandoned by their owners or confiscated for belonging to Batista and his associates. These fell under Che's new authority, and handpicked veterans of the Rebel Army were dispatched to administer them, just as they were being put in charge of the new agrarian cooperatives on the expropriated *latifundios*.

Che now had a small team of economists from Chile and Ecuador working for him. More Cubans came in, some accountants were hired, and plans began to be made for the industrial development of Cuba. In the early weeks of work, Borrego sweated over annual statistical reports to get a grasp of the Cuban industrial landscape, and an an agenda gradually began to evolve. "Very soon the first interventions of factories began," he recalled. "These were interventions, *not* nationalizations. Factories had labor conflicts, or the capitalists running them were doubtful about the revolutionary process and weren't investing, and so we intervened." A resolution adopted by the Ministry of Labor—now in the safe hands of Augusto Martínez Sánchez, Raúl's former aide—enabled Che's department to intervene and administer factories for as long as necessary. Nonetheless, Borrego said, he never imagined the interventions would be permanent. "Of course," he added, "to Che's way of thinking they were definitive, but that wasn't legally declared yet." It was Borrego's job to operate the new properties, and his first headache was finding people to run them. "We started naming some administrators. Basically we chose them from among the members of the Rebel Army whose schooling wasn't too low. When I talk about schooling, I mean men who had completed the sixth grade or more."

Che estimated that more than 80 percent of Fidel's rebels were illiterate. His literacy campaign at La Cabaña had been designed to alleviate the problem, but in late 1959 the military was still made up for the most part of semiliterate or very recently tutored *guajiros,* many of them little more than teenagers. When they were dispatched to run the factories, an inevitable series of disasters and chaos ensued. All the while, Che was cramming to overcome his own lack of economic knowledge. He studied with a Mexican economist, Juan Noyola. Doctor Vilaseca was teaching him advanced mathematics. Beginning in September, Vilaseca began coming over to the INRA office every Tuesday and Saturday morning at eight to give Che, García Vals, and Patojo an hour-long math class. For Vilaseca, the classes were the start of his day; for Che, they were a way to unwind before going home after working through the night. They began with algebra and trigonometry, and soon they went on to analytical geometry.

IV

Che loved telling a story about how he'd gotten the bank job. He said that at the cabinet meeting held to decide on a replacement for Felipe Pazos— who had been ousted after protesting against Matos's arrest—Fidel said that he needed a good *economista.* To his surprise, Che raised his hand. "But Che, I didn't know you were an economist!" he said. "Oh, I thought you said you needed a good *comunista,*" Che replied.

Che's appointment sent a flurry of cold shivers throughout the financial and business community. Few believed Fidel's glib reassurances that Che would be "as conservative as" his predecessor. When he took over at the bank—a colonnaded stone building on a narrow street of Old Havana— he found a lot of empty desks; most of the senior staff had resigned along with Felipe Pazos.* Che called Dr. Vilaseca and asked him to become the bank's administrator, his deputy, but Vilaseca balked. It was not just that he lacked any experience in finance. He was a personal friend of Pazos, whom he described as "someone extraordinarily capable in banking." But Che was adamant; in fact, he was not so much asking Vilaseca as ordering him. "I don't know anything about banks, either, and I'm the president,"

---

*The ministers who sided with Pazos in the Matos affair were unceremoniously fired. They were Justo Carrillo, Manuel Ray, and Che's old antagonist Faustino Pérez. Camilo Cienfuegos's brother Osmany, a longtime PSP member, replaced Ray, and a brother-in-law of Raúl's wife, Vílma Espín, took over Faustino's job. Pazos, Carrillo, and Ray eventually left Cuba, but Faustino Pérez stayed on and soon regained Fidel's favor.

Che told him. "When the revolution names you to a post, you have to accept it, and then do it well." Vilaseca accepted the job.

One of the first people Che called in to the bank was Nicolás Quintana, a thirty-five-year-old Havana architect whose firm had been assigned funds by Pazos to build a new thirty-two-story National Bank building—an American-style skyscraper—on a site overlooking the Malecón in central Havana. It was a huge project, the biggest construction scheme under way in Cuba, and was to cost an estimated $16 million. By late 1959, the building's foundations had just been laid and the first phase of construction begun.

When Pazos was fired and reassigned to an ambassadorship abroad, he had confided to Quintana that he was planning to seek asylum as soon as he got to Europe. "What they are doing to the country is a barbarity," he said. "You're going to inherit a new bank president, and his name is Che Guevara. He's not qualified for the post, and that's one of the reaons I'm going into exile. You're going to have to go, too; it's inevitable." But Quintana was young, he was involved in the biggest architectural project of his career, and he thought that the fact that he had helped the rebels (late in 1958 he provided them with topographical maps of the Escambray area) would help him with Che.

When Quintana went to his meeting with Che at the bank, he was shocked at the way things looked. The once pristine financial building was "dirty and disorganized," with papers lying all over the floor. "In fifteen days, everything had changed," Quintana said. The first thing Che asked him was, "Are you a petit bourgeois?" Quintana answered: "No, I'm not." "No? So, you're a revolutionary." "No, Comandante, I haven't said I'm a revolutionary. I am a *gran* bourgeois. My *shopkeeper* is a bourgeois." Che's eyes warmed, and, looking pleased, he said: "You're the only honest person of your class I've met since I got here." Quintana thought he'd won Che over, and he responded in the same witty fashion, "No, there are many, the problem is that you don't give them a chance to talk." Che's expression froze, and he told Quintana to remember that he was speaking to Comandante Guevara. Quintana realized that he had pushed his limits.

At a second meeting, Quintana and his senior partner presented the building plans and specifications that required Che's approval. They showed him the list of materials that had to be imported and explained that the exposed seafront building would need hurricane-proof windows with rust-proof stainless steel frames. Quintana recommended that the elevators be bought from an American firm, Otis, which had offices in Havana.

Che listened to Quintana's suggestions and finally asked, "Why elevators?" Quintana said that the building would be be thirty-two stories high.

Che said he thought stairs would do; if *he* could climb them, with his asthma, why couldn't everyone else? At this, Quintana's partner got up and left the meeting in disgust, but the younger architect persisted. They returned to the matter of the windows. Che asked Quintana why they had to come from the United States or Germany; why couldn't something cheaper be found, perhaps made from plastic, right in Havana? Next they talked about the number of lavatories proposed; Che looked at the figures and said: "Well, we can eliminate at least half of them."

"But in revolutions," Quintana pointed out, "people go to the bathroom just as much as before it." "Not the *new man,*" Che countered. "He can sacrifice." When the architect tried to return once again to the matter of the hurricane-proof windows, Che cut him off: "Look, Quintana. For the shit we're going to be guarding here within three years, it's preferable that the wind takes the lot."

Quintana finally understood. This wasn't about windows or toilets; Che didn't want the new bank at all. "He was sending me a message that the system was going to change so absolutely that everything we were talking about was unnecessary." The bank was never built. Some years later, the Hermanos Ameijeiras Hospital was erected in its place.

Before long, new Cuban ten- and twenty-peso banknotes were issued. As president of the National Bank, it was Che's job to sign them—which he did, writing simply and dismissively, "Che." To Cuban businessmen, the symbolism of the gesture was quickly understood and bitterly resented. In the new Cuba, money was no longer a hallowed commodity but an onerous vestige of the soon-to-disappear era of capitalist private enterprise.

23

Individualism Must Disappear

I

Huber Matos's sedition trial took place in December 1959, and it quickly turned bitter and ugly. Raúl called for Matos's execution, as did the prosecutor, Major Jorge "Papito" Serguera. Instead, the judges, all handpicked army officers and revolutionary veterans, sentenced Matos to twenty years in prison and gave his junior officers lesser sentences. But several other men were tried, sentenced, and executed for "counterrevolution" in December. Rafael del Pino, Fidel's old friend who had been suspected of betraying a fellow rebel in Mexico City just before the *Granma* left for Cuba, was caught, charged with aiding *batístianos* fleeing the country, and given thirty years.

As he had promised Alexandr Alexiev over vodka and caviar, Fidel began to wage a battle against the "reactionary" press in Cuba. The conservative daily *Avance* was "intervened" after its editor fled the country; Fidel had accused him of siding with the counterrevolution for printing Díaz Lanz's accusations about Communist infiltration of the armed forces. Cuba's second television channel, 12, was intervened, too. *El Mundo* was taken over and put under the editorship of a Fidelista journalist, Luis Wangüemert. The operation to close down the opposition mouthpiece *Diario de la Marina* and the rest of Cuba's independent press would come soon. For now, the editors of *Bohemia* and *Revolución* remained publicly loyal, although they too were becoming nervous about Fidel's accommodation with the Communists. Cuba's international wire agency, Prensa Latina, was up and running under the committed editorship of Jorge Ricardo Masetti, with bureaus opening around the hemisphere. (For a time, a young Colombian writer, Gabriel García Márquez, worked alongside Masetti in Havana.) Prensa Latina tried to combat the reports put out by the AP and UPI, the two U.S. news agencies most galling to Che and Fidel.

Che with his mother, Celia,
who was visiting Havana
in 1960 during the annual
Ernest Hemingway Marlin
Fishing Tournament. Celia
Sánchez, Fidel's confidante,
is at the far right.

The newspaper takeovers were aided by the printers' and journalists'
unions, which were in the hands of Fidelistas and were functioning as pro-
government strike forces in the surviving private media outlets. The CTC
purge had continued over David Salvador's protests, spearheaded by the
Communists now on its executive committee. Even in the Union of Graphic
Artists, there was purging to be done; the Communist actress Violeta Casals,
Alexiev's initial contact for Che, became the head of the union after her predecessor was accused of being a counterrevolutionary and fled the country.

Che's overseas mission of the previous summer had begun paying some
dividends. Official diplomatic and trade delegations from Japan, Indonesia, and Egypt had visited Cuba. A few trade agreements were signed,
although they were more significant for their symbolism than their commercial benefits. Che had kept up a steady stream of blatantly political articles about the countries he had visited. In "America from the Afro-Asian
Balcony," published in the September–October issue of the magazine
Humanismo, he wrote that the common bond between Cuba and the newly
independent former colonial states was the dream of freedom from economic

exploitation. He argued that revolutionary Cuba, personified by Fidel Castro, was a model for change not only in Latin America but in Asia and Africa as well, and he called for an international anti-imperialist alliance. Fidel, he seemed to be saying, could be its leader.

> Might it not be that our fraternity can defy the breadth of the seas, the rigors of language and the lack of cultural ties, to lose ourselves in the embrace of a fellow struggler? . . .
>
> Cuba has been invited to the new Afro-Asian People's Conference. [And Cuba will go] to say that it is true, that Cuba exists and that Fidel Castro is a man, a popular hero and not a mythological abstraction; but it will also go to explain that Cuba is not an isolated event, merely the first signal of America's awakening. . . .
>
> [And when they ask]: "Are you the members of the Guerrilla Army that is leading the struggle for the liberation of America? Are you, then, our allies on the other side of the sea?" I must say [to them] and to all the hundreds of millions of Afro-Asians that . . . I am one brother more, one more among the multitudes of brothers in this part of the world that awaits with infinite anxiety the moment [when we can] consolidate the bloc that will destroy, once and for all, the anachronistic presence of colonial domination.

Since 1957, a dozen nations had won their independence from French, British, and Belgian colonial rule. Others, such as Algeria, were having to wage war for it, but the trend was clear. The days of colonial rule were over, and the future was in the hands of men who had faced down the dying empires, men such as Nasser and Sukarno—and why not Fidel himself? In January, Foreign Minister Roa traveled to Asia and North Africa to extend Cuba's invitation to an international congress of developing nations to be held in Havana.

The first anecdotal accounts of Che's experiences in the guerrilla war had also begun appearing in print. In November, "The Murdered Puppy" was published in *Humanismo*. Coinciding, as it did, with the intensifying pace of land expropriations and the resumption of the revolutionary firing squads, the story's allegorical significance—the necessity to sacrifice innocents in a revolutionary cause—must have made disquieting reading for some Cubans.

II

By January 1960, the architect Nicolás Quintana had come to the conclusion that the future looked bleak for him in Cuba. The revolution's sharp move to the left had alienated him and most of his social class. His dream of building the National Bank had been dashed. A close friend of his, a member of the Juventud Católica, the youth branch of the militantly anticommunist Acción Católica, had just been shot by a firing squad for distributing anticommunist leaflets.

Quintana went to see Che to complain. It was to be a shattering encounter. "Che told me, 'Look, revolutions are ugly but necessary, and part of the revolutionary process is justice at the service of future justice,'" Quintana recalled. "I will never forget that phrase. I replied that that was Thomas More's *Utopia*. I said that we had been fucked by that tale for a long time, for believing that we would achieve something not *now*, but in the future. Che looked at me for a while and said: 'So. You don't believe in the future of the revolution.' I told him I didn't believe in anything that was based upon an injustice."

"Even if that injustice is cleansing?" Che asked.

Quintana replied: "For those who die, I don't believe you can talk of cleansing injustice."

Che's response was immediate: "You have to leave Cuba. You have three choices: You leave Cuba and there's no problem from me; or thirty years [in prison], in the near future; or the firing squad."

Dumbstruck and horrified, Quintana sat frozen in his chair.

"You are doing very strange things," Che said.

"I didn't say anything," Quintana recalled, "but I knew what he was referring to. What surprised me was that he already *knew*, that really surprised me."

Quintana belonged to a group of professionals who had formed an organization they called Trabajo Voluntario (Voluntary Work). It was ostensibly dedicated to carrying out civic works, but the group's real purpose was to organize an anti-Castro opposition. "It was an excuse to meet at night and talk, well . . . you know . . . about what we were going to do about this [the revolution]." After Che's warning, Quintana realized he was not going to be doing very much at all, and, within a few weeks, he fled the island.

Around the same time, José Pardo Llada, the television commentator who had had such a troublesome journey with Che the previous summer, called on the new National Bank president to take up the case of a friend, the tobacco expert Napoleón Padilla. Che had asked Padilla to work for him at INRA, organizing tobacco cooperatives in Pinar del Río. Oddly, in light of his fear and dislike of Guevara's "Communism," which he had already denounced to the U.S. embassy, Padilla had agreed. He had set up cooperatives for INRA, assisted in a large sale of tobacco for export, and, at Che's behest, taught a course in business administration.

Padilla had become increasingly uncomfortable about what he saw at INRA, and he argued with Nuñez Jiménez and the PSP's Oscar Pino Santos, now a top INRA official, over the way they were implementing the agrarian reform. Finally, he exploded and accused Pino Santos of "practicing Communism." From that day on, Padilla felt that he was being frozen out of things. Then, on the evening of January 26, an anonymous phone caller had warned him: "Napoleón, hide yourself right away, they're going to arrest you." The caller had hung up, and, terrified, Padilla drove to the Honduran embassy to ask for political asylum. The ambassador advised him to try to find out what his real status was before he took such an extreme step, and Padilla called Pardo Llada to ask for his help.

At the National Bank offices, Pardo asked Guevara if Padilla had a problem with the authorities. Che showed him a piece of paper. It was an affidavit signed by an army sergeant at the tobacco cooperative where Padilla worked, accusing him of being a counterrevolutionary and of speaking ill of Che's wife, Aleida.

Pardo expressed his surprise that Che paid any attention to such petty gossip, and Che then revealed his hand. He also happened to know, he told Pardo, that Padilla met frequently with the U.S. embassy's agricultural attaché, and that he had spoken negatively about the government in front of INRA officials. Pardo still insisted these weren't reasons to persecute Padilla. "All right," Che told him. "He can resign and leave INRA. And if he wants to leave the country, he can go join his gringo friends." Che's word was good. Six months later—"with Che's express permission," Pardo acknowledged—Padilla was allowed to leave Cuba, taking his car and furniture with him, on the ferry to Miami.

III

Fidel had dubbed 1960 "The Year of Agrarian Reform," but a better label might have been "The Year of Confrontation." The month leading up to Mikoyan's visit in February saw a rapid deterioration in U.S.-Cuban relations and an open acceleration of Cuba's "socialization." A tit-for-tat war began in early January with a note of protest sent by Secretary of State Herter over the "illegal seizures" of American-owned property, for which no compensation had been paid. Cuba responded by seizing all the large cattle ranches and all sugar plantations in the country, including those owned by Americans. More unidentified airplanes flew out of the United States, firebombing Cuban cane fields. The runs were being organized by the CIA, which was now planning to train a Cuban exile force for an eventual guerrilla campaign against Castro.

Che and his protégé Orlando
Borrego doing volunteer labor
on a construction site in 1960.

Reaction in Washington was being fueled by domestic politics. President Eisenhower was in the final year of his second term as president, and the jockeying to succeed him had already begun. Vice President Nixon used Cuba as a rallying cry, warning Castro that he could be punished for his actions. The quota of sugar that the Cubans were permitted to sell to the United States might be cut. Fidel responded defiantly. On January 19, INRA announced the immediate confiscation of "all *latifúndia*," both Cuban and foreign-owned, in the country. The edict put every large remaining agrarian holding in the revolution's hands.

Next, a bizarre altercation between Fidel and the Spanish ambassador, Juan Pablo de Lojendio, occurred on live television. Fidel insinuated during a televised speech that Spain's embassy was implicated in a covert U.S. program to smuggle anti-Castroites out of the island. While Fidel was still on the air, the indignant ambassador stormed into the studio to accuse him of slander. A shouting match ensued, and the apoplectic envoy was forcibly escorted from the building. Fidel resumed his speech with an announcement that Lojendio had twenty-four hours to leave Cuba. Then he veered off into a rant against the United States. Secretary of State Herter reacted by going to Capitol Hill to request passage of a bill that would give Eisenhower the power to alter Cuba's sugar quota. Ambassador Bonsal was recalled to Washington.

There was one final attempt to find a way out of the spiraling crisis. On January 21, Eisenhower issued a statement calling for negotiations to halt further deterioration in the relations between the two nations. That same day in Havana, Daniel Braddock, the deputy chief of mission, asked the Argentine ambassador, Julio Amoeda, to serve as intermediary between his government and Castro. Amoeda went to see Fidel with a proposal from the Americans. If Fidel stopped the anti-American attacks and met with Bonsal in Havana, Washington would consider extending economic aid to Cuba. After first refusing, Fidel relented, telling Amoeda he would halt the press campaign. Osvaldo Dorticós, the Cuban figurehead president, followed up the next day with a declaration that Cuba wished to keep and strengthen its "traditional friendship" with the United States.

The truce held. In Fidel's next speech, on January 28, he did not mention the United States at all. The temporary backing down gave him breathing space before the next round, which he knew would be very soon in coming. On January 31, Cuba's government finally acknowledged the truth of the long-standing rumors and announced the imminent arrival of Soviet Deputy Premier Anastas Mikoyan.

IV

The Soviet trade fair in February turned out to be a great success. More than 100,000 Cubans visited during a period of three weeks. They viewed the Sputnik replica; the models of Soviet homes, factories, and sports facilities; the tractors and displays of farm and industrial equipment. These were the technological achievements of the nation that Nikita Khrushchev had told Americans would "bury" them in the not too distant future. To the average untraveled Cuban in early 1960, such claims were credible. After all, hadn't Russia been the first country to put a satellite—even a live dog—into orbit?

Not all Cubans were impressed. Mikoyan's visit was accompanied by some angry demonstrations, and Cuba's independent media waged an unstinting campaign to expose the inequities and inefficiencies of the Soviet system. Throughout Mikoyan's stay, nocturnal attacks on Cuban sugar mills and cane fields by small planes based in the United States continued without letup. In late February, one of the marauding planes crashed on Cuban soil, killing its occupants, and the identity papers of one of the dead showed him to be a U.S. citizen. Fidel cited this as evidence of U.S. complicity in the attacks. When CIA Director Dulles informed Eisenhower that the dead man and those piloting the other sabotage missions were in fact CIA hirelings, Eisenhower quietly urged Dulles to come up with a more comprehensive plan to overthrow Castro. Eisenhower had only recently ordered customs officials to halt and prosecute any Cuba-bound flights leaving illegally from the United States.

On February 13, the Soviets and Cubans had made public the terms of their new commercial agreement. The Soviets agreed to buy almost 500,000 tons of sugar during 1960, and would buy a million tons per year for the next four years, in return for which Cuba would receive not cash but Soviet products, including oil. In the fifth and final year of the agreement, Moscow would pay cash. Cuba was also to receive $100 million in credit at a bargain-basement 2.5 percent interest rate over ten years, for the purchase of machinery and factory buildings—thus financing Che's industrialization plans. As for Fidel's dream of draining the Ciénaga de Zapáta swamp, which he showed Mikoyan from a helicopter, Mikoyan promised Soviet technical assistance.

Fidel and Che crowed happily about the new deal, calling it a further step toward the economic independence of Cuba. Polish and East German trade delegations arrived and signed their own trade deals with Cuba. The Czechs and the Chinese were not far behind. On February 20, fulfilling another of Che's recent public pronouncements, the era of Soviet-style central planning was ushered into being with the creation of the Junta Central de Planificación (JUCEPLAN). Fidel was its chairman, and Che, its main proponent, was on the management council.

Sergo Mikoyan accompanied his father on most of his peregrinations around the island and was able to observe Cuba's leaders closely. Right away, he noticed the difference between Che and Fidel. He had read about Che, and he recalled that he had expected to meet a "manic guerrilla," a kind of fire-eating Latin American Bolshevik, but Che didn't fit the image. "I now saw a man who was very silent, with very tender eyes," Sergo said. "You feel a little distance when you talk with Fidel [because] . . . he almost doesn't listen to you, but with Che one didn't feel that. Although I had expected him to be the obstinate one, I realized he wasn't stubborn, but inclined to talk, to discuss, and to listen."

The high point of Mikoyan's tour was the obligatory visit to the city of Santiago and Fidel's old Sierra Maestra *comandancia* at La Plata. The whole entourage traveled to Oriente, but only a select group went up to La Plata: Mikoyan, Sergo, and Leonov; Fidel, Che, and their bodyguards. The press corps was left in town.

Fidel had planned for them to spend the night at La Plata, but nothing had been prepared for their arrival. Some workers were there building huts, but they had not finished the job, and there were only a few tents. Fidel was embarrassed and angry. Mikoyan told him not to worry, that he was not averse to sleeping in a tent. Sergo, however, decided to leave and take advantage of the opportunity to see Santiago. He later heard from his father what happened that night. After he had gone, Fidel and Che spoke openly with Mikoyan about their desire to create a socialist revolution, the problems they faced in doing so, and their need for Soviet aid to carry it off.

"It was a very strange chat," Sergo Mikoyan said. "They told [my father] that they could survive only with Soviet help, and they would have to hide the fact from the capitalists in Cuba. . . . [Then] Fidel said, 'We will have to withstand these conditions in Cuba for five or ten more years,' at which Che interrupted and told him: 'If you don't do it within two or three years, you're finished.' There was this difference [of conception] between them."

Fidel then launched into a soliloquy about how the rebels' victory had proved Marx wrong. "Fidel said that according to Marx, the revolution could not have happened except along the paths proposed by his Communist Party and our Communist Party. . . . Mass struggle, strikes, and so forth. 'But we did it,' Fidel said. 'We have overtaken Marx, we have proven him wrong.' My father contradicted him. He said, 'You think this way because your Communists are dogmatic; they think Marxism is just A, B, C, and D. But Marxism is a *way,* not a dogma. So I don't think you have proven Marx wrong, I think you have proven *your* Communists wrong.'"

They didn't talk directly about military aid, Mikoyan said, but they did ask for Soviet economic aid. "They explained that if they didn't receive it they were damned, due to two considerations. First, American imperialism. Second, the struggle with their own capitalists."

After this talk, everyone understood that the commercial agreement they had announced a few days later was merely to be the first step in the reestablishment of full relations between Cuba and the Soviet Union. For now, it was all Fidel dared risk. Nonetheless, Alexiev, who hadn't gone to La Plata, was surprised to learn that Che and Fidel hadn't asked to buy Soviet arms. "They talked with Mikoyan about everything but arms . . . which was a little strange. In Mexico, even Mikoyan said that he thought Fidel might request arms."

It was a logical assumption. Over the past year, Fidel had sent emissaries all over the world to buy airplanes and weapons, but he had managed to buy only some of what he wanted in Belgium and Italy. His requests to Washington for airplanes had been spurned, predictably, and the unwillingness of Great Britain and several other countries to sign arms deals was probably due to U.S. pressure. Lately, defiant phrases such as "Cuba reserves the right to defend itself" and "Cuba will get the arms it needs wherever it has to buy them" had become familar refrains in his speeches.

Very soon, however, the subject was raised. On March 4, the French freighter *La Coubre,* which had just been towed into a dock in Havana harbor, exploded in a horrendous blast heard all over downtown. When the first explosion occurred, Jorge Enrique Mendoza, INRA's chief in Camagüey, was in a meeting with Fidel and the agency's other provincial bosses. They rushed to the port and were starting down the wharf where *La Coubre* was docked when Mendoza saw Che hurry past him toward the burning ship.

Just as Che neared the ship, and with Mendoza, Fidel, and the others about 300 feet back, there was a terrific second explosion. Mendoza and some other men immediately threw themselves on top of Fidel, to protect him. "Fidel began to kick and punch and yell: 'Damnit, you're suffocating me!' Then things began falling from the air," Mendoza recalled. Mendoza turned to Raúl and urged him to take Fidel away. He said that Raúl had to practically take Fidel prisoner to evacuate him. Mendoza then turned his attention to Che, who was still trying to board the burning ship. "I walked quickly over to where he was. Someone, I don't remember who, was trying to stop him from getting on the ship, and I could hear Che say: 'Damnit, don't fuck with me! There's been two explosions; everything that was going to explode has exploded. Let me go on the ship!' And in he went."

It was carnage. Up to 100 people had been killed—mostly stevedores, sailors, and soldiers—and several hundred others had been injured. *La Coubre* was loaded with Belgian weapons, and somehow the cargo had ignited. Fidel accused the CIA of sabotage. The next day, he and Che linked arms at the head of a funeral cortege that wound its way along the Malecón. Later, while Fidel gave a speech—in which he invoked a new battle cry, *Patria o muerte!*—Alberto Korda, a Cuban photographer on assignment from *Revolucíon,* took pictures of the people on the speakers' platform. They included Jean-Paul Sartre and Simone de Beauvoir, who had been invited to Cuba by Carlos Franqui. At one point, Che appeared and Korda shot two frames of him silhouetted against the sky. The photographs of Che weren't used by *Revolución* for its account of the event, but Korda cropped a palm tree and another figure out of one of them and printed it for himself and pinned it to the wall of his studio. He would occasionally give copies to friends and other visitors. (In April 1967, he gave two prints to the left-wing Italian publisher Giangiacomo Feltrinelli, who turned them into thousands of copies of a poster, the first large-scale use of what would become one of the most famous images of the twentieth century.)*

Not long after the *La Coubre* incident, Fidel asked Alexandr Alexiev to meet with him at Nuñez Jiménez's home in La Cabaña. "For the first time," Alexiev said, "Fidel spoke of arms. He said that after the explosion, the American intervention might be inevitable, imminent. 'We have to arm the people,' he said, and he wanted the Soviet Union to sell him some weapons. He spoke of arms such as light machine guns. 'You could bring these arms in a submarine,' he said. 'We have a lot of caves along the coast and we can hide them where nobody can know about them. Send a message to Khrushchev.'"

By then, a Soviet commercial mission had been established in Havana. Among its members was a cryptographer who handled communications with the Kremlin. After his meeting with Fidel, Alexiev went straight to the cryptographer. "I sent the message directly from Fidel to Khrushchev, and I thought that because of our bureaucracy it would take several weeks to get a reply. The very next day the reply came. 'Fidel, we share your worries about the defense of Cuba and the possibility of an attack,' Khrushchev said, 'and we will supply you with the arms you need. But why do we have to hide them and take them in a submarine if Cuba is a sovereign nation and you can buy whatever arms you need without hiding the fact?' That was his reply. And the arms began to arrive."

V

On May 8, Fidel announced the reestablishment of diplomatic relations with Moscow. Faure Chomón, the former Directorio leader, had moved sharply to the left since the rebels' victory, and he flew to Moscow as Cuba's new ambassador. A veteran KGB man who worked under diplomatic cover, Sergei Kudriatzov, was the Soviet envoy. Alexiev, his TASS identity no longer necessary, was made Kudriatzov's first secretary and cultural attaché, his traditional KGB cover.

---

*See Notes for more history of the photograph.

Following the exchange of messages between Fidel and Khrushchev, a Soviet military delegation arrived quietly in Havana. "We talked right away," said Alexiev. "Fidel, Raúl, Che—everyone participated. They outlined everything they needed. Above all they needed antiaircraft guns and planes, artillery, T-34 tanks, old ones that weren't of any use anymore in the Soviet Union. Another delegation came and they talked of prices, although this wasn't really commerce." By June or July, Soviet arms and military advisers were surreptitiously entering Cuba. According to Alexiev, Fidel was still nervous about the U.S. reaction—as were the Soviets—so some of the Soviet advisers came in on Czech passports.

The secret military agreement with the Soviets signed, Fidel felt strong enough to take on the Americans. In fact, immediately after the Soviet trade deal had been signed in February, he had begun pushing on the tentative détente initiated by Washington. In response to the State Department's overture of late January, which had been left in limbo during Mikoyan's visit, Foreign Minister Roa sent a note to Washington giving Cuba's "conditions" for talks. As long as Washington threatened to cut Cuba's sugar quota, there could be no negotiations. The State Department had replied on February 29, refusing to back down and insisting that the United States had the right to take any measures it felt necessary to protect American interests. When *La Coubre* exploded four days later, the exchange turned bitter again. Secretary of State Herter responded angrily to Fidel's charges of CIA complicity in the incident and questioned Cuba's "good faith" in continuing negotiations.

Washington had made one final attempt to reach out to Fidel. In early March, Cuba's finance minister, Rufo López Fresquet, was approached by Mario Lazo, a legal adviser to the U.S. embassy. Lazo told López Fresquet that the United States was willing to offer Cuba military planes and technical assistance. Fidel asked for two days to consider the offer. On March 17, President Dorticós told López Fresquet on behalf of Fidel that he had decided not to accept. Realizing what this rebuff signified, López Fresquet, the last of the old-style ministers, immediately resigned and left for the United States. If Fidel had any qualms about the course on which he was embarked, Nikita Khrushchev's rapid response had dissolved them.

Upon being notified of Fidel's rebuff, Eisenhower approved the CIA's plan to covertly recruit and train an armed force of several hundred Cuban exiles to lead a guerrilla war against Castro. CIA Director Dulles planned to model the operation after the aptly named Operation Success, the undermining of the Arbenz regime in Guatemala in 1954. He put his deputy director for planning, Richard Bissell, architect of the U-2 spy plane project, in command of the Cuba task force. Other members of the team included

Tracy Barnes, a covert operations veteran who had been instrumental in Operation Success, and Howard Hunt, the CIA's gung ho station chief in Montevideo. A skeptical member of the team was the agency's Western Hemisphere division chief, J. C. King, who warned that Cuba was not Guatemala; King preferred a "dirty war" to destabilize the Cuban regime and advocated the assassination of top figures such as Che, Raúl, and Fidel. But Dulles overruled this option in favor of building up the anti-Castro forces and helping them get a foothold in Cuba.

Gerry Droller, aka Frank Bender, the CIA agent who had met with Fidel in New York a year earlier, was sent to Miami to recruit Cuban fighters among the exile community. Droller soon arranged for them to be trained at a secret site in Guatemala, with the collusion of Guatemala's president, General Ydigoras Fuentes.

A few days later, Che denounced the quota on sugar exports to the United States as economic slavery for the Cuban people. By paying a price higher than the market rate for sugar, he argued, the United States obliged Cuba to maintain a single-crop economy instead of diversifying, a vicious cycle that made Cuba dependent on U.S. imports. This attack on the sugar quota system directly undercut one of Fidel's chief battle standards of the moment. He was decrying the Americans' threat to reduce the quota as an example of American "economic agression"—but, significantly, he did not counter Che's remark.

Meanwhile, Fidel kept moving against the media. The owners of the television station CMQ fled the country, and their station became government property. At the same time, the Ministry of Labor had begun to usurp most of the CTC's functions; the ministry, not the unions, now dictated working terms and conditions.

VI

The face of Havana was changing dramatically. The days of privilege for Cuba's upper and middle classes were coming to an end, and increasing numbers of them were leaving on the ferries and shuttle flights to Miami. As many as 60,000 had already fled by the late spring of 1960. The city that had been an American playground of exclusive yacht clubs, private beaches, casinos, and brothels—and whites-only neighborhoods—was disappearing. The roulette wheels were still spinning in the big hotels, but most of the prostitutes were off the streets. Armed, uniformed blacks and *guajiros* chanting revolutionary slogans roamed the city.

In place of tourists, trade and cultural delegations were arriving from socialist-bloc nations, along with a growing stream of current and future

Che talking to Simone de Beauvoir and Jean-Paul Sartre, who visited
him on their trip to Cuba in 1960. Antonio Nuñez Jiménez is at left.

Third World leaders. Left-wing European and Latin American intellectuals flocked to Havana to attend cultural congresses arranged by the revolution. When Simone de Beauvoir and Jean-Paul Sartre visited Cuba in
February, the famous French couple went to see Che, and they talked for
hours. It must have been a very gratifying experience for him, playing host
to the philosopher whose works he had grown up reading. For his part,
Sartre came away extremely impressed. When Che died, Sartre wrote that
he was "not only an intellectual but also the most complete human being of
our age."

    After Fidel's two-hour speech in response to the *La Coubre* incident,
Sartre and de Beauvoir walked through the streets of Old Havana, where
they saw a public fund-raising campaign already under way for a new con-
signment of arms. De Beauvoir was bewitched by the sensual, fervent mood.
"Young women stood selling fruit juice and snacks to raise money for the
State," she wrote later. "Well-known performers danced or sang in the
squares to swell the fund; pretty girls in their carnival fancy dresses, led by
a band, went through the streets making collections. 'It's the honeymoon of

the Revolution,' Sartre said to me. No machinery, no bureaucracy, but a direct contact between leaders and people, and a mass of seething and slightly confused hopes. It wouldn't last forever, but it was a comforting sight. For the first time in our lives, we were witnessing happiness that had been attained by violence."

On March 23, Che gave a televised speech, "Political Sovereignty and Economic Independence." Through the revolutionary seizure of power, he said, Cuba had attained political independence but had not yet won economic independence, without which it was not a truly politically sovereign nation. Some inroads had been made against the foreign, mostly U.S.-owned, monopolies that had previously held sway over Cuba's economic freedom. The electricity and telephone rates had been cut, rents had been lowered, and the large landholdings had been turned over to the people, but the island's oil, mineral, and chemical wealth was still in the Americans' hands.

> It is good to speak clearly. . . . In order to conquer something we
> have to take it away from somebody. . . . That something we must
> conquer—the country's sovereignty—has to be taken away from
> that somebody called monopoly. . . . It means that our road to lib-
> eration will be opened up with a victory over the monopolies, and
> concretely over the U.S. monopolies.

The revolution had to be "radical," and had to "destroy the roots of evil that afflicted Cuba" in order to "eliminate injustice." Those who opposed the revolution's measures, those who resisted losing their privileges, were counterrevolutionaries. The workers of the reined-in CTC were contributing 4 percent of their wages to the "industrialization" program; it was time the rest of society shouldered its fair share of the revolutionary sacrifice.

Lately Che had been driving home the point that Cuba was no longer just Cuba. It was the revolution, and the revolution was the people; going one step further, the people, Cuba, and the revolution were Fidel. It was time to get on board the new ship of state, or get off. Just as the men of the *Granma* had put aside their individual lives, ready to die if necessary in the war against Batista, so now did all Cubans have to sacrifice for the common aim of total independence. The enemy might well retaliate, he warned. And when the counterrevolutionary soldiers came—paid for perhaps by those same monopolies whose interests were being affected—Cuba would be defended not by a handful of men but by millions. All of Cuba was now a Sierra Maestra, and together, Che said, quoting Fidel, "we will all be saved or we will sink."

The "individualistic" university students with their "middle-class" mentalities seemed to especially provoke Che; perhaps in the students he saw his self-absorbed former self, and it rankled him. In early March he went to Havana University to remind the students that they had a duty to perform in the economic development of Cuba. An individual's sense of vocation wasn't justification for choosing a career; a sense of revolutionary duty should and would take its place.

> I don't think that an individual example, statistically speaking, has any importance, but I began my career studying engineering. I finished as a doctor. Later I became a *comandante* and now you see me here as a speaker. . . . That is to say, within one's individual characteristics, vocation doesn't play a determining role. . . . I think one has to constantly think on behalf of masses and not on behalf of individuals. . . . It's criminal to think of individuals because the needs of the individual become completely weakened in the face of the needs of the human conglomeration.

In practical terms, this meant that certain faculties would be expanded; others would be reduced. Humanities, for instance, was a field that would be kept to the "minimum necessary for the cultural development of the country."

In April, Che's guerrilla warfare manual, *Guerra de Guerrillas,* was published by INRA's Department of Military Training. Che dedicated the book to Camilo Cienfuegos, and a photograph of Camilo astride a horse, holding aloft a rifle, his face beaming under a straw hat, was on the cover. "Camilo is the image of the people," Che wrote. Excerpts were widely published in the Cuban media, and before long, not only Cubans but U.S. and Latin American counterinsurgency specialists would be studying the manual with acute interest. In the prologue, "Essence of the Guerrilla Struggle," Che outlined what he believed to be the cardinal lessons for other revolutionary movements seeking to emulate Cuba's success:

1. Popular forces can win a war against the army.
2. It is not necessary to wait for the conditions to be right to begin the revolution; the insurrectional *foco* [guerrilla group] can create them.
3. In underdeveloped Latin America, the armed struggle should be fought mostly in the countryside.

Guerrilla Warfare was Che's own go-to guide for Latin America's would-be revolutionaries. He gave instructions on how to build tank traps and refuges against mortar fire, explained the usefulness of mules as beasts of burden, and emphasized the importance of a constant supply of salt. "If the force is near the sea, small dryers should be established immediately." He wrote that a good working relationship with local peasant farmers was essential for any guerrilla force; the farmers should be encouraged to grow food and livestock to feed the fighters. Cattle "taken from the large land-owners" should be killed for their meat, and their hides should be used to make leather for boots.

Sabotage was an important part of guerrilla warfare, but the use of terrorism should be selective. "Terrorism is valuable only when used to put to death some noted leader of the oppressing forces well known for his cruelty, his efficiency in repression, or for other qualities that make his elimination useful," Che wrote. Wounded prisoners should always be treated decently, unless their past record made them targets for revolutionary justice. Guerrillas had to be willing to lay down their lives at a moment's notice, for the cause. "The essence of guerrilla warfare is that each one of the guerrilla fighters is ready to die, not to defend an ideal but rather to convert it into reality."

A small band of men and women living in the wildnerness and struggling against all odds, fighting and dying together on behalf of the poor and the downtrodden—this was Che's idealized *foco*. It was an almost biblical notion. Over the coming years, the *foco* theory was to be tested again and again, not least by Che himself, and the efforts almost always ended catastrophically. The very success of Cuba's revolutionary experience worked against most future attempts to replicate it. Governments in the region were forewarned and forearmed, and in the coming years, with direct U.S. military and intelligence support, they demonstrated a grimly successful determination to quash Cuban-style insurgencies at the embryonic *foco* stage.

Within Cuba itself, opposition to the revolution was hardening. An underground movement had begun forming under Manuel Ray, who had been teaching at Havana University since his ouster from government. Another openly dissident quarter was the militant Juventud Católica, which was more vociferous than ever since Mikoyan's visit. In the countryside, small counterrevolutionary groups, inflamed by uncompensated land seizures and the general chaos, were becoming active. Many of the counterrevolutionaries were former Rebel Army men. In Oriente, one of Che's old comrades, Manuel Beatón, had taken up arms against the state. He had murdered another of Che's former fighters, evidently for personal reasons, and fled to the Sierra Maestra with twenty armed followers. In Raúl's old turf in the Sierra Cristal, one of *his* former fighters, Higinio Díaz, had gone back to war as well, allying himself with the disaffected July 26 veteran Jorge Sotús, who had led the first rebel reinforcements from Santiago into the mountains in March 1957. They had formed the Movimiento de Rescate de la Revolución (MRR), organizing themselves around Manuel Artime, a former naval academy professor living in exile in Miami. With Artime in Miami, Díaz in the sierra, and a network of underground supporters in Havana, the MRR had quickly come under the benevolent eye of the CIA.

It was not long before Fidel's "listeners" among Cuba's swollen exile community in Miami picked up rumors of the CIA's recruitment drive. In late April, Fidel accused the United States of trying to create an "international front" against him, and he warned that Cuba was not another Guatemala. In Guatemala itself, President Ydigoras Fuentes then accused Che of trying to organize a guerrilla invasion force against his country. On April 25, Cuba and Guatemala broke off relations. Undeterred, the CIA program continued to expand. Anti-Castro propaganda was broadcast to Cuba from a radio transmitter installed on tiny Swan Island, near the Cayman Islands. The man running the station was David Atlee Phillips, who six years earlier in Guatemala had first brought the agency's attention to Ernesto Guevara.

One of the Cuban exiles who joined the CIA's recruitment drive that summer was Felix Rodríguez. He was now nineteen years old. In the aftermath of the failed invasion of Trinidad the year before, he had returned to his military academy in Pennsylvania. After graduating in June 1960, he went to his parents' home in Miami, then ran away to join the CIA program. By September, he would be among several hundred Cuban exiles in Guatemala who were receiving guerrilla training from a Filipino West Point graduate who had fought both the Japanese and the Communists in his country. Their force would eventually be called Brigade 2506.

On May Day, Fidel spoke at the Plaza de la Revolución, which was packed with armed Cubans marching past his podium. He praised the new militias and invoked the threat of an impending invasion; Cubans, like the Spartans, would stand, fight, and die without fear. He also took the opportunity to make two important points clear: If *he* died, Raúl would take his place as prime minister. What's more, there were not going to be any elections; since "the people" ruled Cuba already, there was no need to cast votes. The crowd cheered, repeating the phrase *"Revolución Sí, Elecciones No!"* and a new slogan, *"Cuba Sí, Yanqui No!"*

By then, the United States government estimated that Cuba's armed forces had doubled to 50,000 since January 1959, with another 50,000 civilians already incorporated into the new people's militias—and there was no end in sight. If the training and arming continued unchecked, Cuba would soon have the largest army in Latin America. Washington's private fears that Fidel might already have obtained Soviet military support gained credence on May 3, when the U.S. Senate heard testimony from two officers of the Batista era, former Chief of Staff Tabernilla and Colonel Ugalde Carrillo. Carillo accused Fidel of building Soviet missile bases in the Ciénaga de Zapata. Foreign Minister Roa quickly rebutted the charge, and few gave it credit at the time, but within a year the fantastic notion would become a reality.

Fidel's militaristic May Day rally, and his decision to renew diplomatic relations with the Soviets a week later, sparked the final round between his government and Cuba's last surviving independent media. *Diario de la Marina's* editorials compared Castro to the Antichrist; within days, its offices were attacked and occupied by "workers," and its presses closed down permanently. The editor sought asylum and fled the country. By the end of the month, the two main remaining independent dailies, *Prensa Libre* and *El Crisol,* were also put out of circulation, soon to be followed by the English-language *Havana Post* and *La Calle.*

The first Soviet tankers were already crossing the Atlantic with oil for Cuba, fulfilling part of the barter agreement signed with Mikoyan. The U.S.-owned Esso and Texaco, and British-owned Shell, each of which had refineries in Cuba, had until now been supplying the island with oil from Venezuela. But Cuba had not paid for some time, and the outstanding bill amounted to about $50 million. Che Guevara, as president of the National Bank, was the man to see about getting bills paid. Esso's American manager got a cold reception and no clear answers when he asked Che about the debt.

Che now felt confident enough to take on the U.S. petroleum companies, and he told Alexiev that his plan was to offer them a deal he knew they would have to refuse, which would give him the pretext he needed to seize their installations. Alexiev counseled caution, but Che went ahead anyway. On May 17, he informed the American oil firms that in order for him to pay off the debt owed to them, they each had to buy 300,000 barrels of the Soviet oil that was arriving and process it in their refineries. The companies did not reply right away but sought counsel in Washington, where the government advised them to reject Che's offer.

Opposition activities continued to grow, and so did the government's crackdown. The members of a rebel group in the Escambray, which was made up mostly of students from the University of Las Villas, were captured and shot. The former CTC leader David Salvador went underground and soon joined forces with Manuel Ray's creation, the Movimiento Revolucionario del Pueblo (MRP). The archbishop of Santiago, Enrique Pérez Serantes, a former Fidel supporter, issued a pastoral letter that denounced Fidel's new Communist ties and seemed to bless the spreading antigovernment violence. "Shedding blood is preferable to losing liberty," he wrote. Still wishing to avoid a showdown with the Church, Fidel remained mute. In Miami, the CIA merged the MRR with an anti-Castro group led by Prío's former prime minister, Tony Varona. The result was the Frente Democrático Revolucionario (FDR), which was intended to provide a political front to the military force being trained in Guatemala.

While the dissidents were forming separate groups with different agendas to oppose him, Fidel's revolution had acquired an unstoppable momentum. In June he ordered the seizure of three of Havana's luxury hotels, justifying the action on the same grounds as Che's earlier "interventions" of factories. Their owners were intentionally underfinancing them, making them unprofitable, and therefore a takeover by the state was necessary. Fidel also took up the gauntlet Che had thrown to the American oil companies. They would do as Cuba requested and process the Soviet oil, he declared, or face the confiscation of their properties. Days later, Cuba expelled two U.S. diplomats, accusing them of spying; in response, the Americans expelled three Cuban diplomats.

The war of wills quickly escalated. Fidel warned the United States that it ran the risk of losing all its property in Cuba. If it reduced the quota of Cuban sugar available for export, he would seize one sugar mill for every pound of sugar taken away. On June 29, the day that two Soviet oil tankers docked in Cuba, he ordered Texaco's Cuban installations seized. Twenty-four hours later, Esso's and Shell's installations were taken over. In one fell swoop, Cuba had freed itself of a $50 million debt and gained an oil-refining industry.

On July 3, the U.S. Congress authorized President Eisenhower to cut Cuba's sugar quota. Fidel responded by legalizing the nationalization of all American property in Cuba. On July 6, Eisenhower canceled the Cuban sugar quota for the rest of the year, some 700,000 tons. Calling this an act of "economic aggression," Fidel now dropped broad hints of his arms deal with the Soviet Union, saying he would soon have the weapons he needed to arm his militias; ominously, he also ordered 600 U.S.-owned companies to register all their assets in Cuba.

Khrushchev now entered the game openly. On July 9, he warned the United States—stressing that he was speaking figuratively—that, "should the need arise, Soviet artillerymen can support the Cuban people by missile fire," pointing out that the United States was now within range of the Soviets' new generation of intercontinental ballistic missiles. Eisenhower denounced Khrushchev's threats and warned that the United States would not permit a regime "dominated by international Communism" in the Western Hemisphere. The very next day, Khrushchev announced that the Soviet Union would buy the 700,000 tons of sugar cut from the American sugar quota.

In Havana, Che happily shook his fist at Washington, saying that Cuba was protected by "the greatest military power on earth; nuclear weapons now stand in the face of imperialism." Nikita Khrushchev had insisted that he had been speaking figuratively, but before long, the world would discover that the threat was very real. And Che had been the first to say so.

VII

By July 1960, Che's wife, Aleida, was nearly five months' pregnant with their first child. Their married life had attained a comparative peace and normality. It helped that since Che moved to the National Bank, Aleida and Hilda—who now worked at Prensa Latina—no longer had to see each other every day.

Che and Aleida had moved again, with their permanent guest Fernández Mell in tow, to a pretty two-story neocolonial house with gardens in the residential neighborhood of Miramar, on Eighteenth Street and Seventh Avenue. The Harvard-trained economist Regino Boti, one of the few remaining moderates still at his job in the Ministry of the Economy, lived across the street. The headquarters for Cuban State Security was a block and a half away, in a handsome neocolonial mansion on Fifth Avenue.

To Che's delight, his old friend and traveling companion, Alberto Granado, showed up in time for the July 26 celebrations. It had been eight years since Fuser had said farewell to Mial in Caracas, promising to return after finishing his medical exams. Granado had continued his work at the leprosarium and had married a Venezuelan woman. The birth of their first child coincided with news of the *Granma*'s landing and the false reports of Ernesto Guevara's death. Granado had been visiting his family in Argentina when word of Batista's flight came, and he had celebrated Che's arrival in Havana with the Guevara clan. When he heard that Che would be accompanying Fidel to Caracas in 1959, Granado had eagerly awaited his arrival and was crestfallen when he didn't arrive. They had corresponded, however, and now, finally, Granado and his family had made it to Cuba.

Granado spent as much time as possible with Che and went with him to greet the captain of one of the first Soviet tankers delivering Russian oil to Cuba. With Granado at his side, Che told the captain that he was grateful "for having friends who lend a hand at the necessary time." If Che's words were an oblique hint to Granado, they had an effect; within a few months, he had quit his faculty job in Venezuela, packed up his family, and moved

to Cuba, where he too could lend a hand. He would get a job teaching biochemistry at the University of Havana.

Doctor David Mitrani, Che's friend and colleague from the General
Hospital in Mexico City, also flew in for the July 26 celebrations. Mitrani, who
had been born to European Jewish émigrés and was a Zionist, had gone to
Israel to work on a kibbutz the month before Che boarded the *Granma*. Although they had argued over politics—Che called Zionism "reactionary"—
they had both considered themselves to be committed to socialism. After
meeting Fidel in Mexico, Che had urged Mitrani to join the Cuban revolutionary venture and had ridiculed his plan to "go and pick potatoes" in Israel.
Mitrani had told Ernesto that he thought Fidel was "full of shit" and that the
plan to invade Cuba was crazy. Although their friendship remained intact,
they lost contact after going on their separate adventures. When Mitrani returned to Mexico from Israel on the eve of the rebels' victory in Cuba, he had
sent Che a telegram congratulating him and his comrades.

Since then, Mitrani had established a private medical practice in Mexico
City. He had kept up with news from Cuba and had been shocked to learn
of his friend's role in the revolutionary executions, but when he received
Che's invitation to come to Cuba in 1960, he accepted. Before going, he met
with the Mexican president, Adolfo López Mateos, who asked Mitrani to
bring him back a signed copy of Che's *Guerra de Guerrillas*. The Israeli
ambassador in Mexico asked him to use his contact with Che to see if relations with Cuba could be improved. The Israeli ambassador in Cuba was,
coincidentally, related to Mitrani.

In Havana, Mitrani was lodged in the elegant Hotel Nacional and
summoned by Che for lunch in his private dining room at the National Bank.
Che was in a sardonic mood. "I know you're a bourgeois," he said, "so I've
had a special meal prepared for you, with wine and everything." Mitrani
found Che far more acerbic than he remembered, with a cutting sense of
humor. They met several times, always at the bank, and in their first meetings there were always others present. It wasn't until his third or fourth visit
that Mitrani felt he could talk openly.

Che asked Mitrani if he wanted to go to Oriente, where Fidel was
going to give his July 26 speech, and Mitrani told him no; he'd come to
Cuba to see Che, not Fidel. He didn't attempt to hide his old antipathy
for Fidel. He told Che of Israel's desire for better relations, and Che seemed
supportive. (The days when Cuba would take the Soviet position in favor
of the PLO were still years in the future.) Eventually, Che spoke candidly
with Mitrani about the revolution. "By the first days of August, we're
going to transform this country into a socialist state," he said. At least that
was what he hoped and expected, and he explained that Fidel himself was

not yet totally convinced, because he wasn't a socialist; Che was still trying to persuade him.

Mitrani brought up the issue that had been troubling him the most:
Che's role in the executions. Mitrani told him that he couldn't understand
his involvement, since Che wasn't even Cuban and hadn't suffered at the
hands of the *batistíanos*. Where had this hatred, this desire for vengeance,
come from? "Look," Che said, "in this thing you have to kill before they
kill you." Mitrani let the matter drop but remained troubled by his friend's
logic; it was something he would never learn to reconcile with the Ernesto
Guevara he had known.

Before Mitrani left, Che gave him one of the new Cuban banknotes
with his signature and three inscribed copies of *Guerra de Guerrillas:* for
himself; for Che's old mentor in Mexico, Dr. Salazar Mallén; and for President López Mateos. His dedication to Mitrani read: "To David, in the hope
that you return again to the right path."

VIII

In his triumphant July 26 speech in Oriente, Fidel took up what had until then
been Che's personal vision, warning his Latin American neighbors that unless they improved living conditions for their people, "Cuba's example would
convert the Andean Cordillera into the hemisphere's Sierra Maestra." Fidel
could claim that he was speaking only metaphorically, but of course he wasn't.

The combination of Fidel's adoption of his "continental guerrilla"
scheme and Khrushchev's veiled threat to Washington greatly excited Che.
Two days later, speaking before the delegates of the First Latin American
Youth Congress, he was uncharacteristically emotional.

> This people [of Cuba] you see today tell you that even if they should
> disappear from the face of the earth because an atomic war is un-
> leashed in their names . . . they would feel completely happy and
> fulfilled if each one of you, upon reaching your lands, can say:
>
> "Here we are. Our words come moist from the Cuban
> jungles. We have climbed the Sierra Maestra and we have known
> the dawn, and our minds and our hands are full with the seed of
> the dawn, and we are prepared to sow it in this land and to de-
> fend it so that it flourishes."
>
> And from all the other brother nations of America, and from
> our land, if it still survived as an example, the voice of the peoples
> will answer you, from that moment on and forever: "It shall be
> so: may liberty be conquered in each corner of America!"

Once again, Che invoked the specter of death, now envisioned on a truly massive scale, to extol the beauty of collective sacrifice for liberation. He spoke with the heartfelt conviction of someone with no doubts about the purity of his cause. Che Guevara, age thirty-two, had become the high priest of international revolution. He had plenty of eager listeners, left-wing youths from Chile to Puerto Rico, and he backhandedly thanked Jacobo Arbenz, who was present, for his "brave example" in Guatemala. Cubans had learned from the "weaknesses" of the Arbenz government and had been able to "go to the roots of the question and decapitate in one stroke those in power and the thugs of those in power." In Cuba, he said, they had done what *had* to be done. They had used the *paredón*—the firing squad—and chased out the monopolies, in spite of those who preached moderation, most of whom, he said, had turned out to be traitors anyway. "'Moderation' is another one of the terms the colonial agents like to use," Che said. "All those who are afraid, or who are considering some form of treason, are moderates. . . . But the people are by no means moderate."

In his next breath, Che took on Venezuela's anticommunist president, Rómulo Betancourt, whom he had despised on meeting him in 1953, and with whom Cuba's relations had openly soured. Che said that Betancourt's government was "prisoner to its own thugs." He warned that "the [Venezuelan] people won't remain the prisoners of some bayonets or a few bullets for long, because the bullets and the bayonets can change hands, and the murderers can end up dead." He was alluding to Betancourt's heavy-handed use of security forces to put down the mounting tide of demonstrations against his policies, and the recent upsurge of Marxist political opposition to his government. In May, the leftist youth wing of Betancourt's own party had split off to form the Movimiento de Izquierda Revolucionaria (MIR), inspired by Cuba's revolutionary example, and it would not be long before the *miristas* launched an insurrection against Betancourt with the collaboration of the Venezuelan Communist Party.

Talking to a group of medical students, health workers, and militiamen on the topic of "revolutionary medicine" in late August, Che prepared them for the possibility that Cuba would soon be fighting a massive "people's" guerrilla war. Cuba's new generation of doctors should join the revolutionary militias—"the greatest expression of the people's solidarity"—and practice "social medicine," to give healthy bodies to the Cubans whom the revolution had liberated. Drawing on his own life as an example, Che told the crowd that when he began to study medicine, he had dreamed of becoming a famous researcher. "I dreamed of working tirelessly to aid humanity, but this was conceived as personal achievement," he recalled. It was only when he graduated and traveled through a Latin America riven by misery, hunger, and disease that his political conscience had begun to stir. In Guatemala, he began studying the means through which he could become a revolutionary doctor, but Guatemala's socialist experiment was overthrown. "I became aware, then, of a fundamental fact: To be a revolutionary doctor or to be a revolutionary at all, there must first be a revolution. The isolated effort of one man, regardless of its purity of ideals, is worthless. To be useful it is essential to make a revolution as we have done in Cuba, where the whole population mobilizes and learns how to use arms and fight together. Cubans have learned how much value there is in a weapon and the unity of the people."

At the heart of the revolution, then, was the elimination of individualism. "Individualism as such, as the isolated action of a person alone in a social environment, must disappear in Cuba. Individualism tomorrow should be the proper utilization of the whole individual to the absolute benefit of the community." The revolution was not a "standardizer of the collective will"; rather, it was a "liberator of man's individal capacity," for it oriented that capacity to the service of the revolution.

In his talk to the medical students, Che tried out a phrase that crystallized a concept which he had been developing for some time, and which would soon become synonymous with him: the "new man."

> How does one reconcile individual effort with the needs of society? We again have to recall what each of our lives was like, what each of us did and thought, as a doctor or in any other public health function, prior to the revolution. We have to do so with profound critical enthusiasm. And we will then conclude that almost everything we thought and felt in that past epoch should be filed away, and that a new type of human being should be created. And if each one of us is his own architect of that new human type, then creating that new type of human being—who will be the representative of the new Cuba—will be much easier.

A few days later, Che met with René Dumont, a French Marxist economist who was trying to help Cuba in its difficult conversion to socialism. After extensive travels around the country, Dumont had concluded that one of the biggest problems of the newly established agricultural cooperatives was that their workers did not feel they were owners of anything. He urged Che to consider a scheme whereby the workers who did additional labor during the off-season to maintain the cooperatives would be paid, giving them a sense of co-ownership.

According to Dumont, Che reacted violently to the idea. It was not a sense of ownership that Cuban workers needed, he said, but a sense of responsibility, and he spelled out what this meant. Che had, Dumont wrote, "a sort of ideal vision of Socialist Man, who would become a stranger to the mercantile side of things, working for society and not for profit. He was very critical of the industrial success of the Soviet Union, where, he said, everybody works and strives and tries to go beyond his quota, but only to earn more money. He did not think the Soviet Man was a new sort of man. He did not find him any different, really, than a Yankee. He refused to consciously participate in the creation in Cuba 'of a second American society.'" As far as Dumont could see, Che seemed to be advocating skipping stages in Cuba's socialist transformation of society by going directly from capitalism to Communism, much as Mao had tried to do in China in 1956 with his radical Great Leap Forward forced collectivization. "In short, Che was far ahead of his time—in thought, he had already entered a Communist stage."

Che now openly acknowledged the Communist influences in Cuba's revolution while engaging in some heavy revisionism to prove that they had come about of their own accord. It was only after he and his comrades had fought against the encirclement and annihilation tactics of Batista's army in the Sierra Maestra, he claimed, that "a pamphlet of Mao's fell into our hands" and the rebels discovered they had been fighting with much the same tactics Mao had used against a kindred foe. Similarly, it was seeing the needs of the peasants of the Sierra Maestra that brought the rebel leaders to the threshold of political enlightenment. Was the revolution Communist? he asked rhetorically. "In the event that it were Marxist—and hear carefully that I say Marxist—it would be so because [the revolution] discovered the paths signaled by Marx through its own methods." Che was going much farther than Fidel; it would still be nine months before *el jefe máximo* publicly acknowledged that his revolution had a "socialist nature."

If there was growing disenchantment among some of Fidel's old allies—that summer several more of his former comrades in arms resigned their posts—the disenchantment was also spreading to the PSP. For all the gains it had made since January 1959, it was clear that the Communist Party was becoming increasingly subordinated to Fidel. His preeminence had been blessed by Khrushchev, who reportedly sent him a private note in May to the effect that the Kremlin "does not consider any party to be an intermediary" between Fidel and itself. Communist or not, what was being erected in Cuba was an old-fashioned personality cult.

Bohemia's owner and editor, Miguel Ángel Quevedo, who had experienced a loss of faith since comparing Fidel to Christ the year before, shut down his magazine and fled the country. Before he left, he accused Fidel of delivering Cuba into a shameful state of "Russian vassalage." Miró Cardona, the former prime minister, also left for the United States, where he soon joined the anti-Castro forces. A mass anticommunist rally was held in Santiago by the Juventud Católica; a priest and some of the group's members were captured after a gun battle in which two policemen were killed. Cardinal Arteaga published a pastoral letter that was harshly critical of the government. This time, Fidel responded, complaining of the Church's "systematic provocations."

As the U.S. presidential election entered its final stretch, the fencing between Washington and Havana accelerated. Cuba had become a central issue in the campaign, with each of the candidates—Vice President Nixon and Senator Kennedy—promising to be tougher against Cuba than his opponent would be. Kennedy ridiculed the Eisenhower administration's "do-nothing" policies that had brought about the present crisis; *his* administration, he said, would take firm action to restore "democracy" in Cuba.

Kennedy's charges hit a nerve. The White House pushed through bills to impose sanctions against countries that bought Cuban sugar with American loans and to cut off security assistance to nations that gave *any* aid to Cuba. A debate over "Who lost Cuba?" ensued at the State Department. Then, the United States took its case to the Organization of American States, and, dangling the promise of a new foreign aid handout at a conference of OAS foreign ministers in Costa Rica, pushed through a unanimous declaration condemning any intervention in the hemisphere by "an extra-continental power," a clear reference to Cuba's growing partnership with the Soviet Union.

Fidel reacted to the "San José Declaration" with passionate indignation. On September 2, he made what became known as his Havana Declaration, outlining Cuba's position in the hemisphere as a revolutionary example, and, without using the word "socialist," proclaimed Cuba's determination to defend the rights of the oppressed by fighting against exploitation, capitalism, and imperialism. He added that if the United States dared attack his country, he would welcome Khrushchev's proffered missiles. Finally, he announced, his government would officially recognize Communist China.

Fidel followed up the Havana Declaration with a rowdy trip to New York for the opening session of the United Nations General Assembly. This time, he took pains to be as irritating as possible. He camped out in a hotel in Harlem, the Theresa, on 125th Street, claiming to show solidarity with oppressed black Americans. He played host to Khrushchev, who gave him a bear hug, and met with such "anti-imperialists" as Kwame Nkrumah, Nasser, and Nehru. The Soviet-bloc presidents of Poland and Bulgaria also paid calls on him. In the General Assembly, Fidel and Khrushchev formed a mutual-admiration society. They echoed each other's speeches, lauding the Cuban revolution, accusing the United States of aggression, calling for global nuclear disarmament, and arguing for a revamped, more nonaligned United Nations.

The biggest crisis facing the UN at that moment was in the Congo. Belgium had granted its former colony independence at the end of June, but in the ensuing violent turmoil, Belgian troops had occupied much of the country. The Soviets, the Americans, and the UN itself had intervened in support of various factions. Joseph Mobutu, the Congolese army's chief of staff, who was supported by the CIA, had taken power in a coup on September 14 and ordered the Soviets to leave the country. Khrushchev protested against the UN's involvement in the situation. Essentially, he accused the secretary-general, Dag Hammarskjöld, of being a Western stooge. The Cuban delegation cheered him on. Fidel received attention for giving the longest recorded speech in United Nations history, clocked at well over four hours. He and his bombastic entourage were dubbed "the Greatest Show on Earth" by the press.

Fidel flew back to Havana on a borrowed Soviet Ilyushin after his own aircraft were impounded in consequence of a suit from an ad agency in Miami regarding unpaid bills. He soon began dismantling the last vestiges of American influence while simultaneously tightening the revolution's controls. On September 28, he created the Committees to Defend the Revolution (CDRs)—a nationwide network of civic organizations. The inhabitants of each block in every town and city in Cuba formed a committee to ensure the implemention of revolutionary decrees and to provide grassroots vigilantes for the state security apparatus.

The U.S. embassy in Havana began advising American citizens to leave the island. Recruitment and arms training for the national militia—according to Fidel, already more than 200,000 strong—had become the new national priority.

Ironically, the sheer number of Cuban exiles who now wanted to take up arms *against* Fidel was causing some headaches for the CIA. In Miami, Justo Carrillo resigned from the Americans' anti-Castro alliance, upset at the growing influx of ex-*batistíanos*. There were now some 600 men training in the Guatemalan camps, with smaller groups receiving specialized guerrilla training in Panama and Louisiana. In Havana, Manuel Ray's group carried out a daring assault on La Cabaña and freed some of the officers imprisoned with Huber Matos; afterward, Ray managed to escape to the United States. What was lacking in all these disparate efforts was any degree of cohesiveness or a leader strong enough to unite and bend the others to his will; in short, the anti-Fidelistas didn't have a Fidel.

In early October, a group of armed Cubans and an American were captured in Oriente after a gun battle with government troops, and a few days later Cuban soldiers captured a cache of weapons and ammunition dropped by a CIA plane in the Escambray mountains. There were now as many as a thousand rebels in the Escambray, sustained by CIA airdrops of arms and supplies. They were being helped on the ground by the American expatriate mercenary William Morgan and one of his old comrades, the ex–Second Front warlord Jesús Carreras. Having learned well the lesson of his own ordeal in the Sierra Maestra, Fidel ordered the army and the militias to carry out a mass evacuation of the area's peasantry to isolate the rebels from sources of food and intelligence. Before long, most of the rebels, among them Morgan and Carreras, had been either wiped out or captured and shot by firing squads, although the Escambray would remain a focus of counter-revolutionary activity for several more years.

Che, Raúl, and Fidel attended the eleventh-anniversary celebrations of the founding of the People's Republic of China with the head of China's new trade legation to Cuba. Trade deals were signed with Hungary and Bulgaria. Fidel invited Jean-Paul Sartre and Simone de Beauvoir to visit Cuba again, and they did, but this time they weren't so entranced. "Havana had changed; no more nightclubs, no more gambling, and no more American tourists; in the half-empty Nacional Hotel, some very young members of the militia, boys and girls, were holding a conference. On every side, in the streets, the militia was drilling," de Beauvoir wrote. The atmosphere was tense with rumors of invasion, and a notable air of repressive uniformity was seeping into Cuban life. When Sartre and de Beauvoir asked workers at a clothing mill how their lives had benefited from the revolution, a union leader quickly stepped forward to speak on their behalf, parroting the government's dogma. In the cultural arena, Soviet-style "socialist realism" had arrived; writers told the French couple that they had begun to engage in self-censorship, and the poet Nicolás Guillén said that he considered "all research into technique and form counterrevolutionary." They left after a few days, with de Beauvoir concluding, "[In Cuba there was] less gaiety, less freedom, but much progress on certain fronts." As an example of the latter, she cited a visit to an agricultural cooperative that had impressed her; still, "the 'honeymoon of the revolution' was over."

IX

On October 11, Che summoned Cuba's richest man, the sugar magnate Julio Lobo, to his office. The owner of vast tracts of productive land—now expropriated—and thirteen sugar mills, Lobo was a force to be reckoned with.

He was a cultured man, famous for his collection of art treasures and Napoleonica, and was something of an enigma, having refused to leave Cuba or lend his voice to the flood of anti-Castro protests. Fidel was going to seize the sugar mills in a few days, and Che wanted to persuade Lobo to stay in the country. Alfredo Menéndez, who administered the state's sugar mills for INRA, was advised in advance of the offer Che was going to make Lobo: a monthly salary of $2,000 and the right to keep any one of his palatial homes. "We really didn't want him to leave," Menéndez said. "All that talent was what Che wanted."

The very notion of offering such a wage to a man whose fortune was estimated to be in the hundreds of millions of dollars might appear absurd, but perhaps more than anything else, it reflected Che's singular devotion to his ideal, and his belief that others—even Julio Lobo—might share it. Troubled by the brain drain of experienced technicians and administrators from Cuba, he had often tried to persuade skilled personnel—men such as Napoleón Padilla—to stay, promising to honor their capitalist-era salaries. In terms of the "new Cuba," the salary he was offering Lobo was high; he himself had refused the $1,000 monthly salary due him as president of the National Bank, as a matter of principle, accepting only the $250 paid him in his capacity as a *comandante*.

Che informed Lobo that the time had come for him to make a decision. The revolution was Communist, and Lobo, as a capitalist, could not remain as he was; either he could stay and be a part of it, or he had to go. Lobo gamely pointed out that Khrushchev believed in "peaceful coexistence" between the world's competing political and economic systems, to which Che replied that such a proposition "was possible between nations, but not *within* one."

Che then laid out his offer. Lobo was invited to become the administrator of Cuba's sugar industry. He would lose his properties but be allowed to keep the income from one of his mills. Lobo said he needed time to think about it, but he had already made up his mind. He went home, and two days later flew to Miami. The following day, the government nationalized all of Cuba's banks and large commercial, industrial, and transportation businesses. All of Lobo's sugar mills and homes and their contents were seized, and his Napoleonica collection eventually becoming a state museum.

A second urban reform law banned Cubans from owning more than one home and took over all rented properties, making their inhabitants tenants of the state. On October 19, Washington responded to the latest mass seizures—which had affected many American companies—by imposing a trade embargo on Cuba, prohibiting all exports to the island except food and medicine. On October 25, Fidel nationalized 166 U.S.-owned companies, in effect signing the death certificate for all remaining American commercial interests in Cuba. He boasted that he had both the people and the arms he needed to fight off an invasion. By now, Washington knew this claim was true. On October 28, the U.S. government filed a protest with the OAS, charging Cuba with having received "substantial" arms shipments since the summer from the Soviet bloc. The next day, Ambassador Bonsal was recalled to Washington yet again, this time for "extended consultations." He was never to return to Cuba. By then, Che was in Prague, en route to Moscow.

X

On November 7, Che stood in a place of honor next to Nikita Khrushchev in Moscow's wintry Red Square, overlooking the annual military parade commemorating the forty-third anniversary of the October Revolution. Nikolai Leonov, his interpreter, watched from the stand where the diplomatic corps was assembled. Moments earlier, Che had been at Leonov's side, shivering from the cold, when a messenger had come to inform him that he was invited to join Khrushchev. "Che said no," Leonov recalled, "he didn't feel important enough to be in a place that was so sacred to him." The mes-

In November 1960, Che traveled to Moscow, where he met with Nikita Khrushchev. Che's translator, the KGB officer Nikolai Leonov, is standing next to him.

senger left but soon returned. The Soviet premier was insistent. Che turned
to Leonov and asked what he should do; Leonov told him to go. To Leonov's
knowledge, it was the first time a person who was not a head of state "or at
least a Party chief" had been invited to stand on the hallowed Supreme Soviet
tribune above the red marble tomb where Lenin's embalmed body lay in
state.

José Pardo Llada was also in Red Square that day, as part of a Cuban
press delegation invited by the Soviet Journalists' Union. Seeing Guevara
on the exclusive terrace of the Presidium, with Nikita Khrushchev next to
him and surrounded by the luminaries of the Communist world, he noted
that "Guevara, in the midst of the international paraphernalia of Communism, looked satisfied, radiant, happy."

Che was on his first tour of the Communist bloc, a two-month trip
that took him to Prague, Moscow, Leningrad, Stalingrad, Irkutsk, Beijng,
Shanghai, Pyongyang, and Berlin. The main purpose of Che's trip was to
secure the sale of that portion of Cuba's upcoming sugar crop not already
committed to Moscow, a mission that had taken on some urgency following Eisenhower's decision to halt the purchase of all Cuban sugar for the
rest of 1960. He knew that this was only a prelude to a total American ban
on Cuban sugar imports, but he could hardly have been unhappy about that
prospect; it was, after all, something he had worked hard to bring about ever
since the rebels' victory.

Che had left Havana on October 22, three days after the U.S. embargo
was announced. He was accompanied by Leonardo Tamayo, his eighteen-
year-old bodyguard, who had been with him since the Sierra Maestra; Héctor
Rodríguez Llompart, his messenger for the talks with Mikoyan; and several Cuban, Chilean, and Ecuadorean economists who worked for him at
INRA. At their first stop, Prague, Che toured a tractor factory, gave inter-
views, and obtained a $20 million credit to build an auto assembly plant in
Cuba. In Moscow, between talks with economic, military, and trade offi-
cials and tours of factories, he went sightseeing. He visited the Lenin
Museum and the Kremlin, laid a wreath at Lenin's tomb, attended a
Tchaikovsky concert, and, with Mikoyan, watched a performance at the
Bolshoi Theater. Leonov went with him everywhere.

"He was highly organized," Leonov recalled. "In that sense he was not
at all Latin, rather more like a German. Punctual, precise, it was an amaze-
ment to all of us who knew Latin America. But the other members of his
delegation were really undisciplined. One day, the [sugar] negotiations were
programmed to start at ten in the morning. Che came down to where the
cars were waiting, alone; none of the other members of the delegation had
come down yet, they were all still half-asleep. I asked him: 'Che, shall we

wait? Don't worry, I'll tell the minister to wait for us for fifteen or twenty minutes.' He said: 'No, let's go alone,' and he went off to the negotiations accompanied only by me. When we arrived the Soviets were amazed because they had the whole delegation sitting there, and on the other side was only Che."

The meeting began, and, after twenty minutes or so, the other members of the Cuban delegation started arriving, out of breath and without ties. "Che said nothing, not a single word of criticism, not even the slightest expression altered his face—nothing. But that night, he told me: 'Listen, Nicolás, organize a visit for us tomorrow to Lenin's Museum, and tell the guide to place special emphasis on the discipline Lenin demanded of the Politburo members of that time, tell him to talk about that.'"

Leonov arranged everything, just as Che had requested, and the next day the whole group went off to the museum. "The young woman giving the history began to talk about Lenin's administrative discipline," Leonov recalled. "She explained that when someone was late to a meeting of the Council of Ministers, the first punishment was a very serious warning. The second time they were late, it was a heavy fine and their lapse was published in the Party newspaper. The third time, they were fired." Che's comrades took the hint. Leonov could see the impact on their faces and on Che's, which was "grave, ironic."

Leonov said that after the example of Lenin was suggested at the museum, discipline problems among the entourage ended. Héctor Rodríguez Llompart, however, was punished for having done a sloppy job proofreading the text of a commercial treaty that was to be signed with the government of Romania. Che spotted an error that Llompart had missed and upbraided him furiously. "He said horrible things," Llompart recalled. "I felt crushed, but I had no excuse. I simply hadn't done what I was supposed to do. At first he reacted violently, demanding explanations, but then he became aware of my humiliation and stopped talking. He knew I understood my mistake and that I was ashamed of it." That wasn't the end of it, however. A few days later, Llompart roused himself early to join the rest of the delegation for a sightseeing tour of Leningrad. Che saw him and asked: "Where are you going?" "Well, Comandante," Llompart said, "to Leningrad." "No," Che told him, "first you must learn to fulfill your duty." The group left without Llompart. The sanctions against him lasted for several days.

Che was hardest on those he felt had the ability to become true revolutionaries. If they failed, he could be merciless; if they passed muster, he repaid them with his trust. A few weeks after the proofreading incident, Che named Llompart his representative to visit Vietnam. And when Che returned to Cuba, he appointed Llompart to head the delegation to the remaining Eastern-bloc states on the agenda: Poland, Hungary, Bulgaria, Romania, and Albania.

Che was often blunt to the point of causing offense. When they were in Moscow, Leonov decided to treat him to a private meal. His own apartment was too small for such an occasion, and he arranged with Alexiev's family to prepare a special dinner at their larger, more comfortable flat. They worked hard, preparing sturgeon and other Russian fish delicacies, but when Che arrived, he exclaimed: "*Madre mía!* I'm going to go hungry tonight!" He informed his crestfallen hosts that he couldn't eat fish because of his allergies, and they hastily cooked him some eggs. Later, seated at the magnificently prepared table, Che began tapping on the plates and looking around pointedly at his dinner companions. The Alexievs, who had once lived in Paris, were showing off their best china. Lifting an eyebrow, Che remarked: "So, the proletariat here eats off of French porcelain, eh?"

Che never said so publicly, but those who knew him say he returned from his first trip to Russia dismayed by the elite lifestyle and the evident predilection for bourgeois luxuries he saw among Kremlin officials. Four and a half decades of socialism had not created a new Socialist Man, at least not among the party elite.

Nikolai Leonov spent a good deal of time with Che on the trip, and they spoke of many things, including Che's experience in Guatemala. Che castigated Jacobo Arbenz for having "given up the battle" without a fight. Leadership was a sacred duty granted to an individual "chosen" by the people on the basis of trust. It was a privilege that came with the obligation to honor that trust, if necessary, with one's life. "I don't know if the Cuban revolution will survive or not," he told Leonov. "It's difficult to say. But if it doesn't . . . don't come looking for me among the refugees in the embassies. I've had that experience, and I'm not ever going to repeat it. I will go out with a machine gun in my hand, to the barricades. . . . I'll keep fighting to the end."

Leonov was present for Che's talks with Khrushchev. Among other things, Che wanted Cuba to have its own steel plant—the indispensable cornerstone to industrialization—with a capacity for a million tons of steel. He also wanted the Soviets to fund and build it. "Khrushchev heard him out reservedly and said, 'Well, let's study it,'" Leonov recalled. "And for the several days that the ministerial experts were studying the project, Che became more insistent. Every time he saw Khrushchev, Che asked, 'Well, Nikita, what about the factory?' Finally Nikita told him: 'Look, Che, if you want, we can build the plant, but in Cuba there is no coal, there is no iron, there isn't enough skilled labor, and there's not a consumers' market for a million tons with Cuba's incipient level of industry. Wouldn't it be better if you build a small plant to work from scrap metal, and not spend so much money?' But Che was intransigent. He said: 'If we build that factory we'll train the necessary cadres to [work it]. As for the iron ore, we'll get it from Mexico, or some other place nearby, and we'll find the coal somewhere else; we could bring it from here, on the ships going to pick up sugar from Cuba.'"

Later, when they were on their own, Leonov suggested to Che that perhaps Khrushchev was right. The Cubans might be better off building by stages, more gradually. Such a huge plant might be premature. "Look, Nicolás," Che replied, "there are other factors at stake here—social and political ones. The Revolution must be something big, imposing. We must combat the single-crop economy of sugar, we must industrialize, and anyway, you, here in the Soviet Union, also began your industrialization program without a base." In the end, Leonov said, the idea didn't go anywhere. "It seemed to me," he recalled, "that Che's concept was a bit artificial, with more social and political foundations than economic ones." After consulting with Cuba, Che lost some of his enthusiasm. He didn't push the idea anymore, and the Soviets didn't mention it, either.

Che took Leonov with him on his trip to North Korea, thinking he might need an interpreter, but as soon as they arrived in Pyongyang, they were separated. The Sino-Soviet dispute was in full swing, and North Korea was an ally of Beijing. "They didn't allow me to work with him," said Leonov, who was deposited at the Soviet embassy while Che was taken off to an official government guest house. He remained there throughout Che's trip to China, before they reunited for the return trip to Moscow.

According to Leonov, Che's motives for visiting North Korea and China were twofold: "In the first place, he wanted to see the examples of Asian socialism, and secondly . . . he wanted to secure some sales of sugar there. He resolved the two tasks, because he saw their socialism, a bit despotic, a bit Asian, in that style they have, and he made the sale, I believe, of two hundred thousand tons of sugar to China."

In fact, Che's trip to China had been extremely successful. He had secured the sale of a million tons of Cuba's 1961 sugar crop and obtained a $60 million credit for the purchase of Chinese goods. He had met with Mao Tse-tung and been feted by his deputy, Chou En-lai. Chou had praised the Cuban revolution, and in return Che had lauded China's revolution as an example for "the Americas." No doubt all this irked the Soviets, and their unease must have deepened when, upon leaving China, Che remarked that "in general there was not a single discrepancy" between himself and Beijing.

Che's fraternal remarks did not go unnoticed by the Americans. In a secret U.S. intelligence report about his mission, his Chinese sojourn was

Che with Mao Tse-tung during his 1960 tour of the Communist
bloc.

mentioned with interest. "A noteworthy feature of Guevara's visit to
Peiping [Beijing] was his apparent siding with the Chinese on several key
points in the Sino-Soviet dispute. Speaking at a November 20 reception,
Guevara praised Communist China's commune movement (which has
come under Soviet attack) and two days earlier held up the Chinese Communist revolution as an 'example' that has 'revealed a new road for the
Americas.' Guevara made no such statement about the U.S.S.R.'s example
while in Moscow."

Although Che's statements may have betrayed his personal sympathies,
he and Fidel were taking pains not to take sides openly in the festering quar-
rel. Back in Pyongyang, Che diplomatically expressed his hope to Leonov
that "the differences could be settled" between the two nations, but both he
and Fidel must have been aware that they were in a very good position to
play Beijing and Moscow off against each other. Indeed, after he returned
to Moscow on December 19, the Soviets dramatically expanded their lar-
gesse, agreeing to buy 2.7 million tons of Cuba's forthcoming sugar crop, at
a rate above world market prices. The joint Soviet-Cuban communiqué
issued that day expressed Cuba's gratitude for Soviet economic assistance
and stressed the U.S.S.R.'s "full support" for Cuba's bid to maintain its in-

dependence "in the face of aggression." Echoing Che's plaudits for China, the Moscow communiqué extolled Cuba as "an example for other peoples of the American continent, and also Asia and Africa."

The next day, Che left for Cuba, stopping briefly in Prague and Budapest. He had learned that an old childhood acquaintance, the Spanish Republican refugee Fernando Barral, was living in Hungary. It had been ten years since they had last seen each other, before Barral's arrest for "Communist agitation" and his expulsion from Argentina. Since then, Barral had gone to medical school in Hungary, had become a doctor, and had lived through the 1956 Hungarian uprising and the Soviet invasion that suppressed it. Over the last couple of years, he had read the news about revolutionary Cuba with interest. As for this Argentine-born *comandante*, Ernesto Guevara, called "Che," he wondered, "Could it really be the same *loco* Guevara I knew?" During his brief stop in Budapest, Che had asked the Cuban embassy staff to find Barral, but they were unable to locate him. Che left the following note, which was later delivered.

Dear Fernando:
    I know you had doubts about my identity but you thought that I was I. Indeed, although no, because a lot of water has gone under my bridge, and of the asthmatic, embittered, and individualistic being you knew, only the asthma remains.
    I learned that you had married. I too, and I have two children,* but I am still an adventurer. Only now, my adventures have a just purpose. Greetings to your family from this survivor of a past epoch and a fraternal embrace from Che.
        [P.S.] What do you think of my new name [?]

As it had done for Alberto Granado, the contact with Che was to provide Barral with a new direction in his life. Hungary's entrenched and bureaucratic socialist system no longer held any surprises for him, and the chance to be part of the "new" revolution in Cuba appealed to him greatly; he wrote back to Che, expressing his interest in coming to work in Cuba. In February 1961, Che replied, welcoming him. "The salary will be decorous without permitting great luxuries but the experience of the Cuban Revolution is something that I think would be interesting for people like you, who must begin one day again in their countries of origin." Barral accepted Che's offer and emigrated to Cuba in November 1961. Almost immediately, Che

---

*On November 24, while he was in Beijing, Aleida had given birth to a baby girl that she named after herself.

sent him to see Ramiro Valdés, Cuba's security chief, who, as a test of Barral's revolutionary commitment, dispatched him to the Escambray to fight in the "Lucha contra Bandidos."

Che had met someone new on this trip, someone who would become an important part of his life. A twenty-two-year-old woman named Haydée Tamara Bunke was the interpreter for his meetings with German officials in Berlin. She was the daughter of Jewish Communists who fled Hitler's Germany in 1935 for Argentina, where Tamara was born two years later. She had spent her childhood there, returning with her family to the Communist-run German Democratic Republic when she was fourteen. Her parents had raised her to be a Communist, and she became a faithful child of the socialist state, joining the youth wing of the Communist Party at eighteen. With her Spanish-language abilities, Tamara soon was made an official interpreter, but, according to a signed statement she made to the Party in 1958, her true dream was to return to Latin America—ideally to her birthplace, Argentina—and "help the Party there."

By the time Che met her, the attractive, fair-haired Tamara was already known to some of his comrades. Six months earlier, Che had dispatched Orlando Borrego to Berlin as part of a Cuban trade delegation for which Tamara had interpreted. Borrego recalled that she was avidly interested in Cuba and wanted to go there. Within five months of meeting Che, she had her wish; in May 1961 she flew to Cuba, where she would soon be given a role in Che's program of revolution for Latin America.

As Che flew home from his long trip, he must have felt pleased with himself. He had met the leaders of the socialist world and obtained vital sales and credits for Cuba. Over the last two years, he had been instrumental in welding the Soviet-Cuban alliance. As Alexiev put it, "Che was practically the architect of our relations with Cuba."

On New Year's Day 1961, Fidel called for a general military mobilization and showed off Cuba's newly acquired Soviet tanks and other weaponry in a display of strength on Havana's streets. The next day, he demanded that Washington cut its Havana embassy staff to eleven, which was the number of people in Cuba's embassy in Washington. It was the final straw for Eisenhower, who had only a few more days in office. On January 3, 1961, in one of his last acts before handing the presidency over to John F. Kennedy, he severed diplomatic relations between the United States and Cuba.

24

These Atomic Times

I

On the morning of February 24, 1961, Che left his home on Eighteenth Street in Miramar. His car turned right and headed toward Seventh Avenue. He usually turned left, toward the tree-lined boulevard of Fifth Avenue, then right, driving past State Security headquarters into the tunnel beneath the Almendares River, then down the Malecón to his office at the National Bank, in Old Havana. But that day Che headed for the Plaza de la Revolución. Fidel had turned his INRA department into a full-fledged ministry, and it was Che's first day as Cuba's new minister of industries. The unannounced change of route may have saved his life.

A few moments after he left home, a gun battle erupted just outside his house. Che's bodyguards entered the fray, shooting wildly. Inside the house, Aleida threw herself and three-month-old Aleidita under the first-floor stairwell, where they were joined by the terrified latest addition to the Guevara household, the nanny Sofía Gato, a twenty-five-year-old girl from Camagüey. Afterward, Sofía was able to piece together most of what had taken place. Four or five armed men, *barbudos,* had lain in wait behind some bushes near the corner of Eighteenth Street and Fifth Avenue. When one of the neighbors, a man named Salinas, drove by in his car, they opened fire with automatic weapons. Believing it to be an attack on Che's house, his bodyguards returned the fire. A few minutes later, Salinas lay dead in his car, and one of the assailants, shot in the gut, writhed on the ground.

News of the shoot-out was quickly smothered, although plenty of people heard about it anyway. There was speculation, which was officially denied, that it had been an attempt to assassinate Che. But according to Oscar Fernández Mell, who also lived at the house on Eighteenth Street, Salinas was the attacker's intended target, the victim of an affair of the heart gone bad. As with so many things that have taken place in Cuba, the shooting became cloaked in mystery, and so it has remained for decades.

The notion that the incident on Eighteenth Street was a botched attempt to assassinate Che is entirely credible, considering what was happening in Cuba at the time. All over the country, former *barbudos* like those who fired on Salinas's car that morning had taken up arms against the revolution, against Communism. Che was widely identified as the principal advocate of Cuba's "submission" to the Soviet Union. He was the Red flea in Fidel's ear. At least one other plot to kill Che had already been foiled. One night in early 1960, back in the days before Mikoyan's visit, Alexandr Alexiev was talking with Che at his new office in the National Bank when Che suddenly said, "Look, Alejandro, let me show you the place where the counterrevolutionaries are planning to shoot me from." He pointed to a window across the narrow street from where they sat. Alexiev was alarmed, but Che reassured him that Cuba's intelligence services had already staked out the place and were about to move in.

Whatever the true cause of the shoot-out on Eighteenth Street, Che took new precautions afterward. Visitors to the Ministry of Industries were frisked by guards, and Che carried a cigar box full of hand grenades on the seat next to him in the car. He drove to work by a different route each day.

The last American diplomats had vacated the embassy a month before the shooting, and American citizens were prohibited from visiting Cuba. The Peruvian and Paraguayan governments also broke off relations and pulled out their diplomats. More of Cuba's anti-Castro neighbors would follow their example in the coming months. At least 100,000 Cuban refugees had fled into exile, most of them to Miami, and the U.S. government had set up a resettlement program to house them and give them jobs. Among those who fled was José Pardo Llada, who had made some indiscreet remarks about the Communist Party's infiltration into the government. Humberto Sorí-Marín, the former agriculture minister, was not so lucky. Captured by Cuban troops and accused of CIA-sponsored counterrevolutionary activities, Sorí-Marín was shot by a firing squad.

Soviet technicians, Russian-language teachers, economists, and military advisers were flowing into Havana. The Mongolians, Albanians, Hungarians, Chinese, and North Vietnamese opened up embassies. Eastern-bloc trade and cultural delegations came and went. On January 17, Fidel had announced that a thousand Cuban youths would be sent to the Soviet Union to study "agrarian collectives."

Even working-class Cubans were struck by the difference between the *rusos* and the Americans they had replaced. The Americans had been rich and loud and spoke terrible Spanish, but these newcomers looked and acted like peasants. They were rough-hewn and poorly dressed. The women were fat and wore long peasant dresses and head scarves. The men wore ill-fitting suits of poor-quality cloth. They sweated heavily in Cuba's heat but used no deodorant, and to the finicky Cubans, the Russians smelled bad. They didn't speak any Spanish at all and stuck to themselves. They were trucked through the city to their new residential enclaves like so many cattle. They stared in wonder at the modern city, with its shiny American consumer products still in shop windows—televisions, refrigerators, and air conditioners —and at the swank homes with swimming pools and landscaped gardens. The huge American cars, luxuriant with chrome and fins, had them goggle-eyed.

As representatives of the vaunted socialist "superpower," the Soviets were not inspiring. Che knew about the popular skepticism and addressed it while appearing on Cuban television on January 6 to talk about his recent trip to the Soviet Union. After waxing poetic about all the nations he had visited, singling out North Korea and China for special praise, he turned to the Soviets' evident backwardness in areas many Cubans had long taken for granted:

> We had to bring up some problems there that embarrassed us a little, really. . . . For example, we brought up the problem that the Cuban people needed some raw materials to make deodorant with, and in those countries they don't understand that, because they are nations that are developing all their production for the general welfare of the people and have still to overcome some enormous backwardnesses. . . . They can't be bothered with these things. We too now have to occupy ourselves with more important things.

Che was speaking as diplomatically as he could in the circumstances. He *understood,* he was telling the urbane *habaneros,* but times had changed.

The economic influence of the Soviet bloc had become more visible. The disorganized cooperative farms favored in the early days of land expropriations had been replaced by Soviet-style state farms called *granjas del pueblo.* * Czech and Soviet advisers now worked at Che's ministry alongside the first-generation crew of South American economists. Che organized

---

*Despite the large-scale expropriations, much of Cuba's cultivated land remained in the hands of small farmers, who continued to till their plots without hindrance from the state. In 1963, a new bill reduced the size of private landholdings still further, but the revolution never completely eradicated its fiercely independent *guajiro* farmers.

a weekly Marxism study circle with Anastasio Mansilla, a Hispano-Soviet political economist, for himself and some of his aides. Along with most American influences—such as Santa Claus, who had been banned—the learning of English was now discouraged. Russian was the second language to learn in the "new" Cuba. Che began taking twice-weekly Russian-language classes from Yuri Pevtsov, a philologist sent from Lermonstov University to be his interpreter and personal tutor. They had no Russian-Spanish manual to work from, so the two made do with a Russian-French primer.

Inevitably, in spite of the early popular ridicule of the *bolos,* as the Russians were called, a kind of Sovietization began to seep into Cuban life in ways that were initially superficial. The government spearheaded the transformation. There was already the new central planning board, JUCEPLAN, an imitation of the Soviet Union's GOSPLAN. Streets, theaters, and factories were rebaptized with the names of homegrown and foreign revolutionary heroes and martyrs such as Camilo Cienfuegos and Patrice Lumumba. The old Chaplin Cinema on First Avenue would become the Carlos Marx, and before long, there would be day-care centers named Heroes de Vietnam and Rosa Luxemburg. Since the revolution there had been a spate of Cuban babies named Fidel and Ernesto. Now, more and more Cubans began naming their children Alexei and Natasha. Before long, Che's own newest daughter had a Russian nickname—Aliusha.

In the view of Washington's intelligence analysts, the island's dramatic embrace of the socialist bloc was largely attributable to the efforts of Che Guevara. On March 23, in a secret assessment of Che's recently completed mission abroad, the State Department's Bureau of Intelligence and Research listed the trip's considerable achievements: "By the end of the visit, Cuba had trade and payments agreements and cultural ties with every country in the bloc, diplomatic relations with every country except East Germany, and scientific and technical assistance accords with all but Albania."

Whether or not Che had negotiated additional military assistance for Cuba on his mission wasn't known, but the report deemed it highly likely. "It may be assumed that the subject was discussed and delivery of new weapons agreed upon. According to one report, Guevara, early in his tour, asked Khrushchev for missiles and the Soviet Premier flatly refused, promising instead some automatic weapons from World War II."

II

The pros and cons of assassinating Che, Raúl, and Fidel had been discussed by the CIA for some time. In January 1960, Allen Dulles had rejected an assassination program in favor of the "exile army" scheme, but eventually

Dulles would come around to the view that whatever would get the job done in the most efficient manner was best. If killing Cuba's top leaders helped ensure the success of the invasion plan, then it was an option that had to be pursued. In the intervening months, he had allowed his covert operations director, Richard Bissell, to explore possibilities for assassinations. Already some plots had been hatched, including a bizarre attempt to poison Fidel's favorite brand of cigars. Many more scenarios for killing Fidel and his top comrades would be planned or attempted over the coming months and years, including some in collusion with the American Mafia.*

Assassination was also explored as a remedy for political problems in other areas of the world. In August 1960, with Eisenhower's approval, Dulles had cabled the CIA station chief in Leopoldville, the capital of the Congo, authorizing him to "remove" Prime Minister Patrice Lumumba "as an urgent and prime objective . . . of high priority." Lumumba, the founder of the Mouvement National Congolais, had won the most votes in the first elections held after Belgium agreed to grant the Congo independence, but he had to form a government that included his chief rivals. Joseph Kasavubu became president and Moise Tshombe was appointed head of the provincial government of Katanga, an area rich in copper, uranium, and cobalt. Almost immediately after the independence ceremony at the end of June, the Congo fell into chaos. The army mutinied, the killing of whites was widespread, and Tshombe—backed by Belgian mining interests—declared that Katanga was seceding and would become an independent state. Lumumba severed relations with Belgium, which had flown in reinforcements, and the UN sent in troops from other African countries. The Soviet Union responded to a plea from Lumumba for aid, including arms and military advisers.

Early in September, Kasavubu dismissed Lumumba as prime minister, and a week later Joseph Mobutu, the army chief of staff, who was receiving funds from the CIA, carried out his coup d'état. Lumumba was placed under house arrest, but Allen Dulles reiterated that he must be "eliminated from any possibility [of] resuming governmental position." President Eisenhower was convinced that Lumumba intended to turn the Congo into a Soviet satellite. The CIA station chief in Leopoldville soon received a visitor from headquarters, Dr. Sidney Gottlieb, who had brought a syringe, rubber gloves, a mask, and a vial of poison that was designed to bring on a fatal illness common to the region. A practical solution had been found to

*By 1960, according to Evan Thomas, the author of *The Very Best Men: Four Who Dared—The Early Years of the CIA,* the agency had come up with James Bondish code names for its intended targets: Fidel was AMTHUG; Che, a doctor, was AMQUACK.

"remove" Lumumba. Another idea was that his toothpaste would be poisoned. Before the CIA could get close to him, however, he had escaped from house arrest and was captured by Mobutu's troops. With the support, tacit and otherwise, of the CIA, the UN, and the Belgians, Lumumba was sent to Katanga, where he faced certain death at Tshombe's hands. He was tortured and then murdered on January 17, 1961, although this was not widely known for nearly a month.

When Lumumba's death was finally announced, in mid-February—shortly before the apparently botched attempt to kill Che on his way to work—Khrushchev accused Secretary-General Hammarsjköld of being an accomplice to the murder. Cuba sent a note of protest to the UN and announced three days of official mourning.

By March, preparations for the CIA's Cuban invasion force were well under way. Manuel Ray had been subsumed into the Cuban exile alliance, and the former prime minister, Míro Cardona, had been named to head the Cuban Revolutionary Council as Cuba's future provisional president. The anti-Castro activity had caused major problems, however. The previous November, about 600 Cuban exile fighters of Brigade 2506 had completed a three-month training course in Guatemala, but by then their presence—and the CIA's sponsorship—had been splashed all over the press. The scandal that ensued made life difficult for the Guatemalan president, Ydigoras Fuentes. A sizable group of Guatemalan military officers, angered over the presence of foreign troops on their soil, had staged an uprising. They seized a military garrison in the capital, the Zacapa barracks in eastern Guatemala, and the Caribbean port of Puerto Barrios. But the rebel officers didn't know what to do next, and they turned away hundreds of peasants in Zacapa who asked for weapons to join the fight. The Eisenhower administration had been quicker off the mark. A U.S. naval flotilla was dispatched to stand off the coast, and the CIA's Cuban guerrilla force was deployed to help suppress the revolt. B-26 bombers supplied by the CIA and piloted by exiled Cubans dislodged the rebels from their positions. The show of force worked, and the rebels quickly surrendered.

What looked like a minor sideshow at the time was to have important consequences. Marco Aurelio Yon Sosa and Luis Turcios Lima, two young Guatemalan officers who had been trained by the United States, did not return to their barracks. They went underground, and within fifteen months they would be making their presence felt as the leaders of a left-wing guerrilla insurgency. In time, Turcios Lima would become one of Che's favorite revolutionary protégés.

There had also been trouble in Venezuela that November, with the pro-Cuban *miristas* and Venezuelan Communists launching a violent insurrection in Caracas against Betancourt's regime. The left-of-center URD party of Venezuela's former president, Admiral Wolfgang Larrazábal, which had formed part of the ruling government coalition, deserted Betancourt to join a coalition with MIR and the Communists. They formed the National Liberation Council to overthrow the government. Student demonstrations and street battles with police followed, but the revolt eventually was quashed. By the year's end, constitutional guarantees would be suspended indefinitely, the universities closed, left-wing newpapers banned, and the country's oilfields occupied by troops. The Venezuelan stage was becoming propitious for an armed guerrilla struggle, and, with Cuban backing, it would come before long.

The graduation of the brigade of Cuban exiles in Guatemala coincided with a shift in the CIA's strategy regarding its future role in Cuba. The agency's original idea that the force could fight and survive as a guerrilla army looked increasingly doubtful. While the main force was training in Guatemala, the CIA had run a smaller covert program, dispatching teams of rebels and saboteurs to Cuba. Most of them had been quickly put out of action by Castro's forces. The CIA's airdrops had similarly failed to sustain the rebels in the mountains. A rather more ambitious plan seemed to be in order, and Richard Bissell replaced the guerrilla warfare instruction in Guatemala with conventional training. Under the new plan, the anti-Castro exile brigade would make an amphibious landing on Cuba's coast, supported by air strikes. It would establish a foothold and proclaim a provisional Cuban government, which would be instantly recognized by Washington and friendly Latin American governments. The United States could then, theoretically, intervene to assist the new government. By that time, it was hoped, Fidel, Che, and Raúl would be dead, since the CIA had several schemes under consideration to assassinate the Cuban leaders on the eve of the landing.

Seven separate five-man infiltration groups called Gray Teams had been selected from the Guatemala brigade. They were to meet up with the underground resistance movement on the island and help coordinate the CIA's airdrops of weaponry. The main invasion force was to hit specific targets and lead armed uprisings throughout Cuba. Nineteen-year-old Felix Rodríguez was among those selected for a Gray Team. He and the other team members were moved to a new jungle camp in Guatemala, where they were taught espionage tactics by war-hardened Eastern European anticommunist exiles. A few days after Christmas, his Gray Team was ushered onto an American military transport plane with blacked-out windows and flown to Fort Clayton, one of the American military bases in the Panama Canal Zone. Their training continued, but now they were taught how to handle advanced weaponry of Soviet and Eastern European origin.

In early January, 1961, Rodríguez came up with a plan to assassinate
Fidel that was approved by his American handlers. He and a comrade were
flown to Miami, where he was given a German-made sniper's rifle with a
telescopic sight. The CIA selected the assassination site, a house in Havana
that Fidel was known to frequent. Rodríguez was taken to the Cuban coast
three times in fast boats traveling at night, but each time he failed to rendezvous with his on-ground contacts. After the third failure, the rifle was
taken away, and the CIA told Rodríguez they had changed their minds about
the operation.

The other Gray Teams had been brought to a base camp on the outskirts of Miami. On February 14, the first infiltration team was smuggled
into Cuba. A week later, Rodríguez and his four comrades, with a load of
weapons, explosives, and ammunition, were dropped on Cuba's northern
coast between the Varadero beach resort and Havana. They were picked
up in cars driven by people belonging to the MRR underground.

Over the next month, Rodríguez and his friends met with the underground resistance in Havana and Camagüey, staying in safe houses and
making preparations to receive a large airdrop of weapons from the CIA.
After they got the arms and distributed them, their mission was to largely
replicate what Che and Camilo had done in the last phase of the anti-Batista
war: open up a guerrilla front in northern Las Villas and try to split the island in half, forcing the government to divert forces away from the south
coast, where the invasion force was due to land. At one point in mid-March,
Rodríguez helped the Cuban underground transfer some weapons kept in
a safe house located next door to the State Security headquarters on Fifth
Avenue between Fourteenth and Sixteenth Streets. Rodríguez wasn't aware
that Che Guevara lived less than two blocks away.

None of this activity would have come as a big surprise to Fidel. President Kennedy was determined to show his mettle, and, in the two months
since he had taken office, it seemed clear that preparations were still under
way for some kind of military intervention in Cuba. In fact, Kennedy had
been briefed about the planned invasion soon after he won the election in
November, and he had given CIA Director Dulles the go-ahead. Since taking office, Kennedy had studied the CIA's beefed-up plans with a more
tentative eye, expressing misgivings about their feasibility, but an effective
combination of warnings and reassurances from the CIA had won out in
the end, despite the opposition of some of the president's closest civilian
advisers.

The exile force was well trained and itching to fight, Dulles's people
told Kennedy. D-day had to come soon. As matters now stood, the CIA could
take out Cuba's small fleet of Sea Furies and B-26s before the invasion began,

but that window was rapidly closing. Cuban pilots were being trained to fly Soviet MiGs in Czechoslovakia, and, although no MiGs had yet been delivered to Cuba, some probably would be before long. The CIA had chosen a landing site on Cuba's southern coast near Trinidad, in Las Villas province, but Kennedy thought that landing there would be too "spectacular." He opted for a less visible spot farther west, at a remote beach called Playa Girón on the Bay of Pigs. Kennedy had been assured that if the rebels failed to hold their beachhead, they could make it to the "nearby" Escambray and, after meeting up with the rebels there, begin a guerrilla resistance movement.

The plan had many flaws. The Escambray mountains were actually more than 100 miles away, and the very isolation that made Playa Girón seem ideal for a surprise landing made it a death trap if Castro's forces were able to get there quickly. There were only two ways out: along the narrow roads through the vast Zapata swamp or along the exposed strip of coastal beach. In either case, the invaders could easily be ambushed, pinned down, and massacred. Evidently, none of this occurred to the CIA strategists.

Despite his misgivings, Kennedy agreed to the plan, but he ruled out the direct involvement of U.S. troops or any large-scale American air support once the assault was under way. The CIA men apparently believed that once the action had begun, the president would relent. In any event, this crucial bit of news was not imparted to the Cuban exiles involved; they thought they would be going in backed up by the full weight of America's military power.

The CIA didn't have a clue about the extent to which their "covert" program had already been infiltrated by Castro's intelligence service. At least one of the thirty-five Gray Team members in Cuba was a double agent for the Castro government, and there were undoubtedly others. In Miami, the general outline of the CIA's plans was widely known throughout the exile community, where Fidel had a flourishing spy network. What's more, he now had plenty of armor at his disposal. As Alexandr Alexiev gleefully confided years later, "We already had Soviet arms in Playa Girón. A lot of Soviet arms participated in Playa Girón."

III

During this tense period of a rumored invasion, nocturnal air raids, and a spate of bombing attacks against expropriated stores in Havana, Che continued to give speeches, write articles, and receive foreign delegations. He attended the opening and closing ceremonies of the Chinese Economic Edification Exposition in the Hotel Habana Libre. He cut the ribbon at a new pencil factory and visited the recently nationalized Nicaro nickel mine, urging its workers to "sacrifice to produce more." Che's most recent cause was volunteer labor. He had initiated the practice on a small scale when volunteers helped construct a school in Camilo's memory, but it was the volunteer work brigades in Mao's China that truly inspired him. After he returned from his trip abroad, he devoted his Saturdays to lending a hand in factory assembly lines, cutting sugarcane, and lifting bricks at construction sites. He urged his colleagues at the Ministry of Industries to set an example by volunteering during the sugar harvest. Before long, everyone at the ministry who wanted to remain in Che's good graces began giving up Saturdays at home to join him in these work sessions. The program, which came to be called *emulación comunista,* was based on the idea that by working with no thought of remuneration, the individual takes an important step toward building a true Communist consciousness.

One day, seeing that Che was wearing no watch, his friend Oscar Fernández Mell gave him his own, a fine watch with a gold wristband that he had bought for himself after graduating from medical school. Sometime later, Che handed Fernández Mell a piece of paper. It was a receipt from the National Bank declaring that Oscar Fernández Mell had donated his gold wristband as a contribution to Cuba's gold reserves. Che was still wearing the watch, but it now had a leather wristband.

Che had refused to collect the salary he was due as president of the National Bank, and he continued the practice at the Ministry of Industries, steadfastly drawing only his minuscule *comandante*'s wages. Orlando Borrego, by now a vice minister, felt obliged to draw an equivalent amount of his own salary, donating the rest to an agrarian reform fund; it would have been unseemly to be earning more money than his boss. But self-abnegation and revolutionary showmanship cut particularly close to the bone when Che forced Borrego to give up the car of his dreams. During a visit to an "intervened" cigarette factory, a manager had pointed out a brand-new Jaguar sports car that had been abandoned by its owner, a wealthy Cuban who had fled the country. He suggested that Borrego take it, since no one else knew how to run it. Borrego fell in love with the car and drove it proudly for about a week, until the day Che spotted him in the garage where they both parked. "You're a *chulo*—a pimp!" Che yelled. What was Borrego doing, driving around in a car like that? It was not a car for a representative of the people. Borrego's heart fell, and he told Che he would return it. "Good," Che said, "I'll give you two hours." Back at the office, Che said that Borrego should be driving a car more like Che's own, a modest, year-old green Chevy Impala. Before long, Borrego was given a car exactly like his *jefe*'s, except that his was two-tone. He would drive it for the next twelve years. "Che was superstrict," Borrego recalled, "like Jesus Christ."

The extent of Che's vision of a new society was made very clear to Ricardo Rojo, the Argentinian lawyer who had introduced him to Hilda when they were all living in Guatemala. Rojo now had a diplomatic post in Bonn under the Argentine government of Arturo Frondízi, which had tried, unsuccessfully, to intercede in the intensifying dispute between the United States and Cuba. Rojo had shown up in Havana, evidently hoping to use his relationship with Che to take soundings of Cuba's intentions. He could see that Cuba was preparing for war. He observed militiamen jackhammering Havana's streets to lay explosive charges, and everywhere he looked, uniformed men and women wandered around with weapons. After passing through a crowd of bearded, armed men in the foyer of the Ministry of Industries, he found Che in a half-furnished office. It had been six years since they had last seen each other, in Mexico. Che looked heavier, and Rojo told him so. Che replied that his moon face was a consequence of cortisone treatments for his chronic asthma. He wasn't fat.

No doubt aware that whatever he showed or said to the well-connected Rojo would filter back to Western policy makers, Che took him on a worker's tour of the Cuban countryside: to factories, to the cane fields, and to meet with peasant soldiers fighting in the Escambray against the counterrevolutionaries. He even press-ganged him into a day of volunteer labor cutting cane. Rojo came away certain of several things: that Cuba was definitely on the path to Communism; that the revolution was well armed and enjoyed widespread support among Cubans; and—judging from several comments his old friend had made—that Che was interested in extending the revolution to South America.

Toward the end of March, Che accompanied Rojo to the airport. As they drove past numerous antiaircraft gun emplacements, Che turned to him. "They'll come," he said, referring to the Americans. "But we'll give them a reception. It's a pity you're leaving right now, when the party is about to begin."

On April 3, the White House released a white paper on Cuba. It was the Kennedy administration's call to arms for the military expedition that would soon be known as the Bay of Pigs invasion. Cuba, it said, posed a "clear and present danger" to the Americas.

Five days later, with invasion jitters at a fever pitch, Che published an article in *Verde Olivo* titled "Cuba: Historical Exception or Vanguard in the Anticolonialist Struggle?" Che answered his own question: Cuba was no exception, but merely the first Latin American nation to break the mold of economic dependency and domination by imperialists. Its example was the path for its neighbors to follow to the goal of revolutionary freedom:

> What did we do to free ourselves from the vast imperialist system, with its entourage of puppet rulers in each country and mercenary armies to protect the puppets and the whole complex social system of the exploitation of man by man? We applied certain formulas, [the results] of discoveries of our empirical medicine for the great ailments of our beloved Latin America, empirical medicine that rapidly became part of scientific truth.

This was the "scientific" discovery that Ernesto Guevara had been destined for, the culmination of a search that had begun with his work in medicine. Treating individuals' illnesses had never been his real interest; his motivation had always been that of the researcher looking for a cure, or a means to prevent; and, as it had been with medicine, so it had become with politics. Searching, crossing solutions off the list of possibilities as he went—reformism, democracy, elections—he had found Marx, then Guatemala, then Cuba and the realization that the cure to society's ills was Marxism-Leninism and that guerrilla warfare was the means to achieve it. Before

Che working on the docks in Havana in 1961.

Cuba's revolution, he explained, "Latin America lacked the subjective conditions, the most important of which is consciousness of the possibility of victory through violent struggle against the imperialist powers and their internal allies. These conditions were created through the armed struggle that clarified the need for change . . . and the defeat and subsequent annihilation of the army by the popular forces (an absolutely necessary condition for every genuine revolution). . . . The peasant class of Latin America, basing itself on the ideology of the working class, whose great thinkers discovered the social laws governing us, will provide the great liberating army of the future, as it has already done in Cuba."

Scientific truth is a natural law not malleable by theories. In essence, Che was arguing that his formula for attaining socialism through armed struggle amounted to a scientific discovery, and that the discovery would lead to the end of injustice and the creation of a new form of man.

IV

On April 14, Havana's largest and most luxurious department store, El Encanto, was burned down by one of the underground groups backed by the CIA. Felix Rodríguez had been forewarned by his contacts that "something big" was about to happen and that he might want to leave town, because there would be "a lot of heat."

The next morning, in the predawn darkness of April 15, Sofía, the Guevaras' nanny, awoke to the frightening noise of diving airplanes and exploding bombs. She ran into the hall and called to Che. Still shirtless, he emerged from his bedroom. "The bastards have finally attacked us," he said.

From a window they watched the flashes and explosions; planes were bombing the airfield at nearby Campamento Libertad. Che's *escolta* were running around wildly, yelling and waving pistols. Che shouted out the window, "I'll shoot the first man who fires!" and they calmed down. Within a few minutes he had driven off with them. They went to Pinar del Río, his secret battle station for the invasion. To have the end of the island closest to the United States well covered, Fidel had given Che command of Cuba's western army.

The next day, at the funeral for the victims of the bombing, which had destroyed the greater part of Cuba's minuscule air force, Fidel gave a fiery speech blaming the attack on the United States. The Americans had attacked, he claimed, because they could not forgive Cuba for having brought about a socialist revolution under their noses. For the first time since seizing power, Fidel had uttered the dreaded word. Later, a bronze plaque would be secured on the spot, consecrating the moment when Fidel "revealed the socialist nature of the Cuban Revolution."

Among the crowd listening to Fidel that historic afternoon were a young, prematurely balding artist from the Argentine mountain city of Mendoza named Ciro Roberto Bustos and his wife. They had just arrived in Cuba as volunteers to participate in the Cuban revolutionary experiment. As they walked along Havana's streets, soaking up the tropical atmosphere, the air was charged with portent. The future seemed promising and threatening at the same time—as indeed it was. Before long, Ciro Bustos's life would be completely absorbed, and irrevocably altered, by Che's vision of a continental revolution.

Just after midnight on April 17, the Cuban exile Liberation Army, 1,500 men, came ashore at Playa Girón on the Bay of Pigs. Days earlier, the units based in Guatemala had been transferred to the Nicaraguan port of Puerto Cabezas, where they had been seen off by Nicaragua's dictator, Luís Somoza. He told them to bring him back a hair from Castro's beard. They made the crossing to Cuba aboard ships lent them, as Che had forecast, probably jokingly, by the United Fruit Company, with U.S. naval destroyers as escorts. They were not told exactly where they were to disembark until they were at sea.

Within hours of their landing, which was trumpeted loudly over the CIA's Radio Swan transmitter, Fidel had mobilized his forces. Rather than push inland, the invaders dug into positions on the beach and awaited reinforcements. None came. By mid-morning, the fighting had begun. By dawn the next day, Dulles informed Kennedy that the exiles were bogged down; unless the United States intervened, they would be wiped out. Kennedy refused to authorize more than minimal air support.

In Havana, Felix Rodríguez heard about the invasion on the radio. The CIA had not dared warn anyone in the resistance inside Cuba, for fear of a leak. Cut off from the other members of his Gray Team, he tried to reach his Havana contacts on the telephone. In each case, either there was no reply or strange voices that told him to "come over right away." Realizing that many of the resistance people had probably already been arrested, and that the voices were those of security agents, he stayed where he was. Over the next three days he watched the events unfold on television and wept in frustration.

In Pinar del Río, Che's forces saw no action, but Che himself was nearly killed in a shooting accident. Aleida first learned of it when Celia Sánchez called to tell her that Che had been lightly "wounded," grazed on the cheek and ear when his pistol fell out of its holster and a bullet went off. Celia sent a car to take Aleida to him, and another car to pick up Aliusha and the nanny, Sofía, and bring them to her flat. Celia's flat had become a communications nerve center for the revolutionary leadership. At one point, a weary-looking

Fidel came in, directly from the battleground, and collapsed on the bed where Sofía lay with Che's daughter. As he slept, the baby played with his beard.

The bullet had come within a hairbreadth of penetrating Che's brain. His greatest moment of danger, though, had come not from the bullet, but from the antitetanus injection that medics had insisted on giving him. It had brought on a toxic shock reaction. As Che joked afterward to Alberto Granado, "My friends almost managed to do what my enemies couldn't. I nearly died!"

By the afternoon of April 20, the exile force had bogged down, run out of supplies, and given up. Of the invaders, 114 were dead, and nearly 1,200 had been taken prisoner. At the happy news, Che returned to Havana from his post in Pinar del Río, picked up Granado, and drove to Playa Girón. The Central Australia sugar mill, Fidel's command post during the battle, was a chaos of military equipment, troops, and POWs. Soldiers were still combing the surrounding area for fugitives who had fled into the swamp. Jeeps roared off in all directions.

Che and Granado approached a group of prisoners. One of them was so terrified to see Che that he defecated and urinated in his trousers. Che tried to question the man, but he could not even speak properly. Finally, Che turned away and said to one of his bodyguards, "Get a bucket of water for that poor bastard."

Fidel, of course, was jubilant. He himself had directed the battle at Playa Girón, and he had personally fired a tank cannon at one of the American "mother ships"; his men swore afterward that he had scored a direct hit. All folklore aside, the battle had been a stunning victory for Cuba's revolution. The "people" had stood up to Washington, and they had won.

On the morning of April 26, Felix Rodríguez went from his safe house in Havana to the Venezuelan embassy compound in a chauffeur-driven green Mercedes belonging to the Spanish ambassador. Four months later, he would be granted diplomatic safe-passage to leave the country. But he would soon be back in Cuba; neither he nor the CIA had given up the battle.

V

In August, at a conference held by the Organization of American States in Punta del Este, Uruguay, Che sent a message of gratitude to President Kennedy through Richard Goodwin, a young White House aide. "Thank you for Playa Girón," he said to Goodwin. "Before the invasion, the revolution was shaky. Now, it is stronger than ever."

Kennedy felt morally obliged to secure the release of the 1,200 prisoners taken at the Bay of Pigs, and Fidel had been rubbing his face in his predicament. Fidel offered to free them for 500 bulldozers; Kennedy was willing to give tractors. Fidel insisted on bulldozers, then asked for money. A haggling session had ensued, and talks had broken down in June. The POWs remained in Cuban prisons. (In December 1962 the prisoners were finally released in exchange for $62 million worth of medical supplies.)

Cuba was an open sore in Kennedy's battle of wills with Nikita Khrushchev. The Soviet Union had awarded the Lenin Peace Prize to Fidel in May, and Kennedy worried that the Soviets would consolidate their foothold by installing missile bases on the island. Despite Khrushchev's reassurances to the contrary, Attorney General Robert Kennedy warned of this prospect in April, in a memo to his brother. He urged prompt action. "The time has come for a showdown, for in a year or two years the situation will be vastly worse."

Khrushchev seemed to revel in the Cold War competition. He pressed his advantage wherever he could. For years, Washington and Moscow had fought to assert power in the vacuums left by the retreating European colonial governments in Africa, Asia, and the Middle East, and Moscow seemed to be winning. Washington or its allies had taken beatings in Suez, Lebanon, Indonesia, and Hungary. The Soviet Union had raced ahead with its nuclear arms program, and the ensuing controversy in the United States over a "missile gap" had led Eisenhower to put U-2 spy planes over Russia. Gary Powers had been shot down in May 1960 and then appeared on Soviet television, apologetically confessing that he had been on a spying mission. (Before the end of 1961, U.S. intelligence would determine that the United States was far ahead of the Soviets in nuclear strike capability, but the supposed missile gap continued to influence American policy for decades.)

In 1957, the Soviet Union had become the first nation to put a satellite into space, and in early April 1961—as the Bay of Pigs invasion was being launched—the cosmonaut Yuri Gagarin was sent into orbit. On the eve of Kennedy's decision about whether to go ahead with the invasion, a triumphant Khrushchev had trumpeted his victory in space, daring the West to catch up. JFK grumbled that he didn't like having America come in second.

New flash points continued to erupt around the world. In the Congo, rival factions backed by East and West jockeyed for power. Rwanda, Tanganyika, and Sierra Leone had all gained independence, and in Angola, an armed resistance movement was struggling against Portuguese rule. In Algeria, the war for independence had already cost hundreds of thousands of lives and threatened to ignite a civil war within France itself. Top commanders of the French army, angered over de Gaulle's decision to negotiate Algerian independence with the Front de Libération National (FLN), had staged a revolt. In Southeast Asia, Vietcong guerrillas backed by Ho Chi Minh's Communist North Vietnamese government in Hanoi were harassing the U.S.-backed government of South Vietnam. In neighboring Laos, Soviet and Chinese-backed Pathet Lao guerrillas launched a major offensive against the U.S.-backed Vientiane regime, forcing JFK to consider American military intervention there. In the end, a cease-fire was arranged, but Laos remained tense and unstable.

In the Caribbean, there was one less dictator to worry about after May 30, when Generalissimo Rafael Trujillo's life was cut short by a fusillade of bullets. The assassination team's weapons had been supplied by the CIA; Washington had been under mounting pressure from the Latin American "reformist" governments to do something about Trujillo as a quid pro quo for their backing of Washington's anti-Castro policies.

Kennedy spent summer weekends in 1961 reading both Mao's and Che's writings on guerrilla warfare. He instructed the army to beef up its antiguerrilla capability, and by September a new elite counterinsurgency corps, the Green Berets, was created.

Kennedy and Khrushchev had met for the first time in early June at a tough-talking two-day session in Vienna. They agreed on neutrality for Laos, but their discussions about a nuclear test–ban treaty and disarmament were inconclusive. Khrushchev took the occasion to move another chess piece. Demanding that Berlin be "demilitarized," he threatened to deny the Western occupying powers—France, Great Britain, and the United States— access to the city. The Western governments responded by sending more troops to Berlin. Invoking what he called the "worldwide Soviet threat," Kennedy called for a huge increase in the U.S. military budget. In August, East German and Soviet troops erected the Berlin Wall, sealing off East and West Berlin, and for some tense hours U.S. and Soviet tanks faced off against each other in the newly divided city.

To ensure the United States' continued hegemony in Latin America, Kennedy drew up an ambitious, unprecedented $20 billion, ten-year aid-development package for the region. He called it the Alliance for Progress. It was announced at the OAS conference in Punta del Este, Uruguay, in August. Kennedy sent the treasury aecretary, Douglas Dillon, to represent him. Fidel sent Che.

Punta del Este is a resort city on the Atlantic coast. The staid atmosphere was electrified by the arrival of Che, who immediately stole the show from the other ministers. Photographers and journalists eager for pictures and quotes followed him around everywhere. His adolescent bodyguard, Leonardo Tamayo, lent an exotic touch to the proceedings. While all the

The president of Uruguay, Víctor Haedo (at right, in the white cap),
is among those listening raptly to Che during the OAS conference
in Punta del Este in August 1961.

other ministers attending the conference wore suits, Che wore his olive-drab
military uniform. While the other ministers gave their speeches sitting down,
he delivered his opening speech standing up. Douglas Dillon ostentatiously
looked at the ceiling and yawned as Che lambasted the Alliance for Progress
as a move to further isolate Cuba while extending U.S. control over the
rest of Latin America's nations through financial bribery. Che argued that
the Cuban example of asserting political and economic independence—
carrying out land and housing reform, kicking out the monopolies, and
choosing its own trading partners and creditors—provided a more desirable blueprint for the rest of Latin America. The U.S. estimated that the
Alliance for Progress would spur a 2.5 percent annual economic growth rate
in Latin America. Cuba expected to attain a *10 percent* growth rate within a
few years.

Lest Cuba be seen as a spoiler, Che suggested a series of conditions that
should be set by the countries that joined the proposed alliance: freedom to

export their raw materials wherever they chose; an end to the protectionist American subsidies of its own goods, which kept out competition; and aid to industrialize their economies, the cornerstone of economic independence and prosperity. Then, after a lengthy catalog of the multiple acts of U.S. aggression against Cuba, culminating in the recent Bay of Pigs invasion, Che waved an olive branch to the Americans. Cuba wished no harm to its neighbors, he said, and wanted only to be part of the American family of nations. The Cubans were willing to sit down and discuss differences with the United States at any time, so long as there were no preconditions. All Cuba asked for was a guarantee that it would not be attacked and would be granted the right to be *different* within its own borders. "We cannot stop exporting an example, as the United States wishes, because an example is something that transcends borders. What we do give is a guarantee that we will not export revolutions, we guarantee that not a single rifle will leave Cuba, that not a single weapon will leave Cuba for battle in any other country of America." But he warned that Cuba could not guarantee that its example would not be imitated. Unless its neighbors improved social conditions in their countries, the example of Cuba would inevitably "take fire"and, as Fidel had warned in his July 26 speech a year earlier, "the cordillera of the Andes would be the Sierra Maestra of the Americas."

As Che finished his two-hour-and-fifteen-minute speech, the hall was interrupted by a loud cry of *"Asesino!"* and then, as security guards scuffled with the heckler and dragged him outside, two other strangers climbed onto the podium where Che stood and began insulting him. Ignoring them, Che calmly left the conference room. Later, police informed the press that the hecklers were Cuban exiles who belonged to the Frente Democrático Revolucionario, the CIA-sponsored anti-Castro group.

Che's family had traveled to Uruguay, and for the first time since leaving Argentina, he saw his brother Roberto and his sister Ana María. His father, mother, brother Juan Martín, sister Celia, and aunt Beatriz were there as well. Quite a few friends also came: Julio "Gaucho" Castro, whom Che had tried to get to come to Cuba; Beto Ahumada; Pepe Aguilar; his old business partner, "El Gordo" Carlos Figueroa; and that other *gordo,* Ricardo Rojo, who had resigned his post in Bonn and returned home since seeing Che in Cuba.

Che and his brother Roberto could not have been more different. Roberto had married a woman from one of Argentina's aristocratic families, and, although publicly apolitical, he was a lawyer for the social welfare office of the Argentine navy, one of the most conservative organizations in the country. A family photo taken at Punta del Este shows Che, looking scruffy and dressed in fatigues, surrounded by his family. Standing slightly

behind him to one side, Roberto looks well groomed, conservatively dressed
in slacks, a white shirt, a cardigan, and a tie. His hands are in his pockets,
and he is staring intently at his brother. Roberto has never said if he and
Che discussed their differences in Punta del Este. He would only comment
that he found Che "radically different" from the brother he had seen eight
years earlier: austere, driven, and evidently lacking in humor. When he
remarked about this transformation, Roberto recalled, Che told him curtly.
"I'm no longer interested in witticisms. I have a different sense of humor
now."

Che's bodyguard, Tamayito, said that he witnessed an argument between the brothers. "Che criticized Roberto for serving as an instrument of
repression," he said, "and took the occasion to relate how *he* had evaded the
military draft after graduating from medical school because he wasn't willing to serve in the armed forces of a corrupt regime that was an ally of
American imperialism." Although Tamayito's recollection of what was said
may not be accurate, Che's sermonizing would have rankled his brother.
After all, Ernesto had been turned down by the draft because of his asthma,
not because of any heightened political consciousness.

Roberto Ahumada, who had known Che in Córdoba and who was
still close to the Guevara family, also found his old friend changed. "He had
always been a free man," Ahumada recalled, "and now here he was hooked
into a process with responsibilities . . . a position that implied constant
danger. . . . He was a more reserved man, more careful in the things he said."

After a brusque meeting in public, Che arranged to spend a little time
with his childhood friends in private. He handed out Cuban cigars to everyone, and they all smoked and chatted. According to Ahumada, one by one
they offered their services to Che if he felt their skills could be of use to Cuba.
Che seemed to find this amusing. "He joked with us, pulled our legs,"
Ahumada recalled. "He told Carlitos [Figueroa], who was selling real estate, that in Cuba they didn't need real estate specialists because the state
owned the property, and nothing was for sale. And he ribbed me, telling
me I wasn't needed as a lawyer, either, because in Cuba there were no law-
suits, so what could I possibly do there?"

Carlos Figueroa thought that Che's bantering was a sign that he really
was "the same old Ernesto." He seemed to be trying to impress them with
tales of his thrilling experiences. "You can believe it or not," he boasted, "but
I went hunting on an elephant with Nehru." And he said that when the
Russian cosmonaut Yuri Gagarin had recently come to Cuba, he had been
so excited to meet the first man to go into space that he'd stayed glued to
him for an entire day. Figueroa recalled that one night at dinner, Che's aunt
Beatriz leaned over and asked him about his new wife, Aleida. "She's a

country girl," Che said, "a *guajira*." "And what is that?" Beatriz asked in bewilderment. "A *hacendada*?" Che laughed uproariously. His sheltered aunt seemed to imagine that he had married an aristocratic Cuban landowner's daughter.

Che paid special attention to his youngest brother, Juan Martín, who had just turned eighteen and was still living at home with his mother. Juan Martín was halfheartedly studying journalism in Buenos Aires and had begun going out with a fellow student, María Elena Duarte, who was four years older than he was. He chafed under his father's comparisons of his life with the achievements of his older brothers and sisters. At the same time, he idolized Che and read Marxist texts avidly. Sensitive to his brother's predicament, Che tried to give him some direction during their time in Uruguay and invited him to come to Cuba and go to school there. Juan Martín was enthusiastic, but the decision about exactly when he would go was left up in the air.

While Che was lodged in a nondescript hotel with the rest of his large entourage, his family stayed in a villa rented by a left-wing journalist, Julia Constenla de Giussani, who had become friends with Che's mother after interviewing her for a women's magazine. Together with her journalist husband, Julia now edited a pro-Cuban political magazine called *Che* and worked closely with Alfredo Palacios, the venerable leader of Argentina's socialist party. She had come to Punta del Este with a mission. On behalf of a coalition of Argentinian socialists and left-wing *peronistas*, she was to ask Che if he would be willing to return to his homeland. They wanted to propose his name for a candidacy in the upcoming parliamentary elections.

When Julia finally met with Che alone, he quickly turned down the offer. Cuba still needed him, he explained; he had a destiny there to fulfill, and he didn't see himself as an Argentine politico. Then, looking directly at her, smiling ironically, he asked, "Madame, I am a minister. Do you see me as a parliamentary deputy in Argentina?"

There was quite a bit more to the proposal that Julia was imparting. She explained that they wanted him to lead a "symbolic" candidacy for the left. If a popular front gained power through elections, then he would have helped the effort; but if the elections were canceled and a peaceful solution was seen to be impossible, he could become the leader of a guerrilla movement, "the commander of Argentina's revolutionary transformation." It was up to him, she said; he could remain in Cuba, isolated, or he could help set in motion the process of change in Latin America.

"He asked me for precise details, descriptions of individuals in the various political groups, my analysis about union leaders, and Argentine politics in general," Julia recalled. "It was like he was giving me an exam. I think I reminded him of his youth and what he had once been, and he wanted to find out how that world he had been a part of had changed."

Che went over Julia's proposal point by point, even discussing the relative merits of rural over urban guerrilla warfare, but at no moment did she feel that he wavered on his decision. He seemed to her to be completely pessimistic about the prospects for change through the electoral process in Argentina, and in the ability of its leftists to bring about true social transformation. He asked her how she thought the unions would react to an armed struggle, what the prospects were for mobilizing the urban masses, and which places she thought were best for the installation of a guerrilla force. He mentioned the recent spate of small-scale terrorist activities by the Argentine left and said he was against them. "Every action taken should be something that takes one closer to the seizure of power," Che said, "and after the seizure of power, the goal should be the conquest of the national territory."

Julia recalled that there had been a logic to all his questioning. There were Argentinians in Cuba undergoing military training. She represented the viewpoints of those who had stayed behind; those who, as she put it, "were not within the bureaucratic structure of the export of the Cuban model."

Julia found Che to be a complex and fascinating man with a mean streak. One evening, dining with Che and his family, she reminded him of the dedication he had written in a copy of *Guerra de Guerrillas* that he sent to Alfredo Palacios: "To Dr. Palacios, who, when I was a child, was already talking about revolution." Palacios was thrilled and flattered, but Julia had understood that there was another, ungenerous significance to the words: Palacios had only *talked*. She thought that Che's remark was cruel, and she told him so. Che replied, simply, "That's all he ever did."

"With that he ended the discussion," Julia said. "He could be really disrespectful to some people, and he was capable of saying hurtful things. . . . It was as though the only people who merited his respect were the dispossessed, a hungry worker, a malnourished peasant. Even his parents didn't seem to merit the same respect." (This was a trait that had not gone unnoticed by others. Che had refused to give his parents any financial help that would allow them to visit him. His mother had come to Cuba for a second visit in 1960, and then Ernesto senior had written to Hilda to say he was trying to save up enough money to come. He and Celia wanted to meet their newest granddaughter, Aleidita, and to see Hildita again. When Hilda asked Che why he wouldn't help them, he retorted sharply, "So, you're one of those who don't believe I'm on a fixed salary and can use the public funds as I like?" Hilda denied she meant anything of the kind. "I only suggested you pay your father's passage because he wants to come," she said.

"You can pay it back in installments." Che calmed down, but he put the discussion off.)

Julia thought that Che was immensely attractive, in spite of his apparent character flaws. "As a person he had an incalculable enchantment that came completely naturally," she said. "When he entered a room, everything began revolving around him." Perhaps part of the charm, for a woman, was his physical vulnerability. A few days after arriving at Punta del Este, he had such a severe attack of asthma that he had to spend a night in an oxygen tent. The next day, he was able to walk around, but he was still in great discomfort and breathing with difficulty. At one point he gestured discreetly to Julia that he wanted to meet her in the lobby outside. She went ahead and he appeared a couple of minutes later. He said nothing but leaned close to her, so that no one could see what he was doing. He took out his inhaler, sucked on it, then quickly slipped it back in his pocket. Afterward, whenever Che gave Julia the signal, she immediately went out into the hall. "This happened seven or eight times during the conference," she said. "One time, he was in such a bad state that he leaned against the wall and gestured limply for me to get the inhaler from his pocket. He didn't have the strength."

Another Argentinian at the conference in Punta del Este, Ricardo Rojo, also came bearing a message for Che. Rojo had resigned his post in Bonn to protest President Frondízi's policies, especially the decision to grant U.S. companies oil-exploration rights in Argentina, a move seen by many as an affront to the country's national sovereignty. But Rojo was not the kind of man to burn his bridges entirely, and he now carried a message from Frondízi, who wanted to meet with Che in secret. Rojo had been stunned when approached by an intermediary to deliver the message. Frondízi was already deeply unpopular with the armed forces; there had been numerous coup plots and revolts against him; and such a meeting, if ever made public, could only weaken his already tenuous hold on power.

Che agreed to the encounter. He had already accepted a similar overture for a meeting with the president of Brazil, Janio Quadros. The two South American leaders were vital links in the Kennedy adminstration's proposed Alliance for Progress, and both had been involved in previous unsuccessful attempts to mediate between Cuba and the United States. It was agreed that Che would travel to Buenos Aires after the conference ended, and from there go on to Brasília.

On August 16, in his closing remarks, Che declared that Cuba could not ratify the resolution to support the Alliance for Progress. Few of Cuba's suggestions had been discussed seriously, he pointed out, and few substantive changes had been made in what he considered a seriously flawed document. Finally, because it was, in the end, an initiative aimed at isolating Cuba, his government could not possibly approve it, but he took the occasion to reiterate Cuba's willingness to talk with the United States "on any issue, without preconditions."

The following night, at his behest, and with the connivance of some Argentine and Brazilian diplomats, Che was introduced to Richard Goodwin, who was then President Kennedy's personal assistant and a key member of the U.S. delegation. As Goodwin told President Kennedy later, the encounter came about after he had rejected several prior efforts by the Brazilians and Argentinians to get the two of them together. While having dinner with an Argentine delegate, a pair of Brazilian newspapermen, "and a couple of blonds," Goodwin had been invited to a birthday party for one of the Brazilian delegates to the conference. On the way to the party, he had jokingly asked the Argentine, "You're sure Che won't be there?" His friend had protested vehemently that he wouldn't have set Goodwin up.

"There were about thirty people at the party," Goodwin wrote to Kennedy, "drinking and dancing to American music. I talked with several people and, after about an hour, I was told Che was coming. In a few minutes he arrived. I did not talk to him, but all the women in the party swarmed around him. Then one of the Brazilians said that Che had something important to say to me." They adjourned to an adjoining room, where they talked for the next "20–40 minutes," with interruptions from waiters and autograph-seekers, until Goodwin broke off the conversation.

Goodwin found Che quite different from the daunting public figure he had observed from a distance. As he described the encounter to Kennedy, "Che was wearing green fatigues, and his usual overgrown and scraggly beard. Behind the beard his features are quite soft, almost feminine, and his manner is intense. He has a good sense of humor, and there was considerable joking back and forth during the meeting. He seemed very ill at ease when we began to talk, but soon became relaxed and spoke freely. Although he left no doubt of his personal and intense devotion to Communism, his conversation was free of propaganda and bombast. He spoke calmly, in a straightforward manner, and with the appearance of detachment and objectivity. He left no doubt, at any time, that he felt completely free to speak for his government and rarely distinguished between his personal observations and the official positions of the Cuban government. I had the definite impression that he had thought out his remarks very carefully—they were extremely well organized."

Goodwin said he told Che that he possessed no authority to negotiate, but that he would report what Che said to the relevant officials of the U.S. government. "Guevara began by saying that I must understand the Cuban revolution," Goodwin recalled. "They intend to build a socialist state, and the revolution which they have begun is irreversible. They are also now out of the U.S. sphere of influence, and that too is irreversible. They will establish a single-party system with Fidel as Secretary-General of the party. Their ties with the East stem from natural sympathies, and common beliefs in the power structure of the social order. They feel that they have the support of the masses for their revolution, and that that support will grow as time passes."

Che warned Goodwin that if the United States thought Fidel could be overthrown from within, or believed he was actually a moderate surrounded by fanatics and could be won over by the West, these were false assumptions. The revolution was strong and could withstand such threats. He spoke of Cuba's appeal throughout the hemisphere, and warned that civil war would break out in many countries if Cuba was attacked. He brought up again the contradictions he saw inherent in the Alliance for Progress, which he thought might set loose forces that would escape the Americans' ability to control, leading to Cuba-style revolution. "He spoke with great intensity of the impact of Cuba on the continent and the growing strength of its example."

Che spoke candidly of Cuba's problems: the armed counterrevolutionary attacks; disaffection on the part of the petite bourgeoisie and the Catholic Church; the damage caused by the U.S. embargo; the lack of spare parts or of means to replace them; the inability to import consumer goods; and insufficient currency reserves. He told Goodwin that Cuba "didn't want an understanding with the U.S."—Cuba knew this would be impossible—but a "modus vivendi." In return, Guevara said, Cuba could agree not to make "any political alliance with the East." The expropriated American companies could not be returned, but compensation would be worked out in the form of trade. Cuba would hold free elections once the revolution had been institutionalized. The U.S. naval base at Guantánamo "of course" would not be attacked, Che said, and "laughed as if at the absurdly self-evident nature of such a sentiment." He also hinted "obliquely" that Cuba would be willing to "discuss the activities of the Cuban revolution in other countries."

Che couldn't pass up the opportunity to make a jab about how beneficial the invasion had been for Cuba, saying that it had "transformed them from an aggrieved little country to an equal." But he had come not to goad Washington, but only to propose some form of negotiations. Before their meeting ended, he told Goodwin he would relay the substance of their conversation only to Fidel. Goodwin said he would not "publicize" it, either.

Goodwin saw Che's overture as a sign of weakness. He wrote to Kennedy that he believed the conversation—"coupled with other evidence that has been accumulating—indicates that Cuba is undergoing severe economic stress, that the Soviet Union is not prepared to undertake the large effort necessary to get them on their feet, and that Cuba desires an understanding with the U.S. It is worth remembering that Guevara undoubtedly represents the most dedicated Communist views of the Cuban government—and if there is room for any spectrum of viewpoint in Cuba there may be other Cuban leaders even more anxious for an accommodation within the U.S."

Goodwin outlined a series of actions for Kennedy to take. They included stepping up the economic pressure against Cuba and taking retaliatory measures against anyone doing business with the Castro regime, as well as intensifying anti-Cuban propaganda while simultaneously trying to find "some way of continuing the below-ground dialogue which Che has begun. We can thus make it clear that we want to help Cuba and would help Cuba if it would sever Communist ties and begin democratization. In this way we can begin to probe for the split in top leadership which might exist."

Was Che's offer sincere? Perhaps. He sought a means of stalling Washington's policy of "regional containment." But the offer held little substance. Membership in the Warsaw Pact was a formality Cuba could easily forgo. And if the United States accepted recompensation in the form of trade with Cuba, it could hardly enforce its trade embargo on other countries. As for elections, once the revolution was institutionalized and the remaining malcontents had left the island, this was a process that the revolution could easily control.

Significantly, Che had not said that he would end Cuban support for guerrilla insurgencies in the region. He had promised that "not a single weapon" would leave Cuba for use in other countries, but he had not mentioned training guerrillas, or providing funds or fighters. As for weapons, they could be obtained anywhere, even in the United States.

On August 19, the day after his meeting with Goodwin, Che flew to an airfield outside Buenos Aires. The military officer whom President Frondízi had sent to meet the plane was unaware of the identity of the person he was to take to the presidential residence; when he saw Che Guevara, he was dumbstruck.

Che met over lunch with Frondízi, who plainly wanted to use their meeting to test the waters as to Cuba's intentions. He expressed his hopes for peaceful coexistence. Che assured Frondízi that Cuba had no intention of entering into a formal alliance with Moscow unless it was attacked by Washington.

After lunch, Che asked a favor from Frondízi. Could he see his seriously ailing aunt, María Luisa, who lived in the suburb of San Isidro? Frondízi agreed, and for the first time in eight years, Che saw the streets of

Buenos Aires again, through the windows of a presidential car, a clandestine visitor to his own country. After his visit with María Luisa—it was the last time he would see her—he was driven back to the airfield and flown across the Río de la Plata to Uruguay. He got on board the Cubana plane where his entourage awaited him and flew to Brasília.

The news of Che's "secret" visit spread rapidly, causing consternation in military circles. That night a bomb exploded in Buenos Aires, blowing out the front door of the apartment building on Calle Arenales where Che's uncle, Fernando Guevara Lynch, lived. Fernando told reporters that he had not seen his nephew and had learned about the visit only after it was over. "It was 1953 when he left the country. It would have given me great pleasure to have seen him," Fernando said. Then he excused himself and, with true Guevara aplomb, told the reporters that he was going out for dinner with friends and hoped to make it "if a bomb hasn't been placed under the hood of my car."

The bombing was not the only fallout from Che's visit. Over succeeding days, there were stories in the papers about the "concern" felt in the armed forces, along with photographs of grave-faced generals coming and going from tense meetings with the president. Argentina's foreign minister was forced to resign, and seven months later, when Frondízi himself was overthrown in a military coup, most political observers agreed that his encounter with Guevara had hastened his fall.

Wherever Che alighted, calamities followed. During a speech he gave at the University of Montevideo, there were protests and a shot was fired, killing a Uruguayan professor in the crowd. Tamayito was convinced it had been a plot to kill Che, carried out by anti-Castro exiles flown in by the CIA. At Che's meeting with Janio Quadros, the president of Brazil, he was decorated with the prestigious Orden Cruzeiro do Sol. Five days later, Quadros resigned, his political career suddenly over.

VI

Within a few weeks of the OAS conference in Punta del Este, Washington had sent a clear message that it was not interested in Che's overture to President Kennedy. Congress passed a bill banning U.S. assistance to any nation that dealt with Cuba. Costa Rica broke off relations with Havana, and Betancourt's government in Venezuela followed suit. Latin America's armies were on the alert for signs of Cuban "subversion," and U.S. military aid and specialized training was on offer to deal with the threat. In October 1961, the first Inter-American Counterrevolutionary War Course began at Argentina's Escuela Superior de Guerra. At the inaugural ceremony, echoing the language used by Che Guevara to unite Latin Americans for the common struggle against imperialism, Brigadier General Carlos Turolo invoked the spirit of "international solidarity with the people of the Americas . . . who are faced with the . . . imperative necessity to coordinate action, and to prevent and combat the common enemy, Communism."

Washington was, in effect, going to inoculate the hemisphere. The vaccine was a potent one: counterinsurgency training; coordinated action by the region's military, police, and intelligence agencies; a stepped-up role for the CIA; economic and social development programs through the Alliance for Progress; and military "civic action" projects in backward areas to win the hearts and minds of the civilians who were targeted by the guerrillas.

Allen Dulles had been fired from the CIA after the disaster at the Bay of Pigs, but the new director, John McCone, had a strong hand to play. In November 1961, JFK allocated $50 million for a new covert action program against Cuba. It was code-named Operation Mongoose. Coordinated out of Washington and the CIA's Miami station, the ambitious program aimed to destabilize the Cuban regime through espionage, sabotage, military attacks, and selective assassinations. In time, it would become the CIA's largest covert operation.

The CIA's underground resistance network in Cuba had been devastated in the massive roundup of suspected dissidents by Cuba's security forces after the Bay of Pigs. But in October, only a few weeks after he had left his asylum in the Venezuelan embassy, Felix Rodríguez was on his way back to the island. His mission: to rebuild the CIA's infiltration routes for future paramilitary actions.

By the year's end, Kennedy's containment policy was enjoying some success. In December, an OAS resolution by Cuba's neighbors condemning its alignment with the Soviet bloc was virtually unanimous; only Mexico voted against the resolution. That same month, Colombia, Panama, Nicaragua, and El Salvador severed relations with Cuba. In Havana, Fidel made a speech that definitively sealed Cuba's break with the West. "I am a Marxist-Leninist," he declared, "and will be until I die." At the end of January 1962, the OAS voted to suspend Cuba's membership in the organization and ban arms sales to Cuba by member states. Measures for a joint defense against Cuban actions in the region were adopted. In February, Kennedy tightened the already stringent trade embargo against Cuba, banning all exports except medical supplies.

Edward Lansdale, the director of Operation Mongoose, came up with a rip-roaring schedule for a package of actions, including attacks on key leaders, to culminate in the overthrow of Castro by October. This plan was then scaled down, but the final guidelines for Mongoose, while calling for the CIA to make "maximum use of indigenous resources" to bring about Castro's overthrow, also concluded that U.S. military intervention would be required.

A bomb was discovered and defused by the police outside Che's mother's house on Calle Araoz in Buenos Aires in February. A week later, Argentina severed diplomatic links with Cuba. In March, with agricultural production sharply down in Cuba and consumer shortages in all the shops, mandatory government rationing for foodstuffs and other basic goods was imposed. From now on, Cubans would have to line up to buy food with ration booklets used to record their weekly allowances. It had been only seven months since Che had confidently predicted that Cuba would soon be virtually self-sufficent in food.

Who was to blame for the shortages? Were they caused by the U.S. trade embargo? In part, yes. Had the revolution's radicalization caused the crippling exodus of technicians, managers, and traders from the island? Yes. Were the revolution's leaders incompetent in their attempt to convert a capitalist economy to a socialist one? Yes. Although neither Che nor Fidel would acknowledge the fact, food rationing heralded the end of their illusion of making Cuba a self-sufficient socialist state. As for Che's illusion that a global fraternity of socialist nations could bring about the demise of capitalism, it was about to be dashed to pieces.

VII

In late April 1962, Alexandr Alexiev was urgently summoned back to Moscow by Nikita Khrushchev. No explanations were given, and Alexiev was alarmed. A child of Stalinism, he immediately began thinking the worst and preparing for some kind of punishment while racking his brain to figure out what he could have possibly done wrong. He stalled for time, asking to remain in Havana for the May Day festivities. A million people were expected in the Plaza de la Revolución, and the "Internationale" was to be sung for the first time in the now openly socialist state of Cuba. He was given permission to stay, but told to come to Moscow immediately after the event.

On the third of May, Alexiev flew to Mexico, where the Soviet ambassador said he had orders to lodge Alexiev at the embassy, not in a hotel. It was the same story at his next stop, London. Quite obviously, the Kremlin wanted to keep a close eye on Alexiev, and he arrived in Moscow extremely worried. A department chief of the Soviet Foreign Ministry was waiting for him at the airport. Alexiev was by now truly mystified and was left none the wiser by the official, who would tell him only that he would learn "tomorrow" why he had been called home.

The next morning, Alexiev was escorted into the Kremlin and taken to the office of Mikhail Suslov, Khrushchev's deputy. Suslov wasn't there, but two high-ranking secretaries of the Central Committee were: Yuri Andropov and the KGB chief, Alexander Shelepin, who took Alexiev into his office and explained that he was to be the new Soviet ambassador to Cuba. Nikita Khrushchev himself had made the decision. While they talked, Khrushchev called and asked Alexiev to come to his office. Khrushchev was alone, and the two of them talked for about an hour. Alexiev tried to decline the ambassadorship. What Cuba needed, he said, was an ambassador who knew about economics, and he was an illiterate in that field. "That's not important," Khrushchev told him. "What is important is that you are friendly with Fidel, with the leadership. They believe in you." As for economists, he would give Fidel however many experts he needed. Right there and then, Khrushchev made a call and ordered a team of twenty top-level ministerial advisers from every field of the economy to be assembled. They would accompany Alexiev back to Cuba. He then turned to Alexiev and said that he wanted to see him in a couple of weeks to talk more "concretely."

Toward the end of May, Khrushchev sent for Alexiev again. This time, there were five other officials in the office: Khrushchev's aide, Frol Koslov; Deputy Premier Mikoyan; Foreign Minister Andrei Gromyko; Defense Minister Rodion Malinovski; and a Politburo alternate member, Sharif Rashidov. Alexiev was invited to sit down. "It was a very strange conversation," he recalled. "Khrushchev asked me again about Cuba, the Cuban comrades, and I talked about each one, and then, when I was least expecting it, Khrushchev said, 'Comrade Alexiev, to help Cuba, to save the Cuban revolution, we have reached a decision to place [nuclear] rockets in Cuba. What do you think? How will Fidel react? Will he accept or not?'"

Alexiev was astounded. He told Khrushchev that he thought Fidel wouldn't accept the offer because his long-held public stance was that the revolution had been carried out to restore Cuba's independence. They had thrown out the American military advisers, and if they accepted Soviet rockets on their soil, it would seem to violate their own principles. It would also be viewed through the eyes of international public opinion, and especially by Cuba's Latin American neighbors, as a serious breach of trust. "For these reasons," Alexiev concluded, "I don't think they will accept."

Malinovski reacted angrily. "He attacked me," Alexiev recalled. "What kind of revolution is this that you say they won't accept? I fought in *bourgeois* Republican Spain, which accepted our help . . . and socialist Cuba has even more reason to!" Alexiev was intimidated and kept quiet as another official rallied to his defense, but Khrushchev said nothing, and the argument fizzled. They began talking about other subjects and finally adjourned for lunch in Khrushchev's dining room.

Over lunch, Khrushchev announced that he was going to send a couple of high-ranking officials—Sharif Rashidov and Marshal Sergei Biryusov, commander of the Strategic Rocket Forces—back to Havana with Alexiev to talk with Fidel. "There's no other way for us to defend him," Khrushchev said. "The Americans only understand force. We can give them the same medicine they gave us in Turkey. Kennedy is pragmatic, he is an intellectual, he'll comprehend and won't go to war, because war is war. Our gesture is intended to avoid war. Any idiot can start one, and we're not doing that, it's just to frighten them a bit. They should be made to feel the same way we do. They have to swallow the pill like we swallowed the Turkish one." (Khrushchev was referring to the United States' deployment of nuclear-tipped Jupiter missiles taking place in neighboring Turkey that same month—the culmination of an agreement negotiated by the Eisenhower administration with its NATO partner in 1959 and reluctantly followed through by Kennedy.)

Khrushchev warned that the operation to install the missiles in Cuba would have to be carried out with the utmost secrecy, so that the Americans wouldn't suspect anything until after their upcoming congressional elections in November. It could not be allowed to become a campaign issue. If it was done right, he said, he was convinced that the Americans would be too busy with their campaigning to notice anything before the missiles were in place.

A day or two before he was to leave for Cuba, Alexiev was tracked down by Kremlin officials; Nikita Khrushchev wanted to see him again. They took him to Khrushchev's dacha at Peredelkino in the forested countryside outside Moscow, where he found the premier and the entire Politburo gathered. Khrushchev presented him to the assembled officials, and then announced: "Alexiev says Fidel won't accept our proposal." Khrushchev had thought up an approach that might work, however, and he tried it out on the others. He would tell Fidel that the missiles would be placed only as a last resort; first, the Soviet Union would attempt all other means of persuasion to dissuade the Americans from attacking Cuba, but he would offer his strong personal opinion that only the missiles would do the job. He hoped that would convince Fidel, he said, and told Alexiev to relay the proposal.

A few days later, still convinced that the overture would be rebuffed, Alexiev returned to Cuba with an "agricultural delegation" that included Rashidov and Marshal Biryusov, who was disguised as a simple engineer named Petrov. As soon as they arrived, Alexiev went to see Raúl Castro and said his group was on a mission for Khrushchev and needed to meet with

Fidel immediately. "Engineer Petrov is not engineer Petrov," he told Raúl. "He is a marshal in charge of the Soviet missile program."

Raúl understood and went into Fidel's office. He didn't come out for two or three hours. Then they met with Fidel in Osvaldo Dorticós's office. "I saw that Raúl," Alexiev recalled, "for the first time ever, was writing things down in a notebook." When the Soviets had finished explaining Khrushchev's proposal, Fidel was noncommittal but made favorable noises. He told the Soviets to give him until the next day. The way Alexiev understood it, Fidel wanted to consult with Che.

The next day Alexiev was summoned by Fidel. Once again they met in Dorticós's office, but this time, several others were present, including Che, Dorticós, Carlos Rafael Rodríguez, and Blas Roca. They had considered the proposal and, agreeing that the missiles could stop the Americans from invading Cuba, were willing to go ahead with the program. The conversation then turned to the likelihood of a U.S. invasion, and Alexiev recalled that Che was the "most active" in the discussion that followed, making his opinion on the missile issue clear. "Anything that can stop the Americans," Che said, "is worthwhile."

The Soviets and their Cuban counterparts proceeded immediately with the job of selecting missile sites. Fidel told Alexiev that he wanted a military pact to formalize things, and that he would send Raúl to Moscow to sign it. According to Vitali Korionov, a Central Committee adviser, Fidel outlined for inclusion in the pact a list of objectives he wanted the Soviets to negotiate with the Americans once the presence of the missiles was made public. In addition to securing a commitment from Washington not to invade, he wanted the U.S. naval base at Guantámano Bay dismantled. The Soviets agreed to the pact, and over the next week Alexiev and Raúl worked closely to produce a Spanish-language version. Then, Alexiev said, Raúl and Marshal Malinovski signed each page of the document.

By July 2, 1962, Raúl was in Moscow carrying the treaty draft. Over the next week, according to Alexiev, he met with Khrushchev twice. But Vitali Korionov recalled things differently. He said that when Raúl and his wife, Vílma Espín, arrived, he and Prime Minister Alexei Kosygin met them at the airport. They were taken to a protocol house. Korionov, Kosygin, and Raúl went into the dining room, where there was a grand piano. It was just the three of them. "Raúl put the document on the piano, with Fidel's points, now translated into Russian, and there, without sitting down, Kosygin and Raúl signed the document. Afterward, Kosygin said he was leaving, and he told Korionov to stay and calm down Raúl, who was extremely nervous. "He was in a state of tense expectancy," Korionov said. "As if thinking 'What is going to happen now?' Because the Cuban comrades understood how this could end." Korionov sat up all night with Raúl, talking and drinking Armenian cognac.

Fidel had told Raúl he wanted Khrushchev to answer one question: what would happen if the Americans discovered the operation while it was still in progress? Alexiev said that Khrushchev's reply was short and breezy: "Don't worry, nothing will happen. If the Americans start getting nervous, we'll send out the Baltic Fleet as a show of support." Raúl accepted Khrushchev's answer as a firm commitment of support. Alexiev recalls Raúl saying: "This is great, just great! Fidel will accept everything; he may correct a few things but that's all. In principle he'll accept."

It was a fearsome and hefty military package indeed: twenty-four medium-range and sixteen intermediate-range ballistic missile launchers, each equipped with two missiles and a nuclear warhead; twenty-four advanced SAM-2 surface-to-air missile batteries; forty-two MiG interceptors; forty-two IL-28 bombers; twelve *Komar*-class missile boats, and coastal defense cruise missiles. The arsenal would be accompanied by four elite Soviet combat regiments totaling 42,000 troops. The agreement was renewable every five years. It stipulated that the missiles would be completely under the command of the Soviet military.

Around July 15, even before Raúl had left Moscow or Fidel had seen the agreement, the first missiles were surreptitiously shipped from the Soviet Union's Black Sea ports. They were concealed on cargo ships. Troops also began to leave for Cuba secretly. On July 17, Raúl flew back to Havana; he was followed in three weeks by Alexiev, now the new Soviet ambassador. He brought the agreement that had been ratified by Raúl with him. Khrushchev had told Alexiev that there were "already" Soviet missiles in Cuba, and stressed again the necessity to maintain total secrecy about the operation until November or later. Not one cable should be sent from Havana; if he had something important to discuss, Alexiev should come to Moscow himself or send an emissary.

Khrushchev had not signed the agreement, pending Fidel's final approval. His plan was to travel to Cuba himself for the anniversary of the Cuban revolution in January. There, after he and Fidel had both signed the pact, they would divulge it to the world. By then, everything would be in place, and the fait accompli would give Khrushchev tremendous strategic bargaining power with Washington.

But things did not go as planned. First, Fidel did not like the draft agreement; he though it was "too technical," Alexiev recalled, with not enough of a "political framework." Alexiev said that Fidel took particular issue with the preamble, which read originally, "In the interests of ensuring her sovereignty and to maintain her freedom, Cuba requests that the Soviet

Union considers and accepts the possibility of installing missiles [on her territory]." As Alexiev explained it, Fidel's changes shifted the onus of the decision to install the missiles. In his version, it was a responsibility shared equally between the two nations. He wanted to formalize what Khrushchev had already promised rhetorically—that an attack against Cuba would be considered an attack on the Soviet Union. In Fidel's version, the preamble read, "It is necessary and has been decided to take the necessary steps for the joint defense of the legitimate rights of the people of Cuba and the Soviet Union, taking into account the urgent need to adopt measures to guarantee mutual security, in view of the possibility of an imminent attack against the Republic of Cuba and the Soviet Union."

When the revised draft was ready in late August, Fidel did not send Raúl back to the Soviet Union. He sent Che, and with him Emilio Aragonés, an old July 26 associate and now one of his close advisers. On August 30, they met Khrushchev at his summer dacha in the Crimea. Khrushchev agreed to the amended language of the accord, which was titled "Agreement between the Government of the Republic of Cuba and the Government of the U.S.S.R. on Military Cooperation for the Defense of the National Territory of Cuba in the Event of Aggression." But Khrushchev stalled with regard to signing it, saying he would do so when he came to Cuba in a few months.

Probably concerned that the Soviets were carrying out a double cross, Che argued for the agreement to be made public. Khrushchev refused, insisting that it should remain secret for now. Che and Aragonés then repeated Fidel's nagging worry—one shared by several senior Soviet officials, including Foreign Minister Andrei Gromyko—about a premature discovery of the operation by the Americans. As Aragonés later told it, Khrushchev was as dismissive as he had been with Raúl: "He said to Che and me, with Malinovski in the room, 'You don't have to worry; there will be no problem from the U.S. And if there is a problem, we will send the Baltic Fleet.'" Aragonés recalled that when they heard this, "Che and I looked at each other with raised eyebrows." Neither man was convinced, although there was little choice at this point but to take Khrushchev at his word.

U.S. intelligence was scrutinizing Che's activities in Russia with a wary eye. On August 31, a CIA cable went out noting that the "composition" of Che Guevara's delegation to the Soviet Union "indicates the delegation may have a broader mission than is [sic] announced agenda, which pertains to industrial matters. Guevara is accompanied by Emilio Aragonés, apparently not trained or experienced in economics or industrial matters. The Guevara mission was met at the airport by Soviet economic officials and by First Deputy Premier Kosygin, a member of the Soviet Party Presidium."

By September 6, when Che arrived back in Havana, the Soviet military buildup in Cuba had already been detected. American U-2 reconnaissance planes had discovered the new SAM-2 missile sites and coastal-defense cruise missile installations. Kennedy had been assured by his experts that the weapons were not a threat to U.S. national security, but their presence was a danger sign that could not be disregarded. On September 4, the president had sent his younger brother Robert, the attorney general, to discuss the buildup with the Soviet ambassador to the United States, Anatoli Dobrynin. Dobrynin had relayed Khrushchev's reassurances that no offensive weaponry had been deployed in Cuba. The new weapons were intended purely for Cuba's defense.

The White House remained suspicious. New reconnaissance photos indicated that a Soviet submarine base might be under construction. Kennedy issued a public statement announcing that the United States had detected not only the SAMs but an increased number of Soviet military personnel in Cuba. He admitted that the United States had no evidence of the presence of either Soviet-bloc combat troops or offensive ground-to-ground missiles, but he warned that if they existed there, the "gravest issues" would arise.

The next day, Kennedy asked Congress for approval to call up 150,000 military reservists. The United States announced plans to hold a military exercise in the Caribbean in mid-October, and Cuba denounced this as proof of Washington's intention to invade. Once again, Dobrynin insisted that Moscow was supplying only defensive weapons to Cuba.

Each day brought tension levels higher, as new details of the buildup filtered in. Accusations and denials from the United States, the Soviet Union, and Cuba flew back and forth. Then, on September 9, U.S. intelligence monitors recorded some unsettling remarks made by Che at a reception at the Brazilian embassy in Havana. Speaking to a reporter, Che had called the latest Soviet military aid deal to Cuba a "historic event" that heralded a reversal in East-West power relations; in his opinion, it had shifted the scales in favor of the Soviet Union. As one classified cable paraphrased him, Guevara had said, "The United States cannot do anything but yield."

Che marching with Raúl and Fidel in the 1963 May Day parade in Havana.

25

Guerrilla Watershed

The blood of the people is our most sacred treasure, but it must be used in order to save the blood of more people in the future.

CHE GUEVARA
"Tactics and Strategy of the Latin American Revolution," 1962

One day I reached the summit of a mountain with a rifle in my hand and I felt something I had never felt before—I felt so strong! I had a beautiful feeling of freedom and I said to myself: "We can do it!"

HÉCTOR JOUVE
One of Che's guerrillas in Argentina, 1963–1964

I

In December 1961, Julio Roberto Cáceres (Patojo), Che's young Guatemalan friend and protégé, had left Cuba secretely for his homeland, determined to help launch a Marxist guerrilla struggle there. Che had been especially brotherly with the introverted Patojo and had nurtured his revolutionary aspirations. Patojo was with Che at La Cabaña, INRA, and the Ministry of Industries, and for most of the last three years had been part of the Guevara household. Che helped him get out of Cuba quietly.

Patojo went back to Guatemala at a propitious moment for revolution. Congressional elections had just taken place amid widespread allegations of fraud. Then, in late January 1962, the chief of President Ydigoras Fuentes's secret police was assassinated, and two weeks later the first hit-and-run attacks against military posts were launched near Puerto Barrios by the guerrillas led by Yon Sosa and Turcios Lima. They had named their group the Alejandro de León November 13 Guerrilla Movement, in commemoration of the date of their earlier failed uprising and in honor of a late comrade. In February, the rebels made their aims public in a communiqué that called for rebellion to restore the country to democratic rule. Patojo's group, which was backed by Guatemala's Communist Party, launched its movement independently at around the same time.

In March 1962, only four months after Patojo left Cuba, Che received word that he had been killed in action. A few months later, Myrna Torres[*]

*See Notes.

visited Havana and brought Che a notebook Patojo had left with her in Mexico en route to the battlefield. It included a poem to his girlfriend back in Cuba. Che wrote a eulogy to Patojo that was published in *Verde Olivo* in August, a bittersweet parable of redemption aimed at Cuba's Revolutionary Armed Forces. He gave a brief account of Patojo's life and their relationship—how they had lived and worked together as itinerant photographers in Mexico; how Patojo had also wanted to join the *Granma* expedition but had been left behind; how he had then come to help in Cuba's triumphant revolution:

> After he came to Cuba we almost always lived in the same house, as was fitting for two old friends. But we no longer maintained the early intimacy in this new life, and I suspected El Patojo's intentions only when I occasionally saw him studying one of the native Indian languages of his country. One day he told me he was leaving, that the time had come for him to do his duty. . . . He was going to his country to fight, arms in hand, to reproduce somehow our guerrilla struggle. It was then that we had one of our long talks. I limited myself to recommending strongly three things: constant movement, constant wariness, and constant vigilance. . . .
>
> This was the synthesis of our guerrilla experience; it was the only thing—along with a warm handshake—that I could give to my friend. Could I advise him not to do it? With what right? . . .
>
> El Patojo left, and with time the news of his death came. . . . And not only he, but a group of comrades with him, all of them as brave, as selfless, as intelligent perhaps as he, but not known to me personally. Once more there is the bitter taste of defeat. . . .
>
> Once again, youthful blood has fertilized the fields of the Americas to make freedom possible. Another battle has been lost; we must make time to weep for our fallen comrades while we sharpen our machetes. From the valuable and unfortunate experience of the cherished dead, we must firmly resolve not to repeat their errors, to avenge the death of each one of them with many victorious battles, and to achieve definitive liberation.
>
> When El Patojo left Cuba . . . he had few clothes or personal belongings to worry about. Mutual friends in Mexico, however, brought me some poems he had written and left there in a notebook. They are the last verses of a revolutionary; they are, in addition, a love song to the revolution, to the homeland, and to a

woman. To that woman whom El Patojo knew and loved in Cuba
are addressed these final verses, this injunction:

Take this, it is only my heart
Hold it in your hand
And when the dawn arrives,
Open your hand
And let the sun warm it . . .

El Patojo's heart has remained among us, in the hands of his beloved and in the grateful hands of an entire people, waiting to be
warmed beneath the sun of a new day that will surely dawn for
Guatemala and for all America.

Cuba had become a fully operational "guerrilla central" by 1962, fueling the far-flung substations of armed revolution throughout the hemisphere. Che's dream of a continental revolution now made strategic sense.
The spreading guerrilla threat helped divert American pressure away from
Cuba and simultaneously made Washington pay a high price for its regional
containment policy. Fidel had made support of guerrilla activity government policy. Responding to the expulsion of Cuba from the OAS in January 1962, he issued what he called his Second Declaration of Havana, which
proclaimed the "inevitability" of revolution in Latin America. Jittery Latin
American governments took this to be a tacit declaration of war against their
countries.

Juan Carreterro, aka Ariel, a high-ranking Cuban intelligence officer
at the time, said that he began working with Che in 1962 to create a trans-
continental, anti-imperialist "revolutionary theater in Latin America." Ariel
worked directly under Manuel Piñeiro Losada—Barbarroja—who oversaw the guerrilla programs at State Security as Ramiro Valdés's deputy.* By
that spring, Che was directing a campaign to recruit and organize guerrilla
trainees from among the Latin American students invited to Cuba on revolutionary scholarships. One of them was Ricardo Gadea, the younger brother
of his ex-wife, Hilda. Ricardo had finished high school in Peru and had studied journalism at Argentina's renowned University of La Plata, a magnet
for students from all over Latin America. He had joined the youth movement of the Peruvian nationalist opposition party, APRA, and like many
of his student friends, Ricardo quickly became enamored with the Cuban

*See Notes.

revolutionary cause, seeing it as a model for political change in Latin America. In his spare time he helped out at the July 26 support committee's offices in Buenos Aires, working with Che's father.

In 1960, Ricardo had decided to go to Cuba to finish his studies and to participate in the revolution he sympathized with so strongly. Hilda could help set him up. But when Ricardo arrived, he learned that he wouldn't be able to pursue his career in journalism. The university reform process was under way, and journalism was not a priority profession in the new Cuba. The journalism school at Havana University was, as he put it, somewhat "disorganized." So he began studying economics. The dean of his faculty was the venerable Communist Party leader Carlos Rafael Rodríguez. During the Bay of Pigs invasion, Ricardo and many of his fellow Latin American students volunteered for the revolutionary militias, hoping to be sent to the front, but they were left behind in Havana to guard public buildings.

By early 1962, hundreds of new Latin American students—Bolivians, Venezuelans, Argentines, Uruguayans, Nicaraguans, Guatemalans, Colombians—had arrived in Cuba. There were about eighty students from Peru. Before long, however, a schism opened between those students who were primarily interested in academic pursuits and those who, as Ricardo described it, "wanted to learn from Cuba's revolutionary experience and to return to our own country to carry out our own revolution." Ricardo opted for the latter group. His decision coincided with the March 1962 military coup in Peru that annulled the recent election results, suspended congress, and placed the whole Peruvian political system in doubt. For Peruvians seeking to apply the Cuban model to their nation, it was the time to strike.

Ricardo Gadea and his Peruvian comrades left the university for guerrilla training in the Sierra Maestra. Their instructors were veterans of the Cuban struggle. Fidel himself spoke to them and gave them advice; but it was Che, Gadea said, who was their undisputed revolutionary mentor. "Of all the leaders," Ricardo said, "Che was the most charismatic, sensitive, and involved, as a Latin American. He understood us, knew our difficulties, and helped us overcome many of our problems."

Another country whose revolutionary progress was close to Che's heart was Nicaragua. Since the debacle on the Honduran border in the summer of 1959, the Nicaraguan rebels battling the Somoza dynasty had been going in and out of Cuba. Carlos Fonseca, the group's ideologue, had recovered there from the wounds he suffered during the border ambush. He had returned to Central America to seek a political alliance between his group, which was based in the university, other exiles, and *antisomocistas* within Nicaragua itself. One of his closest disciples, a short, squat, full-lipped former law student named Tomas Borge, traveled to Havana seeking help for the

Juventud Revolucionaria Nicaragüense (Nicaraguan RevolutionaryYouth) group. He and another comrade, Noel Guerrero, joined Che's friend Rodolfo Romero on a visit to Che at the National Bank.

As Borge remembered it, he launched into a flowery greeting "on behalf of Nicaragua's youth," but Che cut him short. "Let's forget the greetings and get down to business," he said. Borge insisted that his speech was not demagogic, and Che let him go on. When he finished, Che embraced him. He also gave Borge and his comrades $20,000 to organize themselves. Rodolfo Romero was designated the military chief of the group, and eventually they had about thirty Nicaraguans in Cuba who were inducted into revolutionary militias and sent off for combat experience in the counterinsurgency war in the Escambray. In 1961, Romero attended the Cuban counterintelligence school. He was the only Nicaraguan there, he proudly recalled. Then he joined Borge, Fonseca, and others at an artillery training course given by Czech advisers at a remote Cuban military base.

By the summer of 1962, Carlos Fonseca was back in Nicaragua, overseeing the anti-Somoza urban underground effort, pulling off bank robberies, and carrying out propaganda and sabotage. Tomas Borge and about sixty other guerrillas under Noel Guerrero's leadership slipped into Nicaragua's northern jungle from Honduras. The group that would eventually call itself the Frente Sandinista de Liberacíon Nacional (FSLN) was ready for action.*

That spring, guerrilla forces had begun operating in Venezuela. In May, troops at a naval base near Caracas had revolted. The Communist Party openly backed the uprising, and President Betancourt banned both the Party and the MIR. In June, a second naval uprising was put down after two days of bloody fighting with loyalist army troops. Dissident officers and troops fled into the hills, where many of them joined the fledgling guerrilla forces. In December, the Party officially endorsed the armed struggle, and two months later a new guerrilla coalition group, Fuerzas Armadas de Liberación Nacional (FALN) announced that it intended to wage war against Betancourt's regime. The FALN called itself a democratic and nationalist movement, but it had a Communist-dominated political front, the Frente de Liberación Nacional (FLN). In communiqués reminiscent of those Fidel sent out while he was fighting Batista, the FLN denied government accusations that it was Communist or anti-American and called for

---

*Unlike all the other Cuban-sponsored guerrilla groups in Latin America, the FSLN went on to seize power, overthrowing the last dictator of the Somoza clan, Anastasio Somoza Debayle, in 1979. Carlos Fonseca did not live to see Nicaragua's "liberation," however. He was killed in the fighting in 1976.

Venezuelans of all creeds to join its united front to make Venezuela "master of her own destiny and her own riches."

Che assisted the new Venezuelan revolutionary organization, just as he was helping the guerrilla movements of Nicaragua, Peru, and Guatemala. With each new rifle raised aloft, his vision of a continental guerrilla struggle against American imperialism was coming one step closer to reality.

II

By now, Che was planning to launch an insurgency in Argentina. He had been cultivating the idea for some time, but it had taken on new vigor after the Argentine military toppled President Frondízi. He had chosen the northern jungle of Argentina, near Salta, not far from the rugged Bolivian border, as an exploratory theater of war. It was the same area he had journeyed through in 1950 on his motorbike trip, during which he had paused to reflect about the meaning of life, death, and his own destiny.

Che asked Alberto Granado for help in recruiting Argentines for the guerrilla venture. In October 1961, Granado had moved with his family from Havana to Santiago to start up a biomedical research school at the university there, and during 1962 he used his job and nationality to assess the potential of his fellow expatriates for Che's Argentine revolution scheme. He became friendly with the Argentine painter Ciro Roberto Bustos, who had arrived in Cuba as a revolutionary volunteer at about the same time as Granado. Bustos had set up a small ceramics factory in the Oriente countryside and was also giving twice-weekly painting classes at Santiago University. When he was in town, Bustos was invited to stay at Granado's house, and their conversations soon broached the topic of armed struggle. When Granado learned that Bustos supported the idea of a Cuban-style revolution in their homeland, he passed along his positive appraisal of the painter to Che. Before long, Granado arranged for them to meet.

Granado also made a trip to Argentina. He journeyed around the country, working through the Argentine Communist Party to recruit technicians and other skilled people to work in Cuba—a plausible cover story for his recruitment of guerrilla cadres. However, as Granado acknowledged years later, the Argentine security services were already suspicious and had evidently monitored his movements. Several of the people he met with were temporarily detained after his visit. Even so, he was able to recruit a couple of men who soon arrived in Cuba for guerrilla training.

Che's plan was for Jorge Ricardo Masetti—the Argentine journalist who had visited him in the Sierra Maestra and then, after the revolution, had become the editor of Cuba's international wire agency, Prensa Latina—

to lead his advance patrol. Masetti had dropped from view after he conducted a televised interrogation of the men taken prisoner during the Bay of Pigs invasion. It was well known that Masetti was no Communist, and, after a long standoff with the doctrinaire Communist Party faction at Prensa Latina, he had been removed. He was said to then be employed by the propaganda department of Cuba's armed forces, but in reality he was working for Che.

After leaving Prensa Latina, Masetti went through an officers' training course to gain military experience. He graduated with the rank of captain and traveled on secret missions for Che to Prague—a new way station for Cuba's overseas espionage—and to Algeria, where he smuggled a huge quantity of American weapons seized at Playa Girón to the FLN insurgents, via Tunisia. One of Granado's recruits, Federico Méndez, an Argentine mechanic in his early twenties who had military experience, accompanied Masetti. For several months, they stayed at the FLN's general staff headquarters, where Méndez gave the Algerians training courses in the use of the American arms. By the time they returned to Cuba, they had established close links with the grateful Algerian revolutionary leadership and its top military officers.

Masetti's mission in Argentina was to become acquainted with the terrain and quietly establish a guerrilla base of operations. Before engaging the enemy, he was to build up support among peasants and a civilian-support infrastructure in the cities. Later on, when the conditions were right, Che would come and lead the force himself.

Che was casting his net wide to take soundings of Argentina's political situation. When Cuba's diplomats were expelled from Argentina in March 1962 and flew home on a plane from Uruguay, he sent a telegram to his friend from Dean Funes high school, the *radicalista* Oscar Stemmelin, inviting him to take advantage of the evacuation flight to come and visit.* Stemmelin and another classmate of Che's took up the invitation and stayed in Havana for about a month. During Stemmelin's stay, he and Che met eight or ten times to talk about old times, Cuba's revolution, and Argentine politics.

On May 25, the Argentine Day of Independence, the 380 members of Cuba's Argentine community in Havana gathered to celebrate with a

---

*Che also saw the flight as an opportunity to get his brother Juan Martín to Cuba. According to María Elena, Juan Martín's wife at the time, he was prepared to go, but there were some last-minute difficulties. In the end, Juan Martín never did return to Cuba while his brother was alive; nor did Che's father or anyone else in the family, except Che's mother.

traditional outdoor *asado,* complete with folk music, traditional dances, and typical Argentine costumes. Che was the guest of honor, and he suggested that the organizers invite the young German-Argentine woman Haydée Tamara Bunke. Since her arrival from Berlin, Tamara, as everyone knew her, had been working as a translator at the Ministry of Education, and she was enthusiastic about everything going on. She joined in volunteer labor sessions, worked as a literacy instructor, and signed up for the militias and her local CDR watch committee. She had become a fixture at the social gatherings of Latin American guerrillas in Havana and expressed great sympathy with their causes.

Tamara and Che's deputy, Orlando Borrego, had renewed the friendship begun in Berlin. She made no secret of her desire to become a fighter in one of Latin America's guerrilla wars and was constantly asking Borrego to take her to see Che. Borrego stalled. There were always lots of people trying to see Che. Tamara finally got her way by arranging to participate in a day's volunteer work alongside him at a school being built near his house. "I underestimated her," Borrego observed wryly.

At the Independence Day *asado,* Che gave his usual speech on the revolutionary struggle in Latin America, putting special emphasis on Argentina. He spoke of the need for Argentina's anti-imperialist forces to overcome their ideological differences, specifically including the *peronistas* in this appeal. According to a Cuban who was present, at one point during the meal, Che scribbled something on a matchbox and wordlessly handed it to an Argentine sitting near him. It bore the word *unidad* (unity). As the matchbox circulated, Che's message was lear. No more sectarian infighting.

It was a significant moment to the group of *peronista* exiles who were present, and their leader, John William Cooke, stood up to echo Che's appeal for revolutionary unity and to laud Cuba for leading the Second Emancipation of Latin America. Cooke, a former Peronist Youth leader and personal representative of Perón, had been in Cuba for several years, but he corresponded regularly with Perón, who was living in Madrid. Cooke had been won over by Cuba's revolution and evoked it for Perón in flattering terms, extending Fidel's invitation for Perón to visit, promising a reception "with the honors of a head of state." Perón never took up the invitation but sent flattering responses back, much as he continued to play kingmaker from exile with all the various *peronista* factions that competed for his approval.

Cooke dreamed of bringing about Perón's triumphal return to Argentina at the head of a revolutionary alliance backed by Cuba. According to Cooke's former comrades, Che became friends with him and his wife, Alicia Ereguren, in spite of Che's lingering skepticism about Perón. In the course of their many conversations, Cooke's arguments gave Che a broader view of *peronismo*'s potential as a revolutionary force, while he in turn was influential in Cooke's assimilation of Marxist-Leninist concepts. This helped to galvanize the revolutionary group that Cooke founded, Acción Revolucionaria Peronista. That summer of 1962, with Che's approval, Cooke's men began receiving guerrilla training to prepare themselves for a future revolutionary war in Argentina.

Stealthily, Che was setting up the chessboard for his game of continental guerrilla war, the ultimate prize being his homeland. He was actually training several different Argentine action groups, distinct in their ideologies but united by a common desire to take to the field. At the right time each group would be mobilized to take its place in a united army in the Argentine campaign under Che's command. Masetti's forward patrol was Che's first move on that chessboard; the others would follow at the right time.*

A number of events that were to have a direct bearing on Che's future had occurred. The previous September, Secretary-General Hammarskjöld had been killed in a suspicious plane crash while visiting the Congo. The new UN secretary, the Burmese diplomat U Thant, had inherited the job of resolving the seemingly insoluble crisis there. The government in the capital of Léopoldville continued to fence for power with the standardbearers of Patrice Lumumba, who were based in the distant northern city of Stanleyville.† And the long-simmering Sino-Soviet dispute had finally become public in October 1961, when Chinese premier Chou En-lai walked out of a Communist Party congress held in Moscow. Both powers now increased their jockeying for global influence, pressuring Cuba and Latin America's Communist parties to choose a side.

In Cuba, the attempt of the "old Communists" in the PSP to control the Organizaciónes Revolucionarias Integradas (ORI)—the new official party, headed by Fidel, which had subsumed the July 26 Movement along with the PSP and Directorio Revolucionario—was publicly denounced by Fidel in March 1962. Accused of favoring Party comrades for a wide variety of government posts, ORI's organization secretary, the former PSP eminence Aníbal Escalante, was the most prominent victim of the purge.

---

*Neither Che, Masetti, nor Cooke would live to see the day, but the forces they helped set in motion eventually brought about a period of revolutionary violence and vicious counterrepression by the military that would drastically alter the political landscape of modern Argentina in the years to come.

†The Congo became the Democratic Republic of the Congo in 1964. It was later renamed Zaire by Joseph Mobutu. The capital, Léopoldville, became Kinshasa, and Stanleyville became Kisangani. When Mobutu was overthrown in 1997, the country became the Democratic Republic of the Congo again.

Publicly castigated, he was sent into exile in Moscow. Afterward, Fidel announced a new name for the reformed party: Partido Unificado de la Revolución Socialista (PURS), the next stage in the creation of a new Cuban Communist Party.

Che was immensely gratified by Fidel's purge. He loathed the holier-than-thou Party apparatchiks who sought to impose their ideological guidelines, and he had defended a number of people whose careers had been damaged, giving them posts—and protection—at his ministry. In May, he forbade "ideological investigations" at the ministry.

"The Sectarianism," as the period of dogmatic Communist Party ideology was called, had affected even non-Cubans such as Ciro Bustos. Taking its cue from the chauvinistic PSP, the Argentine Communist Party had tried to wield control over the Argentines living and working in Cuba. While he was in Holguín, Bustos had been summoned by the Party's representative in Cuba and questioned about his political background and Party affiliations. When he explained that he didn't have an official Communist Party membership, he was warned that if he didn't "regularize" his situation, he would have to leave the country. The "antisectarian" purge had come just in time for him, and he was once again breathing freely when, in the summer of 1962, Granado arranged for him to meet with Che.

Their midnight encounter, which took place at Che's office in Havana late in July, was peremptory. Che explained to Bustos that a group was being prepared to go to Argentina and asked him if he wanted to participate. Bustos said yes. That was all. He was told not to leave his hotel; some people would be coming by to pick him up. In the next stage of his revolutionary metamorphosis, Bustos was first taken to a house in Havana's Miramar neighborhood, where he was greeted by a man he recognized from news photographs to be Jorge Ricardo Masetti, whose book about the Cuban revolutionary war, *Los Que Luchan y los Que Lloran* (Those Who Fight and Those Who Cry), had helped spark his interest in Cuba.

Masetti explained to Bustos that this was Che's project, but since the *comandante* couldn't leave Cuba just yet, Masetti was to lead the guerrilla force in its start-up phase. Then Che would come, and the war would begin. Masetti asked if Bustos was prepared to leave everything to join the project, and once again Bustos said yes. He would return to Holguín until a Ministry of Industries "scholarship" for him to study in Czechoslovakia was arranged to explain his disappearance. His wife would have to stay behind and keep the secret. Later, once the guerrillas had secured a liberated territory, she could undergo training and join him.

By September, Bustos was ensconced in a safe house with three other Argentines: a Jewish doctor from Buenos Aires, Leonardo Julio Werthein;

and two of Granado's recruits—the mechanic Federico Méndez and an athletic man named Miguel, both of whom were from the rural part of northern Argentina known as the *chaco*. Their new home was an elegant villa on Havana's eastern edges. Deserted by the exodus of Cuba's wealthy, the leafy, tree-lined neighborhood of walled compounds was now guarded by Cuban security forces, offering maximum discretion. The Argentines camped in one room of the mansion they occupied, getting to know one another and preparing for the life ahead of them. Their training consisted of hikes and practice at a firing range. For something to do at night, they went out on patrol, trying—with little luck—to catch the gangs of thieves who were breaking into the empty villas and carrying off whatever they could find. "But they were always smarter than we were," Bustos recalled. "We made too much noise."

Masetti, Che, and intelligence officials such as Ariel and Piñeiro came and went. Orlando "Olo" Tamayo Pantoja, who had been one of Che's officers during the sierra war, and Hermes Peña, one of Che's bodyguards, took an active part in their training sessions, and they soon found out that Peña would be going with them as Masetti's deputy commander.

Another person who showed up regularly at the safe house was Abelardo Colomé Ibarra, aka Furry, Havana's police chief. He too would be joining the Argentines as their rearguard base commander and liaison for communications with Cuba. Their chief trainer was neither Cuban nor Argentine, but a Hispano-Soviet general, a man they knew only as Angelito. Ciro Bustos and the others understood that they were not to ask too many questions of him; at this point the presence of Russian military men in Cuba remained a highly sensitive subject. Actually a Spanish-born Catalán, Angelito, also known as Ángel Martínez, was nonetheless an active general in the Red Army, a Spanish Civil War hero whose real name was Francisco Ciutat, one of half a dozen Spanish Republican exiles dispatched to Cuba by the Moscow-based Spanish Communist Party to help train Cuba's militias in the "Struggle against Bandits." "He was a real personality," Bustos recalled. "Tiny, with quite a few years on him, but he could do flips in the air like a gymnast."

As Angelito's deputy, Hermes Peña was their hands-on instructor, reconstructing sierra-war battles for them to study and emulate in their training exercises. Before long, each of the men in the safe house was assigned a specific duty. Leonardo Werthein was to be the expedition medic, Miguel would handle logistics, and Federico Méndez, whom Bustos described as a no-nonsense tough guy of few words, was put in charge of armaments. Bustos was given training in security and intelligence. Hermes Peña assumed responsibility for their military discipline.

Che himself always arrived at the safe house extremely late, at two or three in the morning. "Practically the first thing he told us," Bustos recalled, "was 'Well, here you are: you've all agreed to join, and now we must prepare things, but from this moment on, consider yourselves dead. Death is the only certainty in this; some of you may survive, but all of you should consider what remains of your lives as borrowed time.'" Che was throwing down the gauntlet for his future guerrillas, just as he had done during the Cuban struggle. It was important that each man prepare himself psychologically for what was to come, and Bustos understood the message. "We were going to go and get our balls shot off, without knowing if any of us were going to see it through, or how long it would take." Che let them know he was not sending them off alone to an uncertain fate, however, telling them he planned to join them as soon as he could.

III

The October missile crisis forced Che to accelerate plans for his Argentine guerrilla force. During the crisis, he commanded Cuba's western army based in Pinar del Río. His post was situated in some mountain caves near one of the Soviet missile installations. He took his Argentine guerrilla trainees with him and placed them in a battalion under the command of Cuban officers. If there was fighting, they were to join in.

At the moment of maximum tension—after a Russian SAM missile brought down an American U-2 spy plane, killing its pilot—Fidel cabled Khrushchev, saying that he expected Moscow to launch its missiles first in the event of an American ground invasion; he and the Cuban people, he assured Khrushchev, were ready to die fighting. Only a day later, Fidel learned that Khrushchev had made a deal with JFK behind his back—offering to pull out the missiles in exchange for a promise not to invade Cuba and a withdrawal of U.S. Jupiter missiles from Turkey. Fidel was incredulous and furious, and reportedly smashed a mirror with his fist when he was told. Che tersely ordered his troops to sever his command post's communications line with the adjacent Soviet missile base, and he rushed off to Havana to see Fidel.

Over the coming days, Fidel was consumed with bitter recriminations against Khrushchev, and the hapless Mikoyan was dispatched to Havana to patch things up. Mikoyan did what he could, but Fidel and Che were convinced that Khrushchev had sold them out for his own strategic interests. Their talks went on for several weeks and at times were exceedingly tense. One day, a mistranslation by the Russian interpreter sparked a shouting match. When the misunderstanding was cleared up, Che calmly removed his Makarov pistol from its holster, handed it to the interpreter, and said: "If I were in your place, the only thing left to do . . ." According to Alexandr Alexiev, everyone laughed, including Mikoyan. Che's dark humor had cleared the air.

In public, relations between Moscow and Havana remained "fraternal," but under the surface the situation was extremely tense, and it stayed that way for some time. In the streets of Havana, indignant Cubans chanted: *"Nikita, mariquita, lo que se da no se quita!"* (Nikita, you little queer, what you give, you don't take away!)

"The fate of Cuba and the maintenance of Soviet prestige in that part of the world preoccupied me," Khrushchev acknowledged in his memoirs. "One thought kept hammering away in my brain: what will happen if we lose Cuba? I knew it would be a terrible blow to Marxism-Leninism. It would gravely diminish our stature throughout the world, but especially in Latin America. If Cuba fell, other countries would reject us, claiming that for all our might the Soviet Union hadn't been able to do anything for Cuba except to make empty protests to the United Nations."

In an interview with Che a few weeks after the crisis, Sam Russell, a British correspondent for the socialist *Daily Worker,* found him still fuming over the Soviet betrayal. Alternately puffing a cigar and taking blasts on his asthma inhaler, he told Russell that if the missiles had been under Cuban control, they would have been fired. Russell came away with mixed feelings about Che, describing him as "a warm character whom I took to immediately . . . clearly a man of great intelligence, though I thought he was crackers from the way he went on about the missiles." They also discussed another subject close to Che's heart—global Communist strategy. Che was extremely critical of the Western Communist parties for adopting a "peaceful parliamentary strategy for power." Russell wrote that Che felt this would "deliver the working class bound hand and foot over to the ruling class."

Che was, of course, determined to do something about it. As Ciro Bustos recalled, "When the tension [over the missile crisis] relaxed, we were brought back to Havana and Che told us: 'You're leaving. I want you out of here.' Those were special days. They were still afraid there might be a [U.S.] invasion. There was a very heavy war atmosphere. . . . There was also bad blood with the Soviets. . . . He was very angry with the Soviets." They were told to leave the safe house as they had found it, to remove all traces of their presence. Federico Méndez was sent off for a field-radio training course, and Bustos underwent a weeklong intensive course to learn the art of secret codes and cryptology. He was taught a Soviet code system based on ten never-repeated numbers. "It was James Bond–style," Bustos recalled. "You burned the papers after using the codes."

Piñeiro's passport experts gave each man in the group a different nationality. Bustos, who became a Uruguayan, was unhappy when he saw his passport. "It was unbelievable," he said. "They gave me a really young age and blond hair. I was pretty bald even then, and what hair I did have left was black." When he complained, the expert reassured him that it was to be used only as far as Czechoslovakia, a friendly country where no questions would be asked.

By now the men knew little more than that they were to continue their training until Cuba's security apparatus could prepare a safe rearguard base of operations for them on Bolivia's southern border with Argentina. They also knew that they were to be called the Ejército Guerrillero del Pueblo (People's Guerrilla Army). They were all were given noms de guerre: Bustos was now Laureano; Masetti was Comandante Segundo. The *comandante primero,* of course, was Che, aka Martín Fierro, who for the moment would remain their invisible guiding hand. The mission itself was called Operación Sombra (Operation Shadow). These were all double entendres. Their pseudonyms and the name of the operation corresponded to the Argentine gaucho archetypes, Martín Fierro and Don Segundo Sombra.

In Prague, the group—Masetti, Hermes Peña, Bustos, Leonardo Werthein, Federico Méndez, Miguel, and Abelardo Colomé Ibarra—was met by Major Jorge "Papito" (Little Daddy) Serguera, who was operating out of the Cuban embassy. He drove them to Lake Slapie, about an hour outside the city. They were booked into an exclusive hotel. It was the dead of winter, and there were no other guests—just them and the hotel staff. By agreement with the Czech intelligence services, they were given a simple cover story to explain their presence. "We were a group of Cuban scholarship students," said Bustos, "who were going to stay awhile."

Papito Serguera visited them once or twice, but apart from that, the seven prospective guerrillas were on their own. They had nothing to do, so, to keep fit, they began making cross-country treks through the snow, twelve to fifteen miles in every direction. Finally, growing ever more frustrated as the weeks dragged by, they contacted Serguera at the embassy in Prague to complain. He told them to be patient: the Bolivian farm that was to be their base had not yet been purchased, and more details had to be settled before they could travel. Meanwhile, he told them they were to stop their hiking around. They had apparently been seen wandering into an unauthorized military zone.

Masetti and his men spent another month incommunicado in the hotel at Lake Slapie before Serguera finally allowed them to come to Prague. By now it was December, and the Czechs were becoming increasingly upset over the Cubans' prolonged presence. Finally Masetti could stand it no longer and announced that he was flying to Algeria to arrange for the group to go there to complete its training. The Front de Libération National was now the government of an independent Algeria, and the former Algerian revolutionaries owed him a favor. Ahmed Ben Bella, the new Algerian premier, had been in Havana on the eve of the missile crisis, had met with Che and Fidel, and, before leaving, had signed a declaration of revolutionary fraternity with Cuba.

"Masetti flew off to Algiers and came back two days later," Bustos said. "He told us that Ben Bella and [Houari] Boumédienne [the Algerian minister of defense] had welcomed him at the airport and agreed to help us. We left immediately." But to fly to Algiers they had to lay over in Paris for several days, and this posed a problem for Bustos, who was still traveling on his blond passport. He solved it by putting peroxide in his scarce hair. "Suddenly my hair was yellow," he recalled, laughing ruefully. "I looked like a cabaret transvestite." For three or four days, they stayed in the hotel above the Gare d'Orsay, pretending to be tourists. "We went to the Louvre," Bustos recalled, "and we walked around a lot."

They arrived in Algiers on January 4. The Algerians were still engaged in a "cleansing" process like the one that revolutionary Cuba had applied four years earlier to its *chivatos* and war criminals, and FLN gunmen roamed the city hunting down suspected collaborators or ex-torturers. Suspicious Arab civilians looked upon Europeans or foreigners with open hostility. Conscious of the risks faced by Che's guerrillas in the uncertain climate, Algeria's revolutionary leaders sent two generals and an entire security retinue to meet them at the airport. They were driven to an isolated seaside villa on the city's outskirts and left under armed guard for their own protection. After some time, they were moved to a villa with a walled garden in Algiers itself, but because of the danger of being misidentified as French, they rarely went out. Whenever they did, they were surrounded by Algerian security men.

For the next few months, with a permanent retinue of Algerian revolutionary veterans, the Argentine team practiced their marksmanship, did calisthenics, and took military courses. The Algerians took them to see their former front lines, the ingenious cave-and-tunnel system that had been used to hide fighters and weapons during the war, and also the former French lines. Papito Serguera soon arrived, having conveniently been appointed the new Cuban ambassador. In addition to his other duties, he served as the group's relay for communications with Che.

The Argentines were feted with a banquet, and they reciprocated with a traditional Argentine *asado* attended by Houari Boumédienne. But time was dragging on, and Masetti was anxious to get moving. In answer to his incessant queries, Papito Serguera relayed what Bustos called "strange and contradictory" messages from Havana, supposedly sent by Che. Colomé

Ibarra flew back to Cuba to find out what was going on and returned with some disquieting news. He and Che had gone over the messages the group had received, and Che had identified several that had not originated with him. Since all their communications were channeled through Barbarroja Piñeiro, they speculated about a "malfunction" in his security apparatus. Some, including Bustos, came to suspect there was more to it than that— perhaps even an intentional sabotage of Che's plans. It would remain a mystery that Bustos, at least, was never able to unravel.*

In Cuba, two of Che's bodyguards, Alberto Castellanos and Harry Villegas, who had been sent away to be trained as administrators in the Ministry of Industries, awaited their own marching orders. Many months had gone by and Che had not sent for them. Castellanos had reentered the armed forces and begun a military training course. Arriving home in Havana on a weekend pass in late February 1963, he suddenly received a summons from Che. He assumed that he was going to be punished. "Every time Che sent for you it was to pull your ear about something or other," he recalled. "I said to myself: 'Well, what a coincidence! This weekend I didn't do anything—didn't even get drunk,' so I couldn't imagine what Che wanted to see me about."

When Castellanos walked into Che's office, Che reminded him that several months earlier he had said that if Che was involved in a mission, he wanted to be part of it. "When do we go?" Castellanos asked, excitedly. Che told him to hold on a minute and to listen. Reminding Castellanos that he had a wife to consider, Che warned him that the mission was not to be taken lightly. "This mission is either twenty years fighting, or else you don't come back at all," he admonished. Che told him to think about it seriously before making up his mind. Castellanos remembered that he stood there and "thought" for a moment or two before asking again, "When do I go?"

"OK," Che said to Castellanos. "But don't go getting dressed up as an Indian, because you're not one, and tell Villegas he can't go with you because he's black, and where you're going there are no blacks." Che didn't spell it out any more clearly than that, except to tell Castellanos that he would find some people he knew personally when he arrived at his destination. "You're going to wait for me with a group of comrades I'm sending," he said. "You are going to be the boss until I arrive." He said he intended to join them by the end of the year. Then Castellanos went off

---

*While leaving some of the complaints against him unanswered, Piñeiro rebutted Bustos's version of events, indicating that Masetti's movements were all coordinated out of Havana. "If Masetti went off to Algeria, it was with prior approval from Che and if not, Ben Bella would have asked us for our approval."

to see Piñeiro for his debriefing, his new clandestine identity, and his travel itinerary.

IV

At about the same time, Tamara Bunke began receiving training in espionage by Piñeiro's department. "She approached us and asked to be taken into consideration for a mission," Piñeiro's deputy, Ariel, said, adding that Cuba's secret services had checked her out and cleared her for training. They considered her a prime candidate as a future espionage asset in Argentina, "to be activated when the need arose."

Ariel's pointed mention of Tamara Bunke's security clearance is noteworthy because of the enduring mystery surrounding "Tania," as she later became known. According to East German State Security files, Tamara Bunke was an "IM" (informal informant) for the Stasi, or secret police, before she went to Cuba in 1961. She was also under consideration by its overseas espionage division, the HVA, as a deep-cover agent for insertion first in Argentina, and eventually the United States.

Considering the tightly controlled internal security system of the German Democratic Republic and Tamara's own Marxist-Leninist upbringing, the fact that she became an informant for East Germany's secret services is hardly surprising. To inform on her fellow citizens or foreign visitors on behalf of the Communist state she so fervently believed in was a patriotic duty she would have performed—and evidently did perform—without compunction. But who was Tamara working for when she was in Cuba: the Cubans, East German intelligence, or both? Speaking with the habitual opacity of a lifelong revolutionary *cuadro* still living in Cuba, her friend Orlando Borrego said that he had "no doubt that she worked for the German services," but neither did he have any doubt about her loyalty to the Cuban revolution. Speaking in a vastly altered Moscow nearly three decades after her death, the veteran KGB official Alexandr Alexiev indicated that she had been a German agent seconded to the Cubans for their own use. "The Germans wanted to help," he explained. "They tried to have a friendship with revolutionary Cuba that was as good as ours, and they wanted to do even more, and for that reason they fulfilled any desire or whim of the Cuban leaders—even more than we did."

Pressed for additional details, Alexiev insinuated that when it came to assisting Che in his foreign revolutionary ventures, German and Soviet intelligence had an agreement to divide up the work. "The Germans considered themselves to be more . . . revolutionarily aggressive than us. They were younger; we were older, had more experience and maturity. And if

Tamara Bunke in a Cuban
military uniform and
sunglasses in 1961. She
assumed the nom de guerre
"Tania" in the spring of
1963, when she began
receiving espionage training
from Barbarroja Piñeiro's
agents.

we [the KGB] had gotten involved, there would surely have been even more
risk of failure. Our services were a big bureaucracy, but the Germans were
technically more equipped, the case of Tania being probably the most important." As for Tamara/Tania herself, Alexiev agreed with Borrego, saying that he had no doubt her loyalties were "with the Cubans, with Fidel,
and with Che." He surmised that Che had "conquered her with his ideas;
he was such a convincing and attractive personality."

Another man, an Argentine who worked closely with Che and who
also knew Tamara personally, said that his impression was that she "worked
for the German services and transferred to work for Che's intelligence service, that she asked for license to do it. Neither Che nor the Germans would
have liked her to be sending reports to two places at the same time. Che
wasn't stupid; he wasn't going to permit a double loyalty."

According to the East German files, Tamara Bunke had been recruited
as an informant by a counterintelligence official named Gunter Mannel, who
was in charge of the United States department of the Stasi's HVA. A month
after her departure for Cuba in 1961, Mannel slipped into West Berlin, defected, and before long was working for the CIA. He soon betrayed the
identities of some of his agents, who were arrested in the West, and it might
be assumed that he also informed the CIA about Tamara, the gifted and
fiercely committed young Communist agent who had just gone to Cuba.
Evidently, the HVA made this assumption. Immediately after Mannel's
defection, according to an internal HVA report dated July 23, 1962, Bunke

was sent a letter in Cuba warning her of the danger and requesting that she not attempt to "go to South or North America and that in any case she should consult with us beforehand."

The HVA report states that there had been no further contacts with Tamara, but that she appeared to be "progressively asserting herself" in Cuba, working with a whole series of government institutions, and was always "importuning" visiting GDR delegations to be their interpreter. It added that she had "apparently given up her resolve to go on to Argentina [and] intends to stay in Cuba and also to assume Cuban citizenship. She also has close ties to Cuban security . . . [and] permission to wear a military uniform, and she makes use of it constantly."

The Stasi files suggest that the East German counterespionage agency had an agreement with Tamara Bunke but that she severed contact after she arrived in Cuba. The files, however, give rise to other questions. When Tamara was accepted for service by Cuban intelligence, did she tell her handlers about her prior links with German intelligence or the fact that her recruiter had defected a month after her arrival? If she did tell them, why did Cuba eventually use her in the same region—Bolivia and Argentina—that the HVA had originally planned to use her in? It surely had to be assumed that both Tamara's identity and her intended future espionage role were known to the CIA and its allied intelligence agencies after Mannel's defection.

In response to these questions, Barbarroja Piñeiro said, "I handled Tania directly. And I asked her if she had been recruited by the German [intelligence] services. She said 'no.'" Piñeiro added that if he had known about Mannel and the letter she had been sent, he would have approved her anyway, both because she displayed "excellent qualities" as an agent, and because he trusted his organization's ability to build her an undetectable new false identity.

V

One of the ways Che gathered information and analyzed the situation in Argentina was by engaging Argentine friends and acquaintances—as he had done with Oscar Stemmelin—in long discussions during which he would try out his theories. In February 1963 he sent for Ricardo Rojo. "I want to talk," Che said when Rojo arrived. They didn't see eye to eye politically— Rojo was liberal, an "anti-imperialist," though not a socialist—but the two of them went back a long way, and Che knew him to be both well connected and an acute political analyst. Rojo had first sent Masetti to Cuba and had recently become a close friend of Che's mother. Che put him up in a top-flight government protocol house in Miramar for two months. Rojo wrote later that he found Che depressed about Cuba's growing regional isolation and still upset over the Soviets' "paternalistic" treatment of Cuba in the missile crisis. Che believed that Cuba could not break out of its regional straitjacket until socialist revolutions had taken place in the other Latin American countries, and he made no secret of the fact that he was actively studying how to bring that process about.

One day Che told Rojo that he wanted to discuss Argentina "systematically." As they talked, Che took notes. He showed special interest in the Argentine labor and university movements and was anxious to update his knowledge about who was who among the opposition. They also discussed Perón's enduring popularity with the Argentine working class, and Che showed Rojo a letter he had received from Perón expressing admiration for the Cuban revolution. It seemed to Rojo that Che was weighing the pros and cons of an alliance with the *peronistas* as a means of sparking revolt. There was an unpopular military government in Argentina, and increased labor strife; Che wondered aloud what the "reaction of the masses" would be if Perón came to Cuba to live—something Perón's leftist disciple John William Cooke had been trying to persuade Che to arrange for some time.

In early April 1963, just before Rojo left Cuba, there was a brief but bloody naval uprising in Buenos Aires. It was rapidly suppressed by the army, but Che thought the incident revealed that "objective conditions for struggle" were beginning to appear in Argentina. It was time to follow up with subjective conditions to show the people that they could overthrow their rulers by violent means. Rojo argued that the revolution had worked in Cuba because the Americans had been caught off guard. That day had passed, and the United States and its regional allies were now on the alert. Che conceded the point but, as always, refused to accept that Cuba's success was an exception that could not be repeated elsewhere.

Che never told Rojo explicitly that he was preparing a guerrilla insurgency in Argentina, but there were enough hints for Rojo to draw his own conclusions. He had shared his flight to Havana with a left-wing *peronista* guerrilla, a leader of a short-lived uprising in Tucumán province in 1959. The man was coming to see Che. And then there were Che's last words as Rojo prepared to leave Cuba. "You'll see," he said, "Argentina's ruling class will never learn anything. Only a revolutionary war will change things."*

*In his book *My Friend Che,* Rojo claimed that Masetti was present at some of the sessions with Che, but Ciro Bustos insists that Masetti never left his group except for the short visit to Algeria from Prague.

Back in Algeria, Masetti learned that Piñeiro's people had finally purchased a farm for their use in Bolivia, but there was still no sign that he and his men were about to be moved. Masetti decided he could not wait any longer, and he asked the Algerians to assist them in getting to Bolivia. "The Algerians gave us everything," Bustos recalled. "They would have given us arms, but we couldn't take them, since we were going to have to go through the border controls of several different countries—but they gave us all kinds of military equipment, passports, everything."

In May 1963, seven months after leaving Havana, Masetti's group was finally on its way to South America. But it was minus one man. Miguel, one of Alberto Granado's recruits, had been left behind in rather chilling fashion. (The real name of "Miguel" has apparently been forgotten by his surviving comrades, but they remember him as a well-educated Argentine Jew, a significant detail in light of what happened within the group when it reached Argentina.)

Miguel had become increasingly argumentative and disobedient. One of the strict rules which they had all observed since entering clandestine life—and which Ciro Bustos was supposed to enforce—was that nobody wrote letters home, "not even to their mothers," and Miguel had violated that rule. Bustos had caught him trying to mail some letters when they were in Paris. In Algeria, Miguel had openly questioned Masetti's leadership. The two argued constantly and became fiercely competitive. One day, trying to best Miguel in their physical training exercises, Masetti had strained his back quite badly, an injury that was to cause him great pain in the months ahead.

Matters reached a head as they were preparing to leave Algeria. Miguel announced he didn't want to go if Masetti was the leader, predicting that the two of them would end up shooting each other. "Masetti, who had been in the Argentine navy, and who always tried to be 'the macho of the movie,' did not take it lying down," Bustos recalled. The two men squared off for a fistfight. The other men intervened, but Masetti wanted vengeance. He insisted that a trial be held to decide whether Miguel should stay in the group. Bustos was appointed prosecutor, and Federico acted as Miguel's defense lawyer.

Bustos believed that Miguel had gotten cold feet and provoked the fight with Masetti so that he could drop out of the group. He argued that Miguel's negative attitude posed a security risk, and since they were about to undertake a delicate trip across several foreign borders, the reasonable solution was that he be left behind. Even Miguel's defender, Federico, did not oppose this solution. But Masetti argued that Miguel's wish to withdraw from the group was tantamount to a defection, a crime punishable by death. He proposed that Miguel be executed by a firing squad. He could arrange this with his Algerian military friends.

The group unanimously voted for Miguel to die. Masetti, Papito Serguera, and Abelardo Colomé Ibarra talked with the Algerians, and a military unit took the condemned man away. Bustos was convinced that the decision had been the right one, but he felt bad about it nonetheless. "One of the things that affected us the most," he recalled, "because we were sure they took him away to shoot him, was that the guy left . . . like a man, correctly, without any lamentations or begging for clemency." From that moment forward, Bustos and the others referred to Miguel not by his name, but as El Fusilado (He Who Was Shot), their first sacrifice in the cause for the Argentine revolution.

Traveling in separate groups under false identities, with Algerian diplomatic passports, and accompanied by the two Algerian agents who had been their constant companions of late and who carried their gear in sealed diplomatic luggage, Masetti's men made their way to La Paz, where they got in touch with their Bolivian contacts, all young members of the Bolivian Communist Party. Then they headed to their base of operations. Their cover story was that they were the Argentine and Bolivian partners of a new joint venture, traveling together to set up a farming and cattle ranching operation on a tract of land they had recently bought. They reached their "farm," in a remote area where the Río Bermejo forms Bolivia's border with Argentina and makes a sharp dip south. Their land was strategically set in the middle of this mountainous, forested triangle, with Argentina on either side. There was only one dirt road leading in or out, and they were miles from the nearest neighbors.

A member of the Bolivian Communist Party was on the site, an older man who was to act as caretaker but who spent his days doing not much more than making peanut soup. Piñeiro's people and the Bolivians working with them had bought some gear locally, but it seemed worse than useless. "There were thin uniforms made out of shiny nylon," Bustos said. "Ordinary nylon shirts, and Tom Mix–style holsters with little stars on them. . . . It really seemed like a joke." Their backpacks and boots were of poor quality, as well, but, fortunately, the Algerians had provided them with some good Yugoslav military uniforms, cartridge belts, and field binoculars. And the arsenal that somehow had been smuggled in from Cuba was plentiful and in good condition: Chinese bazookas, pistols, a Thompson submachine gun, automatic rifles, and lots of ammunition. Ciro Bustos acquired a gun with a silencer.

Masetti decided that they were ready to go. Colomé Ibarra, who was to stay behind on the Bolivian side for the time being, drove them to the border, and on June 21, the five-man vanguard of the Ejército Guerrillero del Pueblo crossed into Argentina.

VI

Another Cuban-trained guerrilla force had attempted to cross a Bolivian border a few weeks earlier. In May, the Ejército de Liberación Nacional (ELN), forty guerrillas led by Héctor Béjar, had had been detected and turned back while trying to enter Peru. Béjar's destination was the Valle de la Convención in Peru's southern Andes, where the military was after the Trotskyist peasant leader Hugo Blanco. The small rebel band that Blanco led had attacked a Guardia Civil post the previous November and Blanco had been on the run ever since. The Cubans saw the fracas as a good opportunity for the ELN to go into action.

Bolivia, with its porous and ill-protected borders shared with Peru, Chile, Argentina, Paraguay, and Brazil, was a logical point of entry for both Béjar and Masetti. The government was led by President Víctor Paz Estenssoro of the center-left Movimiento Nacionalista Revolucionario (MNR), and Bolivia was one of the few remaining Latin American countries that still had diplomatic ties with Havana. The Cuban envoy to Bolivia, Ramón Aja Castro, was close to Che. He had accompanied him to the Punta del Este conference, and Piñeiro's man Ariel was on his staff. Since the Bolivian Communist Party (PCB) operated legally, it could assist the Cubans with contacts, safe houses, and transportation for guerrillas. Party cadres helped get Béjar's column as far as the Peruvian border and Masetti's to the Argentine frontier.

The decision by the PCB to assist the Cuban-trained guerrillas was tactical and taken reluctantly. Bolivia's former Communist Party chief, Mario Monje, recalled that he was approached by Cuban diplomats in La Paz. "They told me that they needed help for some young Peruvian Communists who had been trained and wanted to return to their country," Monje said. He told the Cubans that the Cuban experience was unique and couldn't be repeated elsewhere. Like most of the Communist parties in neighboring countries, the PCB eschewed the kind of armed struggle espoused by Cuba—and by Che in particular—in favor of gaining ground through electoral politics. The PCB had established amicable relations with Paz Estenssoro's government and hoped to maintain them.

When Monje told Peruvian Party officials about the Cuban proposal, he found them adamantly opposed. "They did not want to have anything to do with guerrillas," he said. Monje tried to persuade the Peruvians not to precipitate an open break with Havana. He urged them to be flexible and to control the situation. Otherwise, he warned, "this thing [Cuba's export of armed struggle] will hit the fan everywhere and do damage to the Peruvians and everyone else." By then, Monje and his comrades had begun hearing rumors that Havana wanted to get a guerrilla war going in Bolivia as well. The Bolivian Politburo held a meeting and voted unanimously against the notion of an armed struggle in their country, and Monje traveled to Havana with a fellow Politburo member, Hilario Claure. Their mission, according to Monje, was to express the official PCB policy opposing Cuban interventionism in the region generally, while also trying to mediate between Havana and the indignant Peruvians. He met Manuel Piñeiro and reminded him that in the 1930s, under Stalin, the Soviets had backed guerrillas in Latin America and it hadn't worked. "They pushed armed struggle over here, guerrillas over there," he told Piñeiro. "They tried it in different countries and failed, and now you are trying to repeat what they did."

Piñeiro suggested they speak directly with Fidel, and he arranged a meeting in which, Monje said, he once again outlined his and the Peruvian Party's opposition to the scheme. Fidel replied that he could not and would not deny young guerrillas the chance to emulate Cuba's struggle. "We are going to help them," Fidel told Monje. "I'm not asking for the help of the Peruvian Party, but I'm asking for your help." Monje said that he and Claure acceded to Fidel's request because they believed that if they bought Fidel's gratitude he would not authorize guerrilla activity in Bolivia behind the Party's back. They would assist in getting Béjar's group into Peru without informing the Peruvian Communist Party. Monje and Claure also met with Che, who was less friendly than Fidel had been. The atmosphere of the meeting was tense, Monje recalled, and Che expounded his defense of the guerrilla project "aggressively and firmly."

Claure offered a subtly different account of the talks in Havana. He agreed that he and Monje made clear their opposition to a Cuban-sponsored guerrilla war in Bolivia, but he found Fidel noncommittally "diplomatic." Che was "arrogant," and dismissive. "That's what the Communists here told us when we wanted to make the Cuban revolution," Che said. "If we'd listened to them, there wouldn't have been one." Claure recalled that he and Monje returned to La Paz with the suspicion that the Cubans were going to go ahead with whatever they had already planned in spite of the Bolivian Communist Party, and before long, they sensed that their worries were well founded.

On a subsequent visit to Havana, Monje said, he and Che were relaxing outside one day, lying on some grass and talking, when Che turned to him and said, "Hey, Monje, why don't you get a guerrilla war going in Bolivia?" "And why should I?" Monje retorted. "What will it get us?" Che challenged him: "It's because you're afraid, isn't it?" Monje said he shot back, "No, it's that you have a machine gun stuck in your brain, and you can't imagine any other way to develop an anti-imperialist struggle." Che laughed at his retort, and let the matter rest. Monje said that not long after his exchange with Che, a "top Cuban official" told him that "it would be great" if his Party began an armed struggle in Bolivia "because it would distract the imperialists and release pressure on us."

For the time being, Monje kept his relations with the Cubans as fraternal as possible. He even requested permission to send some young Party cadres to Havana "to learn from Cuba's revolutionary experience." Meanwhile, his people began helping Béjar's and Masetti's groups, providing them with safe houses, food, supplies, and transportation. While Masetti and his men were still in Algeria, the Bolivians had located and purchased the rearguard base of operations on the Río Bermejo. After some delays and changes of itinerary, they had moved Béjar's column out of La Paz and on a long river journey toward the Peruvian border.

Béjar's group had reached the border in May, by which time their intentions had evidently become well known to the Peruvian authorities. Béjar sent an advance party across the border, but it was discovered almost immediately by police in the Peruvian town of Puerto Maldonado. One of the fighters, a talented young poet named Javier Herauld, was killed in the resulting shoot-out. Most of the others managed to escape back into Bolivia, whereupon a dozen or so of Béjar's men were captured by local authorities but then released in an apparent goodwill gesture to Cuba by Paz Estenssoro's government. By late May, Hugo Blanco had also been captured and imprisoned in Peru. In early June, Peru's military junta held the elections it had promised after seizing power the year before, and the winner was the center-right candidate Fernando Belaunde Terry, an engineer who had been educated in the United States. The first Peruvian guerrilla venture had failed miserably, but Béjar and his comrades began reorganizing, and before long they would try again.*

Why was the presence of Béjar's group detected so quickly? Béjar himself later accused the PCB of secretly acceding to the Peruvian Party's demands to thwart his effort, pointing out that the Bolivians had delayed their entry by rerouting his force to a point hundreds of miles from where Blanco was operating. Suspicions of internal treachery persisted over the years. As Humberto Vázquez-Viaña, a PCB youth militant at the time, later quipped acidly, the Party had striven to be "good with both God and the Devil."

---

*In the face of the persistent and proven inadequacy of the Cuban security apparatus to successfully implement Che's guerrilla programs, a number of former guerrillas, including Ciro Bustos and several of his comrades, singled out Barbarroja Piñeiro for blame. Piñeiro's task was a thankless one, however. In addition to Béjar's and Masetti's groups, his department was simultaneously assisting the Guatemalan, Colombian, and Venezuelan guerrillas, among others. And there were problems arising on every front, ranging from logistical and communications difficulties to factional splits and military and political setbacks.

Che's former brother-in-law, Ricardo Gadea, missed the Béjar fiasco. After a factional split, he and other would-be guerrillas had formed the Peruvian MIR. They believed they should build up a social and organizational base in Peru before beginning a war. The Cubans did not approve, and Gadea and his comrades were kept on ice in Cuba. While Béjar and his followers were shipped out to Bolivia, Gadea's group was dispatched to the Escambray mountains to fight the counterrevolutionary *"bandidos"* operating there. Their requests to return to Peru were rebuffed or not answered at all for several months, and it wasn't until after Béjar had failed, and after a special trip was made to Havana by the group's leader, Luis de la Puente Uceda, that they were finally allowed to depart. Before he left, Gadea saw Che one last time.

"It was an important conversation for me," Gadea recalled, "because it was the first time Che saw me not just as a student or out of a family obligation, but because of the decision I had made regarding the revolution in Peru." Che made it clear that there was no bad blood and gave Gadea his blessing. "Well, go have your experience," he said. "Everyone has to test himself, and you must learn and gain knowledge through your own experiences." All the members of his group made it to Peru without being arrested, began their work of underground organization, and within two years were ready for war.

VII

Aleida did not want Che to go to Argentina to fight, but she knew she couldn't stop him. From the beginning, he had made clear to her that one day he would carry the revolution to his homeland. This had seemed like an abstraction until Masetti's group was formed and its training was under way.

Che and Aleida's second child, Camilo, had been born in May 1962. The new baby was fair, like his mother. He would grow up to have her blond hair and his father's massive forehead and intense stare. Aleida had become pregnant again during the missile crisis, and they had moved to a new, larger house on Calle 47, in a residential neighborhood in Nuevo Vedado, a few blocks from the zoo and close to the government complex around Plaza de la Revolución. On June 14, 1963—Che's thirty-fifth birthday—Aleida gave birth to a second daughter. They named her Celia, after Che's mother. This was a particularly poignant homage, for at that moment, Celia *madre* was in prison. She had arrived in Cuba in January 1963, had stayed with them for three months, and on her return to Argentina in April had been arrested on charges of possessing subversive Cuban propaganda and of being an agent for Che.

On June 9, Celia wrote to Che from the women's prison in Buenos Aires. "My dear," she began. "I share my present kingdom with 15 people, almost all communists." They were fine companions, apart from their enforcement of an "overly iron discipline and an irredentist dogmatism" that she found trying. She didn't know when she would be freed, "but you know that if there is someone who is well constituted to withstand prison in good humor, that's me. It will also serve me as an exercise in humility. . . . The only thing I find uncomfortable is not having a single minute of privacy in the entire day. We eat, sleep, read, and work in our cell of 14 by 6 [meters] and [exercise] in a gallery where you can see the sky through the bars and from which they throw us out when a common prisoner arrives. It seems we might infect them with a terrible contagious disease." She played volleyball for an hour a day and had also learned some prison crafts, such as making papier-mâché dolls. "They're horrible, but a good way to kill time."

Apart from the lack of privacy, her biggest complaint was about the body searches she was subjected to before and after each visit, and the reading of all her letters, which she found especially humiliating. "The searches include doubtful caresses: almost all the prisoners here are lesbians and I suspect that the guards have elected this wonderful work because they have the same inclinations. . . .

"I don't know, or rather yes I do know why the government has wanted to put me in this place. . . . I'll tell you as a point of curiosity that one of the questions they asked me in the DIPA [Argentine secret police] was 'what is your role in Fidel Castro's government?'" She reassured Che that she hadn't been mistreated. However, prison was "a marvelous deformatory, as much for the common prisoners as for the political ones: if you are lukewarm, you become active; if you're active, you become aggressive; and if you're aggressive, you become implacable." In fact, ever since her son Ernesto had become Che, Celia had undergone a significant political radicalization. She claimed now to believe in "socialism," although she was not a Communist and, according to people who knew her well, she didn't really like or trust Fidel. She particularly didn't like what she saw as his hold over her son, and Che's subservience to him, but in spite of her private qualms about Cuba's disorganization and incompetence, she vigorously defended the revolution.

Whatever the Argentine security forces suspected, there was a bitter irony to Celia's imprisonment along with members of the Argentine Communist Party. Although she downplayed it in her letter, Celia's life was made extremely difficult by her doctrinaire cellmates. According to María Elena Duarte, who was married to Celia's youngest son, Juan Martín, "They imposed rules even the jailers didn't impose. For instance, she liked to read, and as if to persecute her, they turned out the lights. The lights had to be turned out at such and such an hour. If she wanted to play some sport in the patio, they told her no, that was not the correct hour for that sport. It was so cruel . . . and so obviously directed against her."

The leader of the Communist women, and the person María Elena Duarte held chiefly responsible for Celia's ill-treatment, was Fanie Edelman, a veteran Party activist and founder of the Communist-front Argentine Women's Union. Many years later, Edelman acknowledged that she and her comrades had "organized life in the prison" and imposed "very rigorous norms of conduct." But she reacted with indignation at the notion that Che's mother had been in any way singled out for persecution. "We were a harmonious group. On the contrary, we respected her a great deal, precisely because she was Che's mama."*

Not long after she wrote to Che, Celia was released from prison, but she had been cut from her moorings. After the bomb incident the previous year, she and Juan Martín had left the house on Calle Araoz in the care of their Indian maid, Sabina Portugal, and moved into a small, rented apartment. Juan Martín and María Elena were soon married, and while Celia was in prison María Elena had given birth to a baby boy. Celia let them have the apartment and went to live with her daughter Celia in a dark old house on Calle Negro. María Elena and Juan Martín had asked her to stay with them, but she declined. "We have an excellent relationship and I don't want to ruin it by living together," she said. They saw each other frequently, meeting up most weekends at Roberto's house, but Celia had a solitary life. "Celia had her circle of friends, her political activities, but she had compartmentalized her life in a very private, solitary kind of way," María Elena said. "I think in some way she enjoyed the solitude. She read and thought a great deal, and was undergoing a period of reflection, a reevaluation of her political points of view." But being Che's mother had turned Celia's life upside down, just as it had altered the lives of all of the family members in one way or another. As revolution and war had become features of Che's life, bombs, imprisonment, and political

---

*Edelman admitted that the Party at the time was "dogmatic" and "reformist," out of touch with the revolutionary impulse, and rejected outright armed struggle as a means of gaining power. "It was a period in the life of our party in which all guerrillas, all armed groups, were taboo," she said. Indeed, for all its official trumpeting of revolutionary solidarity with socialist Cuba, at home the Argentine Communist Party was a monolithic, well-entrenched bureaucracy that sought political respectability above all else. Like its kindred parties in Bolivia, Peru, and Chile, it was vehemently opposed to the Cuban-inspired calls for armed struggle that had begun issuing from the ranks of its younger militants. Che was aware of this, and for that very reason not only was his bid to install a guerrilla *foco* being conducted behind the Party's back, but he was counting upon Party dissidents to join up and become its fighters.

persecution had entered hers. The unique mother-son bond that Ernesto had severed during his soul-searching years on the road had been strangely restored.

In her letter from prison, Celia had wished Che a happy birthday. She said that she imagined he would spend it "submerged in the Ministry and its problems." Then she added: "I almost forget, can you tell me about the progress of Cuba's economy?" She undoubtedly knew that it wasn't really a matter of progress. Ricardo Rojo's latest trip to the island had coincided with her own visit, and he had noted a marked decline since his earlier stay. The neon signs that had once lit up Havana had been switched off; American cigarettes, no longer available, had been replaced by Cuban brands such as Criollos and Dorados; Cuba's cars and buses looked shabby from lack of spare parts and maintenance, and hundreds of neglected U.S.-built tractors were rusting in the fields for the same reasons.

Cuba's revolutionaries clearly had not thought through the consequences of breaking completely with the United States. The old system had been brought to a screeching halt, and the new one had not caught up with Cuba's present needs—much less its ambitious future plans. Soviet petroleum was highly sulfuric and corroded the piping in the U.S.-built refineries, and the Eastern-bloc technicians had proved ill equipped to take over the modern American-built technology left behind in Cuba. Even the simplest logistic detail caused enormous difficulties: for example, the Soviets' tools were metric and didn't fit the American-manufactured machinery in Cuba.

There were other disappointments. Much of the industrial equipment bought from the Soviet bloc by Cuba had turned out to be shoddy and outdated. Oscar Fernández Mell recalled Che's outrage over the crude file-lathing machines he had purchased from Russia. "Che used to say: 'Look at the shit they've sold us!'" He was beset by a multitude of practical problems. Che told Rojo that to get Cuba's industrialization under way, he needed to produce construction materials, but he had two large kilns standing idle because they didn't have firebricks. "We even have to improvise screws," he said. Textile plants had shut down because the thread they were producing was of uneven quality. And so on. "Were I to draw a conclusion about Guevara's state of mind during those months," Rojo wrote, "I would say that the struggle was undermining his optimism. His ingenuity seemed blunted, his spirit smothered under the mountains of statistics and production methods."

Alberto Granado thought that Che's malaise was also due to his loss of faith in the Soviet model he had embraced with such innocent fervor. Che told Granado that he had been a skeptic about Marxism until his discovery of

Stalin when he was in Guatemala and Mexico. He had been bowled over by what he read. "That was when he began to find a world that was not all slogans and manifestos—an important world—and I think that intoxicated him and made him feel that in the Soviet Union lay the solution to life, believing that what had been applied there was what he had read about. But, in 1963 and 1964, when he realized they had been tricking him—you know Che couldn't stand being lied to—then came the violent reaction."

As Sartre had noted, the revolutionary honeymoon was over by late 1960, and that, in revolutionary terms, was a very long time ago. Che was now, at the threshold of middle age, the father of four children and a government minister at the pinnacle of his career in revolutionary Cuba. He was less lighthearted, and he looked his age. He had shorn the long hair that he had grown in the mountains and worn during the first year of the revolution. He still wore the beret, but his face appeared puffy and swollen. Despite what he had told Ricardo Rojo about cortisone giving him a heavier appearance, he *had* gained weight. So had Aleida, who had grown plump from her string of pregnancies.

Ever the iconoclast, Che steadfastly wore the shirt jacket of his olive green uniform outside his trousers, with his belt on top. He was the only Cuban *comandante* who refused to conform to the military dress code. More often that not, he wore his trousers hanging loose, outside his boots, instead of tucking them in. No one dared reproach him, of course. *"Che es como es,"* his colleagues would say, with a shrug of their shoulders: "Che is the way he is."

When he was home, Che spent hours closeted in his austere little rooftop office full of books. Its only adornments were a bronze bas-relief of Lenin, a small bronze statue of Simón Bolívar, and a large framed photograph of Camilo Cienfuegos. When people asked him why he didn't take a break, he gave work as an excuse. There was never very much time to be with Aleida and the children. More often than not, duty called, and his trips away were invariably long ones. He inspected factories, military units, cooperatives, and schools; gave speeches; received foreign dignitaries; attended diplomatic receptions. Whenever possible, he brought Aleida along to such functions in Havana, but his workweek lasted from Monday through Saturday, including nights, and on Sunday mornings he went off to do volunteer labor. Sunday afternoons were all he spared for his family.

During these afernoons at home, Che would throw himself down on the living room floor and play with his children and his dog, a German shepherd named Muralla who also escorted him to the office. His eldest child, Hildita, now almost eight, was usually there on weekends, and they watched boxing matches and soccer games together on television, pretending to place bets. Occasionally he stopped by to see Hilda. She noted his extreme tiredness, and later recalled how he used to take their daughter in his arms and tell her he wanted to take her on a trip with him someday—but he never did.

At times, Che's disciplinarian streak showed itself at home. Once, when Aliusha had a tantrum, Che walked over and smacked her bottom. Her wails increased. When her nanny, Sofía, tried to pick her up and comfort her, Che said to leave the child alone so she would remember why she had been punished. He was especially severe with his bodyguards, who lived in an annex of the house. One of their fiancées recalled a time when Che made Harry Villegas, his favorite, strip off his clothes before he was locked in a closet as punishment for some misdemeanor. Che's mother was visiting, and she yelled at him, telling him to be more lenient. He told her to keep out of it, that he knew what he was doing.

This was Che the Implacable, Cuba's avenging angel and ultimate political commissar, demanding the impossible of those around him but above reproach himself because he lived up to his own severe dictates. "Che had something of the missionary in him," Manuel Piñeiro said. He was respected and admired, despised and feared, but nobody was indifferent to him.

Perhaps Che's most controversial disciplinary innovation was Guanacahabibes, a rehabilitation camp at the remote, rocky, and devilishly hot westernmost tip of Cuba, where he dispatched transgressors from the Ministry of Industries to undergo periods of self-effacing physical labor to redeem themselves before returning to their jobs. The sanctions were "voluntary," and could last from a month to a year depending on the offense, which was generally a matter of ethics. If someone had practiced nepotism, intentionally covered up a mistake, or had an affair with a comrade's wife, he was called before Che, who gave offenders an opportunity to accept their punishment—a stint at Guanacahabibes—or else leave the ministry. If they did their time and showed that they had learned the error of their ways, they could return with no black mark on their record. If they refused, they were out of a job. In time, due to the excesses of the camp's *comandante,* Guanacahabibes acquired a sinister reputation, a Cuban equivalent of a Siberian gulag.*

Another pet project of Che's was the Ciro Redondo Experimental Farm in Matanzas province. The Ciro Redondo was an agricultural cooperative farm where mostly illiterate *guajiros* from his old sierra column lived and worked communally according to his doctrine of moral incentives. He

*Guanacahabibes remained controversial, and around the time Che left Cuba, it was closed down.

insisted that they better themselves through schoolwork as well and had assigned them a teacher. He often flew there to check up on their progress in the little Cessna airplane he had learned to fly with his private pilot, Eliseo de la Campa. He once took the economist Regino Boti with him to the farm and tested some of the men on their reading comprehension. One man did very badly and Che said, "Well, if you keep studying, maybe you'll get to be as smart as an ox in twenty years." Then he turned on his heel. The poor *guajiro* was so humiliated that he began to cry. Boti talked to Che, persuading him that he had been wrong to be so cruel, that he should go back and speak to the man, to lift his spirits.

Che's tendency to be harsh often had to be tempered by a more diplomatic companion or friend. He seemed to have little sense of the intimidating effects his words could have on others. There were also some comic incidents that served to remind him of his public celebrity, however. He was a notoriously bad driver, and one day he rear-ended a car on the seafront Malecón in Havana. The driver of the car got out, cursing the mother and father of whoever it was who had hit him. When he saw it was Che, he became cravenly apologetic. "Che, Comandante," the man sighed. "What an honor for me to have my car struck by you!" Then, caressing his new dent, he announced that he would never have it repaired, but would keep it as a proud reminder of his personal encounter with Che Guevara.

Such tales became enduring folklore in Havana. Most of the stories concerned Che's famous working hours; his hatred of *adulónes,* or "flatterers"; and his personal austerity. People speak of the time that Celia Sánchez, Fidel's great dispenser of favors, sent Aleida a new pair of Italian shoes. When Che found out, he made Aleida return them. Did the average Cuban wear imported Italian shoes? No. Then she couldn't, either. When they moved from their house on Calle 18 in Miramar to their new home in Nuevo Vedado, Che discovered Aleida fixing decorative lamps. She explained that she had taken them from their previous home, and he blew up and ordered her to take them back. When one of the children was sick, Aleida asked to be allowed to take the child to the hospital in Che's car. He refused, telling her to take the bus like everybody else. The gas in the car belonged to "the people" and was intended for use in his public duties, not for personal reasons.

When food rationing began, and one of his colleagues complained, Che said that his own family was eating fine on what the government allowed. The colleague pointed out that Che had a special food supplement. Che investigated, found that this was true, and had the benefit eliminated. His family would receive no special favors. Rumors circulated about how the Guevaras often didn't have enough to eat, and that Aleida had to borrow money from the bodyguards to make ends meet. Timur Gaidar, a former correspondent for *Pravda* in Cuba, claimed that a sympathetic Soviet embassy official slipped some hors d'oeuvres into Aleida's purse at a diplomatic reception when he was sure Che wasn't looking.

Che's relationship with Aleida was a source of curiosity to many. He was an intellectual, a scholar, and an assiduous reader of books. Aleida preferred movies and social gatherings. He was austere and shunned the good things in life. Aleida, like most people, appreciated them, and aspired to possess some of the comforts enjoyed by most *comandantes'* wives—even in revolutionary Cuba. It was a constant bone of contention between them and produced frequent arguments. Some Cubans close to them have drawn comparisons between their relationship and that of Karl Marx with his unintellectual wife, Jenny Westphalen. While Che had his head in the clouds with his work, his philosophizing, and revolutionary theory, Aleida kept the house running, the bills paid, and the children fed. She was fiercely devoted to him. And, despite their differences, they enjoyed each other's company, had a strong physical attraction for each other, and, by all accounts, were faithful. Both enjoyed an open, earthy repartee; at times it was shared with others. Once, while he was visiting his mother-in-law's house in Santa Clara, she asked him if he wanted a bath. "Not if Aleida's not in it," he quipped.

They were romantics at heart, although Che rarely showed this side of himself in public. At night, in the privacy of their bedroom, he would recite poetry to Aleida. This thrilled her. His favorite poet was Pablo Neruda. Another thing they shared was bluntness of speech. If anything, Aleida was less tactful and even more brutally honest than Che. If she didn't like someone, she would say so to his face. It was, Che used to say, one of the things he liked about her the most. But the main reason Che loved Aleida, their closest friends said, was that she provided him with a home, something he'd never really had in the conventional sense. Che regarded his father warmly but thought he was immature. (Aleida never had much time for Ernesto senior and acknowledged that after Che's death, they had a public falling-out when she heard him tell a gathering that he was responsible for inculcating Che's early socialist leanings. She challenged him, telling him it was a lie, and the old man never forgave her for that.) As much as Che loved his mother, she had never been a physically demonstrative woman. Just as in his adolescence he had gone to his aunt Beatriz for some maternal attention, he sought it as a grown man from Aleida. She recognized this need and responded by mothering him, dressing him, and even bathing him.

Che was notoriously careless about his appearance. The reason he wore his uniform shirt outside his trousers, with the web belt over it, Cossack-fashion, with the top button undone, Aleida said, was that he suffered from the high humidity in Cuba, which exacerbated his asthma. Health reasons also explained why there were no carpets in their home or in his office. He often sat on the floor—where numerous visitors to his office recall finding him—because it was cooler there. Since Che disliked air-conditioning, the solution they came up with for his office was to seal the windows tightly.

Such eccentricities added to the popular myth woven around Che in Cuba. He was aware of it, and he seemed not to care. Indeed, Che stood out in contrast to almost everyone around him. He didn't like parties—a Cuban national pastime—and rarely invited people to his home, or went to theirs, for that matter. Orlando Borrego, one of his closest friends, said that Che dropped by his house only once, although they lived just two blocks from each other. In a country where the people love to dance, and sensual Afro-Caribbean rhythmic music is the heart blood of the culture, Che liked to listen to tangos, but was tone-deaf and didn't dance. On a Caribbean island with beautiful beaches, to which Cubans traditionally escape during the hot summers, Che didn't swim. In a country where rum is the time-honored means of relaxing and passing the time with friends, Che didn't drink. He allowed himself red wine when it was available. Most Cubans do not like wine. In a nation of coffee drinkers, where the average person punctuates his or her day with little cups of hot, sweet espresso, Che vastly preferred his native home-brewed *yerba mate*. Cubans love to eat roast pork, whereas Che preferred a good grilled beefsteak. Cubans have a sense of humor that is straightforwardly bawdy or scatological; Che's was ironic, witty, and acid. The one Cuban habit Che did indulge was smoking Havana cigars—which was disastrous, of course, for his asthma. But even this he did with singular determination, smoking the *tabacos* right down to the nub in order not to waste anything that human labor had helped produce.

Despite his honorary Cuban citizenship and the passage of time, Che was culturally still very much an Argentine. He liked to say, pointedly, that he considered himself a "Latin American." This fit into his scheme to unite the nations of the hemisphere into a socialist fraternity. But his best friends, the people he talked most freely to, such as Alberto Granado, were Argentines. Granado was one of the few people who could criticize Che to his face and get away with it. He challenged him on many things he saw as *irreflexivo,* or overly rigid, in Che's personality, and, although he had helped Che recruit people for the Masetti expedition and evidently also served as his liaison with some of the Venezuelan guerrillas, Granado actually disagreed with Che's belief in jump-starting revolutions in Latin America through guerrilla warfare. It was an issue they argued over frequently, and never resolved.

Granado recalled one conversation with Che in which he pointed out what he believed was the fundamental difference between them. Che could look through a sniper scope at a soldier and pull the trigger, knowing that by killing him he was "saving 30,000 future children from lives of hunger," whereas when Granado looked through the scope, he saw a man with a wife and children.

With his penchant for dance, drink, and good times, Granado fit right into Cuban society, but Che never really did, and even Granado, who was completely loyal to Che, conceded that his friend's caustic nature rubbed some Cubans the wrong way. To many, he seemed altogether too serious about revolution, unrelentingly moralistic, and holier-than-thou. Although many of his subordinates tried to emulate him—unsuccessfully, it must be said—his *austeridad* was a constant reproof to his high-living and philandering fellow revolutionaries.

In a country where many of the men had second and even third "wives" simultaneously with their first marriage, sired children with several women, and had affairs quite openly, Che was, by all accounts, steadfastly monogamous in Cuba, despite the fact that woman flocked to him like groupies to a pop star. One of his aides was at a social gathering where a pretty young woman blatantly flirted with Che. Instead of being flatttered and responding with gallantry or banter, Che primly scolded the woman, telling her to behave herself. A friend recalled being with him at a dinner in a foreign embassy. They had been seated with the ambassador's daughter, and it was implied that the young woman was available to Che. The daughter, said Che's friend, was so beautiful that any man would have forgotten his marriage vows or any commitment to the revolution just to sleep with her. Che was finding it difficult to resist. He finally turned to his companion and whispered, "Find an excuse to get me out of here before I succumb. I can't bear any more."

Che was always suspicious of anyone who did him an unsolicited favor, seeing it as pandering or, worse, a symptom of moral corruption. A classic example is the story of the time a new bodyguard brought Che his boots, freshly shined. Che gave him a kick in the rear and called him a *guataca,* a brownnoser. Then, when the humiliated soldier hurled the boots into the street, Che punished him by docking his pay for a week. Yet Che's devotion to those who earned his trust was reciprocated by fanatical loyalty. Known to everyone as *los hombres del Che,* they included bodyguards, accountants, economists, and revolutionary fighters. Men such as Hermes Peña, Alberto Castellanos, and Jorge Ricardo Masetti had willingly left their jobs, wives, and children to fight in his wars. He personified the revolution for them.

VIII

Masetti and his small band hacked their way through the northern Argentine wilderness for two weeks in late June and early July 1963, trying to reach their target area south of the town of Orán. Their path brought them up against great jungle cliffs, and finally they gave up and returned to the farm in Bolivia to recuperate before trying a different route. When they got back, they discovered that much had changed. The Argentine military had allowed elections to be held on July 7, and since the biggest voting bloc—the *peronistas*—were not allowed to participate, most Argentines had expected the candidate of the armed forces, the right-wing General Aramburu, to win. Instead, the centrist Radical Party of the People's candidate, a respected sixty-three-year-old doctor from Córdoba, Arturo Illia, was elected by a slender majority.

The election results caused a crisis in the fledgling Ejército Guerrillero del Pueblo (EGP). It was one thing to declare war on a military regime that had illegally seized power, but quite another to wage war against a democratically elected civilian president. "Our project disintegrated just like that," Ciro Bustos recalled. "We spent a couple of days doing nothing, with everything on hold." Masetti decided to call the whole thing off. Colomé Ibarra drove to La Paz to advise Havana through the embassy there, and Federico Méndez was sent into Argentina to catch up with Jorge Vázquez-Viaña, the young Bolivian Communist who was coordinating activities with a Trotskyite splinter group. Masetti wanted him to suspend everything.

While Masetti and his men pondered what to do next, Che was in Algeria to attend the first-anniversary celebration of the Algerian revolution. He returned to Havana in time for the July 26 festivities, bringing with him Algeria's minister of defense, Houari Boumédienne, for a public display of the alliance of Algeria and Cuba in the Afro–Asian–Latin American anti-imperialist struggle. By then, Masetti had changed his mind again. Only two days after sending Colomé Ibarra and Federico off with orders to suspend operations, he had reanalyzed the Argentine elections and decided to go ahead.

Masetti wrote what he called a "Letter from the Rebels" to President-Elect Illia. After praising him for his reputation as a civic-minded man worthy of respect, Masetti castigated Illia's decision to "lower himself" and play the military's game by seeking office "in the most scandalous electoral fraud in the history of the country." He urged Illia to resign to restore his reputation and to ally himself with the Argentines who wanted to be free of the military, those "blackmailing gunmen and bodyguards for imperialism and the oligarchy." He announced that the EGP, which was armed and organized, had gone into the mountains. "We are the only free men in this oppressed republic . . . and we won't come down unless it is to do battle." He signed the letter "Segundo Comandante, Ejército Guerrillero del Pueblo, July 9, 1963, Campamento Augusto César Sandino . . . *Revolución o Muerte.*"

Masetti told Ciro Bustos to go after Federico and rescind the suspension order. He was also to take the open letter to Illia and see that it was published, then travel to cities in Argentina where he knew people and lay the groundwork for an urban support network for the rebel force. For the next several weeks, Bustos was on the move between Córdoba, Buenos Aires, and his home city, Mendoza. He managed to have Masetti's letter published, but only in *Compañero,* a leftist *peronista* fringe publication, where it made little impression. He was more successful in establishing a support network. In Córdoba he approached a leftist academic he had known since childhood, Oscar del Barco, a cofounder and editor of the intellectual Marxist journal *Pasado y Presente.* Bustos revealed his mission and asked for help. Within a day, del Barco had assembled a group of people, mostly intellectuals and Communist Party dissidents like himself who worked at Córdoba University's Faculty of Philosophy and Letters. Bustos outlined the EGP's plan of action to them candidly. He told them that the project had Che's backing, that the core group had trained in Cuba and Algeria, and that funds were not a problem. What they needed was recruits, safe houses, urban contacts, and suppliers—in short, a clandestine national urban infrastructure.

It was what these intellectuals had been arguing for—"revolutionary action"—a position that had earned them expulsion from the mainstream Argentine Communist Party. Within days, they had begun to organize enthusiastically, and before long a small but well-coordinated network was being set up in half a dozen cities and towns across the country, from Buenos Aires to Salta, with Córdoba as its center.

By now an important new personality had arrived at the guerrilla base—José María "Papi" Martínez Tamayo, a Cuban army captain who was one of the most valuable assets in Piñeiro's intelligence apparatus. After serving with Raúl during the war, Papi had stayed in the military, and since late 1962 he had been Piñeiro's envoy to various Latin American guerrilla groups. He had joined Turcios Lima in Guatemala, served as an instructor in Cuba for Tamara Bunke's clandestine training, and helped train the Argentine Trotskyite group of Vasco Bengochea. Good-looking, strong, and energetic—"an impassioned conspirator," Bustos remarked, "and a stupendous guy"—Papi had come to see the *foco* through its initial stages and help prepare the way for Che's arrival. He took some of the load off the hard-pressed Colomé Ibarra, who was acting not only as the group's permanent base commander but also as its liaison with Cuba's embassy in La Paz, handling communications, logistics, and arms supplies. With Papi around to do some of these tasks, Colomé Ibarra could safeguard his cover as a pioneering rural *finquero*. Over the coming months, Papi came and went constantly, between Bolivia, Argentina, and Cuba.

By September, it seemed to be time to get moving. Curious Bolivian policemen had already paid the farm a visit, no doubt having heard rumors from locals about the unusual amount of traffic at the newly purchased *finca*. Fortunately, there was only one road to the farm, and a car engine could be heard long before it arrived; the police came, poked around, and left, having seen nothing suspicious. In case they returned, a camp was built for the fighters in the forest a short distance away.

When Papi brought Alberto Castellanos to the farm in late September or early October, Masetti and his men were still there. Masetti had been in Argentina exploring, and had returned to base. Scouts had to be extremely careful and usually traveled by night, for the Argentine police of the Gendarmería Nacional, who had posts throughout the border area, patrolled constantly, on the lookout for smugglers. The rural north was very sparsely settled, and strangers, especially armed, bearded, and uniformed ones, were soon noticed. Castellanos had orders to wait for Che, but seeing that one of Masetti's men was sick, and anxious to get into action himself, he asked Masetti to take him on as a fighter. He wrote a note to Che explaining his decision, and sent it back with Papi.

The group was still tiny. Besides the flap-eared, jovial Castellanos, who became known to everyone as El Mono (The Monkey), there were only one or two newcomers. In light of his initial success at organizing the urban network, Masetti asked Bustos to assume the duty of liaison with the outside and to begin enlisting volunteers. Among Bustos's first recruits were the Jouve brothers from a small town in Córdoba province. Emilio and Héctor were the sons of a French-Basque émigré builder of anarchist leanings. Both in their early twenties and former members of the Communist Youth, they had grown disenchanted with the Party's inactivity and had formed a small action group of their own in Córdoba. They had collected a few guns and had painted graffiti on walls, but had not done much else. They jumped at the chance to go to the mountains when Bustos showed up asking for volunteers. A doctor friend of Bustos, El Petiso (Shorty) Canelo, drove the recruits north. A "bookstore" was opened in the city of Salta as a cover for the storage and transport of supplies for the guerrillas. Three more volunteers arrived from Buenos Aires.

By October, Masetti and his men had moved across the border and installed themselves in a camp in the forest above the Río Pescado, some ten miles from the Argentine border town of Aguas Blancas. The camp lay in the mountains just off the road from Salta, south of Orán. The little force began to grow, and they hiked deeper into the hills looking for peasants to engage in "armed propaganda." This consisted of impromptu consciousness-raising talks in which they explained that they had come to liberate the peasants from poverty and injustice. But their first efforts were discouraging.

"It was shocking," Bustos recalled. "You couldn't even call these people *campesinos.* These lived in little bush clearings full of fleas and dogs and snot-nosed kids, with no links to the real world, nothing. They didn't even live in the conditions of the Indians, who at least have their food, their tribes and things. These people were really lost, marginalized. They could hardly be called a social base for what we were trying to do. They were experiencing problems that were real, but their misery was such that they were completely ruined."

The zone they had selected was sparsely populated, and to reach the isolated settlers they had to hike for hours up and down steep jungle hills, fording rivers in between. It was the rainy season and the rivers were swollen, so they spent much of the time soaked to the skin. Their muscles ached, their feet were blistered, and they were flea-bitten. Swarms of mosquitoes plagued them. With so few farmers around, food was a problem, and they depended entirely on provisions brought to them by truck from the city. This was a task that had to be done carefully, so as not to raise suspicion.

So far, the EGP could hardly be called an indigenous force. Without the help of a peasant strongman such as Crescencio Pérez, who had provided Fidel's tiny rebel force with its first local guides, couriers, and fighters, Masetti and his men were alien transplants on foreign soil. Most of his volunteers were city boys, young middle-class university students impelled by visions of becoming heroic guerrillas and creating a new utopian society. A few had been through obligatory military service, were physically fit, and could handle weapons, and some others adapted; but most were ill-equipped to deal with the rugged terrain, the exhausting marches, the lack of food, and the rigid military discipline demanded by Masetti.

The darker side of Masetti's personality began to appear more and more frequently. His frustration over the slow beginning, exacerbated by the political transformation in Argentina, turned to a kind of simmering rage as he led his greenhorn guerrillas fitfully around the sodden jungle. He channeled his anger mostly against the newcomers who found it tough going, contemptuously calling them *pan blanco* (white bread), and meting out strict punishments for petty errors—extra guard duty, mule work carrying supplies, and in some cases hunger diets for two or three days. Hermes Peña, the tough *guajiro* from Cuba's Oriente and a veteran of war and Che's strict discipline, backed him up.

Masetti had his favorites, such as Héctor "El Cordobés" Jouve, whom he made his political commissar at the same time that he assigned Bustos to continue his role as the coordinator between the *foco* and the city. Jouve was tall, physically fit, and had been in the military; he took to the guerrilla life with ease. Those who didn't, however, soon found themselves under Masetti's brutal scrutiny. Just as he had focused on the unlucky Miguel as the object of his hostility in Algeria, Masetti now cast his gaze among the youths who had joined him, watching for a new potential deserter. He soon found him.

Adolfo Rotblat was a Jewish boy of twenty from Buenos Aires whom they called Pupi. He suffered from asthma and began lagging behind on the marches, complaining about the harshness of guerrilla life. It was obvious he wasn't cut out for it, but instead of letting him leave, Masetti dragged him along. With every day that passed, Pupi's physical and mental state deteriorated. Soon he was completely broken.

When he rejoined the guerrillas in October for a few weeks, Bustos found Pupi in a pathetic condition. He lived in a state of terror, wept, fell behind in the marches, and slowed everyone down. Men had to be sent back to drag him forward. The others were disgusted by him. "A process of degradation began," Bustos recalled. One day he went out with Pupi on a reconnaissance hike and they became lost. Finally Bustos found his bearings at a river, but Pupi refused to cross it. "He wanted me to kill him right there," Bustos said. "Finally I pulled out a pistol and put it against his head and I made him walk like that, more or less by force . . . kicking him in the ass. I made him walk until night fell." Unable to see well enough to continue, they slept in the forest. Bustos tried to console Pupi, who was deeply depressed. The next morning they set out again. Halfway to the camp they found Hermes Peña, who had been sent to look for them. Once again, because of Pupi, the group had been held up.

A few days later, Masetti told Bustos, "Look, this situation is becoming unbearable. No one can stand it anymore. Nobody wants to carry him, and so a measure has to be taken that sanitizes the group's psychology, that liberates it from this thing that is corroding it." Masetti had decided to shoot him.

Masetti decided to kill Pupi the night three new volunteers arrived in camp, and he selected one of them, Pirincho, a student from a wealthy and aristocratic Buenos Aires family, to carry out the task. The way Bustos understood it, Masetti wanted to harden Pirincho, whose gentle, diplomatic personality bothered him. "He wanted hard fighters, guys of steel who responded to him," Bustos said. Pupi had been unwittingly prepared for his execution—given tranquilizers and tied into his hammock, which was hung a short distance from the camp. The others gathered. Masetti explained what had to be done and ordered Pirincho to do it. Pirincho's face told it all—he was terrified—but he complied.

"Pirincho went . . . and we heard the shot," Bustos said. "Then he came back, saying desperately, 'He won't die' . . . and so I go there and see he's got a bullet in the head. He is a dead guy but convulsing, and I decided to end it."

Bustos pulled out his pistol, fired a bullet into Pupi's brain, and returned to his comrades. Pirincho's face showed that he was devastated by his experience, but everyone else was in high spirits. "Suddenly there was euphoria," Bustos said. "It reminded me of when someone dies and everyone feels the necessity to have a lunch and drink toasts. . . . Segundo [Masetti] handed out promotions and began making plans about moving to another zone."

It was November 5, 1963. The raison d'être of the EGP had been consecrated by bloodshed. But it was already too late. The *gendarmería* had picked up the rumors spreading among locals about a group of armed strangers in the forests around Orán. Inquiries were made to local cattle ranchers and rural storekeepers who had sighted them, and a suspicious profile began to emerge; by the year's end, there seemed little doubt that the men in the forest were the same rebels who had sent the communiqué to Illia. The security forces began making plans to infiltrate the area.

Papi told Masetti that he thought they were staying too long in one place, that the zone they were in was not appropriate for building a guerrilla *foco*. He proposed opening up a second front in the *chaco* region, east of the Andean precordillera region they were installed in. Federico Méndez had lived there for years and was well connected. For fighters, Papi suggested activating Vasco Bengochea's Trotskyite group in Tucumán province, which he had trained in Cuba; Papi could be the military chief, and he would take Héctor Jouve with him as the responsible politico.

Masetti angrily rejected the idea and accused Papi and Jouve of trying to undermine his authority. "You've always wanted to be *comandante*," he told Jouve. "But I'm not going to let you—you're staying here."

Papi had brought one of Che's *hombres de confianza*, Miguel Ángel Duque de Estrada, to the Bolivian base camp. He had been *auditor revolucionario*, or judge, in the Escambray and the summary tribunal judge in La Cabaña, and he was the Special Operations man at INRA. Duque's job was to wait at the farm until Che arrived, and then go into the battle zone with him. Meanwhile, Alberto Castellanos had developed a bad throat infection, and by December it became obvious that he needed an operation. Their courier, Dr. Canelo, took him to Córdoba and arranged an operation. For public purposes, Castellanos was Raúl Dávila, a Peruvian. He spent Christmas and New Year's in Córdoba, had his operation, and stayed on in the city through the month of January, convalescing. During that time, Papi showed up in Córdoba to inform Castellanos that Che wasn't coming just yet, and that Duque had been withdrawn from the farm and returned to Havana. Che's orders were for the group to "keep exploring . . . not to recruit peasants until we are ready to fight."

IX

Back in Havana, the ground beneath Che was shifting. He had new enemies, at home and abroad. The Sino-Soviet split was now fiercer than ever, and both Beijing and Moscow were vying for the loyalty of the world's Communist parties. In Latin America, the race for influence had caused open ruptures as *pro-chino* factions broke away to form their own parties. Most of the Latin American Communist parties depended on subsidies from Moscow for their survival and had quickly aligned themselves with the Soviet Union. Put to the squeeze, the Cuban government had finally abandoned its officially neutralist posture, with Fidel himself implicitly supporting the Soviet position during his trip to the U.S.S.R. in the spring of 1963. Khrushchev had treated him like a conquering hero and Fidel had reveled in the acclaim. A joint Soviet-Cuban declaration lauded Cuba as a fully recognized member of the socialist community. Moscow formally pledged to defend Cuba's "independence and liberty," while Fidel reaffirmed Cuba's support for "socialist unity" and for Moscow's policy of peaceful coexistence with the capitalist West. It was a rhetorical vote of support, more tepid than Khrushchev would have liked but just enough to make the Chinese nervous without alienating them completely. Fidel probably thought it was a fair trade, and he came home laden with new Soviet economic commitments for Cuba. Just in time, for Cuba's economy was in dire straits. The 1963 sugar harvest, at less than 4 million tons, was the lowest in years, and the rest of the economy was crumbling.

Che may have been the original architect of the Soviet-Cuban relationship, but his call to armed struggle, his emphasis on rural guerrilla warfare, and his stubborn determination to train, arm, and fund Communist Party dissidents—even Trotskyites—over the protests of their national organizations had led to a growing suspicion in Moscow that he was playing Mao's game. A KGB agent, Oleg Darushenkov, had been assigned to stay close to Che since late 1962. His official cover duty in Havana was as the Soviet embassy's cultural attaché, but he also served as Che's Russian-language interpreter. His sunstroke-prone predecessor, Yuri Pevtsov, had been withdrawn for health reasons after only a year in Cuba, just before the missile crisis. Che's own feelings about Darushenkov aren't recorded, but several people who were part of his inner circle at the time expressed their belief—

in off-the-record interviews—that Darushenkov was a "provocateur" whose real mission was to spy on Che.

Many in the Kremlin, especially after the missile crisis, feared that Cuba's escalating support for guerrilla "adventures," which everyone knew was being spearheaded by Che, might drag the Soviet Union into a new confrontation with the United States. "After the crisis, there was concern over what the Cubans might do," Giorgi Kornienko, Ambassador Anatoli Dobrynin's deputy at the Washington embassy during the crisis, said. "We didn't want our relations with the U.S. complicated further because of those activities."

Feder Burlatsky, a former adviser to Khrushchev, said that in senior circles of the Soviet Central Committee, opinion was divided between officials who supported Che and a more predominant group who distrusted him. Burlatsky counted himself among the latter group. "We disliked Che's position. He became an example for adventurers, which could have provoked a confrontation between the U.S.S.R. and the U.S." Burlatsky said the view that Che was a dangerous character took on added weight because of his remarks after the missile crisis, when he told the Soviets that they should have used their missiles. It was a sentiment that Fidel had also expressed privately, but Che had said so publicly—and whereas Fidel soon modified his rhetoric, few doubted that Che meant what he said. Che echoed the sentiments of many Cubans, but his words were embarrassing since they came from such a high-level revolutionary figure. More pointedly, they echoed Beijing's accusation that the Soviets had capitulated to Washington.

"That's why Che was seen as dangerous, as against our own strategy," Burlatsky said. "But there was still some sympathy for him," he acknowledged. "There was a romantic aura around him; he reminded people of the Russian Revolution. . . . Opinion was divided. . . . Some compared him to Trotsky, or to some of the Bolshevik terrorists. Advisers of Khrushchev like [Mikhail] Suslov, who described themselves as revolutionaries, had sympathy for Che."

The opposition to Che took on real vigor with regard to his guerrilla expeditions in Peru and Argentina. It was spearheaded by Victorio Codovilla's powerful Argentine Communist Party. Kiva Maidanek, an eminent Soviet Communist Party analyst of Latin American affairs, was well aware of the Argentine lobby in Moscow against Che, and its repercussions. She said that the Argentine Party accused Che of being an adventurer, pro-Chinese, and a Trotskyite. "This offended Che a great deal," Maidanek said. "But the view took on weight here, especially in the Latin America section of the Central Committee. Anything to the left of the Soviet line was considered pro-Chinese and pro-Trotskyite. The U.S.S.R. began to incline

toward the [Latin American] Communist parties. Beginning in 1964, the
Latin American area was seen less as a battleground between the U.S. and
the U.S.S.R. and more as a war of influence between China and the U.S.S.R."

Che had continued to test the limits of Soviet tolerance. In September
1963, emboldened by Fidel's Second Havana Declaration (decreeing the
inevitability of revolution in Latin America), which he had begun to cite as
the guiding philosophy of the Cuban revolution, Che had outlined his call
for continental guerrilla war in an ideologically refined sequel to his *Guerrilla Warfare* how-to manual. The sequel was called "Guerrilla Warfare: A
Method." In a rebuke to the Latin American Communist parties' claims to
leadership in the struggle of their countries, Che wrote, "To be the vanguard
of the Party means to be at the forefront of the working class through the
struggle for achieving power. It means to know how to guide this fight
through shortcuts to victory." He bolstered his argument with a quote from
Fidel: "The subjective conditions in each country, the factors of revolutionary consciousness, of organization, of leadership, can accelerate or delay
revolution, depending on the state of their development. Sooner or later, in
each historic epoch, as objective conditions ripen, consciousness is acquired,
organization is achieved, leadership arises, and revolution is produced."

Something palpably new had emerged in Che's call to arms. There
was less reliance on the old Communist euphemism "armed struggle," in
favor of the far more candid "violence." "Violence is not the monopoly of
the exploiters and as such the exploited can use it, too, and, what is more,
ought to use it when the moment arrives. . . . We should not fear violence,
the midwife of new societies; but violence should be unleashed at that precise moment in which the leaders have found the most favorable circumstances. . . . Guerrilla warfare is not passive self-defense; it is defense with
attack. . . . It has as its final goal the conquest of political power. . . . The
equilibrium between oligarchic dictatorship and popular pressure must
be changed. The dictatorship tries to function without resorting to force.
Thus we must try to oblige the dictatorship to resort to violence, thereby
unmasking its true nature as the dictatorship of the reactionary social
classes."

In order to outwit the Yankees, who would do all they could to divide, conquer, and repress the rebelling peoples, the revolution in Latin
America must be of a continental nature. "The unity of the repressive forces
must be met with the unity of the popular forces. In all countries where
oppression reaches intolerable proportions, the banner of rebellion must be
raised; and this banner of historical necessity will have a continental character. As Fidel stated, the cordilleras of the Andes will be the Sierra Maestra
of Latin America; and the immense territories which this continent encom-

passes will become the scene of a life or death struggle against imperialism. . . . This means that it will be a protracted war; it will have many fronts; and it will cost much blood and countless lives for a long period of time. . . . This is a prediction. We make it with the conviction that history will prove us right."

The rich nation of Argentina had long been coveted by the Kremlin, and leaders of theArgentine Communist Party received preferential treatment in Moscow and wielded an unusual degree of influence over Soviet policy in Latin America. With few exceptions, the other regional parties lent their voices to the Argentine position, and by late 1963 their message was the same: Che was intervening in their countries and had to be reined in.

"There was a whole group of comrades who were of the opinion that we had to help the Cuban comrades become Marxists, true Marxists, because they weren't sufficiently prepared theoretically," Nikolai Metutsov, Party Secretary Yuri Andropov's deputy in charge of relations with the non-European socialist states, said. "Among some leaders in the Central Committee department where I worked there was an opinion that we had to embrace our Cuban friends as strongly as possible, to squeeze them so they would not be able to breathe." Metutsov, whose last foreign post had been Beijing, was dispatched to Havana. "For me, for Andropov, for Khrushchev, of course, and other members of the Politburo, the first thing was to clarify the theoretical and ideological positions of the Cuban leaders," Metutsov said. It was imperative in particular, he said, to determine their positions on what he called "the theoretical problems of the global revolutionary process," a euphemism for the rivalry between Beijing and Moscow.

Metutsov traveled to Cuba at the end of 1963 in a Soviet delegation led by Nikolai Podgorny, president of the Presidium of the Supreme Soviet. When he spoke about his mission many years later, he made it clear that neither Fidel nor Raúl was really the issue. "We knew about the process by which they had come to Marxism, how sincere their comprehension of Marxism was. . . . We knew that in essence Fidel was a liberal bourgeois democrat, and we knew that his brother Raúl was closer to the Communists and was in the Party. Now, about Che Guevara: he seemed to me to be the most prepared theoretically of all the political leadership."

That, of course, was the problem. Che had been the guiding hand in moving Fidel toward socialism, to his relationship with the Soviet Union, and now he had become the revolution's foremost revolutionary heretic, an enfant terrible with international aspirations.

During his visit, Metutsov had many conversations with Che, but it was one all-night talk they had together, early in January of 1964, that

Metutsov recalled in special detail. They sat talking until dawn in the library of the Soviet ambassador's residence and, when they had finished, took a swim together in the pool. "The conversation began with a reproach by him," Metutsov recalled. "He said he had heard that in the Soviet Union, in the Party Central Committee, Che Guevara was considered to be pro-Chinese, that is, that he was the person proposing Maoist tendencies within the leadership. And of course, this was the most acute question." Metutsov said that Che then began explaining why he wasn't a Maoist. "I said, 'Che, believe me, someone is weaving a spiderweb. In our Party no such attitude toward you exists; someone is trying to sow discord between us.'"

As he spoke, trying to reassure the younger man, Metutsov said he began to experience a strange sensation. A jowly, beetle-browed man with huge ears and pale blue eyes, Metutsov found himself "falling in love" with Che. "I told him: 'You know, I'm a little older than you, but I like you, I like above all your looks.' And I confessed, I confessed my love for him because he was a very attractive young man. . . . I knew his defects, from all the papers, all the information we had, but when I was talking to him, when we dealt with one another, we joked, we laughed, and we talked about less than serious things, and I forgot about his defects. . . . I felt attracted to him, do you understand? It was as if I wanted to get away, to separate myself, but he attracted me, you see. . . . He had very beautiful eyes. Magnificent eyes, so deep, so generous, so honest, a stare that was so honest that somehow, one could not help but feel it . . . and he spoke very well, he became inwardly excited, and his speech was like that, with all of this impetus, as if his words were squeezing you."

Snapping out of his romantic reverie, Metutsov said that as Che spoke, he became convinced that he was sincere. "He said that according to his ideological and theoretical convictions as a Marxist he was closer to us than to the Chinese . . . and he asked me to keep this in mind, to let my comrades know that he was a true friend of the Soviet Union and the Leninist party."

Still, Metutsov went away with an appraisal that escaped easy definition. "Externally one could truly say that, yes, Che Guevara was contaminated by Maoism because of his Maoist slogan that the rifle can create the power. And certainly he can be considered a Trotskyite because he went to Latin America to stimulate the revolutionary movement . . . but in any case I think these are external signs, superficial ones, and that deep down, what was most profound in him was his aspiration to help man on the basis of Marxism-Leninism."

Che's "peculiarity," Metutsov noted, was his personal commitment to the revolutionary cause. "He understood that his nickname, 'Che,' had become the expression of his personality. In our conversations I had the impression that he knew that his portrait already hung on history's walls, the history of the national liberation movement. He was sufficiently intelligent to understand this, without arrogance, and meanwhile he remained a normal person, looking for ways with his comrades to build socialism in Cuba and to make that historical portrait of his more relevant, more permanent."

The issue of Che's support for the armed struggle may have been a source of worry for some of his comrades on the Central Committee, but Metutsov denied that it was perceived as one by the Kremlin leadership or by Khrushchev personally. "Was the Soviet Union interested in developing the global revolutionary movement? Yes. So what was wrong if Cuba helped and lent its portion of support? It all went into the same piggy bank."

Even as Metutsov and Che had their nocturnal conversation, Fidel was preparing to make a return visit to the Soviet Union. On January 2, 1964, on the fifth anniversary of the revolution and the eve of his trip, he gave a lengthy address to the Cuban people. He spoke with enthusiasm about the future of Cuba's economy and lauded Cuba's partnership with the Soviet Union. He reiterated Cuba's support for the policy of peaceful coexistence and Cubans' desire to live in peace with any country, whatever its political system, including the United States. Fidel's speech was clearly intended for American ears. Only two months earlier, he and President Kennedy had been edging toward a behind-the-scenes détente, sending exploratory messages back and forth with a view to normalizing relations, when Kennedy was assassinated in Dallas.* He was sending a clear signal that he hoped the new American president, Lyndon Johnson, would resume the abruptly severed initiative.

Fidel came back from Moscow with a generous new six-year, 24-million-ton sugar agreement in one hand, and a joint Soviet-Cuban communiqué in the other. This time, he had gone all the way; Cuba and the Soviet Union rejected "factional and sectarian activity" in the world Communist movement; they agreed on Moscow's terms for unity; and, pointedly, Cuba was "ready to do whatever is necessary to establish good neighborly relations with the United States of America, based upon the principles of peaceful coexistence." Khrushchev praised this new Cuban "orientation," which would help "consolidate peace and relax international tensions."

---

*Che Guevara remained a suspect for almost any kind of international skullduggery, evidently, for his name popped up in a number of reports filed during the Warren Commission's investigation into the JFK assassination, including some quite bizarre ones from J. Edgar Hoover's FBI field agents. One, in particular, reported an alleged sighting of Che Guevara and Jack Ruby—Lee Harvey Oswald's assassin—together in Panama.

To Maurice Halperin, an American political scientist and economist who was then teaching in Cuba at Che's invitation, the document Fidel had signed in Moscow was unequivocal. "The endorsement of the Soviet 'line' vis-à-vis China was enormously strengthened by Fidel's signature on a document enjoying the status of a joint communiqué," he said. At the same time, "The message to the United States—and to Latin America, for that matter—was clear: Castro offered to negotiate an accommodation with Washington, Khrushchev approved, and the unavoidable inference for Latin America was that Castro was prepared to abandon the Latin American revolution for the sake of an accommodation."

Of course, like most of Fidel's passionately stated "positions," it was a public posture, one he would revise before long, and then continue to revise in future years. As for his affirmation of support for peaceful coexistence, it was largely intended as a statement of intent to use as a bargaining chip in hoped-for negotiations with Washington. At that very moment, Cuban arms and personnel were directly involved in a number of conflicts in Latin America and at least one in Africa. Masetti's men were prowling the Orán jungle, Héctor Béjar's guerrilla column was busily reinfiltrating Peru, and it had been only two months since Venezuelan authorities had captured a shipment of 300 tons of weapons sent from Cuba for the guerrillas there. Cuba's former revolutionary police chief, Efigenio Ameijeiras, and other Cuban military men were in Algeria, secretly helping command an armored battalion in the border war that had broken out with Morocco.

To Che, the term "peaceful coexistence" was anathema, mere appeasement of the imperialist system dressed up in diplomatic language. For the moment, he kept his mouth shut, but there was no longer any doubt that his and Fidel's paths had begun to diverge. Fidel's goal was to consolidate Cuba's economic well-being and his own political survival, and for that he was willing to compromise. Che's mission was to spread the socialist revolution. The time for him to leave Cuba was drawing near. He put great store in Jorge Ricardo Masetti's abilities to give him the opportunity to do just that.

X

In February, 1964, Alberto Castellanos returned to the "war zone" from Córdoba. He was overweight and out of shape after spending a month in the city drinking beer and eating well. On the six-hour hike up to the guerrilla camp he fainted three times. When he arrived, he learned that Masetti had decided that the EGP was going to become active. The guerrillas were going to *dar un pingazo*—stick the dick in hard. The moment was timed to coincide with the second anniversary of the military coup that had toppled Frondízi: March 18.

Masetti's authoritarian streak had by then become frightening, his paranoia about potential deserters pathological. He was persecuting Henry Lerner, a young medical student from Córdoba who had arrived in camp the night of the execution of Pupi Rotblat. Lerner, like Rotblat, was a Jew, but at the time he didn't think there was a connection. The son of a veteran Communist, and a doctrinaire self-described Stalinist at the time, he was proud of his fortitude and conviction, and he expected military discipline. But as Masetti's remarks toward him became increasingly hostile, and as he was singled out for especially punishing assignments, Lerner began to realize that Masetti thought he was inadequate as a guerrilla and was trying to break him. He despaired.

At Christmas, the urban network had sent up a pile of delicacies for the guerrillas, and after dinner Lerner sat against a tree, smoking a cigarette and feeling nostalgic. His thoughts had turned to his family and the wife he had left back in the city, when Masetti crept up behind him. "Hey, what are you thinking about?" Masetti demanded. When Lerner told him, Masetti said: "So, you're planning to desert, aren't you?" Lerner had heard about El Fusilado, and of course Pupi had been executed the night he arrived. In Masetti's view, to be suspected of even thinking about desertion was punishable by death.

Ciro Bustos noticed the tension on his trips back to camp and became alarmed; he could see another "Pupi situation" developing. Lerner talked to Bustos privately and asked for his help. Bustos interceded, telling Masetti he was wrong; Lerner was a good *cuadro,* committed to the cause, and definitely not a potential deserter. He urged Masetti to give Lerner a chance to prove himself, and Masetti finally agreed. He told Lerner to monitor the behavior of two other fighters he had singled out for punishment. One, Nardo, was a new arrival whose real name was Bernardo Groswald. He was a nineteen-year-old Jewish bank clerk from Córdoba. He had almost immediately fallen apart in the harsh jungle and was exhibiting the same symptoms of distress that had finished off Pupi. Lerner had guided Nardo on his first hike up to the camp, and he recalled that the young man clearly had no idea what he was getting into. "Nardo asked if we gave talks, if we had meetings . . . as if he was coming to some kind of flower show," Lerner said. "He was done for after two days. He had flat feet, was frightened of going down slopes, and he began animalizing. It was truly repellent, and as the days went by he began physically to look more like an animal. To go down a hill he went down on his ass, walked on all fours. . . . He was dirty, unclean, and he was punished, given the hardest jobs, that kind of thing."

The other detainee under observation was "Grillo" Frontíni, a photographer and the son of a well-known and affluent *porteño* lawyer. Grillo had been in charge of coordinating things for the EGP in Buenos Aires but had been profligate and careless with the organization's money. Masetti had ordered Bustos to bring him to the mountains to be tried. He placed both young men under "arrest." Lerner was to guard them at a bivouac in the forest for a week. He was to watch them, talk to them, and determine whether or not they were trustworthy; depending on what he reported back, there would be a summary trial to decide their fates.

Masetti saw enemies all around him. He had become emotionally unpredictable. One moment he was euphoric, and the next he would plunge into a deep depression that could last for days. His sciatic nerve, injured in Algeria in his competitions with El Fusilado, hurt him terribly. Bustos was especially concerned for the fate of Nardo, and he said that he begged Masetti not to do anything until he could make arrangements for Nardo to be evacuated. He would find some people who could be trusted on a farm where Nardo could be kept in custody until it was safe to release him. Masetti promised he would wait.

Meanwhile, Pirincho had left on a special mission. He hadn't been the same since killing Pupi but had managed to conceal his anguish effectively. Having won Masetti's trust, he persuaded Masetti to let him return to Buenos Aires. A Cuban agent was supposed to arrive in Uruguay with a shipment of arms, and Pirincho was to meet him and smuggle the arms across the Río de la Plata in his family's yacht. Masetti wanted the arms for his new plan of action. The CGT, Argentina's huge *peronista*-dominated workers' confederation, was planning a general strike against the Illia government, which had given organized labor the cold shoulder. Masetti's idea was to get arms to Vasco Bengochea's group and launch a series of coordinated lightning attacks against rural military targets in the area where the provinces of Salta and Tucumán joined. The EGP could advertise its presence and show support for Argentina's workers at the same time. The guerrillas would then escape, moving over the Andean cordillera to a new base of operations to the south; Masetti had already carried out some initial exploration of the route. Their disappearance would throw off the security forces by creating the impression that the guerillas were a much bigger force than they really were. It was a tactic Fidel and Che had employed with success in the early days of the sierra war, and Masetti wanted to apply it now.

He was also anxious to get organized. In February, he asked Bustos to make contact with Pirincho in the city and find out how the preparations for the transfer of arms were going. Bustos went to Buenos Aires and arranged a meeting with Pirincho. Pirincho didn't show up. They arranged another encounter: another no-show. Finally, Pirincho agreed to meet Bustos in the Belgrano train station. When Bustos arrived, he saw that Pirincho, clearly afraid of being marked for an "extreme measure," had taken precautions. Not only had he selected a public place to meet; he had several watchful friends stationed nearby, staking out the exits.

"Pirincho told me he had agreed to meet to give me an explanation," Bustos recalled. "He wanted to explain why he wasn't going back because he knew I would understand. Then he told me the whole story, about his breakdown, about how he had lost faith because of the murder of Pupi, and about how he knew the guerrilla thing went beyond the personality of Segundo, and that that was what he respected and would maintain loyal to. He said, 'I want to get out of here. I'm going to Europe. . . . I give my word I won't say anything to anyone.'"

While Bustos was away, Masetti broke his promise about Nardo. After spending his week with Nardo and Grillo, Lerner had returned with them to camp and reported to Masetti on their behavior. Grillo was "recuperable," but there was "nothing to be said" about Nardo, whose behavior had worsened.

"Totally broken, he didn't talk," Lerner recalled. "He got down on all fours, he dragged himself, poor thing, he wept, he masturbated. That was how he cleaned himself, like a primitive form of hygiene."

Masetti ordered a trial for Nardo. Federico was the prosecutor, Héctor was the defense lawyer, and Hermes played the role of tribunal president. Lerner recalled that they all sat around, "like a chorus." Lerner's memory blocked out much of the trial, which lasted ten or fifteen minutes, but he remembered feeling that Nardo had "decided to inculpate himself" because he said nothing to rebut the charge that if they freed him and he was caught by the police, he would tell all he knew.

The verdict was, of course, a foregone conclusion and was quickly delivered. "He was condemned to death," Lerner said, "told that he would be shot by a firing squad, for not complying with the revolutionary laws." Masetti decided that he would be shot at dawn the next day, February 19, and that the newest volunteers would form the *pelotón de fusilamiento,* to toughen them up.

The grave was dug and Nardo was shot beside it. Lerner stood to one side watching. At the last minute, when the order to fire came, he saw Nardo swell out his chest. "He looked straight ahead, he didn't tremble, he didn't fall on his knees, he didn't ask for anything," Lerner recalled. Afterward, nobody said a word. "We all tried to hide from ourselves," Lerner said. Masetti acted as if nothing had happened. "Nardo was buried, his grave covered over, life went on."

The veil of suspicion that had hung over Lerner was now lifted and Masetti's treatment of him improved. It was only many years later that he came to grips with the fact that he himself had come very close to becoming one of Masetti's victims. Lerner reflected on the fact that he, Miguel, Pupi, and Nardo were all Jews, and he wondered about Masetti's political origins as a student member of the ultranationalist and anti-Semitic Alianza Libertadora Nacionalista.

When Bustos arrived back in camp he was upset about Nardo, but there was little to be done about it. They had bigger problems. He told Masetti about Pirincho's desertion, but Masetti refused to believe him. Pirincho was one of his golden boys; he wouldn't desert. He knew Pirincho had a problem with his girlfriend—surely that was all it was—and Bustos had misunderstood him. He ordered Bustos to return to Buenos Aires and bring Pirincho back with him. But it was too late, and not only for Pirincho, who had, as promised, left for Europe and vanished. It was also too late for the Ejercito Guerrillero del Pueblo. A few days after Bustos left again for the city, five new volunteers arrived, forwarded by a dissident Communist Party cell in Buenos Aires. Two of them were undercover agents for the Argentine DIPA, the secret police. Their orders were to infiltrate the EGP, find its base, and return with information.

The DIPA agents' infiltration coincided with the *gendarmerías'* detection of the guerrillas' location. The group's supplier and courier in Salta, the young and cultured Enrique Bolini-Roca, had simply not been a believable provincial bookstore owner; he made too many unexplained trips out of town in his *camioneta,* and he was also too handsome for his own good. The local women chased him: he attracted attention. The gendarmes soon had the remote spot he drove to on the Salta-Orán road staked out. Now they sent their first reconnaissance patrol into the forest.

Almost immediately, the soldiers stumbled into a group of guerrillas at the small supply camp where provisions were stored before being dispatched up to the main group in the mountains. Among them were Castellanos, Lerner, Grillo Frontíni, and another guerrilla known as El Marqués. They claimed they were hunters, looking for wild turkeys in the bush. Nobody believed them. The two DIPA agents were also captured, but soon told the gendarmes their identity and what they had learned. More patrols were sent in, and gradually the EGP began to fall.

By April 18, Che's advance patrol had been liquidated. Hermes was dead, ambushed by a patrol at a peasant's house. With him died Jorge, a philosophy student; their peasant host; and one of the ambushing soldiers. The rest of the guerrillas split up and tried to find a way across the mountains. They climbed and climbed. Before long they were in the cloud forest high in the mountains, at an altitude of more than 10,000 feet. They had no food. They could barely see because of the fog. Three of the newcomers died of starvation in their sleep.

Masetti, barely able to walk because of his injured back, was with Oscar Atilio Altamirano, one of the Argentine recruits; Héctor Jouve; and Antonio Paul. He sent Héctor and Antonio back to find the others. As they climbed down the mountain, Antonio fell off a high cliff above a river; Héctor tried to catch him and fell, too. Antonio hit the rocks and broke his neck. Héctor hit the water. He crawled over to where Antonio lay, gave him an injection of morphine, and stayed with him until he died.

Within a few days the remaining survivors were captured. Bolini-Roca and other members of the urban underground were caught and arrested in Jujuy, Orán, and Buenos Aires. Bustos and the members of the Córdoba network went into hiding, fleeing into Uruguay. Abelardo Colomé Ibarra made it back to Cuba undetected.

Nothing more was heard of Masetti and Atilio. Gendarmes combed the forest for them but came back empty-handed. By the end of April, there were eighteen men in Orán's prison, among them Castellanos, Lerner, Frontíni, and Federico and Héctor Jouve. The group was hermetic and unrepentent. They acknowledged and defended their revolutionary goals, but kept silent about their Cuban links and even managed to keep the true identity of Che's bodyguard, Alberto Castellanos, a secret.

The Cuban connection was soon uncovered, however. Hermes's diary was found, and, from the slang terms he used, police were able to determine that the dead man had been a Cuban. The Argentine security forces checked the origin of the arms seized and learned that their Belgian FAL automatic rifles were from a shipment sold by Fabrique Nationale to Cuba. Some dollars found on the guerrillas were also traced back to Cuba. As for their Soviet-issue weapons, Cuba was the only country in the hemisphere that these could have come from.

The press speculated. Was Che Guevara the driving force behind the EGP? When Hermes Peña was revealed to have been one of his bodyguards, the connections were easily made. When the missing Comandante Segundo was identified as Jorge Ricardo Masetti and Che paid public homage to him as a "heroic revolutionary," the question became academic.

But neither Che nor anyone else involved in the adventure confirmed anything more specific than that. The whole episode of the "guerrillas of Salta" remained something of an enigma, a small incident that was quickly overtaken by larger, more dramatic events. Only a handful of people knew how important the episode had been to Che, or that Masetti's failure had altered the course of Che's life and of history.

Masetti was never found, and his surviving companions believe there are only three possible explanations regarding his fate. One theory is that when Masetti realized it was all over, he and Atilio committed suicide. The second is that they starved to death. The third is that the gendarmes did find them, stole the estimated $20,000 Masetti had in his possession, and then murdered both men to keep the secret.

Before long, the guerrillas were brought to trial. They had a good team of lawyers, including Grillo's father, Norberto Frontíni; a left-wing lawyer from Córdoba named Horacio Lonatti; Ricardo Rojo; and Gustavo Roca—but all the defendants received prison sentences, ranging from four to fourteen years. Federico Méndez was given the longest sentence for his role as the prosecutor in Nardo's execution; Héctor Jouve was given a dozen years for his part in the same trial. Castellanos and Lerner were each given sentences of five years. Their sentences would be appealed, but little could be done for them immediately.

Che was devastated and bewildered by the news of his *foco*'s nightmarish collapse. He learned about it while traveling in Europe, where he had gone to speak at the UN Conference on Trade and Development, which was held in Geneva at the end of March 1964. Afterward, he traveled to Paris, where Gustavo Roca met him and informed him of the unraveling disaster.* After stopping briefly in Algiers and Prague, he returned to Cuba, arriving on April 18, the same day Hermes was killed. As the weeks passed and Masetti wasn't found, Che knew he was probably dead. It was a personal tragedy as well as a major setback to his carefully laid plans to launch the armed struggle in Argentina. Not only had Che lost two of his closest disciples—Hermes and Masetti—but it was obvious that they hadn't heeded his warnings and had committed a number of errors that led to their discovery.

Few people realized the depth of Che's longing for his homeland. An Argentine journalist, Rosa María Oliver, thought she had caught a glimpse of his feelings during a conversation they had in February 1963. They had been sipping *mate* together and talking nostalgically about their country when suddenly Che struck his knee with his hand and exclaimed, almost imploringly, "Enough: Let's not talk about Argentina anymore."

---

*Gustavo Roca was a Marxist, the enfant terrible of an eminent conservative Córdoban clan, a cousin of Che's old love Chichina Ferreyra, and a friend of Che's since adolescence. Over the coming months and years, Roca did what he could to denounce the "human rights abuses" and anomalies in the sentences of the imprisoned guerrillas, but his most important role was as a personal courier between Che, the prisoners, and the surviving guerrilla underground network in Argentina.

"Why, if you love it so?" Oliver asked.

"For that very reason . . ."

Not long after the news of Masetti's disappearance, Alberto Granado went to see Che at his office. He looked depressed. Trying to cheer him up, Granado said, "Che, what's the matter, you've got the face of a dead dog." Che answered, "Petiso, here you see me, behind a desk, fucked, while my people die during missions I've sent them on."

Che continued talking, wondering out loud why Hermes, an experienced guerrilla, hadn't followed his instructions to keep on the move. The group's mistake had been to stay in one place long enough for the Argentine gendarmes to find them. Continual movement was a cardinal rule of guerrilla warfare, and Hermes should have known better, even if Masetti didn't. That was why Che had sent him along, to lend a guerrilla veteran's instincts and expertise to the mission, and it hadn't helped.

The failure of the guerrillas of Salta was a watershed for Che. Once again, "good" but inexperienced men had failed trying to test his theories of guerrilla warfare. It was plain that he would have to demonstrate personally that his ideas could work. Just as the Cuban revolution had been able to count upon Fidel as a figure to rally around and unite disparate revolutionary forces into an effective fighting machine, the success of the continental revolution depended upon the physical presence of a recognized leader, and he was it.

Che and Fidel in 1964.

26

The Long Good-Bye

I

By the summer of 1964, Che had resolved to leave Cuba and return to the revolutionary battlefield. Achieving this goal became his great obsession. He was no longer indispensable in Cuba. The revolution was probably as secure as it would ever be. Although there were still plenty of overflights by U-2 spy planes and counterrevolutionary activities sponsored by the CIA, it seemed unlikely that the Americans would attack anytime soon. In return for the withdrawal of the Soviet nuclear missiles, President Kennedy had promised not to invade. A promise could always be broken, but Lyndon Johnson had his hands full with acrimonious civil rights issues, the upcoming presidential race, and the escalating conflict in Vietnam.

Khrushchev now extolled Cuba as the "daughter" of the Soviet Union, and nobody chanted *"Nikita mariquita"* in public in Havana anymore. Soviet aid flowed more generously than ever to the island. This meant that Cuba was more dependent than ever on Moscow, and the political atmosphere, from Che's point of view, was becoming claustrophobic. Latin America's mainline Communist parties were furious about his export of the armed struggle to their countries. The Salta episode had outraged Victorio Codovilla, the Argentine Communist Party's venerable strongman, and he had vigorously condemned Masetti's *foco,* pointing out that the Communists involved were radicals who had been expelled from the Party. Needless to say, Peru's Communist Party and Mario Monje and his Bolivian comrades shared Codovilla's feelings. Like him, they had made their sentiments known in Moscow.

Despite Che's reassurances, the consensus in the Kremlin was that he was a Maoist, a dangerous extremist, a Trotskyite. Sergo Mikoyan was in Geneva when Che was there for the UN Conference on Trade and

Development, and he tried to arrange an informal get-acquainted meeting between Che and the Soviet foreign trade minister, Nikolai Patolichev. When Mikoyan went to Che's hotel, he noticed that there were Chinese agents in the lobby. Che was happy to see him, immediately agreed to the meeting with Patolichev, and then asked, "Did you see any Chinese downstairs?" When Mikoyan said he had, Che nodded. "In Moscow you think I'm China's agent or connected to them, but I'm not. The truth is they follow me around all the time." They were watching who went up and down the elevator to his floor.

But Che's protestations of innocence sounded disingenuous to most of the Soviet leadership. He had made no secret of his view that the Chinese displayed a truer socialist "morality" than the Soviets. His preference was well known among his aides. Orlando Borrego pointed out that the only Chinese technicians working in Cuba were attached to Che's ministry and worked for free, while the Soviets required salaries and housing, paid for out of the credits Moscow provided to Fidel's government. Che had allied himself time and again with the Chinese. Any attention he received from Beijing could be seen only as having been asked for.

The suspicion had cast a pall over his work in Cuba and his dealings with some of his closest comrades, even Raúl Castro. Since the days in Mexico and the sierra when Raúl had been Che's chief ally and had shown deference to him, their relationship had steadily deteriorated to the point of becoming adversarial. Some say that the turning point was the negotiations over the Soviet missiles in the summer of 1962, when Che had been called in to do "clean-up duty" after Raúl. As Che's own relations with Moscow soured, Raúl had become increasingly pro-Soviet and was reportedly given to cracking jokes about Che's being "China's man" in Cuba.

Che was also engaged in a fierce, if fraternal, ideological debate over the direction and control of Cuba's economy. He advocated a "budgetary finance system," whereby state-owned enterprises shared assets and resources communally instead of competing among themselves in the system of "state capitalism" practiced and advocated by the Soviet Union. His main opponents were Carlos Rafael Rodríguez, whom Fidel had put in charge of agriculture as the INRA chief; and Marcelo Fernández, Che's old July 26 sparring partner, who was now at the Ministry for Foreign Trade.

At the core of the ideological dispute was Che's insistence upon the application of "moral incentives" in addition to "material incentives." The system employed in the Soviet Union had grown out of the New Economic Policy (NEP) adopted by Lenin in 1924 as a way of jump-starting the stagnant Soviet economy after the civil war. It allowed for capitalist forms of competition between factories and individual workers as a means of increasing production. Che believed that the system prevented workers from achieving a true socialist regard for their labor, a regard that only moral incentives could achieve. This was the impetus behind his volunteer labor scheme, which was meant to demonstrate willingness to sacrifice for the common good.

Also at issue was the direction of Cuba's economy. Che's dream of bringing about rapid industrialization in Cuba had soon bogged down. He accepted part of the blame himself for having moved too fast, with an unprepared workforce and insufficient resources, but there were other factors beyond his control: incompetence, lack of technical expertise, and often the poor quality of equipment and materials imported from the Soviet bloc. By mid-1964, with the new Soviet-Cuban sugar deal, and Khrushchev's offer to help invent a cane-cutting machine to mechanize Cuba's sugar harvests, it was fairly clear that agriculture, not industry, was what the future held for Cuba—and this undercut Che's dream of creating the New Socialist Man.

Finally, Che was not a Cuban but an Argentine, and although he never said so publicly, he must have felt that Cuba was "their" country, after all. He had trained loyal cadres who believed in his methods, and they could carry on the battle in his absence; but it was time for him to leave the scene. Perhaps Che was also becoming aware of his age. He was now almost thirty-six; he could still march and fight and lead men. If he waited much longer, it would be too late. The question was, where would he go?

II

The clandestine guerrilla infrastructure in South America had been shaken but not shattered by the fiasco in Salta. With the exception of Alberto Castellanos, the Bolivians and Cubans who were involved had come out unscathed, as had the urban underground in Córdoba, Buenos Aires, and other Argentine cities. Most of the damage had been limited to the guerrillas themselves and to their immediate support network in Salta. Even as Masetti's column collapsed, Che had deployed an important new asset: Tania, as Tamara Bunke was now known. She had adopted the nom de guerre when a mission was proposed to her by Barbarroja Piñeiro in the spring of 1963. She selected the name in honor of the Soviet guerrilla fighter Zoja Kosmodemjanskaja, aka Tania, who was captured, tortured, and hanged by the Nazis in 1941.

When Tania had finished her espionage training, in March 1964, Che summoned her to his office at the Ministry of Industries. One of Piñeiro's top agents, whose pseudonym was Renán Montero, was with him. Renán had participated in several missions, including the ill-fated Nicaraguan guerrilla expedition with Rodolfo Romero in 1959. Che informed Tania that he wanted her to go to Bolivia, to be his deep-cover agent there. She would establish a false identity and become acquainted with as many of the country's leaders as she could. She would remain indefinitely, to be activated when the right moment came. According to Piñeiro, Tania had been selected for Bolivia because, among her other talents, she spoke German, which would be useful for penetrating Bolivia's influential German émigré community. He said she was not informed that Che eventually planned to join her there.

Tania left the meeting with a feeling of pride; Che had recognized her merits and assigned her a vital role in the continental revolution. Shortly afterward, she left Cuba in disguise to travel around Western Europe and acquaint herself with places associated with her false identity, her *leyenda*. For about six months, Tania traveled under various passports and different assumed identities that had been concocted for her by her Cuban handlers. She journeyed to West Germany and Italy, but spent most of her time at various safe houses in Czechoslovakia. Eventually, it was decided that she would "become" Laura Gutiérrez Bauer, an Argentine who had lived for some years in Germany.

Following the meeting with Tania, Che summoned Ciro Bustos to Havana for a debriefing and to issue him new instructions. Since the Masetti debacle, Bustos had been engaged in mopping up while waiting for his marching orders. With the help of the academics in Córdoba, he had put together the legal defense team for the prisoners and had smuggled Abelardo Colomé Ibarra and two other conspirators, "Petíso" Bellomo and Héctor Jouve's brother Emilio, to Montevideo, Uruguay, where he rented a safe house.

Most significantly, Bustos had orchestrated the transfer of arms to two independent groups from the weapons caches intended for the Salta *foco*. One of the groups was the Argentine Trotskyite splinter faction of Vasco Bengochea, which intended to open a new *foco* in Tucumán province, and the other was a nascent group led by Raúl Sendíc, the leader of the Uruguayan *cañeros,* a leftist movement of sugarcane cutters. Bustos's meeting with the latter was cloaked in clandestine drama. "Sendíc asked to meet with me through some contacts of Petíso Bellomo," Bustos recalled. "The meeting took place one Sunday afternoon on a beach of El Cerro, on the industrial outskirts of Montevideo. He was disguised as a poor old fisherman and I as a solitary stroller. Beyond, not far away, some youths—his guys—played soccer on the beach. A little closer, was *el gordo* Emilio, Héctor's brother, serving as my backup 'fisherman.' Sendíc questioned me extensively on the reasons for the Salta failure and asked me for two things: a training course in security and some 'irons' [arms]."

Bustos agreed to train one of Sendíc's men in the basics of security and espionage. (Three decades later, Bustos observed with some irony that his student had become a well-known and respected economist working for the Uruguayan government.) He also authorized Emilio to transfer part of the EGP's arms cache in Uruguay to Sendíc's group. Bustos's decision to aid the Uruguayans was much more significant than he realized at the time. From this humble beginning, Sendíc's organization soon became renowned as the sophisticated Tupamaro urban guerrilla movement, whose actions would shake Uruguayan society to the core.

For his meeting in Havana with Che, Bustos traveled with Pancho Aricó, editor of *Pasado y Presente* and the ideological mentor of the Córdoba support group. Aricó was the only one of the group who had gone to see Masetti in the mountains. Since then he had become convinced—as had his colleagues, Oscar del Barco and Héctor "Toto" Schmucler—that Che's *foco* theory wouldn't work in Argentina. "Pancho went to Cuba to see Che, carrying our critical views, that we thought the rural guerrilla thing wouldn't work tactically," Schmucler recalled. "But when he got there, he couldn't open his mouth. Che talked for two or three hours, and Pancho didn't say anything." Afterward, Aricó told his friends that once he was sitting in front of Che, he was overcome by the force of Che's presence and arguments and was too intimidated to contradict anything. "It was *Che,*" he said.

Bustos, who met with Che several times to go over what had happened in Salta and to decide on a new plan of action, had a similar story. Che said he could not fathom why some of the men had starved to death. Bustos tried to explain the conditions of the jungle around Orán, an area with virtually no peasants and no food; the difficulties of hunting, how at one point the guerrillas had shot a tapir but found it impossible to eat because the meat simply decomposed. "When I told him that, Che said no, they should have boiled it longer, so that the acids converted or something, and then it would have been fine."

Che believed firmly that the creation of a rural guerrilla *foco* was possible if it were done correctly. Bustos had his doubts, but unlike Aricó he had not lost all hope. Any new attempt, he felt, should concentrate on building up infrastructure, spread out over several zones to ensure survival. The guerrillas couldn't expect to live off the land by hunting; nor could they rely, as Masetti's group had, on a flow of canned goods from the city, with pickup trucks coming and going suspiciously in a pattern that ultimately alerted the police. They needed to blend into an area and be as self-sufficent as possible. Bustos said that Che agreed with him. "He told me: 'Tie things up well here, then go back and put your plan in action. Start working with the people. Make use of the [Communist and Peronist] splinter groups, and let's

see what develops.'" Bustos understood that he was to work with which-
ever group was willing to embark on the armed struggle, and simultaneously
to try to forge a coordinated national guerrilla front. There was to be no
politico-military commander named for now, no imminent call-up to the
mountains. The preparatory work was of indefinite duration.

One very big obstacle to all this was going to be money. Bustos said
that Che didn't give him a budget as such but did provide him with "some
help." They discussed fund-raising, and Bustos mentioned an "expropriations" strategy advocated by some of his action-minded comrades: robbing
banks. It was the same proposal Che had made when he arrived to take
command of the revolutionary forces in Las Villas in late 1958, but this was
a different situation; Cuba had been in a full-fledged state of civil war, and
Che had been in command personally. Conditions weren't the same in Argentina, and he didn't want things to get out of hand there before the insurrection had taken root. Che ruled out the bank robbery scheme. "Not at this
stage," he told Bustos. "If you start out by robbing banks you end up as a
bank robber."

Before leaving, Bustos saw Colomé Ibarra, Ariel, and Papi, and they
worked out logistics: entry lines and contact points for receiving and sending messages, people, and money to and from Havana. Uruguay, one of the
last countries in Latin America to maintain diplomatic relations with Cuba,
would remain their relay station for the time being.

On May 20, while he was still in Cuba, Bustos received a cable informing him of an explosion on Calle Posadas in downtown Buenos Aires. Vasco
Bengochea and four of his men had been making bombs on the sixth floor
of an apartment building and had blown themselves to pieces. That was the
end of the Tucumán group. It was another setback, but Bustos recalled that
Che seemed fairly unperturbed about the incident.

After Bustos's departure, Che and Fidel had a temporary falling-out
over strategy. In the midst of sharpening language from the Johnson administration, which tightened trade sanctions and renewed measures by the
OAS to isolate Cuba, Fidel embarked on an appeasement offensive. In July,
he gave a series interviews to a correspondent for *The New York Times,*
Richard Eder, in which he obliquely offered to end Cuba's support for Latin
America's revolutionary movements if the hostilities against Cuba ceased.
For Fidel, it was a matter of realpolitik. He had learned his lesson in the art
of quid pro quo the hard way by watching Khrushchev during and after
the missile crisis. (Khrushchev had pursued talks with Washington and
signed a nuclear test–ban treaty in August 1963.) Fidel hinted strongly to
Eder that he had received advice from the Soviet Union for his gesture, and
he made it clear that he hoped Johnson would defeat the conservative Re-

publican, Senator Barry Goldwater, in the upcoming presidential election. He looked forward to resuming with Johnson the exploratory talks about détente that had begun with John Kennedy.

The day after Fidel's remarks were published, the State Department released a statement flatly rejecting his olive branch. There could be no negotiations with Cuba as long as it was tied to the Soviet Union and continued to "promote subversion in Latin America." Fidel maintained an unusually diplomatic silence despite the rebuff. He even managed to avoid provocation when, on July 19, a Cuban soldier was killed by a gunshot fired by an American from within the Guantánamo base. Raúl spoke at the huge funeral that was held for the dead man and made clear that he was following his brother's cue. The shot fired, he said, was aimed at Cuba and at President Johnson and against the cause of peace. If Goldwater was elected, there would be war.

Within a few days, however, Che made his own uncompromising views public. On July 24, speaking at a factory in Santa Clara, he reminded his listeners that it was their common duty to fight imperialism "whenever it appears and with all the weapons at our disposal." It didn't matter, he said, who the Americans elected as their president; the enemy was the same. This was the closest Che had ever come to a public rebuttal of the doctrine espoused by *el jefe máximo,* and if Fidel took him to task, he did so behind closed doors. Two days later, the OAS voted to impose mandatory sanctions on Cuba and ordered all those member states that had not severed ties with Cuba to do so. One holdout, Brazil, had already broken off relations in May, and now the stragglers followed suit. In August, Bolivia and Chile broke off ties; they were followed in September by Uruguay. Mexico was the only nation that refused to go along with the ruling.

On July 26, as Washington enjoyed its victory, Fidel reiterated his offer of détente. In return for a normalization of relations with its neighbors, Cuba was willing to live within accepted "norms of international law." If attaining peace meant giving up Cuba's "material aid to other revolutionaries," so be it, as long as the gesture was reciprocated. Leaving no doubt that his overture was within the framework of the Soviet Union's existing foreign policy of peaceful coexistence, he concluded, "Our position is that we are disposed to live in peace with all the countries, all the states, of this continent, irrespective of social systems. We are disposed to live under a system of international norms to be complied with on an equal basis by all countries."

That was Fidel's carrot to the Americans, and then came the face-saving stick: "The people of Cuba warn that if the pirate attacks proceeding from North American territory and other countries of the Caribbean basin do not cease, . . . as well as the dispatch of agents, arms, and explosives to

Cuban territory, the people of Cuba will consider that they have an equal right to aid with all the resources at their command the revolutionary movements in all those countries that engage in similar intervention in the internal affairs of our Fatherland." There was no question that Fidel was gingerly offering terms for peace, but, as with Che's overture at Punta del Este in 1961, his gesture was perceived by U.S. policy makers as a sign of weakness, and once again they spurned it. Fidel's placating speech and the OAS ruling put the Americans in a triumphalist mood. The pressure on Cuba was showing results, and by keeping it up they could finally finish Castro off.

They were, of course, quite wrong. Fidel returned to the path of confrontation advocated so unstintingly by Che. Outside events greatly aided his turnaround. On August 5, American planes began bombing North Vietnam in retaliation for alleged attacks by Hanoi's gunboats against American naval forces in the Gulf of Tonkin. Two days later, Congress gave Johnson the green light to escalate U.S. military involvement in Vietnam. The Vietnam War, as it would become known to the Americans, had begun in earnest. Cuba issued a ringing denunciation of the American bombing, calling for unity in the global socialist camp to defend Vietnam against "Yankee imperialist aggression." The crisis in Vietnam afforded a grand opportunity to repair the socialist fraternity that had been damaged by the feud between China and the Soviet Union.

On August 15, at an awards ceremony for outstanding Communist workers who had set records for volunteer labor, Che reassured Cubans that, for all their increased isolation, they were now part of an expanding international community of revolutionary states. In those Latin American nations that had aligned themselves with Washington's policy of containment, revolutionary armed struggles would triumph and extend the socialist alliance still farther. "It does not matter if these are the times when the bad winds blow," Che said, "when the threats increase from day to day, when the pirate attacks are unleashed against us and against other countries of the world. It does not matter if we are threatened with Johnson or Goldwater . . . it does not matter that every day imperialism is more aggressive. The people have decided to fight for their liberty and to keep the liberty they have won. They will not be intimidated by anything. And together we shall build a new life, together—because we are together—we here in Cuba, in the Soviet Union, or over there in the People's Republic of China, or in Vietnam fighting in southern Asia."

Che reminded his audience that in Latin America, there were two revolutionary struggles—in Guatemala and Venezuela—which were making progress, "inflicting defeat after defeat on imperialism." Throughout Africa, national liberation movements were ascendant. In the former Belgian Congo, the inheritors of Patrice Lumumba's revolutionary example were still fighting and would inevitably win. In the Portuguese colony of Guinea, the liberation army led by Amilcar Cabral already controlled half the national territory—soon, it too would be free, as would Angola. Zanzibar had recently won its independence, and Che unrepentantly acknowledged that Cuba had played a part in that happy outcome. "Zanzibar is our friend and we gave them our small bit of assistance, our fraternal assistance, our revolutionary assistance at the moment when it was necessary."

But Che was now ready to go farther than he ever had before in public. He invoked the specter of an atomic apocalypse. He said it was a real prospect, given the inevitability of confrontation between the "liberation movements" and the "forces of imperialism," which could unleash a nuclear war through an error of calculation. "Thousands of people will die everywhere, but the responsibility will be theirs [the imperialists], and their people will also suffer. . . . But that should not worry us. . . . We as a nation know we can depend upon the great strength of all the countries of the world that make up the socialist bloc and of the peoples who fight for their liberation, and on the strength and cohesion of our people, on the decision to fight to the last man, to the last woman, to the last human being capable of holding a gun."

If anyone had missed his point, which he had reiterated and refined over time, Che had said it again, in starker terms. The global battle against imperialism was a struggle between two diametrically opposed historical forces, and there was no sense in protracting the people's agony through doomed attempts to forge tactical short-term alliances with the enemy. The root causes of the problems would remain and inevitably lead to conflict. Moderation ran the risk of giving the enemy an opening where he could seize an advantage. History, science, and justice were on the side of socialism; therefore, it must wage the necessary war to win, whatever the consequences —including nuclear war. Che did not shrink from that outcome, and he was telling others they should not, either. Many would die in the revolutionary process, but the survivors would emerge from the ashes of destruction to create a new, just world order.

For all this to take place, the emergence of the "new socialist man" was essential. A true revolutionary consciousness was the crucial ingredient to bring about a new society. He had begun his speech by quoting from a poem by the Spaniard León Felipe, describing the tragedy of human toil. "No one has been able to dig the rhythm of the sun, . . . no one has yet cut an ear of corn with love and grace":

I quote these words because today we could tell that great desperate poet to come to Cuba to see how man, after passing through all the

stages of capitalist alienation, and after being considered a beast of
burden harnessed to the yoke of the exploiter, has rediscovered his
way and has found his way back to play. Today in our Cuba, everyday work takes on new meaning. It is done with new happiness.

And we could invite him to our cane fields so that he might
see our women cut the cane with love and grace, so that he might
see the virile strength of our workers, cutting the cane with love,
so that he might see a new attitude toward work, so that he might
see that what enslaves man is not work but rather his failure to
possess the means of production.

When society arrives at a certain stage of development and
is capable of initiating the harsh struggle, of destroying the oppres-
sive power, of destroying its strong arm—the army—and of taking power, then man once again regains the old sense of happiness
in work, the happiness of fulfilling a duty, of feeling himself important within the social mechanism.

He becomes happy to feel himself a cog in the wheel, a cog
that has its own characteristics and is necessary, though not indispensable, to the production process, a conscious cog, a cog that has
its own motor, and that consciously tries to push itself harder and
harder to carry to a happy conclusion one of the premises of the
construction of socialism—creating a sufficient quantity of consumer goods for the entire population.

Che's habit of referring to the people, the workers, as bits of machinery affords a glimpse of his emotional distance from individual reality. He
had the coldly analytical mind of a medical researcher and a chess player.
The terms he employed for individuals were reductive, while the value of
their labor in the social context was idealized, rendered lyrically. It was a
conceptual mode that had parallels in his life. Che had found meaning in
his identity as a revolutionary within the large family of socialism. Fraternal guerrilla life was the crucible of his own transformation. The Communist consciousness he had attained was an elusive, abstract, and even
unwanted state of being for many people, however—even those who believed themselves to be socialists and who happily echoed his shout, "Freedom or Death." Willingness to sacrifice material comforts and life itself for
the cause was a state of mind most men and women had not achieved, and
they probably had little interest in trying. Also, of course, the happy global
socialist fraternity of which he spoke was in fact a house bitterly divided.

In Cuba itself, the ill feeling caused by the purging of "sectarianism"
had officially been put to rest after Fidel's rapprochement with the Soviet

Union, but it had not gone away. Aníbal Escalante was moldering in exile in Moscow, but some of his comrades retained influence with Fidel. The previous March, while Che was in Geneva, a former PSP man named Marcos Rodríguez went on trial after being accused of having betrayed some of his comrades to Batista's police in 1957. Because of Rodríguez's links to senior "old Communists," the event at first took on the appearance of a purge trial. Fidel intervened, and a new trial was held. The honor of the Communists was restored, and Marcos Rodríguez—now portrayed as a twisted, resentful loner—was executed by firing squad.

Che had managed to avoid any association with the unsavory proceedings. His distaste for the Communist Party's sectarianism was well known, and he had consistently made a home at the Ministry of Industries for purged or disgraced revolutionaries, whether they were victims of the old Communists' chauvinism or casualties of Fidel's own sometimes fickle purges. He had helped Enrique Oltuski, his old July 26 rival, after Oltuski was ousted as communications minister under Communist pressure in 1961. And he had removed Jorge Masetti from harm's way after Masetti alienated the PSP faction at Prensa Latina. Alberto Mora, the son of one of the martyrs of the Directorio's assault on the palace, became an adviser at the ministry when he was ousted by Fidel as the minister of foreign commerce in mid-1964, even though Mora was one of the most outspoken critics of Che's economic policies.

Another recipient of Che's assistance was the poet and writer Heberto Padilla, who was an old friend of Alberto Mora's. Padilla had worked in the New York and London offices of Prensa Latina and in Havana for *Revolución* under Carlos Franqui and for its now defunct literary supplement, *Lunes de Revolución,* which was edited by the novelist Guillermo Cabrera Infante. Perceived as troublesome nonconformists in Cuba's increasingly repressive intellectual climate, Franqui and Cabrera Infante had been sent into diplomatic exile in Europe. Padilla had just finished a stint at the Spanish-language edition of the Soviet magazine *Moscow News* and was well aware of the intrigues and authoritarianism that had begun to stifle cultural freedom in Cuba. In spite of his own doubts and Franqui's warnings, Padilla decided to go home. Mora arranged for him to meet with Che, who was an admirer of his poetry. Mora was still minister of foreign commerce then and was engaged in a collegial dispute with Che over the economy. Since Padilla had returned with a jaundiced view of what he had seen in the Soviet Union, Mora wanted him to speak to Che.

Padilla and Mora found Che in the midst of a bout of asthma; he was shirtless and prostrate on the floor of his office, trying to regulate his breathing, and he remained there as his visitors began talking. He cut off Padilla's critical appraisal of the Soviet Union right away, saying, "I must tell you I don't need to listen to what you have to say because I already know all of that is a pigsty. I saw it myself." Che said that China, not Russia, was the model to be studied. The Chinese were making a genuine effort toward the realization of Communism. "Many people criticize me because they say I put too much emphasis on sacrifice, but sacrifice is fundamental to a Communist education," he said. "The Chinese understand that very well, much better than the Russians do."

At the end of their talk, Che urged Mora to give Padilla a job in the ministry of foreign commerce. "These are not good times for journalism," he remarked laconically. Padilla became the director general of a department that dealt with cultural matters. When Mora was fired and arranged to leave Cuba on a grant to study political economy with the French Marxist economist Charles Bettelheim (with whom Che had also been debating economic theory), Padilla also arranged to leave, obtaining a post as a roving emissary for the ministry, based in Prague.

Before they left, Padilla and Mora went to see Che again. Mora was unhappy and couldn't conceal it. He explained that he felt depressed when he woke up in the morning. "Che walked up to Alberto slowly," Padilla recalled, "put his hands on his shoulders, and shook him, looking straight into his eyes. 'I live like someone torn in two, twenty-four hours a day, completely torn in two, and I haven't got anybody to tell it to. Even if I did, they would never believe me.'"*

It was a poignant moment of personal revelation for Che, a rare expression of the incredible stress he endured to maintain the persona of an exemplary Communist revolutionary. His father, usually so myopic about Che, had nonetheless perceived this when he wrote that "Ernesto had brutalized his own sensitivities" to become a revolutionary. His mother once told the Uruguayan journalist Eduardo Galeano that from the time of his asthmatic childhood, her son "had always lived trying to prove to himself that he could do everything he couldn't do, and in that way he had polished his amazing willpower." Celia told Galeano that she teased Che for being "intolerant and fanatical," and explained that his actions were "motivated

*Both Padilla and Mora suffered unhappy fates. Mora never recovered from his fall from grace, and he committed suicide by shooting himself in the head in 1972. That same year, after his arrest by State Security, Padilla was put through the humiliating ritual of a public "confession" by the Cuban Writers' Union for alleged crimes as a "counterrevolutionary author." He endured imprisonment, house arrest, and years of official harassment and ostracism before finally being allowed to leave Cuba. He died in Alabama, where he was teaching at Auburn University, in 2000.

by a tremendous necessity for totality and purity." "Thus," Galeano wrote, "he had become the most puritanical of the Western revolutionary leaders. In Cuba, he was the Jacobin of the revolution: 'Watch out, here comes Che,' warned the Cubans, joking but serious at the same time. All or nothing: this refined intellectual must have waged exhausting battles against his own doubt-nagged conscience."

Galeano met with Che in August 1964 and thought he noted symptoms of impatience. "Che was not a desk-man," he said. "He was a creator of revolutions. He was not, or was in spite of himself, an administrator. Somehow, that tension of a caged lion that his apparent calm betrayed had to explode. He needed the sierra." Galeano may have written this appraisal with the benefit of hindsight, but it was accurate nonetheless. As they spoke, Che was searching for a way back to the battlefield, even as he worked himself to the point of exhaustion on Cuba's industrial economy.

Several possibilities existed. Besides the insurgent groups in Guatemala, Venezuela, and Nicaragua, there was now a Cuban-backed guerrilla organization in Colombia, the Ejercito de Liberación Nacional, which had been formed in July. In Peru, Héctor Béjar's guerrilla force and Luis de la Puente Uceda's MIR were both preparing for revolutionary action. But Che had his heart set on the Southern Cone and his Argentine homeland. That posed a problem, for Ciro Bustos and his comrades had a lot of work to do before conditions would be ready for a new attempt at insurrection in this region, and Tania was still traveling in Europe, en route to her post in Bolivia.

Probably the most promising of the potential battlegrounds for the immediate future lay in Africa. All over the continent, rebel movements had formed to do battle with the last colonial holdouts: in the Portuguese colonies of Angola and Mozambique, in white-ruled South Africa, and in the former Belgian Congo. In October 1963, an antigovernment coalition calling itself the National Liberation Council had been formed by a potpourri of former Lumumbist government officials and disaffected regional, often tribally based, strongmen. The council had offices across the Congo River from Léopoldville in the city of Brazzaville, the capital of the Republic of the Congo, formerly French Equatorial Africa. The rebels had managed to attract Chinese and some Soviet aid, and they had sparked revolts in southern, eastern, central, and northern Congo, seizing provincial towns and huge portions of the ill-defended national territory. One Chinese-backed rebel column had seized the distant northern city of Stanleyville in August 1964 and declared a People's Republic of the Congo. By September, the stage was set for a renewed escalation of the Congolese crisis as the government struggled to respond to the rebellion. The ambitious trio that ruled the Congo—Moise Tshombe, President Joseph Kasavubu, and Joseph Mobutu,

commander in chief of the armed forces—took action to bolster their thread-
bare army's fighting strength. They called in the South African mercenary
commander Mike Hoare and asked him to recruit a thousand white fighters from South Africa and Rhodesia.

The African resistance struggles, and particularly the Congolese conflict, had been featured more and more prominently in the Cuban press and
in Che's speeches. In fact, Che had begun to seriously consider temporarily
transplanting his program for continental revolution to the African continent. Barbarroja Piñeiro's agency was given the task of preparing the way.
Although Che had reserved his decision about the best base for a pan-African
guerrilla struggle until he could tour the area and meet with the various
guerrilla leaders himself, the huge Congo, in the middle of the continent,
seemed to offer a perfect setting and conditions for a rurally based guerrilla
war that could "radiate" out to its neighbors.

There were other advantages to fighting in Africa. The Soviets were
less concerned about direct involvement there than in Washington's backyard, Latin America; and the nature of the wars, against foreign, white colonial regimes—or in the Congo's case, against a Western-backed dictator
with little political legitimacy—gave them widespread popular support.
Finally, the continent was already inflamed with conflict; it was not a situation that had to be "created," as had been the case with Masetti's ill-fated
mission to Argentina. The Soviets, the Chinese, and the Americans and their
Western allies were all involved in Africa, providing money, arms, and
advisers. There were also a number of anti-imperialist national leaders
friendly to Cuba whose strategically placed territories could provide invaluable rearguard bases, transshipment points, and access to the zones of conflict. In addition to the regimes holding power in Mali and in Brazzaville,
they included Ben Bella in Algeria, Sekou Touré in Guinea, Kwame
Nkrumah in Ghana, Julius Nyerere in Tanzania, and Gamal Abdel Nasser
in Egypt. These "radical" states were outraged at the specter of white mercenaries and "neocolonial" Western powers intervening on behalf of the
Léopoldville regime, and they openly supported the rebel government at
Stanleyville.

Che saw an opportunity to pursue a long-held dream: to build a Cuban-
led international anti-imperialist alliance to replace the ineffectual Afro-
Asian People's Solidarity Organization, which was based in Cairo. Such an
alliance would give a global dimension to his scheme for the upcoming continental revolution in Latin America. In an ideal world, the alliance would
come under Fidel's political direction, and be bankrolled and armed by the
two socialist superpowers, China and the U.S.S.R. He envisioned repairing
the Sino-Soviet split through the shared burden of waging war.

Throughout the autumn of 1964, Che honed this idea, and he obtained Fidel's approval to travel abroad and take soundings. The notion of projecting himself internationally had always appealed to Fidel, and after his rebuff by the Americans, he had become newly receptive to Che's position. While trying not to appear to take Beijing's side, he once again questioned the value of toeing the Kremlin's line on peaceful coexistence; so far, it had brought him precious little.

In September, the OAS had pushed through yet another resolution, further tightening commercial sanctions against Cuba. The attacks by the CIA-backed Cuban exiles had also intensified. Hijackings, sabotage, and armed commando raids against Cuban shipping were now taking place with alarming frequency. On September 24, a seaborne CIA action team based in Nicaragua attacked the Spanish freighter *Sierra de Aránzazu* as it sailed toward Cuba with a cargo of industrial equipment. The Spanish captain and two crew members were killed in the raid, and the ship was set ablaze and disabled. The incident caused an international outcry and recriminations within the CIA, especially when it was learned that the raiders had attacked the freighter by mistake, believing it was the Cuban merchant marine ship *Sierra Maestra*. The agent back at the base who had authorized the attack was Felix Rodríguez.

Since late 1963, Rodríguez had been in charge of communications for a brigade of anti-Castro commandos based in Nicaragua. They were led by Manuel Artime and bankrolled by the CIA. The group had more than 300 active members scattered across Nicaragua, Miami, and Costa Rica. It was a well-supplied operation. The exiles had at their disposal two 250-foot mother ships, two fifty-foot fast boats, and other craft, as well as a C-47 transport plane, several Cessnas, and a Beaver floatplane. They had a refueling and resupply facility in the Dominican Republic, and for weaponry they could take what they needed from their 200-ton arms cache in Costa Rica, which included 20mm antiaircraft cannon, 50mm and 75mm recoilless rifles, and .50-caliber machine guns. In two years, Rodríguez later claimed, the commandos expended about $6 million in CIA funds and carried out fourteen raids against Cuban targets, one of the most successful being a commando strike against the Cabo Cruz sugar refinery—not far from where the *Granma* had landed—that inflicted serious damage.

By late 1964, however, the operation's budget had been cut back as the Johnson administration's priorities shifted from Cuba to Vietnam. The death knell came after the embarrassing attack on the *Sierra de Aranzazu*. "We subsequently discovered that the ship was carrying a boiler for a Cuban sugarcane facility as well as some Christmas foodstuffs," Rodríguez wrote. "We felt terrible. Soon after the incident, our operations were rolled up. Our

fast boats were taken by the agency and sent to Africa, where they saw service in the Congo. Some of the people who served with me in Nicaragua
volunteered to fight in Africa too." Rodríguez returned to Miami, where
he resumed his work for the CIA.

<h1 style="text-align:center">III</h1>

When Che flew to Moscow from Havana on November 4, 1964, Raúl Castro,
Foreign Minister Raúl Roa, and Emilio Aragonés were at the airport to see
him off. The presence of the chief of Cuba's armed forces, its foreign minister, and the secretary of its official ruling party, the Partido Unificado de
la Revolución Socialista, had great symbolic significance. Once again, Che
was to be the revolution's anointed emissary to the *madre patria* of world
socialism. He headed the Cuban delegation to the forty-seventh-anniversary
celebration of the Bolshevik revolution in Moscow and the opening of the
new Soviet-Cuban Friendship House. Aleida was also there to say good-
bye, along with two of their children. She was visibly swollen, six months
into her fourth pregnancy.

Che's final visit to Moscow came exactly three years after his first. Once
again, he stood in Red Square in a wintry November, but things were different this time. He was not the uncritical Che of 1961, full of hope about
the rosy future of Soviet-Cuban relations; too much contaminated water had
gone under the bridge. A great deal had changed within the Soviet Union
as well. Nikita Khrushchev, discredited by his economic failures at home
and his perceived reckless adventurism abroad—most notably the Cuban
missile crisis—had been ousted from power a few weeks earlier, and Leonid
Brezhnev was the new premier.

There was another reason for Che's visit. Reportedly at the behest of
the Argentine Communist Party chief, Victorio Codovilla, who was still
incensed over Masetti's incursion, the Kremlin had pushed for a first Latin
American Communist Party conference, to be held later that month in
Havana. The Soviet Union's decision to support the conference had a double
significance. On the one hand, it deferred to Fidel, indicating the Kremlin's
recognition of his regional stature; on the other hand, the gesture came with
an implicit expectation that Fidel would put together a pro-Soviet alliance
of regional parties and further isolate Beijing. The Chinese had taken their
dispute with Moscow to new levels lately, aggressively pursuing adherence
to the Maoist line. In January 1964, Peru's Communist Party had been severely weakened after pro-Beijing members broke away to form a rival
party; in Bolivia and Colombia similar factional splits were looming; and in

Guatemala, a Trotskyite faction was emerging that would soon split the guerrilla coalition backed by Cuba.

It was a good time for Che to test the intentions of the new Soviet leadership. He and Fidel were both in a challenging mood. In Cairo in October, at a conference of the new nonaligned countries' association, Fidel's spokesman, President Dorticos, had said that although Cuba supported the Soviet Union's policy of peaceful coexistence as a means of reducing the risk of a nuclear "world conflagration," the policy was worthless while "imperialist aggression against small countries" was taking place. A show of greater solidarity with its Third World partners was needed from the Kremlin, given the escalating intervention by the United States and its Western allies in Southeast Asia, in the Congo, and in the counterinsurgency campaigns in Latin America.

In Moscow, Che made a pro forma appearance in Red Square and cohosted the inauguration of the new Friendship House with the cosmonaut Yuri Gagarin. He also conducted a series of secret meetings with Kremlin officials. He did not have Nikolai Leonov as his interpreter this time. The KGB had reassigned Leonov to Mexico, where he was involved in aiding the Guatemalan guerrillas, among other duties.* Oleg Darushenkov, Che's translator in Cuba, and another Soviet intelligence official, Rudolf Petrovich Shlyapnikov, alternated as his interpreters during this stay. Shlyapnikov worked under Yuri Andropov in the Cuba section of the Central Committee's International Department and was a specialist in Latin American Communist Youth groups; he had been to Cuba on several missions and had met Che previously. During Che's visit to Moscow, Shlyapnikov said, the two of them would sit on the stairs of the protocol house where Che had been installed, playing chess and talking late into the night. Che drank milk and Shlyapnikov drank cognac.† According to Shlyapnikov, Che met with Andropov and Vitali Korionov, the deputy chief of the Soviet Central Committee's Americas Department. Korionov's brief was to handle relations with the Communist parties in capitalist countries, which included all the Latin American parties except Cuba's.

Korionov had received bitter complaints—specifically from Mario Monje in Bolivia and Jesús Faria in Venezuela—about the pressure the Cuban regime was putting on their Parties to enlist in the Cuban "continental revolution" scheme of guerrilla warfare. The Bolivians had formally

*See Notes.

†See Notes.

voted against such an idea, and the Venezuelan Communist Party was re-considering its involvement in the Cuban-backed FALN guerrilla coalition.* Korionov understood Che and Fidel to be proposing nothing less than a modern-day version of the epic liberation wars waged by José de San Martín and Simón Bolívar more than a century earlier. Marxist armies of the northern countries of Venezuela, Colombia, and Ecuador were to sweep south like Bolívar's troops, while those of the south—Chile, Peru, Uruguay, and Argentina—marched north the way San Martín's armies had. Bolivia would be the meeting ground.

According to Korionov, Che wanted to know Moscow's view of the policies of the Latin American parties and was told bluntly that since the Kremlin's official position was to "respect" the regional Communist parties, it was against the Cuban initiative regarding armed struggle. Korionov concluded that Che was determined to push ahead with his plans nevertheless, that he distrusted the Kremlin's policy of peaceful coexistence, and that he was on the Chinese side of the Sino-Soviet schism.

In Havana later in the month, Che's response to the Communist Party Congress convened there could hardly have been heartening, either to the Latin American parties or to the Soviet leadership. He was conspicuously absent from the weeklong forum, traveling instead to Oriente. But he did not remain silent. On November 30, he gave a speech in Santiago castigating Latin America's Communist parties for their reluctance to pursue the path to power.

The Congo also featured prominently in Che's speech; just a few days earlier the Lumumbist revolutionaries had been ousted from their stronghold at Stanleyville by Belgian paratroopers flown in on American planes. Che characterized the "massacres" committed in Stanleyville as an example of "imperialist bestiality . . . a bestiality which knows no frontiers nor belongs to a certain country. Just as the Hitlerian hordes were beasts, so are the Americans and Belgian paratroopers beasts today, as were yesterday the French imperialists beasts in Algeria, because it is the very nature of imperialism which bestializes man, which converts them into bloodthirsty wild animals willing to slit throats, commit murder, and destroy even the last image of a revolutionary or the ally of a regime which has fallen under its boot or struggles for his liberty."

After his speech, Che took Aleida to see Alberto Granado and his wife, Delia, and they all went out to eat pizza at the Fontana de Trevi restaurant.

*Within a few months, in April 1965, the Venezuelan Party plenum voted in favor of giving "priority" to legal forms of political change, leading eventually to a bitter split between the Party and the Cuban-backed guerrillas led by Douglas Bravo.

It was the last time the two old friends Mial and Fuser would see each other. Granado realized later that the visit had been his "silent good-bye." Indeed, although few people in Cuba realized it at the time, Che's absence from the Havana conference was the first sign that something fundamental had shifted. For anyone who cared to notice, Che was already in the process of extracting himself from Cuba's revolutionary government. He had told Fidel he wanted to leave. The trip to Moscow had convinced him that Soviet pressure on Cuba to accept the Kremlin's socialist model was overwhelming. At the Party Congress in Havana, Fidel had approved a resolution that tilted heavily in favor of Moscow's foreign policies, although guerrilla movements were to be backed in nations where neither the parties nor Moscow saw opportunities for open, "legal" political involvement.

A small circle of comrades was privy to Che's decision to leave, and they begged him to stay on for at least two more years, to give time to "prove" that his economc model was better for Cuba than the one the Soviets were trying to persuade Fidel to adopt. Che refused, replying that two more years were not necessary. His ministry was up and running according to his theories and had already proved itself.

A week after returning to Havana from Oriente, Che was gone again, flying this time to New York, the city he had once told his aunt Beatriz he wished to see for himself in spite of his visceral aversion to the United States. But this time he was going as the official spokesman for revolutionary Cuba. His selection as Cuba's representative before the United Nations General Assembly was testimony to the fact that Che continued to have Fidel's support. It was cold when he arrived in New York on December 9, and the photographs of his arrival show him dressed in a winter greatcoat, wearing his beret and the aloof, unsmiling expression of one who knows he has just stepped onto enemy territory. It was to be his second and final incursion into the land of the Yankee.

IV

Che took pains to groom himself for his appearance before the Nineteenth UN General Assembly on December 11, 1964. His boots were polished, his olive green uniform was pressed, and his hair and beard were neatly combed. Nevertheless, he presented a striking contrast to the conservatively attired diplomats who filled the hall, and his defiant speech did not disappoint those who had anticipated a harangue worthy of the famous apostle of revolutionary socialism.

Che had come to sound the death knell for colonialism, to decry American interventionism, and to applaud the "liberation wars" taking place

Che addressing the United Nations, December 11, 1964.

in Latin America, Africa, and Asia. In a bitter reference to the Congolese conflict, he took the United Nations to task for having allowed itself to be drawn in and used there as an instrument of the imperialist West—"a carnivorous animal feeding on the helpless." As for the latest Belgian-U.S. operation in Stanleyville, which had given the city back to Moishe Tshombe's troops at a cost of hundreds of dead, Che declared, "All free men throughout the world must make ready to avenge the Congo crime." He then proceeded to link the "white imperialist" action in the Congo with western indifference to the apartheid regime in South Africa and the racial inequalities in the United States. "How can the country that murders its own children and discriminates between them daily because of the color of their skins, a country that allows the murderers of Negroes to go free, actually protects them and punishes the Negroes for demanding respect for their lawful rights as free human beings, claim to be a guardian of liberty?"

Addressing one of the main themes of the assembly—a debate on global nuclear disarmament—Che expressed Cuba's support for the concept but stressed that it would refuse to ratify any agreement until the United States had dismantled its military bases in Puerto Rico and Panama. Che also reiterated Cuba's determination to follow an independent course in global affairs. Although Cuba was "building socialism," it was a nonaligned country because it identified with those in the new community of states in Africa, Asia, and the Middle East that were fighting against imperialism. Under the circumstances, this could be taken as an implicit dig at the Soviet Union's inaction on behalf of those struggles. In separate references to the feuding socialist superpowers, Che said Cuba strongly supported the Soviet stance in the Congo—and on behalf of China, he argued for its inclusion in the United Nations and the ouster of the U.S.-supported Nationalist Chinese government of Chiang Kai-shek.

Not surprisingly, Che's words provoked vigorous denunciations by the U.S. ambassador, Adlai Stevenson; and by some of the Latin envoys present. Outside the UN building, Cuban exiles angrily protested against his appearance. Some went considerably farther. Several *gusanos* were arrested after firing bazookas at the UN building from across the East River, and a woman was prevented from trying to stab Che with a knife. Throughout the ruckus, Che maintained his composure and seemed delighted at the anger he had aroused. To the shouted insults of the *gusano* protestors, he raised his hand in a universally understood gesture meaning "Fuck you."

Not everyone was displeased with Che's presence. Malcolm X, who had left the Nation of Islam a few months earlier and had been traveling in Africa and the Middle East, was also inflamed over the Congolese conflict, and he also equated white intervention in Africa with racism in the United States. He and Che had found a common cause. During his stop in Ghana, Malcolm X had reportedly discussed with Cuba's ambassador in Accra the idea of recruiting black Americans to help fight in Africa's wars.

On December 13, at a rally at the Audubon Ballroom in Harlem, Malcolm X introduced a special guest: Abdul Rahman Muhammad Babu, whose Cuban-trained political movement had helped seize power on the East African island of Zanzibar. The former sultanate was then fused with the mainland state of Tanganyika to form the new nation of Tanzania. Just before Babu appeared onstage, Malcolm X read a message from Che. "I love a revolutionary," he said. "And one of the most revolutionary men in this country right now was going to come out here with our friend Sheikh Babu, but he thought better of it. But he did send this message. It says: 'Dear brothers and sisters of Harlem. I would have liked to have been with you and Brother Babu, but the actual conditions are not good for this meeting.* Receive the warm salutations of the Cuban people and especially

---

*According to Pedro Álvarez Tabío, Castro's official historian, who accompanied Che's entourage on the UN trip, Che didn't show up because he wanted to avoid an appearance that the U.S. government could claim was an interference in its internal affairs.

those of Fidel, who remembers enthusiastically his visit to Harlem a few years ago. United we will win.' This is from Che Guevara. I'm happy to hear your warm round of applause in return because it lets the [white] man know that he's just not in a position to tell us who we should applaud for and who we shouldn't applaud for. And you don't see any anti-Castro Cubans around here—we eat them up."*

Che did not return to Cuba from New York. On December 17, after giving some colorfully defiant interviews to the American media, he flew to Algiers. It was the start of a three-month odyssey through Africa, to China, and back to Africa again, with stops in Paris, Ireland, and Prague. Officially, Che was acting as Fidel's roving goodwill ambassador to the emerging nations of Africa, but he was also acquainting himself with the continent that was to be the scene of his next adventure. Africa, Che had decided, would be the proving ground for his dream of a "tricontinental" alliance against the West. Between Christmas 1964 and early February 1965, Che traveled from Algeria to Mali; to Congo-Brazzaville, Guinea, and Ghana; to Dahomey; then back to Ghana and Algeria. He met with Algeria's Ben Bella, with Ghana's Kwame Nkrumah, with the Congolese-Brazzaville leader Alphonse Massamba-Débat, and with the leader of the anti-Portuguese Angolan independence movement, Agostinho Neto—to whom he promised Cuban military instructors for the MPLA guerrillas operating out of the adjacent Angolan enclave of Cabinda. (Those instructors soon arrived, marking the beginning of more than two decades of Cuban military involvement in Angola.)

Everywhere he went, Che's message was the same: Cuba identified with Africa's liberation struggles; there should be unity among all of the world's anticolonial and anti-imperialist movements, and there should be common cause between them and the socialist community. The fighting in the Congo featured heavily in his press pronouncements, as did far-off Vietnam, that other former colonial dominion whose people were now fighting American troops.

Che gave an interview to Josie Fanon, the widow of the late Martinican revolutionary Frantz Fanon, author of the fiery anticolonialist manifesto *The Wretched of the Earth*. The interview appeared in the magazine *Révolution Africaine*. Che said that Africa represented one of "the more important fields of struggle against all forms of exploitation existing in the world—against imperialism, colonialism, and neocolonialism." There were, he felt, "great

---

*Two months later, on February 21, 1965, Malcolm X was gunned down by assassins from the rival Nation of Islam while giving a speech in New York. He was thirty-nine.

Che with President Ben Bella in Algiers, 1964.

possibilities for success due to the existing unrest" but also many dangers, including the divisions among the Africans that colonialism had left.

When Fanon asked him about the prospects for revolution in Latin America, Che acknowledged that she had touched on a subject "very close" to his heart, in fact, his "major interest." He thought the struggle there would be long and hard because of the counterinsurgency activities of the United States. "That is why," Che said, "we foresee the establishment of a continental front of struggle against imperialism and its internal allies. This front will take some time to organize, but when it is formed it will be a very hard blow against imperialism. I don't know if it will be a definitive blow, but it will be a severe blow."

In early February, Che flew to China. He was accompanied by Cuba's construction minister, Osmany Cienfuegos—Camilo's older brother—and Emilio Aragonés, who had gone with him to the Soviet Union during the secret negotiations regarding nuclear missiles in 1962 and had seen him off at the airport when he went to Moscow the previous November. Both

Cienfuegos and Aragonés would be heavily involved in the secret Cuban operation in Africa, and their presence with Che at this juncture suggests that they were also involved in its planning stages.

Fidel had already approved a secret Cuban military mission in the Congo; it remained for Che to determine only where Cuba's services could be best directed, and with which of the rebel factions the mission should be carried out. The month before, in January 1965, a group of handpicked black Cubans had been offered the honor of volunteering for an unspecified "internationalist mission," and they were now training at three separate camps in Cuba. Another sign of the impending operation was the recent appointment of Pablo Ribalta—Che's old PSP friend from the Sierra Maestra—as Cuba's envoy to Tanzania, which bordered the Congo.

What happened behind closed doors during Che's trip to China has never been made public by Cuba's government, but according to Humberto Vázquez-Viaña, a well-informed former member of the Bolivian Communist Party, Che's party met with Chou En-lai and other top officials of the People's Republic, but not with Mao himself.* Che must have seen the potential of the Congo plans for turning around the disfavor into which Cuba had fallen with China. Richard Gott, the British historian of Latin American revolutionary movements—who as a journalist covered Che's subsequent guerrilla campaign in Bolivia, and who worked in Tanzania in the early 1970s—believes that Che's mission in China was to talk to the principal backers of the Congolese revolutionaries. "The Chinese were certainly interested in Africa," Gott reasons. "Chou En-lai was to make two visits that year—and they were also at that stage supporting the strategic notions of Lin Pao, the Chinese defense minister. He had made a famous speech advocating the encirclement of degenerate cities by radical revolutionary peasants. This was of course music to the ears of Guevara."

After leaving China, Che stopped in Paris, where he took a few hours off to tour the Louvre. Then he returned to Africa. Over the next month, in Algeria, Tanzania, and Egypt, he met again with Gamal Abdel Nasser, Ben Bella, and Julius Nyerere, and began to take soundings for his ambitious plan for pan-African revolution. Dar es Salaam, where white colonial rule was a very fresh memory, was the crucial stop on his itinerary. Built on a lagoon bordering the Indian Ocean in the 1860s as the site for the Arab sultan of Zanzibar's summer palace, Dar es Salaam had been the

---

*According to one Chinese official, the snub was directed not at Che, who was said to have "behaved correctly," but at Osmany Cienfuegos, who had offended the Chinese by "shouting" and "talking too much" and led them to fear he would provoke an embarrassing incident in Mao's hallowed presence.

capital of the colony of German East Africa until World War I. Then the British had taken over and ruled it as the colony of Tanganyika until granting independence in 1961. Since then, under the leftist president Julius Nyerere, "Dar" had become the headquarters for numerous African guerrilla movements. It was a promising revolutionary outpost. The U.S. embassy had been shut after the two countries had severed relations the previous year, and the Cubans had opened one of their own.

But Che's first encounters with African revolutionaries were disappointing. In what he titled "the first act" of a book—*Pasajes de la Guerra Revolucionaria (Congo)**—that he wrote about his Congolese experience, Che recalled his initial meetings with the men he derisively called, in English, "freedom fighters." These men, he noted, had a common "leitmotif." Almost all were living comfortably in Dar es Salaam's hotels and all invariably wanted the same things from him, "military training in Cuba and monetary help."

The first thing that struck Che about the Congolese rebel leaders was their "extraordinary number of tendencies and diverse opinions." Gaston Soumaliot, the self-styled "president of northeastern Congo," whose forces had liberated a swath of territory in eastern Congo to which they had access from Tanzanian territory across Lake Tanganyika, was vague and inscrutable. Che described him as "little developed politically," and certainly not a "leader of nations." He noted Soumaliot's rivalry with some of his comrades on the National Liberation Council, especially Christophe Gbenye, whose fighters had seized Stanleyville.

A rebel leader who did impress Che was Laurent Kabila, a French-schooled Congolese in his mid-twenties who was the overall military commander of Soumaliot's eastern front. Che found Kabila's exposition about the struggle "clear, concrete, and firm," although Kabila too spoke ill of fellow council leaders, such as Gbenye and even Soumaliot himself. Che later noted that Kabila had lied to him in their first meeting. Kabila announced that he had just arrived "from the interior" of the Congo, but, as Che later learned, he had merely been to the seedy bar-and-brothel port of Kigoma on the Tanzanian shore of Lake Tanganyika. Che chose to ignore Kabila's bluster, however, in light of his avowedly leftist worldview. "Kabila understood perfectly that the principal enemy was North American imperialism," Che wrote, "and

*The manuscript of this book, of which there were reportedly only five copies of the typescript made, was kept under lock and key at the highest levels of Cuba's revolutionary government for nearly three decades until a few leaked copies began circulating to a number of researchers, including me. In 1999, it was published in Spanish. The English title is *The African Dream: The Diaries of the Revolutionary War in the Congo*. The translation here is mine, made from the manuscript.

he said he was consequently ready to fight against it to the end; his declarations and his self-assuredness gave me . . . a very good impression." Finding a receptive ear for the concept upon which his entire African plan hinged, Che told Kabila of his distress at the shortsighted resistance to outside involvement in the Congolese rebellion by many of the African states. "Our viewpoint is that the problem of the Congo is a problem of the world," he said. When Kabila agreed with him, Che offered Cuba's support on the spot. "In the name of the [Cuban] Government I offered some thirty instructors and whatever arms we might have and he accepted with pleasure; he recommended speed in the delivery of both things, which Soumaliot had also done in another conversation, the latter recommending that the instructors be blacks."

Che decided to take the pulse of the other freedom fighters in town. He had planned to meet them in separate groups for informal talks, but "by mistake," he wrote, the Cuban embassy assembled a "tumultuous gathering . . . of fifty or more people, representatives of the movements of ten or more countries, each one divided into two or more tendencies." Che found himself faced with a roomful of guerrillas who almost unanimously requested Cuba's financial support and the training of fighters in Cuba. To their exasperation, Che begged off, arguing that to train their men in Cuba would be costly and wasteful, that true guerrilla fighters were developed on the battlefield, not in military "academies." "Therefore, I proposed that the training should be carried out not in our faraway Cuba, but in the nearby Congo, where the struggle was not merely against a common puppet like Tshombe, but against North American imperialism."

The Congolese struggle, Che insisted, was extremely important. Its victory would have "continental repercussions," as would its defeat. What Che envisioned was a Cuban-led "grand *foco*" in the eastern Congo, where the guerrillas of surrounding countries could come and, by helping in the war to "liberate" the Congo, gain fighting and organizational experience to do battle in their own countries. "The reaction," Che acknowledged, "was more than cold. Although the majority abstained from any kind of commentary, there were those who asked to speak to reproach me violently for my advice. They said their people, mistreated and brutalized by imperialism, would demand an accounting if their men died . . . in wars to liberate another State. I tried to make them see that what we were dealing with was not a war waged within national boundaries, but a continental war against the common master, as omnipresent in Mozambique as in Malawi, Rhodesia, or South Africa, the Congo or Angola."* Nobody in the room agreed with him, Che wrote. "Coldly and courteously they said good-bye." He was left with the clear impression

*See Notes.

that Africa faced a long road ahead before it would acquire a true revolutionary direction. What he was left with, then, was "the task of selecting a group of black Cubans, voluntarily of course, to reinforce the Congolese struggle."

V

In Cairo, according to Nasser's personal adviser, Muhammad Heikal, Che revealed his plans for the Congo, but when he mentioned that he was thinking of leading the Cuban military expedition himself, Nasser told him that it would be a mistake to become directly involved in the conflict, that if he thought he could be like "Tarzan, a white man among blacks, leading and protecting them," he was wrong. Nasser felt it was a proposition that could only end badly.

Despite such warnings, the poor reception his strategies had received in Dar es Salaam, his own doubts about the Congolese rebel leaders he had met, and his lack of hard information about the real situation inside the Congo, Che resolved to push ahead. His last speech on the African continent was also his swan song as a public figure or, as it is sometimes discreetly referred to in Cuba, *su último cartucho* (his last bullet). On February 25, in Algiers, speaking before the Second Economic Seminar of Afro-Asian Solidarity, Che discarded all ambiguity and called upon the socialist superpowers

During his trip abroad in 1964, Che met with the Egyptian president, Gamal Abdel Nasser, a leading "anti-imperialist." Anwar al-Sadat is next to Che.

to support Third World liberation movements and to underwrite the costs of transforming underdeveloped nations into socialist societies.

Che addressed the forty-odd African and Asian delegations—representing a colorful array of Third World states, newly independent nations, and active guerrilla movements—as "brothers." Then "on behalf of the peoples of America," Che defined the cause that united his part of the world with theirs as the "common aspiration to defeat imperialism." Many of those present were from nations either struggling against or recently freed from old-style colonialism, he noted, whereas Cuba had triumphed over the other form of imperialism that dominated the Americas—neocolonialism—the co-option and exploitation of underdeveloped countries through "monopolistic capital." To prevent this from happening in the new societies being forged, he declared, it was "imperative to obtain political power and liquidate the oppressing classes.

"There are no frontiers in this struggle to the death," he said. "We cannot remain indifferent in the face of what occurs in any part of the world. A victory for any country against imperialism is our victory, just as any country's defeat is a defeat for us all. The practice of proletarian internationalism is not only a duty for the peoples who struggle for a better future; it is also an inescapable necessity. . . . If there were no other basis for unity, the common enemy should constitute one."

It was not only in their vital interest but a "duty" of the developed socialist countries to help make the separation between the new underdeveloped nations and the capitalist world effective. "From all this," Che said, "a conclusion must be drawn: the development of the countries that now begin the road to liberation must be underwritten by the socialist countries. We say it in this manner without the least desire to blackmail anyone or to be spectacular. . . . It is a profound conviction. There can be socialism only if there is change in man's consciousness that will provoke a new fraternal attitude toward humanity on the individual level in the society that builds or has built socialism and also on a world level in relation to all the peoples who suffer imperialist oppression."

Che then rebuked the developed socialist states for their talk of "mutually beneficial" trade agreements with the poorer ones. "How can 'mutual benefit' mean selling at world market prices raw materials that cost unlimited sweat and suffering to the backward countries and buying at world market prices the machines produced in the large automated factories of today? If we establish that type of relationship between the two groups of nations, we must agree that the socialist countries are, to a certain extent, accomplices to imperialist exploitation. It can be argued that the amount of trade with the underdeveloped countries constitutes an insignificant part of the foreign trade of the socialist countries. It is a great truth, but it does not do away with the immoral nature of the exchange. The socialist countries have the moral duty of liquidating their tacit complicity with the West."

Che was aiming his attack directly at Moscow, which, along with China, had sent observers to the forum. Although he took care to credit both nations for giving Cuba advantageous trade agreements for its sugar exports, he stressed that this was only a first step. Prices had to be fixed to permit real development in the poor nations, and this new fraternal concept of foreign trade should be extended by the socialist powers to all underdeveloped nations on the road toward socialism.

This was not the first time Che had criticized what he saw to be the Soviet Union's capitalist-style "profiteering" in its trade with Cuba or its relationships with other developing nations—his views were widely known among the revolutionary elite in Havana—but it was the first time he had been critical in an international forum. By doing so, he was consciously and willfully pushing the limits, evidently hoping to "shame" Moscow into action—and he wasn't done yet. He called for a "large compact bloc" of nations to help others liberate themselves from imperialism and from the economic structures it had imposed on them. This meant that weapons from the arms-producing socialist countries should be given "without any cost whatsoever and in quantities determined by their need and availability to those people who ask for them."

Again, Che paused to credit the Soviet Union and China for having followed this principle in giving military aid to Cuba, but then he chastized them once more. "We are socialists, and this constitutes the guarantee of the proper utilization of those arms; but we are not the only one, and all must receive the same treatment." He singled out the beleaguered North Vietnamese—whose country had come under systematic American bombardment just two weeks earlier—and the Congolese as worthy recipients of the "unconditional solidarity" he was demanding.

Not surprisingly, the Soviets were outraged by Che's speech. Calling the Kremlin "an accomplice with imperialism" was an astounding breach of protocol within the socialist bloc, and, considering the degree to which Moscow was already bankrolling Cuba, Che's speech was nothing less than an ungrateful slap in the face.

As Che wound up his long peregrination—from Algiers back to Egypt again before flying on to Prague on March 12—new developments in the Congo seemed to bear out requests by Soumaliot and Kabila for speed in delivering the promised Cuban instructors and arms. The white mercenaries assembled by Mike Hoare had gone into action against the rebels, leading government troops in ground assaults and carrying out aerial bombing raids. They seized several key outposts and quickly threatened the "liberated territory" along the eastern shore of Lake Tanganyika. If Cuba was going to throw itself into the Congolese conflict, the time to act would be very soon.

VI

Just as Kremlinologists looking for signs of power shifts once carefully observed the placement of the Politburo members during celebrations on Red Square, Che's reception in Havana following his provocative speech in Algiers was long scrutinized for evidence of either camaraderie or conflict between him and Fidel.

On March 15, 1965, a little over two weeks after Che gave an inflammatory speech in Algiers that was critical of the Soviet Union, he was met at the airport in Havana by Fidel; his wife, Aleida; the old Communist Carlos Rafael Rodríguez (with the goatee); and Cuban president Osvaldo Dorticós.

When Che arrived at Rancho Boyeros airport on March 15, Aleida was waiting for him, together with Fidel, President Dorticós, and, perhaps most significantly, the old Communist Carlos Rafael Rodríguez. Aleida would not speak about what happened next, nor did Fidel, but it seems that Che went directly from the airport to a closed-door meeting with Fidel that lasted for many hours. Some observers have interpreted the meeting as the fateful climax to the tension that had supposedly built up between the two of them. A knowledgeable Cuban government source said elliptically that there were "probably" some "strong words" from Fidel, but that they would have been less over fundamental differences of opinion than Che's "tactlessness" in his speech in Algiers. In this context, the presence of Carlos Rafael Rodríguez at the airport can probably be interpreted as providing representation on behalf of the ruffled Kremlin.

Maurice Halperin saw it rather differently. "I was astonished when I read the speech a few days later," Halperin wrote. "When I asked a high official in the ministry of foreign trade what the meaning was of Che's blast, he answered with a broad grin: 'It represents the Cuban point of view.'" Halperin concluded that this was quite likely. He thought that Fidel's appearance at the airport to welcome Che back to Cuba personally was his way of showing his approval. Indeed, Che's speech in Algiers was later printed in *Política Internacional,* the official government quarterly, which would seem to erase any doubts about Fidel's own position.

Most evidence suggests that Che and Fidel were working in tandem, even coordinating their public remarks. In a speech on January 2 commemorating the sixth anniversary of the revolution, Fidel had delivered a strong critique of the Soviet socialist model—though without mentioning it by name—and, for the first time ever to the Cuban people, spoke of "problems" existing within the socialist fraternity of nations. Cuba's people had the right to speak with their own voice, he said, and to interpret the ideas of Marx, Engels, and Lenin according to their own perceptions and conditions, and they should be prepared to survive on their own if the current aid received from abroad were to be abruptly halted. It was an unequivocal message to Moscow that Fidel would not accept efforts by the Soviet Union to impose its political model in Cuba.

On March 13, two days before Che's return, Fidel spoke at Havana University, allusively blasting both China and the Soviet Union for their rivalry and for hypocrisy in supporting "people's liberation" while doing nothing to help the Vietnamese in the face of escalating American military attacks. "We propose that Vietnam should be given all the aid which may be necessary! Aid in weapons and men! Our position is that the socialist camp run whatever risks may be necessary!" There was, he reminded his audience, a recent precedent for the kind of solidarity he was referring to: Cuba itself. During the missile crisis, Cuba had volunteered to face the threat of "thermonuclear war" over its acceptance of Soviet missiles on its soil for the purpose of strengthening the socialist camp. Cuba continued to believe its historic duty was to fight against Yankee imperialism, Fidel said, and Cubans felt a bond with those making efforts elsewhere in the world.*

But Che had gone even farther than Fidel in Algiers, saying everything he felt and believed—and damn the consequences. He had issued his challenge, and there was no stepping back. His remarks made it harder than ever for Fidel to defend him to the Soviets. So Fidel "suggested" that he leave Cuba immediately and return to Africa, to lead the Cuban guerrilla contingent already in training for the Congo mission. It was not where Che's heart lay, but the conditions in South America were not yet ready, while the present moment in Africa seemed to offer real revolutionary possibilities. Che agreed to go.

Juan Carreterro—Ariel—said that Manuel Piñeiro and Fidel himself had "urged" Che to go to the Congo. It would be for only a couple of years, and in the meantime, they promised him, Piñeiro's people would continue building the guerrilla infrastructure in Latin America. The Congo war would be an invaluable toughening-up exercise for Che's fighters and would provide a useful screening process for those who would go with him afterward to South America. As Piñeiro recalled it, Che didn't need much convincing. "Che came back really excited by his contacts with the Africans, so Fidel told him: 'Why don't you go to Africa?'"

On March 22, Che gave a speech in the Ministry of Industries, briefing his colleagues about his African trip but making no announcement that he was leaving. A week later, he visited the *guajiro* veterans from his old sierra column who worked on the Ciro Redondo experimental farm in Matanzas and told them that he would be going off to "cut cane" for a while. Back in Havana, he assembled some of his closest comrades at the ministry and told them the same story. Very few people knew that Che was making ready to leave Cuba for good, but that was his intention. His return to Havana amounted to a fifteen-day disappearing act in which he gradually

---

*Fidel also alluded to the irritation he felt over the fact that the Chinese and Soviets had brought their rivalries to his island. Without naming a nation—but he was referring to China—he decried the efforts being made to circulate unauthorized political propaganda on Cuban soil. Only Cuba's ruling party had the right to issue propaganda, he said, and he warned that he would not tolerate it any longer. Despite his warning, however, this problem had yet to reach its climax.

withdrew from sight, avoiding public contact and saying good-bye to a few people who could be trusted to keep the secret. For the Cuban people at large, Che's well-publicized arrival back from Africa at the airport on March 15 was the last time they would ever see him.

Che's children would never see him as their father again, and the youngest of them would retain no memory of him at all. Che had been away for the birth, on February 24, of his last child, a boy Aleida had named Ernesto.

Aleida was upset. She asked Che not to go, but his decision was final. He promised her that when the revolution was in a more "advanced stage," she could join him. Not long before he left, they were eating lunch with their nanny, Sofía, and he asked Sofía what had happened to the widows of the Cubans who had died in the revolution. Had they remarried? Yes, Sofía told him, a lot of them had. Che turned to Aleida and, pointing to his coffee cup, said, "In that case, this coffee you serve me, may you serve it to another."

At dawn on April 1, Che left his home of the past eight years disguised as Ramón Benítez, a staid-looking, clean-shaven man wearing glasses.

The last Guevara family portrait, March 1965. Che is holding his newborn son, Ernesto. He has his arm around Camilo, who is next to Aliusha. Aleida is holding Celia on her lap.

27

The Story of a Failure

I

"One fine day, I appeared in Dar es Salaam," Che wrote in his Congo *Pasajes*. "Nobody knew me; not even the ambassador [Pablo Ribalta], an old comrade in arms, . . . could identify me upon my arrival." He had made a circuitous journey via Moscow and Cairo, accompanied by José Maria "Papi" Martínez Tamayo, his roving guerrilla emissary. Papi had been involved in the missions in Guatemala and in Argentina, and he had assisted in Tania's clandestine training. They traveled with Víctor Dreke, the Cuban officer who had been selected as the official—and acceptably black—commander of the Cuban internationalist brigade. Che was full of high expectations. "Africa for adventuring, and then that's it for the world," he had written to his mother a decade earlier. Since then, Che had seen a great deal of the world, but too often within the restrictions imposed by his role as a government minister and a VIP. Now, he was free once again to be himself.

"I had left behind almost eleven years of work for the Cuban Revolution at Fidel's side, a happy home—to the extent one can call the house where a revolutionary dedicated to his work lives—and a bunch of kids who barely knew of my love," he wrote. "The cycle was beginning again."

II

Che and his companions arrived in Dar es Salaam on April 19, 1965. While they waited for more members of the Cuban brigade, who were traveling in groups using different itineraries, they were housed on a little farm Ribalta had rented on the outskirts of the city. Pulling out a Swahili dictionary, Che chose new names for the three of them. Dreke was henceforth Moja (One); Papi was Mbili (Two); and Che himself was Tatu (Three).

Laurent Kabila and the other Congolese rebel leaders were away in Cairo for a summit meeting. A mid-level Congolese political representative in Dar es Salaam, a young man named Godefroi Chamaleso, who was contacted and introduced to the three men, was told only that they were a Cuban advance party. The explanation for the presence of two white men in the group was that Tatu was a doctor, spoke French, and had experience as a guerrilla. Mbili was there because of his vast and invaluable guerrilla experience. Che told Chamaleso that the number of Cubans coming—130—was greater than that originally planned and that they wanted to enter Congolese territory as soon as possible. Chamaleso went off to Cairo to inform Kabila of their arrival, still unaware that the man he had met was Che.

When to reveal Tatu's true identity, and to whom, loomed as a difficult decision. "I hadn't told any of the Congolese of my decision to fight here," Che wrote. "In my first conversation with Kabila I hadn't been able to do so because nothing had been decided, and after the plan was approved [by Fidel] it would have been dangerous for my project to be known before I arrived at my destination; there was a lot of hostile territory to cross. I decided, therefore, to present a fait accompli and proceed according to how they reacted to my presence. I was not unaware of the fact that a negative response would place me in a difficult position, because now I couldn't go back, but I calculated that it would be difficult for them to refuse me. In essence, I was blackmailing them with my physical presence."

Che had made the same commitment he had demanded of Masetti's followers when they prepared to leave for Argentina. He had told them then that they should consider themselves dead from that moment on. If they survived—though survival was doubtful for the majority—they would probably spend the next ten or twenty years of their lives fighting. This was the nature of the obligation Che had now assumed for himself. He had not just "left Cuba" but truly burned his bridges. He had written a note to Fidel that was at once a farewell letter, a waiver of any responsibility the Cuban government might be perceived as having for his actions, and a last will and testament:

"Fidel," he began:

At this moment I remember many things—when I met you in the [Mexico City] house of María Antonia, when you proposed I come along, all the tensions involved in the preparations. One day they came by and asked me who should be notified in case of death, and the real possibility of that fact struck us all. Later we knew it was true, that in revolution one wins or dies (if it is a real one).

Today everything has a less dramatic tone, because we are more mature. But the event repeats itself. I feel that I have fulfilled the part of my duty that tied me to the Cuban revolution in its territory, and I say good-bye to you, to the comrades, to your people, who are now mine.

I formally resign my positions in the leadership of the party, my post as minister, my rank of commander, and my Cuban citizenship. Nothing legal binds me to Cuba. . . .

Recalling my past life, I believe I have worked with sufficient integrity and dedication to consolidate the revolutionary triumph. My only serious failing was not having had more confidence in you from the first moments in the Sierra Maestra, and not having understood quickly enough your qualities as a leader and a revolutionary.*

I have lived magnificent days, and at your side I felt the pride of belonging to our people in the brilliant yet sad days of the Caribbean [missile] crisis. Seldom has a statesman been more brilliant than you in those days. . . .

Other nations of the world call for my modest efforts. I can do that which is denied you because of your responsibility at the head of Cuba, and the time has come for us to part.

I want it known that I do so with a mixture of joy and sorrow. I leave here the purest of my hopes as a builder and the dearest of my loved ones. And I leave a people who received me as a son. That wounds a part of my spirit. I carry to new battlefronts the faith that you taught me, the revolutionary spirit of my people, the feeling of fulfilling the most sacred of duties: to fight against imperialism wherever one may be. This comforts and more than heals the deepest wounds.

I state once more that I free Cuba from any responsibility except that which stems from its example. If my final hour finds me under other skies, my last thought will be of the people and especially of you. . . . I am not sorry that I leave nothing material to my wife and children. I am happy it is that way. I ask nothing for them, as the state will provide them with enough to live on and to have an education. . . .

Hasta la victoria siempre! Patria o muerte! I embrace you with all my revolutionary fervor.

Che.

*Che was evidently referring to his brief loss of faith in Fidel in the aftermath of the Miami Pact during the revolutionary war.

Che had also left a letter to be forwarded to his parents:

Dear *viejos:*

Once again I feel under my heels the ribs of Rocinante.* I return to the trail with my shield on my arm. Nothing essential has changed, except that I am more conscious, my Marxism is deeper and more crystallized. I believe in the armed struggle as the only solution for the peoples who fight to free themselves and I am consistent with my beliefs. Many will call me an adventurer, and I am, but of a different type, of those who put their lives on the line to demonstrate their truths.

It could be that this will be the definitive one. I don't go looking for it, but it is within the logical calculations of probabilities. If it is to be, then this is my final embrace.

I have loved you very much, only I have not known how to show my love. I am extremely rigid in my actions and I believe that at times you did not understand me. On the other hand, it was not easy to understand me. . . . Now, the willpower that I have polished with an artist's delectation will carry forth my flaccid legs and tired lungs. I will do it.

Remember once in a while this little *condottiere* of the twentieth century. . . . A great hug from a prodigal son, recalcitrant for you.

Ernesto.

For Aleida, he left behind a tape recording of his voice, reciting his favorite love poems to her, including several by Pablo Neruda. And to his five children, in a letter to be read to them only after his death, he wrote:

If one day you must read this letter, it will be because I am no longer among you. You will almost not remember me and the littlest ones will remember nothing at all. Your father has been a man who acted according to his beliefs and certainly has been faithful to his convictions.

Grow up as good revolutionaries. Study hard to be able to dominate the techniques that permit the domination of nature. Remember that the Revolution is what is important and that each one of us, on our own, is worthless.

*Rocinante was Don Quixote's horse.

Above all, try always to be able to feel deeply any injustice committed against any person in any part of the world. It is the most beautiful
quality of a revolutionary.

Until always, little children. I still hope to see you again. A really
big kiss and a hug from Papa.*

Che's contact with his first wife, Hilda, had become formal by then,
limited mostly to his visits to see their daughter. Hilda last spoke to him in
person on the eve of his trip to address the United Nations, in November
1964. When she showed Che a letter she had received from his father, saying he was planning to come to Havana soon, Che seemed surprised. According to Hilda, he blurted out: "Why didn't he come . . . ! What a pity!
Now there's no more time." She didn't understand what Che was referring
to until later, when she realized he must have had his African project already in mind. Eight-year-old Hildita was at the airport to greet him on
March 15, when he returned from Algiers, and he took her home before
going to meet with Fidel. There had been no time to talk with Hilda, but
he told the little girl that he would come back later. He spoke to Hilda on
the phone two or three days after that and said that he was going to the
countryside to cut cane.† Neither she nor their daughter ever saw him again.

For a few of his closest friends, Che had selected books from his office library and written personal dedications inside each of them; he left
them on the shelf to be discovered, without saying anything. For his old
friend Alberto Granado, he left a book on the history of Cuban sugar, *El
Ingenio*. In it, he wrote, "I don't know what to leave you as a memento. I
oblige you, then, to immerse yourself in sugarcane. My house on wheels
will have two feet once again and my dreams no frontiers, at least until
the bullets have their say. I await you, sedentary gypsy, when the smell of
gunpowder dissipates."

Orlando Borrego had asked if he could go with Che to Africa, but Che
had said no. Borrego now had an important job as the minister of sugar,
and Che said his services were too valuable. Che left Borrego his three-
volume set of *Das Kapital*. "Borrego," he wrote on the flyleaf: "This is the

*See Notes.

†Che could not tell Hilda of his secret agenda, for a good reason. According to one of his closest
friends, who was privy to his plans, Hilda had become something of a security risk because
of her penchant for playing "fairy godmother" to any Latin American guerrilla who showed
up in Havana. Some were genuine, others wannabes; and at least one, a Mexican, was later
arrested and unmasked by Cuba's security services as a CIA agent.

wellspring, here we all learned together by trial and error looking for what is still just an intuition. Now that I leave to fulfill my duty and my desire, and you remain behind to fulfill your duty against your desire, I leave you evidence of my friendship, which I rarely expressed in words. Thank you for your constancy and your loyalty. May nothing separate you from the path. A hug, Che."

In addition to the speech he made in Algiers, Che had left behind a final manifesto that can be seen as the crystallization of his doctrine. "Socialismo y El Hombre Nuevo en Cuba" (Socialism and the New Man) was written during his three-month journey in Africa and sent off in the form of a letter to the editor of *Marcha,* the Uruguayan weekly. It appeared in Uruguay in March and had begun to cause a stir in left-wing circles around the hemisphere. It was published in Cuba in *Verde Olívo* on April 11, as Che was en route back to Tanzania. In the essay, he reasserts Cuba's right to a role at the helm of Latin American revolution and issues a stinging disquisition challenging the docile application of Soviet dogmas by fellow socialists. In a further critique of the Soviet model, Che reiterates his argument in favor of "moral" as opposed to material incentives.

Che denied that the building of socialism meant the "abolition of the individual." Rather, the individual was the essence of the revolution: the Cuban struggle had depended on those individuals who fought and offered their lives for it. A new notion of self, however, had emerged in the vortex of that struggle—"the heroic stage" that had been attained when those same individuals "vied to achieve a place of greater responsibility, of greater danger, and without any other satisfaction than that of fulfilling their duty. . . . In the attitude of our fighters, we could glimpse the man of the future."

It is difficult not to feel that Che was rendering an account of his own revolutionary transformation. He had sublimated his former self, the individual, and he had reached a mental state through which he could consciously sacrifice himself for society and its ideals. If he could do it, then so could others.

Finally, Che wrote:

It must be said with all sincerity that in a true revolution, to which one gives oneself completely, from which one expects no material compensation, the task of the vanguard revolutionary is both magnificent and anguishing.

Let me say, at the risk of appearing ridiculous, that the true revolutionary is guided by strong feelings of love. It is impossible to think of an authentic revolutionary without this quality. This is perhaps one of the greatest dramas of a leader; he must combine an impassioned spirit with a cold mind and make painful decisions without flinching one muscle. Our vanguard revolutionaries must idealize their love for the people, for the most sacred causes, and make it one and indivisible. They cannot descend, with small doses of daily affection, to the places where ordinary men put their love into practice.

The leaders of the Revolution have children who do not learn to call their father with their first faltering words; they have wives who must be part of the general sacrifice of their lives to carry the Revolution to its destiny; their friends are strictly limited to their comrades in revolution. There is no life outside it.

In these conditions, one must have a large dose of humanity, a large dose of a sense of justice and truth, to avoid falling into extremes, into cold scholasticism, into isolation from the masses. Every day we must struggle so that this love of living humanity is transformed into concrete facts, into acts that will serve as an example, as a mobilizing factor.

We know that we have sacrifices ahead of us and that we must pay a price for the heroic act of constituting a vanguard as a nation. We, the leaders, know that we must pay a price for having the right to say that we are at the head of the people of America.

Each and every one of us punctually pays his quota of sacrifice, aware of receiving our reward in the satisfaction of fulfilling our duty, conscious of advancing with everyone toward the new man who is glimpsed on the horizon.

III

On April 20, amid mounting rumors that something had "happened" to Che, Fidel announced mysteriously that Che was fine, that he was where he would be of "most use to the revolution." It was all he would say.

That same day, Hildita received a belated birthday letter from her father. She had turned nine on February 15. He told her that he was "a little far away," doing some work for which he had been commended, and it would be "a little while" before he could return. He told her to look after her "other" brothers and sisters, and to make sure they did their homework, and that he was "always thinking" of her.

At around the same time, Che had dispatched a clue to his father that he was fine, hinting strongly which part of the world he was in. It was a postcard, mailed after he had left Cuba, which said simply, "*Viejo:* from the Saharan sun to your [Argentine] fogs. Ernesto renews himself and goes for the third [round]. A hug from your son."

Despite Fidel's reassurances, rumors about Che's fate continued to fly. Some of the earliest speculation was that he was in the Dominican Republic, where a crisis had erupted within days of his disappearance. President Johnson, who had defeated Goldwater in the election in November, had dispatched U.S. marines to quash an armed leftist uprising there. It was the first American military invasion in the Western Hemisphere in decades, and the streets of Santo Domingo had become a battleground between the rebel loyalists of the deposed leftist civilian president, Juan Bosch, and the Dominican military.*

As members of Cuba's secret services have hinted, the rumor about "Che in Santo Domingo" may have been generated in Havana. As long as he was en route to the Congo and vulnerable to detection or capture, it was of paramount importance to keep his whereabouts a secret. As time dragged on, new reports would emerge to suggest that he was in Vietnam or other exotic locations. Some of the reports were disinformation planted by Cuban intelligence; others were probably disseminated by the CIA to cast doubt on the Castro regime. One of the more lurid stories that soon began making the rounds had a Soviet aroma. It was a supposedly secret memorandum reporting that Che had suffered a psychotic breakdown and been interned in a mental clinic, where he spent his time reading Trotsky and writing letters to Fidel promoting his ideas for creating a permanent revolution. (The "R Memorandum," as it was known, pointed with alarming proximity toward Che's true location, claiming that among the places Che mentioned in his letters was Zanzibar, where it was possible to "work with the Chinese.")

As Sergo Mikoyan recalled, the initial reports trickling through Moscow were that there had been a confrontation between Fidel and Che and that Che had been exiled or punished. "The general opinion among the apparatchiks was that there had been a fight between Fidel and Che," he said. "Or maybe not a fight, but that Fidel didn't want Che in Cuba—that he wanted to be the only leader, and that Che was in competition with him."

---

*The fighting was soon over, and the U.S. and allied Latin American troops that had intervened were withdrawn after the OAS mediated a cease-fire agreement. New elections were scheduled and took place the following year. Bosch lost to his rightist rival, Joaquín Balaguer, who dominated politics in the Dominican Republic as an on-again, off-again president for the next thirty years.

Mikoyan stressed that he had never given credence to this scenario. "I knew them both and I knew that Che was absolutely unambitious. . . . He would not even imagine competing with Fidel. That version seemed ridiculous and I didn't believe it. But our people thought of Stalin and Trotsky, then Khrushchev and Brezhnev, who were always fighting—and they thought it was the same in Cuba."

Alexandr Alexiev, who was still the Soviet ambassador in Havana, also heard the rumors, but by now he knew better. In March, Fidel had invited him to a special event. He was going to lead a volunteer labor brigade composed of revolutionaries to cut sugarcane in Camagüey. When Alexiev learned that Che would not be part of the event, he began wondering if the rumors of a split were true. But when the time came, Fidel took Alexiev for a walk at Camagüey and told him the truth. "You have probably noted Che's absence," Fidel said. "He is in Africa. He went there to organize a movement. But I am telling you just for yourself. By no means should you communicate this by cable."

Alexiev interpreted Fidel's warning to mean that he should put nothing in *writing* that might be witnessed by third parties and somehow leak out, but he felt duty-bound to inform his government, and he did. Thirty years after the fact, he found it difficult to recall exactly how he had passed the information along. He believed it was with "someone of great trust" who had come to Havana in a Soviet delegation. He stressed that he had put nothing in writing, although he had followed up when he was next in Moscow by informing Leonid Brezhnev in person.*

Fidel's whispered confidence to Alexiev about Che's mission was no doubt a discreet hint to Moscow that Fidel remained loyal despite his public bearbaiting. Che might be off assisting a predominantly Chinese-backed revolutionary faction in the Congo, but that should not affect relations between the Kremlin and Havana. Indeed, Fidel may have been hoping that the new Kremlin Politburo, which was already giving some aid to the Congolese rebels, might respond with direct support for Cuba's guerrilla program in Africa.

At about the same time that Fidel revealed the secret to Alexiev, the advance column of the Cuban force, led by Che, was preparing to go into action.

---

*Alexiev said that Brezhnev "did not seem very interested" in what he was told. Alexiev gave few additional details of their meeting, but he hinted that Brezhnev would not have let the matter become an issue affecting relations with Cuba. "[Brezhnev] was *with* Fidel," he said. "He was trying to capitalize on Fidel's friendship with Khrushchev and have the same kind of relationship."

IV

At dawn on the morning of April 24, 1965, Che and thirteen Cubans set foot on the Congolese shore of Lake Tanganyika. An expanse of thirty miles of water separated them from the safety of Tanzania and the vast savanna that extended to the Indian Ocean. They had traveled for two days and nights by car from Dar es Salaam and then by boat to the lakeside village of Kibamba. Above them loomed the western edge of the Great Rift Valley, a green jungle escarpment that rose steeply from the lakeshore. Beyond lay the "liberated" territory held by the rebels. Its northern front line began nearly 100 miles away, at the town of Uvira on Lake Tanganyika's northern shore. Uvira had become the rebels' fallback position after they lost the town of Bukavu, farther up the Rift Valley, where the frontiers of the Congo, Rwanda, and Burundi meet. Inland, the territory extended west through the forest for 170 miles, as far as Kasongo on the Lualaba River, just beyond the northern edge of Katanga province. All together, it was a domain that the mercenary leader Mike Hoare described as twice the size of Wales. It included open plains and jungle mountains bisected by untamed rivers. Herds of elephants still roamed there, and a complex mosaic of tribal peoples lived off the land as subsistence farmers and hunter-gatherers. The territory contained few roads or towns, and the few inhabited dots on the map represented native villages, isolated former Belgian colonial garrisons, missions, and trading posts.

Godefroi Chamaleso, the political commissar from Dar es Salaam, had come to help smooth the way for the Cubans; so far, he was the only official link to the revolutionaries Che intended to whip into shape. Kabila had not appeared. He had stayed on in Cairo, sending word that he would return in a fortnight, and in his absence Che had been forced to remain incognito. "To be honest," he acknowledged later, "I wasn't too upset, because I was very interested in the war in the Congo and I was afraid that my appearance would provoke overly sharp reactions, and that some of the Congolese, or even the friendly [Tanzanian] government, would ask me to abstain from joining in the fray."

So far, so good. But already, in Kigoma, the Tanzanian port on the eastern shore of the lake, Che had seen the first evidence that the men he was joining were undisciplined and badly led. A Tanzanian official had complained to him about the Congolese rebels, who regularly crossed the lake to hang out and disport themselves in bars and whorehouses. And Che had had to wait for a day and a night while a boat was made ready for their crossing—nothing had been prepared for him, despite his advance man's efforts. Then, after crossing the lake to Kibamba, he found that the rebels' general staff headquarters was a mere stone's throw up the mountainside, too conveniently close to the village and the safety valve of Tanzania for his liking.

In Kabila's absence, Che found himself dealing with a group of field commanders, the men calling the shots in the various "army brigades" stationed around the rebel zone. Fortunately, some of them spoke French, so Che was able to discern immediately that serious divisions existed among them. In their first meeting with the rebel commanders, Chamaleso enthusiastically tried to help establish rapport between his compatriots and the newcomers by proposing that Víctor Dreke, along with another Cuban of his choosing, be allowed to join in all the meetings and decisions of the general staff. But the Congolese officers were eloquently noncommittal. "I observed the faces of the participants," Che noted drily, "and I could not see approval for the proposal; it seemed that [Chamaleso] did not enjoy the sympathies of the chiefs."

The commanders' displeasure with Chamaleso derived from the fact that he visited the front from Dar es Salaam only occasionally. The military men felt neglected by the head office. There was additional ill feeling between those commanders who stayed in the field and those constantly leaving on errands to Kigoma and its fleshpots. The rank-and-file fighters, for the most part, were simple peasants who spoke only their own tribal languages, or, in some cases, Swahili, and who seemed to Che to inhabit a world completely apart from their officers.

Still another unpleasant surprise for Che was the discovery of the rebels' faith in witchcraft, or *dawa*. They believed that a magic potion protected them from harm. Che learned about this magic in his very first meeting with the Congolese command. A pleasant-seeming officer introduced himself as Lieutenant Colonel Lambert and explained, cheerfully, "that for them, the [enemy] airplanes were not very important because they possessed the *dawa* medicine that makes them invulnerable to bullets." Lambert assured Che that he had been hit by bullets several times, but because of the *dawa*, they had fallen harmlessly to the ground. "He explained it between smiles," wrote Che, "and I felt obliged to go along with the joke, which I believed was his attempt to demonstrate the little importance he conceded to the enemy's armaments. After a little while, I realized the thing was serious, and that the magical protector was one of the great weapons of the Congolese Army."

After the inconclusive initial meeting with the commanders, Che took Chamaleso aside and revealed his true identity. "I explained who I was," Che wrote. "The reaction was devastating. He repeated the phrases 'international scandal' and 'no one must know, please, no one must know'; it had fallen like a lightning bolt in a serene day and I feared for the consequences,

Che, as Comandante Tatu, in the "liberated zone" of the former
Belgian Congo, 1965.

but my identity could not continue hidden much longer if we wanted to take advantage of the influence that my activity here could have."

After the shaken Chamaleso left, heading back to Dar and then to Cairo, this time to inform Kabila of Che's presence, "Tatu" attempted to get his training program under way. He tried to persuade the Congolese *jefes* to let him and his men set up a permanent base more adequate for their mission on the Luluabourg ridge, three miles above them, but the commanders stalled, telling him that the base commander, Leonard Mitoudidi, was away in Kigoma and nothing could be done until he returned. In lieu of that, they suggested he begin an ad hoc training program there at the Kibamba headquarters. Che countered with a proposal to train a 100-man column divided into groups of twenty men over a five- or six-week period, then send them out with Mbili (Papi) on patrol to carry out some military actions; while they were gone, he could train a second column, which would enter the field when the first group returned. After each expedition he could select the truly worthwhile cadres to build up an effective guerrilla force. This proposal too was met with evasions.

The days began rolling by. Boats came and went across the lake, carrying rebels to and from furloughs in Kigoma, but Commander Mitoudidi didn't return. For want of anything better to do, Che began helping out in the rebels' clinic, where one of the Cubans, a doctor rebaptized as "Kumi," had begun working. Che was stunned by the number of cases of venereal disease among the rebels, which he attributed to their visits to Kigoma. A few wounded men were brought in from the various fronts, but they were victims of accidents, not battle casualties. "Almost nobody had the least idea of what a firearm was," Che recalled. "They shot themselves by playing with them, or by carelessness." The rebels also drank a local corn- and yucca-based brew called *pombe,* and the spectacle of reeling men having fights or disobeying orders was distressingly commonplace.

Hearing of the presence of doctors in the area, local peasants began showing up in droves at the dispensary. Its depleting stocks got a boost with the arrival of a cargo of Soviet medicines, which were unceremoniously dumped on the beach along with a great pile of ammunition and weaponry. When Che asked for permission to organize the rebels' logistics depot, that request also fell on deaf ears. Meanwhile, the beach acquired the appearance of a gypsy market, Che wrote, as rebel commanders began arriving and demanding quantities of the new medicines for "fabulous sums of men." One officer claimed he had 4,000 troops, another said 2,000, and so on, but they were "all invented numbers."

By early May, Che had received word that the rebel council's summit in Cairo had been a success but that Kabila wouldn't be returning just yet;

he needed to have an operation on a cyst, and it would be several more weeks before he was back. The Cubans were beginning to feel the first symptoms of malaise brought on by inactivity, and to keep them occupied, Che began daily classes in French, Swahili, and "general culture." "Our morale was still high," Che recalled, "but already the murmurs were beginning among the comrades about how the days were fruitlessly slipping by." The next afflictions to hit them were malaria and tropical infections. Che handed out antimalarial tablets regularly, but he observed that their side effects included weakness, apathy, and lack of appetite, and he later blamed the medication for exacerbating the "incipient pessimism" felt by the Cubans, including, although he was loath to admit it, himself.

Che was getting an ongoing private debriefing about the situation inside the rebel movement from an informant called Kiwe. Kiwe was one of the more voluble general staff officers, "an inexhaustible talker who spoke French at almost supersonic speed" and who had plenty to confide. As was his longtime habit, Che wrote pithy little profiles laced with his own remarks based on Kiwe's information. Kiwe claimed that General Nicholas Olenga, the "liberator" of Stanleyville, had been a soldier whom Kiwe had personally dispatched to make some explorations in the north. Olenga had then begun attacking, giving himself a new military rank with each town he seized. The current president of the rebel council, Christophe Gbenye, was the political leader for whom General Olenga had liberated Stanleyville, but to Kiwe, Gbenye was a dangerous, immoral figure; Kiwe held Gbenye responsible for an assassination attempt against the current council's military chief of staff, Commander Mitoudidi. As for Antoine Gizenga, one of the early revolutionary figures to emerge in the wake of Lumumba's death, Kiwe declared him a left-wing opportunist who was interested more than anything else in using the rebels' effort to build his own political party. As Che wrote afterward, the chats with Kiwe had been enlightening, giving him an idea of the complex internal rivalries within the not so very revolutionary Congolese Liberation Council.

On May 8, Leonard Mitoudidi finally arrived, bringing eighteen new Cubans with him and word from Kabila that for the time being, Che's identity should remain a secret. Mitoudidi left almost immediately, but for the first time since meeting Kabila, Che was favorably impressed with a Congolese officer, finding him "assured, serious, and possessing an organizational spirit." Even better, Mitoudidi approved Che's transfer to the upper base on Luluabourg mountain.

Che took his men up to the huge grassy plateau that began at the top of the escarpment. It was four hard hours of steep hiking and took them to a chilly, damp altitude of more than 8,000 feet above sea level, but as Che looked around and surveyed the scene, he felt renewed optimism. Herds of cattle and the tiny hamlets of ethnic Tutsi Rwandans dotted the plain. Good Argentine that he was, Che wrote that during his stay there, the availability of "wonderful beef was almost a cure for nostalgia."

Che quickly began getting organized, overseeing the building of huts to house his fighters together with about twenty bored and lonely Congolese. Once again he began daily classes to cut through the mounting apathy and listlessness that threatened to consume them, but very soon Che became aware of still more problems he would have to deal with. In addition to the civilian herdsmen living around Luluabourg, he learned, there were several thousand more Tutsi living in the area who were armed and had allied themselves with the Congolese rebels. They had fled their country following Rwanda's independence from France a few years earlier, when their traditional rivals, the Hutu, had begun massacring them. By helping the Congolese to victory, they hoped next to carry the revolution to Rwanda, but despite their marriage of convenience, the Rwandans and Congolese didn't get along at all. This enmity, like *dawa,* was to cause serious problems in the months ahead.

After only a few days, Che developed an extremely high fever and became delirious. It was a month before he regained his strength or his appetite. He was not the only man affected; ten of the thirty Cubans were ill with one fever or another. "During the first month, at least a dozen comrades paid for their initiation into hostile territory with these violent fevers," Che wrote, "the aftereffects of which were bothersome."

Coinciding with Che's return to health, Leonard Mitoudidi arrived back, with ambitious orders for Che to lead a force of two rebel columns in an attack against the enemy bastion at Albertville. "The order is absurd," Che wrote at the time. "There's only 30 of us, of whom 10 are sick or convalescing." But despite his strong misgivings, Che didn't want to start out on the wrong foot, and so he told his men to prepare themselves for battle.

On May 22, as they were thus engaged, a Congolese runner arrived in camp announcing excitedly that a "Cuban minister" had arrived. By now, Che was accustomed to hearing all sorts of wild rumors, the Congolese having a "Radio Bemba" bush telegraph every bit as florid as Cuba's own, but shortly afterward he was stunned to see none other than Osmany Cienfuegos appear before him at the head of a fresh contingent of seventeen new Cubans. A further seventeen had remained behind in Kigoma, awaiting transportation across the lake. This brought the number of Cuban guerrillas on hand to more than sixty.

"In general, the news [Osmany] brought was very good," Che recalled in the Congolese *Pasajes*. "But he brought for me personally the saddest news of the war. Telephone calls from Buenos Aires had revealed that my mother was very sick. The implication was that this was just a preparatory announcement. . . . I had to spend a month in sad uncertainty, awaiting the results of something I could guess but with the hope that the report had been a mistake. Then the confirmation of my mother's death arrived. . . . She never saw the farewell letter that I had left in Havana for my parents."*

The fact that Che included something so personal in his account is an indication of how deeply the episode affected him, but "sad uncertainty" was an understatement. Among Che's personal belongings that later came into Aleida's possession were three pieces of writing, rather like short stories, all very dark and anguished, written in the tortured symbolism of some of his youthful literary efforts, including one that expressed his grief over the loss of his mother.†

Celia had died on May 19, three days before Osmany arrived at Che's base camp. She had succumbed to cancer at the age of fifty-eight. Toward the end, she had been living alone in her little apartment adjoining her daughter Celia's, meeting with a small circle of friends during the week and seeing her children and grandchildren on the weekends. Few people around her realized she was ill. According to her daughter-in-law María Elena Duarte, she had intentionally concealed her illness until the very end, when she collapsed and nothing remained but the deathwatch.

On May 10, Celia had been taken to the exclusive Stapler Clinic in Buenos Aires, where she was placed in a private room with a large picture window. María Elena would find her staring out the window with a look of rapturous longing. "All I ask for," Celia said, "is one more day." Friends such as Ricardo Rojo and Julia Constenla visited her and took turns at her bedside. Desperate to help despite their long estrangement, her ex-husband rushed around trying to find some way to save her, even going to the Soviet embassy after hearing that the Russians had discovered a cure for cancer. His presence must have comforted Celia during those final days. She confided to María Elena that he had been the first and only man in her life, and despite everything, she still felt love for him. But the specter of Che imposed itself even now. When the clinic's managers made evident their displeasure over having the mother of a prominent Communist in their facility, the family moved her to another clinic.

---

*Che noted that the letter to his parents was released in October 1965, when Fidel finally broke silence and divulged Che's farewell letter to him.

†See Notes.

Celia begged Ricardo and Julia to call Havana and ask Aleida where Che was. In March, Che's childhood friend Gustavo Roca had been in Havana and brought back a letter from him to Celia in which he said he was about to resign his jobs, go cut cane for a month, and then work in one of the Ministry of Industries' factories in order to study things from the ground level. But Celia had not received the letter until April 13, by which time Che had vanished and all kinds of rumors had begun to circulate. She wrote a reply to Che's letter, and Ricardo Rojo agreed to send it to Havana with a trusted friend, but the friend was refused a visa.

On May 16, with Celia's death imminent and her anxiety about Che unresolved, Rojo called Aleida, who could say nothing except that Che wasn't in a place where she could contact him quickly. On May 18, Aleida called back and spoke to Celia. Rojo was present. "Celia was in a near-coma," he wrote, "but she sat up in bed as if an electric shock had run through her. It was a frustrating conversation, with a great deal of shouting and a sense of hopelessness." Celia had learned nothing new from the conversation, and so, in a final, futile effort, Rojo sent off a cable addressed to "Major Ernesto Guevara, Ministry of Industries, Havana": "Your mother very ill wants to see you. Your friend embraces you. Ricardo Rojo." No reply came, and the next day Celia died.

Celia's last letter to Che, which was never sent, was published in Rojo's book. In it, Celia expressed her disquiet over her son's fate, obviously assuming that there was truth, after all, to the rumors that he and Fidel had had a falling-out.

My dear one:

Do my letters sound strange to you? I don't know if we have lost the naturalness with which we used to speak to each other, or if we never had it and have always spoken with that slightly ironic tone used by those of us from the shores of the [Río de la] Plata, exaggerated by our own private family code. . . .

Since we have adopted this diplomatic tone in our correspondence, I . . . have to find hidden meanings between the lines and try to interpret them. I've read your last letter the way I read the news . . . , solving, or trying to, the real meanings and full implication of every phrase. The result has been a sea of confusion, and even greater anxiety and alarm.

I'm not going to use diplomatic language. I'm going straight to the point. It seems to me true madness that, with so few heads in Cuba with ability to organize, you should all go cut cane for a month . . .

when there are so many and such good cane cutters among the people. . . . A month is a long time. There must be reasons I don't know. Speaking now of your own case, if, after that month, you're going to dedicate yourself to the management of a factory, a job successfully performed by [Alberto] Castellanos and [Harry] Villegas, it seems to me that the madness has turned to absurdity. . . .

And this is not a mother speaking. It's an old woman who hopes to see the whole world converted to socialism. I believe that if you go through with this, you will not be giving your best service to the cause of world socialism.

If all roads in Cuba have been closed to you, for whatever reason, in Algiers there's a Mr. Ben Bella who would appreciate your organizing his economy, or advising him on it; or a Mr. Nkrumah in Ghana who would welcome the same help. Yes, you'll always be a foreigner. That seems to be your permanent fate.

At Celia's funeral service, Che's framed photograph sat prominently on the coffin. María Elena said that she felt sorry for Celia's other children: "It was as if they weren't there. It was as if she had only one child—Che." And in a way, as painful as it must have been for the others, that was true. The special bond that had always linked Celia and her firstborn son had to some degree excluded the others. And it had endured, as was obvious to everyone, right to the end.

V

In the Congo, Che sat down with Leonard Mitoudidi to discuss their military plans. He managed to convince Mitoudidi that an attack on Albertville was premature. He didn't know the true situation, and neither did the general staff, since they depended on the reports of far-flung field commanders who were often unreliable. Mitoudidi finally agreed with Che's proposal to send out four groups of guerrillas to the various front lines, and within days they began getting the first reports back. At a couple of the fronts, the men seemed well armed and disposed to fight, but everywhere there was passivity and general chaos. The *jefes* often drank to the point of stupefaction, passing out in full view of their troops. The rebels raced back and forth in jeeps, but did little to further the war effort. They occupied fixed positions and didn't train, go out on patrol, or gather intelligence. They forced the intimidated and mistreated local peasants to supply them with food. "The basic characteristic of the Popular Liberation Army," Che concluded, "was that of a parasitic army."

Che found the Congolese lazy. During marches, they carried nothing except their personal weapons, cartridges, and blankets, and if asked to help carry an extra load, whether food or some other item, they would refuse, saying, *"Mimi hapana Motocar"* ("I am not a truck"). As time wore on, they began saying, *"Mimi hapana Cuban"* ("I am not a Cuban"). Víctor Dreke found that the rebels on the Lulimba front were holding a hilltop position about four miles from the enemy post and had not descended from it in months. Instead of launching raids, they spent their days firing off a huge 75mm recoilless rifle in the general direction of the enemy, far out of range. The chief of this front, the self-proclaimed General Mayo, had manifested open hostility to both Kabila and Mitoudidi, seeing them as "foreigners." Mitoudidi had ordered Mayo to come and see him, but the man had refused. Mitoudidi did his best to whip his men at Luluabourg into shape, punishing the *pombe* drinkers by burying them in the earth up to their necks, suspending the distribution of arms, and giving stern lectures.

Che told Mitoudidi that he felt isolated from the Congolese rank and file because of the language barrier, and Mitoudidi lent one of his aides, a teenager named Ernesto Ilanga, to give Che daily Swahili lessons. Nevertheless, by early June Che was getting increasingly claustrophobic. He sent out more exploration groups; but without the approval of Mitoudidi's superior officer, Laurent Kabila, they could undertake no action on their own. There was an erratic flow of notes from Kabila, saying that he was about to come, that he was delayed, that he would arrive tomorrow without fail, or the day after. "And boats kept arriving with good quantities of arms of great quality," Che wrote. "It was really pathetic to observe how they wasted the resources of the friendly countries, fundamentally China and the Soviet Union, the efforts of Tanzania, the lives of some fighters and civilians, to do so little with it."

On June 7, as Mitoudidi made ready to inspect a spot a short distance down the lakeshore where the general staff camp was to be moved, he and Che talked. Che asked him what the truth was behind Kabila's nonappearance, and Mitoudidi confessed that the commander probably wouldn't be visiting just yet. Chou En-lai, the Chinese premier, was coming to Dar, and Kabila had to meet him to discuss requests for aid. Che headed back up the mountain, but before he had reached the top, a messenger caught up with him to report that Mitoudidi had drowned. It was a severe blow, for Che had come to see Mitoudidi as his best hope of achieving anything at all in the Congo. In *Pasajes,* Che titled the chapter in which he wrote of this death "A Hope Dies," and indeed, the murky circumstances of Leonard Mitoudidi's demise seemed to sum up everything that was wrong with this "revolution" Che had come to assist.

According to a couple of Cubans who were in the boat with Mitoudidi, the lake was choppy, with a strong wind blowing, and Mitoudidi had apparently fallen into the water by accident. But Che was suspicious. "From that moment on, a series of strange events occurred, which I don't know whether to attribute to imbecility, to the extraordinary degree of superstition—since the lake is populated by all kinds of spirits—or something more serious." Mitoudidi had remained afloat, calling for help, for ten or fifteen minutes, but two men who dived in to save him also drowned. Meanwhile, the men in the boat had cut the engine, and when they restarted it, "it seemed that some magical force did not permit them to go to where Mitoudidi was; in the end, as he was still crying for help, the boat was steered to the shore and the comrades watched him disappear a little while later."

In late June, after two months of doing "absolutely nothing," the Cubans' war in the Congo finally began. Mudandi, a Chinese-trained Rwandan Tutsi rebel commander, arrived from Dar with orders from Kabila. The plan to attack Albertville had been scrapped, and Che was now to assault the military garrison and hydroelectric plant at Fort Bendera instead. Kabila wanted the Rwandans and Cubans to lead the raiding party, which should take place in a week's time. Che was not enthusiastic about the plan. He had heard from Mudandi's Tutsi that the Bendera garrison was well entrenched, with as many as 300 soldiers and 100 white mercenaries. It seemed too large a target for his ill-prepared force, much less the Congolese. He proposed a smaller target, but in the end decided to go ahead with Kabila's plan, reasoning that any action at all was better than none. But after sending repeated requests to Kabila to be allowed to accompany the attack force himself and receiving no reply, Che was forced to stay behind; in late June a column of forty Cubans and 160 Congolese and Rwandan Tutsi set out for Bendera.

The attack, which begun on July 29, was a catastrophe. The assault leader, Víctor Dreke, reported that at the first outbreak of combat, many of the Tutsi fled, abandoning their weapons, while many of the Congolese simply refused to fight at all. Over a third of the men had deserted before the fighting even began. Four Cubans were killed, and one of their diaries fell into enemy hands, which meant that the mercenaries and the CIA—which had sent anti-Castro Cuban exiles to fly bombing and reconnaissance missions for the government forces—now knew that Cubans were directly assisting the rebels. Indeed, as the mercenary commander Mike Hoare wrote later, the unusually audacious rebel attack had led him to suspect that the rebels were getting outside help; the captured diary, which among other things mentioned Havana, Prague, and Peking as a travel itinerary, was his first conclusive proof of a Cuban guerrilla presence in the region.

The Africans attributed their defeat to bad *dawa,* and said that the witch doctor who had applied it to the fighters had been inadequate. "[The witch doctor] tried to defend himself, blaming it on women and on fear, but there were no women there . . . and not all the men were prepared to confess their weaknesses," Che wrote. "It didn't look good for the witch doctor and he was demoted." The Congolese and Rwandans who had participated in the debacle were humiliated and demoralized, and the Cubans were furious. If the Congolese wouldn't fight for themselves, why should they? The spirit of "proletarian internationalism" was something Che had taken to heart with profound personal conviction, but under these circumstances, it was evident that not all his Cuban comrades had the same level of commitment. A number of them were overheard saying they wanted to return home.

"The symptoms of decomposition among our troops were palpable," Che admitted. "Maintaining morale was one of my main concerns." Hoping for some action, he sent a letter to the general staff officers in Kibamba, expressing his irritation over the performance at Bendera and demanding to know what he was supposed to do with the new Cubans who were arriving. He also wrote to Kabila, arguing that he needed to be allowed to join personally in future military operations.

While wounded men arrived in a steady stream and were carried back from the battle zone, a fourth group of Cubans arrived at the lakeside Kibamba base. Among them was Harry Villegas, Che's former bodyguard, who had been left out of Masetti's mission because he was black. Fidel had handpicked Villegas to provide personal security for Che, and to make sure he came to no harm in the Congo. Villegas had recently married one of Che's secretaries, a pretty Chinese-mulatta girl named Cristina Campuzano, but he had left her and their newborn son to be with his *jefe* and teacher. Villegas was now renamed Pombo, a pseudonym that in time would be famous.

Che took advantage of the newcomers' arrival to give a pep talk and a warning at the same time, appealing to the Cubans' spirit of *combatividad* to try to quash the growing dissension. "I emphasized the need to maintain a rigid discipline," he wrote. He went on to publicly criticize one of the Cubans for making "defeatist remarks." "I was very explicit about what we faced; not just hunger, bullets, suffering of all kinds, but also the possibility of death from our [African] comrades, who didn't have a clue how to shoot properly. The struggle would be long and difficult; I made this warning because at that moment I was prepared to accept that any of the newcomers air their doubts and return [to Cuba] if they so desired; afterward it would not be possible." None of the newcomers showed "signs of weakness," but to his dismay, three of the men who had been in the attack on Bendera did.

"I recriminated them for their attitude and warned them that I would request the strongest sanctions against them."

Che's indignation turned into a sense of personal betrayal when one of his bodyguards, Sitaini, a man who had been with him since the sierra, asked to leave as well. "What made it even more painful was that he used phony arguments about not having heard what I had warned everyone, that the war would last at best three years and with bad luck five," Che wrote. "The duration and harshness of the war had been one of my constant litanies and Sitaini knew it better than anyone because he was always with me. I told him that he couldn't leave because it would be a discredit to both of us; he was obliged to stay." From that moment on, Che wrote, Sitaini was like a "dead man." A couple of months later, Che allowed him to leave, but evidently he didn't speak to him again, and people in Cuba who knew Sitaini say he never recovered from this precipitous and humiliating fall from grace.

More bad news had come from farther afield. On June 19, a coup had toppled Che's friend, the Algerian president Ben Bella. The coup was led by Ben Bella's own defense minister, Houari Boumédienne. This boded ill for the Cuban operations in Africa; Algeria was an essential partner in the multilateral effort to support the Congolese rebels against the regime in Léopoldville. Fidel had immediately condemned the coup and its new leadership, so the hard-won "unity" between the two revolutionary states appeared to have come apart in one fell swoop.

Before Che had even had a chance to organize an effective fighting force, everything seemed to break down. With Mitoudidi dead, he was forced to deal with men who had little political schooling, little sense of mission, and even less fighting spirit. And, after three months in the field, Kabila still hadn't shown up. He had taken to sending barbed notes urging Che to buck up, to "have courage and patience," reminding him in a patronizing manner that he was "a revolutionary and had to withstand such difficulties," and of course repeating the message that he would soon be coming.

Che must have been furious, but he was exquisitely diplomatic in his responses, reiterating his respect and loyalty, both to the Congolese cause and to Kabila as his commander, merely stressing that he needed to talk to Kabila and offering an apology about his covert manner of showing up. Che included this mollification because he now strongly suspected that Kabila resented his presence. He thought this might be why Kabila had not come to the front. "There are serious indications that my presence doesn't give him the least pleasure," Che observed. "It is yet to be known whether this is due to fear, jealousy, or wounded feelings."

Meanwhile, the government troops and mercenaries had begun to probe deeper into rebel territory, sending spotter planes over the lake and

Che instructing his fighters.

making strafing runs against boat traffic and the lakeshore base at Kibamba. This caused alarm at the general staff headquarters, and in response to a plea for help, Che grudgingly dispatched some of his Cubans to man the heavy machine guns in order to provide antiaircraft defense. "My state of mind was very pessimistic in those days," Che acknowledged, "but I climbed down with a certain happiness on July 7 when it was announced that Kabila had arrived. At last the *jefe* was in the field of operations!"

Kabila had indeed come, and he brought with him a commander to replace Mitoudidi, Ildefonse Masengo. But, in a further sign that all was not well within the rebel leadership, Kabila was even more critical of Gaston Soumaliot, his political leader, than he had been when Che first met him in Dar es Salaam. He called Soumaliot a demagogue, among other things. Kabila returned to Tanzania after only five days in Kibamba, explaining that it was important for him to meet with Soumaliot to work out their problems. He had galvanized his troops when he was there, and they set to work digging antiaircraft trenches and building a new clinic, but when he left—some jaundiced Cubans had taken bets on how long he would stay—everything fell apart again. The Congolese put down their shovels and refused to work.

An internal power struggle was taking place among the political leaders who made up the National Liberation Council, each of whom drew strength from alleged power on the military battlefield and from a series of shifting alliances with various regional guerrilla commanders. These men were the visible faces of the Congolese rebellion to the outside world—holding summits; meeting with heads of state such as Nasser, Nyerere, and Chou En-lai—and they had become the privileged recipients of huge amounts of foreign aid. The Chinese were still the primary supplier of the rebels' arms, and in some areas even of military advisers, but the Soviets and Bulgarians were also funneling in aid—such as the Soviet medicines Che had seen dumped on the lakeshore. All three nations were providing military and political training courses in their own countries to Congolese fighters.

Relations between the Rwandan Tutsi and the Congolese had fallen to an all-time low. Mudandi, the Tutsi commander whom Che held responsible for his fighters' pathetic performance at Bendera, had begun airing his grievances. His men had not fought, he said, because the Congolese didn't fight, and it was *their* country and *their* war after all. Over the succeeding weeks, Mudandi's rancor deepened and extended to open hostility against Kabila and the council leadership, whom he accused of willfully neglecting the men at the front.

Things went from bad to worse. Soon, word arrived that Mudandi had shot and killed his own deputy commander, apparently on charges that he was responsible for the bad *dawa* at Bendera. A Congolese rebel officer went to Mudandi's camp to investigate and was unceremoniously expelled; now this officer threatened to leave the Congo unless Mudandi was shot. Mudandi remained defiant and from his zone made it clear he was in a state of virtual rebellion against Kabila and the National Liberation Council, declaring that his men would no longer fight unless the Congolese did.

Matters were not helped by the fact that, in addition to their mistreatment of the peasants and one another, both the Tutsi and the Congolese showed an extraordinary degree of cruelty toward their prisoners. At one point, Che heard that a French mercenary had been captured on the lake and brought to a rebel camp where, by local custom, he had been buried up to his neck in the dirt. When Che sent men to seek the prisoner's release in order to obtain information, they got an evasive reply from the commander, and a day later were told that the prisoner had died.

The dissension in the Cubans' ranks continued to grow. Four more men, including two doctors, asked Che for permission to leave. "I was much less violent but much more hurtful with the doctors than with the simple soldiers, who reacted to things in a more or less primitive way," he recorded. But the growing specter of mass desertion by his own comrades drew him to deeper reflection. "The reality is that at the first serious reverse . . . several comrades lost heart and decided to retire from a struggle that they had sworn to come to and die for, if necessary (what's more, voluntarily), surrounded by a halo of bravura, sacrifice, enthusiasm—in a word, invincibility," he wrote. "What meaning does the phrase 'If necessary, unto death' have? In the answer to this lies the solution to the serious problems we face in the creation of our new men of tomorrow."

As for the military situation, Che had arrived at a crossroads. So far, he had doggedly clung to the hope that he could somehow get the Congolese rebels moving and turn the deteriorating situation around; but after Bendera he knew that unless something dramatic was done soon to improve the rebels' fighting ability, they were doomed. By the end of July, Che realized that his original time frame for seeing the Congolese revolution to victory was unrealistic, and he mused that "five years [now seemed] a very optimistic goal."

Che had been trying to keep up the pressure on the enemy by sending out Cuban-led patrols to lay road ambushes and, since he now knew that the rebels' own information network was worthless, to gather intelligence on the enemy's positions. These efforts produced some tragicomic results. One group, led by a Cuban called Aly, attacked a police unit, but, Che recorded gloomily, "Of the 20 Congolese who went with him . . . 16 ran away." In another, more successful attack, Papi Martínez Tamayo led a combined force of Cubans and Congolese to lay siege to the road between the enemy-held forts at Albertville and Bendera and was able to score a respectable blow, destroying two armored cars and a jeep driven in convoy by a crew of white mercenaries, killing seven. But in another joint Cuban-Rwandan ambush against an army truck, the Rwandans had run away, firing their weapons wildly, and one of the Cubans had lost a finger from this friendly fire. To make amends, the Rwandan commander had pulled out a knife and proposed cutting off the fingers of the culprit, but Papi prevailed upon him not to do so. Then the commander and his men proceeded to drink the whiskey and beer they found in the ambushed truck and got hopelessly drunk before shooting dead a peasant who happened by; they claimed he was a spy.

On August 12, Che issued a candid message to his Cuban fighters, acknowledging that their situation was bad and giving a fairly honest appraisal of the weaknesses of the rebel organization they had come to help. Its leaders, he said, did not come to the front; the fighters themselves did not fight and had no sense of discipline or sacrifice. "To win a war with such troops," he confessed, "is out of the question." As for his original plan of bringing guerrillas from other countries to be trained in the Congolese "school" of guerrilla warfare, such a notion was now unthinkable. When, a few days later, Pablo Ribalta sent word that he was dispatching a group of Cubans to assume the task of organizing a training base for Mozambican and other African guerrillas, Che wrote back to advise against it, citing the "indiscipline, disorganization, and total demoralization" they would find.

Since the defeat at Fort Bendera, Che had redoubled his efforts to persuade the Congolese to adopt his proposals. He outlined a plan for a new unified central military command, a rigorous training program, and a streamlined and disciplined food-supply system and communications network. He proposed that a rebel posse be formed to go after the deserters who were now marauding all over the region and disarm them, both to restore order and to recapture valuable weapons. He had kept up a barrage of petitions to Kabila, which typically received oblique or evasive responses, and he pursued his objectives in frequent conclaves with Masengo. On the surface, the new Congolese chief of staff seemed receptive, but he lacked authority to make decisions, and the situation dragged on without resolution.

Che again asked to be allowed to go into the field himself, but this request, made to Masengo, was met with alarm, ostensibly out of concern for Che's "personal security." Che refused to accept his explanation and demanded to know if the real problem was a lack of trust. Masengo strenuously denied this, and he relented, agreeing to take Che on a visit to some of the regional commands. Writing about this later, Che concluded that both Masengo and Kabila were well aware of the ill feeling their absences had spawned among their fighters, and feared being shown up if he were to visit the fronts where they had never even appeared.

As promised, Masengo took Che on a short inspection trip to nearby bases, but then a message came from Kabila asking his chief of staff to come to Kigoma. The power struggle within the rebel leadership had finally climaxed. In early August, Gaston Soumaliot ousted Christophe Gbenye as the leader of the Congolese National Revolutionary Council, on the grounds that Gbenye had betrayed his comrades by secretly negotiating with the Congo regime. Masengo promised Che he would be back in a day. When he still hadn't returned a week later, Che took off for the rebel front line near Fort Bendera, determined to see the conditions firsthand. It was August 18.

VI

With the enthusiasm of a chess master who senses victory, Fidel was dispatching a regular stream of Cuban fighters to Tanzania. In early September 1965, a fifth group arrived. Among them were the corpulent PURS secretary, Emilio Aragonés—immediately dubbed Tembo (elephant)—and Che's old sierra war sidekick and housemate, now chief of staff of Cuba's western army, Dr. Oscar Fernández Mell, renamed Siki (Vinegar), allegedly for his sour personality.

Fernández Mell had been on vacation at the Varadero beach resort when he got a surprise call from Havana. Although he had been privy to Che's disappearance—he had even taken Che's dental impression so that false teeth could be made for him as part of his disguise for leaving Cuba—he had not known, or asked, Che's destination, and had assumed it to be South America. "It was something he had talked to me about, and that he had proposed as far back as the Sierra Maestra," Mell recalled. "He had said that after liberating Cuba he was going to liberate his own country. It was his final objective—that's the great truth.... When they called me, I thought it was for *that,* but when I was told it was for Africa, I didn't even think about it. I said, 'Well, if he's there, that's where we go.'"

Fernández Mell said that in Cuba the general feeling toward Che's African mission was euphoria. "They said that everything was all right, that everything was marching along and they had had some victorious battles, et cetera. And that our mission was to lend Che a hand and help in everything and to serve as a kind of backup." He and Aragonés had gone off with enthusiasm, even though Fidel had expressed concern that Che seemed "overly pessimistic" about the prospects. It hadn't taken them long to realize that things on the ground were not as had been painted for them.

In Dar es Salaam, they met Kabila, who was driving around in a Mercedes Benz. Then, in Kigoma, Kabila's men refused to let them cross the lake in what they called "Kabila's launch," a new fast motorboat that the Cubans and Soviets had provided. They had to cross in a larger, slower boat. When they reached Kibamba, Kumi, the Cuban doctor at the base dispensary, told them, "You'll see what this is: a piece of shit." Pombo came down the hill to meet them as they struggled on the climb up, and from him they heard more details of just how bad things really were, and that Che, fed up with being "retained" at the base, had taken off. Knowing Che as he did, Mell was not surprised. "Underneath that calm demeanor he had, always writing, reading, and thinking, Che was a man of enormous activity," he said. "He was an erupting volcano who wanted to do things, and in the Congo, he wanted it to be like it was in the Sierra Maestra, he wanted to fight, he wanted to go to where the mercenaries were."

Che headed back to base when he heard that Fernández Mell and Aragonés had arrived. He was worried that they had orders to bring him back to Cuba and was relieved and gratified to learn he was mistaken. They had both volunteered to come, out of a desire to be a part of his mission.

The brief trip had revived Che's spirits. For the first time, he had entered into friendly contact with the peasants, and had reveled in it. "Like peasants anywhere in the world, they were receptive to any human interest taken in them," he wrote. He had carried out a little "social action," handing out vegetable seeds for planting and promising to send doctors on regular medical visits to the area. He briefly even returned to his old profession of doctoring, giving injections of penicillin against the most "traditional" disease he found, gonorrhea, and dispensing antimalaria pills. In one place, the villagers dressed up as bush devils and danced around a stone idol and sacrificed a sheep for him. "The ritual seems complicated, but it boils down to something very simple: a sacrifice is made to the god, the stone idol, and afterward the sacrificed animal is eaten, and everyone eats and drinks profusely."

Wherever he went, Che had tried hard to get the commanders to agree to send their men to his base for training, but invariably he found that they wanted the Cuban instructors to be sent to *them*. Their presence was seen as a sign of prestige. He had even set up some ambushes in which, for the first time, some of the Rwandans hadn't run but actively participated. These were slim grounds for optimism, but after so many months of gloom and inaction Che felt that headway had been made.

September brought him back to reality. The Tanzanian government was now throwing obstacles in the way of the Congolese, and it was becoming difficult for them to move men and supplies out of Kigoma. In the Congo itself, a pro-Gbenye faction had begun causing problems in some of the outlying rebel areas, and there were a few armed standoffs between pro- and anti-council factions. Masengo was shot at in a couple of pro-Gbenye villages and had to beat a retreat. The situation was becoming dangerous for the Cubans, who no longer knew who was friend or foe. Still, Che was anxious to pull together some coordinated actions against the mercenaries before they took the initiative. After sending units out to reinforce rebel defenses, he went to the town of Fizi, the domain of the rebel strongman General Moulana, where he found the general's antiaircraft defenses to consist of a single machine gun manned by a Greek mercenary prisoner. Che tried to persuade Moulana to bring his men to the lake for training, but the general refused. The trip wasn't a total waste, however, since Moulana provided Che with one of the more colorful spectacles of his time in the Congo. Taking his distinguished visitor to his home village, Baraka, Moulana put on a special outfit. "It consisted of a motorcycle helmet with a leopard skin on top, which gave him a really ridiculous appearance," Che observed. His bodyguard, Carlos Coello—now Tumaini, or Tuma—dubbed Moulana "the Cosmonaut." In Baraka, the Cubans had to endure a "Chaplinesque" parade ceremony. The saddest thing about it, Che noted later, was that the Congolese fighters seemed to enjoy parading around more than learning how to fight properly.

Next Che moved on to the house of General Lambert, a rival of Moulana's and the man who had introduced Che to *dawa*. Lambert promptly got smashed on *pombe,* and was such a funny drunk that Che did not even bother to lecture him. He left after securing Lambert's promise of 350 men for an operation against the Lulimba garrison. (Predictably, Lambert never produced such a force.)

By early October, Che realized that it was going to be impossible to organize a successful attack unless he altered his approach radically—and when Masengo finally returned, he had come up with a plan. To avoid having to deal with the existing—and to Che's mind, completely incorrigible—rebels, he wanted to recruit fighters from among the local peasantry, for an independent fighting column, which he would command. "We would create a kind of fighting school," Che explained later. "Also, we would organize a new and more rational General Staff that would direct operations on all fronts."

While Che was in the midst of his meeting with Masengo, "trying to raise the Liberation Army from the ruins," as he described it, one of the Cubans in camp dropped a burning lighter, and in a flash a fire began. One after the other, their straw huts burst into flames. Pombo managed to save Che's diary and a few other things from their hut, but then everyone fled as grenades left in the huts began exploding. Che punished the unlucky culprit, an otherwise good cadre, by ordering him to go three days without food.

"In the midst of this party of bullets and exploding grenades," he wrote, "Machadito, our minister of public health, arrived, with some letters and a message from Fidel."

José Ramón Machado Ventura—Machadito—the doctor who had extracted the M-1 bullet from Che's foot in the sierra, had come to assess the health needs in the rebel territory as the result of a remarkable request made by Gaston Soumaliot for fifty Cuban doctors. When, a few weeks earlier, Che had learned that Fidel was planning to host Soumaliot on a visit to Havana, he had sent a message advising him not to receive the rebel leader, and certainly not to give him any material assistance. Che's missive either arrived too late or was ignored, for Fidel had feted Soumaliot, who had painted an idyllic picture for him of the Congolese revolution; when asked for the fifty Cuban doctors, Fidel had quickly agreed. After hearing Che's adamant objections and seeing the situation for himself, Machadito promised to relay Che's assessment to Fidel.

"I had already learned through Tembo that the feeling in Cuba was that my attitude was very pessimistic," Che wrote. "This was now reinforced by a personal message from Fidel in which he counseled me not to despair, reminded me of the first stage of the [Cuban] struggle, and to remember that these inconveniences always happen."

Taking advantage of Machadito's prompt departure, Che wrote a long letter to the *jefe*. "Dear Fidel: I received your letter, which provoked contradictory feelings in me, since in the name of international proletarianism we commit errors which can be very costly. Also, it worries me personally that, whether for my lack of seriousness in writing, or because you don't comprehend me totally, it could be thought that I suffer from the terrible sickness of undue pessimism. . . . I'll just tell you that here, according to those around me, I have already lost my reputation as an objective observer, as the result of maintaining an entirely unwarranted optimism in the face of the existing situation. I can assure you that if I was not here, this beautiful dream would have dissolved long ago in the general chaos."

Che went on to give Fidel a brutally realistic picture of the way the foreign aid was being wasted by the Congolese. "Three brand-new Soviet launches arrived little more than a month ago and two are now useless and the third, in which your emissary crossed, leaks all over the place," he wrote. All he wanted was 100 more Cubans—"they don't all have to be black"— and some bazookas, fuses for their mines, and R-4 explosive. As for the requested doctors, Che told him, "With 50 doctors, the liberated zone of the Congo would have an enviable proportion of one for every thousand inhab-

Che; José Ramón Machado Ventura, the Cuban minister of health;
Emilio Aragonés ("Tembo"), the organization secretary of the
Partido Unificado de la Revolución Socialista; and Che's friend
Oscar Fernández Mell.

itants, a level that surpasses the U.S.S.R., the U.S., and the two or three other
most advanced nations of the world. . . .

"Have a little faith in my criteria and don't judge by appearances," Che
finished, adding that Fidel should "shake up" the people supplying him with
information, who, he said, "present utopic images which don't have anything to do with the truth. I've tried to be explicit and objective, concise and
truthful. Do you believe me?"

Indeed, the efforts of Cuba and the other nations helping the Congolese rebels were being squandered. A group of Congolese fighters had
recently arrived at the lake, fresh from six months of training in Bulgaria
and China, but Che noted with sarcasm that their first concern was to ask
for fifteen days of vacation to visit their families. "Later they would stretch
it because it had been too short. In any case, they were trained revolutionary cadres, they couldn't risk themselves in the fighting, it would have been

irresponsible; they had come to inundate their comrades with the mountain of theoretical knowledge they had accumulated in six months, but the revolution should not commit the crime of making them fight."

Che turned to the task at hand: creating his envisioned "fighting academy," which in its latest genesis would be made up of 210 men, including peasants and rebels from the three main fronts. After what he had seen there, he was also doubtful about General Moulana's ability or willingness to defend the strategic Fizi plain, a certain attack route in the event of a government offensive. He sent Mell with some men to try to "talk sense" to the Cosmonaut-General, with orders to do what he could to organize Fizi's defenses.

Once again Che had to lecture his grumbling Cuban troops. "I told them that the situation was difficult," he wrote. "The Liberation Army was falling apart and we had to fight to save it from ruin. Our work would be very hard and unpleasant and I could not ask them to have faith in the triumph; personally I believed that things could be fixed although with a lot of work and a multitude of partial failures. Nor could I ask them to have confidence in my leadership ability, but, as a revolutionary, I could demand that they show respect for my honesty. Fidel was aware of the fundamentals, and the incidents that had occurred had not been concealed from him; I had not come to the Congo to win personal glory, nor would I sacrifice anyone for my personal honor." The important thing now was for the men to obey him, but Che realized that his words were not convincing. "Gone were the romantic days when I threatened to send the undisciplined ones back to Cuba; if I had done that now, I would have been lucky to keep half the troops."

On top of everything else, malaria as well as gastroenteritis continued to plague the Cubans. Che was also afflicted, as he wrote with black humor: "In my field diary I had recorded the statistics, in my case, of more than 30 depositions [defecations] in 24 hours, until the rigors of my runs vanquished my scientific spirit. How many more there were, only the bush knows."

Meanwhile, it did not appear he was making any headway in getting through to the Congolese fighters. One day, when they refused to do some work he had ordered, Che blew up. "Infuriated, I talked to them in French, I told them the most terrible things I could find in my poor vocabulary, and in the heights of my fury, I told them that I would put dresses on them and make them carry yucca in a basket (a female occupation) because they were worthless, and worse than women; I preferred to form an army with women rather than have individuals of their category. As the interpreter translated my outburst to Swahili, all the men looked at me and cackled with laughter with a disconcerting ingenuousness."

There were some other cultural barriers that simply never came down. One of them was the *dawa,* and Che finally opted for a pragmatic approach, hiring a witch doctor for his Congolese troops. "He occupied his place in the camp and took charge of the situation immediately," Che noted.

By mid-October, the onset of the rainy season, the long-awaited government offensive began. Che and his men were still unprepared. Backed up by a fleet of gunboats and fast launches, and a small air force of bombers, helicopters, and spotter aircraft, Mike Hoare's mercenaries began moving in on the rebel domain in a three-pronged encirclement manuever. They took General Moulana's front at Baraka and Fizi with ease, then Lubonja. General Lambert's defenses collapsed, and his men and the Cubans with them escaped in headlong flight toward the lake. Che sent Mell and Aragonés with Masengo to the lake to take charge there, while he dug in at a new camp at the edge of the foothills.

VII

The noose was being drawn tightly around Che, and then it was given another tug—not by Hoare's mercenaries, but by a political settlement reached between the Congolese government in Léopoldville and the Congolese Liberation Army's backers in the Organization of African Unity (OAU), which included Tanzania.

The OAU had blacklisted the Congo regime of Prime Minister Moise Tshombe because of his unholy alliance with the Belgian and white mercenary forces. On October 13, President Kasavubu ousted Tshombe, and in a meeting of African presidents in Accra ten days later, he announced that the white mercenaries would be sent home. It was to be a quid pro quo, however. If the mercenaries went, those states aiding the rebels would have to end their support as well. All foreign intervention in the Congo was to cease—and that meant the Cubans too.

Mike Hoare was not pleased when he heard the news and, in a meeting with Joseph Mobutu, the Congolese army chief, insisted that his men's contracts be honored. Mobutu prevailed upon Kasavubu to let the mercenaries stay until the rebellion had been completely crushed.

Che had been forewarned about the mounting external pressure for a negotiated settlement, and he knew from Masengo and others that the Tanzanians had become increasingly uncooperative. But in the field, events now took place in rapid succession, too quickly for Che to react effectively, let alone concentrate on the political machinations taking place. On the morning of October 24, the six-month anniversary of his arrival in the Congo, his base camp was overrun by government troops. Che had time to order that the huts be torched, but in the confusion of the retreat his men left behind large stocks of weapons and ammunition, communications equipment, food stores, papers, and two pet monkeys Che had kept.

As they withdrew, Che castigated himself for having been caught unaware. He had not posted sentries on the route the enemy had taken to approach, not believing they would come that way. He was even more bitter when he discovered that the initial panicked reports of the approaching enemy vanguard had been mistaken: they had actually been peasants fleeing the advancing government troops. If he had waited and found out the truth, Che could have mounted a good ambush and struck an important blow against the enemy. Now, it was too late.

"Personally, my morale was terribly depressed; I felt responsible for that disaster through weakness and lack of foresight," he wrote. As Che and his Cubans retreated, the Congolese fled past them, finding their own escape, and when Che reached a hilltop where he had ordered some Cubans who had gone ahead to wait for him, he found they had gone on. Che looked around at the little band of men who were still with him: it included Víctor Dreke, Papi, and his bodyguards Pombo and Tumaini—and Chamaleso, his original Congolese contact. "I made the bitter reflection that we were thirteen in number," Che wrote. "One more than Fidel had at a certain moment [after the *Granma*'s landing], but I was not the same leader."

Che and his men marched on through a desolate landscape of abandoned hamlets whose peasant inhabitants had joined the rebels' flight toward the lake. They hiked on through the night and at dawn reached a village where they found one of the Cubans, Bahaza, gravely wounded with a bullet in the lung.

After doing what he could to alleviate Bahaza's condition, Che ordered the column forward, leaving the valley to find safer refuge in the hills. Under a heavy rainfall, and up a steep mountain trail slippery with mud, with the men taking turns carrying Bahaza, everyone experienced the next six hours as a grinding ordeal. From the heights, they observed a terrible spectacle: on adjacent hills were fleeing peasants, while in the valley below columns of smoke rose from burning huts as the advancing government troops burned everything in their path. Reaching a small village filled with hungry refugees, Che was berated by angry peasants who said the soldiers had carried off their wives, but they had been helpless to save the women because they had only spears; the rebels had not given them guns to defend themselves.

Bahaza died at dawn the next day. "Bahaza was the sixth man we lost and the first whose body we were able to honor," Che wrote. "And that body was a mute and virile accusation, as was his conduct from the moment of his wounding, against my . . . stupidity." Che gathered his men around and gave what he described as a "soliloquy loaded with self-reproach."

"I recognized the errors I had committed and I said, which was a great truth, that of all the deaths that had occurred in the Congo, Bahaza's was the most painful for me, because he had been the comrade I had seriously reprimanded* for his weakness and because he had responded like a true Communist [by acknowledging it] . . . , but that I hadn't been up to my responsibilities, and I was guilty of his death. For my part, I would try to do everything I could to erase that error, through more work and more enthusiasm than ever."

But it was not to be. As Che dug in at his new site, the recriminations began. Word came that Congolese commanders such as Lambert were saying the defeat was Che's fault, that the Cubans were cowardly and had betrayed them. Fernández Mell and Aragonés kept up a flow of messages to Che from the lakeside base at Kibamba, urging him to abandon his position; an enemy attack could be expected at any moment, and he could easily be cut off from escape to the lake.

The Congolese government was now trying to press its advantage by forming alliances with some of the rebel leaders. Masengo had informed Aragonés and Fernández Mell that President Kasavubu had sent him a secret message, offering him a government ministry if he abandoned the struggle. "If they've approached Masengo," Aragonés and Mell warned Che, "they must also be working on Soumaliot and Kabila."

On October 30, they sent Che a new urgent note, begging him to join them on the lake. Planes had begun firebombing positions around Kibamba, and they feared that this was just the prelude to a final assault. The base was becoming chaotic, a refuge for all kinds of "deserters, criminals, and traitors," and there was no control. "The thing is really alarming," they stressed. "We think we've been writing you quite enough and have kept you abreast of the international situation as well as the one here. We almost seem like two gossipy old ladies. We beg you to do the same as us since we are always anxious for news (then we can be three gossips)."

Che finally decided to heed their advice. Leaving Papi with a group of Congolese at his new village base with orders to continue the military training sessions, he headed down to Kibamba. Although virtually everyone around him believed the so-called Congolese revolution to be in its death throes, Che refused to give up hope, and even now was trying to shore up

*Che had censured Bahaza only days before for abandoning a weapon in the exodus from Lambert's front.

the outlying fronts that had not yet been overrun. In his habitual end-of-month summary, he concluded that October had been a "month of disaster without qualifiers. . . . In summary, we enter a month [November] which may be definitive."

But even as Che was writing, the rug was being pulled out from under him. On November 1, Ambassador Ribalta was called in by the Tanzanian government and informed that, because of the agreements reached at Accra, Tanzania had decided to end "the nature of its assistance" to the Congolese National Liberation Movement. An urgent message was sent to Che, telling him the news.

"It was the coup de grâce for a moribund revolution," Che wrote. Given the delicate nature of the information, he decided not to tell Masengo, and to base any decision he made on how matters developed over the next few days. Then on November 4, Che received a telegram from the embassy giving him an advance summary of a letter from Fidel, the full text of which was being brought to him by courier. It was Fidel's response to the letter Che had sent with Machadito a month earlier. The summary of Fidel's points was as follows:

1. We must do all we can short of the point of absurdity.
2. If in Tatu's [Che's] judgment, our presence is becoming unjustifiable and useless, we should think about retiring. You should act according to the objective situation and the spirit of our men.
3. If you think you should stay, we will try to send as many human and material resources as you deem necessary.
4. We are worried that you erroneously fear that your attitude has been considered defeatist or pessimistic.
5. If you decide to stay, Tatu can maintain status quo returning here or remaining in another place.
6. We support any decision you take.
7. Avoid annihilation.

Using the field radio, Che dictated a message to Dar es Salaam to be relayed to Fidel, briefing him on the current situation. A few days earlier, he told Fidel, when rumors were spreading of a mass escape by the Congolese rebel leaders to Tanzania, he had resolved to stay behind with twenty handpicked men. They would have continued to try to assemble a guerrilla force; if they failed, he would go overland to another front or seek political asylum in Tanzania. That option had ended, however, with Tanzania's decision to suspend its support.

Che proposed that a high-level Cuban delegation be sent to Tanzania to speak with Nyerere and outline the Cuban position, which was that "Cuba [had] offered its aid subject to Tanzania's approval. It was accepted and the aid became effective. We comprehend Tanzania's present difficulties but we are not in agreement with its proposals. Cuba does not retreat from its promises, nor will it accept a shameful escape leaving its [Congolese] brothers in disgrace at the mercy of the mercenaries. We will only abandon the struggle if, for well-founded reasons or force majeure, the Congolese themselves ask us to, but we will continue fighting so that this does not come to pass."

Che also asked Fidel to solicit a minimum of continued support from Tanzania: to allow them to keep open their communication with Dar es Salaam, and permission to continue using the lake for food and arms supply runs. Finally, he advised Fidel to pass a copy of his letter along to the Chinese and the Soviets "to forestall any discrediting maneuver."*

By November 10, the situation was continuing to unravel on the perimeter of the reduced rebel territory. One of the Rwandan Tutsi positions was overrun and the enemy was advancing steadily toward the lake. With food and medical supplies running low at Kibamba, Che sent a telegram to the Cuban stations in Kigoma and Dar es Salaam. "Enemy pressure increases and the [Tanzanian] lake blockade still in place. Substantial quantities of Congolese currency are urgently needed in event of isolation. You have to move quickly. We are preparing to defend the base."

On November 14, Che's Cuban launch captain, Changa, crossed the lake from Kigoma carrying food and a Cuban intelligence official from Dar with a new message from Fidel. He advised Che that the Tanzanian government was showing no sign of moderating its position. The emissary from Dar asked if he should begin preparing a "clandestine base" for Che in Tanzania, given the current official posture, and Che told him he should.

---

*A Cuban intelligence official who was directly involved in the Cuban operation in the Congo at the administrative level told me that Soviet rivalry with the Chinese exerted a direct influence in the Congolese denouement. "I think the Soviets wanted to be rid of Che," he said. He indicated that the Soviets, while cooperating with the Cuban- and African-backed rebel alliance, had done so primarily in order to compete in an area staked out by the Chinese; that when the winds shifted, Moscow had thrown its weight behind the negotiated settlement, thus dooming the Congolese revolutionary cause—and Che's personal effort. Bolstering this analysis, a senior Cuban official acknowledged seeing something in Che's notes (presumably his original, handwritten, Congo diary) alluding to his suspicion that the Soviets had "pressured" the Tanzanian president, Nyerere, into calling for a Cuban withdrawal.

In a ludicrous sideshow, the boat captain had also brought over forty new Congolese rebel "graduates," fresh from a training course in the Soviet Union. Like their Bulgarian- and Chinese-trained predecessors, they immediately requested two weeks of vacation, while also complaining that they had nowhere to put their luggage. "It would be a little comic if it weren't so sad," Che wrote, "to see the disposition of these boys in whom the revolution had deposited its faith."

Despite the efforts of Cuban commanders in the field, the rebel defenses continued to crumble. On November 16, Che sent an SOS to the Cuban embassy in Dar es Salaam requesting arms supplies from the cache in Kigoma. He accused the Tanzanian authorities of intentionally blockading his logistics pipeline, and asked the embassy to demand a clear response as to what their intentions were. Enemy gunboats were patrolling the lake, and he needed action now.

That same day, Papi, still in the mountains, sent word that he needed reinforcements urgently. The Rwandans with him had deserted en masse that morning, taking their weapons with them, and now the Congolese were leaving, as well. It was devastating news: without sufficient men at the front there was no way to hold back the enemy advance.

Che held a conclave to discuss strategy with the Congolese leaders at hand: Masengo, Chamaleso, and a couple of others (despite repeated entreaties, Kabila had still not crossed the lake). As they saw it, there were only two alternatives: a fight to the end in their present position or a breakout attempt, cutting through enemy lines and escaping either north or south. The first option was discarded because of the unreliability of their fighters, and they tentatively decided to make a break for the south, through an area called Bondo. Che ordered Dreke and another of his officers, Aly, to make a quick reconnaissance trip there to see what the possibilities were.

As Che recorded it, Aly exploded, saying it was time to stop "running over hills without having these people's cooperation." "I answered him cuttingly that we would organize the evacuation from Bondo and he could leave with the group that left the struggle; he replied immediately that he would stay with it to the end."*

Deciding that it was unfair to keep the secret any longer, Che now told Masengo of Tanzania's decision to end its support, telling him to draw his own conclusions. Evidently, the news was definitive for Masengo and his comrades; that night, Chamaleso came to tell Che that all the rebel officers in camp had decided to end the campaign. Che took the news badly, telling

*See Notes.

Chamaleso that if that was the case, he wanted their decision in writing. "I told him that there was something called history, which is made up of much fragmentary data and which can be twisted." Che wanted documentation in case the Congolese later said that it had been a Cuban decision to withdraw. Chamaleso said he didn't think Masengo would agree to sign such a letter, but went off to confer.

Just then, a field telephone call informed Che that his upper base had fallen. His men had retreated without a fight, and the enemy was advancing in large numbers. Che reacted swiftly, proposing an immediate retreat, which Masengo accepted. Chamaleso took the occasion to inform Che that he had talked again with the officers and they were still unanimous in their desire to withdraw "definitively" from the battlefield. That was an academic point now, as Che noted: "Within five minutes, the telephone operators had disappeared, all the military police had run away, and chaos took over the base."

VIII

When Che decided to withdraw, on November 18, night had already fallen on the camp. Che radioed Kigoma to prepare the boats for an evacuation. He ordered his men to burn the huts and conceal what equipment they could, and to bring the heavy weapons, in case they had to make a last stand. They began slowly walking toward the lakeshore at dawn, straining under their loads, abandoning some pieces of equipment by the side of the trail. Che noted that his men's faces showed "a centuries-old weariness," and he tried to hurry them along. Behind them, explosions shot fire and smoke up into the sky: someone had set fire to their ammunition stores. Most of the Congolese had fled, and Che let them go, knowing that when they reached the lake, there would not be enough boats to transport everyone.

They had decided on a rendezvous point on the lakeshore about six miles south of Kibamba, and during their march, Che sent new radio messages to Kigoma, asking for the launches to meet them that night. By afternoon they had reached the evacuation point; Che radioed again, saying he and his men were in place, the war was over, and it was urgent that they be withdrawn. His calls finally got a response: "Copied." Che wrote, "When they heard the 'copied' from the lake, the expression of all the comrades present changed as if a magic wand had touched their faces."

But the boats did not arrive that night, or the next day. While they waited with increasing anxiety, Che set up ambushes to protect their perimeter, and sent men back to look for the missing. One man appeared the next morning, hobbling on a sprained ankle, but two other Cubans were still unaccounted for. That afternoon, November 20, Che radioed his launch captain, Changa, in Kigoma, saying he had 200 men to evacuate. Changa radioed back to explain that he had been detained by the Tanzanian authorities but would cross that night.

At this news, wrote Che, "the people were euphoric." He had already talked with Masengo and his general staff, and they had agreed that one of the Congolese commanders would stay behind with his men; Masengo and the others would be evacuated with the Cubans. But for the plan to work, those escaping had to deceive the Congolese fighters, and Che and Masengo decided to use various "pretexts" to embark the stranded fighters on a boat that would take them to a nearby village. When they were out of sight, the "real" evacuation would take place.

Things did not turn out so smoothly. While they managed to coax a good portion of the Congolese onto the first boat that arrived, those who remained "smelled something," recalled Che, and announced that they wanted to stay where they were. On the spot, Che ordered his men to carry out a selection of those Congolese who had shown the "best behavior" to be taken with them "as Cubans."

As he stood on the lakeshore, overseeing the final evacuation of the Cuban mission in the Congo, Che continued to mull over the possibility of staying behind to carry on the struggle. "The situation was critical. Two men who I had sent out on a mission would be abandoned unless they arrived in a few hours. As soon as we left all the weight of calumnies would fall upon us, inside and out of the Congo. I could extract, according to my research, up to twenty men who would follow me, although at this point with knit brows. And afterward, what would I do? The chiefs were all retreating; the peasants were displaying more and more hostility toward us. But the idea of evacuating completely and leaving behind defenseless peasants and practically defenseless armed men in defeat, and with the sensation of having been betrayed, I found deeply painful."

One of the options Che had been toying with in the last few days was the possibility of crossing the Congo to try to join up with the rebel force led by Pierre Mulele, but Mulele's territory was hundreds of miles away through the jungle, and it would be a feat just to survive the odyssey, much less organize an effective guerrilla force.

As they waited for the boats, Che continued to weigh his options, none of them good. "In reality," he acknowledged, "the idea of staying behind continued to circle around in my head long into the night." He was disturbed by the demeaning manner of his retreat and by thoughts of how he and his comrades would be remembered by the Congolese fighters left behind. "I passed the last hours solitary and perplexed," he wrote, "until, at two in the morning, the boats arrived." First the sick and wounded boarded, then

Masengo, his general staff, and about forty Congolese men they had selected to go with them. Finally, Che and the Cubans climbed aboard.

"It was a desolate, sobering, and inglorious spectacle," Che wrote. "I had to reject men who pleaded to be taken along. There was not a trace of grandeur in this retreat, nor a gesture of rebellion. The machine guns were prepared, and I had the men ready in case the [abandoned fighters] tried to intimidate us with an attack from land, but nothing like this happened. There was just some sobbing as I, the leader of the escapees, told the man with the mooring rope to let go."

28

No Turning Back

I

Within a couple of days of the Congo disaster, Che was safely concealed inside a small apartment in the Cuban embassy residence on the outskirts of Dar es Salaam. Ambassador Ribalta cleared out all the employees except for his cryptographer-telegraphist, a male secretary, and a cook, who never knew that there was a stranger living upstairs.

The other Cubans on the ill-fated expedition had been ferried by truck to Dar es Salaam and then were sent to Moscow and on to Havana aboard their own aircraft. Fernández Mell was left behind in Kigoma to organize a search-and-rescue mission for the two missing Cubans, and to evacuate the Congolese who had been left behind. It would be four months before he found the Cubans, in an odyssey that was to take him almost all the way to Rwanda.

Che and his men had had a close encounter with an armed Congolese government cutter on their way across Lake Tanganyika. Che bluffed his way out of the situation by having his men mount their 75mm recoilless rifles on the prows of the boats to give the appearance that they were well armed and prepared for battle. It was an audacious move. If the weapons had been fired, the afterblast alone would have killed many of those on board. In any case, the gunboat did not approach.

A small motorboat piloted by Cubans was waiting for Che when they neared the Kigoma shore. To ensure his safety, he was to be separated from the others and transported secretly to Dar es Salaam.

Taking Papi, Pombo, and Carlos Coello with him, Che boarded the small boat. He bade farewell to the rest of the fighters, telling them that he hoped to see them again. He said that some of them would go on to fight in other lands. It was an awkward and emotional moment. The

Cubans, although overjoyed to be going home, had mixed emotions about their experience.

Pombo said that when they got to shore, Che turned to his three young companions and said, "Well, we carry on. Are you ready to continue?" They understood then that Che was not going back to Cuba. "Where?" Pombo asked. And Che replied, "Wherever."

Pombo was twenty-five and Tuma was just a year older. Both of them had been close to Che since 1957, when they were teenagers and had joined him in the Sierra Maestra. Papi was twenty-nine and had been Piñeiro's point man in Che's guerrilla programs since 1962. They were among the half dozen or so men Che believed he could call upon to follow him "without knit brows," and he was not disappointed; in reply to his question on the Tanzanian shore, all said yes.*

"He could not return to Cuba without having achieved success," Pombo explained. "He thought that the best thing was to continue. Through his own efforts, with whatever possibilities, he had to continue the struggle."

Che had planned to be fighting for five years, but after only six months it was all over. Fidel had made Che's farewell letter public a month earlier, at the inaugural ceremony of the Cuban Communist Party. (The new Party replaced the Partido Unificado de la Revolución Socialita (PURS) as the country's single ruling party, complete with a new, offical Soviet-style central committee and Politburo.) In the farewell letter, Che had committed himself before the world to lend his hand in "new battle-fronts," and for reasons of pride, he felt he could not go back. Getting out of the Congo, however, was a good idea for several reasons. Even if the CIA did not already know where Che was, presumably it had put the Congo on the short list of possibilities after the capture of the Cuban guerrilla's diary at Bendera in June. Che had to assume they would be looking for him. As of late November 1965, he was probably the world's best-known Marxist revolutionary, a man for whom the goal of "proletarian internationalism" knew no frontiers. But for now, he had nowhere to go. He was truly a man without a country.

II

On November 25, four days after Che and his men left the Congo, Joseph Mobutu, the chief of staff of the armed forces, overthrew President Kasavubu. Mobutu's despotic regime, backed by the West, would endure for the next three decades. The Congolese revolution was over.

*See Notes.

After a few days in Dar es Salaam, Tuma and Pombo had flown to Paris and then to Moscow and Prague, where they were installed in a safe house provided by the Czech intelligence service. Holed up in his little apartment in the Tanzanian capital, visited only by Pablo Ribalta and the Cuban telegraphist, who took dictation, Che set to work on his Congolese memoirs. Just as he had measured his final actions in the Congo with an eye to history, Che set about writing this account with the intention of its eventual publication—"at the convenient time"—as his contribution to the annals of global socialist revolution. The title he chose, "Pasajes de la Guerra Revolucionaria (Congo)," echoed the title of his book on the Cuban revolutionary war and made the point that the Congo was just one more stage in a historic struggle that had as its final goal the liberation of the world's oppressed.

There was a marked difference between the two accounts. The book on the Cuban war contained many blunt reminders of mistakes and sacrifices, but it was primarily a paean to the heroism of the Cuban guerrillas, an exaltation of Fidel's unerring leadership that had taken them to victory, and a moral tale. The second memoir was a starkly negative reflection of the first, as Che made clear in his opening pages when he wrote, "This is the story of a failure." The dedication, "To Bahaza and his comrades, looking for a meaning to the sacrifice," indicated that Che was determined to expunge his sins in classic Marxist self-criticism. At the end of the book, he listed his own faults. "For a long time I maintained an attitude that could be described as excessively complacent," he said, "and at other times, perhaps due to an innate characteristic of mine, I exploded in ways that were very cutting and very hurtful to others."

Che wrote that he felt the only group with whom he had maintained good rapport had been "the peasants," but he chastised himself for his lack of willpower in not learning Swahili well. By relying on his French, he had been able to speak to the officers but not with the rank-and-file soldiers.

> In my contact with my men, I believe I showed enough commitment to prevent anyone from impugning me in the personal and physical aspects. . . . The discomfort of having a pair of broken boots or only one change of dirty clothes, or to eat the same slop as the troops and live in the same conditions, for me is not a sacrifice. But my habit of retiring to read, escaping daily problems, did tend to distance me from the men, without mentioning that there are aspects of my character that don't make intimate contact easy.
>
> I was hard, but I don't believe excessively so, nor unjust; I utilized methods that a regular army doesn't apply, like making

men go without food; it is the only effective punishment method I know of in times of guerrilla warfare. At the beginning I tried to use moral coercion, and failed. I sought to make my troops have the same point of view as I did regarding the situation and I failed; they were not prepared to look optimistically into a future that had to be viewed through a gloomy present.

Finally, another thing that weighed in my relations with the others . . . was the farewell letter to Fidel. This caused my comrades to view me, as they did many years ago, when I began in the Sierra, as a foreigner. . . . There were certain things in common that we no longer shared, certain common longings that I had tacitly or explicitly renounced and which are the most sacred things for each man individually: his family, his nation, his habitat. The letter that provoked so many eulogistic comments inside and out of Cuba separated me from the combatants.

Perhaps these psychological musings seem out of place in the analysis of a struggle that has an almost continental scale. I continue to be faithful to my conception of the nucleus; I was the leader of a group of Cubans, no more than a company, and my function was to be their true leader, their guide to a victory that would speed the development of an authentic popular army. But at the same time my peculiar status turned me into a soldier representing a foreign power, an instructor of Cubans and Congolese, a strategist, a high-flying politician on an unknown stage, and a Cato the Censor, repetitive and tiresome. . . . With so many strands to deal with, a Gordian knot formed which I didn't know how to untie. . . .

I have learned in the Congo; there are errors I won't commit again. Maybe there are others I will repeat, and new ones I will commit. I have come out with more faith than ever in the guerrilla struggle, but we have failed. My responsibility is great; I will not forget the defeat, nor its most precious lessons.

III

From the moment he left the Congo, Che became totally dependent on Cuba's secret services for his protection and survival. For the first time in his adult life, he was not the master of his own destiny.

The intelligence and guerrilla-support network run by Barbarroja Piñeiro now operated throughout Africa just as it did in Latin America and other parts of the world, often under the cloak of diplomatic cover. The

Cuban chargé d'affaires in Cairo, José Antonio Arbesú, was one of Piñeiro's operatives, as was Ulíses Estrada, chief of his Africa and Asia section. Ulíses was a tall, thin black man who had been Tania's lover in Cuba and also Masetti's controller before he left for Argentina. Throughout Che's time in the Congo, Ulíses was a primary liaison, constantly traveling between Cuba and Tanzania to coordinate the flow of arms, men, and intelligence. Since the debacle, he had been responsible for getting the Cuban fighters back to Havana and for coordinating Che's future movements. Fidel wanted Che to come back to Cuba, but he refused to do so, saying he wanted to go directly to South America. Piñeiro's chief deputy, Juan Carretero—Ariel— who had helped implement the Béjar and Masetti expeditions in Peru and Argentina, was drawn into the dilemma and found that Che was not an easy man to deal with. "He was very hard to argue with," Ariel said. "He had a very ascetic mentality. He didn't want to come back to Cuba publicly after the [farewell] letter because of his obligation to the revolutionary cause. It simply was not a possibility."

Christmas and New Year's came and went, and Che remained in seclusion. In early January 1966, at Che's request, Aleida was brought to Tanzania. She was rushed straight from the car into the embassy building in Dar es Salaam, and, once inside, quickly upstairs. She and Che shared two rooms. One was a tiny photographic darkroom with a bed, where they slept, and the other was a small living room where they spent their days. For the next six weeks, neither she nor Che left those rooms, and the curtains on the windows were permanently drawn. Just once, Aleida dared to peek out. She saw a grove of trees. No other houses were in sight. Their only visitor was Pablo Ribalta, who brought their meals upstairs. In a communications room on the same floor were the cryptographer and Che's typist, a Cuban named Coleman Ferrer. Nobody else knew who they were or even saw them.

Che didn't seem bothered by the confinement, Aleida said, because he had plenty to do. He had already finished his Congo memoirs by the time she arrived and had begun two other projects: "Apuntes Filosóficos" (Philosophical Notes),* and "Notas Económicas" (Economic Notes), which was based on his critical review of the Soviet *Manual of Political Economy,* the standard socialist bible since Stalin's day. When he wasn't writing, Che spent his time reading, including poetry and fiction for mere enjoyment. When Aleida arrived, he set her a curriculum of books to read, like homework, which they

---

*Che eventually bequeathed the outline for a manual on philosophy to Armando Hart, then the Cuban minister of education, who had moved sharply to the left politically since the rebel victory. Che's letter to Hart and the outline appeared in a Cuban magazine, *Contracorriente,* in 1997.

discussed at the end of each day. They clearly relished the time together. Che took some fanciful, romantic photographs of the two of them in which he looks younger, slimmer, and more handsome than he had in several years. His dark, wavy hair has grown back and he has a thin mustache. In some of the photographs he is bare-chested. In one of them, Aleida is reading a play by Strindberg while Che looks on with a playful expression. In another he is wearing a dark suit and kneeling by Aleida, holding her hand.

Aleida recalled that their Tanzanian interlude was the closest thing she ever had to a honeymoon. It was the first time they had been alone together. In a giggling allusion to their bed in the darkroom, Aleida hinted that they had made up for lost time. She said that in the past they had often talked about one day visiting Mexico and Argentina together, but "there was no time, and there was not to be any." When she returned to Cuba at the end of February, Aleida left in the same way she had come: down the stairs, out the front door, into a waiting car, and straight to the airport. She rued the fact that she had been to East Africa and seen nothing, not even the fabled game parks. "Later I saw what I had missed," she said, "in a movie starring Yves Montand and Candice Bergen."*

IV

By the time Aleida left, Ariel had persuaded Che to go to Prague, where he would be safer and could wait things out.† But before he left Tanzania, sometime in March, Fernández Mell came to see him. He had finally rounded up the missing Cubans, rescued the abandoned Congolese fighters across the lake, and helped wind up the Cuban operation in Kigoma. Che showed his friend the passages in his memoirs where he referred to him critically, and said, "See how I dump on you?" Fernández Mell retorted that anything Che criticized him for was a direct reflection on him, since he had only followed Che's orders.

The Congo experience had distanced them. They were still friends, but they no longer believed in the same things. Fernández Mell had done a lot of thinking about Che's notions of continental guerrilla war and had begun to doubt the wisdom of the strategy, at least for Africa. He thought Che was stubbornly deluded about it. "In the Congo, Che had said things to us that I am convinced he knew weren't realistic," Fernández Mell explained, "although he wasn't a man who said things he didn't feel. . . . He

---

*Claude Lelouch's *Vivre pour vivre* (1967).

†See Notes.

had it stuck deeply in his head that he had found the path to liberate the people and that it would be successful, and he expounded it as an absolute truth. So he could not accept that the attempt in the Congo ruined that strategy he had thought out so well."

Fernández Mell knew that Che was probably going on to South America, and ultimately to Argentina. It had always been understood that Fernández Mell would join him there, but now the subject didn't come up. He didn't inquire about Che's plans or volunteer himself to be a part of them. Their mutual silence said it all. It was a parting of the ways between two friends. A few days later, Fernández Mell returned to Havana, taking Che's latest "Pasajes de la Guerra Revolucionaria" with him to deliver to Fidel. He would never see Che again.

V

Che arrived in Prague accompanied by Papi. They were met by Pombo and Tuma at the safe house, a large, stately villa on the outskirts of Prague, discreetly screened by a row of tall juniper trees. The Czechs had turned over a number of safe houses in Prague for Cuba to use as it saw fit. According to Ariel, they were run by the Cubans independently of the Czechs. "Che was brought in as just another Latin American revolutionary under a false identity," he said. "The Czechs never knew he was there." Pombo recalled that they lived quietly in the villa, killing time and keeping their skills honed with shooting practice. Aleida rejoined Che for a few weeks. Piñeiro's agent Ulíses Estrada came and went from Havana bearing messages. (Eventually, Ulíses was replaced by Ariel at Che's request. Ulíses was black, and he attracted too much attention in Prague.)

According to both Ariel and Pombo, Fidel continued trying to persuade Che to return to Cuba, but Che wouldn't budge. "Che didn't want to return under any circumstances," said Pombo. Those who were close to Che suggested that, in addition to his pride, a decisive factor was his recognition that he had become a political liability for Fidel with the Soviets, who were now bankrolling the Cuban ship of state. Che was more useful to Fidel abroad, where he could carry forward Cuba's revolutionary foreign policy, with Fidel discreetly backing him on the grounds that he was aiding an old comrade.

Che's departure from Cuba had coincided with Fidel's swing back to an aggressively internationalist stance. It had become explicit in his May Day speech in 1965, when he blasted the concept of peaceful coexistence. In January 1966, at the first Tricontinental Conference, an outgrowth, promoted by Cuba, of the Cairo-based Afro-Asian People's Solidarity Organization—attended by hundreds of delegates from more than eighty Latin, Asian, and

African states; sundry armed national liberation movements; and the Soviets and Chinese—Fidel had once again played the feuding socialist superpowers off against each another. He had disturbed Moscow by pushing through a resolution lauding the guerrilla movements fighting in Venezuela, Guatemala, Colombia, and Peru, while simultaneously tweaking the Chinese by mentioning the "misunderstandings" between Havana and Beijing over China's decision to reduce Cuba's badly needed rice imports. (In February, Fidel would abandon his diplomatic language and come out publicly with a list of grievances against China, accusing the Chinese of trying to meddle in Cuba's politics and seeking to use rice as a bludgeon to secure political obeisance.)

The Tricontinental Conference provided a platform for dampening the continuing rumors of a rift between Fidel and Che, and for creating an opening for Che to enter a new battlefield. Fidel proclaimed 1966 the Year of Solidarity and pledged common cause with the guerrilla struggles taking place against imperialism around the globe. And he instructed Piñeiro to find a place for Che to go.

In early 1966, the Latin American revolutionary panorama was vibrant and in a violent state of flux. There were now pro-Chinese Communist Party factions in Bolivia, Peru, and Colombia, and guerrilla groups were popping up all over the place. There were some senior Cuban agents in place with the guerrillas in Venezuela and Colombia, but the situation in those countries was tenuous; along with the guerrilla upsurge had come an increased American military and CIA presence.

In Guatemala, the Cuban-backed rebel coalition was being riven in two by a Trotskyite breakaway movement, but, in spite of their internal splits, the guerrillas had pulled off some spectacular attacks, including the assassination of the head of the U.S. military mission, and, a few months later, that of the Guatemalan deputy defense minister. Then, in March 1966, when Che was in Prague, Guatemalan security forces swooped down on a secret meeting of the Guatemalan Communist Party leadership, murdering the twenty-six top officials it captured. Their deaths temporarily decapitated the Cuban- and Soviet-backed guerrilla leadership.

The Peruvian MIR guerrillas led by Luis de la Puente Uceda and Guillermo Lobatón had finally gone into action in June 1965, after two years of underground organizing. In September, the Cuban-backed ELN in Peru led by Héctor Béjar began fighting as well. Peru's government had suspended constitutional guarantees, and Peruvian troops, supported by the United States, had begun a fierce counterinsurgency war. By October 1965, they had killed Luis de la Puente Uceda; then they killed Lobatón only three months later, leaving the MIR leaderless and its combatants on the run. By December, the ELN was in a similar situation; before long, Béjar himself was captured and imprisoned.

In Colombia, the picture was similar. An official state of siege had been imposed in May 1965 following the appearance of the Colombian ELN guerrillas, who were also backed by Cuba, at the beginning of the year. By December, an outspoken revolutionary Catholic priest, Camilo Torres, had joined the Colombian ELN, lending its effort a charismatic blend of social vision and potentially broader appeal. By February 1966, Torres was dead, but the Colombian insurgency would continue, with the appearance of new offshoots and mutations, for many years to come.

Problems were brewing in Venezuela's FALN guerrilla organzation. The Communist Party, which had initially supported the armed struggle, was now stepping back in the wake of the imprisonment of many of its leaders. In April 1965, in a move openly criticized by Fidel, the Venezuelan Party plenum had voted to alter course in favor of "legal struggle," and a year later the Party leaders were released from prison. The guerrillas backed by Cuba repudiated the Party and continued the fight.

A military junta in Bolivia had overthrown Víctor Paz Estenssoro, the civilian president, in November 1964, and the charismatic president of the powerful Bolivian workers' union, Juan Lechín, had led a vociferous campaign against the junta. In May 1965, Lechín was exiled, a general strike was called in protest, and a state of siege was declared. Still, the pro-Moscow Bolivian Communist Party, led by Mario Monje, was hesitant about undertaking an armed struggle. A pro-Chinese breakaway faction of the Party, formed in April 1965 in a movement spearheaded by the student leader Oscar Zamora, had previously sought Che's backing to launch a guerrilla war and been given the go-ahead, but during Che's time away in the Congo, Cuban-Chinese relations had soured, and little had been done to push this option by either Piñeiro's agency or Zamora.

According to Pombo, the first possibility proposed by Che as his next destination was Peru, but to go there he would need the help of the Bolivians. Che sent Papi to Bolivia in April, and he planned to follow if Papi gave the all-clear. "The first thing," Pombo explained, "was to establish contact with the Peruvians, see what state their movement was really in, and [get] the support of the Bolivian Communist Party. The Bolivian Party had helped us with the Masetti thing and the Puerto Maldonado thing [with Héctor Béjar's ELN group]. There were people who were loyal to the ideas of the revolution, who had worked with us before, and, what's more, had been trained in Cuba."

The loyal Bolivian cadres Pombo was speaking about were a group of young Bolivian Communist Party members. Among them were the Peredo brothers, Roberto, who was known as Coco, and Guido, who was called Inti. They came from a large and prominent family in Bolivia's northeastern Beni province. A younger brother, Osvaldo, or Chato, was studying in Moscow. There were also the Vázquez-Viaña brothers, Humberto and Jorge, the European-educated sons of a well-known Bolivian historian. Jorge, or Loro (the Parrot), had worked closely with Abelardo Colomé Ibarra and Masetti in the Salta campaign of 1963–1964. Rodolfo Saldaña, a former miner and unionist, had helped hide Ciro Bustos and his companions at his home in La Paz after their arrival from Algeria. Loyola Guzmán, a young woman of predominantly Quechua Indian blood, was the daughter of a Communist teacher in Bolivia's mining communities and a graduate of the elite Communist Party political cadres' training school in Moscow. She too had helped the Argentine and Peruvian guerrillas. These, and a few other Bolivians, some of whom were already training in Cuba, were the hard core of activists that the Cubans could count upon to support a war in Peru or to get a war going in Bolivia itself.

There has long been a degree of murkiness about the true target of Che's next—and last—war-making effort. Pombo said that it wasn't until after he and Tuma arrived in Bolivia that plans changed and Bolivia itelf came under consideration. Ariel had a different story. He said that he, Piñeiro, and Fidel had Bolivia in mind when they managed to lure Che out of his confinement in Tanzania.* "One of the ways we convinced him to come to Prague was by getting him enthusiastic about the possibilities in Bolivia, where some agreements had been made and conditions were being prepared," Ariel said. "Venezuela and Guatemala were previously under consideration, but Bolivia offered many advantages. First, because of its proximity to Argentina, which was very important to Che. Next, because of the agreements, the prior experience there, the human assets, and the

---

*Pombo told me that Papi was sent to Bolivia from Prague to talk with Monje about facilitating their entry into Peru and to set things in motion for Che's arrival; and that Pombo and Tuma were then dispatched to Bolivia to assist Papi. He said that it was only after they were in Bolivia that the Peruvian guerrillas began falling apart and were suspected of being "penetrated," at which point the idea of beginning a war in Bolivia itself was discussed. One problem with this version—in addition to its being contradicted by Ariel—is that Pombo didn't arrive in Bolivia until July 1966. The disintegration of the Peruvian guerrillas had begun months earlier with the deaths of the MIR leaders Luis de la Puente Uceda and Guillermo Lobatón, followed by the arrest of Ricardo Gadea. And the ELN leader Héctor Béjar, who was aligned with Havana, had been arrested in March.

Party's militant traditions. And finally, because of its geographic location, which offered good possibilities for the later 'irradiation' of guerrillas trained in the Bolivian guerrilla front to the neighboring countries of Argentina, Peru, Brazil, and Chile. He became enthusiastic over this possibility and agreed to go to Prague."

This is perhaps the most crucial single question about the life of Ernesto Che Guevara that still remains unsatisfactorily answered: *who* decided he should go to Bolivia; and when and why was that decision made? Fidel always said that Che selected Bolivia himself, and that he had tried to stall him, urging him to wait until conditions were more "advanced." Manuel Piñeiro concurred. He said that Fidel persuaded Che to come back to Cuba after they learned from Papi that Che was ready to head straight to Bolivia without anything prepared for his arrival there. Fidel offered him Cuba's help in selecting and training his men, as well as laying the groundwork for a Bolivian guerrilla *foco*. Fidel's and Piñeiro's explanations do not exactly mesh with the accounts given by Ariel and Pombo, but then, *their* versions don't match up, either. How to explain the contradictions between the versions of Ariel and Pombo—one a senior Cuban intelligence official and diplomat, the other a high-ranking military general and an officially recognized "Hero of the Revolution"—let alone between them and the version offered by Piñeiro and the *jefe máximo*? The true answer might lie in the unpublished preamble to Pombo's diary, which was begun in Prague and written up later on the basis of his notes.

> Seven months following the termination of the guerrilla operations in African territory and in the midst of an intense period of preparation and organization for our next adventure, conceived to take place in Peruvian territory . . . Ramón [Che]* gathered Pacho [Alberto Fernádez Montes de Oca], Tuma, and myself and read us a letter he'd recently received, in which Fidel analyzed [the situation] and urged him to coldly reconsider his decision, and as a consequence of that analysis he proposed: [Che's] return to Cuba for a short period of time, and at the same time he pointed out the prospects for fighting in Bolivia, the agreements reached with Estanislao (Mario Monje) to launch the armed struggle.

---

*Che's name had changed again, from Tatu in Africa to Ramón in Prague—one of several names, including Mongo and Fernando, he would use in Bolivia.

[Che] told us that, faced with the correctness of these proposals, he had decided to send Francisco* to La Paz, to explore
the possibilities of the struggle. . . . We anxiously awaited the return of Francisco. This took place in the first days of June. His
report is that the results are positive. Papi affirmed that the conditions were propitious, even for our arrival there [in Bolivia]. Not-
withstanding that, Francisco told Ramón he wanted to abandon
ship, asking him not to tell us because he felt ashamed; as a reason
he cited his feelings about dying far from Cuba.†

So, it would appear that Fidel himself persuaded Che to start the
struggle in Bolivia, sometime in the spring of 1966—and that the plan was
set into motion soon after Francisco's return from La Paz and his and Papi's
positive assessments of the situation.

    Che sent Pombo and Tuma ahead to La Paz, while he and Pacho made
their way back to Cuba, arriving there around July 21. Che had been away
for more than a year, but he was not returning "home." He was lodged in a
safe house on the rural fringe of eastern Havana, and his presence there was
known to only a few people.

VI

One aspect of the secret planning for Che's Bolivian mission that most parties involved concur on is that, at a certain point, an "agreement" was reached
between Cuba and the Bolivian Communist leader Mario Monje. Almost
everyone concurs, that is, except Mario Monje. Speaking at length from his
self-imposed exile home in wintry Moscow nearly three decades later, Monje
offered a lengthy and candid explanation of his own tangled and often duplicitous dealings with Piñeiro, Fidel, and Che.

    Monje's relationship with the Cuban revolution extended back to its
early days, and, as he told it, he had approved his Party's help for Béjar's

---

*The identity of "Francisco" has never been disclosed; he is referred to in the published ver-
sion of Pombo's diary as "a Cuban liaison" who had decided not to continue in the venture.
Piñeiro says Francisco was a brave man, seasoned in urban combat, and that unexplained
"psychological reasons" were behind his desire to withdraw.

†I obtained a partial copy of Pombo's original handwritten diary, the typewritten manuscript
that he made later, and a copy of the editing corrections he made. The above excerpt is taken
from the typed document. In 1996, after being suppressed for three decades, the *edited* version of Pombo's diary was published in Cuba and Argentina with the approval of the Cuban
government, minus this key passage.

and Masetti's guerrilla groups in hopes that Cuba would not try to start a guerrilla war in his own country. Even after the Masetti and Béjar episodes, however, Monje remained suspicious of Cuban intentions, keeping a watchful eye on their activities and, most especially, on Che Guevara.

When Che disappeared from Cuba in 1965 and rumors began circulating as to his whereabouts, Monje took notice. He said he never believed the stories of a rift between Fidel and Che. He knew that they shared the goal of revolutionary expansion, and he suspected that Che was probably somewhere in Africa. Then, in September 1965, the Bolivian Party received an invitation from the Cuban government for three of its members to attend the Tricontinental Conference convening in Havana in January 1966. Monje soon learned, however, that Oscar Zamora, leader of the rival Maoist Communist Party of Bolivia, had also been invited to attend and was being allowed to head a larger delegation. It appeared clear to Monje and his comrades in the Politburo that, for whatever reasons, the Cubans were favoring the pro-Chinese party. In November, Monje's comrades urged him to travel to Havana ahead of time and get to the bottom of the mystery.

The Cuban overture to Zamora's group raised the disquieting possibility in Monje's mind that the Cubans were still plotting an insurrection in Bolivia. Zamora was known to have offered his forces to the Cubans for this option, and, significantly, Zamora was friendly with Che. At this point, Monje said, he began wondering: "Where is Che? What is his role in this?" From then on, he recalled, he began to study news reports closely, looking for clues as to Che's whereabouts. Meanwhile, he told his comrades that when he went to Havana, he would be as conciliatory as possible and would ingratiate himself with the Cubans in order to learn what they were up to. His idea was to tell the Cubans that the members of his Party weren't opposed to "preparing themselves," with Cuba's help, for an eventual armed struggle, and he would even offer himself and other Party members to personally receive Cuban military training.

Feeling "somewhat cautious," in December 1965 Monje left for Prague, where many of the foreign delegations heading to the Tricontinental Conference were assembling for the flight to Havana. On the plane to Havana he recognized Régis Debray, a young French Marxist theoretician whom he knew to be closely linked to Fidel and Cuba's security apparatus, and who had visited Bolivia the year before. By now, Debray was known—largely on the strength of a series of articles he had written—to be an active proponent of the Cuban revolutionary model in Latin America.*

*See Notes.

When he arrived in Havana, Monje told the Cuban security service that he was there not only for the Tricontinental Conference but to discuss "another matter." He was quickly transferred from his hotel to a safe house run by Cuban intelligence. There he was joined by two Bolivian Party comrades previously selected as escorts. He would later be joined by the other two Tricontinental delegation members still on their way.

Monje got in touch with the circle of young Bolivian "students" in Havana, all members of the Bolivian Communist Youth, and discovered that many had been receiving military training without Party approval. Instead of confronting them, he "joined" them, as it were. Meeting officials of with the Cuban Interior Ministry—Piñeiro's people—Monje told them of his interest in undergoing military training along with some other comrades. "They were very happy," Monje recalled—so happy, in fact, that Monje was able to thoroughly outmaneuver Zamora's group. In what he proudly described as a game of brinksmanship, Monje demanded that the Cubans choose between granting official status at the conference to his group—now disposed to take up arms—or Zamora's. His delegation was accepted as the official one, while, as Monje put it, Zamora's group was sent on a "tour" of the Cuban countryside.

Monje quickly realized that what was important was not the speeches being given at the conference, but what was happening behind the scenes. "The Cubans began seeking out contacts with this group and that," he recalled, "but always with the intention of seeing about creating new guerrilla *focos* in Latin America. They gave most attention to the more radical groups, the more defiant groups, those who to a certain degree were at odds with the more traditional Communists."

Monje knew that the Soviets were uncomfortable with the Cuban guerrilla recruitment campaign, and when the Tricontinental was over he decided to make a quick trip to Moscow to "take soundings." To his surprise, he was ushered straight through to Boris Ponomoriov, the supreme boss of the Central Committee's International Department. "We began talking about Bolivia," Monje said, "and he asked me about the Tricontinental, and what the thinking of the [Bolivian] Communist Party was about what [Cuba] was preparing. I gave him my critique, more or less, and told him what we were planning to do, and then he asked me if I knew where Che was. I told him that I knew that he had been in Africa, but that he had already left." Monje said he had the distinct impression that this was news to Ponomoriov.*

---

*Monje was giving himself a little more credit than was due. Alexiev had informed Brezhnev where Che was, and the Soviets had only recently helped evacuate the Cuban fighters from Tanzania.

Monje said that the Soviets wanted to know what role Che played in the conference, where the Cubans had encouraged "the most radical groups." They had come to the same conclusion as Monje: the driving force behind the Tricontinental Conference had also been its most conspicuous absentee— Che Guevara.

After his briefing at the Kremlin, Monje returned to Cuba to begin military training. He had decided to ask the Bolvian students who had already been trained to stay in Cuba until he and the other newcomers had finished their own military training, at which point he would try to ship them all off to Moscow for "theoretical training." He reasoned that he could thus forestall any surreptitious Cuban plan to put the youths in the field behind his Party's back, as he suspected the Cubans were anxious to do. Monje knew that his training would take three or four months to complete, giving him time to alert his Party comrades back in Bolivia about what was happening.

As he was about to begin his training, in late January 1966, Monje was summoned to a meeting with Fidel. Several other people were there, including Piñeiro and some of his agents. According to Monje, Fidel asked him what his intentions were regarding his Bolivian cadres in Cuba. He gave Fidel a less than sincere answer, but one that sounded credible. Reminding him that Bolivia had a history of popular uprisings, he told Fidel that the current situation, with the nation again under military dictatorship, indicated the possibility of another insurrection. "If there is one," he told Fidel, "we'll be able to take control of the situation." With the active backup of his Cuban-trained cadres, he explained, he could push for elections, in which the Communists would emerge in a strengthened position.

It was not the answer Fidel wanted to hear. What about the possibilities for a guerrilla struggle? Monje explained that he didn't see that as a realistic possibility in Bolivia. At this point, several of Piñeiro's agents leaped in to offer their own opinions; from what they said, Monje knew they had been to Bolivia and had been studying it closely. After the meeting, Monje recalled, Piñeiro buttonholed him. "Fidel didn't like the interview," Piñeiro said. "He doesn't like your plan because you're not thinking of the guerrilla struggle, and these people in training are destined for the guerrilla struggle. You have two or three months. Revise your points of view, and then start a guerrilla war."

Using the excuse that he hadn't realized he would be away so long, and that he had left certain situations unattended back in Bolivia, Monje asked Piñeiro to send for Ramiro Otero, the Bolivian Communist Party's representative in Prague. "I played that game," explained Monje, "because I knew they couldn't let me leave." When Otero arrived in February, Monje took him into the garden of the safe house and gave him explicit instructions: "Go to Bolivia, ask for a meeting with the Politburo, and tell them the Cubans are preparing for a guerrilla war in Bolivia."

With Otero hurrying back to La Paz, Monje's training began. At thirty-five, he was the oldest in the group—most of the others were in their mid- to late twenties—but he tried to keep up. Then Otero returned with bad news. He hadn't been able to talk to the Central Committee; he had talked only to members of the lesser Secretariat, and they hadn't believed Monje's story. They sent word that the military training should end and Monje should return immediately. Serious doubts had been cast on his activities during his absence, and he was in danger of losing his post.

Monje felt caught between a rock and hard place. According to his own slightly tortuous explanation, he had gone along with the Cuban plan for war in Bolivia only as a means to forestall that war, but now his Party compatriots were thoroughly alarmed. He needed to return to Bolivia to explain what was going on to the right people in his Party and clear up the misunderstandings, but the Cubans would be highly suspicious if he did so. It was also too late for his original plan—to keep the cadres away from Bolivia by sending them all to the Soviet Union—because his own training had almost ended and the cadres were now itching to go home. In desperation, Monje arranged to meet with Fidel, along with a visiting member of the Bolivian Politburo, Humberto Ramírez, to define the situation. In May, they flew to Santiago so that they could talk with Fidel in his car during the drive back to Havana.

In the car, Monje said, Fidel talked about everything other than Bolivia. "He would stop the car and explain to us how he had carried out ambushes. . . . He was interested in having us see how a guerrilla struggle is waged. We even stopped to shoot along the way, testing marksmanship and weapons."

Their car journey ended in Camagüey, where they stayed overnight. They still hadn't spoken about Bolivia. The next day they boarded a plane for Havana. Monje, who was seated with Ramírez, began to fear that his mission had failed. Then Papi walked down the aisle to tell Monje that Fidel wanted to speak to him alone.

He sat down next to Fidel, who asked how Monje "saw things." Before Monje could answer, however, Fidel started talking again: "You know, you've been a good friend of ours. You have developed an internationalist policy with us. Frankly I want to thank you for all the help you've given us, and now it turns out that a mutual friend wants to return to his country, someone whose revolutionary caliber nobody can question. And nobody can deny him the right to return to his country. And he thinks the best place to pass through [to get there] is Bolivia. I ask you to help him pass through your country."

Monje didn't need to ask who the "mutal friend" was, and he immediately agreed to help. At that, Fidel added: "Look, as for your own plans, just keep developing them as you see fit. If you want us to help in training more people, send us more. . . . We are not going to intervene in your affairs." Monje says he thanked Fidel and repeated his willingness to help in the "transit" of their mutual friend.

Then, using his trademark combination of flattery and enigmatic language, Fidel said, "You've always been good at selecting people; I'd like you to choose the people that will receive [Che], accompany him in the country, and escort him to the border. If you and your party agree, they could accompany him within the country to gather experiences, or just go to the border and that will be the end of it."

He then asked Monje to give him some names. Monje named four cadres he had authorized for training in Cuba: Coco Peredo, Loro Vázquez-Viaña, Julio "Ñato" Mendez, and Rodolfo Saldaña. Papi, who was listening, commented, "Excellent." Fidel noted down the names and told Monje: "That's it." Their business was finished. Monje felt greatly relieved and told Humberto Ramírez that they needn't worry—the Cubans' plans were different from what they had suspected—but they still needed to inform the Party.

Monje completed his training in June. He sent his four handpicked comrades back to Bolivia but told the original group of students to stay and continue their studies in Cuba until the Party decided what was to be done with them. He wrote a letter to Jorge Kolle Cueto, his substitute in La Paz, explaining his promise to Fidel that the Party would assist their "mutual friend" in passing through Bolivia. Before returning to Bolivia himself, Monje decided to take another short trip to Moscow. The Cubans suggested he stop over in Prague en route, so that "someone" there might look him up, but Monje decided to avoid Prague, suspecting that the Cubans were laying a trap for him. "They waited for me in Prague. What for?" Monje surmised that the Cubans were planning to present him with a fait accompli, telling him that by undergoing training he had in effect approved the option of an armed struggle for his country, and that he had no choice but to go forward with it.

Monje revealed neither why he went to Moscow on this trip nor whom he met with there, but, to judge from his earlier admissions, one can reasonably assume he spoke in the Kremlin about Fidel's request and revealed Che's next destination. And in view of the Kremlin's increasing impatience with the "fire-starters" in Cuba, its reaction can also be surmised. Undoubtedly,

Monje was advised to stand up for his rights as the Bolivian Party chief and told not to let Che or Fidel push him around. As things turned out, that is exactly what Monje would try to do.

VII

With Fidel's help, Che was putting his chess pieces in motion. He wanted eventually to go to Argentina, but Argentina was not ready just yet. Conditions would have to be prepared from Bolivia. Che envisioned guerrillas from neighboring countries coming to join the fighting and then fanning out to form allied guerrilla armies in their own countries. When the Argentine rebellion was up and running, he would leave Bolivia and take command.

It was with this goal in mind, the Cubans say, that Che had placed Tania in La Paz. She could provide them with valuable intelligence about the regime and the political situation in Bolivia, but she was also to be used as a liaison with the evolving insurgencies in the neighboring countries, especially Argentina. So far, her selection as an agent seemed to be paying off handsomely. As Laura Gutiérrez Bauer, an Argentine ethnologist of independent means, Tania was able to make quick headway in penetrating the small and racially stratified social environment of La Paz. She was an attractive, single white woman, and within two months she had established a circle of valuable contacts in the political and diplomatic community, obtained her Bolivian residency and work permit, and even found a volunteer job in the Ministry of Education's Folklore Research Committee. On the side, she taught German to a small group of students.

One of her best contacts was Gonzalo López Muñoz, President Barrientos's press secretary, who gave her documents with his office's letterhead and credentials as a sales representative for a weekly magazine he edited.* By late 1965, she had also found a suitable husband, a young Bolivian engineering student. Marriage to him would help her obtain Bolivian citizenship, and he could be gotten rid of by being sent abroad on a study scholarship, an idea she had already implanted in her guileless groom's mind.

In January 1966 she was visited by one of Piñeiro's men, Carlos Conrado de Jesús Alvarado Marín, a Guatemalan who had been working with the Cuban intelligence agency since 1960. His code name was Mercy,

---

*Later on, after the guerrillas were discovered, López Muñoz was arrested and charged with aiding them. He claimed he had been duped and was released, but he was in fact a willing partner in the guerrilla plan, recruited by Inti Peredo, whose wife was his wife's cousin.

and he was posing as a businessman.* He brought Tania her mail, carried inside a false shoe heel, and the news that she had been honored with membership in the new Cuban Communist Party. Explaining to her acquaintances that she had been offered some interpreting work, she slipped out of La Paz to meet up with Mercy in Brazil, where he gave her a counterintelligence refresher course. In April, she traveled to Mexico. Another Cuban agent gave her a new Argentine passport, and she debriefed him on the politico-military situation in Bolivia. She returned to La Paz in early May with instructions to lie low until she was contacted again.

Meanwhile, Mercy wrote an extensive and detailed report of the time he had spent with Tania. He found her deeply committed to the cause and the work she was doing, but under extreme nervous tension and emotional strain, throwing fits on several occasions. He decided that her behavior was caused by the stress of being so long alone in a capitalist country, but concluded on a bright, sloganeering note: "I believe she is aware of the honor of being a link in a chain that in the not-too-distant future will strangle imperialism, and she is proud of having been chosen for special work to aid the Latin American Revolution."

But, as a poem she wrote in April showed, Tania was in a melancholy frame of mind. The poem, titled "To Leave a Memory," seems to question the cost of her clandestine existence and the effacement of her real identity.

So I must leave, like flowers that wilt?
Will my name one day be forgotten
And nothing of me remain on the earth?
At least, flowers and song.
How then, must my heart behave?
Is it in vain that we live, that we appear on the earth?

To protect Tania's false identity, Che had passed along orders for Papi to minimize his contacts with her; he didn't want Papi to blow her cover by spending too much time around her. He also sent orders that Tania not be used in the setup phase of the guerrilla war. She was too valuable as a deep-cover asset to risk losing; Che needed her as a courier who could come and go without detection to Argentina, Peru, and the other countries where he planned to recruit fighters. By the time Pombo and Tuma arrived carrying Che's orders in late July, however, Papi had been in regular contact with Tania since May. He had not only briefed her on the plans for the guerrillas

---

*Mercy's identity was not known for many years, even after he died in 1997. It was revealed in Ulíses Estrada's book *Tania la Guerrillera*, which was published in 2005.

but introduced her to the man dispatched to be the mission's permanent liaison with Havana, Renán Montero, also known as Iván. Tania recognized Renán from the meeting in Havana two years before, when Che had told her of her mission.

As always, Argentina loomed large in Che's mind, and with his arrival in Bolivia only a matter of months away, he tried to get things moving on that front. In May 1966, while Che was still in Prague, his Argentine lieutenant, Ciro Bustos, was summoned to Havana by Piñeiro. The last time Bustos had seen Che was in the summer of 1964, six months before Che went off on his world tour and then vanished from sight. Che had ordered Bustos to return to Argentina and keep up his organizing work, to "lean on the schisms," as he put it—that is, to avoid the Argentine Communist Party and recruit cadres from disaffected factions. Bustos had spent the intervening two years doing just that. With no firm timetable for action in hand from Che with which to draw potential recruits, however, it was not an easy job, although Bustos had had some success. When Che disappeared in April 1965, Bustos was unperturbed, knowing that he was involved in revolutionary work somewhere, and that he would reappear one day to assume control of the guerrilla network Bustos was building for him.

When Bustos arrived in Cuba, he assumed he would be meeting with Che, but instead he was placed alone in a safe house, a mansion in the Marianao district of Havana. A special provisions truck came by regularly and left him food and cases of beer. He spent several weeks there waiting, with no explanation offered about how long he was to wait or exactly why he was there. Finally, boiling with impatience and hearing that his friend Abelardo Colomé Ibarra was now the army commander in Oriente, Bustos flew to Santiago. He found Colomé Ibarra at a military base in Mayarí.

Bustos gave vent to his litany of complaints, and Colomé Ibarra immediately got on a radio-telephone in his office and had a long, cursing conversation with someone—Bustos believed it was Piñeiro—demanding that he attend to Bustos "properly" and fix up his meeting with "the man," presumably Che. It was a strange scene that Bustos recalled vividly. As Colomé Ibarra made his call, "Soviet officers passed back and forth nervously outside in the fog at five in the morning."

Once he was back at the safe house in Havana, Bustos said, "everything changed." Bustos was told that Che wanted a report from him and needed it quickly; a secretary was brought in to take shorthand. "I dictated a report about our work and the national [Argentine] political situation, predicting a military coup, which did in fact take place before I returned to the country." Finally, Bustos was informed that he would not be seeing Che on this visit; he should await a "contact" in Córdoba, but he wasn't told when it would take place or who it would be.

Before returning to Argentina, Bustos was involved in a very strange odyssey. On an invitation from Mao's government, he flew to China, where he spent three weeks being grandly feted as Che's chief Argentine guerrilla lieutenant. Over the course of a series of meetings, Chinese government officials offered to give military training to "Che's men" and to provide them with unspecified material and financial support. The tantalizing offer came with a catch, however, as Bustos discovered during a meeting with the vice president of the National People's Congress in Beijing, when he was asked to publicly denounce Fidel Castro for having "allied with imperialism." A stunned Bustos quickly refused, and his "goodwill tour" ended shortly afterward.*

Back in Córdoba, Bustos put on a wig to disguise himself and went into the Salta prison, where he and his incarcerated comrades held a whispered "general staff council." Their cases were all on appeal, but it would be some time yet before they had a resolution, and under the new military regime that had seized power while Bustos was away, their prospects looked bleak. In Cuba, Bustos had explored the possibility of organizing a breakout to free them, and Ariel, Piñeiro's deputy, had promised to look into it.† For now, all Bustos could do was go home to his family, resume the routine of "normal life," and await the promised contact that would lead him to Che.

VIII

By the end of summer, the troops for Che's Bolivian mission had been selected and were assembled at a secret training camp in the eastern Cuban province of Pinar del Río. It was in an area called Viñales, distinguished by a peculiar geological formation, called *mogotes,* a series of large bulbous jungle-covered hills that rise steeply like great green puffballs from the

---

*When they met up in Bolivia later, Bustos told Che about his uncomfortable encounter. Che laughed and said, "You were lucky. It was the beginning of the Cultural Revolution; it could have cost you your balls." Che never clarified for Bustos if *he* had engineered the trip, or what his own dealings with the Chinese had been; because of the quick sequence of events that followed their talk, this was to be the only time they discussed it.

†Ariel told me that he did speak to several left-wing Argentine underground groups, including the leaders of a small "rather terroristic group," about the idea of a breakout. In the end, it was deemed too difficult to pull off, and Cuba fell back on the "legal option," supporting the efforts of Gustavo Roca and the other lawyers to get the prisoners' sentences reduced.

red-earth tobacco fields and river valleys. Their base camp was an ironic choice. Nestled on top of one of the *mogotes* was a luxurious country villa with a stream-fed swimming pool, which had formerly belonged to an American accused of being a CIA agent. It had been expropriated, and now it was serving as the launching pad for Che's next anti-Yankee expedition.

Che had chosen an eclectic group. It included a few men who had been with him in the Congo, others who had been with him in the sierra war, and members of his bodyguard corps. From different parts of Cuba, they had been put on planes to Havana, where they were taken to Raúl Castro's office. There they recognized old friends they hadn't seen for some time. None of them knew why they were there. Finally, Raúl told them they had the honor of being selected for an "internationalist mission." For most of them, it was a dream come true—to be an internationalist revolutionary had become one of the highest aspirations for Cubans serving in the armed forces.

Dariel Alarcón Ramírez (Benigno), a tough, lean *guajiro* in his late twenties, had shown his mettle as a hardy fighter in the sierra and as a member of Camilo's invasion column; most recently he had been in the Congo with Che. Eliseo Reyes (Rolando), twenty-six, was another veteran of the sierra who had been on Che's long march to the Escambray. Smart and loyal, he had served for a time as the head of police intelligence, then fought against counterrevolutionaries in Pinar del Río. Thirty-three-year-old Antonio "Olo" Pantoja had been one of Che's rebel officers in the sierra and an instructor for Masetti's group. Papi Martínez Tamayo's younger brother, René, or Arturo, was a veteran of clandestine work for State Security and the military. Twenty-nine-year-old Gustavo Machín de Hoed (Alejandro) had come out of the Directorio Revolucionario and joined Che in the Escambray; later he had been one of Che's vice ministers of industry. "Manuel" or Miguel Hernández Osorio, was thirty-five and had led Che's vanguard squad during the march to the Escambray.

Pacho, or Pachungo, thirty-one-year-old Alberto Fernández Montes de Oca, had been Che's traveling companion from Prague and his personal courier with La Paz. Pacho had been a teacher before joining the July 26 urban underground during the war. There were three black men besides Pombo. Octavio de la Concepción de la Pedraja—who was known as Morogoro in the Congo—was a thirty-one-year-old doctor, an anti-Batista veteran, and a career officer in Cuba's armed forces. One of Raúl's veterans, thirty-three-year-old Israel Reyes Zayas (Braulio), another military careerist, had been with Che in the Congo as Azi. And Leonardo "Tamayito" Tamayo, or Urbano, as he was now called, had been with Che since 1957 as a member of his bodyguard corps.

The heavy-set, forty-one-year old Juan "Joaquín" Vitalio Acuña was the oldest of the men. He had been in Che's column in the war and had become a *comandante* himself during the final push to power. Another Central Committee man and career officer, Antonio Sánchez Díaz, also called Marcos or Pinares, had been one of Camilo Cienfuegos's officers and had been promoted to *comandante* after the rebels' victory. And finally, there was the thirty-year-old, extroverted Jesús Suárez Gayol, or Rubio, Orlando Borrego's friend since the Escambray and currently his deputy in the Ministry of Sugar.

Nobody knew where they were going to fight or who their commander would be until the day a stranger in civilian clothes, balding and middle-aged, showed up at their camp. "Ramón" began walking up and down before the assembled men, caustically insulting them. It was only when he had taken the joke quite far with Eliseo Reyes, who grew offended, that Ramón revealed his true identity: Che. From then on, Che lived with his men, overseeing their physical training and target practice, and, as always, giving daily classes, this time in "cultural education," French, and a new language— Quechua.

By August, a base of operations had been located in Bolivia, a remote 3,700-acre tract of wilderness in the backward southeastern region, with a seasonal river, the Ñancahuazú, running through it. It lay in a hilly, forested area abutting the eastern foothills of the Andean cordillera and at the edge of the vast tropical desert of the *chaco* that spreads eastward to Paraguay, the nearest border. It was about 150 miles south of Santa Cruz along a dirt road, and a similar distance from the Argentine border; the nearest town, an old Spanish colonial outpost called Lagunillas, was about twelve miles away. A few hours' drive farther south lay the oil-drilling and army garrison town of Camiri.

Since his return from Cuba, Mario Monje had complied with his promise to Fidel, assigning his Cuban-trained Party cadres to help make the arrangements for Che's arrival, buying equipment and weapons, renting safe houses, and lining up transportation. Papi, who had gone to Bolivia with no clear directives about where he should establish a base, had agreed to the Ñancahuazú purchase based on Monje's recommendation.

Years later, Monje admitted that it was an almost arbitrary choice and certainly not a strategic one. He sent Coco, Loro, and Saldaña off to look for a good base near the Argentine border—assuming that this was where Che was headed—and two weeks later, Loro returned, having located Ñancahuazú; Monje says he looked at a map, decided that it seemed close enough to Argentina, and gave the go-ahead. On August 26, Loro and Coco, posing as prospective pig breeders, bought the land.

When Pombo and Tuma arrived in late July and told Monje that their plans had changed, that the "continental" guerrilla operations would begin in Bolivia rather than Peru, Monje told them he was in agreement. When the Cubans sounded him out on the possibility that Che might be personally involved, Monje expressed his willingness to go to the field himself and agreed to give them more men to set up a rural guerrilla front, while still stating his preference for a popular uprising.

A few days later, Monje had changed his tune, saying he did not remember promising the Cubans more men, and reminding them that he could withdraw the Party's help altogether. He had to be in control of what was happening in his country, he said, and he resented the way the Cubans were trying to dictate terms to the Bolivians. In an attempt to pull rank, he alluded to conversations he had had in Moscow detailing his own plans, and said he would request aid from the Soviet Union at the appropriate moment. He had, he said, agreed to lend the Party's help in getting Che to Argentina and assisting the guerrilla efforts in Brazil and Peru, but Bolivia itself had never been under discussion. The Cuban advance team remonstrated with him and Monje backed off, but from that time forward the air was full of mutual distrust.

One of the reasons for Monje's demurral was the outcome of Bolivia's general elections in July. The Communist Party was given permission to field candidates, and Monje and his fellow Politburo apparatchiks had opted to participate while simultaneously telling Cuban-trained Young Turks such as Coco Peredo that they were only delaying, not abandoning, the option of an armed struggle. The Party had picked up some votes, a mere fraction of the total, but still the biggest number it had ever obtained. For Party moderates, it was an argument for continuing to work within the system.

In early September, while Monje continued to vacillate and send mixed signals, Che dispatched Pacho to La Paz to assess the situation. The Cubans began taking soundings among the Bolivian Party cadres to determine their affinities; would they join the Cubans if a guerrilla war was launched independent of the Party? Coco Peredo, for one, told them he would fight with them to the death, but some of the others, loyal to the Party hierarchy, clearly could not be counted on. Meanwhile, Che sent word that he wanted the guerrilla base to be in the Alto Beni, a tropical farming region in the upper Amazonian watershed, northeast of La Paz and at the other end of the country from Ñancahuazú. He told his men to purchase land there, and to transfer the weapons they had stored in Santa Cruz.

Meanwhile, Monje learned from Party informants that Régis Debray had been sighted moving around the Bolivian countryside—in Cochabamba, in the Chaparé, and in the Alto Beni—all regions that had been under discussion by the Cubans as possible guerrilla sites. He also heard that

Debray had met with Moisés Guevara, an action-minded, dissident miners' leader, who had broken off from Oscar Zamora's pro-Chinese Communist Party faction. Monje accused the Cubans of operating behind his back and demanded to know if they were having any dealings with the *fraccionalista* Guevara. The Cuban advance team denied any knowledge of Debray's presence and assured Monje that there had been no contact with Moisés Guevara. Both assertions were, of course, untrue. In fact, Che had sent the Cubans a message explaining Debray's mission: to recruit Moisés Guevara's force, and to make an assessment of the Alto Beni area he had chosen as the war's launching ground.

Pombo, Papi, and Tuma were caught in the middle. They already had a guerrilla base, but it was in the southeast. They had a semblance of support from the Bolivian Communist Party and a whole network established. All of it had come about through their dealings with Monje, they told Che, and as difficult as the Party leader was to read, he was all they had at the moment. As for Moisés Guevara, he had promised to join the armed struggle, but so far had produced no men and was demanding money. They urged Che to reconsider his choices.

To complicate things further, they were also dealing with the Peruvian guerrillas who had expected to be the primary focus of Cuba's guerrilla assistance efforts in the area. The Peruvians were led by a Peruvian-Chinese Mao look-alike, Juan Pablo Chang, an old friend of Hilda Gadea's, who was now trying to rebuild the clandestine infrastucture shattered after the deaths of Lobatón and Uceda and the imprisonment of Ricardo Gadea and Héctor Béjar. Chang had a man with the Cubans in La Paz, Julio Danigno Pacheco—alias Sánchez—but he and his comrades were upset about the Cubans' change of focus to Bolivia. The Cubans held a meeting with Sánchez to placate him and explain the new strategy.

Che's lieutenants were finding it difficult to oblige him about the place in the Alto Beni. They sent him a long report lobbying in favor of the Ñancahuazú property already purchased, and pointed out that the Beni was heavily populated; the large amount of land they would need was not available, and if they set up camp on a smaller farm, they ran the risk of early detection. At last, Che relented, sending word that the present farm would do for the moment.

It was now October, but many issues still hung inconclusively in the air. In a new twist, Monje announced that his Central Committee had voted in favor of the armed struggle but, as usual, emphasized that it would have to be led by Bolivians. He intended to go to Havana to make this policy understood. Despite the obvious need for urgency, however, Monje first made a visit to Bulgaria; he would not arrive in Havana until late November.

There he would discover that the man who was becoming his nemesis was nowhere to be found. In fact, Che had already left for Bolivia, having decided to arrive unannounced except to his closest circle of Cuban comrades.

Monje recalled that Fidel would not confirm or deny that there had been a change of plans. He let Monje make his point that in Bolivia the revolution had to be directed by Bolivians, but deferred the issue, suggesting that he and Che "get together and talk." Where was Monje going to be around Christmas? Fidel asked. In Bolivia, Monje replied. Fidel said that a meeting would be arranged around that time, somewhere "outside" Bolivia, but near the border. By now, Monje said, he knew where that place was—not outside Bolivia at all, but in Ñancahuazú. He returned to Bolivia in mid-December, more certain than ever that the Cubans had deceived him.*

IX

Che had lain low until the final days of his stay in Cuba. Aside from Fidel, the men in his training camp, and some high-ranking revolutionary leaders, Orlando Borrego was one of the few people who knew of his presence. Still only in his late twenties, Borrego was keen to accompany Che to the battlefront—as he had wanted to go to Africa—even though he had responsibilities as the Cuban minister of sugar. When Che sent word that he had selected Jesús Suárez Gayol, Borrego's deputy, to go to Bolivia with him, Borrego asked to go, too. Che refused, but promised that he could join them at a future stage, when the revolution was more secured.

There was another reason why Che wanted his protégé to stay. After one of Aleida's clandestine reunions with Che abroad, she had returned with a special present for Borrego. It was Che's own heavily marked-up copy of the Soviet *Manual of Political Economy* that he had begun working on in Dar es Salaam. The manual had for years provided the "correct" interpretation and application of the teachings of Marx, Engels, and Lenin in the construction of a socialist economy. Accompanying Che's copy was a ream of notations and comments, many of them highly critical, in which he questioned some of the basic tenets of scientific socialism as codified by the Soviet Union. He also sent an outline of his theory for the "budgetary finance system" that he favored over the established Moscow line. What Che had in mind was a new manual on political economy, better suited to modern times, for use by the developing nations and revolutionary societies of the Third World. As

*Although Monje would not say he had done so, it is believed in Cuba that he traveled to Moscow as part of his return trip to Bolivia for the express purpose of complaining to his handlers in the Kremlin about the Cubans' plans for his country.

for his economic theory, he wanted it expanded into book form. He knew he was not going to have time to finish either project and was now entrusting Borrego with completing the tasks for him. In a letter attached to the material, addressed to Borrego by his pet name, "Vinagreta" (Sourpuss), Che joked that he was sending it via Tormenta (Storm), meaning Aleida. He urged Borrego to do his best with it and told him to be patient about Bolivia, but to be ready for the "second phase."

In Che's critique of the Stalinist manual, he pointed out that since Lenin's writings, little had been added to update the evaluations of Marxism except for a few things written by Stalin and Mao. He indicted Lenin—who had introduced some capitalist forms of competition into the Soviet Union as a means of kick-starting its economy in the 1920s—as the "culprit" in many of the Soviet Union's mistakes, and, while reiterating his admiration for and respect toward the culprit, he warned, in block letters, that the U.S.S.R. and Soviet bloc were doomed to "return to capitalism." When Borrego read this, he was stunned. "Che is really audacious," he thought to himself. "This writing is heretical!" He thought Che had gone too far. With the passage of time, of course, Che would be proved right.

In his notes, Che softened the criticism of Lenin by pointing out that his errors did not make him an "enemy," and that Che's own criticisms were "intended within the spirit of Marxist revolutionary criticism," in order to "modernize Marxism" and to correct its "mistaken paths" to help underdeveloped countries that were struggling for freedom. Che anticipated attacks against him from fellow socialists. "Some will take this writing as counterrevolutionary or reformist," he said, and he stressed that for this reason the arguments needed to be well elaborated and based on airtight scholarship. Some of the remarks he scribbled in the margins of the Soviet manual, however, were very irreverent. Regarding a passage that read, "Socialism need not come about through violence, as proven by the socialist states of Eastern Europe, where change came through peaceful means," he quipped, "What was the Soviet army doing, scratching its balls?" Borrego assumed that Che meant to have his work come to light in one fashion or another. "Even if he realized that the new path he was proposing could not be implanted here, for a variety of reasons," Borrego said. "He probably hoped he could get something going and try it out for himself if he were able to take Bolivia or one of those countries."*

*In the increasingly Sovietized Cuba of subsequent years, however, Borrego had difficulty finding the "right time" to push for the publication of Che's writings. Reportedly, Fidel considered them too sensitive to be made public. Borrego finally received approval to publish excerpts of Che's economic critique in a memoir he wrote, *Che: El Camino del Fuego*, in 2001. A complete version of Che's critiques, *Apuntes Criticos a la Economica*, was published in 2006.

While Che had been in the Congo and Prague, Borrego and Enrique Oltuski had worked around the clock for months on his "collected works"; in the end, they had produced a seven-volume set, *El Che en la Revolución Cubana,* compiling everything from *Guerra de Guerrillas* and *Pasajes de la Guerra Revolucionaria* to Che's speeches and a sampling of letters and articles, including some that were previously unpublished. Che was both surprised and pleased when Borrego showed him the final result, but with characteristic dryness, he looked through the books and cracked, "You've made a real potpourri."

Borrego had an edition of 200 sets printed, and he gave the first set off the press to Fidel, but the Cuban public never saw them. The books went to the revolutionary *dirigentes* and to individuals on a special list that Che composed, one of the last things he did before leaving Cuba. In the end, only some 100 sets were sent out; the remainder were stored in a warehouse where they presumably remain, if they haven't succumbed to water damage and silverfish.*

X

Che's impending departure was very hard for Borrego, and he tried to spend as much time as possible with Che in the last days. He made frequent trips to the house in Pinar del Río, as did Aleida, who stayed for the weekends and cooked meals for everyone. Borrego even accompanied Che to a session with the "physiognomy specialist" from Cuban intelligence who plucked out the hairs on top of Che's head one by one in order to give him the severely receding hairline of a man in his mid-fifties. When Che was in his full disguise, Fidel introduced him to a few of the highest-ranking ministers of Cuba as a visiting foreign friend and nobody, according to Fidel, recognized him. "It was really perfect," Fidel recalled later.

One day in October, not long before Che was due to leave, Borrego took four gallons of his favorite strawberry ice cream to the men in training. A special feast had been prepared, and everyone sat at a long picnic table. When Borrego got up, intending to get a second helping of the ice cream, Che called after him in a loud voice, "Hey, Borrego! You're not going to Bolivia, so why should you have seconds? Why don't you let the men who *are* going eat it?"

Che's criticism, heard by everyone, lacerated Borrego; tears began running down his cheeks. Without saying a word, he walked away, burn-

---

*In 1997, in commemoration of the thirtieth anniversary of Che's death, an "abridged" version of Borrego's special edition of Che's works was finally approved by Cuba's government for public consumption.

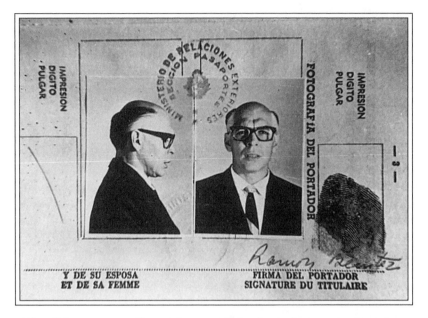

One of the passports Che used to travel clandestinely.

Fidel with the disguised Che before he left for Bolivia.

ing with shame and indignation. He sat on a log listening to the rough-and-ready guerrillas titter and break into guffaws behind his back. After a few minutes, he heard steps. A hand was placed softly on his head and tousled his hair. "I'm sorry for what I said," Che whispered. "Come on, it's not such a big thing. Come back." Without looking up, Borrego said, "Fuck off," and stayed where he was for a long time. "It was the worst thing Che ever did to me," Borrego recalled.

The last few days were emotional for everyone, but the most poignant moments were Che's final encounters with Aleida and his children, who were brought out to the *finca* to see him. Che did not reveal himself as their father. He was "Uncle Ramón." He had seen their father recently, he said, and he was there to pass on his love, along with little pieces of advice for each of them. They ate lunch together, with *tío* Ramón sitting at the head of the table, just as Papá Che used to do.

Che's three-year-old daughter, Celia, was brought separately to see him. Borrego described the visit as wrenching. There was Che with his child, unable to tell her who he was or to touch her and hold her as a father would, for she could not be trusted to keep the secret. Of course, it was the ultimate test of his disguise. If his own children could not recognize him, nobody would.* During another visit, five-year-old Aliusha came up to give him a peck on the cheek and then ran back to Aleida's side to exclaim in a loud whisper: "Mama, I think that old man's in love with me." Che overheard the comment, and tears welled up in his eyes. Aleida was devastated but managed to contain her own tears until she was out of sight of the children.

The time had finally come. The operation to liberate South America was beginning. All the men present at Che's farewell banquet the night before he left felt the momentousness of the occasion. Special food had been prepared—a cow cooked *asado* style, red wine, and a roast pig and beer—for Che had wanted it to be an Argentine-Cuban meal. But as Fidel talked and talked, giving advice and encouragement to Che, reminding him of past times and moments shared in the sierra, everyone forgot the food and sat listening raptly. Benigno, one of the guerrillas who were present, recalled that hours passed in that way. Finally, realizing it was time to go to the airport, Che leaped up.

Che and Fidel met in a quick, short embrace, then stood back looking at each other intently, their arms outstretched on each other's shoulders, for a long moment. Fidel later described his good-bye with Che as a manly *abrazo* befitting two old comrades in arms. Since both were reserved men

*Hildita was the only one of his children Che did not see. She was ten, old enough to see through his disguise.

when it came to public displays of emotion, their hug, he said, had not been very effusive. But Benigno remembered it as a deeply charged moment.

Then Che got into his car, told the driver: "Drive, damnit!" and was gone. Afterward, said Benigno, a melancholy silence fell over the camp. Fidel walked away from the men and sat by himself. He was seen to drop his head and stay that way for a long time. The men wondered if he was weeping, but no one dared approach him. At dawn, they heard Fidel call out and saw him pointing to the sky. Che's plane was heading away from Cuba.

A self-portrait taken by Che in the mirror on a door in his room at the Hotel Copacabana in La Paz, Bolivia, in November 1966. He was disguised as a middle-aged Uruguayan economist, Adolfo Mena González.

29

Necessary Sacrifice

Bolivia must be sacrificed so that the revolutions in the neighboring countries may begin.

CHE
December 1966, speaking to his guerrillas in Bolivia

Wherever death may surprise us, let it be welcome.

CHE
April 1967, in his "Message to the Tricontinental"

I

In his postmortem of the Congo fiasco, Che acknowledged that one of his greatest mistakes was to have attempted a *chantaje de cuerpo presente,* blackmail by physical presence. He had foisted himself unannounced on the Congolese rebels, causing animosity and suspicion among the leadership. It was one of the mistakes he had vowed to learn from. Yet when he went to Bolivia in early November 1966, he neatly replicated his Congo *chantaje,* once again appearing on alien turf without an invitation, convinced that the Bolivian Communist Party leaders wouldn't back out of the impending guerrilla war once he presented them with the fait accompli of his presence.*

Things began well enough. When Che—or rather Adolfo Mena González, a middle-aged Uruguayan businessman on an economic fact-finding mission for the Organization of American States—arrived with Pacho in La Paz on November 3, he was met by his closest aides: Papi, Pombo, Tuma, and Renán Montero. He checked into a third-floor suite of the Hotel Copacabana on the graceful, tree-lined Prado boulevard of central La Paz. His favorite mountain, Illimani, snowcapped and blue, overlooked the scene. Che took a photograph of himself in the mirror of his wardrobe door. The pudgy-looking man sitting on the bed stares back at the viewer with an intense, inscrutable expression.

The reflective interlude was brief, for Che was not in a mood to waste time. Tania provided him with the letters of introduction that he had asked her to obtain for him. Using her newfound friendships within the Bolivian government, she had secured an official document signed by none other than the president's chief of information, Gonzalo López Muñoz. It identified

*See Notes.

Adolfa Mena as a special envoy of the OAS and requested "all possible cooperation" from the "national authorities" as well as "private individuals and institutions."

Two days later, Che had descended from the bright chill of the altiplano into the dry-season dust and swelter of the *chaco*. Accompanied by Pombo, Tuma, Papi, Pacho, and the Bolivian Loro Vázquez-Viaña, he set out on a three-day drive to Ñancahuazú. During one roadside stop to eat lunch, Che revealed his true identity to Loro, asking him not to let the Party know he was in the country until he had spoken with Monje. "He told Loro that his decision to come to Bolivia was because it was the country with the best conditions for a guerrilla base in the continent," Pombo wrote. Che then added, "I've come to stay, and the only way that I will leave here is dead, or crossing a border, shooting bullets as I go."

II

By New Year's Eve, Che's hair had begun to grow back and he had a sparse beard. His Cuban comrades and a Peruvian guerrilla, "Eustaquio," had arrived at Ñancahuazú, joining the Bolivians who had been in training there. He had an army of twenty-four men. Only nine were Bolivians. Two of them, Coco Peredo's older brother Inti and Freddy Maymura, a Japanese-Bolivian former medical student, had just undergone training in Cuba. The men had built a proper base camp and a secondary bivouac concealed in the forest above a steep, red-stone canyon several hours' hike upriver from the place they called the Casa de Calamina—a tin-roofed, mud-brick house, their legal "front" for the future Ñancahuazú pig and timber farm. They had a mud oven for baking bread, a meat-drying hut, and a rustic medical dispensary, even crude log tables and benches for eating. They had dug a latrine, and tunnels and caves for storing their food, ammunition, and most compromising documents. In one cave they had set up a radio transmitter for sending and receiving coded communications to and from Havana, or "Manila," as it was now referred to.

The urban underground in La Paz was taking shape. Bolivians such as Rodolfo Saldaña, Coco Peredo, and Loro Vázquez-Viaña—the "owner" of the farm—came and went to buy supplies, carry messages, ferry newcomers, and transport weapons. But Che was already worried about the preponderance of foreigners in his "Bolivian army."* Signs of competitive

---

*In the end, the breakdown of nationalities in Che's guerrilla force—excluding the members of his urban network—would be as follows: one Argentine (Che), one German (Tania), three Peruvians, sixteen Cubans, and a total of twenty-nine Bolivians.

discord between the Cubans and Bolivians were showing. Che tried to remedy the situation with lectures about discipline and by announcing that the Cubans would temporarily be the officers of the little troop, until the Bolivians had gained more experience. This measure, obviously, was not popular with the Bolivians. When word came from Juan Pablo Chang that he wanted to send twenty Peruvian fighters to the camp, Che stalled him, concerned about "internationalizing" the struggle before Monje was involved. What Che needed was a solid base of Bolivian support, and he wanted to have at least twenty Bolivians with him before beginning operations. To do that, he needed Monje.

Despite precautions, the presence of newcomers soon provoked the interest of their few neighbors in this backwoods region—just as it had done at Masetti's base near the Río Bermejo, farther south. Even before Che had arrived, in fact, his advance men had learned that Ciro Algarañaz, their only immediate neighbor, was spreading the word that he suspected the newcomers were cocaine traffickers, a budding profession in this coca-producing nation. Algarañaz's house and pig farm lay at the roadside on the approach to their own *finca*, and they had to pass it to get to Casa de Calamina. Although Algarañaz lived in Camiri during the week, his caretaker lived on the property permanently.

By late December, Monje was expected at the camp, and before he arrived, Che talked to his men about the proposals he would make. First, Che would insist that he should be military commander, and in charge of finances; he had no interest in being the political chief, however. For outside support, he proposed asking both the Soviet Union and China for aid, and he suggested that Moisés Guevara could go to Beijing with a letter from him to Chou En-lai to ask for help with "no strings attached," while Monje could go to Moscow "together with a comrade who could at least say how much he was given." Che's proposal shows that even at this late date, he thought he could hammer out the differences between the pro-Chinese and pro-Soviet Communists in Bolivia. If he could achieve a local peace in South America, then perhaps there was still hope for socialist unity on a larger scale.

From his crude camp in the Bolivian outback, Che foresaw an astonishing, even fantastic sequence of events. "Bolivia must be sacrificed so that the revolutions in the neighboring countries may begin," he said. "We have to create another Vietnam in the Americas with its center in Bolivia." Starting the war and spreading it to neighboring nations were the first two stages of his plan. In the third stage, wars in South America would draw in the North Americans. This would benefit the guerrillas by giving their campaigns a nationalistic hue; as in Vietnam, they would be fighting against a foreign invader. And by deploying forces in Latin America, the United States would be more dispersed and, ultimately, weaker on all fronts, in Bolivia as well as in Vietnam. Finally, the spreading conflagrations would lead China and Russia to stop their feuding and align their forces with the revolutionaries everywhere to bring down U.S. imperialism once and for all. To Che, what happened in Bolivia was to be no less than the opening shot in a new world war that would determine whether the planet was to be socialist or capitalist. First, though, he had to deal with Mario Monje.

On December 31, Tania accompanied Monje to Ñancahuazú, and at long last the two rivals had their showdown. They sat in the forest to talk. Two very poor photographs have survived as evidence of the encounter. In one, Che lies on the ground, looking archly toward the seated Monje, who is talking with his legs drawn up defensively.

Monje demanded overall leadership of the armed struggle in Bolivia for himself. He also demanded that no alliance be formed with the *pro-chinos*. Che said he could forgo an alliance with the pro-Chinese Communists, but on the question of command he was unbudging. He would be the military commander because he was better qualified. And he also thought he could handle political decisions better than Monje. But he offered to make Monje the "nominal chief" of the guerrilla operation if that would help him "save face."

Afterward, Monje told the men in camp that he would resign his post as Party chief and come and proudly fight with Che—not as Party secretary, but as "Estanislao," a simple combatant. He would now return to La Paz and inform the Party about the imminent guerrilla war so its members could take precautionary measures. He would return to join the band within ten days.

Either this was a bluff intended to provoke Che into making an additional face-saving gesture, or Monje was simply lying. The next morning, before leaving, he assembled the Bolivians and told them that the Party did not support the armed struggle, that they would be expelled if they stayed on, and that the stipends to their families would be suspended. Only four men—Coco, Saldaña, Ñato, and Loro—had the Party's permission to be there, and that would be honored, but for the rest the choice now was between Party and war. They chose the latter. Monje left and did not return.

Rafael Segarra, a Communist Party official in Santa Cruz, said that Monje stopped to see him on the return trip from Ñancahuazú. "The shit's going to hit the fan," Monje warned. "This thing is going ahead and either we bury it or it'll bury all of us." He urged Segarra to lie low or to disappear. In the coming days, Monje gave the same advice to Party people everywhere.

Monje's actions remain cloaked in the web of intrigue and suspicion that he helped create. Pombo insists that what Monje perpetrated was an act of "conscious treason." Thirty years after the event, Che's widow, Aleida, still considered Monje—*"ese índio feo"* (that ugly Indian)—the man who betrayed her husband.

The meeting between Che and Monje had culminated in disaster, and Che's tactlessness had played as great a part in the unhappy ending as had Monje's duplicity and indecision. The die was cast. As of January 1, 1967, Che and his two dozen fighters were, to all intents and purposes, on their own.

III

Content that a number of young Bolivian Communists had remained loyal to him, and trusting in Fidel's superior powers of persuasion to sort things out with the Party hierarchy, Che refused to allow the rupture with Monje to affect his vision of the future. In a coded message to Fidel, or "Leche" (Milk), as he was now referred to, Che told him what had happened in unalarmed tones.*

Indeed, it seemed that things were progressing fairly smoothly for Che. He had dispatched Tania to Buenos Aires to summon Ciro Bustos and Eduardo Jozami—a young journalist, law student, and leader of a dissident faction of the Argentine Communist Party—with an eye to getting the Argentine guerrilla movement up and running. Meanwhile, his people were busy organizing his underground network throughout Bolivia. When Moisés Guevara came calling, Che told him that he would have to dissolve his group and join Che as a simple soldier, that there could be no more factional activity. At first taken aback, Moisés agreed. He would return to the Bolivian highlands and recruit some men before returning himself.

Che's men were now patrolling the area around Ñancahuazú, and a semblance of military discipline had been achieved. The fighters did sentry duty, fetched water and firewood, and took turns cooking and washing. Regular porters' missions, or *gondolas,* were organized to carry supplies into the camp. Some men hunted, bringing in turkeys and armadillos for the cooking pot, and Quechua classes began again. There were, of course, the discomforts of life in the bush—pernicious insects, cuts and scrapes, men falling ill with malaria—but Che took it all with aplomb. "Boron day," he wrote on January 11. "Larvae of flies removed from Marcos, Carlos, Pombo, Antonio, Moro, and Joaquín."

*A short while later, Fidel wrote back that the Bolivian union leader Simón Reyes was in Cuba, and that Jorge Kolle Cueto, the number two Bolivian Communist Party official, was on his way there for talks to amend the crisis.

There were also the usual behavior problems, and Che returned to his old strict self in laying down the law. Loro was operating a little too freely, finding time to seduce women on his trips to buy supplies, and Papi was moping around, feeling he had fallen into Che's disfavor. After scolding Papi for what he had called his "many mistakes" in the Bolivian advance work— including making unwanted advances to Tania—Che ordered him to stay with him in the field. The man he had designated his deputy, Marcos, had been abusive with the Bolivians, and Che publicly upbraided and demoted him, naming the oldest man, Joaquín, in his place.

Their neighbor, Ciro Algarañaz, was continuing to be an irritation. He and another man had been snooping around, and one day Algarañaz approached Loro, saying that he was a friend and could be trusted. He wanted to know what Loro and his companions were up to. Loro brushed him off, but a few days later some soldiers arrived at the forward camp, questioned Loro, and took away his pistol, warning that he and his friends were under observation. Clearly, the locals believed the guerrillas were contrabandists and wanted a piece of the action. After this incident, Che mounted lookouts to keep an eye on Algarañaz's house.

On February 1, Che left a few men in camp and took most of the others off for what he intended to be a fortnight's conditioning trek into the surrounding *chaco*. The fortnight turned into a grueling forty-eight-day ordeal. They got lost and endured torrential rain, hunger, thirst, and exhausting marathon hikes. They were reduced to eating palm hearts, monkeys, hawks, and parrots, and with the men worn-out and demoralized, there had been several quarrels. There was also tragedy. Two of the young Bolivians drowned in the swollen rivers—a coincidence, Pombo noted, eerily reminiscent of how their stay in the Congo had begun, with the drowning death of Leonard Mitoudidi. For his part, Che lamented the deaths, but also the loss of six good weapons in the second drowning incident.

Even before returning to camp on March 20, Che knew that something had gone awry in his absence. A small plane was circling the vicinity of Ñancahuazú. He soon learned why from an advance party that had come out to meet him. While he was gone, some of Moisés Guevara's Bolivian recruits had arrived and had quickly become disenchanted with camp life. The Cubans left in charge had relegated them to menial chores. Two of the Bolivians had deserted, had been captured by the army, and had confessed everything they knew, including stories about Cubans and a *comandante* named Ramón. A few days earlier, Bolivian security forces had raided the Casa de Calamina. Nobody had been there at the time, but the army was rumored to be on the move in the area. The aircraft Che had seen circling overhead was a spotter plane; it had been up there for the past three days.

Walking on, Che was met by runners with more bad news. The army had just returned to the farm and had confiscated one of their mules and their jeep and captured a rebel courier—one of Moisés Guevara's men. Che quickened his pace to reach the camp. When he arrived, he observed a mood of defeat, some more new arrivals, and complete chaos and indecision among his men. On top of everything else, Che had to attend to visitors. Régis Debray, Ciro Bustos, Tania, and Juan Pablo Chang were all there to see him. After bringing Monje to the camp on New Year's Eve, Tania had been busy. She had traveled to Argentina on Che's orders, she had ferried Chang and two Peruvian comrades to Ñancahuazú, and she had gone back to La Paz and picked up Debray and Bustos and brought them to the camp.

Che dealt first with Chang, who had been to Cuba and asked Fidel for help in setting up a new Peruvian guerrilla column. Fidel had told him to get Che's approval. "He wants $5,000 a month for ten months," Che wrote. "I told him I agreed on the basis that they would go to the mountains within six months." Chang's plan was to lead a band of fifteen men and begin operations in the Ayacucho region of Peru's southeastern Andes. Che also agreed to send him some Cubans and weapons, and they discussed plans for maintaining radio contact.

As they spoke, Loro arrived. He had been doing forward sentry duty downriver from the camp and had killed a soldier he caught by surprise. Clearly, the war was about to begin, whether Che wanted it to or not. He hastened to polish up details with Chang, then conferred with Debray, who said he wanted to stay and fight, but Che told him that it would be better if he worked on the outside, promoting his cause with a European solidarity campaign. Che would send him out with news for Cuba and would write a letter for Bertrand Russell, asking for help in organizing an international fund in support of the Bolivian Liberation Movement.

It was Ciro Bustos's turn. Bustos had been waiting for his "contact" in Argentina, and after five months it had come in the form of Tania. She had told Bustos to go to La Paz, thus giving him the first inkling that Che was in Bolivia. Bustos had begun to question the wisdom of Che's theory of rurally based guerrilla war, and he sought out the advice of his most trusted comrades in Córdoba, who urged him to express his doubts, which they shared, when he saw Che. Using a hastily prepared false passport, he had flown to La Paz in late February. He was instructed to board a particular bus leaving for the city of Sucre, and when he got on the bus he spotted another European-looking man—Régis Debray, he would soon learn. As the bus was leaving the city, a taxi raced up, and out of it and into the bus came Tania. Bustos thought her actions and their form of transportation a reckless public display that could only attract notice.

Che and some of his fighters in the Ñancahuazú camp. From left, Alejandro, Pombo, Urbano, Rolando, Che, Tuma, Arturo, and Moro.

From left, Che's Argentine emissary, Ciro Bustos; the Peruvian Juan Pablo Chang; Che; and the French writer Régis Debray, whose code name was "Dantón."

"There we were, the only three foreigners on the bus, like three flies, looking around but not talking to one another," he recalled. "I wasn't very pleased about things."

According to Bustos, the rest of the journey was characterized by amateurish behavior on Tania's part. She spoke loudly and used Cuban slang in the roadside restaurants they stopped in. She had hired a car in Sucre, and the driver was both drinking and driving too fast; Tania thought this was funny, but it made Debray and Bustos mad. When they arrived in the camp, Che and most of the Cubans were gone, still out on their trek. Almost immediately, Bustos said, Tania pulled out some photographs she'd taken on her earlier trip and had brought to show everyone. There they were, virtually all of them, posing with their rifles, hamming it up, cooking, reading, and standing around and talking. Bustos was incredulous. He spoke to Olo Pantoja, the Cuban left in charge of the camp, who quickly ordered the photos gathered up.

In Che's prolonged absence, matters had slipped out of Olo's grasp. The day after Tania, Bustos, and Debray arrived in the camp, two of Moisés Guevara's men went out with their guns to hunt but did not return. Alarm bells rang. The two men had seen all the photographs and heard everyone talking openly about Cuba and other delicate topics. When a search party didn't locate the men, Olo ordered the camp evacuated. They went to a hiding place farther into the hills. Within a couple of days, when the plane began buzzing around, it was clear their worst fears had been well founded. The deserters had been picked up by the army. It was then that the first men from Che's expedition began returning.

Bustos was stunned when he saw Che. "He was torn apart," he said. "His shirt was in shreds, his knee poked out of his trousers, and he looked really skinny. But imperturbable. He gave me an *abrazo,* which was very moving for me. There were no words or anything." Bustos hung back, watching as Che simultaneously ate and took charge of the situation. He harangued Olo and the other men who had been responsible for the camp, using a degree of verbal violence that surprised Bustos. Later, he would see that it was a pattern in Che's behavior. "Afterward, [Che] would become calm, he would go read, serenely, while the guys he'd punished went around hangdog, turned into shit."

When it came time for Che and Bustos to talk, the first thing Che wanted to find out was why Bustos hadn't come earlier. Bustos told him Tania had not given him a specific time frame for his visit. Calling Tania over, Che tongue-lashed her for misrepresenting his instructions. "Damnit, Tania, what did I tell you to tell El Pelao [Bustos]?" he demanded. "What the fuck do I tell you things for!"

"I can't remember exactly what he said to her, but they were strong and violent things, and she started to shake," Bustos recalled. "She went away crying." Later, Che told Bustos to try to comfort her. But Che was already unhappy with Tania for having risked exposure by coming to the camp again. After her first visit, with Monje at the end of December, he had told her not to return.* What's more, Eduardo Jozami, the young Argentine dissident he had wanted to meet with, had come to Bolivia and gone home again when she hadn't shown up for a rendezvous with him.

Turning back to his business with Bustos, Che told him what he had in mind for Argentina. "My strategic objective is the seizure of political power," he said. "For this I want to form a group of Argentines, to prepare a couple of columns, season them in war for a year or two over here, and then enter. I want this to be your mission. And I want you to hang on as long as possible until you have to join up [in the mountains]. I want you to be the coordinator sending me people." Che added that the work had to be done well, "not like this shit here, where everyone does what they want." He said Bustos should work together with Papi on the means of transporting men, and with Pombo on the question of provisions, and he reeled off names of others he should coordinate with for specific issues. Che said his intention was to form a central command divided into two columns totaling about 500 men, including Bolivians, Argentines, and Peruvians, who would later split off and take the war to other zones.

As Che talked, Bustos wondered how he was going to arrange a food-supply line between Ñancahuazú and Argentina. And how was he supposed to coordinate with Pombo, when Pombo was in the bush with Che? These details weren't discussed, but it didn't sound realistic to Bustos. "It was like something magical," he said. "Out of this world." Che told Bustos that his first priority was to see Bustos safely out of the mountains so that he could get to work in Argentina, but a dense air of uncertainty hung over everything. The guerrillas' presence had been detected. A soldier had been killed. It was only a matter of time before an army patrol came looking for them.

IV

It came two days later, on March 23, a day Che recorded in his diary as one "of warlike events." Che had sent out men to prepare ambushes, creating a

---

*Loyola Guzmán, Che's new "national finance secretary" and a member of his urban network in La Paz, explained that Tania's first return trip, with the Peruvians, was really the fault of her group, which had decided to send Tania as an escort because the others were all too busy to go.

defensive perimeter, and at 8:00 A.M. Coco came running in to report that they had ambushed an army unit, killing seven soldiers and taking twenty-one prisoners, four of them wounded. They had also seized a nice bunch of weapons, including three mortars, sixteen carbines, two bazookas, and three Uzi submachine guns. And they had captured a document that showed the army's operational plans. Seeing that it called for a two-pronged advance, Che quickly dispatched some men to the other end of the river canyon to lay another ambush. In the meantime, he sent Inti Peredo—whom he was impressed by and was beginning to groom as a leader for the Bolivians—to interrogate the two captured officers, a major and a captain. "They talked like parrots," Che reported later.

Che recorded the victory tersely. He was worried about food supplies now that the approaches to Ñancahuazú were cut off and they had been forced to leave their camp with their stores behind. Another problem, and a serious one, was that their radio transmitter was malfunctioning. They could receive broadcasts and "Manila's" messages, but they could not send.

The next day brought no new ground troops, but a plane flew over and dropped bombs around the Casa de Calamina. Che sent Inti back to interrogate the officers again, then ordered the prisoners to be set free. The soldiers were ordered to strip and leave their uniforms behind, but the officers were allowed to keep their uniforms. The major was told he had until noon on March 27 to return and collect his dead.

After the prisoners had gone, Che turned his attention to his men. Marcos had been repeatedly insubordinate and had continued to mistreat some of the Bolivians. He had already been warned that he risked expulsion, and Che now demoted him again, naming Miguel to take his role as chief of the vanguard. Since the desertions, tension between the Bolivians and the Cubans had increased. The revolutionary fortitude of the four remaining Bolivians that Moisés Guevara had recruited—Paco, Pepe, Chingolo, and Eusebio—was openly questioned, and the men found themselves treated with contempt and suspicion. On March 25, Che told them that if they didn't work, they wouldn't eat. He suspended their tobacco rations and gave their personal belongings away to "other, needier comrades." He criticized another Bolivian, Walter, for being "weak" on their trek, and for the fear he had shown during the previous day's aerial bombardment. To another couple of men, he gave words of encouragement; they had performed well in the last few days. Finally, Che chose that day to name his little army: the Ejército de Liberación Nacional (ELN), or National Liberation Army, adding to the ranks of the similarly named Cuban-backed guerrilla *focos* in Peru and Colombia.

Over the next few days, the guerrillas concentrated on looking for food. Scouts came back having sighted groups of soldiers not far away, while others observed a group of about sixty soldiers and a helicopter stationed at Algarañaz's house. On March 27, Che wrote, "The news exploded, monopolizing all the space on the radio and producing a multitude of communiqués including the Barrientos press conference." He noted that the army was making wild claims of having killed fifteen guerrillas and taken four prisoners, including two "foreigners." He resolved to write the first guerrilla communiqué to refute the army's claims and announce the guerrillas' presence at the same time. "Obviously, the deserters or the prisoners talked," Che wrote. "But we do not know exactly how much they told and how they told it. Everything appears to indicate that Tania is spotted, whereby two years of good and patient work are lost. . . . We will see what happens."

V

What happened was a whirlwind of bellicose activity that threw all of Che's plans out the window and forced him to pursue the war he had begun, almost inadvertently, through a cumulative series of errors and and mishaps. Within a few days of the ambush, news reports became more and more exaggerated as the government mobilized its available troops. After first doubting the existence of the guerrillas, President Barrientos seized upon evidence found at their camp, including photographs, to decry the foreign invaders as agents of "Castro-Communism" and to call upon the patriotism of his fellow citizens in resisting the outsiders. In this intensely nationalistic country, the appeal to xenophobia was an effective way to isolate the civilians from the guerrillas; the foreign nature of the "Reds" was something Barrientos would now propound ceaselessly. There was little Che could do to combat the propaganda except write communiqués. His immediate priority was to avoid being wiped out. Che surmised from the radio reports that the army knew exactly where his band was located. He ordered men to dig new caves for storing weapons at a smaller camp that they called El Oso, since an anteater, or *oso hormiguero,* had been shot there.

In Cuba, the two dozen or more guerrillas who were preparing for the "second phase" did not include Orlando Borrego, but he and his brother-in-law, Enrique Acevedo, begged Fidel to be allowed to go to Bolivia. Their request was refused. The guerrillas had been prematurely discovered, Fidel said, and the situation was too volatile; what's more, direct contact with Che had been lost, so there was no way to insert them safely into the field any longer. As the months passed, Borrego and his comrades read the reports from Bolivia with increasing anxiety. The situation of Che and his band seemed to slide irrevocably toward disaster.

In his end-of-the-month summary for March, Che wrote laconically, "This month was full of events." After analyzing his troops and the current situation, he wrote, "Evidently we will have to get going before I had thought. . . . The situation is not good but today begins a new phase to test the guerrillas, which should do them much good once they get over it."

Their days were now spent on the move, alternately looking for or hiding from the army, which seemed to be everywhere around them in large numbers. On April 10 they fired upon a platoon of soldiers as they came down the river. "Soon the first news arrived, and it was unpleasant," wrote Che, who had stayed at his command post. "Rubio, Jesús Suárez Gayol, was mortally wounded; he was dead on arrival at our camp, a bullet in his head." Che had lost his first man in action, a Cuban, but three soldiers had been killed, and several others wounded and taken prisoner. After interrogating the prisoners and determining that more enemy forces were on their way, Che decided to leave his ambush in place. By the afternoon, more soldiers appeared and they too fell into the trap. "This time," he wrote, "there were seven dead, five wounded, and 22 prisoners."

That night, Bustos recalled, Che did something he found very strange. Rubio's body was placed on the ground in the middle of the camp and remained there until morning. It was, Bustos said, like a kind of wake. Nobody referred to the body, but it was right there, unavoidable, a grim reminder of what could await each of them. The next day, after Che made some remarks about Suárez Gayol's bravery—and his carelessness—he was buried in a shallow grave and the prisoners were set free. The captured enemy officer was sent off with Che's "Communiqué No. 1" announcing the commencement of hostilities by the ELN. Che noted the motley composition of the men sent in against him. "There are Rangers, paratroopers, and local soldiers, almost children."

Reluctantly, Che was forced to concede that there might be truth to what the news media were reporting: that the army had found their original camp and uncovered photographs and other evidence of their presence. A group of journalists had been taken there, and on April 11 Che listened to a reporter on the radio describe a photo he had seen in the camp of a beardless man with a pipe. It sounded like a photo of Che, although he wasn't identified. Two days later came the news that the United States was sending military advisers to Bolivia. This move was said to have nothing to do with the guerrillas: it was only part of a long-standing military assistance program between the two countries. Che didn't believe it for a second and made a hopeful note: "We may be witnessing the first episode of a new Vietnam." He was partly right. The United States *was*, of course, sending advisers to help the Bolivians quell the guerrilla threat, but if he thought it would spark off a campaign of national resistance as in Vietnam, he was wrong.

The question of what to do with Bustos and Debray had remained unresolved as Che's band reacted to the emergency at hand. It had already been decided that Juan Pablo Chang would stay on for the time being, as would Tania, whose cover had been blown since the discovery of her jeep, which she had left in Camiri, along with her identity papers as Laura Gutiérrez Bauer. Debray, meanwhile, had become increasingly nervous. Che observed on March 28, "The Frenchman stated too vehemently how useful he could be on the outside." A few days later, as Che tried to move his band out of the dragnet, he spoke to Bustos and Debray, outlining their options: to stay with them, to try to leave on their own, or else to stay on until the guerrillas reached a town where they could be left safely. They settled on the final option. Three dramatic weeks had passed since then, with more clashes and constant movement. The government had outlawed the Communist Party and declared a state of emergency in the southeastern region.

Applying the tactics he and Fidel had used in the first days of the sierra war, Che had decided to surprise the enemy by operating in a new area, around the village of Muyupampa; if possible, Bustos and Debray would leave from there. Then he and his men would move north to the eastern Andean foothills. He prepared his "Communiqué No. 2" for Debray to take out, as well as a coded message to Fidel informing him of the present situation. According to Bustos, Che stressed to him the importance of getting news of the guerrillas' actual circumstances to the island. He needed a new radio urgently, and Fidel should dispatch the men in training in Cuba to open a new front, farther north, to distract attention from his group.*

As they approached Muyupampa, Che joined the vanguard column and left Joaquín behind at a river crossing to wait for him. In order to make faster progress, Che had decided to split the column in two, leaving Joaquín

---

*Fidel had sent word that he was doing what he could to help. He'd met with the union leader Juan Lechín, who had promised his help and men for the cause. Lechín would be returning secretly to Bolivia in a few weeks. But Lechín ran into problems of his own and, as with so many of the Bolivians who at one time or another had promised their support, did little to help in the end. Previously, Fidel had sent Che a message saying that his meetings with Kolle Cueto and Simón Reyes from the Bolivian Party had gone well; they were "understanding," he said, and had promised their help. Kolle was supposedly going to visit Che; now, of course, that was out of the question. The army had flooded the area, picking up any civilian suspected of dealings with them, and, since Barrientos's ban on their activities, the Party leaders had had to go underground.

in charge of the rearguard column, made up of those who were sick—both Tania and Alejandro had a high fever—or malingering, such as the Bolivian *resacas*. Joaquín was ordered to make his presence felt but avoid frontal combat and to expect Che's return in three days. Che, Bustos, Debray, and the rest moved on, through an area inhabited by peasants who were clearly terrified by their arrival. When they approached Muyupampa on April 20, they found that the army had taken up positions there, and civilian spies had been sent out to look for them. Che's advance men captured the civilians, who were accompanied by a suspicious character, an Anglo-Chilean reporter named George Andrew Roth. He had come, he said, for an interview with the rebel leader.

Inti Peredo gave Roth an interview, and then Bustos and Debray decided to use him as a cover for their escape. They would try to outsmart the soldiers by separating from the guerrillas and walking into the village posing as journalists. The ruse failed, and they were immediately arrested. When Che learned what had happened, he calmly noted the odds of their survival; both Bustos and Debray had been carrying false documents. Che thought it "looked bad" for Bustos, but he speculated that Debray "should come out all right."*

Che now concentrated his efforts on rejoining Joaquín and the rearguard column, and exploring the route they would have to take to reach the Río Grande, beyond which lay the mountains of central Bolivia, their gateway to the Andes and, he hoped, escape from the army dragnet. Over the next few days, however, they ran into more enemy patrols and took more losses. In one clash, Loro disappeared. In another ambush, Eliseo Reyes (Rolando), a comrade since his days as an adolescent courier for Che's sierra column, was mortally wounded. He died as Che tried to save him, and for the first time since his arrival in Bolivia Che's diary reflected a real sense of loss. "We have lost the best man in the guerrilla band," he wrote. "Of his unknown and unheralded death for a hypothetical future that may materialize, one can only say: 'Your valiant little body, captain, has extended to immensity in its metallic form.'" (A line from Neruda's "Canto para Bolívar.")

The scouts Che had sent out to search for Joaquín's group returned with more bad news. They had run into the army, losing their rucksacks in

---

*When, the next day, the radio reported ominously that "three foreign mercenaries" had been "killed in battle," Che made a note in his diary to launch a revenge mission if it turned out they had been murdered by the army. Luckily for the three men, however, a local newspaper photographer had taken pictures of them alive in custody. The publication of that photograph may have saved their lives, for by the end of the month they were reported to be in prison in Camiri.

a firefight, and still had no idea where the rearguard column was. Judging from where the skirmish had taken place, near the Ñancahuazú, Che concluded that their only two river exits toward the Río Grande were now blocked. They would have to go over the mountains.

Still desperate to find Joaquín's group, Che and his band began moving north, cutting their way with machetes through the dense brush of the mountains. At the end of April, his summary presented an overwhelmingly bleak outlook. After describing the deaths of Rubio and Rolando and Loro's still unexplained disappearance,* he concluded, "[Our] isolation appears to be complete, sicknesses have undermined the health of some comrades, forcing us to divide forces, which has greatly diminished our effectiveness. As yet we have been unable to establish contact with Joaquín. The peasant base has not yet been developed, although it appears through planned terror we can neutralize some of them; support will come later. Not one [Bolivian] enlistment has been obtained."

The hard-nosed use of force to gain a civilian constituency had always been a part of guerrilla warfare, and Che and Fidel had employed it in the sierra, although in Che's public writings about the Cuban struggle he had never used the word "terror." The alliance between guerrilla and peasant had been rendered as a kind of idyllic mass wedding, an organic symbiosis. But this was now bare-bones survival, and there was no time to wax poetic; Che would have to use whatever tactics seemed necessary in order to survive. On the bright side, he noted that the public "clamor" about the guerrillas' activity was being matched by propaganda efforts in Cuba. Before he left Cuba for Bolivia, Che had written an undated call to arms addressed to the organization formed in the wake of the Tricontinental Conference. It had been published on April 16 in a special issue of what would become *Tricontinental* magazine. "After the publication of my article in Havana there must not be any doubt about my presence here," he wrote. "It seems certain that the North Americans will intervene heavily." (His references in the article to where "the struggle was going on" would have provided clues to where he was.) Che also noted in his journal that while the army was performing better in the field against them, it had not so far mobilized the peasants, but only some spies, who were "bothersome" but could be "neutralized."

The capture of Debray and Bustos was a heavy blow. They had been his only chance to get word to the outside world, and he now had no means of contact with La Paz or Cuba. "Dantón [Debray] and Carlos [Bustos] fell

---

*Jorge Vázquez-Viaña was reported captured and wounded, but later the army said he had "escaped." In fact, he had been removed from his hospital bed and executed; his body was taken up in a helicopter and hurled into the forested mountains near Lagunillas.

victim to their own haste, their near desperation to leave," he wrote. "And to my own lack of energy to stop them, so the communication with Cuba (Dantón) has been cut and the plan of action in Argentina (Carlos) is lost." Che and his men were truly on their own now. The enemy was alerted; Che's forces were cut in half and on the run; he had no backup from Cuba or Bolivia's cities, and no peasant support. Things could not be much worse. And yet, faced with this harsh reality, Che ended his April summary with a strangely optimistic conclusion. "In short: a month in which everything resolved itself in the normal manner, considering the necessary hazards of guerrilla warfare. The morale is good among all the combatants, who have passed their preliminary test as guerrillas."

VI

According to his former interrogators, it was Régis Debray who provided the final confirmation of Che Guevara's presence in Bolivia.* At first, Debray claimed he was a French journalist and had nothing to do with the guerrillas, but after his interrogation became tougher, he succumbed, confirming that the guerrilla *comandante* known as Ramón was in fact Che. Debray could not have held out for long in any case, since his links to Cuba were already well known. Just a few months earlier, his book *Revolution in the Revolution?* had been published in Cuba, and it was circulating around Latin America, causing a storm of controversy in leftist circles. *Revolution in the Revolution?*—based on his notes from conversations with Fidel, on Che's writings and speeches, and on his own observations from the guerrilla battlefields of the region—sought to give a theoretical foundation to Cuba's argument for the "guerrilla option." Debray's position, which was more explicit than Che's or Fidel's, was that the rural guerrilla *foco* should be the elite vanguard of the revolutionary struggle, from which the future leadership would be born. (Debray had brought Che a copy of the book, and Che read it from cover to cover in one sitting, condensing it in his own notes, which he used to give a few classes to his fighters.)

Bustos, meanwhile, was pretending to be a traveling salesman with leftist leanings who had somehow gotten mixed up in things, but who knew very little about what was going on. After several weeks, however, his true identity was ascertained when Argentine police forensic experts arrived to take

---

*At the end of June, General Ovando Candia confirmed publicly that Che was in Bolivia. Writing in his diary on June 30, Che observed, "Ovando's declaration is based on the statements made by Debray. It appears the latter said more than was necessary, although we cannot know the implications this may have, nor the circumstances in which he said what he did."

his fingerprints for comparison with those on file in Buenos Aires. When the results came back and Bustos was confronted with his lie, he said, he confessed. Learning that he was an artist by profession, his interrogators asked him to draw profiles of the members of the guerrilla band. He did so, and also drew maps of the Ñancahuazú camps and cave complexes. Fortunately, however, his identity as Che's Argentine guerrilla liaison was never revealed, so the people in his underground network in Argentina remained safe from arrest.

The Americans were now directly involved in Bolivia. The interior minister, Antonio Arguedas, was already on the CIA's payroll.* Working closely with him was a Cuban-American agent who operated under the name of Gabriel García García and who was present during some of the interrogations of Debray and Bustos. After the news of Che's presence in Bolivia broke, a group of American Special Forces Green Berets arrived in Bolivia to create a counterinsurgency Rangers Battalion, and the CIA began interviewing men on its payroll for a new mission: to find Che and stop him from getting a foothold in Bolivia.

One of those interviewed was Felix Rodríguez, the young Cuban-American CIA paramilitary operative who had been with the CIA's covert anti-Castro program since the beginning. He had been working for its Miami station since his withdrawal from Nicaragua in 1964. Until the summer of 1967, the CIA had been frustrated regarding the issue of Che's whereabouts. "As I remember it," Rodríguez said, "there were some high-ups in the Agency who had reported that Che had been killed in Africa, and so . . . when people started saying he was in Bolivia, well . . . [there were those] who said 'no, he's not there.' When the evidence was confirmed by Debray that he *was* there, that's when they really decided to move forward and put out a maximum effort in Bolivia." (According to Rodríguez, the CIA would have moved more quickly if not for the "Congo" theory, and he attributed this to the fact that the man who defended it was a senior CIA official who had staked his reputation on the story.)

Rodríguez got a telephone call from his CIA control officer in June 1967. He went to his office, where he was introduced to a CIA division chief who explained the project to find Che. Would Rodríguez be willing to go on the mission? Rodríguez immediately said yes. It was the mission of his life, and Rodríguez knew it. He also knew that the Agency had given it a

*The enigmatic Arguedas was not only working for the CIA. He was a former member of the Communist Party and a friend of Mario Monje's, and over the next several years, he functioned as a triple agent. He worked for the CIA, the Bolivian Communist Party, and eventually the Cubans. Thirty years later, none of his former colleagues in these various services could say with certainty where his true loyalties lay at any given time. (See Notes.)

high priority. "It feared [what might happen if] Che grabbed Bolivia," he recalled. "With a secure Cuban base there, they could easily expand the revolution to important countries like Brazil, Argentina." Adding to those anxieties, he said, was the clear impression that Che's operation was being directed out of Havana, and the language coming from there was all about creating "various Vietnams" in Latin America.

Indeed, Che's "Message to the Tricontinental" had caused a sensation. He had appealed to revolutionaries everywhere to create "two, three, many Vietnams." Opening with a quote from José Martí, "Now is the time of the furnaces, and only light should be seen," Che questioned the validity of the so-called peace of the postwar world and demanded a "long and cruel" global confrontation to bring about the destruction of imperialism and a new socialist world order. In a litany of the qualities that would be required for this battle, he cited hatred as a prime element: "a relentless hatred of the enemy, impelling us above and beyond the natural limitations that man is heir to, and transforming him into an effective, violent, seductive, and cold killing machine. Our soldiers must be thus; a people without hatred cannot vanquish a brutal enemy."

It would be a "total war," to be carried out against the Yankee first in his imperial outposts and eventually in his own territory. The war had to be waged in "his home," his "centers of entertainment"; he should be made to feel like a "cornered beast," until his "moral fiber begins to decline," and that would be the first symptom of his "decadence," and of victory for the popular forces. Che urged men everywhere to take up their brothers' just causes, as part of the global war against the United States. "Each spilled drop of blood, in any country under whose flag one has not been born, is an experience passed on to those who survive, to be added later to the liberation struggle of his own country."

We cannot elude the call of the hour. Vietnam is pointing it out with its endless lesson of heroism, its tragic and everyday lesson of struggle and death for the attainment of final victory. . . . How close we could look into a bright future should two, three, many Vietnams flourish throughout the world with their share of death and their immense tragedies, their everyday heroism and their repeated blows against imperialism, impelled to disperse its forces under the sudden attack and the increasing hatred of all the peoples of the world!

If we, at a small point on the world map, are able to fulfill our duty and place at the disposal of this struggle, whatever little of ourselves we are permitted to give; our lives, our sacrifice, and

if some day we have to breathe our last breath on any land, already
ours, sprinkled with our blood, let it be known we have measured
the scope of our actions. . . . Our every action is a battle cry against
imperialism, and a battle hymn for the peoples' unity against the
great enemy of mankind: the United States of America. Wherever
death may surprise us, let it be welcome, provided that this, our
battle cry, may have reached some receptive ears and another hand
may be extended to wield our weapon and other men may be ready
to intone the funeral dirge with the staccato singing of the machine
guns and new battle cries of war and victory.

Apocalyptic language had been present in Che's manifestos before, but this
one, which synthesized his true convictions implacably, was all the more
chilling and dramatic for the fact that everyone knew Che was somewhere
in the battlefield, trying to do exactly what he proposed: sparking another—
and he hoped definitive—world war.

    During a briefing in Washington, Felix Rodríguez was shown the pile
of evidence that Che was in Bolivia, including the "confessions" made by
Debray and Bustos, as well as Bustos's drawings. Rodríguez left for La Paz,
traveling undercover as a businessman, Felix Ramos. He arrived there on
August 1 and joined another Cuban-American agent, Gustavo Villoldo
Sampera (aka Eduardo González), a veteran of the CIA's recent antiguerrilla operation in the Congo, who had been in Bolivia since March.*

VII

By August, Che was sick and exhausted, and so were many of the two
dozen men still with him. On August 7, the nine-month anniversary of
the guerrilla army's birth, he noted, "Of the [original] six men, two are
dead, one has disappeared, two are wounded, and I with a case of asthma
that I am unable to control." Since the capture of Debray and Bustos three
months earlier, Che and his men had hacked their way with machetes
through the brutal spiny bush of the southeast, alternately enduring sear-
ing cold winds, rain, and blistering heat, vainly trying to make contact with
the rearguard column led by Joaquín. They often got lost and occasionally skirmished with army patrols. Radio Havana was their sole link to
the outside world.

    When they were bivouacked, Che spent much of his time reading,
writing in his diary, and filling his notebooks with thoughts about socialist

*See Notes.

economics, as if divorced from the reality around him. A new fatalism laced with dark humor appeared in many of his daily diary entries. He observed, from a curious distance, the continual bickering and petty thievery of food among his men; occasionally, he took charge and issued warnings and lectures. Much of the time, however, he was simply too weak to be stern anymore. Once, in early June, he had even let an army truck carrying "two little soldiers wrapped in blankets" go by without opening fire on it. "I did not feel up to shooting them, and my brain didn't work fast enough to take them prisoner." Another time, after capturing a policeman posing as a merchant, who had been sent out to spy on them, Che considered killing him but let him go with a "severe warning." On June 14, his official thirty-ninth birthday, Che reflected, "I am inevitably approaching the age when my future as a guerrilla must be reconsidered. For now, I'm still in one piece."

An attempt to send a friendly peasant youth out from the mountains as a courier with messages to fetch help ended in failure. Che's tape recorder was lost in a skirmish, so he could no longer decode the messages received via Radio Havana. He also lost his notes on Debray's book and a volume by Trotsky he had been reading, and he rued having given the army another propaganda tool to use against him.

What remained of Che's support network had crumbled. In March, Piñeiro had evacuated Renán Montero from La Paz because his passport had expired, and no replacement for him had been sent.* This left the tiny urban cell that included Loyola Guzmán, Rodolfo Saldaña, and Humberto Vázquez-Viaña without a means of communicating with Havana—or with the guerrillas in the field. They were uncertain what they should do, and had resorted to listening to commercial radio in the vain hope of hearing a message from Che. They even considered, then abandoned, an idea about posing as itinerant merchants and traveling into the war zone, hoping to bump into the guerrillas. Under pressure from Fidel, Monje's comrades in the Communist Party had adopted a more conciliatory attitude toward the cadres who had joined Che's efforts, but their aid did not go much beyond rhetorical expressions of solidarity and offers to help the urban cell in printing propaganda leaflets.

---

*According to Manuel Piñeiro, it was important to bring Renán back to Cuba to provide him with new documentation and to debrief him in order to assess whether or not he had been "detected." Ariel says Renán was withdrawn because he was extremely ill with "acute parasites." Whatever the case, Piñeiro did not allow Renán to return to Bolivia, apparently out of fear for his security. Piñeiro conceded that the decision did not make him popular. "Renán blames me for denying him his chance to have been part of a historic mission," he said. (See Notes.)

In Cuba, a second group of several dozen guerrillas was in training, but with Che out of contact, there was no point in dispatching them. "After we lost contact with Che, we felt a tremendous uncertainty," Piñeiro said, "but we were also confident he would pull through." The confidence was misplaced. By the summer of 1967, Che's Bolivian guerrilla operation was fragmented into four groups, each incommunicado from the other: Che's group, isolated and on the run, out of contact with Havana and the city; Joaquín's group, wandering separately from Che's column and equally cut off from the outside; the urban group, which had no idea what was happening anywhere; and finally, Cuba itself, where the security apparatus was reduced to monitoring events in Bolivia through news reports.*

Whenever possible, Che traveled on mules or horses, which the guerrillas took from the army or bought from peasants, but the *campesinos* for the most part remained frightened of them. Already sick and emaciated, Che had begun suffering from asthma in late June, with no medicine to treat it. Once, he became so ill with vomiting and diarrhea that he lost consciousness and had to be carried in a hammock for a day; when he awoke, he found he had defecated all over himself. "They lent me a pair of trousers but without much water my stench extends for a league," he wrote. Despite the stench, Che had reverted to his nonbathing Chancho days. On September 10, he would record a historic moment. "I almost forgot to mention that I took a bath today, the first in six months. It is a record that many others are attaining."

Fatigue, hunger, and vitamin deficiencies had weakened all of them, and the pressing concerns of food and health gradually began to dominate the men's thoughts and Che's diary entries. Once, after they had eaten some pork bought from a peasant, Che wrote, "We remained completely immobilized, trying to digest the pork. We have two cans of water. I was very sick until I vomited, and then I felt better." The next day, he called an assembly to discuss the "food situation": "I criticized Benigno for having eaten a can of food and then denying it; Urbano for having eaten jerky on the sly."

They even slaughtered and ate their own horses and mules. At one point, the men were so hungry that they began coveting Che's mount, a jack mule, but he refused to kill it. Their hopes were given an unexpected boost one day when the mule took a spectacular head-over-heels tumble down a steep incline. The men held their breath, hoping it would break its neck in the fall, but to their disappointment, and Che's relief, it survived.

The strain of command and Che's disabilities showed up in dramatic form another time, when he stabbed the mare he was riding because she was

*See Notes.

Che was too ill to walk for much of the time during the Bolivian campaign. He rode mules or horses whenever possible.

moving too slowly. He made a big gash in her side, and afterward Che assembled the men and spoke about the incident. "We are in a difficult situation," he told them. ". . . I am a mess and the incident of the mare shows that there are moments in which I lose control of myself; that will change, but we must all share alike the burden of the situation, and whoever feels he cannot stand it should say so. This is one of those moments in which great decisions must be made, because a struggle of this type gives us the opportunity to become revolutionaries, the highest step in the human ladder, and also allows us to test ourselves as men." Some of the guerrillas remained silent, but most announced their willingness to continue.

No rapport had been established with the locals, and the "lack of enlistment" was a problem. To expand, they needed to make their presence felt in a more populated area, but to do that, they needed more men. At the moment, Che had barely enough manpower to get through each day, much less engage in political tasks of consciousness-raising and recruitment. Civilians often reacted to their arrival with fear and panic, and to obtain food and information they frequently had to resort to coercion, adopting the practice of holding people hostage while a relative or friend was sent off on errands for them. A couple of times, they hijacked pickup trucks belonging to the state petroleum company based in Camiri and were able to exult in the unaccustomed luxury of covering distances quickly, until either the gas or the engines gave out.

On July 6, six of Che's men had hijacked a truck on the main road between Santa Cruz and Cochabamba and driven into the town of Samaipata. The site of an ancient Incan temple, Samaipata was a roadside way station for travelers, large enough to have its own hospital and a small army detachment. Paradoxically, their most daring mission to date did not have a military objective. It was to secure badly needed medicines for Che's asthma, remedies for the other sick men, and some food and other supplies. They took over the garrison after some brief cross fire in which one soldier died; and then, before the stunned civilian onlookers, they went to a pharmacy to buy medicines. They left town with ten soldiers as hostages and, after stripping them of their clothes, left them at the roadside.

The action at Samaipata represented a propaganda victory for the Ejército de Liberación Nacional, but it had been a failure from Che's point of view; the guerrillas had not found any asthma medicine. A few days later, he recorded that he had given himself "various injections in order to continue," but worried that they might have to return to Ñancahuazú to retrieve his asthma medicine hidden there. Even this possibility was dashed in mid-August when the radio carried news of the army's discovery of their remaining supply caches at Ñancahuazú. "Now I am doomed to suffer asthma for an indefinite time," he wrote. "They also took all types of documents and photographs of every type. It is the hardest blow they have ever given us. Somebody talked. Who? That is what we don't know."

Inevitably, more men had died. On June 26, Carlos "Tuma" Coello, caught in cross fire, was shot in the stomach. Che tried desperately to save him, but Tuma's liver had been destroyed and his intestines were punctured. Tuma died in Che's arms. "I lost an inseparable companion of many years' standing, whose loyalty survived every test, and whose absence I already feel almost like that of a son," Che wrote. He took Tuma's watch and slipped it onto his own wrist, planning to give it to the newborn son back in Cuba whom Tuma had never seen.

On July 30, José María Martínez Tamayo—Papi—was killed when an army patrol took the guerillas by surprise, practically walking into their camp before dawn. In the firefight that followed, one of Moisés Guevara's men, Raúl, was also killed, by a bullet in the mouth. Pacho escaped with a graze across his testicles. In his diary, Che remembered Papi as "the most undisciplined" of his Cubans, but "an extraordinary fighter and old comrade in adventure." As for the Bolivian, he wrote, "Raúl hardly needs to be counted. He was an introvert, not much of a worker or fighter."

By the end of July, the new losses had reduced Che's force to twenty-two, two of whom were wounded. Che's asthma was "going full speed," he noted. But he also observed with satisfaction that he had successfully internationalized the Bolivian conflict. Argentina's military president, General Juan Carlos Onganía, had closed the border with Bolivia as a security precaution, and Peru was reported to be taking measures along its border as well. "The legend of the guerrillas is acquiring continental dimensions," Che wrote in his end-of-the month summary for July. On the other side of the coin, he observed that some things hadn't changed. Radio Havana carried news of a Czech condemnation of his Tricontinental message. "The friends [Czechs] call me a new Bakunin and deplore the blood that has been shed and that will be shed if there are 3 or 4 Vietnams."

Ever alert for news of Joaquín, Che listened closely for reports of skirmishes or rebel activity elsewhere. He had been searching for the lost column north of the Río Grande, assuming it had headed in that direction, but Joaquín had actually remained south of the river. Finally, in mid-August, the radio reported a clash near Muyupampa in which a guerrilla had been killed, and his name was divulged. It was a man from Joaquín's group. A few days later, Eusebio and Chingolo, two Bolivians who had deserted from Joaquín's column—and who had led the army to the Ñancahuazú camp—were produced in public by their government captors, and Che realized Joaquín had remained in the south. He began heading in that direction to find him. Coincidentally, Joaquín began heading north to search for Che.

At dusk on the evening of August 31, after reaching the home of one of their few peasant collaborators, Honorato Rojas, Joaquín's group of ten, including an ailing Tania, waded into the Río Grande not far from its confluence with the Masicuri River, near a place called Vado del Yeso. What Joaquín did not know was that Honorato Rojas had been arrested, pressured, and "turned." The man who now commanded his loyalties was Captain Mario Vargas Salinas of the Eighth Army Division. As Rojas led the unsuspecting guerrillas downriver, Vargas Salinas waited until they were within close range, then signaled his men to open fire.

It was a massacre. At the cost of one soldier dead, Joaquín's column was wiped out. The dead included Tania; Che's former vice minister of industries, Gustavo Machín; Moisés Guevara; and Joaquín himself. The bodies of the men were recovered and taken to the army's field headquarters in the town of Vallegrande for public display. Tania's body was found downstream, blackened and disfigured, some days later. The only visible survivors were a Bolivian, José Castillo Chávez—Paco—and Freddy Maymura, the Japanese-Bolivian medical student trained in Cuba. But

within a few hours Maymura was murdered by the soldiers.* A third survivor, the Peruvian doctor José "El Negro" Cabrera, was caught and killed
four days later.

When Che heard the news that an entire guerrilla column had been
"liquidated" nearby, he refused to believe it, suspecting it to be army
disinformation. Over the coming days, however, as the names and descriptions of the members of Joaquín's group began to filter out, he knew it was
true. Remarkably, the two groups had almost met up. On September 1, the
day after the massacre, Che's group had crossed the river, reached the house
of the traitor Honorato Rojas, and moved on after finding signs of the army's
recent presence. Honorato and his family were gone.

The ambush meant the loss of a third of Che's fighting force. But he
was now released from the moral obligation of searching for Joaquín; he
could concentrate on saving himself and his remaining men by escaping to
a more populated area and making contact with his support network in La
Paz and with Cuba. For the Bolivian military, meanwhile, the so-called Vado
del Yeso massacre was a morale-boosting triumph, celebrated with parades
and a visit to Vallegrande by President Barrientos and his top generals and
their wives. Barrientos promoted Captain Vargas Salinas, the hero of the
day, to major, and publicly congratulated the "civilian hero" of the episode,
Honorato Rojas—an unwise move that the peasant would pay dearly for
later on.†

After lying on gruesome display in the laundry house of the Nuestro
Señor de Malta Hospital, the guerrillas' bloated and ravaged bodies were
secretly buried at night on the outskirts of Vallegrande under the direction
of Lieutenant Colonel Andrés Selich. A tall, thin mustachioed man of
Yugoslav ancestry who was a dedicated anticommunist, Selich was the
deputy commander of the Pando Regiment of military engineers, based in
Vallegrande.

When Tania's unrecognizable body was brought in on September 8,
President Barrientos personally ordered that as a woman she be honored

*According to Vargas Salinas, he assented to the execution when his soldiers demanded to
take the life of one of the two prisoners in revenge for the death of a fellow soldier. As he
tells it, Maymura was "defiant," and Paco was terrified. While Vargas Salinas pondered what
to do, he could feel Paco, who had been sitting next to him, squirm underneath his legs for
protection. At that moment, Vargas Salinas said, he made a motion with his head toward
Maymura, who was immediately shot to death by his men. Paco's life was spared.

†Late in 1969, Honorato Rojas was executed by a group of Cuban-trained Bolivians who had
returned to their country to continue Che's guerrilla war.

with religious rites and given a Christian burial. For the devout Communist Tamara Bunke, Barrientos's "honor" was ironic in the extreme. Her body was placed in a coffin and an army chaplain officiated at a small service that was held at the army post across from the graveyard. But Tania was not buried there, and it is probably safe to assume that Barrientos never intended her to be, despite his gallant public gesture. At eleven o'clock that night, Selich took charge of the operation to bury her secretly, as he had done with the others, carrying out the military's secret decision to "disappear" the dead guerrillas, a morbid policy that endured to the end of the antiguerrilla campaign.

The military men liked to take keepsakes from the dead guerrillas as personal talismans. Most of the captured documents, address books, and letters were forwarded to Army Intelligence, and to Interior Minister Arguedas and his CIA adviser, Gabriel García García, but many other items remained in the hands of individual military officers. Among those that found their way into Lieutenant Colonel Selich's possession—along with snapshots of the bullet-riddled bodies of the guerrillas and photos of himself posing with prisoners—was a piece of paper with the handwritten lyrics to "Guitarrero" (Guitar Player), a melancholy Argentine ballad:

> *Don't leave,* guitarrero
> *for the light in my soul goes out*
> *I want to see another dawn*
> *To die in the* cacharpayas.*

Bedraggled, filthy, and with a long tangled beard, the young Bolivian Paco had been taken to Vallegrande along with the bodies of his comrades. He was paraded there like a trophy. Officers had pictures of themselves taken with him, looking like a wild man from the forest. Terrified and completely broken psychologically, Paco began to talk.

The Cuban-American CIA agents Felix Rodríguez and Gustavo Villoldo were now intimately involved with the antiguerrilla operation in the field. (In fact, according to Villoldo, he and Rodríguez had themselves participated in the ambush of Joaquín's column with Vargas Salinas's troops, camouflaged in Bolivian army uniforms.) Felix Rodríguez said he had immediately perceived Paco's usefuless. Over the opposition of Paco's initial interrogator, Lieutenant Colonel Selich, who wanted to execute him,

---

*A *cacharpayas* is an Andean farewell party, with singing, dancing, and drinking. The poem was confiscated by Selich, whose widow showed it to me.

Rodríguez said, he was given custody of the prisoner. For the next few weeks, Rodríguez worked on Paco daily, gradually obtaining a clearer picture of life in the guerrilla ranks. From his information, Rodríguez said, he was able to learn who had died and who was still likely to be alive in the field, as well as their relative strengths and weaknesses, and their relationships with Che.

After a few days of trying to sort out what had happened to Joaquín's column, Che and his men decided to head back north. On September 6, they left the Río Grande and began climbing into the mountains, out of the region that had been their home, and their graveyard, for the last ten months.

VIII

North of the Río Grande, the forested land rises massively toward the sky, climbing away in blue mountain eddies toward the brown lunar scree of the Andean highlands in the far distance. Above the tree line, the great denuded hills and chilly plateaus give way to swooping ravines, dotted sparsely with rustic hamlets linked to one another by footpaths and the occasional dirt road. The inhabitants, mostly Indians and mestizos, live by tending pigs or cows, their corn patches and vegetable gardens forming geometric patterns on hillsides around adobe houses. There is little foliage, and the natives can spot a stranger coming from miles away.

For two weeks, Che's band climbed steadily upward, fording rivers, climbing cliffs, running once or twice into army patrols with tracker dogs. By now, the men were all showing symptoms of a breakdown of one sort or another. They squabbled over things such as who had eaten more food, accused one another of making insults, and, like children, came to tell Che their grievances and accusations. The most alarming symptom of all was displayed by Antonio—Olo Pantoja—who one day claimed to see five soldiers approaching; it turned out to be a hallucination. That night, Che made a worried note about the risk this troubling apparition of war psychosis might have on the morale of his men.

Che continued to listen attentively to the radio. Barrientos had now put a price on Che's head—a mere $4,200—while at the same time announcing his belief that Che was dead. Debray's pending trial, which was attracting international media attention, had been suspended until September 17. "A Budapest daily criticizes Che Guevara, a pathetic and apparently irresponsible figure, and hails the Marxist attitude of the Chilean Party for adopting practical stands," Che recorded. "How I would like to take power just to unmask cowards and lackeys of every sort and to rub their snouts in their own filth."

Perhaps because of his powerlessness to alter the course of events, his acid humor returned. Radio Havana reported that "a message of support had been received from the ELN" at the recently convened Organización Latinoamericana de Solidaridad conference in Havana, a message, Che noted, that must have been received through "a miracle of telepathy." At the conference, Che's emblematic visage had dominated the proceedings in huge posters and banners, and he was spoken of as a hero by Fidel.

In mid-September, news came of the arrest and attempted suicide in La Paz of Loyola Guzmán. During a pause in her interrogation session on the third floor of the Interior Ministry, Guzmán had hurled herself out of the window to avoid being forced to betray her comrades. She was badly hurt but survived.

On September 21, the group reached an elevation of more than 6,000 feet, the highest altitude they had yet experienced. Walking along a dirt road under bright moonlight, they headed toward Alto Seco, an isolated hamlet of fifty houses perched on a great rocky dome of a mountain. As they marched toward it the next day, Che noticed that "the people are afraid and try to get out of our way." When they reached Alto Seco that afternoon, they were received with a "mixture of fear and curiosity," and discovered that the local mayor, or *corregidor,* had gone off the day before to tell the army they were approaching. In reprisal, Che seized the food supplies in the man's little grocery store and was deaf to his weeping wife's entreaties that she be paid something in return.

Instead of leaving immediately, Che and his men stayed in Alto Seco that night, organizing an assembly in the little schoolhouse, where Inti gave a speech explaining their revolution to a "group of 15 downtrodden and silent peasants." Only one man spoke up, the schoolteacher, who asked provocative questions about socialism, and whom Che profiled as "a mixture of fox and peasant, illiterate and guileless as a child."

The bearded, dirty, and armed men who appeared in their midst were bewildering to these isolated people. Some even thought they were supernatural creatures. After a visit by the guerrillas, who were looking for food, a peasant woman who lived near Honorato Rojas told the army that she believed they were *brujos,* sorcerors, because they seemed to know everything about everyone in the area. When they paid her with paper money for her food, she thought the money was enchanted and would become worthless in her hands.

The government had been doing a good job of psychological warfare. In addition to its large-scale "civic action" program, which consisted of building roads, distributing antiguerrilla propaganda, granting land titles to peasants, and handing out school supplies in rural areas, the army and police had been actively ferreting out intelligence from the peasant communities for months. Even before the guerrillas began moving away from Ñancahuazú and operating north of the river, the town of Vallegrande, with its civilian population of 6,000 and its military garrison, had been put on a war footing. In April, the military had declared the entire province an emergency zone, imposing martial law and advising the population that "groups of Castro-Communist tendency, mostly foreigners, have infiltrated our country, with the sole objective of sowing chaos and halting the Progress of the Nation, carrying out acts of *bandolerismo,* pillage, and assault against private property, especially among the peasantry. . . . The Armed Forces, conscious of its specific obligations, has been mobilized to detain and destroy the foreign invasion, as malicious as it is vandalous."

Since late summer, Vallegrande had become the main base for the army's counterinsurgency operations, and an atmosphere of war hysteria had taken over. A public megaphone blared out antiguerrilla information in the public square, the few local leftist students were arrested, and foreign-looking strangers were detained and questioned. On August 23, according to Lieutenant Colonel Selich's daily log, the entire population of Vallegrande had been "mobilized in the face of a possible Red attack."

On September 1, when the army command in Vallegrande had made radio contact with Captain Vargas Salinas after his ambush of Joaquín's column the night before, there was euphoria—and confusion—at his initial list of *exterminados,* for it included the name "Guevara." As the assembled chiefs of staff of the armed forces listened in from La Paz, there was palpable excitement in the voice of army chief General David La Fuente as he pressed Vallegrande for clarification: "Does he mean *Che* Guevara?" They soon discovered that the dead man in question was Moisés Guevara, not the legendary *comandante guerrillero*.

It was now known that Che was hungry and sick, with a greatly reduced force of men. A soldier, Anselmo Mejía Cuellar, one of three taken prisoner by the guerrillas for a five-day period in August, told Selich that they walked little and moved slowly, gradually cutting their own path through the bush with machetes—and that they were "very dirty." He described their weapons and each of the guerrillas' duties, and made some interesting observations about Che. "The *jefe* travels by horse . . . and the others serve him like a God, they made his bed and brought him *yerba mate.* He smokes a pipe, of silver . . . and travels in the center of the column with the wounded man [Pombo, recovering from a leg injury]; he has green trousers and a camouflaged shirt with a coffee-colored beret . . . and wears two watches, one a very large one." Cuellar's fellow ex-prisoner, Valerio Gutiérrez Padilla, said that although Che never complained, he was obviously "bad off" because his men had to dismount him from his horse.

By the time the guerrillas reached Alto Seco, the army already knew they were coming and had began mobilizing to go after them. On September 24, the garrison in Vallegrande dispatched a regiment of soldiers to establish a forward base of operations at the village of Pucará, some ten miles northwest of the advancing guerrillas.

From Alto Seco, the guerrillas moved on, meandering for the next two days through the open landscape at a leisurely pace. Che, sick with what he called a "liver attack," seemed almost in a reverie as he observed a "beautiful orange grove" where they stopped to rest. Approaching the next village, Pujío, he casually noted that he had bought a pig to eat "from the only peasant who stayed home. . . . The rest flee at the sight of us."

Reading these passages, one can't help concluding that Che had become strangely detached from his own plight, an interested witness to his inexorable march toward death. He was breaking every rule sacred to guerrilla warfare: moving in the open without precise intelligence about what lay ahead, without the support of the peasants, and knowing that the army was aware of his approach.*

Something Che wrote during his odyssey suggests that he knew his time was running out. It was a poem meant for Aleida as a last will and testament. He titled it "Against Wind and Tide."

> This poem (against wind and tide) will carry my signature.
> I give to you six sonorous syllables,
> a look which always bears (like a wounded bird) tenderness,
> an anxiety of lukewarm deep water,
> a dark office where the only light is these verses of mine,
> a very used thimble for your bored nights,
> a photograph of our sons.
> The most beautiful bullet in this pistol that always accompanies me,
> the unerasable memory (always latent and deep) of the children
> who, one day, you and I conceived,
> and the piece of life that remains for me.
> This I give (convinced and happy) to the Revolution.
> Nothing that can unite us will have greater power.

As peasants spread the news of their slow approach, the *corregidores* of the villages went ahead to alert the army. On September 26, reaching the

*See Notes.

miserable little hamlet of La Higuera, in a bowl of land between two ridges, they found only women and children; all the men had left, including the *corregidor* and the telegraph operator. Che sent his vanguard ahead to scout the way to the next village, Jagüey, but when they reached the first rise of land leading out of La Higuera, they walked straight into an army ambush. Two Bolivians, Coco Peredo and Mario "Julio" Gutiérrez, and the Cuban Miguel Hernández were killed instantly. Two other Bolivians, Camba and Léon, seized the opportunity to desert. Benigno, Pablo, and Aniceto Reinaga survived and returned to La Higuera, but Benigno was wounded and Pablo had a badly hurt foot.

The soldiers who had struck the devastating blow were from Villegrande. At his base there, Lieutenant Colonel Selich listed the three dead guerrillas and then crowed that his soldiers "had not suffered a single death, or injury, or even a scratch. A crowning victory won by the Third Tactical Group for the Bolivian Army." With the smell of victory in the air, different army units began to compete to see which would claim the ultimate prize. Colonel Joaquín Zenteno Anaya, commander of the Eighth Army Division; Colonel Arnaldo Saucedo, his intelligence chief; and the CIA adviser Felix Rodríguez had arrived in Vallegrande. Various army units patrolled out of bases both in front of and behind the guerrilla band, in Alto Seco and Pucará. Fresh from their weeks of training by the Americans, the new Bolivian Army Rangers now entered the field.

After the ambush outside La Higuera, Che and the survivors exchanged fire with soldiers positioned on the heights above them, then withdrew, escaping into a canyon. The next day they tried to find a way out of their predicament, climbing up to a higher elevation, where they found a small patch of woods to hide in. For the next three days, they remained there, anxiously watching the army pass back and forth on a road that cut across the hill just in front of them. Other soldiers were posted at a nearby house. When there were no soldiers in sight, Che sent out scouts to fetch water, gain a sense of the enemy's movements, and find an escape route back down to the Río Grande. For the moment, though, they were surrounded.

In Vallegrande, the three new dead guerrillas had been brought in by mule and jeep and laid out in a bloody row in the Nuestro Señor de Malta Hospital. On September 27, Selich noted that "the astonished people of Vallegrande dared to look at them only from a distance." The next night, the troops who had carried out the ambush returned to base and were "rendered tribute" at a special party given by Colonel Zenteno Anaya. After a government commission arrived from La Paz to identify the bodies, Selich once more performed burial duty. At eleven o'clock on the night of September 29, he noted, "In absolute secrecy and in some place, the remains of the Red mercenaries killed in the action at [La] Higuera were buried."

On September 30, bringing with him a large retinue of officials and the press, President Barrientos returned to Vallegrande to share in the latest triumph. That same night, only thirty miles away, an exhausted Che and his men stole from cover and began making their way cautiously into the canyon below, careful to avoid contact with any of the peasants whose little farms dotted the area. The radio carried news of the large military mobilization under way; one report said 1,800 soldiers were in the zone; another said that "Che Guevara is surrounded in a canyon"; still another gave the news that when Che was caught he would be "brought to trial in Santa Cruz." Then the capture of Camba and León was reported. Both men had obviously talked, even telling their captors that Che was sick. "So ends the tale of two heroic guerrillas," Che remarked disgustedly in his diary.

By October 7, the guerrillas were in a steep ravine near La Higuera, where a narrow natural passage leads down toward the Río Grande. Their progress had been slow because Juan Pablo Chang, whose glasses were broken, was almost blind at night, and he held them back considerably. Still, Che was reasonably upbeat, beginning his diary entry that day with apparently intentional irony, for their circumstances were now truly desperate: "We completed the 11th month of our guerrilla operation without complications, in a bucolic mood."

At midday, they spotted an old woman grazing goats and seized her as a precaution. She said she knew nothing about soldiers—or anything else, for that matter. Che was skeptical and sent Inti, Aniceto, and Pablo with her to her squalid little farmhouse, where they saw that she had a young dwarf daughter. They gave the woman fifty pesos and told her not to speak to anyone about their presence, although they did so, Che noted, "with little hope that she will keep her word."

There were seventeen of them left now. It was, coincidentally, the same number of men that his and Fidel's original band of guerrillas had been reduced to in the hard days after the catastrophic landing of the *Granma*, a little less than eleven years before. That night they set off downhill again, under a "very small moon," walking through a narrow stream gully whose banks were sown with potato patches. At two in the morning they stopped because of Chang, who could not see well enough to walk farther. That night, Che listened to an "unusual" army report on the radio that said army troops had encircled the guerrillas at a place between the "Acero" and "Oro" rivers. "The news seems diversionary," he observed. He wrote down their present altitude: "2,000 meters [about 6,500 feet]." It was the final entry in his diary.

IX

Early the next morning, October 8, a company of freshly trained Bolivian Army Rangers led by a tall young captain, Gary Prado Salmon, took up positions above Che and his men. They had been alerted to the guerrillas' presence by a local peasant. As daylight broke, the guerrillas spotted the soldiers on the bare ridges hemming them in on either side. They were trapped in a brushy gully called the Quebrada del Churo, which was about 1,000 feet long and not more than 200 feet wide, in places much narrower than that. Their only possible escape was to fight their way out. Che ordered his men to take up positions, splitting them into three groups. Several tense hours passed. The battle began at 1:10 in the afternoon, when a couple of the guerrillas were detected by the soldiers as they moved around. The soldiers opened up on the men below with mortar and machine-gun fire, and the Bolivian Aniceto Reinaga was killed.

In the the prolonged firefight that ensued, Arturo Tamayo and Olo Pantoja were both killed and the guerrillas lost track of one another. Partially concealed behind a large rock in the middle of a potato patch, Che fired his M-2 carbine, but it was soon hit in the barrel by a bullet that rendered it useless. The magazine of his pistol had apparently already been lost; he was now unarmed. A second bullet hit him in the calf of his left leg; a third penetrated his beret. Helped by the Bolivian Simón Cuba—Willy— he tried to climb up the bank of the gully in an attempt to escape. Some soldiers watched them approach. When they were a few feet away, a short, sturdy highland Indian named Sergeant Bernardino Huanca broke through the brush and pointed his gun at them.

A moment later, alerted by Huanca's yells that he had captured two guerrillas, Captain Prado arrived. Without preamble, Prado asked Che to identify himself. Just as bluntly, Che told him. Prado pulled out one of Ciro Bustos's sketches and positively identified Che by his pronounced brow and the bullet scar near his ear—from the accident that had nearly killed him during the Bay of Pigs invasion. Then he tied Che's hands with his own belt. After sending out a radio message to Vallegrande, he told his men to guard Che and Willy closely, and he returned to the combat.

At 3:15 P.M., Lieutenant Colonel Selich was informed by radio of the "bloody combat" the Rangers were fighting with "the group of Reds commanded by *Che Guevara!*" Hearing that Guevara himself was a casualty, Selich excitedly boarded a helicopter and flew to La Higuera. When he arrived, he headed immediately for the battlefield.

Taking La Higuera's helpful *corregidor* with him, Selich climbed down into the canyon where Che was being held as the fighting continued in different parts of the *quebrada* between the soldiers and the rest of Che's men. As they descended, they met soldiers bringing up a mortally wounded comrade, and Selich was told there were two more army dead still below. When he reached the place where Che was being held, Selich had a short dialogue with him, which he would later record in a confidential report. "I told him that our army wasn't like he imagined," Selich wrote, "and he replied that he had been wounded and that a bullet had destroyed the barrel of his carbine, and in those circumstances he had no alternative but to surrender himself."

With night approaching and the combat continuing in the *quebrada,* Selich led his two prisoners, Che and Willy, toward La Higuera. By now, he had been joined by Captain Prado and his commanding officer, Major Miguel Ayoroa. For the steep hike out of the ravine, Che had to be helped by two soldiers because he could bear down only on his unhurt right leg. Bringing up the rear, some peasants carried the bodies of Arturo Tamayo and Olo Pantoja.

Later that evening, Che lay bound hand and foot on the dirt floor of a room in the mud-walled schoolhouse in La Higuera. Next to him lay the bodies of Arturo and Olo. In the other room, still alive and unhurt, Willy had been imprisoned. Because of the darkness, the army pursuit of the fugitive guerrillas was suspended until 4:00 A.M., but Selich took precautionary measures in La Higuera, posting guards in case Che's comrades tried to rescue him. At 7:30 P.M. Selich radioed Vallegrande, asking what to do with Che, and was told to "keep him in custody until new orders." Then he, Prado, and Ayoroa went into the schoolhouse to talk with Che. Selich recorded their forty-five-minute dialogue in some abbreviated private notes.

"Comandante, I find you somewhat depressed," Selich said to Che, according to his notes. "Can you explain the reasons why I get this impression?"

"I've failed," Che replied. "It's all over, and that's the reason why you see me in this state."

Selich then asked why Che had chosen to fight in Bolivia instead of his "own country." Che evaded the question but acknowledged that "maybe it would have been better." When he proceeded to praise socialism as the best form of government for Latin American countries, Selich cut him off. "I would prefer not to refer to that topic," he said, claiming that in any event Bolivia was "vaccinated against Communism." He accused Che of having "invaded" Bolivia and pointed out that the majority of his guerrillas were "foreigners." According to Selich, Che then looked over at the bodies of Arturo and Olo.

"Colonel, look at them. These boys had everything they could want in Cuba, and yet they came here to die like dogs."

Lieutenant Colonel Andrés Selich's photograph of the schoolhouse in
La Higuera where Che was held and then executed.

Selich tried to elicit some information from Che about the guerrillas still on the run. "I understand Benigno is gravely wounded since the
[September 26] La Higuera battle, where Coco and the others died. Can you
tell me, Comandante, if he is still alive?"

"Colonel, I have a very bad memory, I don't remember and don't even
know how to respond to your question."

"Are you Cuban or Argentine?" asked Selich.

"I am Cuban, Argentine, Bolivian, Peruvian, Ecuadorian, etc. . . . You
understand."

"What made you decide to operate in our country?"

"Can't you see the state in which the peasants live?" Che asked. "They
are almost like savages, living in a state of poverty that depresses the heart,
having only one room in which to sleep and cook and no clothing to wear,
abandoned like animals . . ."

"But the same thing happens in Cuba," Selich retorted.

"No, that's not true," Che said. "I don't deny that in Cuba poverty
still exists, but the peasants there have an illusion of progress, whereas the

Bolivian lives without hope. Just as he is born, he dies, without ever seeing improvements in his human condition."*

The officers began going through the documents captured from Che and, finding the two volumes of his Bolivian campaign diaries, stayed up until dawn reading them.

At 6:15 A.M. on October 9, a helicopter flew into La Higuera carrying Colonel Joaquín Zenteno Anaya and the CIA agent Felix Rodríguez. No doubt owing to their earlier clash over the custody of the prisoner Paco, Selich was not pleased to see the CIA man arrive and scrutinized him closely, observing that Rodríguez, who was wearing a Bolivian army uniform and was referred to as Captain Ramos, had come with a powerful portable field radio and a camera with a special lens for photographing documents. The group went into the schoolhouse, where Selich noted that Zenteno Anaya "chatted with the *Jefe Guerrillero* for approximately 30 minutes."

Rodríguez recorded in detail the grim encounter with his archenemy. Che was lying on his side in the dirt, his arms still tied behind his back and his feet bound together, next to the bodies of his friends. His leg wound oozed blood, and to Rodríguez he looked "like a piece of trash."

"He was a mess," Rodríguez wrote. "Hair matted, clothes ragged and torn." He no longer had boots; his mud-caked feet were encased in crude leather sheaths, like those a medieval peasant might have worn. As Rodríguez stood silently observing, "absorbed in the moment," Zenteno Anaya asked Che why he had brought war to this country. He received no reply. "The only sound was Che's breathing."

Immediately afterward, as Selich watched suspiciously, "Mister Felix Ramos [Rodríguez] . . . set up his portable radio set and transmitted a coded message . . . to an unknown place." Then Rodríguez began photographing Che's diary and the other captured documents on a table set outside. Taking Ayoroa with him, Zenteno Anaya headed off for the *quebrada*, where the military operations had resumed, leaving Selich in charge of La Higuera. When they returned, at around 10:00 A.M., Felix Rodríguez was still taking photographs. By eleven o'clock, he had finished his task and asked Zenteno Anaya permission to speak to "Señor Guevara." Selich was distrustful and, "considering my presence necessary in this talk," went into the schoolhouse

---

*In 1996, Selich's widow, Socorro, allowed me to review and copy her late husband's documents, which had not been seen by anyone else. They included photographs, cables, internal army memorandums, Selich's daily log of military activities for 1967, the uncompleted notes of his talk with Che Guevara, and a secret report he filed to General La Fuente about the events and circumstances of Che Guevara's execution. (See Notes.)

with Rodríguez. Selich's notes reveal only that the talk dealt with "diverse themes of the Bolivian Revolution as well as the Cuban Revolution."

In his memoirs of the encounter, Rodríguez does not mention that Selich was in the room with him, but, like Selich, he noted Che's proud defiance. When he first entered, Che warned Rodríguez that he would not be interrogated, and relented only when the CIA man said he merely wished to exchange views. According to Rodríguez, Che acknowledged his defeat, blaming it on the "provincial" mind-set of the Bolivian Communists who had cut him off. Whenever Rodríguez tried to glean from him information about specific operations, however, Che refused to answer. He especially refused to "speak badly about Fidel," although Rodríguez tried to coax him.

Finally, Che asked Rodríguez a question. Rodríguez was clearly not Bolivian, he observed, and to judge from his knowledge of Cuba, Che guessed that he was either a Cuban or a Puerto Rican working for U.S. intelligence. Rodríguez confirmed that he was born in Cuba and had been a member of the CIA-trained anti-Castro 2506 Brigade. Che's only response was, "Ha."

At 12:30 a radio message for Colonel Zenteno Anaya came from the Bolivian high command in La Paz, and he relayed the order to Selich. According to Selich's notes, it was to "proceed with the elimination of Señor Guevara." He pointed out to Zenteno that it was Major Ayoroa's duty to take charge of the executions, since he was the commanding officer of the unit that had captured Guevara. In Selich's words: "Ayoroa then ordered the fulfillment of the order."

Immediately afterward, leaving Ayoroa and Rodríguez behind, Selich and Zenteno Anaya boarded a helicopter to fly back to Vallegrande with their booty of captured documents and weaponry. Upon their arrival at about 1:30 P.M., they were advised from La Higuera that the execution of Che Guevara had been carried out.*

In his version, Felix Rodríguez claimed it was he, not Zenteno Anaya, who had received the coded message ordering Che's death, and that he had taken Zenteno Anaya aside to dissuade him. The U.S. government, he claimed, wanted to "keep the guerrilla leader alive under any circumstances." He said that U.S. aircraft were on standby to evacuate Che to Panama for interrogation. According to Rodríguez, Zenteno Anaya said that he could

---

*According to Selich's report, none of the officers at La Higuera—including himself and Felix Rodríguez—agreed with the decision to execute Che. "We believed it would be better to keep Sr. Guevara alive because in our judgment it would be more advantageous to present him before world opinion in defeat, wounded and sick, and to then obtain compensation [from Cuba] to offset the expenses incurred by fighting the guerrillas, and to compensate the families of the soldiers murdered by the Guerrilla Band."

not disobey the order, which had come directly from President Barrientos and the joint chiefs of staff. Zenteno Anaya said he would send a chopper back at 2:00 P.M. and wanted Rodríguez's word of honor that Che would be dead by then, and that he would personally bring back his body to Vallegrande.

After Zenteno and Selich left, Rodríguez pondered his options. He had relayed word to the CIA that morning after positively identifying Guevara, asking for instructions, but no reply had come, and now it was too late. He could disobey Zenteno and spirit Che away, but he knew that if he did, he might be making a historical mistake of huge proportions; at one time Fidel Castro had been imprisoned by Batista, and that obviously hadn't put a stop to him. In the end, he wrote, "It was my call. And my call was to leave it in the hands of the Bolivians." While still debating, Rodríguez heard a shot from the schoolhouse. He rushed first into Che's room. Che was alive and looked up at him from his place on the floor. Rodríguez went into the next room, where he saw a soldier, his gun smoking, and beyond, Willy "collapsing over a small table." "I could literally hear the life escape from him." The soldier told Rodríguez that Willy had tried to escape.

Rodríguez then went to talk with Che again and at one point took him outside to take his picture. Those photos, kept secretly by the CIA for years, have survived. In one, a youthful-looking and plump-faced Rodríguez stands with his arm around Che, who resembles a wild beast brought to heel, his emaciated face grimly turned downward, his long hair tangled, his arms bound in front of him.

Rodríguez took Che back inside the schoolhouse and they resumed their talk, only to be interrupted by more gunfire. This time the executed man was reportedly Juan Pablo Chang,* who had been captured, wounded, and brought in alive that morning; by now the bodies of Aniceto and Pacho, who had been killed in the ravine, were also there. "Che stopped talking," Rodríguez recalled. "He did not say anything about the shooting, but his face reflected sadness and he shook his head slowly from left to right several times. Perhaps it was at that instant that he realized that he, too, was doomed, even though I did not tell him until just before one P.M."

---

*Rodríguez's account contains certain claims that are contradicted by the Bolivian officers who were also present in La Higuera—just as there are numerous discrepancies among the officers' versions. According to Miguel Ayoroa, for instance, Willy and Juan Pablo Chang were held together in the second room of the schoolhouse and executed at the same time. This testimony coincides with the most widely believed version of events, which is that Che's photo session with Rodríguez came *before* Willy's execution, and that afterward, he and Willy and Juan Pablo Chang were executed almost simultaneously, by Bolivian army "volunteers."

The Cuban-American CIA agent Félix Rodríguez took Che outside the schoolhouse in La Higuera so that they could have their picture taken. Soon afterward, Rodríguez told Che that he was about to die.

According to his chronology of events, Rodríguez then went outside. He was shuffling documents and "postponing the inevitable" when the village schoolteacher came up to ask when he was going to shoot Che. He asked her why she wanted to know, and she explained that the radio was broadcasting the news that Che had died of combat wounds.*

Rodríguez realized that he could stall no longer and went back into the schoolhouse. He entered Che's room and announced that he was sorry, he had done everything in his power, but orders had come from the Bolivian high command. He didn't finish his sentence, but Che understood. According to Rodríguez, Che's face turned momentarily white, and he said, "It is better like this. . . . I never should have been captured alive."

Rodríguez asked if he had any messages for his family, and Che told him to "tell Fidel that he will soon see a triumphant revolution in America. . . . And tell my wife to remarry and to try to be happy."

At that, Rodríguez said, he stepped forward to embrace Che. "It was a tremendously emotional moment for me. I no longer hated him. His moment of truth had come, and he was conducting himself like a man. He was facing his death with courage and grace."

Rodríguez then left the room. A man had already responded to Major Ayoroa's request for an executioner, a tough-looking little sergeant named Mario Terán, who waited expectantly outside. Rodríguez looked at Terán and saw that his face shone as if he had been drinking. He had been in the firefight with Che's band the day before and was eager to avenge the deaths of his three comrades who had died in the battle.

"I told him not to shoot Che in the face, but from the neck down," Rodríguez said. Che's wounds had to appear as though they had been inflicted in battle. There was to be no evidence of an execution when the body was displayed to the press. "I walked up the hill and began making notes," Rodríguez recalled. "When I heard the shots I checked my watch. It was 1:10 P.M."

There are different versions, but according to legend, Che's last words, when Terán came through the door to shoot him, were: "I know you've come

---

*Although her story has been impugned by military officers who were present, the woman, Julia Cortéz, who was then twenty-two years old, claimed that Che had asked to see her and that she had been permitted into the room where he was held. She had been nervous, and when she entered, Che fixed her with a penetrating stare that she found impossible to meet. He motioned to the blackboard and pointed out a grammatical error in what she had written, then told her that the squalidness of the school was shameful and that in Cuba it would be called a prison. After a short talk, she left. According to her, Che asked to see her again shortly before his execution, but she had felt too afraid to go.

to kill me. Shoot, coward, you are only going to kill a man." Terán hesitated, then pointed his semiautomatic rifle and pulled the trigger, hitting Che in the arms and legs. As Che writhed on the ground, biting one of his wrists in an effort to avoid crying out, Terán fired another burst. The fatal bullet entered Che's thorax, filling his lungs with blood.

On October 9, 1967, at the age of thirty-nine, Che Guevara was dead.

Epilogue: Dreams and Curses

I

During the night of October 8, 1967, as Che lay trussed on the floor of the schoolhouse in La Higuera, Aleida awoke suddenly with a feeling that her husband was in grave danger. For several months, the news from Bolivia had made Aleida anxious. On October 8 she was staying in the Escambray mountains, where she and Che first met, doing field research for a social history project. After Che had left for Bolivia, Aleida had gone back to school and was studying at Havana University. It was something Che had urged her to do, to "keep herself occupied." Fidel had been coming to her home regularly to update her about Che's situation, which she knew was bad. So she was almost expecting the men who appeared at her doorstep late in the day on October 9. Fidel had sent them.

For weeks, Fidel had been reviewing the news reports coming out of Bolivia with both suspicion and mounting concern. On October 9, Che was reported to have been captured, then to be "dead of his wounds." When the first photograph of the body said to be his came over the wires, there was some resemblance, but it was hard for Fidel to imagine that the emaciated corpse was that of the man he had last seen eleven months earlier. After Aleida arrived in Havana, she and Fidel pored over the reports and the new photographs that came in. At first, neither wanted to believe the worst, but soon there was no doubt.

II

On the afternoon of October 9, Che's blood-drenched body had been placed on a stretcher, tied to the landing skids of a helicopter, and flown over the bleak hills to Vallegrande. Felix Rodríguez, wearing his Bolivian army

captain's uniform, accompanied it. Soon after they touched down, he melted
into the waiting crowds and disappeared. Within a few days, Rodríguez was
back in the United States for debriefings with his bosses at the CIA. He had
brought some relics from his trip, among them one of several Rolex watches
found in Che's possession, and Che's last pouch of pipe tobacco, half-smoked,
which he had wrapped in paper. Later, he would put the tobacco inside a
glass bubble set into the butt of his favorite revolver. The strangest legacy
of all, though, was the shortness of breath he developed soon after arriving
in Vallegrande. "As I walked in the cool mountain air I realized that I was
wheezing, and that it was becoming hard to breathe," Rodríguez wrote
twenty-five years later. "Che may have been dead, but somehow his
asthma—a condition I had never had in my life—had attached itself to me.
To this day, my chronic shortness of breath is a constant reminder of Che
and his last hours alive in the tiny town of La Higuera."

Slung onto the concrete washbasin of the laundry house in the rear
garden of Vallegrande's Nuestro Señor de Malta Hospital, Che's body lay
on view that evening and throughout the next day. His head was propped
up and his brown eyes remained open. To prevent decomposition, a doctor
had slit his throat and injected him with formaldehyde. As a procession of
people including soldiers, curious locals, photographers, and reporters filed
around the body, Che looked eerily alive. Some of the hospital's nuns, the
nurse who washed his body, and a number of local women surreptitiously
clipped off clumps of his hair and kept them for good luck. Later, the military ordered a doctor at the hospital to perform an autopsy on Che. The
doctor's report detailed the nine bullet wounds Che had suffered "in combat"
—in the area of his collarbone, chest, and ribs; in both legs; and in his right
arm—and stated that the cause of death was "wounds in the thorax and the
resulting bleeding."

Lieutenant Colonel Andrés Selich and Major Mario Vargas Salinas
posed for photographs next to the body. Along with Che's leather port-
folio, Selich kept and one of his watches, as did Captain Gary Prado.* The
executioner, Mario Terán, kept his pipe. Colonel Zenteno Anaya claimed
Che's damaged M-2 carbine as his personal trophy. He allowed Prado to
distribute the money found in Che's possession—several thousand American dollars and a large quantity of Bolivian pesos—among his junior officers and soldiers.

---

*Fidel gave all of the Cubans Rolexes—Oyster Submariners with stainless-steel cases and red
and blue faces—when they departed for the battlefield. If a fighter was killed, one of his
comrades often kept the watch in his honor. Che had kept Tuma's watch, intending to give
it to his widow, but in the meantime he wore it as a cherished memento.

Che's body lying on public display in the laundry house of the Nuestro Señor de Malta Hospital in Vallegrande.

By then the decision had been made to deny Che a burial site. His body, like those of his comrades who had died previously, would be "disappeared." To counter the initial reactions of disbelief coming out of Havana, General Alfredo Ovando Candía wanted to decapitate Che and preserve the head as evidence. Felix Rodríguez, who was still in Vallegrande when this solution was proposed, claimed to have argued that it was "too barbaric," and suggested that they just sever a finger. Ovando Candía compromised: they would amputate Che's hands. On the night of October 10, two wax death masks were made of Che's face, and his fingerprints were taken; his hands were sawed off and placed in jars of formaldehyde. A pair of Argentine police forensic experts arrived to compare the fingerprints with those on file in Buenos Aires for Ernesto Guevara de la Serna. The identification was positive. In the early morning hours of October 11, Che's body was disposed of by Lieutenant Colonel Selich, with a couple of other officers, including—according to him—Vargas Salinas, acting as witnesses.

Che's brother Roberto arrived in town later that morning, hoping to identify the body and retrieve the remains, but it was too late. General

Ovando Candía said he was sorry: Che's body had been "cremated." It was only one of several versions of the story of his remains that would circulate in coming days as the Bolivian generals contradicted one another. The real whereabouts of Che's body would remain an unsolved mystery for the next thirty years.

For Roberto, grim-faced, wearing a dark suit—looking very much like his famous brother, and yet so different—there was nothing to do but return home to Buenos Aires, where his father, brothers, and sisters waited. Now they too accepted the sad news, although Che's aunt Beatriz refused ever to acknowledge her favorite nephew's death or even discuss the matter.

With Cuba awash in rumors, Fidel addressed the nation on television on October 15. He confirmed that the reports of Che's death were "painfully true," decreed three days of national mourning, and announced that henceforth October 8, the day of Che's last battle, would be known as the Day of the Heroic Guerrilla.*

Aleida suffered an emotional breakdown. Fidel took her and the children to his house, and, over the next week, he comforted her. Then he moved her to another house, where she and the children lived incommunicado, out of public view. While Aleida was recovering, Fidel came every day to see her.

Orlando Borrego also went through an emotional crisis that lasted for several months. Che's death affected him, he said, more than his own father's had. His grief had been suspended at first as he rallied to comfort Aleida and the children, but it finally hit him. "It was as if my equilibrium had been thrown off," he recalled. "I couldn't come to terms with the idea that Che was dead, and I had recurrent dreams in which he appeared to me, alive."

On the night of October 18, in Havana's Plaza de la Revolución, Fidel spoke to one of his largest audiences. Nearly a million people had gathered for a national wake for Che. His voice raspy with emotion, Fidel gave an impassioned tribute to his old comrade, extolling him as the incarnation of revolutionary virtue. "If we want the . . . model of a human being who does not belong to our time but to the future, I say from the depths of my heart that such a model, without a single stain on his conduct, without a single stain on his behavior, is Che. If we wish to express what we want our children to be, we must say from our very hearts as ardent revolutionaries: we want them to be like Che!"

_____

*The date of Che's death, October 9, was assiduously ignored, and the photographs of his body were not allowed to circulate in Cuba for decades to come.

A banner with Alberto Korda's soon-to-be-famous image of Che was hung in the Plaza de la Revolución in Havana at Che's wake on the night of October 18, 1967.

III

Over the succeeding days, four more of the fugitive guerrillas—Moro, Pablo, Eustaquio, and Chapaco—were tracked down and killed; their bodies too were buried secretly around Vallegrande. Incredibly, three Cubans (Pombo, Benigno, and Urbano) together with three Bolivians (Inti Peredo, Darío, and Ñato),* had managed to escape from the ravine. The army continued to track them, and on November 15 they were caught in a firefight with army troops. Ñato was gravely wounded and asked his comrades to kill him. Benigno said it was he who delivered the coup de grâce. The remaining five men fled their encirclement, and three months later, with the help of members of the Bolivian Communist Party, who belatedly mustered their courage to save the survivors of Che's insurgency, they emerged in Chile, on the other side of the snow-covered Andes. There, under the auspices of the Chilean socialist and Communist parties, the Cubans were taken in. The socialist senator Salvador Allende flew with them to Easter Island, in the Pacific Ocean, from where they traveled home via Tahiti, Addis Ababa, Paris, and Moscow.

Benigno and others would later claim that Fidel "abandoned" Che and his guerrillas in Bolivia, but the evidence suggests that Fidel did what he could, although it wasn't much. After Che's presence was discovered and the Americans arrived in force, Cuba's agents in Bolivia had almost no room for maneuvering. With Bolivia's borders either sealed or under heavy surveillance, and the Communist Party outlawed, a new guerrilla who tried to bolster Che's effort would have been easily detected. As it was, the Bolivian military detained any suspicious foreigner who was spotted.

Cuba's support for the guerrilla war in Bolivia did not end with Che's death. Inti Peredo and Darío, the Bolivians who survived the debacle and made it to Cuba, returned home in 1969 with a new contingent of Bolivian volunteers. Later that year, Inti was gunned down in a safe house in La Paz. Not long afterward, Darío was caught and murdered. Inti's younger brother, Chato, became the new leader, taking seventy-odd mostly untrained young Bolivian students to launch a guerrilla war near the mining outpost of Teoponte, north of La Paz, on the headwaters of the Río Beni. After a few months in the field, the disorganized, hungry ELN was surrounded by the

---

*Moro and Morogoro were both noms de guerre of the Cuban doctor Octavio de la Concepción de la Pedraja; Pablo and Chapaco, who were both Bolivians, were Francisco Huanca Flores and Jaime Arana Campero. Eustaquio's real name was Lucio Edilberto Galván Hidalgo. He was a Peruvian citizen. Dario and Ñato were David Adriazola Viezaga and Julio Méndez Korne.

army. The group's second attempt to build a guerrilla *foco* expired in a miasma of blood and wasted lives.*

After impassively observing the fatal denouement of Che's attempt at guerrilla warfare, the Bolivian Interior Minister, Antonio Arguedas, inexplicably rediscovered his Marxist leanings. In 1968, with the help of several Bolivian Communist friends, he smuggled a microfilmed copy of Che's diary to Cuba, where it was soon published. He later arranged for Che's amputated hands and death mask to be taken to Cuba. When he was suspected of being the person who had leaked the diary, Arguedas fled Bolivia, reappearing eventually in Cuba and presenting himself as a kind of secret hero of the whole episode. In a mystifying series of about-faces, he later left Cuba, reinitiated contact with the CIA, and returned to Bolivia, where he narrowly escaped an assassination attempt. In the 1980s, Arguedas was accused of belonging to a gang of kidnappers, and he spent three years in prison. In the late 1990s, he led a semi-clandestine life in La Paz, where he was, reportedly, involved in drug trafficking. He died in February 2000. According to the Bolivian police, a bomb in his possession accidentally exploded. Like so much of Arguedas's life, the circumstances of his death remain mysterious.

Mario Monje lost his position as leader of the Bolivian Communist Party and went into exile in Moscow. Upon his arrival there, he said years later, he was instructed by Soviet intelligence officials not to talk, and he didn't talk until the 1990s, when the Soviet Union had ceased to exist. For several decades, Monje was subsidized by the Latin America Institute, a Party-run policy-research office. After the collapse of the Soviet Union, however, Monje became a man without a country or a big brother to look after him.†

Most of the survivors of Masetti's guerrillas who were incarcerated in Salta were released in 1968 through the efforts of their lawyer, Gustavo Roca. During their time in prison, some of them got the shock of their lives when El Fusilado, the man Masetti had condemned to death in Algeria, showed

*Chato Peredo told me that in the summer of 1967, when Che and Chato's brothers, Coco and Inti, were still alive and in the field, and he was studying in Moscow, he asked the Soviets to give him and other Bolivian students military training so they could go to Bolivia and help in the struggle. He was turned down, he said. The Soviets told him that such a request could only be channeled—or approved—through the Bolivian Communist Party. Chato survived the massacre of the ELN and went on to become a successful psychotherapist in the city of Santa Cruz. He specialized in taking his patients "back to the womb."

†During a meeting with me in 1993, Monje mentioned an interest in the trade in precious gems as a possible livelihood.

up one day as a visitor. According to him, the Algerians had spared his life, and instead of shooting him had locked him in a prison cell. He had remained there, cut off from the outside world, for a year or two, until one day he was inexplicably freed and sent to Cuba. He believed that his predicament may have been brought to the attention of Che during Che's visits there in 1965, and that Che had ordered his release. Back in Cuba, he was sent to fight counterrevolutionaries in the Escambray, and then, having been deemed rehabilitated, he was dispatched to Argentina to explore the possibilities of organizing a breakout for his former comrades. He told them he bore them no grudge for what had happened to him; he was thankful merely to be alive. According to Henry Lerner, who met him for the first time, El Fusilado was a fellow Jew.

After spending three years and eight months in prison, Che's bodyguard Alberto Castellanos was spirited out of the country and made it back to Cuba. The appeals for Héctor Jouve and Federico Méndez were denied; their fourteen- and sixteen-year sentences were extended to life imprisonment. When Juan Perón returned to Argentina in 1973, however, they were given amnesty. Perón died the following year, and his second wife, Isabela, became president. She was deposed by a military junta in 1976, initiating a wave of anticommunist repression that became known as Argentina's Dirty War, and Jouve and Méndez soon fled the country. They returned home when civilian rule was restored, in the early 1980s. Jouve lived with his family in Córdoba, where he worked as a psychotherapist. Federico Méndez died of cancer.

Henry Lerner, who nearly died at Masetti's hands, was captured by the Argentine military. He was said to have "disappeared," but in fact he was slated for execution. After being incarcerated for three years, he was saved in an unusual deal arranged by the Catholic Church, whereby the lives of 100 people in government detention were spared. They were then expelled from Argentina. Lerner was accepted for asylum by Israel. Later, he emigrated to Madrid, where, like his old comrade Héctor Jouve, he became a psychotherapist.

Harry Villegas stayed on in the Cuban Revolutionary Armed Forces and became a commander of the expeditionary troops in Angola. Promoted to general, he was awarded the rare official distinction of Hero of the Revolution. He continued to live in a modest apartment not far from Che's old house in Havana. Leonardo "Urbano" Tamayo remained in the Cuban military with the rank of colonel; he apparently suffered a nervous breakdown after returning to Cuba, but recovered and went on to live a quiet life in Havana. Dariel Alarcón Ramírez—Benigno, Che's able *machetero* in Bolivia—moved on to a career in Cuba's prison system, and, into the late

1980s, as a trainer of guerrillas from a variety of Latin American countries. Over time, however, he became disenchanted with the Revolution. In 1994, while on a trip to France, he asked for asylum. In 1997, he published a book harshly critical of Fidel's regime. Knowing that he had become an official traitor to the Revolution and that he faced a probable execution by firing squad if he returned home, Benigno became a permanent exile in Paris.

During the Dirty War against the left in Argentina, the Guevara family soon found themselves to be targets. Che's father fled for Cuba with his new bride, Ana María Erra, a painter some thirty years his junior. They raised a family in Havana and named one of their boys Ramón, Che's Bolivian nom de guerre. After his brother's death, Roberto was radicalized, and both he and Juan Martín became active in a "Guevarist" Argentine guerrilla movement. Roberto moved between Cuba and Europe, but Juan Martín made the mistake of returning to Argentina, hoping to fight in the guerrilla underground there. Within a month he had been arrested, and he spent nine years in prison. His sister Celia spent most of that time in London, working through Amnesty International to secure his release. With the end of the *Proceso*, as the Dirty War became known, Che's siblings gradually returned to Argentina, where Roberto went to work as a lawyer for leftist labor unions. Juan Martín ran a bookshop in Buenos Aires and eventually opened a restaurant. Che's youngest sister, Ana María, died in 1990. Celia Guevara also returned from exile and lived a quiet life in Buenos Aires. Their father died in Havana in 1987, at the age of eighty-seven. He spent his final years producing books based on Che's letters and diaries. His wife, Ana María, and their children—Che's half-brothers and sisters—remained in Cuba.

In 1970, nearly three years into the thirty-year sentences they had been given at their trials, Ciro Bustos and Régis Debray were released from prison on the orders of Bolivia's new military ruler, the reformist General Juan José Torres. They were flown to Chile, where Salvador Allende was then president. Debray, whose celebrity had increased during his public trial in Bolivia, remained an active voice in European leftist intellectual circles. In the 1980s, he became an adviser on Latin American policy to the French president, François Mitterrand. Gradually, however, his infatuation with Cuba's revolution soured. In 1996, he published a memoir that was highly critical of Fidel Castro, whom he called a "megalomaniac," and of Che Guevara, whom he described as "more admirable" but less "likable" than Castro, accusing him of being harsh and unfeeling to his men in Bolivia.

Of those who survived the Bolivian affair, perhaps none suffered more emotional anguish than Ciro Bustos. He took the brunt of the blame for "betraying" Che's presence in Bolivia. Drawing the portraits of Che and the other members of his guerrilla band was an act of disloyalty that would torment Bustos for the rest of his life. Vilified by Debray and frozen out by his former comrades in Cuba, Bustos worked for a time in Chile before fleeing the CIA-backed coup of General Augusto Pinochet in 1973. He returned home to Argentina and resumed painting, only to flee once more, to Sweden, when the Dirty War began. When it ended, Bustos did not return home but remained living in a kind of self-imposed exile in the southern port city of Malmö, where he made paintings of people without faces.

Loyola Guzmán, Che's Bolivian "national finance secretary," was freed from prison in 1970 after her comrades in the ELN took two German engineers hostage to force her release. She made her way to Cuba, where she met Che's widow, Aleida, who took her under her wing, since nobody in Cuba's secret services seemed to want to see her or offer her an explanation for what had gone wrong in 1967. By that time, Che had become almost unmentionable in Cuba. The Soviets had finally clasped Fidel in a bear hug. That hug would last for the next seventeen years, and "adventurism" like Che's was discredited, at least for the time being.

Guzmán and some of her comrades returned unaided to Bolivia, intending to continue with the guerrilla effort, but in 1972, she, her husband, and a few other guerrillas were tracked down and surrounded by the military at a safe house in La Paz. Her husband and the others escaped, only to be killed and "disappeared" later. Guzmán, who was pregnant, was caught and spent the next two years in prison, where she gave birth to her first son. She named him Ernesto, in honor of Che. As Latin America's U.S.-backed armies became ever more brutal in their efforts to quell the spreading Marxist insurgencies that Che had helped inspire, Guzmán became a spokesperson for the families of the disappeared. She remained in La Paz, a tireless champion of the efforts to locate the bodies of Che and the other guerrillas who were killed in 1967, as well as those of the approximately 150 people who disappeared under the Bolivian military regimes of the 1970s and 1980s.

Many of the men who were associated with Che's death in Bolivia went on to die violently, leading some people to believe in "the curse of Che." The first to die was Bolivia's president, General René Barrientos, whose helicopter fell out of the sky in unexplained circumstances in April 1969. In 1971, Colonel Roberto Quintanilla, Antonio Arguedas's intelligence chief at the Ministry of Interior, the man who had made Che's fingerprints, was murdered in Germany. The populist president General Juan José Torres—who as a member of Barrientos's joint chiefs of staff had cast his vote in favor of Che's execution in 1967—was murdered by Argentine death squads in 1976. Only two weeks earlier, General Joaquín Zenteno Anaya was gunned down in Paris, in an action claimed by the obscure "Che Guevara International

Brigade." Captain Gary Prado rose rapidly within the armed forces, eventually becoming a colonel. But during an operation to suppress an armed revolt in Santa Cruz in 1981, he was shot and left paralyzed from the waist down. After retiring from the army as a general, he went into politics, aligning himself with the center-left, and for a period he served as Bolivia's ambassador to London. Mario Vargas Salinas also became a general and a government minister for the dictator General Hugo Banzer Suárez in the 1970s.

Lieutenant Colonel Andrés Selich fared the worst of those who were directly involved in the capture and execution of Che Guevara. In 1971, Selich led a military revolt that ousted President Juan José Torres and brought Hugo Banzer to power. After serving as Banzer's interior minister for only six months, Selich was sidelined and sent into diplomatic exile as ambassador to Paraguay. He soon began conspiring against Banzer and, after secretly reentering Bolivia in 1973, preparing for a new revolt, was caught and beaten to death by army thugs on Banzer's orders.

After retiring from the military with the rank of colonel, Miguel Ayoroa lived discreetly in Santa Cruz. He denied having anything to do with Che's death, laying the blame on the late Selich's shoulders.

The executioner, Mario Terán, became a pathetic figure, a man who for many years lived in hiding—at times wearing wigs and other disguises—out of fear for his life, convinced he was targeted for assassination by Cuba or its allies. Although the army continued to employ him in a series of jobs—including one as a bartender in the officers' club of the Santa Cruz Eighth Army Division headquarters—Terán became deeply embittered. He resented his superior officers, who wrote books and gained glory through their participation in Che's defeat. He periodically offered (as he did with me) to speak about the events that took place in La Higuera on October 9, 1967, but he wanted to be paid for it. (I refused.) Stout and rumpled, with a face marred by a curving scar that cut across his upper lip, Terán exploded with rage when I asked if he regretted having killed Che. "What do you think?" he exclaimed. "You imagine that I just walked into that room and pulled the trigger? I was down in the *quebrada* the day before. I was there! I saw three of my friends die that day."

Felix Rodríguez also believed he was targeted by the Cubans for assassination. He spoke of an incident in the 1970s when he was warned by American intelligence about a plot to hijack a plane he was planning to travel on. His career in the CIA continued in Vietnam, El Salvador, and other war-torn countries, but his cover was finally blown in the late 1980s when he had to appear before the Senate committee investigating the Iran-Contra affair. Rodríguez had worked as Oliver North's point man in providing illegal aid to the Nicaraguan contras, and in operations against the Salvadoran Farabundo Martí guerrillas. In his later years, Rodríguez was a heavyset man who seemed to live largely in the past. The den of his house in suburban Miami was filled with the necromantic talismans and ornaments of his long career as a CIA hireling: framed in glass, the brassiere he confiscated from a Salvadoran female guerrilla *comandante* he once captured; grenades; rifles; honorary plaques and diplomas from numerous counterinsurgency forces; a letter from the first President Bush thanking him for services rendered. The largest space on Rodríguez's crowded wall was occupied by the framed portrait of him standing next to the wounded, doomed Che Guevara. He also showed me a photo album filled with gruesome pictures of dead bodies, including those of Che and Tania.

Whether they had fought with him or against him, a curious bond united those who had known Che. Over the years most of them had come to realize that if their own obituaries were ever to be published, it would be because of their relationships to Che.

Ricardo Rojo, Che's occasional companion and political sparring partner, wrote his best-selling book, *My Friend Che,* in the immediate aftermath of Che's death. It earned him fame and some wealth on the one hand, but bitter condemnation by Cuba and some of Che's comrades on the other, for Rojo perpetuated the story that Che had had a falling-out with Fidel. Rojo fled Argentina in the 1970s, returning home to live only after the restoration of civilian rule in 1983. He practiced law and remained active in political and media circles. A charming and sharp-tongued ranconteur, Rojo died of cancer in Buenos Aires in 1996.

Che's friend Alberto Granado stayed on in Cuba, raising his family and working in the biochemical research industry. In 1980, he published his account of the road trip he had taken with the young Ernesto Guevara, but it got little attention. After Che's *Motorcycle Diaries* was published in the mid-1990s, however, Granado became rather famous. By then in his seventies, he relished the limelight, assuming his role as Che's old road buddy with amiable panache, giving interviews and traveling abroad to hold forth at Che-themed events.

Che's children grew up under the protective eyes of *tío* Fidel and *tío* Ramiro Valdés. His sons, Ernesto and Camilo, both spent five years in Moscow, which included a stint at a KGB training academy. For a time, Camilo worked in the Cuban Ministry of Fisheries under Che's old friend Enrique Oltuski. Ernesto worked for Ramiro Valdés in a state-owned electronics firm, but he eventually quit that job and thereafter devoted himself to fixing up and riding vintage Harley-Davidson motorcycles. Aliusha became a doctor with a specialty in allergies. Against her mother's wishes, she volunteered for duty in Nicaragua and Angola in the 1980s, at the height of Cuban military involvement in those countries. For a time, she was married to a son of Gustavo Machín de Hoed, one of the men who died with Che in Bolivia. Che's daughter Celia became a marine biologist and worked with dolphins and sea lions at Havana's Seaquarium. Aliusha, who bore a striking resemblance to her father—with his penetrating eyes and sharp tongue, if not his quick wit or sense of humor—emerged as the family's spokesperson and defender of her father's legacy, a role hastened by her mother's withdrawal from public life. Eventually, her brother Camilo joined her in this task, and the two frequently traveled abroad to public events where they were expected to speak about their father.

A few years after Che's death, Aleida remarried, as Che had said he wished her to. She moved out of the house on Calle 47 to a new one in Miramar, just down the street from Alberto Granado and directly across from Ana María, the widow of Che's father. Aleida's new husband was a foreign ministry official. He proved to be bitterly jealous of Che, and his periodic mistreatment of Aleida and her children led to several separations, but Aleida always returned to him. Her example of less than noble widowhood was frowned upon in Cuba's ruling circles but was not discussed openly. For years she was active in Cuba's Communist Party Congress as a deputy, and in the Cuban Women's Federation, which was headed by Raúl's wife, Vílma Espín. But Aleida gradually relinquished her public duties to dedicate herself to her family and the perpetuation of Che's legacy, eventually opening a research center across the street from their old home.

La Casa del Che, as it is called, is painted marine blue. Its roof garden and entryway are covered with red and purple bougainvillea. In the 1990s, when I lived in Havana and visited the house frequently, paintings of Che adorned the walls of the foyer, although they were threatened by water damage from the perpetually leaking roof. Upstairs, Che's little office remained as it was when he left Cuba, with his small white Formica-covered desktop built into varnished plywood and his vinyl-backed office chair on wheels. The double windows at either end of the room looked out to the same view of the neighborhood Che had seen. His books were still there, just as he'd left them: the works of Marx, Engels, and Lenin, their margins messy with his jottings; Stefan Zweig's biographies of Marie Antoinette and Joseph Fouché, one of the most bloodthirsty Jacobins, who became Napoléon's minister of police. In a little alcove under Che's desk were the books he was reading last: several about Bolivia, Africa, and Algeria's revolution, many of them in French, and one about the assassination of John F.

Kennedy. A portrait of Camilo Cienfuegos hung behind Che's desk, and on top of the bookcase that stretched across the front there was a bust of Simón Bolívar and a bronze bas-relief of Lenin. A carved ornamental *yerba mate* gourd and a silver sipping straw were on a side shelf, and on the floor, a bronze statue symbolizing "New Soviet Man" gathered dust. On the shelf of a narrow closet were some of the belongings Che left behind: an olive-green army backpack, a web belt, and other military apparel, all disintegrating in the Cuban humidity.

When Che's first wife, Hilda, died of cancer in 1974, their daughter, Hildita, went to Europe. It was a kind of escape: she did not have a good or close relationship with her stepmother, Aleida. Hildita worked at odd jobs and led the life of a hippie in Italy and other European countries. She later lived in Mexico and married a Mexican guerrilla named Alberto. They came to live in Cuba, but Alberto's conspiratorial activities against Cuba's staunchest regional ally made Fidel's regime uneasy, and he was asked to leave. Hildita went with him, but they eventually divorced. Returning to Cuba in the mid-1980s with two young sons, she worked at La Casa de las Americas as an archivist and researcher and began to compile a bibliography of her father's writings.

Loyal to Cuba's revolution but outspoken about what she saw as its defects, Hildita earned the quiet disapproval of the regime for her views and personal conduct. When her older son, Canek, then a teenager, made remarks to the foreign press that were critical of Fidel's government, opprobrium fell more heavily over her little clan. In 1995, Hildita died of cancer at the age of thirty-nine, the same age her father was when he was killed. Neither Fidel nor Raúl appeared at her wake, although both sent large wreaths. At the funeral in the vast Cementerio Colón, where she was interred in the Pantheon of the Revolutionary Armed Forces, no one spoke.

IV

Che's unshakable faith in his beliefs was made even more powerful by his unusual combination of romantic passion and coldly analytical thought. This paradoxical blend was probably the secret of the near-mystical stature he acquired, but it seems also to have been the source of his inherent weaknesses —hubris and naïveté. Gifted at perceiving and calculating strategy on a grand scale, yet at a remove, he seemed incapable of seeing the small, human elements that made up the larger picture, as evidenced by his disastrous choice of Masetti to lead the Argentine *foco*. There, and in Cuba, the Congo, and Bolivia, the men he believed in consistently failed him, and he consistently failed to understand how to alter the fundamental nature of others and get them to become "selfless Communists." But, along with his mistakes, what is most remembered about Che is his personal example, embodying faith, willpower, and sacrifice.

As a veteran Cuban intelligence official in Havana observed, "Toward the end, Che knew what was coming, and he prepared himself for an exemplary death. We would have preferred him to remain alive, with us here in Cuba, but the truth is that his death helped us tremendously. It's unlikely we would have had all the revolutionary solidarity we have had over the years if it weren't for Che dying the way he did."

The island went through many shifts in political position under Fidel's long tenure as *jefe máximo*. In the immediate aftermath of Che's death, relations with the Soviet Union went into a deep freeze. Angered over Moscow's implicit backing of the Bolivian Communist Party line, and because of harshly critical articles on Che and the "export" of revolution published in *Pravda,* Fidel shunned the Kremlin. As an expression of his displeasure, he sent his lowly health minister to attend the annual festivities in Red Square in November 1967. Ambassador Alexandr Alexiev, who was seen as too close to Fidel, was withdrawn from his post in 1968 and dispatched to, of all places, Madagascar. Fidel launched a new purge of the pro-Soviet "old Communists" after allegedly uncovering a dissident faction engaged in a talking conspiracy against him with members of the Soviet embassy staff. Like the purge of "sectarianism" in 1962, this plot featured the redoubtable Aníbal Escalante; this time, he was not sent to Moscow but was given a fifteen-year prison sentence. Among Escalante's and his fellow conspirators' tape-recorded crimes was criticism of Che.

Invoking Che's spirit, Fidel made a desperate attempt to make Cuba economically self-sufficient. After proclaiming that the nation would produce an unprecedented 10 million tons of sugar in 1970, he poured all of Cuba's hard-stretched resources into reaching that goal. When Orlando Borrego, the minister of sugar, warned Fidel that it could not be done, he was fired. It was *not* done, and the Cuban economy was left in a state of near-total collapse. For all intents and purposes, Fidel's disastrous *zafra de los diez milliones*—the 10-million-ton harvest—as it was known, represented the end of any hope for Cuban autonomy, and the Soviets, who were already buoyed by Fidel's declaration of support for their invasion of Czechoslovakia, swiftly asserted themselves. Che's Ministry of Industries was divided up into many smaller ones and was gutted of his loyalists; many of the foreigners who had come to work for him soon left Cuba. The rehabilitation camp, Guanacahabibes, and the Ciro Redondo experimental farm were both shut down. Che's "department of control," with more than 40,000 archives on individuals cataloging their revolutionary aptitude and work records, was destroyed. Orlando Borrego remained loyal to Fidel and the revolution, but he never again held a senior government position. For years, he worked as an adviser to the Ministry of Transportation and, after it was inaugurated in 1995, to the Che Guevara Faculty at the University of Havana.

Che's officially induced "hibernation" lasted for a decade and a half. He reemerged as a revolutionary touchstone in Cuba only after the Soviet Union itself began to change in the late 1980s under Mikhail Gorbachev. Fidel opposed the liberal reforms of glasnost and perestroika with what he called a "rectification" process, which reinstituted Che's ideas as the correct ones for Cuba's Communists to follow. This coincided with the precipitous collapse of the Soviet bloc and the end of the long flow of Moscow's subsidies to Cuba. Forced to allow limited foreign capital investment and other "market reforms" to rescue Cuba's battered economy, while instituting austerity measures, Fidel managed to pull Cuba back from the brink of disaster. Throughout the difficult "Special Period," as Fidel defined the post-Soviet era, he encouraged Che's resurrection as a popular hero who best represented the ideals of revolutionary Cuba.

That Che and guerrilla warfare had not lost their allure as models for political action was demonstrated by the Zapatista uprising that erupted in 1994 in Chiapas, in southern Mexico. The Zapatistas' less than aggressive military tactics and avowed political goals—to win autonomy for Chiapas's indigenous peoples—were far more modest than Che's, but his legacy was apparent in the guerrillas' repudiation of Mexico's subservience to U.S. capital interests and their appeals for sweeping social, political, and economic reforms. The charismatic figure of their gun-wielding, pipe-smoking, reflective, ironic, lyrical leader, Subcomandante Marcos—the thinking man's guerrilla fighter—captivated the popular imagination as Che once had. Indeed, it was hard not to see Marcos as a reborn Che Guevara, adapted to modern times—less utopian but still idealistic, still willing to fight for his beliefs—perhaps having learned from his predecessor's mistakes but modeled on him nonetheless. To a degree, the Zapatistas represented a successful implementation of the *foco* theory. Marcos had spent years undetected among indigenous communities in the forests of Chiapas, organizing and training its cadres, before going public with the insurgency.*

V

Che's rehabilitation as a saintlike presence in Cuba reached its apotheosis with the return of his remains to Cuban soil. I was with the joint Cuban-Argentine forensic team in November and December 1995, during the first

*See Notes.

weeks of its search for Che's body on the airstrip in Vallegrande. The team had been assembled after Mario Vargas Salinas broke his long silence and told me what happened the night Che disappeared. They rather quickly discovered the bodies of Octavio de la Concepcíon; of the two Bolivians, Pablo and Chapaco; and of the Peruvian, Eustaquio. But then the trail went cold, and I left to go home for Christmas. I remained in touch with the searchers by telephone over the following year.

In June 1996, the head of the Argentine forensic team, Alejandro Inchaurregui, met me in Paraguay, where I interviewed Socorro Selich, the widow of Lieutenant Colonel Andrés Selich. She and her husband had moved to Asunción in the early 1970s, when he was the Bolivian ambassador there. His family had stayed when he went back to Bolivia to foment a coup and was murdered. Selich was a mysterious figure. Very little was then known about his role in the death of Che, although there were vague, somewhat sinister, stories about his presence in La Higuera and Vallegrande during the period when the bodies disappeared. Socorro had been a widow for twenty-three years and was deeply immersed in the culture of Alfredo Stroessner's Paraguay. The dictator had protected her and her several daughters, one of whom had dated a son of Stroessner. She was more or less apolitical herself, but I think that after we talked for a few days she felt that perhaps her husband's name would be cleared if she told what she knew and shared the documents and mementos she had saved.

Socorro confirmed Mario Vargas Salinas's story about Che's burial. She said that the body had been dumped in a secret grave dug by a bulldozer somewhere in the brushy land near the Vallegrande airstrip and that a mass grave was dug nearby to bury six of Che's comrades. Her husband had shown her the map coordinates of the grave sites. The coordinates had since vanished, but she was sure that Che had been buried separately. (Vargas Salinas, on the other hand, had told me that Che and his comrades were buried together, in a single mass grave.) Interestingly, the logbook in which Selich normally recorded his burial duties was blank from 3:45 P.M. on October 9 until 9:00 A.M. on October 11, omitting all mention of Che Guevara or what was done with his remains.* Socorro allowed me to study her late husband's notes, among other things, including transcripts he had collected of the military interrogations of the peasants in the areas where Che and his

---

*To add to the contradictions, a few days after the repatriation of Che's remains to Cuba, in July 1997, the former Cuban-American CIA agent Gustavo Villoldo emerged from years of obscurity to summon me to a meeting in Miami, where he insisted that he had presided over Che's burial with several of Selich's men, but denied that either Selich or Vargas Salinas was present.

guerrillas were roaming. Before I left Asunción, Socorro promised to cooperate personally with the search for Che's body by making a trip to
Vallegrande, incognito, to see if she could identify his burial spot from her
memory of the coordinates. She later did go there but was unable to pinpoint a spot.

Alejandro Inchaurregui had promised to let me know immediately
when Che's body was found, and he was as good as his word. In early July
1997, I was in Miami—coincidentally, speaking about Che and giving interviews to journalists—when Alejandro telephoned me. In a quiet voice
that was taut with excitement, he said, "We've found him. Come."

I flew to Santa Cruz the next day and then drove to Vallegrande.
Nothing had yet appeared in the press, but rumors of a discovery had begun
to circulate. The bodies had been found by a team of Cuban and Bolivian
forensic experts. They, in turn, had quietly summoned the Argentines.
Alejandro and two colleagues had flown in a couple of days earlier. A few
journalists had also arrived, but were being kept at bay, and in the dark.
Out at the airstrip, a mere fifteen feet from the last of the holes dug there in
November 1995, was a new pit. The area around it was roped off, and some
Bolivian soldiers guarded the approaches. Alejandro walked me over to the
far edge of the pit. It was about six and a half feet deep. At the bottom, a
skeleton lay on its back. The body had been laid out, apparently with some
respect, just a few feet away from a tangled heap of six other cadavers. They
were later identified as Pacho, Aniceto, Willy, Juan Pablo Chang, Arturo,
and Olo.

The skull of the body that had been laid out neatly was covered by an
olive-green military jacket. One of the arms, cocked at the elbow, pointed
skyward. The hand had been amputated at the wrist; the bone appeared to
have been cut with surgical precision. Alejandro and the other experts had
few doubts that the body was Che's. They had found plaster of Paris in a
pocket of the jacket—traces from the death mask that was made when Che's
hands were amputated. Alejandro had also found some pipe tobacco, which
Che was known to have been given to smoke the night before his execution. All that was left to do, he said, was to check the dental records.

Things moved quickly after that. Within a day, the news was out and
a media frenzy had begun. Fearful of an order to halt the proceedings by
the former military dictator, Hugo Banzer (who had won Bolivia's recent
presidential election and was due to assume office in a few weeks), the
Cubans and their Bolivian counterparts decided not to waste any time. On
the night of July 5, they evacuated the bodies of Che and his comrades from
Vallegrande in a lightning operation involving a convoy of vehicles. The
bodies were taken to a hospital in Santa Cruz, where they were kept under

guard and examined further. Che's teeth were matched with the plaster mold that the Cubans had made before he left for the Congo. A few days later, the remains were put on a plane and flown to Cuba. In keeping with the revolutionary tradition of giving each year an official title, 1997 was consecrated as the Year of the Thirtieth Anniversary of the Death in Combat of the Heroic Guerrilla and His Comrades.

VI

Manuel Barbarroja Piñeiro died in 1998, at the age of sixty-eight, after losing control of his car while returning home from a diplomatic reception in Havana. Barbarroja, who had retired from his post as the head of the Americas Department a few years earlier, had remained faithful to Fidel. An affable man and a great raconteur who still wore his trademark long beard, he liked to spend long evenings gathered with friends in the kitchen of his book-crammed home in Miramar, smoking, drinking whiskey, and discussing international affairs. Despite his love of conversation, Barbarroja kept a lot of secrets to himself, and he took the majority of them with him to his grave.

Aleida finally published her memoirs. Her book, *Evocación*, contained some of Che's private letters and poems dedicated to her. By the fortieth anniversary of Che's death in 2007, Aleida had gradually released most of Che's writings and diaries for publicaton. Living in Europe, deeply estranged from Cuba, Hildita Guevara's son, Canek, meanwhile, wrote a reflective, melancholy blog called "Diaries without a Motorcyle."

In Latin America, history seemed to have come around in a big circular loop. By January 2009, when Barack Obama replaced George W. Bush as president of the United States, more than a dozen Latin American countries had acquired left-of-center governments. Most of them were demanding a new relationship with the United States, and several were downright hostile. Three of them had recently ousted their U.S. ambassadors, and one, Venezuela, had been host to Russia in joint naval war games in the Caribbean. Things had begun to change a decade earlier, in 1999, with the electoral victory in Venezuela of Hugo Chávez, a former army paratrooper, whose call for a "Bolivarian revolution" and willingness to confront "the Empire," as he called the United States, helped accelerate a deterioriation in American influence in the region. Chávez regarded Fidel as his political mentor and Che Guevara as one of his greatest heroes. Using Venezuela's vast oil resources, Chávez became the primary economic sponsor for Cuba, and for Bolivia as well. In 2006, one of his political protégés, Evo Morales, an indigenous Aymara, was sworn into office as Bolivia's president. For some, the alliance between Chávez, Fidel, and Evo Morales represented a resuscitation of Che's dream of a continental revolution—only this time carried out without weapons. That was certainly Chávez's aspiration.

Evo Morales attended a ceremony held in La Higuera on June 14, 2006, to commemorate Che's seventy-eighth birthday. Standing next to him were Che's son, Camilo, and the ambassadors of Cuba and Venezuela. After asking for a moment of silence in Che's memory, Morales said, "We will never betray the struggle of Che Guevara, of Fidel, or of Chávez, and we say this on the spot where our elder brother lost his life." Two months later, Chávez and Fidel paid a joint visit to Che's boyhood home in Alta Gracia, Argentina. They were feted by the townspeople and toured the recently inaugurated Casa-Museo del Che, in the former Guevara family home, Villa Nydia. Calica Ferrer was there, as was Carlos Figueroa. On the flight back to Havana, Fidel fell ill and vanished from public view for a long period. He was replaced in office by his brother, Raúl, who succeeded him formally as Cuba's president in February 2008. Fidel's illness did not prevent him from receiving some foreign dignitaries and from appearing in short video clips that were periodically released to the public. He could be seen talking, and often laughing, with his most frequent vistor, Hugo Chávez.

Around the time Che's body was exhumed, a scrawl of graffiti in Spanish had appeared on the wall of the Vallegrande public telephone office. It said: "Che—Alive as they never wanted you to be."

Notes

Sources

Selected Bibliography

Maps

Chronology

Acknowledgments

Notes

Chapter 1, page 8: According to Julia Constenla de Giussani, who was a friend of Che's mother and of the astrologer who drew up Che's astral chart, Celia said that she gave birth on May 14, 1928, the same day, and at the same hour, as a striking dockworker called "Diente de Oro" (Gold Tooth) died of gunshot wounds. The yellowing archives of Rosario's daily newspaper *La Capital* confirm the story. In May 1928, a strike by dockworkers escalated into violence. Stabbings and shootings took place almost every day, most of them carried out by armed scabs working for the stevedores' hiring agency, the Sociedad Patronal. At 5:30 P.M. on Tuesday, May 13, 1928, a twenty-eight-year-old stevedore named Ramón Romero, alias "Diente de Oro," was shot in the head during a fracas at the Puerto San Martín. At dawn the next day, May 14, he died in the Granaderos a Caballo Hospital in San Lorenzo, about twelve miles north of Rosario.

Chapter 7, page 99: In 1968, Rojo wrote a book, *My Friend Che,* in which he gave his account of Che's life and their friendship. Perhaps because it was written in a rush to publish following Che's highly publicized death, the book has a number of inaccuracies. Rojo also made somewhat more of their relationship than was actually there, but he was not alone in seeking a vicarious limelight among the posthumous horde of former Guevara friends and acquaintances. The fact is, they did know each other and were friendly, and therefore Rojo's book has some historically salvageable aspects. In his book Rojo claimed that after they first met, he traveled with Calica and Ernesto for most of their journey northward from La Paz. This is untrue. They met again in Lima, in Guayaquil, Costa Rica, Guatemala, and Mexico, but always traveled separately. He later visited Che a couple of times in Cuba.

Chapter 8, page 119: "Note on the Margin" was published as part of *Notas de Viaje* by Guevara's widow, Aleida March, although her husband had instructed her to burn this and other early writings after his death. Fortunately, she decided not to. She believed that the enigmatic person he described might have been a fictional composite of several people encountered along his journey or a literary device that he employed to evoke the scene of self-revelation.

Alberto Granado did not recall meeting anyone of this person's description during their journey. He was mystified at the notion that Ernesto had such thoughts so long before his adoption of Marxism became known to his friends and family.

Chapter 9, page 140: A number of men whose careers were to become enmeshed with Ernesto Guevara's emerged out of Operation Success. Among them was Daniel James. As the editor and chief Latin American correspondent of the anticommunist weekly *New Leader,* James was involved in the U.S. media campaign against Arbenz. In mid-1954 he wrote *Red Design for the Americas,* a book that lobbied for the overthrow of the Arbenz government. According to the authors of *Bitter Fruit: The Untold Story of the American Coup in Guatemala,* James's forceful arguments that Communists were in control of Guatemala were "so convincing" that the CIA bought hundreds of copies of the book and distributed them to American journalists and other "opinion molders." In 1968, James was given exclusive access to publish the documents captured by the CIA that belonged to Che's guerrillas in Bolivia, including Che's diary. He followed up this book a year later with a highly caustic biography of Che. Che's original diary is in Bolivia's central bank, in La Paz.

Chapter 13, page 184: Miguel Sánchez later turned against Castro. I met him in 1997, when I was promoting the first edition of this book. Sánchez appeared in a bookstore and identified himself. He carried a cloth bag, out of which he pulled a large, framed black-and-white close-up photograph of Che's amputated hands. The fingertips were black with ink. He explained that the picture had been given to him by his "good friend" Felix Rodríguez, the Cuban-American former CIA agent who was present at Che's execution in Bolivia in 1967. Rodríguez had autographed the picture and added a personal note to Sánchez.

Chapter 15, page 227: Che examined a document brought by the National Directorate visitors outlining the July 26 Movement's ideological platform. He was guardedly impressed. "In it, a series of quite advanced revolutionary decrees were proposed," he wrote, "although some were very lyrical, such as the announcement that no diplomatic relations would be established with the [Latin] American dictatorships." He was probably referring to the latest issue of *Revolución*, the clandestine organ published by Carlos Franqui, a former Communist who worked as a journalist in Havana and secretly handled underground propaganda for the July 26 Movement. The February 1957 issue of *Revolución* carried an article, "Necessity for Revolution," extracted from a draft pamphlet titled *Nuestra Razón*. Franqui had commissioned the manuscript from Mario Llerena, a political writer, intending it to become "The Manifesto-Program" of the July 26 Movement. In the article, the "Revolution" was described as: "A continuous historic process. . . . The Revolution is struggling for the complete transformation of Cuban life, for profound modifications in the system of property and for a change in institutions. . . . In accordance with its goals, and as a consequence of the historic, geographic, and sociological reality of Cuba, the Revolution is democratic, nationalist, and socialist."

When *Nuestra Razón* was published a few months later, Fidel distanced himself from it, evidently anxious to avoid any ideological pronouncements that might alienate potential July 26 adherents.

Chapter 17, page 281: In his letter to Daniel (published in Carlos Franqui's *Diary of the Cuban Revolution*), Che wrote, "Because of my ideological background, I belong to those who believe that the solution of the world's problems lies behind the so-called iron curtain, and I see this Movement as one of the many inspired by the bourgeoisie's desire to free themselves from the economic chains of imperialism. I always thought of Fidel as an authentic leader of the leftist bourgeoisie, although this image is enhanced by personal qualities of extraordinary brilliance that set him above his class. I began the struggle with that spirit: honestly without any hope of going further than the liberation of the country; and fully prepared to leave when the conditions of the later struggle veered all the action of the Movement toward the right (toward what all of you represent). What I never counted on was the radical change in his basic ideas in order to accept the Miami Pact. It had seemed impossible, and I later found out that it was. . . . Fortunately, Fidel's letter arrived during the intervening period . . . and it explained how what we can call a betrayal came about."

As to the issue of supplies, he said, neither he nor Fidel was getting what was needed quickly enough, and so he would continue to make his own arrangements. His main supplier might be a "shady character," but he considered himself capable of dealing with him without risk. *He* did not compromise his values, he told Daniel pointedly, unlike those who had gone along with the Miami Pact, where "all that happened was that an ass was yielded up in what was probably the most detestable act of 'buggery' in

Cuban history. My name in history (which I mean to earn by my conduct) cannot be linked with that crime, and I hereby put that on record. . . . If this letter pains you because you consider it unfair or because you consider yourself innocent of the crime and you want to tell me so, terrific. And if it hurts you so much that you cut off relations with this part of the revolutionary forces, so much the worse."

Four days later, Daniel responded in an eloquent rebuttal of his own; he too was writing to leave "proof of his revolutionary integrity." As for keeping Che's letter private, as Che had requested, Daniel informed him that he had shared it with the rest of the Directorate; Che could therefore consider his reply as coming from all of them. "I am not the slightest bit interested in where you situate me, nor will I even try to make you change your personal opinion of us. . . . Now is not the time to be discussing 'where the salvation of the world lies.' . . . Our fundamental differences are that we are concerned about bringing the oppressed peoples of 'our America' governments that respond to their longing for Liberty and Progress. . . . We want a strong America, master of its own fate, an America that can stand up proudly to the United States, Russia, China, or any other power that tries to undermine its economic and political independence. On the other hand, those with your ideological background think the solution to our evils is to free ourselves from the noxious 'Yankee' domination by means of a no less noxious 'Soviet' domination."

Chapter 17, page 285: After the rebels' victory in 1959, *Revolución* became a daily newspaper and *Lunes de Revolución* was edited by the novelist Guillermo Cabrera Infante. Both Cabrera Infante and Carlos Franqui eventually fell out with Castro and went into exile. *Revolución* was closed down.

Chapter 18, page 304: By divulging details of the sierra-llano dispute in his article, published just before he left Cuba, Che broke silence on a topic that had been officially taboo since the revolutionary triumph. In it, Che chose to skip over Faustino Pérez's disagreement with the decisions reached at the May summit, and to give the impression that the rift had been definitively settled.

It must be remembered that at the time Che wrote his article, not only were he and Faustino on the "same side," but Faustino was also a prominent member of Cuba's revolutionary leadership, and their past differences had become as irrelevant as they were inconvenient to rehash extensively in public.

Faustino Pérez's later career showed that in addition to his other virtues enumerated by Che, he was an inveterate survivor. The former opponent of Fidel's caudillismo became one of the grand viziers of *fidelismo;* the former anticommunist became a member of the Central Committee of the reconstituted Cuban Communist Party when it was officially inaugurated by Fidel in 1965, and remained a leading apparatchik until his death in 1993.

Chapter 18, page 313: In his letter, Fidel warned Raúl, "We must consider the possibility that elements of the dictatorship, exploiting this incident, are hatching a plan for physical aggression against North American citizens; given Batista's hopeless situation, this would turn international public opinion against us, as it would react with indignation to the news, for example, that several of those North Americans had been murdered by the rebels. It is essential to declare categorically that we do not utilize the system of hostages, however justified our indignation may be against the political attitudes of any government. . . . You must keep in mind that in matters that can have weighty consequences for the Movement, you cannot act on your own initiative, or go beyond certain limits without any consultation. Besides, that would give the false impression of complete anarchy in the inner circles of our army." (From Franqui's *Diary of the Cuban Revolution*.)

Chapter 19, page 324: By the end of 1958, Che had already recruited or was acquainted with most of his future guerrilla comrades. Eliseo Reyes, later "Rolando"; Carlos Coello, aka "Tuma"; Orlando "Olo" Pantoja, later "Antonio"; and Manuel Hernández Osorio, aka "Miguel," were all with him on the march to Las Villas. Also, Harry Villegas, "Pombo,"one of his bodyguards, and Leonardo Tamayo, "Urbano," in El Vaquerito's "Suicide Squad." The third Cuban survivor of the Bolivia campaign, Dariel "Benigno" Alarcón Ramírez, was with Camilo's invasion column, as was Antonio "Pinares" Sánchez. José María "Papi" Martínez and Octavio de la Concepción Pedraja, "El Moro," were with Raúl in Oriente. Juan Vitalio Acuña, aka "Joaquín" in Bolivia, had stayed behind in the Sierra Maestra and been made a *comandante* by Fidel. Three more future fighters would soon join Che in the Escambray: Alberto Fernández Montes de Oca, "Pachungo"; Gustavo "Alejandro" Machín de Hoed; and Jesús "Rubio" Suárez Gayol.

Chapter 23, page 443: The story of how the Korda photograph of Che came to be disseminated so widely is complicated. It was not used in *Revolución* to illustrate the article about the *La Coubre* rally, but it appeared months later, printed quite small, in an advertisement for a conference that Che was to speak at. Korda certainly gave a copy of the photo to Feltrinelli in 1967, before Che died, and Feltrinelli reproduced it as a black-and-white poster for the October 1967 Frankfurt Book Fair. Feltrinelli is said to have been trying to get attention for Che's plight (he was then fighting a losing battle in Bolivia) and thus save his life, but Che was killed that month, three days before the opening of the book fair, in fact.

It seems, however, that reproductions of the Korda photo began to appear in various versions some months before the fall of 1967. It was apparently used on posters in Havana in May 1967, at the Salon de Mayo, which was attended by many French artists, and also in July, for a conference of the Organization of Latin American Solidarity. In Europe, it appeared in the August 19, 1967, edition of *Paris Match*, illustrating a story by Jean Lartéguy about Che that asked the question, "Where is he now?"

The version of the image that became most widespread is based on a black-on-red graphic by the Irish artist Jim Fitzpatrick, who said that he got the photograph itself from some Dutch activists who may or may not have gotten it from Jean-Paul Sartre. Fitzpatrick said he also saw the photo in *Stern*. He made many versions of the image, first in 1967, apparently completely independently of the Feltrinelli poster. It was a version of Fitzpatrick's version that became the banner for the 1968 student demonstrations and then was taken up by innumerable T-shirt manufacturers. Fitzpatrick's version is also the model for the mysterious "Warhol Che," a nine-panel silk screen that is not by Warhol. The author of that version remains unidentified. In February 1968, the American journal *Evergreen* published on its cover a painting by Paul Davis based on the pop-art graphic versions of the Korda picture. That image was used on the cover of the first edition of this book and on many subsequent editions.

The most complete accounts of the journey of the Korda image are in Trisha Ziff's *Che Guevara: Revolutionary and Icon* (Abrams, 2006) and Michael Casey's *Che's Afterlife: The Legacy of an Image* (Vintage, 2009).

Chapter 25, page 507: Myrna Torres, the friend of Ernesto and Hilda Gadea during their days in Guatemala, moved to Cuba in the early 1960s. Her house in Havana became a sanctuary for a whole generation of Central American revolutionaries. Humberto Pineda, her first husband and the father of her two children—one of two brothers Che had described in the diary he kept in Guatemala in 1954 as having "a real pair of balls"—was one of the founders of the Guatemalan guerrilla movement. He was captured, tortured, and murdered in 1966, and in 1975, his brother, Luis Arturo, was "disappeared." Myrna returned to Nicaragua in 1979, after the Sandinista guerrillas ousted Anastasio Somoza, and she worked for the new government in their press office. When the Sandinistas fell from power, in 1990, she returned to Havana to live. An elegant and vivacious woman, Myrna retained a keen interest in regional politics. Between trips to Mexico and Costa Rica, where her sons lived, she claimed to be writing her memoirs.

Chapter 25, page 509: The Latin American guerrilla program had Fidel's early support. The secret agency known as the Liberation Department was set up under Manuel Piñeiro as a vice ministry—the Viceministerio Técnico—within Ramíro Valdés's State Security agency. "I was responsible for the intelligence organizations and the Dirección Nacional de Liberación Nacional, which handled Latin America and Africa," Piñeiro explained. In that capacity, he said, he sustained "an active and intense relationship with Che," joining in his many predawn conclaves with revolutionaries from around the world. Valdés is said to have concentrated more on counter-espionage directed against the United States, while he also had "some involvement" in implementing the guerrilla programs. Raúl's role was evidently less direct; in a pattern established early on by Fidel, he was deferred to by being allowed to select his own cadres from within the army for the operations. But Che was the true overseer. "From day one, Che was in charge of the armed liberation movement supported by Cuba," explained a Cuban government source with access to the relevant classified files.

Chapter 26, page 579, top: In November 1962, Leonov came face-to-face with Lee Harvey Oswald, who had arrived at the Soviet embassy in Mexico City and asked to speak to an official. According to Leonov, he was called out to deal with him. But Oswald was both armed and agitated, and Leonov quickly called other embassy personnel to help remove him from the premises. Leonov said that he was stunned when, soon afterward, he realized that the "psychotic and dangerous" man who had come to the embassy was the man who had been arrested in Dallas and was accused of murdering the American president. In a conversation about the various JFK assassination theories, Leonov dismissed the notion that Oswald might have acted on the KGB's orders, citing the "psychotic" behavior he had witnessed firsthand. He said that, theoretically, even if the KGB *had* wanted to kill JFK, it would never have used someone so unbalanced and so difficult to control.

In the course of three separate conversations with Leonov in Moscow during 1993, we discussed his intelligence career and his relationship to Che Guevara and other figures. During one session, Leonov spoke passionately of the Guatemalan revolutionary cause in particular and of the murders of Guatemalan Communist Party "friends" by military death squads. He did not go into detail about what kind of relationship he had with the friends, other than to say he had supported their cause. But the well-informed Argentine Isidoro Gilbert, a former TASS correspondent, wrote in his 1995 book *El Oro de Moscú* that Leonov actively assisted the Guatemalan revolutionary cause, and suggested that he did so as part of an officially approved, if covert, KGB program. More elliptically, Manuel Piñeiro told me that

Leonov "always showed solidarity toward Latin America's revolutionary fighters and the Cuban revolution."

To judge from a declassified memorandum that the KGB chief, Alexander Shelepin, sent to Khrushchev on July 29, 1961, the Soviets did not have a problem with guerrilla wars in the countries where the local Communist Party was outlawed and sometimes gave their support to such actions. According to extracts published in *Inside the Kremlin's Cold War: From Stalin to Khrushchev,* by Vladislav Zubok and Konstantin Pleshakov, Shelepin's memo proposed a series of covert activities around the world to distract the United States from the confrontation in Berlin. "Shelepin advocated measures 'to activate by the means available to the KGB armed uprisings against pro-Western reactionary governments.' The subversive activities began in Nicaragua, where the KGB plotted an armed mutiny through an 'internal front of resistance,' in coordination with Castro's Cubans and with the 'Revolutionary Front Sandino.' Shelepin proposed making 'appropriations from KGB funds in addition to the previous assistance of 10,000 American dollars for the purchase of arms.' The plan also envisaged the instigation of an armed uprising in El Salvador, and a rebellion in Guatemala, where guerrilla forces would be given $15,000 to buy weapons." (Khrushchev approved this plan, and it was passed by the Soviet Central Committee on August 1, 1961.)

Chapter 26, page 579, bottom: Shortly after Che's visit to Moscow, Rudolf Shlyapnikov traveled to Cuba to take up a post at the Soviet embassy, as the official in charge of the thousands of Soviet Komsomol "volunteers" working in Cuba. In February 1968, accused of colluding with the unrepentant Aníbal Escalante and other disgruntled "old Communists" in a plot to undermine Fidel's revolutionary authority, Shlyapnikov and several other Soviet agents were expelled from Cuba; Escalante was sentenced to fifteen years in prison. From his embassy post in Havana, Oleg Darushenkov rose rapidly in Party ranks to become head of the Central Committee's Cuba department. In the 1980s, he became the Soviet ambassador to Mexico. After the fall of Communism in the U.S.S.R., he resigned his post but remained in Mexico, working as an executive for the Mexican television conglomerate Televisa. (Shlyapnikov's last diplomatic post, as Soviet consul in Veracruz, Mexico, also coincided with Darushenkov's tenure as ambassador to Mexico.)

These men are considered to have represented the anti-Guevarist Soviet line. Che's widow, Aleida March, said she believed that Oleg Darushenkov was a "provocateur." She was rankled by the fact that after Che's death, when Darushenkov came to her house and offered his condolences, he undiplomatically asked her, "Why did Che go to Bolivia, when he was a foreigner?"

She took offense and cited the precedent of the Dominican general Máximo Gómez, who helped in Cuba's war of independence against Spain. Finally, she asked Darushenkov how he dared to pose such a question in Che's house.

Orlando Borrego agreed with Aleida's assessment of Darushenkov, whom he knew well, and described him as extremely bright, capable, and highly ambitous, but also "wicked," given to bad-mouthing people and making provocative comments in a pattern that seemed to indicate an ulterior motive.

Chapter 26, page 588: Among those in the room, according to Che's widow, Aleida, was the young Chinese-trained Angolan resistance leader Jonas Savimbi, who later founded the UNITA guerrilla movement. In the multi-sided battle against the Portuguese, which finally culminated in Angola's independence in 1975, Savimbi's forces lost out to the rival Cuban- and Soviet-backed MPLA, which seized power and installed a Marxist regime. Savimbi turned to the West and continued to wage war with military support from the CIA and South Africa. During the the 1980s, Savimbi's UNITA had lavish offices in Washington, D.C., and he was lauded by President Ronald Reagan as an anticommunist freedom fighter in the best Western tradition. But after participating in and losing national elections following an internationally brokered cease-fire agreement in 1992, Savimbi returned to war; countless thousands of Angolans died in the renewed fighting, which left much of Angola destroyed. In 1996 he was briefly involved in power-sharing negotiations with the regime. In 2002, Savimbi was finally surrounded and killed in battle. With his death, Angola's long war finally ended.

Chapter 27, page 600: Aleida told me that in addition to the tape-recorded poems, Che wrote her a special poem that, at the time we spoke, she had not made public. "The world can read it after I'm dead," she said. Aleida always guarded the details of her life with Che with an almost obsessive zeal. Her eldest daughter, Aliusha, said it wasn't until she was in her twenties, prepared to follow in her father's footsteps by going off to Nicaragua to serve as a doctor, that fear of losing her had made her mother open up. At that point, Aleida read to her a love letter Che had written, kept under lock and key in a special desk at their home. And, while Aliusha was in Nicaragua, Aleida sent her a copy of the tape-recorded love poems he had left. (In her memoir, *Evocación*, which was published in 2008, Aleida printed a poem written to her by Che that may be the one she spoke to me about.)

In addition to the "public" farewell letter to his children, Che also sent them some postcards from Africa, and a tape recording of his voice telling them how he felt to be their father. "Che was a *machista,* like most Latins,"

Aleida said, in an affectionately chiding tone, explaining that in a letter to his two sons, Camilo and Ernesto, excluding the girls, he told them that at the end of the century—if he was still alive and if imperialism still existed—they would have to fight it together, and if not, they would "go together to the Moon on a spaceship." In a letter to his daughters, he told them to look after their brothers, especially Camilo. They should get him to stop using bad words.

Chapter 27, page 611: For many years, Aleida refused to publish the three dark stories Che wrote, arguing that they were too intimate to be shared with the public. She finally relented, however, and two of them, "La Duda" (Doubt), and "La Piedra" (The Stone), appeared. "La Duda" is an undated meditation on the Congolese belief in *dawa*, or witchcraft. "La Piedra" is also undated but was clearly written after Osmany Cienfuegos gave Che the news that Celia was dying. "He told me as one would speak to a strong man, to someone in authority," the story begins, "and I thanked him. He didn't feign anguish and I tried not to show it either. It was so easy. The confirmation had yet to arrive that would allow me to be officially sad. I asked myself if I could cry a little. No, I shouldn't, because the *jefe* is supposed to be impersonal; it is not that he should not be allowed the right to feel, but that he shouldn't show it, except, maybe, on behalf of his soldiers."

The rest of the story revolves around the small, indispensable things Che always took with him: his pipe for smoking tobacco, his lighter, his notebook and pens, his asthma inhaler. The title has to do with a little stone attached to a key chain that his mother had given him. The stone had become separated from the chain and Che carried it in his pocket. He also speaks about a linen handkerchief that Aleida had given him before he left home. "She gave it to me in case I was wounded in the arm," he wrote. "It would be a loving sling." Then he speculates about what might happen if something more drastic occurred—if his head was split open and he was killed. He imagines the handkerchief tied around his jaw. He muses that "they might exhibit me, and maybe I would appear in *Life* with a look of agony and desperation, frozen at the moment of maximum terror. Because one feels it. Why lie about it?"

Chapter 27, page 633: In unpublished notes dated November 21, 1965, from the diary of Harry "Pombo" Villegas Tamayo, sections of which I obtained in Cuba, Villegas wrote about problems that Che omitted in his own account.

"After making the decision to retreat from that place and return to the neighboring country of Tanzania, open discrepancies began to appear between Tatu [Che] and the other high-ranking leaders of the Party who had been designated to collaborate with him in the exercise of such a difficult duty (Tembo, Siki, Uta, Karim).

"The fundamental root of the aforementioned divergences lies in the attitude of the *compañeros* toward the reality in which we found ourselves, their poor comprehension of the attitude taken by Tatu in the face of the situation on the ground, due to the fact that [they] . . . didn't trust him as a national leader of our revolution and as a leader of our detachment designated to fight in those distant lands.

"They felt that Tatu was being willful in his determination to stay there, and that he hadn't been able to appreciate the fact that the subjective conditions didn't exist to carry out the revolution; that even if the insurrection were to win, the [Congolese] revolution did not have leaders to take it forward because they were all pseudo-revolutionaries, without principles, and it could even be said that they had few morals.

"But the reality is that Tatu was aware of this, aware about the impossibility of carrying out a social revolution; it was something he had told all of us, except for Siki [Fernández Mell] and Tembo [Aragonés], who weren't present because they were at the base, where it wasn't sent." (Pombo was referring to Che's August 12 "Message to the Combatants.")

"I personally said that his position of sacrifice was due to his conviction that the withdrawal of the Cubans should be a decision that should come from the Cuban government . . . [and] that we should never [beg or] shout asking to be authorized to withdraw. . . ."

Chapter 28, page 638: When Pombo joined Che in the Congo, he left behind a bride of less than three years; they had an infant son, Harry Jr. His wife, Cristina Campuzano, had been Che's secretary early on at the Industrialization Department of INRA. She was a friend of both Hilda Gadea and Aleida. The families of Che's men were extremely close in those days. Tuma had been the best man at the wedding of Pombo and Cristina.

It was "terribly hard" for the wives, Cristina said, because they rarely saw their husbands. "When they were in Cuba they were up at all hours with Che, then they went to the Congo, then Bolivia." The families were "withdrawn" from circulation for security reasons when the men were on a mission with Che. A group of them lived in a semi-communal apartment building in Miramar. At one point, Cristina was to have joined Pombo and was given a *leyenda*—a false identity—to study so she could join him. At the time, she says, Pombo was living in seclusion in the Cuban embassy in Paris.

After Pombo's departure to Bolivia, Cristina was told that she could go there when "the conditions were right." Pombo had argued that their son, Harry, was too young to be left, and that she should not come until the "ground was secured."

Papi also left behind a wife and young son. Only Tuma was childless, but after returning to Cuba from Prague, he impregnated his wife; their son, whom he would never know, was born after he left for Bolivia.

Chapter 28, page 642: Since there has been no extensively documented Cuban clarification of Che's exact movements, meetings, and whereabouts between the time he left the Congo and reappeared in Cuba, I based my account on the most credible sources available to me: Aleida March; General Harry Villegas (Pombo); Manuel "Barbarroja" Piñeiro; Juan Carreterro, the senior Cuban intelligence official and diplomat, alias Ariel; and Oscar de Cárdenas, who was Ulíses Estrada's deputy in charge of the African department of Cuban intelligence at the time Che left the Congo. All of them said that Che went from Tanzania to Prague, and from there back to Havana.

But there are other versions. Mario Monje, the former Bolivian Communist Party secretary, told me that he had learned, without naming his sources of information, that Che, after leaving Tanzania, went to the German Democratic Republic, where he lived "under the protection of the German intelligence services." A knowledgeable Cuban source indicated the possibility that Che did spend "some time" in the GDR during his underground period, but that this followed his secret return trip to Cuba, while he was en route to Bolivia in the fall of 1966. This source also added that Aleida "may" have visited him there. Bolstering the possibility of Che's presence in the GDR is the circumstantial evidence that Che himself provided upon his capture. The first of his two Bolivian diaries, which he began writing in during November 1966, was manufactured in East Germany. Aleida March told me that she had joined Che abroad, clandestinely, on three separate occasions. The first, in January–February 1966, in Tanzania; the second time, in Prague, before his return to Cuba in mid-1966; and a third time that she did not specify. In her memoir, *Evocación*, she mentions two times: the Tanzanian and Prague visits.

Added to the rather complex mosaic of chronologies is the account provided by Che's "official" Cuban biographers, former Ministry of Interior agent Froilán González and his wife, Adys Cupull, who were given access by the Interior Ministry to false passports that were allegedly used by Che to travel following his disappearance from public view in April 1965. According to them, Che left Tanzania on December 28, 1965, for an unspecified country in Eastern Europe and stayed there until July 14, 1966, when he traveled to Prague; between July 19 and 20 he traveled from Prague to Vienna, Geneva, Zurich, and Moscow, and then he immediately left for Havana.

But Ariel, Manuel Piñeiro's deputy, told me that "the various passports held by Cuban intelligence with different stamps on them showing different countries don't mean anything. Various *leyendas* would have been prepared for him, and the stamps applied by us, here in Cuba." Ariel also said that at the time Che left for Prague from Tanzania, Ariel was personally involved in spreading "disinformation" about him so as to confuse Western intelligence agencies and help throw them off his scent.

Manuel Piñeiro confirmed that Che did not stay rooted in Prague. At one point, he acknowledged, Che took a trip to Paris, to put his latest *leyenda* through a test.

Chapter 28, page 649: According to my sources in Cuba, Régis Debray, like Tania, was part of the intelligence network run by Barbarroja Piñeiro. He was handled directly by Ulíses Estrada and by Juan Carretero—Ariel—who implemented Cuba's guerrilla programs. These sources said that Debray's involvement in the program began when he came to Havana as a graduate student in philosophy in 1961. His public cover for his trip to Bolivia, as a French journalist, was both genuine and useful, for he did write about Latin America for the French publisher Maspéro. But he was also an underground courier for Barbarroja. It is said that Debray was regarded as useful by the Cubans in this latter capacity—as a propagandist and courier for the cause—rather than as a theorist and ally at the command level.

Chapter 29, page 669: "Che was not in command of the situation into which he was inserted," a Cuban government source acknowledged, speaking of the Bolivian expedition. "It was the Department of the Americas [the name later chosen for Piñeiro's restructured Liberation Department] that studied the conditions for revolution in other countries and made the recommendations to Fidel."

Piñeiro's people seem to have overplayed their hand in assuring Fidel that the conditions were right for Che to come to Bolivia. People close to Che in Cuba still privately blame Piñeiro and his men for "fucking things up." Few suggest that there was a betrayal, but rather shoddy work and *guaperia*—a Cuban term meaning bully-boy arrogance—that brought about the chain of multiple errors that characterized the Bolivian operation.

Chapter 29, page 686: Arguedas's name came up at a meeting in La Paz between Pombo, Papi, and Mario Monje on the night of August 8, 1966. In Pombo's published diary, he recorded the meeting and Monje's boast of having key allies placed inside Bolivia's government but omitted their names for security reasons. In some unpublished notes, however, Pombo scribbled, "He spoke to us of Arguedas who had been named minister [of Interior]. . . . He explained that, as a member, he [Arguedas] had been authorized to occupy said post by the [Bolivian Communist] Party, that he was situated in a key post, [to which] we expressed our worries over the method applied and our belief that it was a double-edged sword. He stressed that [Arguedas] was a colleague who was easy to dominate (but he was very wrong)."

Chapter 29, page 688: In July 1997, Gustavo Villoldo Sampera—who had previously not come forth in public—told me that the CIA had additional intelligence sources in Bolivia, most importantly an informant who was an active member of the Bolivian Communist Party. Villoldo would not disclose the identity of the traitor, whom he described as "someone close to the Peredo brothers." He said this person was still alive. Villoldo also said that Mario Monje informed regularly to Colonel Roberto Quintanilla, the intelligence chief at Antonio Arguedas's Interior Ministry. He said that Quintanilla passed Monje's information along to the CIA.

As for Bustos and Debray, Villoldo said that both men broke down during their first days in captivity and told what they knew. He added that anyone would have done the same thing in their situation. He said that they were threatened with death and were in fact going to be killed by the Bolivian military, but that he and his CIA colleagues saved them in order to obtain their information.

Chapter 29, page 689: Most of the survivors of the Bolivian episode agree that withdrawing Renán from La Paz was an error. Why was he pulled out at such a crucial moment? Piñeiro said it was to renew his documentation, and run a check on his cover identity. But Loyola Guzmán, who met with Renán several times in 1967, got the distinct impression in her last rendezvous with him that he was "running scared," that he was afraid of being caught. Ariel said that Renán was "extremely ill." They were preparing another man to replace him, Ariel said, but events in Bolivia disrupted that plan. By the time the other agent was ready to go, it was too late. But Guzmán was puzzled. She sent two letters by couriers to Havana, stressing the urgent need for a substitute for Renán; and later, after Che's diary was captured and published, she found that the messages had arrived, because in August he wrote that he had received a coded message from Havana essentially retransmitting her remarks, and advising him that a replacement was on his way. "How is it possible that they could get my letter, retransmit it to Che, and still take no action?" she asked.

By late August, Guzmán and her companions in the city had resolved that she would go to Havana to explain the urgency of their situation. First, she followed up a message that the Party was reconsidering its position and was willing to meet her in the city of Cochabamba. Before setting out, she began to feel that she was being followed. She told Humberto Vázquez-

Viaña, who ran a test to see if her suspicions were true. She spent a day moving around the city, getting on and off buses, with Humberto following at a discreet distance, watching. At the end of the day, he confirmed it. She was being followed.

A couple of days later, she was arrested.

Responding to the accusations thrown in the direction of him and his agents, Piñeiro was adamant that Che's survival and ultimate success had been their main concern. He rejected as "repugnant" any suggestions to the contrary.

Chapter 29, page 690: In the spring of 1967, Régis Debray had smuggled out word about Che's situation to Cuba's secret services via his Venezuelan girl-friend, Elizabeth Burgos, who was allowed to visit Debray in jail in Camiri. Ciro Bustos also asked his wife, Ana María, to get word to Havana that Che desperately needed new radio equipment and added his recommendation that a second guerrilla *foco* be started so as to distract attention away from Che. Ana María wrote a letter, but, owing to a number of problems, it did not reach Havana until the eve of Che's capture. In September 1967, Bustos's friend Hector Schmucler was asked by Cuban intelligence agents in Paris to travel to Argentina, and then to Bolivia, to find out what he could about Che's situation. Schmucler said he got the impression that the Cubans were very worried. He agreed to go, but by the time he arrived in Argentina in early October, it was already too late. (Schmucler studied semiotics with Roland Barthes in Paris, and in the 1970s he was a cofounder, with Ariel Dorfman, of the Chilean journal *Communicacíon y cultura.* He went on to have a long and distinguished academic career. His son, Pablo, who was a Montonero guerrilla, disappeared in Argentina in 1977. In 2005, when Schmucler was still teaching at the University of Córdoba, he and his old friend Oscar del Barco had a public exchange of letters in which they repudiated the violence they had endorsed when they were young.)

Chapter 29, page 699: Among some of his friends and associates in Cuba, it is acknowledged off the record that Che's Bolivian operation was a catastrophe from beginning to end. They point out that Che never had the support of the peasants in Bolivia; that the Cuban and Bolivian guerrillas never established good rapport; and that Che, older and weaker than his tougher former sierra self, was loath to act against the slackers in his ranks. "This humanity cost him in the end," one Cuban official said. "A lesser man would have carried out some executions, but Che didn't; he didn't want to scare people off; he wanted to get people to join him, and he knew he was, after all, a foreigner."

Manuel Piñeiro defended Che's efforts in Bolivia and the Congo, calling them "heroic exploits" and quoting Fidel on the issue of whether or not

Che's final battles were failures: "I always say that triumph or failure does not determine the correctness of a policy."

Chapter 29, page 705: In my rendition of their encounter, I used extracts from Selich's notes from his talk with Che. The following exchange was not included:

> Selich: What do you believe is the reason for your failure? I think it was the lack of support of the peasants.

> Che: There may be something of truth [in that], but the truth is that it is due to the effective organization of Barrientos's political party, that is to say, his *corregidores* and political mayors, who took charge of warning the army about our movements.

Selich's notes end, inexplicably, with an unanswered question he posed to Che: "Why didn't you manage to recruit more national [Bolivian] elements, such as the peasants of the zone?"

Epilogue, page 726: Che's ghost periodically reappeared in the unreconciled conflicts that persisted after his death. In December 1996, the seizure of hostages in the Japanese embassy in Lima, Peru, by a "Guevarist" guerrilla group, the Movimiento Revolucionario Tupác Amaru, focused the attention of the world on a previously obscure cause and rattled the confidence of a regime that had thought of itself as secure. Only a few weeks earlier, far away in Africa, with regional tensions rising from the presence of several million Rwandan Hutu refugees and the armed militias hiding in their midst in eastern Zaire, a previously unknown Zairean rebel movement made a spectacular appearance, forcing the refugees back into Rwanda, seizing Zairean towns, and putting the Hutu militias on the run. The man leading the rebellion soon made his appearance. It was Laurent Kabila, the rebel leader whom Che had unsuccessfully tried to assist in the Congo three decades earlier. In an extraordinary comeback, Kabila emerged from obscurity to raise the battle standard once again. By May 1997, after a stunningly rapid military campaign, he had overthrown Mobutu's thirty-one-year-old dictatorship, assumed power himself, and renamed the country the People's Democratic Republic of the Congo. Kabila had shown himself to be a canny survivor, but he proved to be little better than his corrupt predecessor. He soon plunged his country into a war that cost the lives of more than 4 million people. Kabila was assassinated in 2001 by one of his own bodyguards, but that, sadly, did not end Congo's bloodletting. It was a reminder that some of the battles that had begun while Che was alive had no resolution.

Sources

Part One: Unquiet Youth

Field Research and Interviews

To research Che's childhood and family history, I spent three months in Argentina in 1994, much of the time traveling in the company of Che's friend Alberto Granado. Roberto and Celia Guevara were extremely helpful with clarifications of the family history, as well as in their personal reflections on their brother. Julia Constenla de Giussani, a friend of Che's mother, provided me with the account of Che's birthdate. Ana María Erra, Ernesto Guevara Lynch's second wife, also helped with details of Guevara family history.

Alberto Granado and I traveled together to Misiones and found the Guevaras' old Puerto Caraguataí homestead. We interviewed a number of people who remembered Che's parents, including Gertrudis Kraft and Johann Fahraven; others who helped with local history were Emiliano Rejala, Dr. Oscar Darú, and Leonor and Epifanio Acosta.

With Alberto Granado and "Calica" Ferrer, I traveled to Alta Gracia and Córdoba; Carlos Figueroa let us stay in his old family house on Calle Avellaneda in Alta Gracia, just down the street from the Guevaras' former homes, Villa Chichita and Villa Nydia. I was able to gain a privileged glimpse into the past as these men reminisced and took me to meet Guevara's other childhood friends and acquaintances. They included Rodolfo Ruarte, Sarah Muñoz, Enrique Martín, Paco Fernández, Carlos Barceló, Mario and Chicho Salduna, Blanca de Alboñoroz, Juan and Nelly Bustos, José Manuel Peña, Alberto Ferrer, and Ofelia Moyano. I also met Rosario López, the Guevaras' former housekeeper; and Elba Rossi, Ernesto's third-grade school-teacher at the Escuela Liniers.

In Córdoba and Buenos Aires, I interviewed a number of Che's school-
mates at Dean Funes, among them Raúl Melivosky, Oscar Stemmelin,
Roberto "Beto" Ahumada, Osvaldo Bidinost, Carlos López Villagra, Jorge
Iskaro, and José María Roque. Among his teenage acquaintances were
Miriam Urrutia, Nora Feigin, Betty Feigin (the widow of Gustavo Roca),
Tatiana Quiroga de Roca, Jaime "Jimmy" Roca, Carlos Lino, and "Chacho"
Ferrer. In Spain, I interviewed Carmen González-Aguilar and her brother
"Pepe." In Cuba, Fernando Barral gave me his own reminiscences. Chichina
Ferreyra and I exchanged e-mails in 2009.

In Rosario, Alberto Granado and I were assisted by the journalist
Reynaldo Sietecase of *Pagina 12*, a Che aficionado, and together we ex-
plored the city where Che spent his first month of life. Granado's cousin
Naty López recalled for us the day long ago when, as "Mial" and "Fuser,"
Alberto and Che had roared through town on "La Poderosa," on their
"escape to the north."

For Che's years in Buenos Aires and on the road, I talked with Ricardo
Rojo, Carlos Infante, Dr. Emilio Levine, Fernando Chávez, Adalberto Ben-
Golea, Nelly Benbibre de Castro, Andro Herrero, Anita García (Gualo
García's widow), and Mario Saravia. Alberto Granado and Calica Ferrer
shared with me their memories of the trips they took with Ernesto.

For Che's Guatemalan and Mexican periods, I was assisted greatly by
the journalist Phil Gunson, who arranged all of my interviews and con-
ducted a number of them on my behalf. Those interviewed included Ricardo
Romero, Edelberto Torres Jr., Antonio del Conde ("El Cuate"), Yuri
Paporov, Alfonso Bauer Paiz, Fernando Gutiérrez Barrios, Dr. David
Mitrani, Dr. José Montes Montes, Dr. Baltazar Rodríquez, and others. I
interviewed Nikolai Leonov in Moscow on three separate occasions in 1994.
Myrna Torres also helped me with details of Che's life in Guatemala.

Material Sources

For Che's childhood and youth I referred to *Mi Hijo el Che,* the memoir written by Che's father, Ernesto Guevara Lynch. The extracts from Che's account
of his first trip around Argentina, in 1950, are taken from this book. The translation is mine. The short story "Angustia," which Che wrote while he was at
sea in 1951, was published in the Argentine newspaper *Primer Plano* in 1992.

For Che's travels with Alberto Granado in 1951–1952, I referred to
Granado's book *En Viaje con el Che por Sudamerica,* and Che's own *Notas de
Viaje,* which was published in English as *The Motorcycle Diaries,* first by
Verso in 1995 and then by Ocean Press in 2004. I made extensive use of
Ernestito, Vivo y Presente, the book of oral testimony encompassing Che's life
from 1928 to 1953, compiled by the Cuban Guevara historians Froilán

González and Adys Cupull. Their chronology of Che's life, *Un Hombre Bravo,* was a useful reference for this and subsequent periods. Also, *El Che y los Argentinos,* by Claudia Korol, and *Testimonios Sobre el Che,* edited by Mírta Rodríguez. Quotations by Dolores Moyano are taken from an article she wrote for *The New York Times Magazine* in 1968.

Che's widow, Aleida March, shared with me the full collection of Che's "Diccionario Filosófico," reflecting his reading in philosophy, religion, mythology, and psychology between the ages of seventeen and twenty-eight; and the "Indice Literario," his reading list covering the same period.

For Che's life from mid-1953, when he left Argentina, through to his meeting in Mexico with Fidel Castro, I based much of my narrative on his diary, "Otra Vez," which had not been published when I was working on this book but which was provided to me by Aleida March. The translations here are mine. After my book appeared, Aleida March authorized the publication of the journal under its original title. In 2001, an English-language translation, *Back on the Road*, was published together with a selection of Che's letters home. In 2005, Calica Ferrer published his own version of the trip, *De Ernesto al Che: El Segundo y Ultimo Viaje de Guevara por America Latina.* It has since been published in English as *Becoming Che.* Fernando Barral gave me an original manuscript of *Aquí Va un Soldado de las Americas,* Che's letters home compiled by his father in book form. The manuscript contained letters not included in the published version.

Calica Ferrer gave me copies of his letters written home while he was traveling with Che in 1953. Anita de García also shared her late husband "Gualo" García's letters, and Andro Herrero gave me excerpts from his own diary, as well as letters he received from Che, Gualo García, Oscar Valdovinos, and Ricardo Rojo after they left him in Guayaquil and traveled north to Guatemala.

I was able to review original materials covering Che's life from his infancy to his Mexico City period—including some previously unpublished family letters and early writings—at Cuba's Council of State Historical Archives, with permission from its director, Pedro Álvarez Tabío. Heberto Norman Acosta, a specialist in the pre-*Granma* "exile" period of the July 26 Movement, allowed me to review Che's censored testimony from his interrogation by the Mexican police and other materials. Lionel Martin lent me the late Harold White's copy of the Marxist anthology that the young Ernesto Guevara helped him translate in Guatemala.

I employed Hilda Gadea's book *Ernesto: A Memoir of Che Guevara* for her account of their relationship, which includes a number of short memoirs by others, including Myrna Torres, Harold White, Lucila Velásquez, Juan Juarbe y Juarbe, and Laura Meneses de Albizu Campos.

Che's *Reminiscences of the Cuban Revolutionary War* refers to his time on the road in Mexico and Guatemala as well. On October 17, 1967, Cuba's official Communist Party newspaper, *Granma*, dedicated a special edition to Che, and I drew a number of quotations from this publication, including the recollections of Mario Dalmau and others. The Cuban house of culture, Casa de las Americas, also published a number of special editions devoted to Che; the quotations from Alfonso Bauer Paiz, referring to the Guatemala-Mexico period, are taken from them. Phil Gunson obtained articles published in 1956–1957 on the Cuban revolutionaries from Mexican press archives of that period.

Tad Szulc's biography, *Fidel: A Critical Portrait,* and Hugh Thomas's *Cuba: The Pursuit of Freedom* were invaluable resources for this period. Lionel Martin provided me with a treasure trove of index cards from his personal archive including quotations from many primary interviews he conducted in the 1960s, when he was planning to write a biography of Che Guevara.

Part Two: Becoming Che

Field Research and Interviews

In Cuba I interviewed a number of people who fought with Che in the Sierra Maestra, among them Harry Villegas ("Pombo"), Ricardo Martínez, Jorge Enrique Mendoza, Dariel Alarcón Ramírez ("Benigno"), and Oscar Fernández Mell.

Aleida March, Lolita Rossell, Miguel Ángel Duque de Estrada, and Orlando Borrego also gave details of Che's Escambray period, the battle for Santa Clara, and the drive on Havana.

Material Sources

I based most of my narrative for Part Two on Che's then-unpublished "Diario de un Combatiente," his private journal from 1957 to 1959. A typescript copy of the manuscript was provided to me by Aleida March, who said that the only other copy then in existence belonged to Fidel. At that time, the diary was being sanitized, with a view toward its eventual publication in Cuba. That is, the names of certain Cuban government officials who were mentioned critically, or antagonistically, were being removed. The journal encompassed almost the entire span of the two-year Cuban guerrilla war, but in the middle, an eight-month period was inexplicably missing. The first section of the text given to me began on December 2, 1956, and ended on August 12, 1957. The middle section (August 13, 1957, to April 17, 1958) was missing; the second section ran from April 18, 1958, through December 3, 1959, one month before the war's end. For information on the missing months, I relied on interviews and other published material, including Guevara's own writings dealing with the relevant periods. I used his published account of the war, *Pasajes de la Guerra Revolucionaria*, in both the English- and the Spanish-language editions. An English-language version had been published in 1968 as *Reminiscences of the Cuban Revolutionary War* and then in 1996 as *Episodes of the Cuban Revolutionary War*. The Che Guevara Studies Center in Havana announced that it would publish the full journal as *Diarios de la Sierra*.

Hugh Thomas's *Cuba*, Tad Szulc's *Fidel: A Critical Portrait*, Lionel Martin's *The Early Fidel*, Carlos Franqui's *Diary of the Cuban Revolution*, and Robert Quirk's *Fidel Castro* were all invaluable reference tools that I used extensively. I also used Jorge Ricardo Masetti's *Los Que Luchan y Los Que Lloran*, Robert Taber's *M-26: Biography of Revolution*, Herbert Matthews's *The Cuba Story*, and Heinz Dieterich's *Diarios Inéditos de la Guerrilla Cubana*. For the rebels' internal correspondence and Che's letters written in this period, I relied upon Franqui's *Diary*, Guevara Lynch's *Mi Hijo el Che*, and the Casa de las Americas commemorative compilation of Cuban army and July 26 reports, memos, and cables. I also made use of *Descamisado* by Enrique Acevedo, and the Cuban *comandante* Juan Almeida's own series of autobiographical books on the sierra war.

The Cuban historian Andrés Castillo Bernal provided me with his extensively researched unpublished manuscript on the war, and I also drew from the Cuban oral histories *Ellos Lucharon con el Che, Los Doce, Testimonios Sobre el Che,* and *Entre Nostoros*.

Part Three: Making the New Man

Field Research and Interviews

I interviewed Orlando Borrego, Alfredo Menéndez, and Oscar Fernández Mell for the post-triumph La Cabaña period and the early revolutionary period. Aleida March, Alberto Castellanos, Enrique Viltres, Colonel Ricardo Martínez, and Nicolás Quintana also shed light on this time.

Doctor Salvador Vilaseca and Alfredo Menéndez both shared their accounts of Che's 1959 trip to the nonaligned countries. For Che's work at the National Bank, the Ministry of Industries, and the Central Planning Board, I was helped by Aleida March, Orlando Borrego, Dr. Salvador Vilaseca, Regino Boti, Nicolás Quintana, Nestor Laverne, Tirso Saenz, Juan Gravalosa, Cristina Campuzano, Ángel Arcos Vergnes, and others who gave me insiders' accounts. For Che's 1961 trip to Punta del Este, Julia Constenla, Ricardo Rojo, Roberto Guevara, and Carlos Figueroa shared their recollections.

In three visits to Moscow, I interviewed a number of former Soviet officials who spoke about the relationship between Cuba and the Soviet

Union and Che's dealings with Moscow. Che's role in forging Cuba's links
with the Soviet Union was explained to me in depth by Alexandr Alexiev,
Giorgi Kornienko, Sergo Mikoyan, Nikolai Leonov, and Yuri Paporov,
among others.

I conducted other interviews with Yuri Pevtsov, Vladimir Bondarchuk,
Timur Gaidar, Feder Burlatksy, Nikolai Metutsov, Kiva Maidanek, Yuri
Krasin, Yvgeny Kosarev, Marat Muknachov, Vitali Korionov, Rudolf
Shlyapnikov, and the former Soviet generals Gribkov and Garbus.

The most comprehensive accounts of Che's life in all its facets, both
public and private, during his time in Cuba, came from his widow, Aleida
March, and his friend Orlando Borrego. Other details came from Lolita
Rossell, Sofia Gato, and Che's daughters Hilda Guevara and Aliusha
Guevara; and from Alberto Granado, Fernando Barral, Pepe Aguilar, Harry
Villegas, and Alberto Castellanos. For his relationship with his family in
Argentina, Aleida March, Ana María Erra, and María Elena Duarte were
especially valuable sources.

To document Che's guerrilla activities, I interviewed people in Mos-
cow, Havana, Argentina, Paraguay, Bolivia, Spain, and Sweden. They in-
cluded Aleida March, Orlando Borrego, Manuel Piñeiro, Juan Carreterro
("Ariel"), Osvaldo de Cárdenas, Regino Boti, General Harry Villegas
("Pombo"), Dariel Alarcón Ramírez ("Benigno"), Alberto Castellanos,
Ricardo Gadea, Rodolfo Saldaña, Ciro Roberto Bustos, Héctor Jouve, Henry
Lerner, Alberto Granado, Oscar del Barco, Hector Schmucler, Alberto
Coría, Alberto Korn, Nestor Laverne, Loyola Guzmán, Marlene Lorjiovaca,
Humberto Vázquez-Viaña, Ana Urquieta, Chato Peredo, Antonio Peredo,
José Castillo ("Paco"), Oscar Zalas, Jorge Kolle Cueto, Simón Reyes, Juan
Lechín, Gustavo Sánchez, and others. I interviewed Mario Monje on two
separate occasions in Moscow.

Among Che's enemies, I met with the former CIA agents Felix
Rodríguez and Gustavo Villoldo; former Bolivian generals Reque Terán,
Gary Prado Salmon, and Mario Vargas Salinas; ex-sergeant Mario Terán;
and the former Bolivian army majors Rubén Sánchez and Miguel Ayoroa.
The former CIA station chief in La Paz, John Tilton, spoke to me by tele-
phone from his home in Georgia. In Asunción, Paraguay, the widow of
Colonel Andrés Selich, Socorro Selich, provided me with her account of her
late husband's activities in the campaign against Che.

Material Sources

A great many books have been written on the Cuban revolution, and I had
access to most of them. Among those I found most useful were Hugh
Thomas's *Cuba,* Tad Szulc's *Fidel: A Critical Portrait,* Richard Gott's *Rural*

Guerrillas in Latin America, Carlos Franqui's *Diary of the Cuban Revolution* and his *Family Portrait of Fidel,* Robert Quirk's *Fidel Castro,* K. S. Karol's *Guerrillas in Power,* and Maurice Halperin's *The Taming of Fidel Castro.* I also used Hilda Gadea's *Ernesto: A Memoir of Che Guevara,* Ricardo Rojo's *My Friend Che,* Ernesto Guevara Lynch's *Mi Hijo el Che,* and José Pardo Llada's, *El "Che" Que Yo Conoci.*

Other resources were Régis Debray's *Revolution in the Revolution?* and his *Castroism: The Long March in Latin America* and *La Guerrilla del Che en Bolivia.* Also, *El Che y los Argentinos* by Claudia Korol; *Tania: Misión Guerrillera en Bolivia* by Marta Rojas and Mírta Rodríguez; Simone de Beauvoir's memoir *All Said and Done; A Thousand Days* by Arthur Schlesinger Jr.; Che's own *Diario del Che en Bolivia;* the seven-volume set of Che's collected works edited by Orlando Borrego, *El Che en La Revolución Cubana;* Casa de las Americas' two-volume selected works, *El Che Guevara: Obras 1957–1967;* Gianni Miná's *An Encounter with Fidel;* Harry Villegas's memoir, *Un Hombre de la Guerrilla del Che,* and Humberto Vásquez-Viaña's monograph, *Antecedentes de la Guerrilla del Che en Bolivia;* the five-volume collection of documents and interviews *El Che en Bolivia,* edited by Carlos Soria Galvarro. Paco Ignacio Taibo II, Felix Guerra, and Froilan Escobar's book, *El Año Que Estuvimos en Ninguna Parte,* is the first to be written on Che's time in the Congo. Gary Prado's *La Guerrilla Immolada,* General Arnaldo Saucedo Parada's *No Disparen Soy el Che,* and General Reque Terán's *La Campaña de Ñancahuazú* were insightful accounts of the Bolivian military's view of Che's campaign in Bolivia, as was Richard Dindo's extensively researched documentary *The Diary of Che in Bolivia.*

In addition to interviews and published sources, I had access to a good deal of previously unpublished documentation, including a review of Che's critique of the Soviet Manual of Political Economy, his "Notas Económicas"; unexpurgated sections of Pombo's 1966–1967 Prague-Bolivia diary; Inti Peredo's original draft manuscript for his book *Mi Campaña Junto al Che,* written in Cuba following his escape from Bolivia; interrogation transcripts, photographs, and army propaganda from the archives of General Reque Terán; and assorted documents and photographs from the personal archive of the late Colonel Andrés Selich, including his field log during the 1967 antiguerrilla campaign, his question-and-answer session with the captured Che Guevara, and his private report on the capture and execution of Che Guevara to the Bolivian general David La Fuente.

Selected Bibliography

Since this book was first published, in 1997, a vast amount of new material has been published on Che, and more of Che's own writing has come to light. Most significantly, some of the unpublished material that I was given access to by Che's widow, Aleida March, has since been published—although often in expurgated form—in Spanish and sometimes in English as well. This includes Che's diary, *Otra Vez*, detailing his movements from the time he left Argentina in 1953 until his meeting with Fidel Castro in Mexico in 1956; his Congo journal; and his polemical critique of the Soviet manual on political economy. No doubt the outpouring of work on Che will continue. This bibliography is not intended, therefore, to be exhaustive or definitive. It includes the works cited in the first edition of my book plus new translations, new editions, and new books that seem to me to have some special significance or interest.

By and about Ernesto Che Guevara

Adams, Jerome R. *Latin American Heroes*. New York: Ballantine, 1991.

Alexandre, Marianne, ed. *Viva Che*. London: Lorrimer, Third World Series, 1968.

Álvarez Batista, Gerónimo. *Che: Una Nueva Batalla*. La Habana: Pablo de la Torriente, 1994.

Anderson, Jon Lee. "Bones Now Seem to Prove That Che Is Dead." *The New York Times*, July 5, 1997.

———. "Where Is Che Guevara Buried? A Bolivian Tells." *The New York Times,* November 21, 1995.

Ariet, María del Carmen. *Che: Pensamiento Político*. La Habana: Editora Política, 1993.

———. *El Pensamiento del Che*. La Habana: Editorial Capitán San Luis, 1992.

Borrego, Orlando. *Che: el camino del fuego*. La Habana, Cuba: Ediciones Imagen Contemporanea, 2001.

———. *Che, recuerdos en rafaga*. La Habana, Cuba: Ciencias Sociales, 2004.

Bourne, Richard. *Political Leaders of Latin America*. London: Pelican, 1969.

Bruschtein, Luis. *Che Guevara: Los Hombres de la Historia*. (Magazine supplement.) Buenos Aires: Pagina 12, Centro Editor de America Latina, 1994.

Bustos, Ciro. *El Che quiere verte: La historia jamas contada del Che*. Buenos Aires, Argentina: Vergara Grupo Zeta, 2007.

Candía, Gen. Alfredo G. *La Muerte del Che Guevara*. La Paz, Bolivia: La Liga Anticomunista de los Pueblos Asiaticos, Republica de China, 1971.

Casey, Michael. *Che's Afterlife: The Legacy of an Image*. New York: Vintage, 2009.

Castro, Fidel. *Che: A Memoir by Fidel Castro*. Melbourne, Australia: Ocean Press, 1994.

Centro de Estudios Sobre America. *Pensar al Che,* Tomo I and 2. La Habana: Editorial José Martí, 1989.

"Che." La Habana: Casa de Las Americas No. 43 (January–February 1968).

"Che": Edición Especial de *Moncada*. La Habana: Ministerio del Interior, October 6, 1987.

Constenla, Julia. *Celia, la madre del Che*. Buenos Aires, Argentina: Editorial Sudamericana, 2004.

Cupull, Adys, and Froilán González. *Cálida Presencia: Su Amistad con Tita Infante*. Santiago de Cuba: Editorial Oriente, 1995.

———. *Canto inconcluso: Una vida dedicada al Che*. La Habana: Editora Politica, 1998.

———. *La CIA contra El Che*. La Habana: Editora Política, 1992.

———. *El Diario del Che en Bolivia*. La Habana: Editora Política, 1988.

———. *Entre Nosotros*. La Habana: Ediciones Abril, 1992.

———. *Ernestito: Vivo y Presente*. La Habana: Editora Política, 1989.

———. *Un Hombre Bravo*. La Habana: Editorial Capitán San Luis, 1995.

———. *De Ñancahuazú a La Higuera*. La Habana: Editora Política, 1989.

Debray, Régis. *La Guerrilla de Che*. Barcelona: Siglo Veintiun Editores, 1975 (orig. Paris: Maspéro, 1974).

Deutschmann, David, ed. *Che Guevara Reader*. Melbourne, Australia, and New York: Ocean Press, 2003.

Elizundia, Alicia. *Bajo la Piel del Che*. La Habana, Cuba: Ediciones la Memoria, Centro Cultural Pablo de la Torriente Brau, 2005.

Escobar, Froilán, and Félix Guerra. *Che: Sierra Adentro.* La Habana: Editora Política, 1988.

Espinosa Goitizolo, Reinaldo, and Guillermo Grau Guardarrama. *Atlas Ernesto Che Guevara: Historicó Biográfico y Militar.* La Habana: Editorial Pueblo y Educación, Ministerio de las Fuerzas Armadas Revolucionarias, 1991.

Estrada, Ulises. *Tania la Guerrillera.* Melbourne, Australia, and New York: Ocean Press, 2005.

———. *Tania: Undercover with Che Guevara in Bolivia.* Melbourne, Australia, and New York: Ocean Press, 2005.

Ferrer, Carlos "Calica." *De Ernesto al Che: El segundo y ultimo viaje de Guevara por Latinoamerica.* Buenos Aires, Argentina: Marea Editorial, 2005.

Gadea, Hilda. *Ernesto: A Memoir of Che Guevara: An Intimate Account of the Making of a Revolutionary by His First Wife, Hilda Gadea.* London and New York: W. H. Allen, 1973.

Galvarro, Carlos Soria. *El Che en Bolivia: Documentos y Testimonios,* Vols. 1–5. La Paz, Bolivia: CEDOIN Colección Historia y Documento, 1994–1996.

Gambini, Hugo. *El Che Guevara: La Biografía.* Buenos Aires: Grupo Planeta, 1968, rev. ed., 1996.

Garcés, María. *Materiales sobre la Guerrilla de Ñancahuazú: La Campaña del Che en Bolivia (1967) Atravéz del la Prensa.* Quito, Ecuador: Editorial La Mañana, 1987.

García Carranza, Araceli, and Joseph García Carranza, eds. *Bibliografía Cubana del Comandante Ernesto Che Guevara.* La Habana: Ministerio de Cultura Biblioteca Nacional José Martí. Dept. de Investigaciónes Bibliográficas, 1987.

González, Luis J., and Gustavo A. Sánchez Salazár. *The Great Rebel: Che Guevara in Bolivia.* New York: Grove, 1969.

Granado, Alberto. *Con el Che Guevara de Córdoba a la Habana.* Córdoba, Argentina: Opoloop Ediciones, 1995.

———. *Con el Che por Sudamerica.* La Habana: Editorial Letras Cubanas, 1980.

———. *Traveling with Che Guevara: The Making of a Revolutionary,* trans. Lucía Alvarez de Toledo. New York: Newmarket, 2004.

Granma: Edición Especial. "Dolorosamente Cierta La Muerte del Comandante Ernesto Guevara." La Habana: Comité Central del Partido Comunista de Cuba, October 17, 1967.

Guevara, Ernesto Che. *The African Dream: The Diaries of the Revolutionary War in the Congo,* trans. Patrick Camiller. New York: Grove, 2000.

————. *America Latina: Despertar de un Continente,* eds. Maria del Carmen Ariet and Javier Salado. La Habana, Cuba: Centro de Estudios Che Guevara, Ocean Press, 2003.

————. *Apuntes criticos a la economia politica.* La Habana, Cuba: Centro de Estudios Che Guevara, 2006.

————. *Back on the Road: A Journey to Latin America,* trans. Patrick Camiller. New York: Grove, 2001.

————. *The Bolivian Diary: Authorized Edition.* Melbourne, Australia, and New York: Ocean Press, 2006.

————. *Bolivian Diary,* trans. Carlos P. Hansen and Andrew Sinclair. London: Jonathan Cape/Lorrimer, 1968.

————. *Bolivian Diary.* New York: Pathfinder, 1994.

————. *Che Guevara and the Cuban Revolution: Writings and Speeches of Ernesto Che Guevara.* New York: Pathfinder/Pacific and Asia, 1987.

————. *El Che Guevara en la Revolución Cubana,* ed. Orlando Borrego. La Habana: Ministerio de Azúcar, 1969.

————. *Che Guevara Speaks.* La Habana: Pathfinder/José Martí, 1988 (orig. 1967).

————. *Che Periodista.* La Habana: Editorial Pablo de la Torriente, Unión de Periodistas de Cuba, 1988.

————. *Che: Reminiscences of the Cuban Revolutionary War,* trans. Victoria Ortíz. New York: Monthly Review Press, 1968.

————. *Che: Selected Works of Ernesto Guevara,* eds. Bonachea and Valdes. MIT Press, 1969.

————. *Diario de Bolivia, Edición anotada,* Canek Sanchez Guevara and Radamés Molina Montes eds. Barcelona: Linkgua ediciónes, 2008.

————. *Diario del Che en Bolivia.* Buenos Aires: Editorial Lagasa, 1994.

————. *Ernesto Che Guevara (Obras).* La Habana: Editorial de Ciencias Sociales del Instituto Cubano del Libro, 1972.

————. *Ernesto Che Guevara: Obras 1957–1967.* La Habana: Casa de las Americas, 1970.

————. *Ernesto "Che" Guevara: Scritti scelti,* Vols. 1 and 2, ed. Roberto Massari. Rome: Erre Emme, 1993.

————. *Ernesto Che Guevara: Temas Economicós.* La Habana: Editorial de Ciencias Sociales, 1988.

————. *Episodes of the Cuban Revolutionary War.* New York: Pathfinder, 1996.

————. *El Gran Debate sobre la economia en Cuba, 1963–1964.* La Habana, Cuba: Editorial de Ciencias Sociales, 2004.

————. *Guerrilla Warfare.* Lincoln and London: University of Nebraska Press, 1985.

————. *Ideario Político y Filosófico del Che.* La Habana: Editora Politica/ Olivo Colección, 1991.

————. *La Guerra de Guerrillas.* La Habana: Talleres de INRA, 1961.

————. *The Motorcycle Diaries,* trans. Ann Wright. London: Verso, 1994.

————. *The Motorcycle Diaries: Notes on a Latin American Journey,* trans. Alexandra Keeble. Melbourne, Australia, and New York: Ocean Press, 2004.

————. *A New Society: Reflections for Today's World.* Melbourne, Australia: Ocean Press, 1991.

————. *Notas de Viaje.* La Habana: Editorial Abril, 1992.

————. *Otra Vez.* Milan, Italy: Sperling e Kupfer Editori, 2000.

————. *Pasajes de la Guerra Revolucionaria.* La Habana: Ediciones Unión/ Narraciones, UNEAC, 1963.

————. *Pasajes de la Guerra Revolucionara: Congo.* Milan, Italy: Sperling e Kupfer Editori, 1999.

————. *Punta del Este: Proyecto alternativo de desarollo para America Latina,* eds. Maria del Carmen Ariet and Javier Salado. Melbourne, Australia: Ocean Press, 2003.

————. *Reminiscences of the Cuban Revolutionary War.* Melbourne, Australia, and New York: Ocean Press, 2006.

————. *Self-Portrait Che Guevara,* ed. Víctor Casaus. Melbourne, Australia, and New York: Ocean Press, 2004.

————. *Venceremos: The Speeches and Writings of Che Guevara,* ed. John Gerassi. London: Panther Modern Society, 1969, 1972 (orig. Weidenfeld and Nicolson, 1968).

Guevara, Ernesto Che, and Raúl Castro. *La Conquesta de la Esperanza: Diarios Inéditos de la Guerrilla Cubana,* eds. Heinz Dieterich and Paco Ignacio Taibo II. Mexico: Editorial Joaquín Mortiz. Grupo Editorial Planeta, 1995.

Guevara Lynch, Ernesto. *Aquí Va un soldado de América.* Buenos Aires: Sudamericana-Planeta, 1987.

————. *Mí Hijo el Che.* La Habana: Editorial Arte, 1988.

————. *Young Che: Memories of Che Guevara by His Father,* trans. Lucía Alvarez de Toledo. New York: Vintage, 2008.

Harris, Richard L. *Death of a Revolutionary: Che Guevara's Last Mission.* New York: Norton, 1970 and 2007.

Hart, Joseph, ed. *Che: The Life, Death, and Afterlife of a Revolutionary.* New York: Thunder's Mouth, 2003.

Hodges, Donald C. *The Legacy of Che Guevara: A Documentary Study.* London: Thames and Hudson, 1977.

James, Daniel. *Che Guevara: A Biography.* New York: Stein and Day, 1969.

————. *The Complete Bolivian Diaries of the Che Guevara and Other Captured Documents.* New York: Stein and Day, 1968.

Korol, Claudia. *El Che y los Argentinos.* Buenos Aires: Ediciones Dialéctica, Colección Testimonial, 1988.

Lartéguy, Jean. *Los Guerrilleros.* Mexico: Editorial Diana, Mexico. 1979.

Lavretsky, I. *Ernesto Che Guevara.* Moscow: Progress, 1977.

Lopez, Coco. *Mate y ron (de Rosario a La Habana): el Che en la vision de argentinos y cubanos.* Rosario, Argentina: Ameghino Editora S.A., 1997

Maestre Alfonso, Juan. *Ernesto Che Guevara: Antología del Pensamiento Político, Social y Económico de America Latina.* Madrid: Ediciones de Cultura Hispánica, 1988.

March, Aleida. *Evocación, mi vida al lado del Che.* Bogata, Colombia: Espasa, 2008.

Martínez Estévez, Diego. *Ñancahuazú: Apuntes para la Historia Militar de Bolivia.* La Paz, Bolivia: Transcripción e Impresión Laser "Computacion y Proyectos," 1989.

Martínez Heredia, Fernando. *Che, el Socialismo y el Comunismo.* La Habana: Ediciones Casa de las Americas, 1989.

Massari, Roberto, Fernando Martínez, et al. *Che Guevara: Grandeza y Riesgo de la Utopia.* Txalaparta, 1993.

————. *Che Guevara: pensiero e politica dell'utopia.* Roma: erre emme, 1993.

————. *Guevara para Hoy.* La Habana: Centro de Estudios Sobre America/ La Universidad de Camilo Cienfuegos, Matanzas/erre emme edizioni, 1994.

————. *Otros Documentos del Che en Bolivia.* La Paz, Bolivia: Ediciones Katari (undated).

Moyano Martin, Dolores, "The Making of a Revolutionary: A Memoir of Young Guevara." *The New York Times Magazine* (August 18, 1968).

Pardo Llada, José. *El "Che" que yo conoci.* Medellín, Colombia: Editorial Bedout, 1969.

Peredo, Inti. *Mi Campaña con el Che.* Mexico: Editorial Diogenes S.A., 1972.

Pérez, Galdos, Víctor. *Un Hombre Que Actua Como Piensa.* La Habana: Editora Política, 1988.

Prado Salmon, Gen. Gary. *La Guerrilla Inmolada: Testimonio y Análisis de un Protagonista.* Santa Cruz, Bolivia: Co-Edición Grupo Editorial Punto y Coma, 1987. (Published in English as *The Defeat of the Che Guevara.* Westport, Conn.: Greenwood, 1990.)

Ray, Michele, "In Cold Blood: How the CIA Executed Che Guevara," *Ramparts* (February 5, 1968).

Rodríguez Herrera, Mariano. *Con la Adarga al Brazo.* La Habana: Lectura para Jovenes, Editorial Política, 1988.

————. *Ellos Lucharon con el Che.* La Habana: Ediciones Políticas, Editorial de Ciencias Sociales, 1989.

Rodríguez, Spain. *Che: A Graphic Biography.* London: Verso, 2008.

Rojas, Marta. *Testimonios sobre el Che, Autores Varios.* La Habana: Colección Pablo de la Torriente, 1990.

Rojo, Ricardo. *My Friend Che.* New York: Grove, 1969 (orig. Dial, 1968).

Ryan, Henry Butterfield. *The Fall of Che Guevara: A Story of Soldiers, Spies, and Diplomats.* New York: Oxford University Press, 1998.

Sáenz, Tirso W. *El Che: ministro, testimonio de un colaborador.* La Habana, Cuba. Editorial de Ciencias Sociales, 2005.

Sánchez Otero, Germán. *Los enigmas del Che.* Caracas, Venezuela: Ediciónes Ko'ey, 1997.

Saucedo Parada, Gen. Arnaldo. *No Disparen Soy El Che.* Santa Cruz, Bolivia: Talleres Gráficos de Editorial Oriente, 1988.

Sinclair, Andrew. *Guevara.* London: Fontana/Collins, 1970.

Soria Galvarro, Carlos. "Tras Las Huellas del Che en Bolivia." *La Razon* (October 9, 1996).

"The Spirit of Che." *Evergreen Review,* No. 51 (February 1968).

Tablada, Carlos, Jack Barnes, Steve Clark, and Mary-Alice Waters. *Che Guevara: Cuba and the Road to Socialism (Che Guevara, Carlos Rafael Rodríguez).* New York: New International, 1991.

Tablada Pérez, Carlos. *El Pensamiento Economicó de Ernesto Che Guevara.* La Habana: Ediciones Casa de las Americas, 1987.

Taibo, Paco Ignacio II. *Ernesto Guevara: también conocido como El Che.* Mexico: Editorial Joaquín Mortiz, Grupo Editorial Planeta, 1996.

Terán, Gen. Reque. *La Campaña de Ñancahuazú: La Guerrilla del "Che" Visto por el Comandante de la IV Division del Ejercito Boliviano.* La Paz, Bolivia: 1987.

Vargas Salinas, Gen. Mario. *El Che: Mito y Realidad.* La Paz/Cochabamba: Los Amigos del Libro, 1988.

Vázquez-Viaña, Humberto. *Antecedentes de la Guerrilla del Che en Bolivia.* Research Paper Series, No. 46. Stockholm: Institute of Latin American Studies, September 1987.

Vázquez-Viaña, Humberto, and Ramiro Aliaga Saravia. *Bolivia: Ensayo de Revolución Continental.* Bolivia (privately published, undated).

Vicioso, Chiqui. *Le decian Lolo: Presencia del Che en las mujeres guerrilleras.* Dominican Republic: Editora de Colores, 1999.

Villegas, Harry (Pombo). *Un Hombre de la Guerrilla del Che.* Buenos Aires and La Habana: Ediciones Colihüe. Editora Política, 1996.

Vicent Monzo, Josep, ed. *Che fotógrafo.* Valencia, Spain: Centro de estudios Che Guevara, 2007.

Ziff, Trisha, ed. *Che Guevara: Revolutionary and Icon*. New York: Abrams, 2006.

About Cuba, Fidel Castro, and Che

Acevedo, Enrique. *Descamisado*. La Habana: Editorial Cultura Popular, International Network Group, 1993.

Almeida Bosque, Juan. *Atención, Recuento!* La Habana: Editora Política, 1988.

———. *La Sierra*. La Habana: Editora Política, 1989.

———. *La Sierra Maestra y Mas Allá*. La Habana: Editora Política, 1995.

———. *Por las Faldas del Turquino*. La Habana: Editora Política, 1992.

Arenas, Reinaldo. *Before Night Falls: A Memoir*. New York: Viking Penguin, 1993.

Beschloss, Michael R. *The Crisis Years: Kennedy and Khrushchev, 1960–1963*. New York: HarperCollins, 1991.

Borge, Tomas. *Fidel Castro: Un Grano de Maíz. Conversación con Tomas Borge*. La Habana: Oficina de Publicaciónes del Consejo de Estado, 1992.

Blight, James G., Bruce J. Allyn, and David A. Welch. *Cuba on the Brink*. New York: Pantheon, 1993.

Blight, James G., and Philip Brenner. *Sad and Luminous Days: Cuba's Struggle with the Superpowers after the Missile Crisis*. Oxford, England: Rowman and Littlefield, 2002.

Brugioni, Dino A. *Eyeball to Eyeball: The Inside Story of the Cuban Missile Crisis*. New York: Random House, 1991.

Cabrera Infante, Guillermo. *Mea Cuba*. New York: Farrar, Straus, and Giroux, 1994.

———. *Vista del Amanecer en el Trópico*. Barcelona: Seix Barral, 1974.

Castro, Fidel. *La Historia Me Absolverá*. La Habana: Oficina de Publicaciónes del Consejo de Estado, 1993.

Castro, Fidel, with Ignacio Ramonet. *My Life: A Spoken Autobiography,* trans. Andrew Hurley. London: Allen Lane, 2007.

Castro, Fidel, and Che Guevara. *To Speak the Truth*. New York: Pathfinder, 1992.

Chang, Lawrence, and Pete Kornbluh, eds. *The Cuban Missile Crisis 1962*. New York: New Press, 1992.

Chaviano, Julio O. *La Lucha en las Villas*. La Habana: Editorial de Ciencias Sociales, 1990.

Chomsky, Aviva, Barry Carr, and Pamela Maria Smorkalloff, eds. *The Cuba Reader: History, Culture, Politics*. Durham and London: Duke University Press, 2003.

Cuervo Cerulia, Georgina, ed. *Granma—Rumbo a la Libertad*. La Habana: Editorial Gente Nueva, 1983.

Darushenkov, Oleg. *Cuba, El Camino de la Revolución.* Moscow: Editorial Progreso, 1979.

Debray, Régis. *Prison Writings.* London: Pelican Latin America Library, Penguin, 1973.

——. *Revolution in the Revolution?* London: Pelican Latin America Library, Penguin, 1968 (orig. Paris: Maspéro, 1967).

——. *Strategy for Revolution.* London: Pelican Latin America Library, Penguin, 1973.

DePalma, Anthony. *The Man Who Invented Fidel: Castro, Cuba, and Herbert L. Matthews of the New York Times.* New York: PublicAffairs, 2006.

Draper, Theodore. *Castroism: Theory and Practice.* New York: Frederick Praeger, 1965.

Dumont, René. *Cuba: Socialism and Development.* New York: Grove, 1970.

Ediciónes Políticas. *Cinco Documentos.* La Habana: Editorial de Ciencias Sociales, Instituto Cubano del Libro, 1971.

Edwards, Jorge. *Persona Non Grata: An Envoy in Castro's Cuba.* London: The Bodley Head, 1977.

English, T. J. *Havana Nocturne: How the Mob Owned Cuba . . . and then Lost It to the Revolution.* New York: William Morrow, 2007.

Franqui, Carlos. *Diary of the Cuban Revolution.* New York: A Seaver Book, Viking, 1980.

——. *Family Portrait with Fidel.* New York: Vintage, 1985.

——. *The Twelve.* New York: Lyle Stuart, 1968.

Galeano, Eduardo. *El Tigre Azul y Otros Relatos.* La Habana: Editorial de Ciencias Sociales, Editora Política, 1991.

Geyer, Georgie Anne. *Prince: The Untold Story of Fidel Castro.* New York: Little, Brown, 1991.

Gosse, Van. *Where the Boys Are: Cuba, Cold War America, and the Making of a New Left.* London and New York: Verso, 1993.

Gott, Richard. *Cuba: A New History.* New Haven, Conn.: Yale University Press, 2004.

Habel, Janette. *Cuba: The Revolution in Peril.* London: Verso, 1991.

Halperin, Maurice. *The Taming of Fidel Castro.* Berkeley: University of California Press, 1979.

Hinckle, Warren, and William Turner. *The Fish Is Red: The Story of the Secret War against Castro.* New York: Harper and Row, 1981.

Iglesias, Joel. *De la Sierra Maestra al Escambray.* La Habana: Letras Cubanas, 1979.

Jenks, L. H. *Nuestra Colonia de Cuba.* La Habana: La Empresa Consolidada de Artes Gráficas (orig. published 1928).

Karol, K. S. *Guerrillas in Power.* New York: Hill and Wang, 1970.

Kennedy, Robert. F. *Thirteen Days: A Memoir of the Cuban Missile Crisis*. New York: A Mentor Book, Penguin, 1969.

Lara, Jesús. *Guerrillero Inti Peredo*. Cochabamba, Bolivia: Edición del Autor, 1980.

Lazo, Mario. *Dagger in the Heart: American Policy Failures in Cuba*. New York: Funk and Wagnall, 1968.

Llovio-Menéndez, José Luis. *Insider: My Life as a Hidden Revolutionary in Cuba*. New York: Bantam, 1988.

Lockwood, Lee. *Castro's Cuba, Cuba's Fidel*. New York: Westview, 1990.

Mallin, Jay. *Covering Castro: The Rise and Decline of Cuba's Communist Dictator*. New Brunswick, N.J.: U.S.-Cuba Institute, Transaction, 1994.

Martin, Lionel. *The Early Fidel: Roots of Castro's Communism*. New York: Lyle Stuart, 1977.

Martínez Víctores, Ricardo. *RR: La Historia de Radio Rebelde*. La Habana: Editorial de Ciencias Sociales, 1978.

Masetti, Jorge Ricardo. *Los Que Luchan y Los Que Lloran*. Buenos Aires: Puntosur, 1987.

Matthews, Herbert L. *Castro: A Political Biography*. London: Pelican, 1970.

————. *The Cuban Story*. New York: George Braziller, 1961.

Meneses, Enrique. *Hasta aqui hemos llegado*. La Coruña, Spain: Ediciones del Viento, 2006.

Minà, Gianni. *An Encounter with Fidel*. Australia: Ocean Press, 1991.

Nuñez Jiménez, Antonio. *En Marcha con Fidel*. La Habana: Editorial Letras Cubanas, 1982.

————. *Patria o Muerte*. La Habana: INRA, 1961.

Padilla, Heberto. *Self-Portrait of the Other: A Memoir*. New York: Farrar, Straus, and Giroux, 1990.

Pérez, Louis A. *Cuba: Between Reform and Revolution*. New York: Oxford University Press, 1988.

Quirk, Robert E. *Fidel Castro*. New York: Norton, 1993.

Reid-Henry, Simon. *Fidel and Che: A Revolutionary Friendship*. London: Sceptre, 2008.

Robbins, Carla Anne. *The Cuban Threat*. New York: ISCHI, 1985.

Rojas, Marta, and Mírta Rodríguez. *Tania la Guerrillera Inolvidable*. La Habana: Instituto del Libro, 1970. (Published in English as *Tania: The Unforgettable Guerrilla*. New York: Random House, 1971.)

Rodríguez, Felix I., and John Weisman. *Shadow Warrior: The CIA Hero of a Hundred Unknown Battles*. New York: Simon and Schuster, 1989.

Salkey, Andrew. *Havana Journal*. London: Penguin, 1971.

Sarabia, Nydia. *Médicos de la Revolución*. Apuntes Biográficos. La Habana: Editorial Gente Nueva, 1983.

Stubbs, Jean. *Cuba: The Test of Time.* London: Latin America Books, 1989.

Sweig, Julia E. *Inside the Cuban Revolution: Fidel Castro and the Urban Underground.* Cambridge, Mass: Harvard University Press, 2002.

Symmes, Patrick. *The Boys from Dolores: Fidel Castro and His Generation, From Revolution to Exile.* London: Robinson, 2007.

Szulc, Tad. *Fidel: A Critical Portrait.* New York: Morrow, 1986.

Taber, Robert. *M-26: The Biography of a Revolution.* New York: Lyle Stuart, 1961.

Thomas, Hugh. *Cuba or The Pursuit of Freedom.* London: Eyre and Spottiswoode, 1971.

Timossi, Jorge. *Los cuentos de Barbarroja: testimonio de la vida de su protagonista.* Madrid: Edicíones Libertarias, 1999.

Timmerman, Jacobo. *Cuba.* New York: Vintage, 1992.

"Una Leyenda llamada Tania," by Mario Rueda and Luis Antezana Ergueta. *La Razón* "Ventana" (October 15, 1995).

Welch, Richard E., Jr., *Response to Revolution: The United States and the Cuban Revolution, 1959–1961.* Chapel Hill: University of North Carolina Press, 1985.

Wyden, Peter. *Bay of Pigs.* New York: Simon and Schuster, 1979.

About Argentina

Barnes, John. *Evita: First Lady—A Biography of Evita Perón.* New York: Grove, 1978.

Baschetti, Roberto, ed. *Documentos 1970–1973: De la Guerrilla Peronista al Gobierno Popular.* Buenos Aires: Editorial de la Campana, Colección Campana de Palo, 1995.

Crasweller, Robert. *Perón and the Enigmas of Argentina.* New York: Norton, 1987.

Gilbert, Isidoro. *El Oro de Moscú: La Historia Secreta de las Relaciones Argentino-Soviéticos.* Buenos Aires: Planeta/Espejo de la Argentina, 1994.

Luna, Felix. *La Argentina: De Perón a Lanusse, 1943–1973.* Buenos Aires: Planeta, Espejo de la Argentina, 1993.

Main, Mary. *Evita: The Woman with the Whip.* London: Corgi, 1977, 1978.

Rock, David. *Authoritarian Argentina: The Nationalist Movement, Its History and Its Impact.* Berkeley: University of California Press, 1993.

Scobie, James R. *Argentina: A City and a Nation.* New York: Oxford University Press, 1971.

Tulchin, Joseph S. *Argentina and the United States: A Conflicted Relationship.* New York: Macmillan, 1990.

About Latin America

Aguilar, Luis E., ed. *Marxism in Latin America: A Borzoi Book on Latin America.* New York: Knopf, 1968.

Borge, Tomas. *The Patient Impatience.* New York: Curbstone, 1992.

Brown, Michael F., and Eduardo Fernández. *War of Shadows: The Struggle for Utopia in the Peruvian Amazon.* Berkeley: University of California Press, 1991.

Cajías, Lupe de. *Juan Lechín, Historia de una Leyenda.* La Paz, Bolivia: Los Amigos del Libro, 1994.

Castañeda Jorge G. *Utopia Unarmed: The Latin American Left after the Cold War.* New York: Knopf, 1994.

Dunkerley, James. *Rebellion in the Veins: Political Struggle in Bolivia 1952–1982.* London: Verso, 1984.

Gerassi, John. *The Great Fear in Latin America.* New York: Collier, 1963.

Gott, Richard. *Guerrilla Movements in Latin America.* London: Thomas Nelson, 1970. (Reissued as *Rural Guerrillas in Latin America.* London: Pelican Latin America Library, Penguin, 1973.)

————. *Land without Evil: Utopian Journeys across the South American Watershed.* London: Verso, 1993.

Gunson, Chamberlain, Thompson. *The Dictionary of Contemporary Politics of Central America and the Caribbean.* New York: Simon and Schuster, 1991.

Herrera, Hayden. *Frida: A Biography of Frida Kahlo.* New York: HarperCollins, 1984.

Lindqvvist, Sven. *The Shadow: Latin America Faces the Seventies.* London: Pelican Latin America Library, Penguin, 1969.

Miná, Gianni. *Un Continente Desaparecido.* Barcelona: Ediciónes Península, 1996.

Pendle, George. *History of Latin America.* London: Penguin, 1963, 1990.

Schlesinger, Stephen, and Stephen Kinzer. *: The Untold Story of the American Coup in Guatemala.* New York: Anchor/Doubleday, 1983.

Szulc, Tad. *Twilight of the Tyrants.* New York: Holt, 1959.

Ydigoras Fuentes, Miguel. *My War with Communism.* New York: Prentice-Hall, 1963.

About Cuba and Africa

Barreto, José. "Comrade Tato." *Prensa Latina* (June 1993).

Bridgland, Fred. *Jonas Savimbi: A Key to Africa.* New York: Paragon House, 1987.

Carrasco, Juana. "Tatu: Un Guerrillero Africano." *Verde Olivo* (June 1988).

Galvez, William. *Che in Africa: Che Guevara's Congo Diary.* Melbourne, Australia, and New York: Ocean Press, 1999.

García Márquez, Gabriel, and Jorge Risquét, Fidel Castro. *Changing the History of Africa, Angola, and Namibia.* Australia: Ocean Press, 1989.

Gleijeses, Piero. *Misiones en conflicto: La Habana, Washington y Africa, 1959–1976.* La Habana, Cuba: Editorial de Ciencias Sociales, 2002.

Gott, Richard. "Che's Missing Year: Che Guevara and the Congo." *New Left Review,* No. 220 (1996).

Heikal, Mohammed Hassanein. *The Cairo Documents.* New York: Doubleday, 1971.

Jiménez Rodríguez, Limbania. *Heroinas de Angola.* La Habana: Editorial de Ciencias Sociales, 1985.

Moore, Juan Carlos. *Castro, the Blacks, and Africa.* Berkeley: Center for Afro-American Studies, University of California Press, 1988.

Risquet Valdés, Jorge. *El segundo frente del Che en el Congo: Historia del Batallón Patricio Lumumba.* La Habana, Cuba: Casa Editora, Abril 2000.

Taibo, Paco Ignacio II, Froilán Escobar, and Felix Guerra. *El Año Que Estuvimos en Ninguna Parte.* Mexico: Editorial Joaquín Mortiz, Grupo Planeta, 1994.

About the Cold War

Andrew, Christopher, and Oleg Gordievsky. *KGB: The Inside Story.* London: HarperCollins, 1990.

Frankland, Mark. *Khrushchev.* Lanham, Md.: Madison Books, 1969.

Goodwin, Richard. *Remembering America: A Voice from the Sixties.* Boston, Mass.: Little, Brown, 1988.

Grose, Peter. *Gentleman Spy: The Life of Allen Dulles.* New York: Houghton Mifflin, 1994.

Kwitny, Jonathon. *Endless Enemies: The Making of an Unfriendly World.* New York: Viking Penguin, 1986.

Schlesinger, Arthur Jr. *A Thousand Days: John F. Kennedy in the White House.* New York: Houghton Mifflin, 1965.

Steele, Jonathon. *World Power: Soviet Foreign Policy under Brezhnev and Andropov.* London: Michael Joseph, 1983.

Ranelagh, John. *The Agency: The Rise and Decline of the CIA.* London: Weidenfeld and Nicolson, 1986.

Thomas, Evan. *The Very Best Men: Four Who Dared—The Early Years of the CIA.* New York: Touchstone, Simon and Schuster, 1995.

Weiner, Tim. *Legacy of Ashes: The History of the CIA.* New York: Doubleday, 2007.

Wickhan-Crowley, Timothy P. *Guerrillas and Revolution in Latin America: A Comparative Study of Insurgents and Regimes Since 1956.* Princeton, N.J.: Princeton University Press, 1993.

Zubok, Vladislav, and Constantine Pleshakov. *Inside the Kremlin's Cold War: From Stalin to Khrushchev.* Cambridge, Mass.: Harvard University Press, 1996.

Miscellaneous

Allaine, Marie-Françoise. *Conversations with Graham Greene.* London: Penguin, 1991.

Anderson, Benedict. *Imagined Communites.* London: Verso, 1991 (orig. 1983).

Armiño, Mauro, ed. *Lucha de Guerrillas: Según los Clásicos de Marxismo-Leninismo.* Madrid: Biblioteca Jucar, 1980.

Bottomore, Tom, ed. *A Dictionary of Marxist Thought.* Oxford: Blackwell's, 1991.

Cantor, Jay. *The Death of Che Guevara.* (Fiction.) New York: Knopf, 1983.

De Beauvoir, Simone. *All Said and Done.* London: Penguin, 1977 (orig. Paris: Gallimard, 1972).

————. *The Force of Circumstance.* London: Penguin, 1968 (orig. Paris: Gallimard, 1963).

Debray, Régis. *Loues Soient Nos Seigneurs: Une Éducation Politique.* Paris: Gallimard, 1996.

Desmond, Adrian, and James Moore. *Darwin.* New York: Warner, 1992.

Fanon, Frantz. *The Wretched of the Earth.* New York: Grove, 1982 (orig. Paris: Maspéro, 1963.)

Greene, Graham. *Fragments of Autobiography.* London: Penguin, 1991.

————. *Our Man in Havana.* London: Heinemann, 1958.

Harris, Nigel. *National Liberation.* London: Penguin, 1990.

Malcom X. *Malcolm X Speaks,* ed. George Breitman. New York: Grove Weidenfeld, 1990 (orig. 1965).

Mao Tse-tung. *Mao Tse-Tung on Guerrilla Warfare,* trans. Samuel B. Griffith. New York: Praeger, 1961.

Nehru, Jawaharlal. *The Discovery of India.* Oxford University, 1985 (orig. Calcutta: Signet, 1946.)

Neruda, Pablo. *Five Decades: A Selection (Poems 1925–1970),* ed. and trans. Ben Bellit. New York: Grove, 1974.

Payne, Robert. *The Life and Death of Lenin.* New York: Simon and Schuster, 1964.

Salisbury, Harrison. *The New Emperors: China in the Era of Mao and Deng.* New York: Avon, 1992.

Schama, Simon. *Citizens: A Chronicle of the French Revolution.* London: Penguin, 1989.

Snow, Edgar. *Red Star over China.* New York: Grove Weidenfeld, 1973 (orig. Random House, 1938).

Taber, Robert. *War of the Flea: The Classic Study of Guerrilla Warfare.* New York: Lyle Stuart, 1965.

Vives, Cristina, and Mark Saunders, eds. *Korda: A Revolutionary Lens.* Göttingen, Germany: Steidl, 2008.

Westoby, Adam. *The Evolution of Communism.* New York: Free Press, Macmillan, 1989.

Maps

Prepared by Matthew Ericson

The "Motorcycle Diaries" Trip, 1952

"Otra Vez" Trip, 1953–1954

The Sierra Maestra, 1956–1959

Cuba

Congo, 1965

The Bolivian Odyssey, 1996–1967

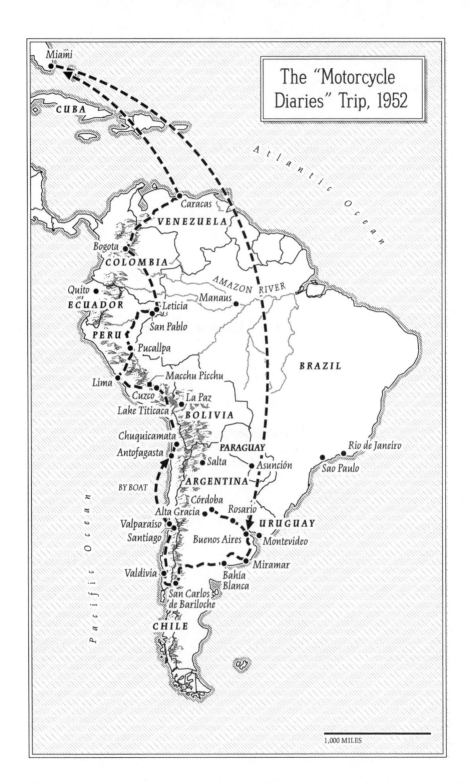

The "Motorcycle Diaries" Trip, 1952

1,000 MILES

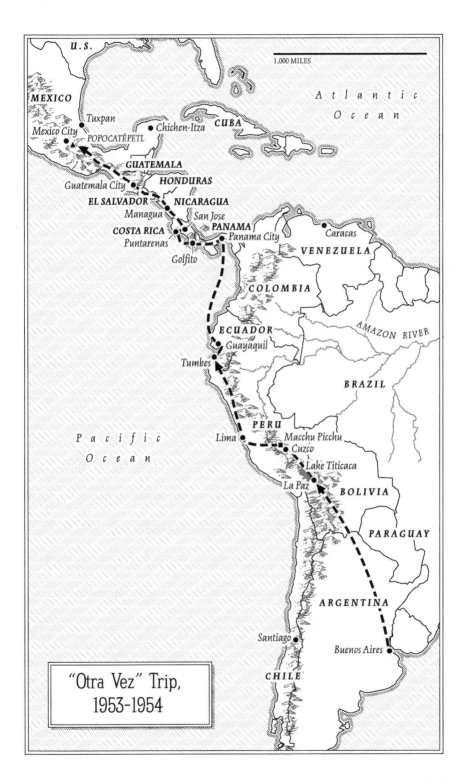

"Otra Vez" Trip, 1953-1954

The Sierra Maestra,
1956–1959

Caribbean Sea

Manzanillo •

C U B A

• Niquero

Purial •

El Lom[
La Derecha
ALTOS DE ESPINOSA

• Las Coloradas

• Alegría de Pío

Pilón •

Cabo Cruz

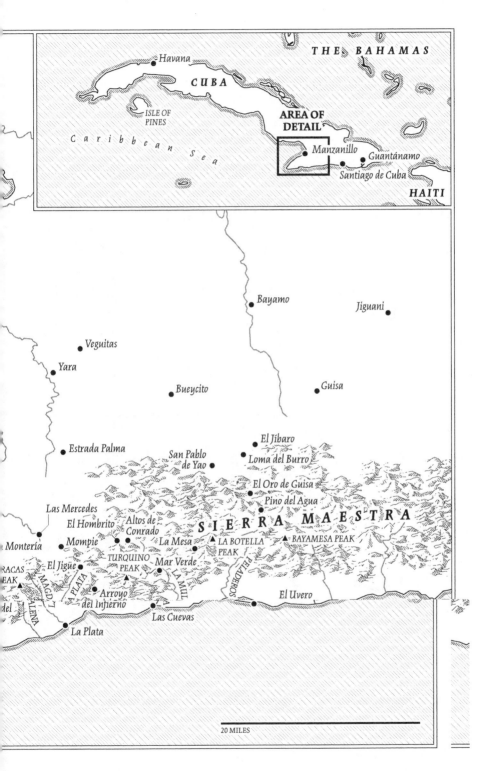

THE BAHAMAS

CUBA

Havana

ISLE OF
PINES

C a r i b b e a n   S e a

AREA OF
DETAIL

Manzanillo

Guantánamo

Santiago de Cuba

HAITI

Bayamo

Jiguani

Veguitas

Yara

Bueycito

Guisa

Estrada Palma

El Jíbaro

San Pablo
de Yao

Loma del Burro

El Oro de Guisa

Pino del Agua

Las Mercedes

El Hombrito

Altos de
Conrado

SIERRA MAESTRA

Monteria

Mompie

La Mesa

LA BOTELLA
PEAK

BAYAMESA PEAK

RACAS
EAK

El Jigüe

TURQUINO
PEAK

Mar Verde

del

Arroyo
del Infierno

Las Cuevas

El Uvero

La Plata

20 MILES

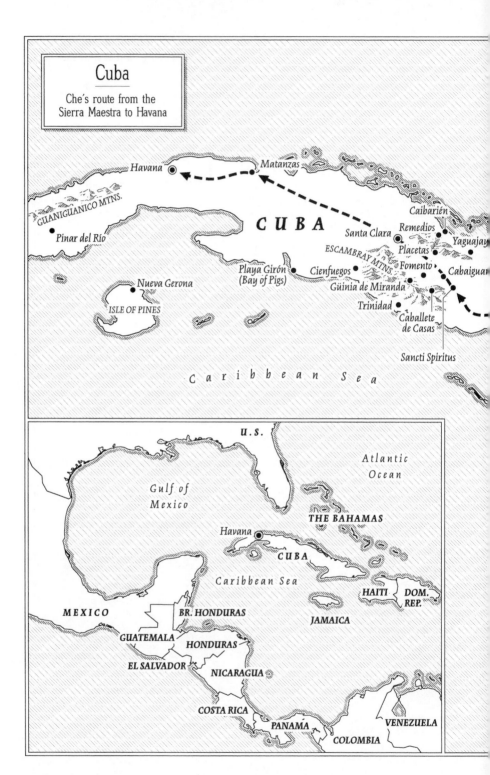

Cuba

Che's route from the
Sierra Maestra to Havana

GUANIGUANICO MTNS.

Havana

Matanzas

Pinar del Río

C U B A

Caibarién

Santa Clara

Remedios

Yaguajay

ESCAMBRAY MTNS.

Placetas

Nueva Gerona

Playa Girón
(Bay of Pigs)

Cienfuegos

Fomento

Cabaiguan

ISLE OF PINES

Güinia de Miranda

Trinidad

Caballete
de Casas

Sancti Spiritus

C a r i b b e a n   S e a

U.S.

*Atlantic
Ocean*

*Gulf of
Mexico*

THE BAHAMAS

Havana

C U B A

Caribbean Sea

HAITI

DOM.
REP.

MEXICO

BR. HONDURAS

JAMAICA

GUATEMALA

HONDURAS

EL SALVADOR

NICARAGUA

COSTA RICA

PANAMA

VENEZUELA

COLOMBIA

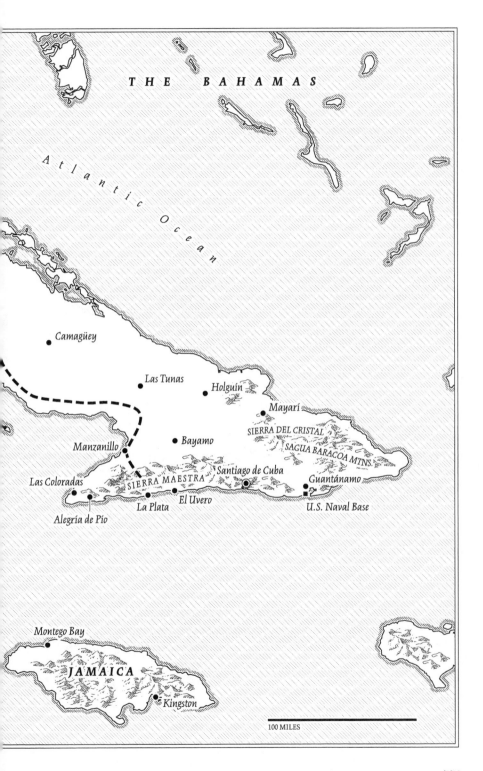

THE BAHAMAS

Atlantic Ocean

Camagüey

Las Tunas

Holguín

Mayarí

SIERRA DEL CRISTAL

SAGUA BARACOA MTNS

Manzanillo

Bayamo

Las Coloradas

SIERRA MAESTRA

Santiago de Cuba

Guantánamo

La Plata

El Uvero

U.S. Naval Base

Alegría de Pío

Montego Bay

JAMAICA

Kingston

100 MILES

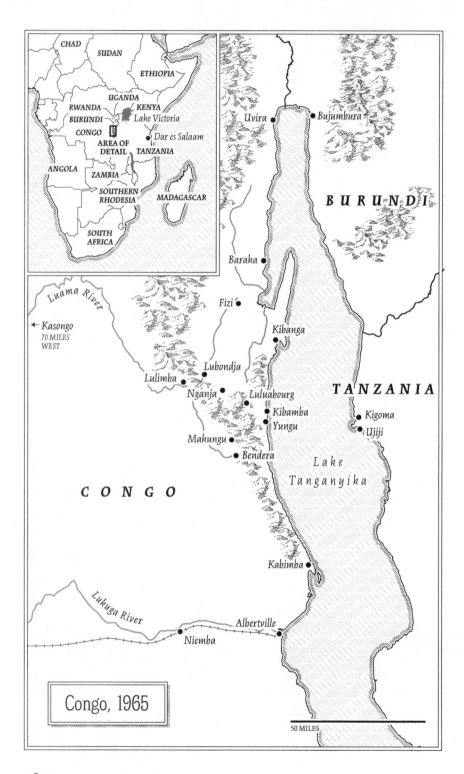

CHAD

SUDAN

ETHIOPIA

UGANDA

RWANDA   KENYA
BURUNDI   Lake Victoria
CONGO
            Dar es Salaam
AREA OF   TANZANIA
DETAIL

ANGOLA

ZAMBIA

SOUTHERN
RHODESIA   MADAGASCAR

SOUTH
AFRICA

Luama River

← Kasongo
70 MILES
WEST

Uvira   Bujumbura

B U R U N D I

Baraka

Fizi

Kibanga

Lubondja

Lulimba   *T A N Z A N I A*

Nganja   Luluabourg
            Kibamba   Kigoma
            Yungu   Ujiji

Makungu

Bendera   *Lake
            Tanganyika*

C O N G O

Kabimba

Lukuga River

Albertville

Niemba

Congo, 1965

50 MILES

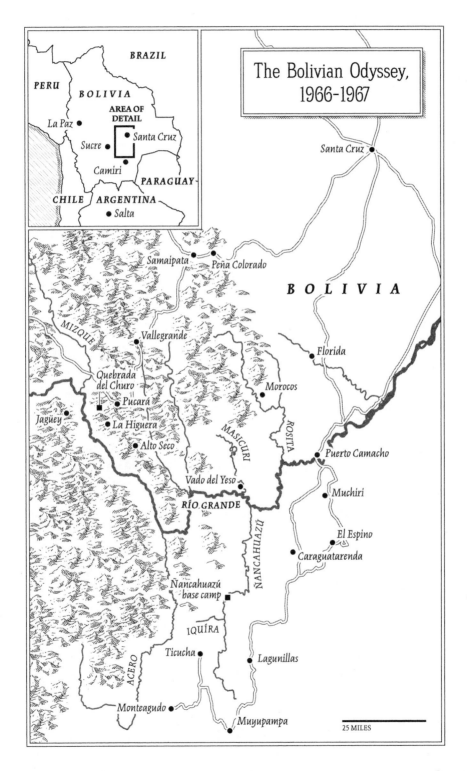

BRAZIL

PERU

BOLIVIA

AREA OF
DETAIL

La Paz

Sucre

Camiri

Santa Cruz

PARAGUAY

CHILE   ARGENTINA

Salta

Santa Cruz

Samaipata   Peña Colorado

B O L I V I A

MIZQUE

Vallegrande

Florida

Quebrada
del Churo

Pucará

Morocos

Jagüey

La Higuera

MASICURI

ROSITA

Alto Seco

Puerto Camacho

Vado del Yeso

Muchiri

RÍO GRANDE

ÑANCAHUAZÚ

El Espino

Caraguatarenda

Ñancahuazú
base camp

IQUÍRA

ACERO

Ticucha

Lagunillas

Monteagudo

Muyupampa

25 MILES

Chronology

May 14, 1928 Ernesto Guevara de la Serna is born in Rosario, Argentina, to Ernesto Guevara Lynch and Celia de la Serna. (Birth certificate is falsified to indicate June 14 birth date.)

1932 Family moves to Alta Gracia.

1943 Family moves to Córdoba.

1946 Ernesto graduates from Colegio Nacional Dean Funes in Córdoba.

March 1947 Family moves to Buenos Aires.

1947 Ernesto enters Faculty of Medicine at the University of Buenos Aires.

January 1, 1950 Ernesto takes off alone on first motorcycle trip, around Argentina.

February 9, 1951 Ernesto ships out to sea on an oil tanker.

January 4, 1952 Ernesto and Alberto Granado set out on "Motorcycle Diaries" trip.

March 10, 1952 Fulgencio Batista takes over as president of Cuba in a coup d'état.

August 1, 1952 Ernesto returns to Buenos Aires.

April 1953 Earns medical degree.

July 7, 1953 Ernesto and Calica Ferrer leave Buenos Aires for Bolivia. "Otra Vez" trip.

July 26, 1953 Fidel Castro leads an attack on the Moncada army barracks in Santiago de Cuba. He is captured, tried, and imprisoned.

December 1953 Ernesto arrives in Guatemala City. Meets Hilda Gadea.

June 18–27, 1954 U.S.-sponsored coup in Guatemala.

September 1954 Ernesto arrives in Mexico.

May 1955 Fidel is freed from Isle of Pines prison in an amnesty signed by Batista.

July 1955 Ernesto meets Fidel in Mexico City.

August 18, 1955 Marries Hilda Gadea.

February 15, 1956 First child, Hilda Beatriz Guevara, born.

June 24, 1956 Ernesto, who has begun training for revolution with Fidel's band of Cuban exiles, is arrested by the Mexican police. He is imprisoned for nearly two months.

November 25, 1956 *Granma* sets off from Mexico for Cuba.

December 2, 1956 *Granma* arrives at Playa las Coloradas on Cuba's southeastern coast.

December 5, 1956 Rebels are attacked and dispersed at Alegría de Pío.

January 17, 1957 Successful attack on La Plata army barracks.

February 17, 1957 Herbert Matthews of *The New York Times* interviews Fidel in the Sierra Maestra.

February 17, 1957 Che executes the traitor Eutimio Guerra.

May 28, 1957 Rebel attack on army garrison at El Uvero.

July 22, 1957 Che made *comandante*.

August 31, 1958 Che leads Rebel Army column toward the Escambray mountains of Las Villas province.

October 16, 1958 Rebel Army column led by Che reaches Escambray.

December 28, 1958 Che's column of the Rebel Army begins the battle of Santa Clara.

January 1, 1959 Batista flees Cuba. Santa Clara falls.

January 2, 1959 Che and Camilo Cienfuegos begin advancing on Havana. When Che arrives in the city, he occupies La Cabaña fortress, where, as Supreme Prosecutor, he will oversee numerous trials and executions.

January 8, 1959 Fidel arrives in Havana.

February 9, 1959 Che is made a Cuban citizen.

February 16, 1959 Fidel becomes prime minister.

May 22, 1959 Che and Hilda divorce.

June 2, 1959 Che marries Aleida March.

June 12–September 8, 1959 Che travels through Europe, Asia, and Africa.

October 8, 1959 Che is made director of the new Industrialization Department of the Instituto Nacional de Reforma Agraria (INRA)

November 1959 Che becomes president of the National Bank of Cuba.

March 5, 1960 At a funeral service for the victims of an explosion on the ship *La Coubre*, in Havana harbor, Alberto Korda photographs Che on the speakers' platform.

April 1960 Che's guerrilla warfare manual, *La Guerra de Guerrillas*, is published by INRA's Department of Military Training.

October 19, 1960 The United States imposes a trade embargo on Cuba, prohibiting all exports except food and medicine.

October 22, 1960 Che leaves Havana to visit the Soviet Union, the German Democratic Republic, Czechoslovakia, China, and North Korea.

November 24, 1960 Che and Aleida's first child, a daughter, Aleida (Aliusha), is born.

January 3, 1961 Eisenhower breaks off diplomatic relations between the United States and Cuba.

February 23, 1961 Che becomes minister of industry.

April 17–20, 1961 Bay of Pigs invasion.

August 1961 Che represents Cuba at the OAS economic conference at Punta del Este, Uruguay. Meets privately with President Kennedy's adviser Richard Goodwin.

February 1962 President Kennedy tightens trade embargo.

May 20, 1962 Che and Aleida's first son, Camilo, born.

August 27–September 7, 1962 Che visits Soviet Union.

October 1962 Cuban missile crisis.

June 14, 1963 Che and Aleida's third child, Celia, born.

March 1964 Tamara Bunke ("Tania") is sent from Havana to Europe to establish a false identity before infiltrating Bolivia as an agent for guerrillas attempting to foment revolution.

April 1964 The guerrilla band sent by Che to launch an armed struggle in Argentina is destroyed in the mountainous Salta region of northeastern Argentina. Their leader, Jorge Ricardo Masetti, disappears. Most of the survivors are arrested and imprisoned.

July 26, 1964 The OAS imposes sanctions on Cuba. Mexico is the only member state that does not sever ties with Cuba.

August 5, 1964 The United States begins bombing North Vietnam.

November 4–9, 1964 Che visits the Soviet Union.

December 9, 1964 Che embarks on a visit to the United States, Algeria, Mali, the Congo, Guinea, Ghana, Tanzania, China, France, Ireland, Czechoslovakia, and Egypt. He will be away for three months.

December 11, 1964 Che addresses the United Nations General Assembly in New York City.

February 24, 1965 Che and Aleida's fourth child, Ernesto, born.

February 25, 1965 Che addresses the Second Economic Seminar of Afro-Asian Solidarity in Algiers.

March 15, 1965 Che returns to Cuba but soon drops from public view.

April 1, 1965 Che leaves Havana in disguise, bound for Africa.

April 19, 1965 Che arrives in Dar es Salaam, Tanzania, en route to the Congo to lead a Cuban brigade in support of the Congolese rebels.

May 19, 1965 Che's mother, Celia, dies in Buenos Aires.

October 3, 1965 Fidel reads Che's "Farewell Letter" publicly.

November 21, 1965 Che and his men flee the Congo.

November 1965 to March 1966 Che lives secretly in the Cuban embassy in Dar es Salaam, where Aleida visits him.

March–July, 1966 Che moves to Prague, where he alternates between safe houses in the city and in the countryside. Aleida visits him again.

July 1966 Che returns to Cuba, secretly, and prepares for the Bolivian expedition.

November 1966 Che arrives in Bolivia disguised as a middle-aged Uruguayan businessman. Within a few days, he leaves La Paz for a camp established for his guerrillas in a remote wilderness area in the southeastern part of the country.

April 16, 1967 Publication of Che's "Message to the Tricontinental," which calls for "two, three, many Vietnams."

August 31, 1967 A rearguard column of guerrillas, including Tania Bunke, is intercepted and massacred by Bolivian forces at a place on the Masicuri River known as Vado del Yeso.

October 8, 1967 Che's last battle. He is wounded and captured by Bolivian soldiers.

October 9, 1967 Che is executed in the hamlet of La Higuera after spending the night in captivity. His body is transferred by helicopter to the town of Vallegrande, where an autopsy is performed. The body is displayed to the public for the next twenty-four hours.

October 10, 1967 Death masks are made of Che's face. His hands are amputated.

October 11, 1967 Che's body is secretly buried in the early morning hours.

July 1997 Che's body is unearthed at the burial site at the airport in Vallegrande, Bolivia.

October 17, 1997 Che is interred in a mausoleum in Santa Clara, Cuba. A memorial was built there to honor him as the Heroic Guerrilla.

Acknowledgments

A biography is achieved with the collaboration of many people, and since this project spanned five years, I have a great many to thank. Some of them may not approve of the final result. To them, I can say only what I have always said: My sole loyalty in this book was to write the truth, as I saw it, of Che Guevara's life; his truth, not anyone else's.

In Cuba, where the bulk of my time was spent and research done, I owe gratitude to Che Guevara's widow, Aleida March, who emerged from three decades of hibernation to open up to an impertinent, prying American. I know that there were many who advised her against it. I appreciate her trust. She allowed me to draw my own conclusions about what I learned. To María del Carmen Ariet, Aleida's aide-de-camp and probably the world's foremost Che scholar, I owe a great deal. Orlando Borrego, Che's protégé, shared his knowledge and his archives and also treated me as a friend. For that I am forever grateful. Cuba's former spymaster, the late Manuel Piñeiro Losada, alias "Barbarroja," helped shed light on Che's clandestine activities. Also many thanks to Aleida Piedra, my assistant and faithful friend, who practically became a member of our family.

Thanks to Denís Guzmán, the Central Committee official who channeled my initial request to work in Cuba and who tried to smooth over the early glitches of our stay; María Flores, Roberto de Armas, and the late Jorge Enrique Mendoza; Julie Martin and her father Lionel Martin, a wonderful man and good friend who shared his thoughts, years of experience, and personal archives with me; Manuel, Alejandro, Katia *y toda la familia* Gato; Lorna Burdsall, Pascal and Isis Fletcher, Lisette, Ron Ridenour, Veronica Spasskaya, Roberto Salas, Encarna, Fernando and Laly Barral, Leo and Michi Acosta, Micaela and Fernando, Miguel and Tanja, Julio and Olivia, Marta and Carmen, Isaac and Ana, Dinos and Maribel Philippos, Ángel

Arcos Vergnes, Juan Gravalosa, Tirso Saenz, Cristina Campuzano, Alberto Castellanos, Alberto Granado, Osvaldo de Cárdenas, Ana María Erra, María Elena Duarte, Estela and Ernesto Bravo, Mariano, Gustavo Sánchez, Jesús del Valle, Paco Usallan, Marta Vitorte, Cari and "la profe [Margarita]." At Cuba's Council of State, the late Pedro Álvarez Tabío allowed me into the "Che" archives, where I was helped by Efraín González; also, Heberto Norman Acosta. Andrés Castillo Bernal let me examine his own extensively researched manuscript on the Cuban revolutionary war and other documents.

In Argentina, I must thank Calica Ferrer, the late Carlos Figueroa, Chicho and Mario Salduna, Pepe and Chuchi Tisera, Roberto and Celia Guevara, Julia Constenla, Rogelio García Lupo, Reynaldo Sietecase, Hector Jouve, Alberto Korn, Héctor "Toto" Schmucler, Oscar del Barco, Benjamín and Elsa Elkin, Nelly Benbibre de Castro, Emiliano Acosta, Tatiana and Jaime Roca, and everyone in the Equipo Argentino de Antropología Forense—Anahi, Patricia, Darío, and Mako—and especially Alejandro Inchaurregui, a good friend and an admirable man. Also, Roberto Baschetti, Julio Villalonga, María Laura Avignolo, and Claudia Korol.

In Bolivia, special thanks to Loyola Guzmán and Humberto Vázquez-Viaña. Also, to Rosa and Natalí Alcoba, Martín and Matilde; Ana Urquieta, Juan Ignacio Siles, Chato Peredo, Rene Rocabado, Carlos Soria, Clovis Díaz, Miguel Ángel Quintanilla, and Tania at the Hotel Copacabana. Retired General Reque Terán generously shared his time, documents, and collection of captured photographs.

In Paraguay, Socorro Selich and her daughters, especially Zorka, took me in on trust, unveiling the secrets of the late Colonel Andrés Selich, a key figure in the final hours of Che Guevara's life. I thank them for their confidence and their hospitality, and also Tilín for his help in making copies of thirty-year-old tapes and photographs.

In Mexico, my research was either coordinated or conducted by Phil Gunson, an excellent journalist, veteran Latin America hand, and good friend of many years. To him I owe a special debt of gratitude for his tireless help in ferreting out people and archives in Mexico, Guatemala, Nicaragua, and Panama.

In the United Kingdom: Richard Gott and the late John Rettie gave their encouragement, information, and contacts, all of which were invaluable. Thanks also to Duncan Green and Raquel at LAB, Pedro Sarduy and Jean Stubbs; Noll Scott, Landon Temple, Muhammad, Helena Poldervaart, Carlos Carrasco, Ashok Prasad, and Peter Molloy.

In Moscow: Irina Kalinina, Anatoli, Esperanza, Volodya, Mario Monje, and Alexandr Alexiev. In Spain, Henry Lerner, Carmen González-Aguilar, and her late brother, Pepe, who gave me time on his deathbed. In

Sweden, Ciro Bustos opened up his home and heart in our long talks. In Cairo, Carol Berger kindly and selflessly tracked people down for me. In Germany, Peter Müller helped with the Stasi files and in other ways as well. The Swiss filmmaker Richard Dindo generously gave me contacts and tips for Bolivia and some photographs for the book.

In Washington, thanks to Peter Kornbluh at the National Security Archive, Scott Armstrong, David Corn, Sergo Mikoyan, and Phil Brenner. In Miami, many thanks to my friends and repeat hosts—Rex and Gabriela Henderson, David and Inés Adams, and José and Gina de Córdoba.

These and other friends and relatives, spread around the world, made this long endeavor a much warmer experience. They include Vanadia Sandon-Humphries, Doris Coonrad, the late David Humphries, Jonathon Glancey, Michelle, Tina, Meim, Nohad Al-Turki, Nick Richards, Christopher and Monique Maxwell-Libby, Colin Pease, David Ridd, Simon Tucker, Rosalind Bain, Laurie Johnston, Cathy Booth, Tim Golden, Jeff Russell, Chuck and Bex, Michele Labrut, Bertha Thayer, Mike and Joan Carabini-Parker, Janet and Terry Parker, Maria Elena, the late Matilde Stone, Martin and Eva Barrat, Ingrid Vavere, Colin Lizieri, and Jos and Kien Schreurs-Timmermans. Jan Hartman has been a wise counselor and generous friend.

My mother, Barbara Joy Anderson, who was my first mentor and dear friend, passed away suddenly while I was in Cuba. I miss her still. Sofía Gato, who helped raise Che's children and then did the same for us, died while I was still writing this book. She will always be remembered with great affection.

It is fitting that this book is published by Grove Press, which first introduced many of Che Guevara's writings to readers in the United States. Grove's offices were bombed in the Sixties after its "radical" magazine, *Evergreen,* was published bearing the same painting of Che on its cover that now graces the cover of this book. Grove's publisher, Morgan Entrekin, has stood by me throughout the years. Thanks also to Carla Lalli and Elisabeth Schmitz, Anton Mueller, Kenn Russell, Muriel Jorgensen, Miwa, Judy, and everyone else at Grove Press who made me feel at home; Joan, Eric, Jim, Scott, Lissa, Kirsten, Tom, Lea, and Ben—many thanks. Special thanks to Amy Hundley, Lauren Wein, and Andrew Robinton. Patty O'Connell sorted out my tangled syntax and lapses into Spanglish. My thanks also to Deborah Schneider; Ursula Mackenzie at Transworld, Robert Feith at Objetiva, and Jorge Herralde at Anagrama. At the Wylie Agency, my thanks to Sarah Chalfant, Andrew Wylie, and Edward Orloff.

Few writers are fortunate enough to have a brother and a close friend, who also happen to be authors, as their editors, and yet I was uniquely privileged to have Scott Anderson and Francisco Goldman as the slashers of my once overwhelmingly ponderous tome. Sharon DeLano oversaw the revision and updating of this edition, a gargantuan task that has improved the book immensely and, I hope, also extended its life-span. I shall be forever grateful to her dedicated spirit and her incomparable editing skills.

My wife, Erica, has been my unflagging companion and bolster throughout the entire "Che" odyssey. With true British aplomb, she accepted our move from Oxford to Havana in 1993 and proceeded to set up a home there, even as that society seemed to crumble around us. She withstood my many foreign trips, most of them lasting several months, without complaint, and always gave me a healthy and boisterous family to return to. For our children, Bella, Rosie, and Máximo, this book became an inextricable part of their lives. Rosie and Máximo's first language was Spanish, while Bella began her morning classes with the hymn "Seremos como el Che": We will be like Che.

Index

Montand, Yves, 642
Montané Oropesa, Jesús, 173, 178, 210
Montero, Renán "Iván" (pseudonym), 565, 656, 669, 689, 746
Moore de la Serna, Edelmira (aunt), 5, 108
Moore de la Serna, Juan Martín, 50
Mora, Alberto, 573–74
Mora Valverde, Manuel, 115
Morales, Calixto, 188–89, 215, 268, 356, 381
Morales, Evo, 729–30
Morales, Ramón Villeda, 418
Morán, "El Gallego" José, 223–25, 233, 245, 278
Morán, Rolando. *See* Ramírez, Ricardo
Moreno, Dr. Carlos, 112
Morgan, William, 290, 336, 415, 461
Moscow News magazine, 573
Motorcycle Diaries, The (Guevara), 70*n*., 722, 750
Moulana, "General" (Congolese rebel), 624, 627, 628
Movimiento 26 de Julio. *See* July 26 Movement
Movimiento de Izquierda Revolucionaria (MIR), 456, 511, 575, 644
Movimiento de Rescate de la Revolución (MRR), 450, 452, 478
Movimiento Nacionalista Revolucionario (MNR), 96, 98, 100, 126, 529
Movimiento Revolucionario del Pueblo (MRP), 451
Moyano, Dolores, 28–30, 35, 50, 52, 54, 64–67, 295
MRP. *See* Movimiento Revolucionario del Pueblo
MRR. *See* Movimiento de Rescate de la Revolución (MRR)
Mudandi (Rwandan Tutsi), 615, 619–20
Mujíca, Nicanor, 120
Mulele, Pierre, 635
"Murdered Puppy, The," 435
Mussolini, Benito, 32, 34, 49
My Friend Che (Rojo), 526*n*., 722, 733

Nasser, Gamal Abdel, 409, 435, 459, 576, 586, 589, 619
National Association of Small Farmers (ANAP), 318

National Conference of Sugar Workers, 328
National Directorate of July 26 Movement. *See* July 26 Movement, National Directorate
National Institute for Agrarian Reform. *See* Instituto Nacional de Reforma Agraria (INRA)
National Liberation Army. *See* Ejército de Liberación Nacional (ELN)
National Liberation Council (Venezuela), 575, 587
National Liberation Council (Congo), 619, 620. *See also* Congolese Liberation Council
National Press Club, 395
"Necessity for Revolution," 735
Nehru, Jawaharlal, 38, 51, 409–10, 459, 490
Neruda, Pablo, 36–38, 110, 292, 539, 599
Neto, Agostinho, 584
New China (Mao), 129
New Leader magazine, 734
New York Times, The (newspaper), xiii, 224, 228, 235–36, 244, 287, 292*n*., 295, 372, 568
Nicaragua, 110, 136, 498, 575, 721–22
  Che's 1953 travels through, 115
  plans to spread the revolution to, 376–79, 397–98, 417–18, 510–11, 740
Nicaro nickel mine, 313, 326, 480
Ñico López training school, 334
Nicolardes Rojas brothers, 372
Nixon, Richard M., 155, 160
  1960 election campaign, 438, 459
  Castro and, 396
Nkrumah, Kwame, 459, 576, 584
Nogues, "Gobo," 97–99, 103
Nogues, Isaías, 96–99
North Korea, 467, 473
North Vietnam, 465, 472, 487, 570, 591
Notas de Viaje (Guevara), 70*n*.
  "Note on the Margin," 118–19, 734
  personal transformation noted in, 91
"Notas Económicas" (Economic Notes), 641
"Note on the Margin," 118–19, 734
Noyola, Juan, 430
nuclear weapons, 100, 571, 582
  missiles in Cuba. *See* Soviet Union, missiles in Cuba
Nuestra Razón, 735

Credits for Photographs

Pages x, 369 (top), 438, 506, 562, and 715: Salas; pages 14, 17, 19 (top and bottom), 42, 46, 55, 59, 66, 164, 168, 173, 182, 191, 197, 204, 226, 240, 284, 294, 320, 337, 345, 350, 369 (bottom), 383, 402, 434, 446, 595, 607, 618, 626, and 665 (bottom): Cuban Council of State Office of Historical Affairs; page 25: Courtesy of Carlos Barceló; pages 106 and 122: Courtesy of Carlos "Calica" Ferrer; pages 355 and 358: Burt Glinn, Magnum Photos; page 403: Agenzia Contrasto; page 463: TASS/Prensa Latina; pages 468 and 592: Prensa Latina; page 482: Liborio Noval; pages 488 and 585: AP/Wide World Photos; page 524: courtesy of Thomas Billhardt; pages 582 and 589: UPI/Corbis-Bettmann; pages 665 (top), 668, 676 (top), and 691: courtesy of Richard Dindo; page 676 (bottom): Che Guevara's confiscated film, courtesy of General Luis Reque Terán; page 704: courtesy of Socorro Selich; page 708: courtesy of Félix Rodríguez; page 713: Freddy Alborta.